A Passion for Government

A Passion for Government

The Life of Sarah, Duchess of Marlborough

FRANCES HARRIS

CLARENDON PRESS · OXFORD

1991

Oxford University Press, Walton Street, Oxford OX2 6DP
Oxford New York Toronto
Delhi Bombay Calcutta Madras Karachi
Petaling Jaya Singapore Hong Kong Tokyo
Nairobi Dar es Salaam Cape Town
Melbourne Auckland
and associated companies in
Berlin Ibadan

Oxford is a trade mark of Oxford University Press

Published in the United States
by Oxford University Press, New York

British Cataloguing in Publication Data
(data available)

Library of Congress Cataloging in Publication Data
Harris, Frances.
A passion for government: the life of Sarah, Duchess of
Marlborough / Frances Harris.
Includes bibliographical references and index.
1. Marlborough, Sarah Jennings Churchill, Duchess, 1660–1744.
2. Great Britain—History—Anne, 1702–1714—Biography. 3. Great
Britain—Political and government—1660–1714. 4. Great Britain—
Politics and governement—1714–1760. 5. Great Britain—Court and
courtiers—Biography. 6. Favorites, Royal—Great Britain—
Biography. I. Title.
DA462.M4H37 1991
941.06'9'092—dc20 [B] 91–6295
ISBN 0–19–820224–5

Typeset by Pentacor PLC
Printed and bound by
Courier International Limited
East Kilbride

ACKNOWLEDGEMENTS

Quotations from the Stuart Papers at Windsor Castle are included by the gracious permission of Her Majesty the Queen I am indebted to the Marquess of Tavistock and the Trustees of the Bedford Estates for allowing me to use and quote from their family papers, and to the great kindness of their archivist, Mrs M. P. G. Draper, during my visits to the Bedford Office. Quotations from the Portland and Coventry Papers at Longleat are included by kind permission of the Marquess of Bath, Longleat House, Warminster, Wiltshire. I also owe grateful acknowledgements to the following individuals and institutions for allowing me to make use of manuscripts in their ownership and custody: the Governor and Company of the Bank of England; the Bodleian Library, Oxford; the British Library Board; the Syndics of Cambridge University Library; the Manager, Child's Bank, Fleet Street, London; Mr H. J. R. Wing, Assistant Librarian of Christ Church, Oxford, and the Trustees of the Will of Major Peter George Evelyn (Evelyn MSS); the Archivist of Churchill College, Cambridge, and H. W. Drax, Esq. (Erle-Drax MSS); the County Archivist, Devon Record Office, and Mrs P. Gordon-Duff-Pennington (Seymour of Berry Pomeroy MSS); the Librarian, Dr Williams's Library; East Sussex County Library (Wolseley MSS); the County Archivist, East Sussex Record Office (Frewen MSS); the County Archivist, Hertfordshire Record Office, and Lady Ravensdale (Panshanger MSS); the Librarian and Curator of Manuscripts, the Huntington Library, San Marino, California; the County Archivist, West Kent Archives Office (Stanhope MSS); the County Archivist, Leicestershire Record Office (Finch MSS); the Keeper of Manuscripts, National Library of Wales; the Librarian, the Newberry Library, Chicago; the County Archivist, Northamptonshire Record Office; the Director, Pierpont Morgan Library, New York; the Public Record Office, Chancery Lane, London; the Archivist, Suffolk Record Office, Bury St Edmunds Branch, and the National Trust (Ickworth MSS); the Librarian, Westminster City Libraries; Yale University Library and Mr Stephen Parks, Curator of the Osborn Collection.

Quotations from *The Marlborough–Godolphin Correspondence*, ed. H. L. Snyder (Oxford, 1975), are included by permission of Oxford University Press. The first part of Chapter 16 contains a modified version of my article, 'Parliament and Blenheim Palace', first published in *Parliamentary History*, 8 (1989). It is included here by permission of the Parliamentary History Yearbook Trust.

Dr Robert Beddard, Dr Joanne Finkelstein, Andrea Goldsmith, Professor Edward Gregg, Helen Hudson, Louis Jebb, Clyve Jones, Professors Pat Rogers and Henry Snyder, and Edwin Welch have all given me the benefit of their advice and help at different stages of my research, and I owe a particular debt to Esther Hardware and to my colleagues at the British Library for a variety of personal and professional kindnesses, support, and assistance in preparing this book.

F. H.

CONTENTS

viii CONTENTS

LIST OF ILLUSTRATIONS

(between pp. 214 and 215)

NOTES ON DATES

In general these are given according to the Old Style (Julian) calendar current in England; in the seventeenth century this was ten days, and in the eighteenth century eleven days, behind the New Style (Gregorian) calendar used on the Continent. For letters written from the Continent and for the dispatches of foreign envoys in London both Old and New Style dates are given in the notes. The New Year is always taken to begin on 1 January (not 25 March as in Old Style reckoning), but both years are given in the notes when only the Old Style year appears on the document.

INTRODUCTION

'THIS is a World that is subject to frequent Revolutions.' So wrote Sarah, Duchess of Marlborough, from the vantage-point of approaching old age.[1] Her life, which began in the year monarchy was restored after a period of unstable commonwealth rule and ended on the eve of the second Jacobite rebellion, is a panorama of this insecure, faction-riven era. In the course of it she was the favourite of the Queen of England, the wife and partner of that Queen's most powerful subject, the associate, tool, friend, or enemy of most of the leading politicians of her day; in her twenty-two years of strenuous and embattled widowhood the effective head of one of England's great families; and at the end of her 'fourscore years of arrogance' a legend and a curiosity to the coming generation. Her life has been written many times, but the focus has usually been on her tempestuous personal relationships—with her husband, with her children and grandchildren, with Queen Anne, and with a handful of her more famous contemporaries—without a full appreciation of how these related to the major preoccupations of her life: her passionate involvement in politics and her colossal administrative labours to consolidate the fortunes of her family.

The Duchess of Marlborough was a woman with a 'Passion for Government'[2]: a compulsion to wield power, not only in the affairs of her own family, but in public life as well, as far as her influence could reach; for government in the institutional sense—the struggle for power between the political parties and between the sovereign and Parliament—was in many ways the most powerful and enduring interest of her long life. It began with her support of the first Whigs during the Exclusion crisis when she was a girl in her teens, and continued into her seventies and eighties when she became the matriarch, gadfly, and 'immortal, undecaying Toast' of the patriot opposition to Walpole. These, needless to say, were unusual preoccupations for one who belonged to 'the simple sex' (her own wry version of the contemporary estimate of feminine capacity). As a woman, the only official role in public life which was open to her was that of professional courtier, and this she performed, with only one brief interval, for the better part of forty years. But the formalities and constraints of Court life were always profoundly uncongenial to her, and after the first few years she tolerated them only for the opportunities her position gave her to advance her family's interests and act in a wider sphere.

The Duchess of Marlborough was fond of claiming that 'tho a Woman', she had done all she could to promote the Whig cause and preserve the liberties of England.[3] Certainly no woman outside the royal family had a comparable role in the politics of her age. She came from a social class of middling county gentry for whom participation in government was a birthright. As the last of her father's line, only her sex prevented her from succeeding him and her grandfather as one of the MPs for St Albans. Her husband, himself bred in the Tory principles of a royalist father, was perceptive in calling her 'the true born Whig'. As the descendant of men who had sided against Charles I, she claimed to have imbibed a hatred of tyranny before she had ever read a line on the subject. It was her lifelong conviction that no sovereign was to be trusted and that Parliament remained the true guardian of the constitution by its power to punish erring ministers, 'and by that means oblige weak or bad Princes to keep their coronation oaths'.[4]

Having become the favourite servant of James II's younger daughter Anne, she was able to take an active role in that central and definitive event of Whig historiography, the Revolution of 1688; and in the following reign her intimacy with the Princess enabled her husband and their friend Godolphin to establish themselves as Anne's confidential advisers. When Anne herself came to the throne in 1702, the two men succeeded as her chief ministers and Sarah emerged again into public life, determined to do her utmost with them and with the new Queen to advance the cause of the Whigs. This was not just a matter of personal allegiance; she was never on good terms with any of the five members of the Whig Junto for very long. She was simply convinced that it was only under a Whig government that the Revolution settlement, for which she and her husband had risked their lives and fortunes, could be securely maintained and the country kept safe from the prospect of a Jacobite restoration.

As the favourite of the monarch and the wife and friend respectively of her two chief ministers, Sarah was better better placed than any female subject in England at the beginning of Anne's reign to support the government and exercise influence—if only she had been willing to recognize that the essential prerequisite for doing so was to maintain her personal friendship with the Queen. Instead she was determined to act in her own right, sacrificing the royal favour if necessary to achieve her political ends. Very quickly her loud, intolerant, and unremitting attempts to impose her views on government first alienated the Queen, whose natural sympathies were with the Tories, and then gradually undermined Anne's confidence in her two ministers as well. Although Sarah still had a role to play in mediating between them and the Junto, her loss of favour left the way open for rival influences at Court and allowed the Whigs to claim by the end of the reign that she had helped to bring about their downfall by her calamitous mismanagement of the royal friendship.

It was her ageing husband's determination to regain his former power that gave Sarah a renewed role in the Hanoverian era. When Marlborough was incapacitated by a stroke within two years of George I's accession, it was she who acted and spoke for him in public affairs for the remainder of his life. By the time of his death in 1722, just as Walpole was beginning to establish his twenty-year grip on the treasury and Parliament, her outspoken disapproval of the conduct of the Whigs once they were in power had placed the Marlboroughs at odds with almost all of their former allies. For the rest of her days Sarah 'detested courts and courtiers', and was one of Walpole's most vociferous opponents. Having had a hand in turning out James II to save English liberties, she declared, she would sooner die than give them up to any minister.[5] For the sake of her wealth, her electoral interest, and such influence as she could command (chiefly by threat of disinheritance) over the political conduct of her grandsons, the opposition leaders cultivated her, although some of them, like Queen Anne's Whigs, eventually came to see her as more trouble than she was worth.

In the final reckoning, Sarah's chief significance in Augustan politics lay in the influence she exercised through her male relations and associates, rather than in her more famous role as 'Mrs Freeman' to Queen Anne's 'Mrs Morley'. Yet it took her many years to accept the limitations of her position as a woman in this respect, to acknowledge bitterly that 'the things that are worth naming will ever be done from the influence of men'.[6] Her husband, greatly as she loved him, never fully shared her commitment to the Whigs, and even those politicians who did, constrained by the need to translate their principles into day-to-day action, were seldom energetic or disinterested or uncompromising enough to satisfy her. In their turn, the grandsons through whom she sought to act vicariously after her husband's death all completely failed in one way or another to fulfil her ambitions and expectations as public men. She never ceased to chafe against this sense of 'insignificance' as a woman in the world of affairs, or to wish in moments of national crisis that she could take an independent part in parliamentary government: 'I am confydent I should have been the greatest Hero that ever was known in the Parliament Hous, if I had been so happy as to have been a Man.'[7]

The story of her political involvement is in many ways one of passionate wrong-headedness, of an arrogant, driven, opinionated woman constantly at odds with the constraints of her situation, and in her frustration as often as not damaging the very cause she wished to promote. Yet her family connections, her money, her sheer force of personality, and her compulsion to act meant that she was seldom without influence of some kind. And if nothing else, hers was an extraordinary life span: the old woman who as a girl had witnessed the rise of the first Whigs lived long enough not just to rejoice in Walpole's fall, but to denounce the turncoat patriots of the opposition who then joined with the Court, and finally (it is pleasant to note) to die at peace with Pelham's administration.

In private life, though her sex could still be a handicap, there were fewer obstacles to her exercise of power. It was her repeated boast in old age that no woman had ever been so useful to her family. Her favour with Queen Anne was the foundation of her husband's spectacular European career and therefore of her whole family's fortunes. All her life she continued to labour 'like a packhorse' on their behalf: educating, nursing, match-making, electioneering, building and furnishing houses, investing capital and buying estates, and all the while waging a constant campaign of litigation against the inroads of maladminstration and fraud; it was difficult, she admitted, 'for a Woman to get the better of so many people in the profession of cheating', but she never let this difficulty deter her.[8] As her husband's principal executor and trustee, she devoted her widowhood to administering his estate (worth well over a million pounds), investing it in land and national securities. This financial control not only gave her an influence over government interest rates, but also confirmed her position as virtual head of her own family: a most unusual one for a dowager where the heirs were of age. For good measure, she amassed a huge fortune of her own in land and investments and used it to endow one of her younger grandsons, thus establishing a second, independent branch of the family in the next generation.

As Sarah admitted towards the end of her life, she had had her share 'of what is thought most valuable in this world': beauty which endured well into old age, such vitality of mind and body that, as one of her friends commented, it looked 'as if the maker had designed both [to be] immortall, had he not been engaged to the contrary',[9] a remarkable capacity for inspiring love and friendship, and, from her middle years onwards, all the privileges of wealth and rank. Yet 'what do I dream of satisfaction', she wrote in a moment of bleak self-knowledge, 'when there are not two things upon earth at so impossible a distance as satisfaction and me?'[10]

Those who suffered at her hands likened her to some elemental, destructive, and unstoppable force of nature: a hurricane, perhaps, or a volcano (one of her enemies dubbed her 'Mount Aetna'). She lived her whole life, even her crippled and bedridden last years, in a continual bustle of energy and hyperactivity. She was extravagantly emotional in love and hate, liable to violent and unpredictable swings from one to the other, and from tearing high spirits to the depths of pessimism, depression, and disillusion. Confrontation, what she called 'a perpetual warr' with the knaves and fools of the world, was her constant state.[11] She was unable to govern her temper or her tongue, or to bear control, opposition, or criticism in any form. 'Dissembling is so great a force to my nature that I could never bring myself to it,' she declared in her high-handed way, although she acknowledged that 'perhaps by doing it I might have prevented a great many mischiefs that have happened to me'.[12] Yet she never ceased to value herself on this devastating 'sincerity', even when she had to face the full extent of the damage it had done, and when an acquaintance pointed out that if everyone behaved as she did, it would destroy society and there would be no living in the world. In the end she outlasted all those she had most cared about, and died almost universally unregretted.

Most commonplace pleasures had inevitably eluded her, and conventional religion could bring no comfort to such a restless and undisciplined spirit. She put her faith in personal relationships: 'I have always thought that the greatest happiness of life was to love and value somebody extremely that returned it and to see them often.'[13] Yet what happiness she could derive from this source could only come from the few whose love for her was strong enough to survive her violent and domineering humours and her insistence upon making compliance and agreement the test of personal feeling. Her relations with her children and grand-children all suffered in one way or another by these means, and her intimacy with Queen Anne utterly failed, in the last resort, to withstand the intolerable stresses she placed on it. It was the two ministers, Marlborough and Godolphin, whose common love for Sarah helped to cement their long political partnership, and whose careers were built on her friendship with the Queen, who then stood by her despite the incalculable damage which its disintegration wrought in their public lives.

She knew what she owed to them. The Lord Treasurer Godolphin, who always understood and brought out the best in her, and finally refused to abandon her even to save his ministry, she called 'the truest friend to me & all my family that ever was, & the best man that ever lived'.[14] From her husband, who learnt that 'a man must bear with a good deal to be quiet at home', she had unfailing love and forbearance. Indeed, some thought her 'too happy for any one mortall' if only for this reason.[15] But love, Sarah once commented, could be as uneasy a companion as hate, and marriage itself was a form of bondage for a woman. Marlborough could only give her the freedom she craved in a practical way by placing all her personal fortune in trustees' hands for her sole use. 'Till hee made me an executor, I never had any thing to do with his fortune, nor hee with mine,' she recalled in her widowhood: 'this was a very uncommon thing to give to a wife, but hee had experience enough of me to know that I would make no ill use of the power.'[16] Reflecting on the hostility of her surviving daughters, inexplicable (as it seemed to her) after all she had done for them, she added, 'I am sure I was a much better mother in all respects than I was a wife, in which I had no occation to shew any vertue, because never any man deserved so much from another as the Dear Duke of Marlborough did from me.'[17] Dedicating her widowhood to fulfilling his wishes for his family was her way of repaying him. Two of her own comments may be borne in mind as the story of her life unfolds: 'my case is in many things different from other wemens,' and 'I could say Something to every Part of my Life that would convince you that 'tis only a new Sceen of Trouble.'[18]

Family Fortunes

IN old age the Duchess of Marlborough was accustomed to profess
herself 'very little concerned about pedigree of family'. In some
moods she would even say that 'we were all Adham's children, and
'twas no matter for birth'. Having come across an account of her Jenyns
ancestry in an unauthorized biography of her husband, she acknowledged that it was accurate, 'but I don't know what it signifies to have it
mentioned'. Nevertheless, she was careful to point out that her father's
family had been 'reckoned a good one', and that he had estates in
Hertfordshire, Somerset, and Kent worth £4,000 a year.[1] The statement
is true as far as it goes, but the implication that her childhood
environment was that of a prosperous and secure landed family is
thoroughly misleading.

The Hertfordshire estate consisted of the manor of Sandridge, a few
miles north of St Albans, and property on the southern outskirts of
St Albans itself, including a mansion house called Holywell set in several
acres of grounds. Puzzling over the oldest deeds in her possession, she
found that these lands had come to the Jenynses through marriage with a
family called Rowlett, 'and that might have been in William the
Conqueror's Time for ought I know'.[2] In fact the transaction was more
recent and more prosaic. They had been acquired by Ralph Rowlett,
goldsmith and Merchant of the Staple, at the dissolution of the
monasteries, when the lands of St Albans Abbey were sold off and the
Abbey itself dwindled into a parish church. In due course they
descended to his grandson, Ralph Jenyns, child of Elizabeth Rowlett and
Bernard Jenyns, a wealthy merchant of London. It was this Ralph who
added the manor of Churchill in Somerset to the family estates. In the
second decade of the seventeenth century his grandson, Sir John Jenyns,
married Alice Spencer, daughter of the Hertfordshire landowner Sir
Richard Spencer of Offley. These two, part of a great network of
substantial county gentry, were the grandparents of Sarah, Duchess
of Marlborough.[3]

Up to this point the family was well-to-do. One reason for the drastic
reduction in their circumstances by the time Sarah was born in 1660 was

undoubtedly what Sir John Jenyns himself (when making excuses for not paying his Ship Money) called his 'great charge of children'. As his granddaughter explained, he had twenty-two of them, 'by which means the estate of the family . . . came to be divided into small parcels'.[4] Even so, it is worth noting that a number of the children died very young in the lifetime of their father, and there was therefore some point in the retort of a hostile mayor of St Albans that Sir John's 'charge of children is the case of most of his neighbours who have not a sixth part of his estate'.[5] It will be seen that the reasons for Sir John's reluctance to pay his Ship Money were not purely financial.

Richard Jenyns, the eldest son and father of Sarah, was born in 1618 or thereabouts. In December 1643, shortly after his father's death, he married Frances Thornhurst, the only child of a Kentish baronet, Sir Gifford Thornhurst, and his wife Susanna Temple, in her youth a celebrated beauty at the Court of James I, and one of the many descendants of the Temples of Stowe.[6] The marriage portion which Frances brought to the Jenyns family was the Kentish manor of Agney on the Romney marshes, which her mother held on a lease from the Dean and Chapter of Canterbury.[7] The Duchess of Marlborough's statement that her parents had lands in Hertfordshire, Somerset, and Kent was therefore quite true. What she did not add was that from the very beginning of their married life they scarcely knew where to turn for money. For Richard Jenyns had inherited not only his father's estates (less a third of the income to which the widowed Alice was now entitled by law), but also his extensive debts, and responsibility for the twelve surviving brothers and sisters who all had the right to a portion or annuity from the Hertfordshire land. Indeed, the charges on this estate now exceeded its income. And the manor of Churchill, the most valuable of Richard's possessions, was near Bristol and so hard hit by the disruption of the Civil War that it yielded no rents at all at this period. His mother summed up the parlous situation with some desperation in 1644, in the face of a persistent assumption by the tax authorities that the family had a large surplus income: 'if I had the money,' she added, 'I would willingly pay all that is demanded.'[8]

At first Richard simply ignored his commitments. The result was a series of acrimonious lawsuits initiated by his mother, his brother Ralph, and two of his sisters, which offer some clue to the origin of the Duchess of Marlborough's notoriously litigious temperament. Richard, who had succeeded his father as one of the MPs for St Albans, tried unsuccessfully to evade these proceedings by claiming parliamentary privilege.[9] He was already under pressure from his other creditors, and the income from the much poorer Kentish estate can scarcely have been enough to support his own growing family. His first child, Susanna, was born in 1645, followed quickly by a son, John, and two more daughters, Frances and Barbara.[10]

The Duchess of Marlborough is usually said to have come from a royalist family. In fact Sir John Jenyns, although he died before the Civil War broke out, was a supporter of Pym, and his eldest son followed his lead.[11] Sarah's assertion of the rights of Parliament over 'weak or bad Princes', and her admission that she was 'born of a principle never to have any remorse for the deposeing of any King that became unjust', were a natural part of her legacy from her family.[12] Yet by 1650 Charles I had been executed and Richard Jenyns's allegiance, like that of many of his contemporaries, had shifted. In May that year he embarked on a mysterious journey, first to Holland and then 'into very far and remote parts'. It emerged after the Restoration that he had gone to the West Indies with Lord Willoughby of Parnham, the former leader of the Presbyterian party who had fled to Holland to be appointed governor of Barbados by the exiled Charles II. Richard presumably made his peace with the King as well, and this was to stand him in good stead after the Restoration; but if he hoped that his estate in Antigua would restore his fortunes he was disappointed. By the end of the year he was back in England to find his affairs in even greater disorder than before.[13] To raise the ready money he now desperately needed, he set about selling his Somerset estate.

The buyer he found in 1652 was a young lawyer named John Churchill. Of quite humble Dorset origins and the son of a London tradesman, the latter may nevertheless have shared the grandiose belief of his cousin Winston, also a lawyer but with an antiquarian turn of mind, that the manor of Churchill had ancestral connections with their family.[14] At the time of the purchase this Winston Churchill, a former royalist army officer living uncomfortably in the household of his Puritan mother-in-law, had an infant son, another John Churchill, who was destined for a much closer connection with the Jenyns family.

The sale of Churchill did not restore Richard Jenyns to solvency. There were a number of subsequent proceedings against him for debt,[15] and in 1654, being again 'in great want of money', he took the further serious step of persuading his wife to dispose of her lease of Agney manor, to a buyer who had acquired the reversion when the lands of the Dean and Chapter of Canterbury were disposed of by Act of Parliament in 1649.[16] He then settled down to see out the Protectorate as quietly and economically as possible, cultivating the orchards at his house in St Albans. In 1653 and 1654 two more sons were born, neither surviving more than a few months. The eldest child, Susanna, died in 1655. But Ralph, born in 1657, survived; and so, most notably, did Sarah, a child of the Restoration year, 1660. The parish registers of St Albans Abbey record that she was born on 5 June and baptized twelve days later. The picturesque and persistent tradition that her birth date was really 29 May, the very day of Charles II's restoration, is disproved by incidental evidence given in a lawsuit shortly after her death. The testimony of her secretary, who had lived in her household for twenty years, that 'on 17 May 1738 the late Dutchess of Marlborough wanted only 19 Days of completing her 78th year', confirms the accuracy of the parish register date.[17]

There has been unnecessary confusion about the place, as well as the date, of Sarah's birth. Since the late nineteenth century, claims have often been made on behalf of Water End, a Jacobean house which still stands on the Sandridge estate,[18] and a number of Sarah's biographers have painted an idyllic picture of her childhood there. In fact Water End, although within the manor of Sandridge, was a freehold in the occupation of the Gerrards, another substantial local family, and remained so throughout the seventeenth century.[19] It has no connection with the Jenyns family. At the time of Sarah's birth her father was rated for a large property in the middle ward of St Albans which is readily identifiable as Holywell,[20] and her birth and baptism, as well as those of her four elder brothers and sisters, were all recorded in the registers of the Abbey parish in which the house was situated. It is beyond reasonable doubt that this was where she was born and spent her early childhood.

The house, at the foot of Holywell Hill with the Abbey looming above, was half in the town and half in the country. The west front was on the very edge of the road, while the last cottages of the town almost touched the boundary wall on the north side. But to the east and south were twenty acres or more of gardens, orchards, and pasture, intersected by a trout stream, and beyond was open countryside. In structure the building was Tudor if not earlier, with an open cloister on the garden side, a long gallery above, and a great bedchamber which in Sarah's childhood was still known as 'the Queen's Chamber', in memory of the fact that Queen Elizabeth had once spent the night there. By the 1660s the house was showing signs of age and of the family's straitened circumstances, but an inventory of the contents taken when Sarah was 8 years old suggests that it retained a certain tattered and outmoded grandeur. The nursery, of which she was to be the last occupant, had some old hangings on the walls, two 'foot carpets' for the floor, a curtained bedstead, an old table, a few stools, and a pair of little dressing tables. It sounds shabby but comfortable.[21]

The disposal of the Churchill and Agney estates meant that at the time of his youngest daughter's birth Richard Jenyns had nothing like the income of £4,000 which she afterwards claimed for him. Nevertheless he was a member of the Convention Parliament which summoned back Charles II, and the Restoration gave him the opportunity to regain at least a portion of his lost wealth. The sale of Agney had been conditional on the Jenynses' having the right to recover it in the event of a restoration of Church lands. In 1663 they did so, and the negotiations brought them into contact with the King's brother, James, Duke of York, and his favourite, Charles Berkeley. When one of the Duchess of York's maids of honour had to resign her post in haste to marry Berkeley in 1664, the vacancy was filled by Richard Jenyns's 16-year-old daughter, Frances.[22]

Like her grandmother before her, Frances Jenyns was an immediate success at Court. Her radiant youthful prettiness and scatterbrained manner hid a firmness of character which preserved her from many dangerous attentions, including those of the Duke of York himself. Always inclined to regard his wife's maids as 'part of his property', he had to console himself with the less attractive but less scrupulous Arabella Churchill,[23] by coincidence a cousin of the purchaser of Churchill manor and daughter of the royalist Winston. In 1666 Frances Jenyns resigned her post to marry George Hamilton, a well-connected Irish Catholic army officer and former page to the King; but his religion was a bar to the couple's otherwise promising future. Later in the same year he and his fellow Roman Catholics were required by Parliament to resign their commissions. This provided Arabella Churchill's young brother John with his long-awaited chance of an ensign's post in the Guards, but for Hamilton it meant the loss of his livelihood. He had no choice but to accept the offer of military service under Louis XIV, though before he left he had the compensation of a knighthood from Charles II. His wife, who became a convert to his religion, joined him in France early in 1668,[24] leaving behind a younger sister dazzled by her success at Court and longing to emulate it.

In the meantime the restored Agney estate was proving a very mixed blessing to their parents. Seeing that Sandridge was too encumbered with debt to provide the maintenance which her marriage settlement had specified, Mrs Jenyns tried to ensure that part of the income from Agney would be received by trustees for her own benefit and that of the three younger children, Barbara, Ralph, and Sarah. But she was soon complaining that her husband and his brother Ralph (the latter still trying to secure the arrears of his annuity) were diverting the income for the payment of Richard's debts 'without any regard to her'.[25] Embittered by a married life of constant financial anxiety, she too began legal proceedings against her husband, who again tried to delay them by claiming parliamentary privilege.[26] The only reason the affair went no further was that by the end of the session Richard Jenyns was dead; he was buried in St Albans Abbey on 8 May 1668.

While the lawsuit was in preparation Mrs Jenyns had been living in London lodgings, apparently separated from her husband,[27] and there seems to have been no reconciliation between them before his death. In her will twenty-five years later she asked to be buried in St Albans Abbey, as near as possible to the children who had predeceased her. There is no mention of her husband.[28]

Her difficulties continued into her widowhood. Administration of Richard's estate had to be surrendered to his principal creditor,[29] while the Hertfordshire lands were entailed on the eldest son, John. In the course of the next six years he too raised large mortgages on both Sandridge and Holywell. Meanwhile he and his uncle Ralph continued to lay claim to Agney. It was not until 1671 that Mrs Jenyns reached an agreement with them which gave her back control of this estate,[30] and even after this, her son seems to have remained very much under the influence of his uncle: in 1672 he made a will in which he effectively disinherited his younger brother in favour of the elder Ralph. When John Jenyns died suddenly two years later the family was plunged into a fresh round of lawsuits in order to win back the family property for the younger Ralph; but in the course of these proceedings he too fell foul of his mother, who accused him of trying to appropriate Agney along with the other lands.[31]

In this quarrelsome and insecure atmosphere the youngest member of the family was growing up undisciplined and unstable in temperament. In later life Sarah never mentioned her parents' embittered marriage and parlous circumstances or the effect these had on her childhood, but they must have made her determined to put herself and her own children out of the reach of such anxieties. Her lifelong obsession with the financial independence of women suggests that her mother's struggle to wrest control of her marriage portion from the men of the family had impressed her profoundly. And Mrs Jenyns's truculent, suspicious, and disillusioned personality probably left its mark on her in other ways. For all her restless vitality, Sarah, as she confessed herself, was never in her life 'one that could easily believe or hope in any thing'; and it was probably from her mother also that she derived the flaring temper which would come upon her uncontrollably 'like a fit of a Fever', and the outspokenness which began to get her into trouble from her earliest childhood.[32]

Yet despite the inevitable clashes of personality, there was no lack of affection between Mrs Jenyns and her 'litell Sairey'.[33] Nor was it any indication of neglect that while Sarah's brothers took their turns at St Albans grammar school, she herself, for all her naturally sharp wit, 'had litle if any advantage from Education'.[34] Many of her female contemporaries, including the Duke of York's two young daughters, shared this deficiency. But in Sarah's case it helped to aggravate an existing indiscipline, and for all her later efforts at self-improvement her intelligence was to remain essentially untrained and immature all her life: 'what a girl you are,' Alexander Pope told her when she was 82. Her self-devised system of arithmetic always looked 'as if a child had scrabbled over the paper, setting down figures here and there at random' (although it was noticed that the sums came out right in the end 'in defiance of Cocker').[35] For many years she continued to 'hate writing of all things', and 'never read any Book as she used to say but the World'.[36] But this last was an education which began before she was well out of the nursery.

Maid of Honour
1673–1678

FROM an early age Sarah's eyes were turned away from her quarrelsome, improvident family and towards the Court: the centre of the nation's affairs, and the place with which all her future fortunes and those of her family, for good or ill, were to be bound up. She already had the chief qualifications for success there: precocious self-assurance and a vivid prettiness, which unlike her sister's was to mature into lasting good looks. (Not otherwise vain of her appearance, Sarah herself considered that her hair, a reddish gold in colour and magnificently abundant, was 'the best thing I had'.)[1]

She afterwards gave her age at her first coming to live at Court as 12 or 13,[2] but there is no doubt about the date of her official appointment as maid of honour. The Duke of York's first wife died in 1671, and his second marriage to the 15-year-old Mary Beatrice d'Este, sister of the Duke of Modena, took place by proxy in September 1673. By the time of the new Duchess's arrival in England in November most of the appointments to her household had been settled. The unpopularity of a popish match did not diminish competition for places. At last, 'after virgins have allmost scratched out one an other's eyes to be maides of honor', as it was reported in October, these four posts were bestowed on Mary Kirk, Isabella Boynton, Eleanor Needham, and Sarah Jenyns.[3] Sarah was a few months past her thirteenth birthday. They were a representative group: the pretty daughters of minor courtiers and gentry, whose families were prepared to risk their chastity at the disreputable Restoration Court in the hope of attracting better matches for them than they might otherwise have hoped for.

Even so the appointments were not cheap to hold. Sarah later recalled crossly that she had been paid 'a ridiculous sum' (£20 a year) by way of salary, 'at the same time that I spent four or five hundred [pounds] a year for having that service'.[4] It cost this sum to follow the Court from place to place, to keep a personal maid and to provide elaborate clothing for the round of royal birthdays, mournings, plays, and balls. It is not surprising that Mrs Jenyns soon had to have lodgings in the Duke's residence, St James's Palace, as a refuge from her creditors, nor that this supervisory presence very quickly became irksome to her daughter. 'I will constran myself as much as is possible,' Sarah wrote ominously to Frances Hamilton at this time, in her large unformed scrawl, 'but som times she would provoke a sant.'[5]

'I came extream young into the Court,' she recalled years later, 'and had the luck to be liked by manny in it.'[6] Her closest friendships in these early years were not with the other maids of honour, but with two families just as closely associated with the Court, the Fortreys and the Villiers. The four Fortrey sisters, the daughters of Samuel Fortrey of Kew, had relatives in France, and it was while on a visit there that one of them wrote the charming letter which describes a vision of 'Miss Ginnings' at St James's: 'a young beuty coming down the great walk' amid a crowd of admirers, 'with rayes about her head like a sun'.[7] The eldest Fortrey sister, Mary, had 'a great deal of Sense', Sarah remembered, 'and I must own she gave me the best Advice I ever had, when I was so young and ignorant, that it was of great Use to me'.[8]

As for Barbara Villiers, who had inherited a full share of her famous family's charm and wit, Sarah recalled, 'I loved her . . . when I was but a child'; and as they grew older, ''tis certain I had more fondness and inclination for [her] then any body I ever knew in my life, except such as is not necessary to name'.[9] As the daughters of Lady Frances Villiers, governess to the Duke of York's children, Barbara and her sisters were brought up in the royal nursery at Richmond, where they were also neighbours and friends of the Fortreys at Kew. Sarah therefore fitted readily into the circle of young female courtiers who grew up alongside the Duke's daughters, the Ladies Mary and Anne; the former three, the latter five years younger than herself. Since the King had no legitimate children and the Duke no surviving sons, it was foreseeable that his daughters would one day succeed to the throne. Yet in the informal surroundings of the Restoration Court, the two girls associated freely with the children of their father's courtiers, adopting romantic nick-names so that they could be on equal terms with particular friends. When Barbara Villiers married Captain John Berkeley and incurred her mother's displeasure, it was Sarah who carried secret messages to her from Mary and Anne, under the very nose of their suspicious lady governess,[10] and at the beginning of 1675 she was chosen to act with the royal children in the masque *Calisto*, staged with elaborate costumes and scenery in the Great Hall of Whitehall Palace.[11] Even at this early period, she recalled, Anne expressed 'great kindness' for her, although their close friendship was still well in the future.[12]

Yet in spite of congenial companions and glamorous amusements, it did not take Sarah long to see 'the senceless parade of the Court' for what it was:

I think anyone that has common Sense or Honesty must needs be very weary of Everything One meets with in Courts . . . I protest I was never pleased but when I was a Child, and after I had been a Maid of Honour some Time, at Fourteen I wished myself out of the Court as much as I had desired to come into it before I knew what it was.[13]

In fact the life of a professional courtier, described by one onlooker as a state of 'extreame slavery & subjection',[14] could not have been more unsuited to her temperament. John Evelyn's biographical tribute to Margaret Blague, Sarah's fellow player in *Calisto*, gives some insight into the less attractive aspects of a maid of honour's existence: the constant dependence on the whims of royalty, the long hours in waiting in the drawing-room and bedchamber, the interminable card-playing and gossip. Of the formal gatherings in the drawing-room, Sarah herself remarked in old age, 'for my own part I never was young enough to like any thing of that sort'.[15] Yet there was no question of her leaving the Court prematurely. One of the attractions of a maid of honour's place in her case had been the customary provision of a dowry by the Court. By the terms of her parents' marriage settlement she and her sisters were entitled to portions of £2,000 apiece.[16] Frances and Barbara (the latter now married to a law student named Edward Griffith) were settled, but the continuing family quarrels and financial difficulties made it by no means certain that Sarah's share would be forthcoming. The bounty of the Court was therefore all she had to depend on to establish herself securely in life.

Conventionally, a maid of honour was expected to resign her post after a year or two in order to marry, and of those appointed with Sarah, Isabella Boynton did achieve this respectable end when she married the Duchess of York's master of the horse in 1674. But the atmosphere of the Restoration Court was more often conducive to what a friend of Sarah's described as 'dangerous and modish galantries' than to marriage, and the maids of honour were the most notorious victims of this state of affairs. In June 1675 Mary Kirk gave birth to a son in the maids' lodgings at St James's Palace. Since the Duke of York, the Duke of Monmouth, and the Earl of Mulgrave had all been rivals for her favour, the paternity of the child was in some doubt, but any dispute was prevented by its failure to survive. The only midwife had been the 'mother of the maids', an older woman who was supposed to exercise some sort of supervision over the morals and welfare of the girls. Mary Kirk retired in disgrace to

France.[17] 'Her Royal Highness has very ill luck with her maids of honour,' the Duchess's secretary reported only a few weeks later; for the Duke of Monmouth, 'ever in some amour', had now transferred his attentions to Eleanor Needham. The first to stumble on the secret was Isabella Boynton's replacement, Mary Trevor; then Sarah became involved, as Mary of York reported to her friend Frances Apsley, the daughter of the Duke of York's treasurer:

thay both beged very hartely that thay wold not tel, the duke of munmoth that thay wold not tell his wife & Mrs Nedham that thay wold tel no body of it but espetialy Mrs. Jenings, so thay all promising her thay wold not tel but mrs trevors maid sa[i]d the divel take her if she did not tel Mrs. Jenings the frist time she see her . . . Mrs Jinnings came hom and Mrs trevors maid was as good as her word, then the duches [of York] hering of it was mighty angry at it & now Mrs Needam is gone away & says nobody shal never hear of her more.[18]

Sarah, with her usual sincerity, had evidently made her opinion of such affairs quite clear. In fact she was the only one of the Duchess's maids not to be touched by scandal. 'Since I can remember,' she wrote in old age, 'though I can give no account how it came to be so, I never feared anything so much as to do the least thing that, I imagined, could possibly bring any shame upon me.'[19] Afterwards she was proud of having preserved her reputation at 'a Court where Vice and folly had all those marks of honour and approbation as might dazell the eyes of young persones'; and this in spite of the fact that she 'had as much, if not more, wit and beauty, than any of those whose unhappy conduct made their names more remarkable'.[20] There is no doubt that she had admirers. 'In a desart you could not want intruigs,' Mary Fortrey told her, 'and in a Court tis impossible.'[21] One of them was the young Lord Willoughby or Eresby, who in later years became Marquis of Lindsey and was jokingly dubbed 'the Duchess of Marlborough's lover', because he was once 'like to have thrown himself away on her'. At the time, however, Willoughby was a boy of Sarah's own age, well under the control of his parents, and in the end they chose to dispose of him to a Welsh heiress with a vast fortune.[22] However much he admired Sarah Jenyns, it is unlikely that he would have been permitted to think seriously of marrying her. Sarah had every reason to share her sister's maxim, that 'in so dangerous a situation, she ought to use her utmost endeavours not to dispose of her heart until she gave her hand'.[23] When at the age of 15 she fell in love with John Churchill, her future husband, she was to need all her strength of character to achieve this end.

Churchill, at 25, was chiefly remarkable for his good looks and the 'inimitable sweetness and gentleness' of his manner. From his appearance, a contemporary wrote, 'no expectations were given of the accomplished officer & soldier. His complexion was fine & delicate, the whole fabric of his body . . . indicated nothing like strength & vigor.' At an early stage of his youthful affair with the notorious Duchess of Cleveland, the knowing gossips of the Court predicted that 'he had too indolent an air, and too delicate a shape, long to maintain himself in her favour'.[24] His promotions at Court and in the army were put down to her influence and that of his sister Arabella.

These were always very sore subjects for Sarah. She pointed out quite truthfully that at the time his sister was seduced by the Duke of York, John Churchill had been a boy at St Paul's School, and therefore quite unable to prevent her dishonour.[25] Yet the unpalatable fact remained that he had largely owed his first appointments, as page in the Duke's household and ensign in the Guards, to Arabella's position—although it is equally true that she was to procure him no unearned advancement beyond that. Churchill's intermittent liaison with the Duchess of Cleveland, nearly ten years his senior and a superannuated mistress of the King, was too distasteful a matter for Sarah ever to mention directly. Its most famous episode, of which differing versions were bandied about for years afterwards, occurred early in 1672, when the King surprised the couple together and banished Churchill from the Court.[26] 'My poore son Jack . . . has bin very unfortunate ever since, in the continuance of the K[ing']s displeasure,' Sir Winston lamented in October, 'who notwithstanding the service he did in the late fight [the battle of Sole Bay] . . . would not give him leave to be of the D[uke']s bedchamber, allthough his highness declared he would not dispose of it to any body els.'[27]

Abandoning his career at Court for the time being, Churchill went abroad to serve in the French army at the end of 1672, and remained there for most of the next two years. During the campaign of 1674, as a youthful colonel of 24, he commanded an English regiment under Turenne, who recognized his promise and from whom, as he afterwards told Sarah, he learnt a great deal. In company with her brother-in-law, Sir George Hamilton, he earned the general's commendation for his conduct at the battle of Entzheim against the Imperial forces in October, and it was also in Hamilton's company that he returned to England at the end of that year.[28] Amid growing disapproval at the use of English troops to further the ambitions of Louis XIV, Churchill now put his French service behind him for good. His earlier indiscretions forgiven, he was made lieutenant-colonel of the Duke of York's regiment and finally allowed to take up his post as groom of the bedchamber. It was probably as a friend and colleague of her brother-in-law that he first became known to Sarah, but as members of the same household they now had many opportunities, in London and during the Court's summertime idyll at Windsor the following year, of furthering their acquaintance.[29]

Early in 1676 the Duchess of Cleveland left the Court altogether to live in Paris, taking with her a brood of illegitimate children of disputed paternity, the youngest of whom, a daughter, was supposed to be Churchill's. Court gossip reported that it was he who had put an end to the affair, having taken so much money from her that she was obliged to go abroad to recover her finances.[30] These rumours were hardly an auspicious basis for his courtship of Sarah, which began almost at once, when she was 'not more than fifteen'.[31] 'If I had as little love as yourself, I have been told enough of you to make me hate you,' she reminded him spitefully during one of their premarital quarrels. Yet it is clear that the relationship was as much of her seeking as his. 'You must give me leave to beg you will not condemne me for a vaine foole that I did believe you did love me,' Churchill protested, 'since both you and your actions did oblidge me to that belief.'[32] Of course it is not remarkable that Sarah should have fallen in love with a young man whom she afterwards described as 'handsome as an angel'; but in later life she insisted that it was not simply 'blind unreasonable passion' which had drawn her to her future husband, 'but the effect of Judgment, at an age when few exercise that faculty, [for] she then saw that good understanding and those excellent qualities that have since made him the wonder of the world'.[33]

They met constantly, in public at the balls, plays, and drawing-room gatherings of the Court, and in private in the maids' lodgings. Many of Churchill's early love letters relate to these assignations:

The reason that I writt thus early to you is for feare you should be gone abroad, and this would be a very long day, if you should be soe unkind as not to writt. I hope, althofte you do go to Mrs Fortrey, that you will be dressed att night, so that I may see you in the drawinge room. Pray writt t[w]o wordes before you goe. You aught to doe itt, for I love you with all my hart and soull.

And:

I was last night att the balle, in hopes to have seen what I love above my owne soull, but I was not soe hapy, for I could see you noe wher, soe that I did not stay above an hour . . . Pray lett me hear from you, and att what time you will be soe kind as to lett me com to you tonight. Pray, if you have nothing to doe, let 8 be the latest for I never am trully hapy but when I am with you.[34]

During the summer and autumn of 1676 the hospitality of the new French ambassador, Honoré de Courtin, and his compatriot, the Duchess Mazarin, helped to compensate the English courtiers for the lack of their usual summer recess while Windsor was being rebuilt. In the blazing hot weather the Duchess and her band of musicians lured the courtiers away from their usual haunts to take the air on the river, while Courtin made himself popular by indulging the young people's insatiable appetite for dancing. Sarah, as the sister of 'Madame Hamilton', who was well liked at the French court, was welcome at his select gatherings. In September, for example, Courtin gave a small entertainment for

Madame Mazarin, Madame de Sussex, Madame Hamilton's sister, and Mademoiselle Trevor, who is the prettiest of the Duchess of York's maids of honour and is not displeasing to the Duke. . . . The young ladies' admirers will be there too, and the girls will praise me for my good nature and are sure to declare that I know how to live. The door will be firmly closed. I shall play at ombre with Madame Mazarin, and we shall let the young people dance as much as they like.[35]

Churchill, whom Courtin wished to observe, would certainly have made one of the party. A new lieutenant-colonel was needed to command the Royal English regiment in French service, and Courtin, who knew that the Duke of York wanted the post for Churchill, did not consider him at all suitable. With his voyeuristic interest in the love intrigues of the English Court, he retailed to the French war minister all the details of the Cleveland affair and likened Churchill's current pursuit of Sarah Jenyns to Monmouth's seduction of the two maids of honour during the previous year; it was obvious to him that the young man preferred 'to serve the very pretty sister of Madame Hamilton' than to accept the post.[36]

But a week later Courtin added that Churchill had actually proposed to marry Sarah, only to find that his parents would not consent.[37] The family property in Dorset was burdened with debts, and they were already negotiating a match for him with the heiress of the playwright and notorious libertine, Sir Charles Sedley. Women in such a society, as Frances Hamilton once remarked, were commodities to be 'bought and sold'; it was a process in which Sarah herself was to engage readily and efficiently where her own children and grandchildren were concerned. But this did not prevent her from objecting to it very strongly when her own future was at stake, and certainly, although her expectations as a maid of honour would not bear comparison with her rival's, the Churchills had made a disconcerting choice. Katherine had a sharp wit but none of Sarah's beauty, and it was well known that her mother had been kept under restraint for many years. At 19 she already had the reputation of being 'as mad as her mother, and as vicious as her father'.

To Sarah the matter was plain: the Churchills were trying to marry their eldest son 'to a shocking creature for money'.[38]

Churchill was in love with Sarah Jenyns. But he was able and ambitious as well as a dutiful son, and he knew that not only the clearing of the family estates, but also his own advancement would depend on his command of large sums of money. The conflicting pressures preyed on his health so much that he talked of being in 'a consumption' and of going to France to recover. Courtin cynically commented that he only wanted an excuse to resume his less complicated relations with the Duchess of Cleveland in Paris. As for Sarah, Courtin noted that at one of the Duchess of York's balls in November, she had 'far more wish to cry than to dance'.[39] Characteristically her distress manifested itself, not in illness, but in violent irritation against the nearest objects to hand. When her mother tried to intervene, Sarah turned on her furiously, demanding that she be turned out of St James's altogether. But Mrs Jenyns, seeing her daughter involved with a man who was apparently not free to marry her, refused to go without her. In a blunt reference to Mary Kirk and Eleanor Needham, she declared that 'two of the maids had had great bellies att Court, and she would not leave her child there to have the third'. It took some weeks for Sarah to win this battle, her mother being 'commanded to leave the Court and her daughter in itt . . . the girle saying she is a mad woman'. It was an unedifying episode, and one which was remembered to Sarah's discredit long after the participants, who understood each other's flaring tempers only too well, had forgiven and forgotten it.[40] What it did demonstrate was that Sarah, at 16, was already determined to take control of her own life and happiness.

She dealt with her vacillating lover just as summarily. Her letters to him during this crisis are copies which she made herself in old age, presumably in order to suppress the uneducated handwriting and spelling of the originals. Yet their survival in any form is noteworthy, since she insisted on the destruction of all her other letters to her husband. Obviously she was proud of her handling of this difficult episode. 'As for seeing you,' she wrote to Churchill,

I am resolved I never will in private, nor in Publick if I could help it & as for the last I fear it will be some time before I can order it so as to be out of your way of seing me, but surely you must confess that you have been the falsest creature upon earth to me. I must own that I beleive I shall suffer a great deal of trouble, but I will bear it, and give God thanks, tho too late I see my error.

To punish him, she refused the letters in which he tried to explain himself, dismissed his complaints of ill health ('out of any bodys power to ease until the next new play'), and snubbed him in public so unmercifully that he at last grew resentful in his turn, protesting at being treated 'like a footman' and reminding her that she had led him to believe that she loved him.[41]

Eventually Sarah did consent to give him a hearing ('not that I can be persuaded you can ever justifye yourself'), but her message was plain, and remarkably forceful and articulate for a girl of 16 with no formal education: 'if it were true that you have that passion for me which you say you have, you would find out some way to make yourself hapy, it is in your power,' she wrote, and ''tis to no purpose to imagin that I will be made rediculous in the world when it is in your power to make me otherwise.'[42] Finally, in May 1677, the Sedley match was formally broken off, Churchill agreeing in return to join with his father in breaking the entail on the family estates to enable him to pay his debts.[43] Katherine Sedley, apparently with no regrets or hard feelings, went on to succeed Arabella Churchill as the Duke of York's mistress.

By this time Sarah had the moral support of her sister Frances. Sir George Hamilton had been killed in action during the campaign of 1676, leaving his widow grief-stricken and overwhelmed by debts. With her four small daughters she came over to England the following March to beg a pension from the Court.[44] It might have seemed a timely warning to Sarah of the perils of marriage to a professional soldier of small fortune. Then in the summer of 1677 there was an unexpected change in the circumstances of both sisters. Their brother Ralph died, leaving them, together with Barbara Griffith, co-heiresses of the family property in Hertfordshire. For all its burden of debts, this was a substantial inheritance. A contemporary called it 'a brave lordship', while Sarah herself, after years of experience in the acquisition and management of estates, later described it as 'one of the best manors I know anywhere and when it is well looked after, worth fifteen hundred pounds a year'.[45] The fact that she was now an heiress in her own right must have helped to reconcile Churchill's parents to the match. Sir Winston's only lingering regret was that Richard Jenyns had chosen to sell off the manor of Churchill, for that as well as Sandridge 'had come to my son in right of his wife, had it not been so unfortunatly alianated by her said father'.[46] Since Sarah was still a minor, her share of the inheritance had to be administered for her, probably by the family lawyer Anthony Guidott, who was to become one of her most trusted friends.[47]

Although the marriage with John Churchill was now agreed, Sarah was warier and more exacting than before, and even talked at one point of going back with her sister to France. Churchill was negotiating with the Duchess of York (who was no doubt glad to see one of her maids respectably disposed of) for an increased income with which to begin their married life, but when he tried to discuss his plan with Sarah, she told him capriciously to 'say nothing of it to the Dutches upon my account, & your own interest when I am not concernd in it will probably compass what will make you hapier then this can ever do'. Perhaps she relished this reversal of their former situations, when it was he who had talked of going to France. But the protracted and difficult courtship had left him incapable of responding lightly to this new crisis:

My hart is redy to breake. I wish 'tware over, for since you are growne so indifirent death is the only thing [that] can ease me. If that the dutchess could not have efected this, I was resolved to have maid another preposall to her, which I am confedent she might have efected, but itt would not have brought soe mutch mony as this. But now I must think noe more of it since you say we cannot be hapy . . . I wish with all my soull my fortune had bene so considerable as that it might have made you hapyer then your goeing out with your sister into France will doe, for I know tis the joye you prepose in that, that makes you think me faulty.

Sarah, realizing that the defensive ritual had been carried far enough, made him a more straightforward and reassuring reply:

if your intentions are honourable & what I have reason to expect you need not fear that my sisters coming can make any change in me, or that it is in the power of any body to alter me but yourself, & I am at this moment satisfyed that you will never do anything out of reason, which you must do if you ever are unjust to me.[48]

In November 1677 William of Orange was married to the Duke of York's daughter Mary at a private ceremony at St James's which Sarah attended. The Duke's master of the robes was to go to Holland as a member of the couple's new entourage, and by the Duchess's influence Churchill was allowed to buy his post.[49] The Churchills' own marriage must have taken place shortly after this, although its exact time and place are still unknown. At Court only the Duchess of York was in a secret which was not publicly acknowledged until well into the following year.

In these early difficulties Sarah's strength and independence of mind had stood her in good stead; whatever afterwards befell her, she had obtained what she described as 'the greatest comfort of this life, a very kind husband'.[50] Churchill's notorious carefulness about money, regarded with derision by his more spendthrift contemporaries, gave her a security which she had never known in her own family. 'From the very Beginning of his Life,' she wrote afterwards, 'he never Spent a Shilling beyond what his Income was.' Clearing the debts on his wife's inheritance and making proper provision for their future family was his absolute priority.[51]

In fact, in their preoccupation with financial security, the Churchills have been represented as beginning their married life in a state bordering on poverty. This is a considerable exaggeration. John had his regimental income, and even after he sold his groom's place in 1678 he continued to receive the income of £200 a year in the form of a pension, in addition to his salary as master of the robes.[52] He also had two private annuities, amounting to £600, supposedly bought with the proceeds of his affair with the Duchess of Cleveland.[53] Since his return from France he had lived in some style, keeping at least seven servants at his house in Jermyn Street; and purchases in the months before his marriage of a coach, embroidered harness, furniture, and gold lace for servants' liveries confirm that he could afford to provide his young wife with all the trappings of a fashionable existence.[54] As a former maid of honour Sarah was entitled to a pension of £300 a year, which she continued to receive regularly for the next ten years, until the Revolution put an end to it.[55] And her share of Sandridge was a valuable future asset, independent of the uncertainties of Court favour.

The secret marriage was in itself no particular indication of financial difficulties. Many marriages involving couples who were independent of their families took place privately at this period for no other reason than a desire to avoid publicity, or because of some uncertainty in their situation. This last particularly applied to the Churchills. The marriage of William of Orange to Mary of York had drawn England almost at once into his war with France. The Duke of York immersed himself in military preparations, intending to take command on the Continent in the event of hostilities, and John Churchill was given the colonelcy of one of the newly raised regiments. The prospect that he might have to go abroad at short notice probably made him and his wife decide to keep their marriage a secret while they waited on events.

When Churchill did travel to the Continent in April 1678, Sarah remained at Court, still addressed by her maiden name. 'I believe I was married,' she wrote of this awkward interlude later, '. . . but it was not known to anyone but the Duchess.'[56] She was therefore an eyewitness of the fresh scandal which now broke out in the maids' quarters. Gossip had it that the Duke of Monmouth, holding Mary Trevor responsible for the disclosure of his affair with Eleanor Needham, had encouraged the wealthy Thomas Thynne of Longleat to seduce her. As Sarah recalled the episode,

[Lady Trevor] persuaded Her Daughter to trust Mr Thynne and to go to Bed to him, because he said he wou'd not Marry any Body, till he knew whither he could have a Child. This Design succeeded, but he did not keep his Word. And I saw my self This Woman go out of the Gallery where the Maids Liv'd with

Infamy, wringing her Hands and saying, her Mother had undone her by her Advice.[57]

The affair can only have confirmed Sarah's distaste for Court life.

Churchill returned to England on 26 April, and in the following weeks the prospect of war receded.[58] Once his marriage was acknowledged, he intended that he and his wife should live near London so that he could continue his duties there, but that Sarah should have no contact with the Court.[59] The Jermyn Street lodgings, within a stone's throw of St James's, were hardly suitable. His parents' house at Minterne, in the remote and peaceful Dorset countryside, was to be their temporary home for the summer while he looked for a more suitable place to rent. Some time in May or June 1678 Sarah declared herself a married woman and resigned her maid's post to one of the Fortrey sisters.[60]

She found out very early what it was to be the wife of an ambitious courtier and soldier. Early in July there was a sudden flare-up of hostilities on the Continent, and Churchill was summoned up to London by the Duke.[61] Although he was not sent abroad immediately, for the rest of the summer he regularly made these long journeys to and fro between Minterne and London, writing to Sarah at every opportunity, as he was to do during the many separations of their married life. 'I will not complaine,' he reproached her gently on one occasion, 'but itt is now 3 weeks and above a goe sence you writt to me,' and 'when you writt you are afraid to tell me that you love me.' Sarah felt insecure, and with some reason. 'You are very unjust to me in makeing a doute of my love,' he protested to her: 'if I could followe my owne inclinations, I would never be from you . . . Here is noe talke but of warr, but I hope itt will end in a peace, soe that I may have my desier of being with you'; while to his colonel he had written only a week before, hoping that it would not be long before he had orders to come over.[62] But when he did travel to the Low Countries again in September, it was not, as he assured Sarah, to go into danger, but to supervise the dispersal of the army into winter quarters pending the conclusion of the treaty of Nijmegen. After a hard-working fortnight he was able to return to England, only to find the Court and the country in the grip of a crisis that was to disrupt his married life even further for the next four years.[63]

If Sarah had married a less able and ambitious man, a mere courtier or a country gentleman, her life would have been more secure and less remarkable. Afterwards, in times of stress, she was sometimes to reproach her husband for his ambition, and to claim that a quiet existence as mistress of a small country house would have been the life of her choice. Yet these moods, though genuine enough, were never more than passing. In reality, as she admitted herself, it was the qualities which

singled her husband out from his contemporaries that had attracted her
to him, and the dominant side of her nature was to rise to the
opportunities he provided: to join with him in founding a great family,
and to make a role for herself in the disturbed and divided times in which
they lived.

3

'True Born Whig'
1679–1684

THE Duke of York's conversion to Roman Catholicism had aroused suspicion and alarm from the moment of its first announcement in the early 1670s, presenting as it did the prospect of a successor to the throne who might try to re-establish his hated and feared religion in England and emulate the absolutist regime of his cousin, Louis XIV. In August 1678 this hostility was immeasurably sharpened when a dubious clergyman, Titus Oates, came forward with information of a plot to assassinate the King and subvert the government. Two circumstances helped to give credibility to his fabrications: the violent death in October of the magistrate before whom he had sworn his depositions, and the discovery among the papers of Edward Coleman, the Duke's former secretary, of evidence that he at least, with or without his master's consent, had been intriguing to extirpate the 'pestilent heresy' of Protestantism from England. On 3 December, the day Coleman was executed for high treason, Sarah remembered:

I dined with several of the Duke's old servants at St James's. And they were transported with Joy when they brought word he was dead without confessing any Thing. . . . The reason of that Joy was because they knew the Duke would have been hurt if Coleman had made any Discovery by his Confession. To prevent which . . . Coleman had been promised to be saved by a Reprieve before he was turned off the Ladder.[1]

The Duke might have been saved from Coleman, but by the end of the year he was fighting a powerful opposition party in Parliament, soon to be dubbed the Whigs, who sought to exclude him altogether from the succession. On 24 January 1679 the 18-year-old Cavalier Parliament was dissolved and the King yielded to pressure to send his brother into exile before the new Parliament met on 6 March.

When the Duke and Duchess reluctantly embarked for the Low Countries on 3 March, the skeleton staff they took with them did not include the Churchills. Having been elected to the new House of Commons, John Churchill was excused personal attendance while the session lasted, and when he travelled over with leave of absence early in May to report to his master, Sarah still did not go with him. By this time she was expecting their first child, and he was not the only member of the household who wanted to avoid the expense and upheaval of transporting his family to Brussels while the length of the Duke's stay there remained uncertain.[2] Meanwhile the Duke himself, his right to the succession under attack from the new House of Commons, constantly urged his brother to call him home to take part in the civil war which he now regarded as inevitable. Instead the King dissolved the first Exclusion Parliament in July 1679 and called another. The Duke had to resign himself to spending the winter in Brussels, and Churchill, who did not intend to stand for re-election, returned to England to fetch over Sarah and their household. They arrived in Brussels on 28 August and were joined a few days later by the Duke's daughter, Anne, on a visit to her father.[3]

The Duke worked off his frustrations in his usual fashion with violent hunting expeditions into the surrounding countryside, but for the women the only amusements were walking or driving about the streets in the long evenings. In one respect, however, the experience made a lasting impression on Sarah. 'I had alwaies . . . hated Popery, before I had ever looked into a booke of divinity,' she wrote in later life.[4] Anne, who was forbidden to visit the Roman Catholic churches and monasteries, found enough to affront her Protestantism in 'theire images, which are in every shope & corner of the street'.[5] Sarah's sight-seeing was not so restricted. Accustomed only to the proscribed and fugitive Catholicism of England, she had her strongest prejudices confirmed by what she saw. In justifying her part in the Revolution of 1688, she explained that 'I had seen so much of the cheats & nonsense of that Religion abroad, that it gave me a greater prejudice to it, then it is possible for any body to have that has never been in a Catholick Country'.[6]

The Churchills had barely settled in Brussels, however, when the King was taken seriously ill, and his brother immediately set out for England to safeguard his right to the throne. He travelled in disguise with only a tiny entourage, Churchill representing 'the best man in the company'. After a gruelling journey on horseback they arrived in London on 1 September, only to find the King already out of danger. Four days later Churchill was off again: to Paris, bearing a message from his master to Louis XIV. From there he returned to Brussels at the end of the month, shortly before the Duke arrived to escort his family back to England in person;[7] for their place of exile had now been changed to Edinburgh. At the end of October the Duke left London on his slow progress north, with the promise that he would be allowed to return after the prorogation of Parliament in January. But he still insisted on having Churchill with him, although Sarah's confinement was now only a matter of days away.

By this time Churchill was beginning to form close ties with the three youngish men—Robert, Earl of Sunderland, Laurence Hyde, and Sidney Godolphin—who now made up the King's inner ministry. With Hyde, the Duke's Protestant brother-in-law and most unquestioning supporter, he had the common bond of their personal allegiance. Godolphin, 'the silentest and modestest man that was perhaps ever bred in a Court',[8] was soon to become the Churchills' closest friend. In 1675, after a nine years' courtship, he had married Margaret Blague, Sarah's fellow player in *Calisto*, only to lose her tragically at the birth of their first child. Lady Sunderland, bustling, intriguing, and kindly, had taken the widower and his motherless little son under her wing.[9] Now Sarah's plight, facing the dangers of childbirth for the first time in her husband's absence, also aroused her protective instincts. 'Lady Sunderland . . . told me that she toke itt very unkindly that I had not left [you] in her caire,' Churchill wrote to Sarah as he set out on the first stage of his journey north, 'but however she saide, she would take caire of you in spite of me, therefor pray when you see her be very sivell to her, for as things now stand itt is very fitt you should be well with her.'[10]

By the time he reached Edinburgh he had the news that Sarah had been safely delivered of a daughter, Henrietta, or Harriet as they always called her. But again Sarah reacted badly to the separation, evidently suggesting that he was finding greater attractions in Edinburgh than in London. In return he poured out a succession of the clumsy, ill-spelt, eloquent, and moving love letters which she could never bring herself to destroy, even when she read them over in extreme old age, intending to do so before she died. 'I am not soe unreasonable as to exspect you should not be concerned if I waire cockett, and maid love to anny other woman,' he protested, 'but sence I doe not, and love only you above my owne life, I cant but think but you are both unjust, and unkind, in having a suspition of me, after soe many ashurances as I have given you to the contrary.' He was suffering from the violent headaches that affected him all his life at times of stress: 'all my misfortunes I attribute to my being from you, which after this time, I hope never to be soe long absant as long as I live'; and

althofte I belive you love me, yett you doe not love soe well as I, soe that you can not be trully sensable how mutch I desier to be with you. I swaire to you the forest [first] night in which I was blesed in having you in my armes, was not more earnestly wish'd for by me, than now I doe, to be againe with you, for if ever man loved woman trully well I now doe you, for I swaire to you waire we unmaryed, I would beg you on my knes to be my wife, which I would not doe, did I not estime you, as well as love you.[11]

It was not until 24 February that the York household returned to London, and he was reunited with his wife and saw his daughter for the first time.

But their troubles were by no means over. By the summer of 1680 the Exclusionists had renewed their attacks on James, and with the meeting of Parliament imminent, Sunderland and Godolphin forced the issue. If the Duke did not go back into exile voluntarily, the latter predicted, 'he will be forced to leave within fourteen days, and the King with him'.[12] When the Duke and Duchess left for Edinburgh again on 20 October, Churchill, who was now seen to have supplanted his cousin George Legge as 'the only favorite of his master', had no choice but to abandon his small family again and go with them. As long as the exile lasted, James wrote inexorably, 'I would not willingly have Churchill from me'.[13] With Sunderland and Godolphin now declaring for Exclusion, Churchill drew closer to Hyde and George Legge, and spent his time travelling to and fro between London and Edinburgh to concert measures with them for the Duke's return. He made his first visit in late January and early February 1681, when he was involved in the secret negotiations for the subsidy from Louis XIV (afterwards denounced by his wife with Whiggish fervour), which was intended to reduce Charles II's dependence on his troublesome Parliaments. Dispatched again after the dissolution of the brief third Exclusion Parliament in March, he spent the greater part of May and June in London, pressing unsuccessfully for an end to his master's exile.[14]

Sarah was now expecting another child, and by ill luck her husband's departure for Scotland on 22 June meant that she had to cope alone with the death of their daughter Harriet a few days later.[15] He immediately returned to London, arriving in time for the christening on 29 July of another daughter, also called Henrietta.[16] Before he left London again ten days later he arranged for Sarah to join him in Edinburgh as soon as she was able to travel, and she set out early in September, leaving the baby behind to be nursed in the south. At Berwick Churchill came to meet her, accompanied by Laurence Hyde on his return from a fruitless mission to persuade the Duke to conform outwardly to the Church of England as a condition of his return to Court. James's adamant refusal left him and his household with no foreseeable end to their difficulties.[17]

To a friend who was about to set out for Scotland many years later, Sarah recalled the country as she had known it at this time, telling him that it was 'not very agreable, but she hoped it was mended since'.[18] Certainly Edinburgh was primitive in comparison with London. Yet the

Duke himself assured one of his correspondents with defensive cheerfulness that 'we here do not passe our tyme so ill as you in England thinke we do, for we have plays, ride abroad when tis good weather, play at Basset, and have a great deale of good company'.[19] His daughter Anne, now 16, had arrived in Edinburgh shortly before Sarah for a prolonged visit. The next eight months spent together in the isolated Court at Holyrood were to give the two young women every opportunity to renew their childhood acquaintance.

Yet Sarah's intelligence was never fully engaged by Court pastimes, and this political crisis which was affecting her own life so intimately now made her take her first serious interest in the trials of strength between King and Parliament, in which her father and grandfather had played an active part. And in spite of the threat which the policies of the first Whigs posed to her personal fortunes, there appears to have been no doubt where the sympathies of this 'true born Whig' lay. In the last years of Queen Anne she was prepared to defend their conduct on the basis of 'more than thirty yeares' observation, that is from the very beginning of the Exclusion crisis.[20] Later still she became disillusioned with political parties and their leaders,

[but] I am persuaded that I shall never change as to that principle which I saw very good reason for as soon as I could understand anything at court. I knew that King Charles and King James were both Roman Catholicks, taking mony from the King of France to betray their own truth and country . . . and at the same time I saw that neither of these Kings could indure a whigg, and were very fond of the torys . . . [and] as to what is called the whigg notion that I will never part with. That Parliaments should punish ill ministers and by that means oblidge weak or bad Princes to keep their coronation oaths . . .[21]

These were remarkably independent opinions for the young wife of a professional courtier, and what she saw and heard in Scotland only served to confirm them. Shortly after her arrival, six Scottish dissenters were brought to trial for declaring that Charles II was not their lawful sovereign and calling him a tyrant and a covenant-breaker. Five were hanged and their heads impaled on one of the city gates. Even the Duke, who loathed their principles, could not help pitying their fate.[22] But Sarah's comments in old age indicate that her sympathies had been with the Covenanters' opinions as well as with their sufferings:

I . . . was much grieved at the Trials of several People that were hang'd for no Reason in the World, but because they would not disown what they had said, that King Charles the Second had broke his Covenant. I have cried at some of these Trials, to see the Cruelty that was done to these Men only for their choosing to die rather than tell a Lye.[23]

Early in 1682, when Sarah had been about six months in Edinburgh, the Duke was allowed to make a visit to the Court at Newmarket, where he at last induced the King to put an end to his exile. In May he set out again for Scotland to escort the rest of his household home. But on the outward voyage the frigate *Gloucester* on which he was embarked went aground on a sandbank off the East Anglian coast and sank with the loss of most of those on board. Churchill and George Legge were among the few saved. Called at the last minute into the Duke's long boat, they were ordered to use their swords to keep off others who were struggling frantically to save their lives. When her husband arrived in Edinburgh, Sarah recalled later, he 'blamed the Duke to me excessively for his Obstinacy and Cruelty. For if he would have been persuaded to go off himself at first, when it was certain the Ship could not be saved, the Duke of Marlborough was of the Opinion that there would not have been a Man lost.'[24]

Back in England, the Court retired to Windsor for the summer, but Sarah, who was again in what she called 'whimsicall circumstances', remained behind when her husband's duties required his attendance there.'I hope in God you are out of all dainger of miscarying,' he wrote on one of these occasions, 'for I swaire to you I love you better then I doe all the rest of the world putt together.'[25] When the Court returned to London for the winter, he was rewarded for his four years of arduous service with the Scottish title, Lord Churchill of Eymouth, and he and his wife left their Jermyn Street house to take up new lodgings in St James's Palace.[26] Clearly he was not following his resolution of keeping Sarah away from the Court. The reason, probably, was her growing favour with Lady Anne, in which there was now a decisive development.

At the end of October 1682 the Earl of Mulgrave was dismissed from Court for what was alleged to be a clandestine courtship of Anne, and along with him went her chief female favourite, Mary Cornwallis, accused of having acted as go-between in the affair.[27] This young woman was a Roman Catholic and the daughter of Katherine Cornwallis, one of the Duchess of York's bedchamberwomen;[28] yet the friendship had been allowed to go unchallenged until now, despite Anne's strictly Protestant upbringing. By 1682, according to Sarah, it was of three or four years' standing, during which time Anne had written, 'it was believed, above a thousand letters full of the most violent professions of everlasting kindness'; indeed, 'K[ing] Charles us'd to say, No man ever loved his Mistress, as his niece Anne did Mrs Cornwallis'. Sarah told this story at the height of her bitterness after her own loss of favour. Omitting all mention of Mulgrave, she attributed Mary Cornwallis's dismissal to the Duke of York's distaste for the fervid feeling between the two girls, improved by the Hydes, who feared the consequences of Anne's friendship with a papist; and she went on to describe how Anne, for all her professions of friendship, 'in a fortnight after this separation, seem'd as perfectly to have forgot this Woman, as if she had never heard of Her'.[29]

From George Legge, however, comes another version of the story which implicates Sarah:

Mrs. Cornwallis, a Roman catholic, was in great favour with the princess Ann, and had introduced her friend Mrs. Churchill . . . who soon found, if she could get rid of her introductress, she should have the entire confidence to herself: and bishop Compton was made use of, to take notice at the council of the dangerous consequence such a woman's being about the princess might have; upon which Mrs. Cornwallis was ordered never to come into her presence more.[30]

Sarah was certainly well acquainted with Mary Cornwallis, who was a close friend of the Fortreys and a distant relation of the Churchills. Nevertheless her own friendship with Anne had come about not by this means, but as a natural result of her family's long association with the York household. In any case it is clear that neither Anne nor Mary Cornwallis regarded Sarah as their betrayer. She continued on visiting terms with the cast-off favourite until the Revolution, and twenty years later they were still in intermittent contact.[31]

In fact Legge was not a reliable witness against Sarah by this time, because he had a powerful grudge against the Churchills for supplanting him in the Duke of York's favour. The alliance between them and Laurence Hyde (now Earl of Rochester), which had served the Duke well in adversity, was breaking up. Legge told an avid and credulous Samuel Pepys 'of the Duke of York's hardness to him and how Churchill was made what he is by my Lord Rochester, only to lessen him; and that all he knows Churchill recommends himself by, is his lying with their wives, which he says is most certain as to my ladies Rochester and Sunderland'.[32] The letters of Lady Sunderland show that even Sarah did not take this gossip seriously. 'My service to Lord Churchill,' she concluded one of them at this time; 'tell him my Lady Rochester says she has now health and good humour enough to do any thing. I hope hee'l thanke me for this timly good advice.'[33] All the same, the disappearance of Mulgrave and Mary Cornwallis left a gap in Anne's emotional life which Sarah was quickly able to fill. When a third daughter was born to the Churchills in February 1683, Anne stood godmother to the child, who was named after her. John Churchill encouraged the friendship, realizing, if his wife did not, that the favour of a Protestant member of the royal family was an asset to be carefully cultivated. 'Lady Anne askes for you very often,' he prompted her shortly after the baby's birth, 'soe that I think you would doe well if you writt to her to thanke her for her kindnesse in inquiring after your helth.'[34]

If nothing else, the Mulgrave affair had demonstrated that it was high time for Anne to be suitably married. Early in 1683 a bridegroom was found for her in the person of Prince George, brother of the King of Denmark, and in June John Churchill was sent to escort him to England. Blond good looks and a soldierly reputation redeemed an otherwise unremarkable personality, but there was no getting away from the fact that the Prince was 'heavy' both mentally and physically. Yet he and Anne found each other agreeable enough, and after a token period of courtship, during which Sarah acted as one of the chaperones, the marriage took place on 28 July. Anne's household was now remodelled on an adult pattern, though on a scale which suited her limited income. She was to have a groom of the stole and one other lady of the bedchamber, the former with a salary of £400 a year and the latter with £200. Her governess, Lady Rochester, was to retire, but in her place, much to Anne's disgust, the Hydes put forward Rochester's sister-in-law, Lady Clarendon, to be groom of the stole. 'She lookt like a Madwoman, & talked like a Scholar, which the Pr[incess] thought agreed very well together,' was Sarah's dry summing-up of this utterly uncongenial relationship. The candidate for the other post was Lady Thanet, another guardian of the Hyde interest, and another middle-aged great lady with whom Anne could have nothing in common. In Sarah's words, 'the P[rincess] begd she might not have her, & the Duke comply'd with her'.[35]

It was at this point that John Churchill prompted his wife to offer her services, and used his influence with the Duke to have them accepted.[36] In itself the post was not inviting; as Sarah pointed out, it involved 'a good deal of trouble & attendance' in return for 'so small a sallary that people that were either usefull or agreeable did not care for it'.[37] Yet in the jockeying for power and influence at Court which was going on at this time it was not without significance, and for this reason, as Sarah records, the Hydes did all they could to prevent her getting it. In spite of his support for Exclusion, Sunderland had been allowed to return to Court, and Rochester was discontented at his declining status. 'My Lord Rochester wanted to have one in my Place that would be intirely obedient to Him: Which he had experienced I would not be,' Sarah wrote afterwards, 'And this was really all the Offence I ever gave Him, or any of his Family.'[38] It was the beginning of a long personal and political rivalry between them for influence over Anne.

Sarah's Whig sympathies must have added to the Tory Hydes'

uneasiness about her. Shortly before Anne's marriage the leading Exclusionist, Lord Russell, was executed for alleged complicity in the Rye House assassination plot against the King. Sarah, who was friendly with his widow, wrote afterwards of the horror she felt at this Court revenge against the Whigs, and (the first hint of political differences which were to become so important in the future) of her disappointment that Anne showed no similar feelings: 'all I could prevaile on my selfe to doe was to say nothing but I could not commend & flatter & raile at the unfortunate sufferers.'[39] At a time when the most vigorous denunciation of Russell and his associates was expected of all Court supporters, this would have been enough to show where her sympathies lay.

When Anne showed signs of weakening over Sarah's appointment, in the face of the Hydes' opposition and her father's irritation at the whole affair, Sarah made it clear that she was not pleased; the Hydes had evidently aroused her combativeness. Anne's urgently self-justifying reply demonstrates the hold Sarah already had over her affections:

Oh deare Lady Churchill lett me beg you once more not to beleeve that I am in fault . . . I will try once more be he never so angry; but oh donot lett this take away your kindnes from me for I asure you tis the greatest trouble in the world to me & I am sure you have not a faithfuller freind on earth that loves you better then I do. My eyes are full, I canot say a word more . . .[40]

In the end Sarah was confirmed in the post. The accident of having attracted Anne's friendship and the advantage her husband made of it had returned her to the role of professional courtier: not the one she would have chosen for herself, nor one for which she was at all suited by temperament, but the only means open to her as a woman to contribute to her family's advancement and provide against the difficulties that might lie ahead in the divided Court. She and Anne were to remain bound together as mistress and servant for the next twenty-seven years, and as professed friends for all but the last few years of that time. Since both the friendship and its eventual break-up were to have the most momentous consequences for the fortunes of the Churchills and their political allies, it is worth pausing for a moment to examine the basis of the relationship at this early stage.

Although none of Sarah's letters for this period survives, there is no reason to question her later testimony that she felt a genuine affection and sense of duty towards her mistress.[41] Nevertheless, it is unlikely that she ever fully reciprocated the Princess's intense feeling for her. What Anne chiefly craved was a friend with whom, in private at least, she could keep up the illusion of equality.[42] But for Sarah, who had no need of these fantasies, the relationship with a daughter of the heir to the throne could never be other than a public one. It involved her in time-consuming and ill-paid Court duties which took her away from her family, and was to subject her increasingly to the pressures and conflicts of public life. In return she expected not just the personal intimacy of this rather dull girl five years her junior, but the tangible benefits of royal favour for herself and her husband and children.

In her private life she had much that was more rewarding than her relationship with Anne: a successful marriage and a growing family, as well as her many friendships among the more sophisticated adult society of the Court. Always ready to 'tumble out' her own mind in waspish, energetic talk, she set a high value on being entertained in her turn. Her closest friends at this time were Frances Bathurst (the former Frances Apsley, now married to one of the Duke's household officers) and the irrepressible Barbara Berkeley, both of them known as witty talkers. Anne was well aware of this competition and wistfully jealous of it. 'I hope that next to Lord Churchill I may claime the first place in your heart,' she wrote; 'I know I have a great many Rivalls which makes me sometimes feare loosing what I so much value.'[43] Her preferred method of enjoying her favourite's company was therefore to be shut up with her in solitary tête-à-têtes, and there is no doubt that Sarah found these something of a strain. Whatever the Princess might pretend, the difference in rank was always to be a barrier to friendship on genuinely equal terms. It was not until Sarah had been in the household for more than a year that Anne asked her 'not to call me Your Highness at every word',[44] and the famous Morley–Freeman nicknames lay well in the future. Sarah wrote later of the tedium of being so much alone with one who had to be treated with deference despite the 'Insipid Heaviness' of her talk. This was written in great bitterness after the break-up of their friendship; but even in old age, when she had retracted all other criticisms of her former mistress, Sarah still insisted that 'nobody can maintain that she was wise or entertaining in conversation', and many of Anne's surviving letters bear her out.[45]

Shared problems of motherhood would soon provide a temporary bond between them: Anne had the first of many miscarriages a bare nine months after her marriage, and Sarah also had her griefs and anxieties on this score, though they were not to be so tragically frequent. Opposition to the Court in the two following reigns was also to draw them closer together and bury their political differences for the time being. But in its inequality and (on Sarah's part) its large and inevitable element of constraint and self-interest, as well as in the essential incompatibilities of temperament and political outlook between the two women, the friendship always contained the seeds of its own destruction. Less surprising than its eventual break-up is that it should have lasted as long as it did.

Charles II's reign was now well into its peaceful last phase, Tory-dominated and untroubled by the challenges of Parliament. Whatever Sarah's misgivings about this method of government, it was a time for settling down after the disruption of the past five years. While Godolphin had risen to be a treasury commissioner, there was no question of a ministerial appointment for Churchill. Rumours that he was a candidate for the secretaryship of state were greeted with hilarity, and said to be occasioned by his attempts to learn to write.[46] In peacetime his military duties were largely ceremonial, and he appeared very much as a family man, touchingly devoted to his wife and two little daughters. 'You can not imagine how I am pleased with the children,' he wrote to Sarah while she was at Tunbridge with Anne in the summer of 1684,

for thay having noe body but ther maid thay are soe fond of me that when I am att home thay will be always with me, a kissing and huging me . . . Mis is pulling me by the arme that she may writt to her dear mama, soe that I will say noe more, only beg that you will love me always soe well as I love you, and then we can not but be hapy.[47]

In the winter the Churchills left St James's Palace to move into new lodgings in the Cockpit, the portion of Whitehall Palace next to St James's Park which had been assigned to Anne after her marriage.[48] This was to be their London home for the next seven years. Although not yet wealthy, they were gradually becoming people of substance, able to maintain a considerable bank balance and make the first of many loans to the exchequer.[49] By this time Sarah was beginning to take control of their day-to-day affairs. Her husband's attitude to money, reassuring in the first years of their marriage, was becoming an irritant; she found that he continued to make her 'uneasy . . . in little expences in his family' long after it had ceased to be justified by their circumstances, while at the same time, sooner than have the trouble of scrutinizing a tradesman's or steward's account, he would let himself be 'intolerably cheated'. By this curious mixture of frugality and 'indulgent gentleness', she wrote, 'he could not manage matters so as was convenient for our Circumstances, [and] this obliged me to enter into the management of my family'.[50]

Their next step was to acquire land, the most secure form of property in an unstable society. Having joined with Sir Winston Churchill in breaking the entail on his Dorset estates, they no longer had expectations from this quarter, so that it was Sarah's inheritance which now provided them with a country estate suitable to their rank. Barbara Griffith and

her only child had died within a few months of each other in 1679,
bringing her share of the Jenyns property back into the family.[51] When
Frances Hamilton made a second marriage to Richard Talbot, another
Roman Catholic of military background and one of the Court's chief
advisers on Irish affairs, the time was ripe to resolve the ownership of the
estate. In the autumn of 1684 the Churchills were able to buy out
Frances's one remaining share of Sandridge and Holywell at the cost of
£11,000.[52] This gave them not only land, but useful electoral influence in
St Albans and a house conveniently near London, where they could raise
their children in country air. Within the year they engaged an architect of
rising reputation, William Talman, to remodel the dilapidated Tudor
mansion, retaining the picturesque gallery and cloisters but adding a
modern three-storied wing facing north towards the town. Using their
influence in the borough, they had the highway diverted away from the
west front to accommodate these somewhat makeshift alterations and
give their new home more of the air of a country house.[53]

Having now acquired a title and an estate, they must have looked
forward to the birth of a son and heir. On at least one occasion they were
disappointed, as Sarah recalled in this cautionary tale when her favourite
granddaughter was expecting her first child:

I have a great dread of your driving a chaise, because I know the reaching out
your arm to whip the horse is a very improper motion at this time. . . . What
makes me so apprehensive of reaching out your arms, is, because I miscarried of
a son myself from follies which I committed when I was very young . . . [54]

Exactly when this happened is not clear, but it was probably in the
otherwise unexplained interval between the birth of Sarah's daughter
Anne in February 1683 and that of her first surviving son nearly four
years later. In October 1684, at a time when outdoor pastimes were very
popular with the ladies of the Court, she was reported to be 'in a fair way
of recovery' from an unspecified illness or accident which may have been
connected with a miscarriage.[55] Whatever the reason, there was to be an
anxious and prolonged interval before her next pregnancy.

The first disturbed years of Sarah's married life were an important
formative period for her, not only forcing her to take stock of her
political views, but bringing her, unexpectedly, royal favour and an
independent position at Court; and with these came the possibility of a
partnership with her husband in furthering his career and providing for
their young family. The next reign was to be a testing time for these new
allegiances and roles.

'Arbitrary Power & Popery'
1685–1688

WHEN Charles II succumbed to a stroke on 6 February 1685, having lingered just long enough to be received into the Roman Catholic Church, Sarah for one shed no tears for the merry monarch, under whose reign her whole life to date had been passed. To her he was simply the pensioner of France, the King who during the Popish Plot had 'suffered many People to be hang'd that he knew to be innocent', and who had connived at the judicial murder of the Whig leaders after the Rye House plot; in short, he had done 'everything that was wrong'. She was among the many who were convinced that he had been poisoned by the Jesuits to allow his brother to succeed.[1] Yet the short reign of James II, which she recollected as a time of almost continuous fears and apprehension, opened promisingly enough. Even with hindsight she always preferred him to his brother; he was at least open about his Catholicism, and 'his having a mind to establish his own religion was natural & well ment to save so many wicked peoples souls'. Although he lacked the easy charm and quick wit of Charles II, he was more conscientious and hard-working, and a better 'manager for the public'.[2] Whitehall under his rule became a markedly less disreputable place to live.

Despite past opposition, James succeeded to the throne amid demonstrations of loyalty.[3] Most people were reassured by his initial readiness to ally himself with the Anglican Tories, for at the beginning of the reign, as Sarah noted, 'next to the Roman Catholics', the Hydes 'had all the power'.[4] Yet although Rochester and his brother Clarendon were reassuringly staunch Protestants, their relations with the Churchills had gone sour. The latters' friendship was now entirely with the Sunderlands and their inseparable ally Godolphin. Sunderland remained as secretary of state, while the more dispensable Godolphin was demoted from the treasury, where Rochester now reigned supreme. For Churchill there was still no prospect of a ministerial appointment, but he received an English peerage, and remained James's favourite personal servant.

Although he told a leading French Protestant that if the King should ever attempt to alter the established religion, he would serve him no longer,[5] for the time being he joined the throng of courtiers pressing forward to pledge their loyalty.

James was therefore in a strong position to face the first major challenge of his reign, when the Duke of Monmouth and a handful of followers sailed from Holland to Lyme Regis in June 1685 and summoned the west country dissenters to rebellion against their popish King. Churchill was sent with a detachment of troops to put down the rising. It was his first independent command, and he was anxious to use it to demonstrate his zeal and competence. In his letters to Sarah he complained of the continual rains, which 'makes us not press the Duke of Monmouth so much as I think he should be'.[6] Sarah's attitude was less straightforward. With Monmouth himself, the seducer of maids of honour, she can have had little sympathy; but his cause was a different matter. The following winter Lord Grey, the Duke's only aristocratic accomplice, was able to save his life by giving evidence against his associates. 'I remember a tryall where I saw my Lord Gray a witnesse, who had great honours don him in King William's Reign,' she wrote years later, 'but indeed I thought it a sad thing to appear against ones friends after being ingaged in a cause that I shall allways think glorious, to defend the libertys of England from Arbitrary power & popery.'[7]

But this was with hindsight. At the time there was the complication that these defenders of English liberty were putting her husband's life at risk. When the strain of keeping up appearances at Court became too great, she took refuge at St Albans, where Lady Sunderland and Barbara Berkeley kept her informed by letter of the progress of the western campaign. The crisis drew Sarah so close to these two friends that Anne grew uneasy. When the news came of Monmouth's defeat at Sedgemoor on 6 July and of Churchill's emergence from the battle with safety and credit, she hastened to assure Sarah that 'nether of your other t[w]o freinds who writt can be half so glad of any thing of good that happens to you as I am tho may be they can expres themselves beter'.[8] Churchill, on his way home from the west country, begged Sarah to come to town to meet him, for 'I shall be at no ease till I am in your arms'.[9] When Anne left shortly afterwards to take the waters at Tunbridge Wells, the couple remained behind together in London. Sarah was just beginning to recover from the effects of her illness or miscarriage of the previous autumn. 'I long mightely to see my dear Lady Churchill,' Anne reassured her, 'but I hope you dont think me so unreasonable as to take any thing ill that you do when tis on your Lords account,' and 'since you have what you have not had so long I beleeve you must not yet begin the purging waters.'[10]

Her absence left Anne in the unrelieved company of Lady Clarendon, who, as she told Sarah, 'growes more & more naucious every day'.[11] She was therefore delighted when Sunderland, as part of his campaign to undermine the Hyde interest at Court, had Clarendon appointed Lord Lieutenant of Ireland, and his wife was obliged to resign her post as groom of the stole in order to accompany him. The Princess immediately promoted Sarah into her place, thus doubling her salary from £200 to £400 a year. Although this remained a modest return for the attendance involved, there were now opportunities for making more substantial profits. Anne delayed the appointments of two pages until after Lady Clarendon's departure, expressly so that Sarah could have the advantage of them. Although the practice of selling Court appointments afterwards fell into disrepute, at the time, as Sarah explained defensively, 'every body that had the disposal of places look'd upon it as their right . . . and were no more asham'd of doing it, than of receiving their Salarys, or their Rents out of the Country. And upon this establish'd custom and direction from the Princess I must own I did sell these two places, which . . . came to twelve hundred pounds.'[12]

The appointment as groom of the stole to the Princess marks Sarah's real entry into public life. Anne was now the only Protestant member of the royal family in England, and the only member of it, Protestant or Catholic, believed to be capable of producing an heir to the throne. While the Queen was constantly ailing in health and Mary's marriage to William of Orange remained childless, Anne had given birth to a daughter in the spring of 1685 and by the autumn was pregnant again. The senior appointments to her household had therefore become matters of public concern, and particularly so in the case of Sarah, who was seen to have a virtual monopoly of her mistress's friendship and confidence. It was at this period that the first assessments of her character and influence began to appear in the dispatches of the foreign envoys.[13]

Yet at the time Sarah herself appeared to be less concerned with her new status than with the inroads her Court duties were making into her private life. To fill the vacancy left by her promotion, Sunderland sought to consolidate his position further by putting forward his elder daughter, Lady Anne Spencer. An unmarried girl would not normally have been considered a suitable candidate, as he and his wife were well aware. 'Thers twenty objections to be answerd . . . ,' Lady Sunderland admitted to Sarah, 'but wee are all resolved to pursue this pretension and to owe the favor of it to you.'[14] Sarah also had ends of her own to serve. To outside observers it appeared that the Spencer appointment had been forced on the Princess by her father at Sunderland's instigation.[15] On the evidence of Lady Sunderland's letters to Sarah, however, it had also come about as the result of a private agreement by which Sarah sought to lighten the burden of her own Court duties. Lady Sunderland acknowledged that it had been bestowed on condition that 'whenever the princess went any Jurneys I would go to[o] . . . and that my daughter would gladly wait whenever you would have her'.[16]

In fact the appointment was not a success for any of them. The Princess, whose personal jealousy of Lady Sunderland soon grew into a violent distrust on political grounds, felt that she had to be constantly on her guard in the presence of her new lady, 'knowing from whence she comes'.[17] The girl herself had not been in the post for more than a few months when she had a prolonged fit of illness which left the whole duty of attendance on Sarah, who was irritable and out of sorts herself at this time. In fact by the spring of 1686 she was at last expecting another child—her first since she had entered the Princess's service—but for some months she remained a prey to 'dismall thoughts', refusing to believe that her constant sickness was a sign of pregnancy, rather than simply of ill health.[18] As a result she picked an unreasonable quarrel with Lady Sunderland about her daughter's failure to perform her duties. 'I must needs own I am extremly out of humour and troubled, having once belived I should live easyly in the place I am in,' she burst out when Lady Sunderland asked the reason for her coldness, '[but] I am disapointed of that and likly to be a slave . . . for I cannot belive it possible that you ever designed going Jurneys as the princess may do and then am I, sicke or well, to wait and be weary of my life.'[19] The matter was patched up, and did not prevent Sarah from spending part of the summer of 1686 with Lady Sunderland at Althorp. By this time she was reassured about the reality of her pregnancy, and the jealous Princess, left behind once more at Tunbridge, pointed out that she risked a miscarriage by going on so long a journey.[20]

Sarah's discontent with her situation had now become acute; she complained afterwards that if she were expected to wait constantly in public as well as to keep the Princess company in private, she would never have had a moment to do anything for herself.[21] On her return from Althorp she paid Anne a brief visit at Tunbridge and had the matter out with her, evidently with some heat. 'I must desire you to pardon what I said the night before you went away,' Anne wrote, in a letter which acknowledged that their relationship had passed beyond that of mistress and Court servant, '. . . for I now see my errour & . . . desire nothing more but to have you live as easily with me as you would with any body els.'[22] By the autumn of 1686, although her income was already overstretched, she agreed to the appointment of a third lady of the bedchamber, 'that you may have more ease & have no just cause to grow weary of me.'[23] In any case, with the height of the season at Court approaching, Sarah, as she freely admitted, was hardly a figure to grace a ceremonial occasion:

> . . . I remember when I was within three months of my reckoning, I could never endure to wear any bodice at all; but wore a warm waistcoat wrapped about me like a man's, and tied my petticoats on the top of it. And from that time never went abroad but with a long black scarf to hide me, I was so prodigious big.[24]

The choice fell on Lady Frescheville, a middle-aged widow who had been rejected in favour of Anne Spencer the year before. The Princess wrote of her to her sister Mary in terms which incidentally highlighted more than one of Sarah's shortcomings as a Court servant:

> . . . I never having heard no ill of this woman, I thought I could not have a better, she being a single woman, very well at her ease, and consequently would need less lodging, and was like to prove a good waiter, which was one of the chief reasons of my taking her. For Lady Churchill, when she is with child, can't wait so much as I have occasion for her, and the other lady is not wholly at her own dispose.[25]

That Anne was called upon to justify the appointment at all was a sign of the change that had taken place in her position during the previous year. The honeymoon period for James and his Parliament had not lasted long. The first serious differences came in November 1685, when the King declared his intention of retaining the Roman Catholic officers who had been temporarily commissioned to deal with the Monmouth rebellion, thus overriding the laws which barred Catholics from holding office. Ultimately his aim was to repeal the anti-Catholic legislation altogether. The fear then was that he would try to force Anne's conversion and change the succession in her favour, bypassing Mary, whose husband was already establishing himself as the champion of the Protestant interest in Europe.

Since Sarah's brother-in-law Talbot, recently created Earl of Tyrconnel and already pursuing James's pro-Catholic policies on a large scale in Ireland, had explicitly sounded her out on this subject, she and the Princess could be forgiven for sharing these fears. But James himself was a kindly father, and his efforts to convert Anne, as Sarah admitted afterwards, never went further than giving her appropriate books to read.[26] Her Protestantism was more than proof against these gentle methods, as no doubt it would have been against harsher ones. Young and inexperienced as she was, she had a strong sense of her own position and a full share of her father's and grandfather's immovability in the face of coercion. Yet this was an age particularly inclined to suspect and exaggerate the influence of favourites; new appointees to her household were therefore carefully watched by William and Mary for signs of

Catholic infiltration, and existing ones to ensure that they remained suitable associates for the head of the Protestant interest in England. As a result Sarah now began to find herself under increasingly searching scrutiny, not only from William and Mary, but from the King and his supporters as well.

She had begun a correspondence with Mary in May 1686 in order to give her news of Anne's health after the birth of her second daughter. At the time Mary had replied affably enough, reminding Sarah of their 'old acquaintance' and commending her attachment to her mistress.[27] Yet by the following December Anne had to write a long letter defending her favourite against her sister's criticisms. The main source of the trouble was Sarah's laxness in religious matters. As impatient of formality and control in this as in everything else, she was openly contemptuous of ostentatious Anglicans such as Lady Clarendon, who 'made a great rout with prayers'.[28] Anne had already had to take her to task about this. When Sarah apologized for writing a shorter letter than usual because she was about to go to church, the Princess replied that she would not complain, 'for indeed I think you donot go to that place so often as you should do'.[29] To her sister, Anne had to admit that Sarah was 'not so strict as some are', but assured her that she 'has a true sense of the doctrine of our Church', and also that she 'abhors all the principles of the Church of Rome'; and 'as to this particular,' Anne added, 'I assure you she will never change'.[30]

This was not the only reservation harboured by the court at The Hague about Anne's favourites. William and his circle, having long since formed a low opinion of John Churchill, now feared that the profits he was making from his military posts would cause him to fall in with the King's schemes,[31] and these suspicions can only have been increased by the Churchills' continuing friendships with James's Catholic advisers. The end of 1686 saw Sunderland's final victory over the Hydes, the deciding factor being that he was prepared to accept conversion to Catholicism and they were not. Rochester was dismissed from the treasury and replaced by a commission which included Godolphin, whom Anne did not trust because of his close alliance with Sunderland. Clarendon was recalled from Ireland to leave the field free for Tyrconnel. Yet Sarah allowed her personal dislike of the Hydes to override her disquiet at this weakening of the Protestant interest, and when her long-awaited son was born in January 1687, Godolphin and Tyrconnel were asked to stand godfathers.[32] Only one thing can have prevented Anne from becoming as suspicious of Churchill as she was of Godolphin and Sunderland, and this was her intimacy with Sarah. It gave her the confidence to assure William and Mary that Churchill was as staunch a Protestant as his wife, despite his attachment to the King.[33] It is clear already at this point how much the special relationship with Anne, on which Churchill's whole future career was to be built, owed to his wife's position.

In February 1687 William dispatched his personal envoy, Dijkvelt, to report on the alarming situation in England. This year, which had begun well for the Churchills with the birth of their son and heir, opened disastrously for the Princess. A miscarriage was followed by the serious illness of her husband and the deaths in quick succession of her two little daughters. Retiring to Richmond with Sarah in attendance, she authorized Churchill to speak to Dijkvelt on her behalf. The envoy returned to The Hague in May, having antagonized the King by his constant fraternizing with the opposition, and leaving behind him the beginnings of an association against James. At the same time Churchill wrote directly to William, emphasizing his own and the Princess's determination to remain firm Protestants.[34] Whatever the appearances of favour and friendship, co-operating in the establishment of Catholicism in England was never an option for either of the Churchills. William and Mary were now satisfied on this score, although they still remained uneasy about the extent of Anne's reliance on her favourites.

They were not the only ones to be so. The King, who shared the mistaken belief that Sarah governed his daughter entirely, suspected her of instigating Anne's planned visit to The Hague at this time (which he immediately forbade), and of constantly playing on the Princess's fears that he would try to force her conversion.[35] In fact, Anne's letters to her sister indicate that if anyone was responsible for keeping up her hostility to her father, it was Mary and not Sarah. 'Because you think in my last I seemed too much at ease,' Anne wrote to her sister in August 1687, 'I must justify myself and tell you that I don't think that I am at all the more secure for the kindness the K[ing] has showed me lately.' She did not believe, she added, that he would proceed with such sweeping measures in favour of the Catholics unless he had hopes of converting one or other of them.[36] But this fear was soon pushed into the background by a more alarming development.

Despairing of Anglican co-operation in the repeal of the anti-Catholic laws, James II now sought an alliance with the dissenters. In April 1687 he issued his Declaration of Indulgence, granting general liberty of conscience to Catholic and Protestant alike. Then in July he dissolved his unco-operative Parliament and set about campaigning for another which would make his policies into law. Anne, thoroughly alienated by this time, spent the summer with Sarah at Windsor, while the King, with Churchill in attendance, departed on an electoral progress through the

north-western counties. The Queen was left behind at Bath, in the hope
that the waters might improve her health and give her the prospect of
further pregnancies. When the first rumours began to circulate in
October that she was indeed expecting another child, the loudly
proclaimed confidence of the Roman Catholics that this would prove to
be a son aroused immediate suspicion. The Princess was foremost in
asserting that a Catholic conspiracy was afoot to provide the King with
the male heir he needed to ensure the long-term success of his policies.[37]

In the course of this winter the Churchills' position became more and
more insecure. When the King demanded the dismissal of Prince
George's Protestant groom of the stole Lord Scarsdale, who had refused
to co-operate in his electioneering, they retired to St Albans to avoid the
charge that they were solely responsible for Anne's refusal to obey. Yet
having declared that he would not vote for the repeal of the anti-Catholic
legislation, Churchill himself was now seen to be losing favour with the
King from day to day.[38] In fact it was becoming clear 'to all the World',
as Sarah put it, '& more particularly to those at Court, that every body
must be ruin'd sooner or later that would not be a Roman Catholick'.[39]
The fixing of allegiances among the divided Stuart dynasty was no safe or
easy matter, and the Churchills now had their young family to think of
as well. Just before Christmas they took the precaution of conveying
Sandridge into the trusteeship of Anthony Guidott for safe-keeping.[40]

With the King's Catholic advisers now pressing him to dismiss Sarah
from Court altogether,[41] she used the excuse of a far advanced pregnancy
to keep herself out of the public eye as much as possible. Yet it is
significant that when she gave birth to her third daughter, Elizabeth, in
March 1688, the baby's godmother was Lady Lumley, the wife of one of
William's most active supporters in England.[42] In fact by the spring of
1688, on condition that he received a formal invitation from a sufficiently
representative group, William had taken the decision to invade England
in the autumn to preserve his wife's inheritance and draw the nation into
his European coalition against France.[43] When the Queen was brought
to bed of a son in St James's Palace on 10 June, it was clear that there was
no more time to be lost.

Anne, who had retired to Bath allegedly to re-establish her health after
a recent illness, was not among the many witnesses in the overcrowded
royal bedchamber. The Jacobites, keeping up the fiction that she was
incapable of acting for herself, afterwards claimed that Sarah and Barbara
Berkeley had first persuaded her to absent herself 'that she might not be
an eye-witness of the birth of her brother', and then reported that the
King had sent her away so that he could more safely foist an imposter on
the nation. The King himself maintained with more truth that Anne had

insisted on going, in order to avoid being 'a witness, to what she was resolved to question'.[44] In later life Sarah, like the Princess, kept up the convenient pretence of doubting that the Prince of Wales really was the child of the King and Queen. 'I was an ey witness of all that proceeding for about seven months,' she wrote in 1704, '& I must say there was great cause given for Jealousys. If it was a true Child it was certainly very ill orderd, but if it was not I don't see how it could be better.' But some years later, when she heard the Duchess of Somerset refer with Whiggish bluntness to 'that Bastard the Pretender', she objected to this slight on the Queen, who 'had no fault but being govern'd by the Priests'.[45] Although she had not been present at the birth, both her sister and Godolphin were, and she must have known from their evidence that there was no real cause for doubt.

On 30 June 1688 Admiral Herbert secretly left for The Hague with the famous document signed by 'the immortal seven', urging William to come over before it was too late, and pledging their support for his undertaking. Churchill was fully involved. Although his motives and the extent of his personal commitment to William are still by no means clear, he undertook to work with other officers to bring the army over to the Prince at his landing, and promised the support of Anne and Prince George.[46] Sarah was also informed of what was afoot and had no reservations. Ever since the birth of the Prince of Wales, she recalled, 'the insolence of the Roman Catholicks' had been 'insupportable', giving an indication of what the Protestants could expect if James were allowed to proceed unchecked; 'this consideration made me very well pleased at the Prince of Orange's undertaking to rescue us from such slavery.'[47] All the same it was a nerve-racking secret to be trusted with. She was only too aware of the 'Train of Hazzards and Accidents' to which 'the attempt of succeeding in the Revolution was subject', and that failure meant incurring the penalties of high treason. When the King and Queen went to Windsor and the Princess to Tunbridge at the end of July, the Churchills stayed behind in London to settle their affairs. In what was apparently their first formal marriage settlement, Churchill conveyed £7,000 to his wife, and placed all his property in trustees' hands for the benefit of her and the children in case the worst should happen.[48]

It was not until September that the incredulous King could be brought to acknowledge the prospect of his son-in-law's invasion. As he put his navy in readiness and spent day after day drilling his troops in Hyde Park, Churchill was seen to look on and laugh. Through his connections in the army and the Princess's household, he was the centre of a network of conspiracy in both forces, neither of which, if all went according to plan, would be of any use to the King in a confrontation. After one false start, William put to sea on 1/11 November. Borne down the channel by the Protestant wind, he landed at Tor Bay with his invasion force on 5 November, and moved forward as far as Exeter. The defections from the royal army which Churchill had promised now began. James was at first badly shaken, then reassured by the return of a significant number of the rank and file of the regiments to their posts. On 17 November he finally set out for the west, taking with him Prince George and Churchill, newly promoted lieutenant-general. In their absence Sarah and the Princess would have to act for themselves. The following day Anne wrote to William of Prince George's intention to join him 'as soon as his friends shall think proper'; and she added, 'I am not yet certain if I shall continue here or remove into the City; that shall depend on the advice my friends will give me.'[49]

In mentioning the City, the traditional place of refuge for opponents of the Court, Anne probably had the town house of the Bishop of London in Aldersgate Street already in mind. The Bishop, Henry Compton, was a militant Protestant who had been active all through the autumn in organizing support for William in the midlands and the north.[50] Now, while his associates gathered in the northern towns, he remained in London to provide for the Princess's safety. Sarah was to be the link between them. A note of his whereabouts, at a secret address in Suffolk Street just north of Whitehall, was left with her, so that she could find him quickly, 'in case the Princess should have any occasion to make use of any friends'.[51]

When the King arrived at Salisbury on 19 November, William was still at an inconvenient distance for would-be defectors, who urged him to come closer. Meanwhile Churchill and his fellow conspirators used doubts about the army's loyalty in a vain attempt to persuade the King to open negotiations with the Prince.[52] In fact it is possible that at this stage they still hoped to hold the balance of power between the two and force the King to accept a settlement. Then came the news that Compton's allies, Danby at York and Devonshire at Nottingham, had declared for the invaders. Weakened by copious nosebleeds and beset by well-founded doubts about his army's reliability, James was incapable of firm action. Although Churchill urged an advance towards the Prince, by this time the King did not trust him, and decided to return to London. Churchill's loyalty had become so widely suspected that it was not safe for him to remain longer in the King's camp, nor was there now any point in his doing so.[53] In the early hours of the morning of 24 November he slipped out of Salisbury with a few officers and as many men as they could bring with them, and presented himself at the Prince's headquarters at Axminster later the same day. Although matters had not gone entirely as he had led William to believe, or perhaps as he himself had hoped, his desertion completed the King's demoralization, and more defections followed. The remaining officers advised the King that he could no longer rely on the army.

It was not until the evening of 24 November that Prince George could safely get away to join William. He was not missed until the following morning, and it was a further twelve hours before the news was sent to London.[54] This delay was to be useful to Anne and Sarah; for in the meantime, on the morning of 25 November, an order was sent ahead for the seizure of Churchill's goods. This reached London early the same afternoon, and his papers and valuables were duly sealed up and guards placed on the doors of his Cockpit lodgings.[55] Sarah, as she admitted afterwards, was thrown into a panic by this development. In the overwrought atmosphere at Whitehall it was easy to imagine that her husband's part in the events at Salisbury, regarded by the King as the blackest of all acts of betrayal, was about to be avenged on her. 'Some of my acquaintance', she wrote, 'had made me believe that the rage of the Roman Catholicks would expose me to some thing or other that was very shamefull.'[56]

By this time the Princess had also had private notice of Prince George's desertion.[57] With the King himself now only a day's journey from London, it was time for her to take advantage of Bishop Compton's offer of a place of safety. Sarah's lodgings communicated directly with hers by means of a new set of backstairs, said to have been built as a possible escape route. In Sarah's words, 'she sent for me to tell me the news & to desire I would goe to the Bishop of London to ask where she should be, for her Father was coming back, & rather then see him, she would jump out at window'.[58] Both Churchill and Prince George afterwards expressed surprise that their wives had not taken this decision earlier,[59] but it is hard to see how they could have done so. Reliable news from the west was difficult to come by, and the course of events far from predictable. The women could not have left the Cockpit prematurely without the risk of exposing their husbands' plans.

Even so, the presence of the guards on Sarah's door suggested that their escape might indeed have been left too late; but there were disputes about the legality of the warrant issued by the Lord Chief Justice, and uncertainty as to whether Churchill's wife was automatically included in an order to seize his goods and chattels. The Lord Chamberlain Mulgrave, who had jurisdiction at Court, was also said to have succumbed to a personal appeal from the Princess not to put her favourite under restraint until she had had an opportunity to appeal to the Queen. With more justice Mulgrave himself blamed the inadequacy of the King's instructions: an order to seize Churchill's property, 'before he had secur'd either his Lady or the Princess . . . was only frightening the one, and disobliging the other.'[60] At all events Sarah's fears of being kept a close prisoner were not realized. 'In all this trouble I got out,' her narrative continues,

for the guards were very easy, & went to a house in Suffolk Street where I found the Bishop of London. He told me he would go to his friends in the City to advise what would be don, & that he would come to the Cockpit at Twelve that night & carry the Princess where she should be private.[61]

That evening Anne went to bed early, telling her servants that she was not to be disturbed until she rang in the morning. A little after midnight, still in her night clothes, she crept down the backstairs with Sarah to their meeting with the Bishop. With them went Barbara Berkeley, whose husband had gone over to the Prince with Churchill, and who also wanted to put herself out of reach of reprisals. Undetected, they were taken up in a hackney coach by Compton and his nephew Lord Dorset, and driven east across London to Aldersgate Street. It was none too soon. At three o'clock in the morning came an order from the King that the Princess was to be placed under guard; Mrs Berkeley was also to be confined to her father's house, and Sarah to her sister's vacant apartments in St James's Palace. It was only the guards' instructions not to disturb the Princess until she woke in the morning that concealed her absence for the few hours needed to complete her escape.[62]

Sarah afterwards chose to represent her part in the Revolution as a very minor one.[63] Nevertheless, in helping to bring about Anne's escape from Whitehall she was held by some to have performed as great a service to the Prince of Orange as her husband; it was noticed that 'the Papists reckon the loss of the Princess as great as that of the army.'[64]

Meanwhile the placing of the guards had convinced the fugitives that they were not safe while they remained in London,[65] and since the royal army lay between them and William's headquarters, it was natural for Compton to suggest that they join his associates at Nottingham. Sarah's insistence that 'the Princess going as she did to Nottingham was purely accidental, for there was nothing of that matter concerted,'[66] has been more scoffed at than any other statement in her memoirs. Of course she was on the defensive, having been accused after the Revolution of deliberately frightening the Princess into an undutiful desertion of her father. Even so, her claim is true as far as it goes. Although the possibility of Anne's leaving the Court had certainly been considered in advance, she then had no thought of going further than the City, and recent research concerning the northern risings has confirmed that the decision to go to Nottingham was indeed made at the last minute under the pressure of events.[67]

By morning the Princess and her party were on their way out of London, bound for Copt Hall, Dorset's mansion in Epping Forest. There they stayed one night, and the next day set out through Hertfordshire and Bedfordshire, gathering an escort of local people as they went. At Hitchin, where they stopped to change horses and take refreshment at an inn, Sarah and Barbara Berkeley perched themselves on a cart in the yard as if they were common malefactors going to their execution, 'saying that but for their flight it might have been their lot'.[68] This was not mere play-acting for Anne's benefit, as the Jacobites afterwards maintained. The hysterical reaction at Whitehall to the Princess's disappearance was an indication that the Roman Catholics were thought capable of anything.[69]

As soon as the party reached Nottingham, the local gentry came flocking in, bringing their wives with them; in Sarah's words, 'the country gathered about the Princess,' and she felt safe for the first time since leaving London.[70] Devonshire, who welcomed her presence as a sanction for his activities, gave a banquet in her honour at which the young son of a Danish sculptor employed at Chatsworth was pressed into service to wait at table. Posted behind Lady Churchill, all he could recall of the conversation on that historic occasion was her request for some wine and water: 'except at that single Sound, all my Senses were collected into my Eyes, which during the whole Entertainment wanted no better Amusement, than of stealing now and then the Delight of gazing on the fair Object so near me.'[71]

On 5 December, as he was about to open negotiations with the King's commissioners, William ordered the Nottingham insurgents to march south to join him at Oxford. But they had got no further than Warwick when they were met by the news that James, rather than make the concessions to the Prince which his Protestant supporters urged, had fled to the Kent coast, intending to make his escape to France and leave the country without a government.[72] William had already turned aside from Oxford to head for the capital, so that it was only Prince George who met the Princess in Christ Church quadrangle, 'with all possible demonstrations of love and affection'. Sarah had to wait a few days longer for a reunion with her own husband, who had been sent to London ahead even of the Prince of Orange.[73] He was too useful to William in reassembling the disbanded royal army, and too uncertain of his position under the new regime, to turn aside at this critical time for any personal consideration. It was only a temporary setback to William that the King was detained at Faversham by a gang of seamen in search of absconding Jesuits, and briefly returned to Whitehall. The Prince's response was to send him back to the coast under safer escort, so that he could complete his escape unhindered. By 18 December William was installed in St James's Palace and in effective control of events.

When Anne had the news of her father's flight, her reaction was simply one of relief that she was now safe and could return to London.[74] Sarah was also overwhelmingly relieved to see England freed from the threat of 'Arbitrary power & popery', and the memory of the risks she had run and the ties she had broken to help bring this about were to determine most of her future political attitudes. Even so, the King's removal, and, still more, the ease with which it had been accomplished, were unexpected and disconcerting. For the rest of her life she was haunted by the recollection that 'King James, who would have been a very good King, if it had not been for Popery, was drove out of England without shutting up a shop, tho' he had many Friends'.[75] It was a chilling demonstration of the insecurity of any government. With this in mind, the forming of new allegiances was not to be an easy or straightforward process, especially for those, like the Churchills, who had personal obligations to the old King, and no particular reason to like those who came in his place.

Rival Courts
1689–1692

O N 22 January 1689 a Convention met to consider the best means of governing in the King's absence. The alternatives were: a regency, by which the government could be carried on in James's name; the succession of Mary (or of Mary and William together); or the recognition of William as *de facto* ruler for life. But the last choice meant setting aside the superior claims of his wife and sister-in-law; and while Mary, as a dutiful wife, was quite prepared to submit, there was no such overriding obligation on Anne, who resented William's desire to supersede her. The Prince had been in London only a few days when a reminder of her attitude and of the Churchills' possible influence in the matter caused his old antagonism towards them to flare up; he remarked ominously that 'Lord Churchill could not governe him nor my Lady, the Princesse his wife, as they did the Prince and Princesse of Denmark'.[1]

Anne's position complicated the Churchills' already ambivalent attitude to the settlement. For all their active participation in the Revolution, neither at first supported William's claims to the crown. On 31 January Lord Churchill gave his vote against declaring the throne vacant, causing the Whigs to mutter that 'he that has been false once may be so againe'.[2] In a very significant (and inexplicably ignored) passage in her memoirs, Sarah maintained that once the ends of the Revolution had been achieved, her husband intended that 'the Army would make the Prince of Orange go back'. As for herself, 'I do solemnly protest that . . . I was so very simple a creature that I never once dreamt of his being King'; she imagined that his 'sole design was to provide for the safety of his own country by obliging King James to keep the laws of ours, and that he would go back as soon as he had made us all happy'.[3]

When William's Tory opponents urged Anne to form a party to press her claim, Sarah therefore at first tried to assist them, her loyalty to the Princess temporarily overriding her natural political allegiances. It was her first foray into parliamentary politics, and she conducted it with more zest than discretion or sense, talking to several MPs and taking 'a great deal of pains (which I believe the King and Queen never forgot) to promote my mistress's pretensions'.[4] Yet it soon became apparent that such efforts on behalf of either sister were simply unrealistic. On 3 February William summoned a group of leading peers, and declared to them that he would accept neither a regency nor a position subordinate to his wife. Mary might be named jointly with him as Queen, but unless the government were vested in him for life, he would return to Holland. Since the country had to have an effective government, this settled the issue. In her canvassing Sarah found 'that all the principal men, except the Jacobites' were for William, 'and that the settlement would be carried in Parliament, whether the Princess consented to it or not'. But these were awe-inspiring constitutional issues for a young female courtier to meddle in, and being 'fearful about everything the Princess did, when she was *thought to be* advised by me', Sarah brought in John Tillotson, William's future Archbishop of Canterbury, to second her advice that Anne must yield precedence in the succession to her brother-in-law.[5] On 6 February Churchill carried a message to the House of Lords that the Princess was prepared to do so, and himself voted that the crown be offered to William and Mary.[6] This was duly done on 13 February.

Churchill's contribution to the Revolution was rewarded with an earldom (he took the title of Marlborough from an extinct peerage in his mother's family). He was also confirmed in his post as gentleman of the bedchamber, given the lucrative task of remodelling the army, and put in command of the English forces which were sent to the Continent when war was declared against France in May. Yet the personal favour he had enjoyed under James was conspicuously lacking. A young Irishman, afterwards a leading Jacobite, who attended him at Court at this time, remembered that even by the low standards of William's personal relations with Englishmen, Marlborough was treated with particular neglect, and that when he returned home his wife would tell him, 'it was what he deserved. He ought to have considered how good his settlement was, some months before.'[7] However necessary it had been to defeat James's schemes, it was galling to reflect on what they had forgone.

Although Sarah had a much more cordial reception from Mary, she was one of those who found the new Queen's display of forced gaiety when she first arrived at Whitehall distasteful.[8] Nor did the warmth of the reunion between Mary and Anne last long. Many, not least the Queen herself, were to blame Sarah for this, and it was true that her hold on the Princess's affections left room for no more than a token friendship between the sisters. But in other respects her responsibility for the bad feeling which soon flared up between them has been greatly exaggerated.

Differences of temperament now made it difficult for Mary and Anne to resume their childhood intimacy; and at the root of the problem was the inevitable friction between monarch and successor, aggravated by Anne's lingering resentment at the Revolution settlement, which William's graceless demeanour did nothing to remove. As Sarah put it, his treatment of the Princess and still more of the Prince made it clear that he thought they 'had been of more use to him than they were ever like to be again'.[9]

Seeing William's first Parliament dominated by Whigs who supported his title to the throne, the Princess and the Tories who regarded her as the head of their party were determined to exact a price for the postponement of her rights in William's favour. Anne had an income of £30,000 a year, on which she always found it difficult to manage. The question of an increased parliamentary settlement for her first came up for consideration on 17 July 1689, and three weeks later her supporters proposed that she should be granted an additional revenue of £40,000 a year for life. Although in the interval she had greatly contributed to the stability of the new regime by giving birth to a son, William, Duke of Gloucester, opposition from the Court caused the matter to be further postponed until the winter.[10]

Again, it was not Sarah who initiated this dispute. In July she was confined herself with the birth of her fourth daughter, Mary, and since the Queen and her groom of the stole, Lady Derby, both stood godmothers, it is clear that nothing had happened up to this point to disturb her apparent favour at Court.[11] It was not until the question of the Princess's income came to a head during the next session that she became seriously involved. The Court evidently hoped that, as in the matter of the succession, Sarah might be persuaded to influence her mistress to accept political realities. Their chief emissary for this purpose was Barbara Berkeley, who now had a foot in both camps. While she was still Sarah's closest friend and governess to Anne's son, her adolescent friendship with Mary had revived, and her sister, Betty Villiers, was the King's mistress. 'Sometimes she attacked me on the side of my interest,' Sarah wrote,

telling me that if I would not put an end to measures so disagreeable to the King and Queen, it would certainly be the ruin of my Lord and conseqently of all our family. When she found that this had no effect, she endeavoured to alarm my fears for the Princess by saying that those measures would in all probability ruin her. For nobody, but such as flattered me, believed the Princess would carry her point, and in case she did not, the King would not think himself obliged to do anything for her. That it was perfect madness in me to persist, and I had better ten thousand times persuade the Princess to let the thing fall . . . [12]

Sarah was certainly impressed by these arguments, but her uneasy alliance with Anne's Tory supporters was pushing her in the opposite direction. While she maintained that their chief motive was not to benefit the Princess but to thwart the King, they accused her of having already betrayed her mistress in the matter of the succession in order to curry favour at Court;[13] and she knew that if she tried to persuade Anne to drop the financial settlement, these accusations would be redoubled. 'I really thought I should have been madd,' she remembered, 'between the uncertainty of the Princess's succeeding & the reflections it might bring upon me if she ded not indeavour it, by giving her interest up to make my court, which I would have dyed ten thousand times reather than have don'.[14]

On 17 December a committee of the House rejected the proposed income of £70,000 a year for Anne.[15] The next morning the secretary of state, Lord Shrewsbury, was sent to the Marlboroughs with a compromise proposal: if Anne would now allow the matter to drop in Parliament, the King would grant her £50,000 a year once his own revenue was settled. Marlborough, by the Queen's account, told Shrewsbury he could do nothing: 'his wife would by no means hear of it, but was like a mad woman and said the princess would retire if her friends would not assist her.'[16] Although the report is from a hostile source, the substance is very similar to Sarah's own account of her state of mind. There is also the significant indication that Marlborough's influence with Anne at this stage was still very much subordinate to his wife's.

Shrewsbury then tackled Sarah directly, assuring her that he was confident the King would keep his word, and 'that if he did not, he was sure he would not serve him an hour after he broke it'. Sarah, who had been told by Godolphin that William considered even £30,000 an extravagant income for the Princess, was unimpressed by this posturing. Shrewsbury's longing for an excuse to resign was well known; in any case, as she pointed out, his resignation would be no compensation to the Princess for the loss of money. Anne herself told him that since the business had now gone so far, she thought it reasonable 'to see what her friends could do for her',[17] and on 18 December the King was recommended by parliamentary address to make an annual provision for the Princess of £50,000. Although this result was not very satisfactory to either side, both claimed a victory. Sarah, still fearful of seeming lukewarm in Anne's interest, wondered if they should continue to press for £70,000, but her political sense told her that the power of the Court in Parliament was so great that it would be better not to take the matter any further.[18]

Afterwards Mary quarrelled openly with the Princess about her rejection of the King's offer, and the coldness between them continued well into the following year. Mary claimed that she would have made overtures of reconciliation to her sister, 'but I saw plainly she was so absolutly governed by Lady Marlborough that it was to no purpose'. In fact, when the Queen fell ill in April, it was Anne who made the first approach. But when she went on to ask that the £50,000 recommended by Parliament should now be settled securely, Mary was suspicious of her sincerity: 'This was all an efect of a conference she had had with the Speacker, whoes advise it was . . . ; but to speack more plainly this was done by Lady Marlborough who, finding it could be carried no other way, had with much ado, rather then lose it, brought her self to give my sister this advise.' A token reconciliation was patched up, but Mary remained convinced that there was 'no hopes of a lasting kindness', since it seemed on Anne's side 'to depend so much on anothers humour'.[19]

Sarah was well aware that she had damaged her own position at Court, and probably her husband's as well, by her support of the Princess over this issue, and although she took pride in her loyalty to her mistress the situation made her uneasy. What she particularly resented was being held solely to blame for Anne's poor relations with the Queen, and for this there was some justification; it is clear both from Anne's letters to Sarah and from Mary's memoirs that the sisters were quite capable of keeping up the quarrel without her. In fact it was Sarah herself, for her own sake as well as the Princess's, who now made some attempt to improve matters by taking Anne to task for not having 'a proper behaviour' to the Queen, and for making no effort to conceal her preference for her favourite's company.[20]

For the time being the quarrel had no outward effect on Marlborough's situation. When the King went to take command of the army in Ireland in June 1690, he was left behind as commander-in-chief of the forces in England, and one of the Council of Nine appointed to advise the Queen. Yet his divided allegiances had certainly undermined his position. Mary in particular considered that he could 'never deserve either trust or esteem', and the Lord President, Carmarthen, contemptuously dismissed him as a 'general of favour':[21] a sneer at his early career, and perhaps also a reference to the rumour that his wife had secured his appointment by cancelling a large gambling debt owed her by the King's mistress. (Sarah afterwards admitted that she had always been 'very civill' to Betty Villiers, but 'without the least design of making any use of her interest, which is seldom the case with such sort of acquaintance'.)[22]

By the beginning of July Sarah's sister Frances was entertaining the beaten King James in Dublin on his way back to France after the battle of the Boyne. But the simultaneous defeat of the English fleet off Beachy

Head left the country for some weeks in fear of invasion. For Sarah, expecting another child within the month, the long weeks of July when a landing was expected on the coast at any moment must have been a nightmare, and a French invasion remained a terror that haunted her into old age. Nottingham and Carmarthen wrote to William, imploring him to return and questioning Marlborough's ability to deal with the crisis.[23] Both the King and Marlborough reacted more coolly. As soon as the immediate danger was over, the latter proposed that he should go to Ireland with a detachment of troops for the taking of Cork and Kinsale. This would give him an opportunity to demonstrate in the most practical way that he was not simply a general of favour. William agreed, and on 26 August Marlborough left for Portsmouth to embark his troops.

'As little reason as I have to care for his wife,' Mary wrote to William, 'yet I must pity her condition, having lain in but eight days; and I have great compassion for wives when their husbands go to fight.'[24] Sarah had given birth to a second son, Charles, on 19 August. In the will which she wrote out carefully in her own hand the day before, disposing of the £7,000 settled on her at the Revolution, her chief concern was for the financial independence of her daughters. They were to receive their shares of the capital at 21 or on marriage, but from the age of 15 they were to have the interest paid 'into their own hands' by the trustees. Her mother, her trustee Anthony Guidott, and her two closest friends, Barbara Berkeley (now Lady Fitzhardinge) and Lord Godolphin, were to have mourning rings, and there was a large bequest of £500 'to release poor people out of prison'.[25]

As soon as she had recovered from her confinement, Sarah again took refuge at St Albans. Until the Revolution, as she frankly admitted, she had never read books or passed her time at anything but card-playing.[26] Now she began to use her country leisure to make strenuous efforts at self-education. Her handwriting and spelling improved markedly and she was also discovering a new interest in reading. Not only did she devour every work of political controversy, 'great and little', that she could lay hands on, but she began to make forays into literature as well. Besides a predictable collection of devotional tracts and manuals of family medicine, her small library at St Albans in the 1690s included the plays of Shakespeare and Dryden, Milton's *Paradise Lost*, and the poems of Suckling, Waller, and her 'beloved Mr Cowley'. With most of these she became so familiar that she could quote them readily in letters and conversation in later life; but there were also several works of a more unexpected and speculative turn: Sir Thomas Browne's *Religio Medici*, Burton's *Anatomy of Melancholy*, and, in translation, the works of Seneca and the essays of St Evremond and Montaigne.[27]

Her friends, to whom she was inclined to parade this new interest, reacted with amusement or incomprehension. Lady Scarborough, sending her regular bulletins of news from Ireland, urged her to leave her books and come to town to join in their card parties: 'Lady Fitzharden tells me you will come outt . . . soe wise and larned that you will dispise us poor mortalls and a pack of Cards, and will sit Reading in your Chamber all day, but I hope you are not soe changed.'[28] For the Princess this new bookishness was simply another unwelcome rival claim on her favourite's attention. When Sarah's letters became intermittent, Anne reminded her sharply that if she had 'spare minutes to look on Seneca', she might also find time to keep up their correspondence.[29]

Having reduced Cork and Kinsale to surrender with an admirable display of competence, Marlborough was back in England before the end of October. Yet William's grudging acknowledgement made it clear that he was still considered essentially unproven, and the unrealistic rewards he now expected, the Garter and the mastership of the ordnance—Sarah had taunted him before he left with being over-ambitious[30]— were not forthcoming. The negotiations he opened during the winter as an insurance against the restoration of his old master were a sign both of his personal discontent and of his general sense of insecurity, and the latter at least must have been fully shared by his wife.

When the Jacobite agent, Henry Bulkeley, met Marlborough and Godolphin in St James's Park one day in January 1691, he was invited back to dine with them at the Cockpit.[31] There he also had a warm welcome from Sarah, for they were very old friends. 'It was his interest that made him a Jacobit,' she wrote after his death, 'his understanding was very far from it, & having known me from twelve year old & allways professed a great deal of kindnesse for me . . . hee had so good an opinion of me that hee would say anything to me that hee thought.'[32] Bulkeley was not her only contact with the exiled Stuarts. She was still in correspondence with her sister Frances, who had left Ireland to take up her old post as lady of the bedchamber to Queen Mary at St Germains. Other Jacobites were also encouraged by Sarah's declining favour at Court to sound her out for signs of a change of heart. One of these, Lord Ailesbury, had paid her a clandestine visit at St Albans while Marlborough was away, where he hinted at matters 'of the highest moment' which were 'not yet ripe but might be soon', and had to be hastily ushered out through the woodyard at the back when Lady Fitzhardinge and Lord Godolphin arrived by coach from London to dine with her.[33]

Through his contacts with Bulkeley and other agents, Marlborough now opened a correspondence with King James himself, giving promises of support if occasion should arise, and offering 'to abandon Wife,

Children and Country' to regain the King's esteem. He asked for a
pardon for himself 'and other great offenders who by their future
behaviour should give proofs of deserving it, which he said would
influence [the Princess her]self, My Lady Churchill and others'. Not that
James was under any illusions about these undertakings; 'in fine they
were all to be pardoned and secure in case the King returned,' he
commented bitterly, 'but to give only bare promises in return.'[34]

Although Sarah could not afterwards remember whether the episode
occurred before or just after the Revolution,[35] it was at about this time
also that she took responsibility for her four young cousins, the children
of her father's youngest sister Elizabeth, quite unaware that by this act of
charity and family duty she was contributing towards her own eventual
downfall at Court. Elizabeth Jenyns had been brought up as the ward,
and eventually became the heiress, of her brother Ralph, with whom
Sarah's mother and brother had disputed the inheritance of the family
estates in the 1670s, and it was under Ralph's auspices that she married a
prosperous merchant, Francis Hill, to whom she bore the four
children.[36] The estrangement between the two branches of the family
accounts for Sarah's otherwise improbable assertion that she had been
brought up in ignorance that 'there were such people [as the Hills] in the
world'.[37] It was not until the failure of Francis Hill's business ventures
had reduced them to destitution that they were brought to her notice by
Marlborough's cousin, Anne Chudleigh. Sarah often gave money in such
cases, and there could be no doubt that the Hills had a particular claim
on her. Having sent a few guineas for their immediate relief, she set
about providing for the children in such a way as to make the family self-
supporting. At her request Godolphin found a place for the elder son in
the customs service, while she herself clothed the younger boy Jack, 'for
he was all in rags,' and put him into St Albans grammar school.[38] The
school records, which show that he was entered as a scholar in the year
1690/1, enable her first contact with the Hills to be pinpointed more
exactly than her wayward memory would afterwards allow.[39] He
remained at St Albans for a year or two, until she was able to find a place
for him as page to Prince George.

Sarah hoped to find posts in the Princess's household for the two
daughters as well, but suitable vacancies for women were slow in
occurring. In any case the elder girl, Abigail, had been forced by her
family's plight to go into domestic service, and was now in such a low
state of health that her life seemed to be in danger. Sarah's powerful
nursing instinct was aroused, and she bore her cousin off to St Albans to
recuperate. Abigail remained in the house for some time, probably very
much as a poor relation. Sarah never let her forget that she had lost caste

by going into service, and the brief statement, 'she lived with me and my children', probably indicates that she was expected to make herself useful in the crowded nursery at Holywell.[40]

In May 1691 Marlborough left with the King to take up his command against the French in the Low Countries, and almost at once Sarah and Anne were again embroiled with the Queen. What precipitated the quarrel this time was the Prince's desire to take some part in the war by serving as a volunteer on board the fleet. Interpreting this as a rival bid for popularity, Mary tried to persuade Sarah to use her influence to prevent it, without revealing at whose instigation she was doing so. She refused, and the Prince would not submit until he was publicly forbidden to go, thus reviving all the bad feeling between the two Courts.[41] In July the Prince and Princess went to take the waters at Tunbridge Wells, where they were joined after a week or two by Sarah. Godolphin was also there. Although he was one of the few Englishmen whom William both liked and trusted, he had scruples about serving under the new regime: 'hee was no way concernd in making the revolution & disliked it very much,' Sarah wrote afterwards.[42] In the autumn of 1690 he had been far enough advanced with negotiations for a second marriage to offer this as an excuse for his resignation from the government, but in the end nothing came of the match; indeed, although various other romantic attachments were reported of him, he never remarried. William enlisted Marlborough's help to persuade him to stay at the treasury (Marlborough, with his unerring insight in such matters, told the King he must appeal to Godolphin's friendship, not simply to his sense of duty), and from this time on his private life became increasingly bound up with that of the Churchills.[43]

Godolphin's friendship was as close with Sarah as with her husband. Like the King, she recognized a fundamental honesty and disinterestedness in his nature; it was both curious and impressive to her that 'he did not love money' or appear to value any of the other rewards of public life.[44] Her affection and respect for him grew with the years, until she came to rely on the soundness of his advice in every matter from the investment of her fortune to her conduct at Court. He in his turn responded to her beauty and vitality, her tough, impetuous talk, and 'the reason and understanding by which', as he once told her, 'you are most justly distinguished from the rest of your sex'.[45] His growing attachment to the Princess's service by means of this friendship did not pass unnoticed. Many years later Sarah recalled how she and her husband had brought him in at this time to counsel Anne in her difficulties with the Court, when she had formerly had no acquaintance with him and indeed had distrusted him because of his association with Sunderland.[46] Like

Marlborough, Godolphin owed his first informal introduction into
Anne's service to Sarah's special relationship with her mistress.

Sarah did not go to Tunbridge in the summer of 1691 simply to attend
the Princess. Four pregnancies in as many years, together with the
'continuall bustle' and stress of her life at Court, had taken their toll even
of her resilient good health. She complained of the 'vapours' and a
continual weight on her eyes.[47] For some time, in fact, she had been
talking seriously of resigning her post altogether.[48] She already had six
children to attend to, and at 31 no reason to suppose that her child-
bearing was over; Lady Scarborough predicted 'the Effect Tunbridg
watters will have of you when your Lord comes home'.[49] Having lost
her annuity of £300 at the Revolution, she had only her salary of £400
from the Princess, and the demands of her post were greater than ever, in
terms of both public and private attendance. More importantly, by
remaining at Court she was attracting the displeasure of the King and
Queen not only to herself but to her husband, at a time when the
Princess seemed unlikely to outlive her sister, and when, as Sarah bluntly
put it, there was very little pleasure in her service, 'or prospect of any
great advantage'.[50] It cannot have been coincidence that just at this time
Anne wrote to offer her an extra income of £1,000 a year from the privy
purse.[51] The part Sarah had played in securing the Princess's increased
revenue was the ostensible reason, but the payments were probably
intended chiefly as an inducement to her to stay in her post.

Sarah, who sought Godolphin's approval before accepting, afterwards
justified herself on the grounds that her family's circumstances were 'not
very great' at the time.[52] In fact the Marlboroughs were generally
reputed to have grown wealthy after the Revolution (the result, it was
said, of Marlborough's sale of commissions during the reorganization of
the army), and their bank account confirms that they had amassed a good
deal of capital.[53] Yet they still regarded themselves as having much to
achieve by the standards of the class to which they had risen. To her
Jacobite friend Lord Ailesbury, who taxed her on the subject, Sarah
exclaimed, ' "Lord" (a common word with her), "they keep such a noise
at our wealth. I do assure you that it doth not exceed seventy thousand
pounds, and what will that come to when laid out in land, and besides we
have a son and five daughters to provide for." '[54] It was not long before
the payments became known to the Queen (though they were assumed
to be gambling debts), and contributed to her disapproval of the
relationship.[55]

This year also saw the inception of the famous names, Mrs Morley and
Mrs Freeman, by which Anne and Sarah were to correspond for as long
as their friendship lasted.[56] The idea was the Princess's: not only to

enable them to write to each other on terms of equality, but also to provide a practical safeguard against prying eyes in case their letters should be opened. Offered her choice of the names, Sarah's 'frank open temper' led her to pitch on Freeman, 'and so the Princess took the other'.[57] And to begin with, there was one other member of this charmed circle, although very grudgingly admitted on Anne's part: Lady Fitzhardinge figured in their letters as Mrs Hill. At one point in the summer of 1691, much to Anne's relief, she and Sarah seemed to have quarrelled irrevocably, and when 'Mrs Hill' sought a reconciliation, the Princess urged her favourite not to be taken in. Yet Sarah continued to find Barbara's company irresistible, and so 'by degrees', as Anne wrote sadly, 'you weare made up till at last you weare as much bewitched by her as ever'.[58] It was a tribute to Barbara's charm that something of this bewitchment lingered, even after it was reported that by relaying private talk from the Cockpit to the ears of the King and Queen, she was partly to blame for the disaster which overtook them all during the coming winter.

The crisis began without any warning on the morning of 20 January 1692, with a message from the secretary of state, Lord Nottingham, that Marlborough was dismissed from all his posts. Although no official reasons were given, the King caused it to be put about that there were three causes of Marlborough's disgrace. The first was the discovery of his correspondence with the Jacobite Court, to which common talk added that a secret design against France had been betrayed by Sarah to Lady Tyrconnel; or, according to another version, that she had gossiped about it to Lady Fitzhardinge, by whom the breach of confidence had indirectly come back to the King. The second reason was Marlborough's outspoken criticism of William for his promotion of foreigners to senior military posts. The third was the use of Sarah's influence with the Princess to alienate her from the Court and encourage her to set up a party of her own.[59]

About the first and second of these reasons Sarah was always reticent, although the accusation of betraying state secrets to her sister was to dog her for years. In fact the few fragments of letters which survive do support Lady Tyrconnel's claim that their correspondence was quite innocent.[60] Sarah was also reluctant to accept that her beloved Barbara had deliberately betrayed them. She did admit that they had all talked too freely in the presence of Betty Villiers, but claimed that 'it was nothing that ought to have don the Duke of Marlborough any prejudice'. She was much more inclined to blame 'the malice of the torrys' (always her readiest scapegoats) or William's detested favourite Portland, for turning the King against her husband.[61] Finally, however, she did admit to the third reason. 'There can be no doubt but my stubbornness in all that concern'd the Princess did Prejudice to the Duke of Marlborough,' she conceded in one account. In another, this became 'the true cause' of her own and her husband's loss of favour, until finally she claimed that Marlborough had been dismissed simply to provide an excuse for getting rid of her.[62]

Although there was certainly a good deal more to it than that, at the time it was expected that Sarah's dismissal or resignation must quickly follow, and there followed a fortnight's lull, during which she refused to go near a Court 'which, as I thought, had used my Lord Marlborough very ill'. But eventually her 'best friends' persuaded her to wait on the Princess as usual in her formal visits to the King and Queen. Godolphin, she remembered, urged that 'it would give some Handle for Complaint against me, if I did not,' and argued that 'it could not be thought I made any mean court to the King and Queen, since to attend the Princess was only paying my duty where it was owing'.[63] Accordingly, on 4 February Sarah accompanied Anne on a visit to Kensington.

In fact this simply precipitated the crisis. William, and Mary in particular, were determined that she should not remain about the Princess 'to feed the dissatisfaction that was too visible on that side'. The King sent a message to this effect via Godolphin, while the Queen wrote to her sister, pointing out that 'never anybody was suffered to live at Court in my Lord Marlborough's circumstances,' and that if his wife were allowed to remain, it would give him too good an excuse for 'being where he ought not'. When Anne asked them to reconsider, the response was a direct order from the Lord Chamberlain to Sarah to leave the Cockpit.[64] All the Princess's combativeness was roused. In the first heat of her indignation, she assured Sarah that she would keep her 'in spite of their teeth', and 'go to the utmost verge of the earth rather than live with such monsters'.[65] Sarah had no choice but to leave the Court, but only temporarily, for Anne was already taking steps to go, if not 'to the utmost verge of the earth', at least to Sion House in Brentford, a private residence borrowed from the Duke of Somerset, where the Lord Chamberlain had no jurisdiction.

It was one thing for Sarah to toy with the idea of resignation of her own accord, but as she admitted herself, 'the being turned out is something very disagreeable to my temper,' and she was at first as defiant as Anne.[66] Nevertheless, she had a clear duty to offer her resignation, and she made sure that it was known that she had done so. Of course there was no question of Anne's accepting it. Whenever Sarah raised the subject, the Princess 'fell into the greatest passion of tenderness and weeping that is possible to imagine', and implored Sarah never to leave her, for 'I . . . had rathere live in a cottage with you then reinge [*sic*] Empresse of the world without you'.[67] There was more to this attitude than extravagant devotion to a favourite. Anne was well aware of her own share in Marlborough's dismissal: 'Can you think either of us so wretched', she asked Sarah, 'that . . . we should forsake those we have such obligations to, and that we are so certain we are the occasion of all their misfortunes?'[68] In fact there were now powerful reasons apart from her defiance of the Court to keep Sarah from pressing her resignation. Although she and her family were in no danger of starving, Marlborough's dismissal meant a substantial loss of income, and in the circumstances her revenue of £1,400 a year from the Princess was not lightly to be thrown away. And now that Marlborough had overreached himself by his outspoken opposition to the King, Sarah's relationship with Anne, however unpromising at this moment, was their only remaining foothold at Court.

When Anne left the Cockpit for Sion on 19 February Sarah was in attendance, but she remained there only for a day or two. She needed to re-establish her household at Jermyn Street, and to take advice about her health; for she had come away from Sion ill and reportedly pregnant. By the second week in March she and her husband were back at Sion, but from there came further reports of Sarah's serious ill health.[69] It is not clear whether she had suffered a miscarriage or simply mistaken the symptoms of illness for the early stages of pregnancy. At all events, although she was only in her early thirties, there were to be no further children. The atmosphere at Sion during the bitterly cold and backward spring was not calculated to restore her health. Several members of Prince George's household, resenting their isolation and fearing the withdrawal of Anne's income, urged the Prince to persuade his wife to let Sarah go.[70] Feeling herself beset by hostility and criticism, she herself now began to talk in earnest of resignation. Anne had to beg her not to 'vex & torment your self at all the malitious storys you heare', and not to 'lett the ill returns you meet with all from others make you deprive me of one of the greatest comforts of my life'.[71]

A hostile account suggests that Sarah had no confidence in Anne's professions of devotion, and feared being forgotten in a fortnight, like Mary Cornwallis, if she parted from her even temporarily. She herself admitted that her friends had urged this on her.[72] Yet as the quarrel continued and the pressures on her built up, she was to spend long periods away from Court. While she remained in attendance on the Princess she was bound to be held responsible for the continuing breach between the two Courts, and there were times, for all her defiance and Anne's significant assurance that 'all this would have come upon me if you had not been', when she believed herself to be so.[73] Looking back on the experience, she commented with obvious sincerity, 'it was soe uneasy to my own temper, that if I could have known it would have lasted soe long I am confydent I should have gon to the Indies reather then have indured it.'[74]

It was at Sion on 17 April, after a difficult labour, that Anne gave birth to a son who died almost at once. The same afternoon the Queen paid her a visit, but as Anne reported to Sarah, 'never asked her how she did, nor expressed the least concern for her condition', but said without preamble, 'I have made the first step by coming to you, and I now expect you should make the next by removing my Lady Marlborough.' When Anne refused, the Queen left without another word. Sarah herself poured scorn on the assumption that 'a visit, which the Queen made to every Countess, was so extraordinary a grace to a sister that it should oblige her to do what she had retired from Court to avoid', and she attributed Anne's slow recovery to the agitation of the episode.[75] These outspoken opinions did not help her situation. Shortly afterwards, in order to justify the continued insistence on her dismissal, Nottingham declared publicly that Lady Marlborough, 'setting aside all her past behaviour and the circumstances of her lord, has so misrepresented the Queen's affection to the Princess, in this visitt as to deserve her Majesties displeasure'. A few days later the Queen herself forbade all members of her own Court to visit the Princess.[76] With a Jacobite invasion fleet now at sea and the country in the grip of consternation and panic, the rival Court at Sion was not merely in disgrace, but under suspicion.

By this time both Sarah and her husband had again returned to Jermyn Street, and it was there, amid mass arrests of Jacobite suspects, that Marlborough was taken into custody on 4 May and committed to the Tower on suspicion of high treason. His Jacobite contacts were of course known to the government, but Sarah assured Anne that he was confident they could have nothing specific against him on this occasion,[77] and indeed the only concrete evidence which did come to light proved to be counterfeit. In order to secure his release from Newgate, a professional criminal, Robert Young, concocted an 'association' in favour of James II, to which he forged the signatures of a random selection of supposed Jacobite sympathizers, including Marlborough and the Bishop of Rochester. He then concealed it, by means of an accomplice, in a flower-pot in the Bishop's palace at Bromley. If it had been found by the royal messengers who first searched the palace on 7 May, the fabrication would have been exposed at once; for as Nottingham himself admitted when the document did at last come to light, it was so manifestly silly in its contents that it could not possibly have been accepted as genuine. Yet despite strong hints from Young to pay particular attention to the flower-pots, the messengers overlooked it.[78]

Young, however, had also produced forged letters from Marlborough, in which reference was made to the association, and in which his handwriting was so expertly counterfeited that the victim himself could afterwards scarcely believe that they were not genuine. Accepting these as conclusive evidence of his guilt, Nottingham ordered him to be kept a close prisoner until the invasion panic was over and he could be brought to trial.[79] This meant that his wife could have access to him only by agreeing to share his imprisonment. Although she was willing to do so, Marlborough reportedly got word to her 'not to ask it, but to stay with the Princesse and take her fortune'.[80] In this crisis her position was their one remaining asset. It was not until five days after his committal that she was given leave for a visit or two or three hours 'for this time only'.[81]

The next weeks were very difficult for her. The Princess was careful to make no demands at a time 'when you have so many things to do and think of',[82] but at Jermyn Street Sarah was isolated and frightened. She complained that friends who had formerly 'lived in the family like near relations' (meaning chiefly Barbara Fitzhardinge) were now afraid to come near her, and if a Dutch intelligence agent in London is to be believed she could not go about the streets without being jeered at by the mob.[83] As if these were not troubles enough, within a fortnight of Marlborough's imprisonment their younger son Charles was taken ill, and although Sarah rushed to St Albans, she was unable to save his life. On the same day, 21 May, came the news that the invasion fleet had been defeated at La Hogue. Visiting restrictions on the prisoners in the Tower were at once relaxed, and with the beginning of the law term approaching Marlborough began to take steps to secure his release, a process in which 'one of his best friends', as Sarah recalled, 'was a paper . . . which I had often kissed, the Act of Habeas Corpus'.[84] But this also meant that the government was free to proceed against the prisoners. On 25 May Young was released from Newgate so that he could give evidence, and Marlborough's attempt to gain his release three days later on the first day of term was unsuccessful. At Westminster Hall it was reported that he was shortly to be indicted for high treason.[85]

On Sarah, dividing her time between her children, her husband in the Tower, and the Princess at Sion, the strain was now beginning to tell badly. 'My dear Mrs Freeman was in so dismal a way when she went from hence, that I cannot forbear asking how she does,' Anne wrote anxiously when Sarah returned to London early in June: '. . . For God's sake have a care of your dear self, and give as little way to melancholy thoughts as you can.' But at the end came the joyful postscript: 'I had no

sooner sealed my letter but I received my dear Mrs Freeman's . . . and am
overjoyed at the good news you send me, which I hope will cure you of
everything.'[86] The good news was that Young's forgeries had at last been
exposed. This meant that Marlborough could neither be brought to trial
nor detained beyond the end of the law term.[87] Even so, he was kept in
the Tower until the very last day, and then only released on bail. Sarah
remained in London, chafing at the delay, and when he was finally freed
on 15 June she retired for an interval alone with him and their children at
St Albans. The Princess paid them several visits there, before leaving Sion
for good in the middle of August to go to Bath.[88]

For Sarah, who never liked Bath at the best of times, this was another
disagreeable interlude. Anne's household had been infiltrated by
government spies, and the local dignitaries were under orders not to pay
their usual respects to her. Again Sarah found that she could not show
herself in public without attracting the attention of the mob.[89] When
they left Bath on 14 October, the Prince and Princess went temporarily
to the Duke of Gloucester's nursery at Camden House, while Berkeley
House, a private mansion in Piccadilly which they had exchanged for the
Cockpit, was being prepared for them. Marlborough stayed in London
in order to get his bail discharged. But Sarah went straight to St Albans.[90]
She returned to Berkeley House in November, while her husband took a
leading part in opposition attacks on the government in the House of
Lords; but after a few weeks she left again for St Albans, where she was
to remain for the greater part of the next two years. In January Anne
wrote wistfully to her that Marlborough, who came regularly to pay his
respects, 'does not give me any hopes of seeing you & knowing how
happy you are at St Albans I dare not propose it'.[91]

For five or six years Sarah had played a more active part in public
affairs than she could have dreamt of when she first came to Court, and
she had found the experience, for all its fascination, overwhelmingly
stressful and complicated. Her husband's career had been curtailed
partly as a result of her situation, and with the quarrel at Court no nearer
a solution even her beloved Whigs were 'violently against her': enough in
itself to make her doubt the rightness of her position.[92] Her passionate
interest in their fortunes remained, but for the time being she had had
enough of personal involvement. Although she retained her official post
in Anne's household, for the immediate future, as her brother-in-law
remarked, she was 'no longer a courtier'.[93]

A Retired Way
1693–1701

AT St Albans Sarah thankfully put aside her Court finery with its long trains, and adopted the short skirts of a countrywoman. To be in her own house with her family and the company of a few 'easy & agreeable friends without ceremony', she always maintained was 'the best injoyment that one can have in this life',[1] and it was a large group that gathered about her at Holywell in the spring of 1693. Apart from Marlborough, there were the five surviving children, 'four daughters and a son, all like litle angils',[2] of whom the eldest, Henrietta, was at this time rising 12, and the youngest, Mary, not quite 4 years old. Mrs Jenyns, now elderly and frail in health, had a house of her own up the hill in the town. There was also Sarah's favourite niece, Lady Rosse (Lady Tyrconnel's eldest daughter), her two cousins, Abigail and Jack Hill, and various other friends and relations who came and went as temporary guests. Edward Griffith, returning from a visit in May, sent his service to 'Lady Rosse, Lady Harryett, Lady Anne, litle Lord, and the other half dozen'.[3]

Among the first visitors to Holywell in the spring of 1693 were Lord and Lady Sunderland.[4] After his disgrace and exile at the end of the previous reign, Sunderland had made a remarkable and unforeseeable return to politics and was now William's 'minister behind the curtain'. His friendship with the Churchills had quickly revived. He 'had really a great many good Qualitys, with some bad ones', Sarah wrote afterwards;[5] and no doubt he now redeemed himself a good deal in her eyes by using his influence with William strongly in favour of the Whigs. He also undertook, as a matter of political necessity, to try to reconcile the two estranged Courts. Indeed he may well have recommended Sarah to keep in the background as much as possible with this end in view. Since he had no influence with the Queen, by whom the quarrel was chiefly kept up, she believed he had little hope of success, but she was grateful for his support. On all occasions relating to the Princess, she noted, he 'showed himself a man of sense and breeding.'[6]

Sarah's days were occupied in looking after her large household (in spite of her extreme short-sightedness, she was an exacting mistress of a house, seeing 'immediatly any thing that is arye, a hole or a spott which often vexes me'), and in superintending the education of her children.[7] In spare moments she worked copious quantities of fringe, a monotonous and matronly occupation which brought her a good deal of teasing from her friends. Marlborough meanwhile turned to gardening. Under his direction ten of the twenty or so acres at Holywell, hitherto taken up with orchard and pasture, were gradually converted into formal gardens. Water was diverted from the Ver on the southern boundary to form an elaborate system of canals and ponds, which provided both the centre-piece for the garden layout and fish for the table.[8]

Sarah admitted that flowers were 'a very innocent pleasure' and liked to have a well-stocked kitchen garden from which to supply her household and practise her considerable skills as an amateur apothecary, but an elaborate pleasure garden for its own sake was not to her taste. The dirt and disruption, as well as the expense of Marlborough's operations bothered her.[9] Even so, she could not help responding to his delight in his creation and to the beauty of the gardens once they became established. In later years, when he was absent on campaign, he would remind her of their pleasure in walking alone together there, listening to the nightingales in the 'wilderness' at the far end of the garden.[10] Enough pasture remained for the cow that kept the whole household supplied with milk, and for the family's horses. Godolphin sent Sarah a new mare, with anxious injunctions not to ride her 'till some of your women has tryed her whether she will endure a woman's saddle', and 'never to ride her through the town of St. Albans, where there are twenty things every moment that will make any horse shy'. Visiting or taking exercise she rode out a good deal, sometimes long distances into the surrounding countryside.[11] In this settled routine, with her family and friends about her, she was able to relax, regain her usual robust health, and forget the stresses of the previous years.

The only real disturbance to her peace came in the summer of 1693, when Mrs Jenyns suffered a paralytic stroke. While the Princess dispatched medical help from London, Sarah at once took charge in the sickroom. There she nursed her mother devotedly, scarcely leaving her even to eat or sleep, until she died on 27 July. The fits of 'disorder and ill humour' between the two had not decreased with the years, although they were always quickly made up, and it took Sarah some time to come to terms with her loss. For weeks she continued to brood over the details of her mother's illness, and to reproach herself, of all things, with not having done enough for her in her last days. Perhaps she was really blaming herself for the past frictions of their relationship. At her insistence the Princess questioned Dr Radcliffe as to whether anything further could have been done to save Mrs Jenyns, and received the characteristically blunt reply that the case had been hopeless from the first, but that Sarah had managed to keep her mother alive longer than anyone could have expected.[12]

Throughout August Sarah remained at St Albans winding up her mother's affairs, for Mrs Jenyns had left her sole heir and executrix.'I fear by what deare Mrs Freeman says it will be a great while before she will com to town,' Anne wrote, '& you may be sure exsept I should be dying or something extraordinary should happen, I would not be so unreasonable [as] to desire you to com till your busines is over.'[13] Nor apparently did Sarah go with her husband to the much publicized political 'congress' at Althorp towards the end of August.[14] Although it was widely believed to presage the reinstatement of Sunderland, Shrewsbury, and Marlborough himself, and the reconciliation of the two Courts, Sarah remained rightly sceptical about Sunderland's ability to bring all this about, and she prolonged her stay at St Albans for some days after Marlborough had gone up to town for the opening of Parliament on 7 November. Apart from her distaste for London and the Court, it was a wrench to part from her children. She told a friend how the sight of Henrietta at the window of Holywell as she drove away drew her love.[15]

Unlike his wife, however, Marlborough was by no means content with the indefinite prospect of a quiet country life. He hoped that his friend Shrewsbury's reappointment as secretary of state in March 1694 would lead to his being restored to his former commands. In anticipation he even wrote to the exiled King James to ask his permission to accept. When this prospect faded, his trafficking with the Jacobites took a more serious turn; as Shrewsbury himself commented, 'it is natural for a man that is very ill on one side, to desire not to be so on the other'.[16] Early in May, in order to give some evidence of his commitment to his old master, Marlborough disclosed the secret destination of a forthcoming expedition against the French naval installations at Brest. The project failed disastrously and its leader, General Thomas Talmash, died of his wounds. It has now been established that this failure was owing to advance information received by the French of an earlier date than Marlborough's, and to Talmash's misjudgement in pressing the attack despite the obvious preparations to meet it.[17] Nevertheless this betrayal has remained the most difficult charge for Marlborough's apologists to deal with, particularly as he immediately pressed for his own reappointment in Talmash's place. It did him no good. 'As to what you wrote in your last letter concerning lord Marlborough,' William coldly replied to Shrewsbury, 'I can say no more, than that I do not think it for the good of my service to entrust him with the command of my troops.'[18]

It is unlikely that Sarah knew much of this. She always had some sympathy with those who suffered for their Jacobite allegiances, and particularly with the women: with Anne Merryweather, for example, who had been arrested for distributing a printed declaration of King James three years before, but had refused to reveal her source even under repeated threat of execution; or Susanna Counter, the imprisoned wife of a Jacobite conspirator, to whom Sarah was still paying a small annuity at the time of her own death more than forty years later.[19] The quarrel between the two Courts certainly threw her a good deal into Jacobite company. Once the Queen had forbidden normal visits to her sister, Sarah recalled, 'nobody but two or three Jacobitt ladys came near the Princesse, & it was easy to observe that all of that interest rejoyced much at this difference'.[20] Among these ladies were Lady Sandwich and her witty companion, Elizabeth Higgons, whose father and brothers were active Jacobites, and they also became Sarah's close friends for a time. But the only reference to Jacobite intrigues in their letters is joking. In the late summer of 1694 Sarah paid a visit to her mother's estate on Romney Marsh, an area of the Kent coast notorious for clandestine comings and goings; and this happened to coincide with the escape from the Tower and subsequently to France of the Jacobite agent, Colonel John Parker. On her return Elizabeth Higgons wrote slyly, 'I heard in towne yesterday twas tould a privie counsellour you convey'd away Parker when you were in Kent. I conclud my Lord Lucas [the Governor of the Tower] is in love & takes this way to gett you into his hands.'[21]

No doubt when Sarah was with her Jacobite acquaintances she adapted her conversation to her company. When taxed to her face with having encouraged the Princess in her flight to Nottingham, she would lay the blame on Lady Fitzhardinge. Lady Sandwich, wishfully misinterpreting Sarah's detestation of William, believed that she had quickly come to repent her own and her husband's part in bringing the Revolution about, while a government *agent provocateur* who visited the Princess's household in 1692 reported a certain 'brisk and bitter lady' as saying that she hoped James would soon return to depose William and avenge his daughter's ill treatment.[22] But against this dubious information ('the brisk and bitter lady' may well have been Lady Sandwich rather than Sarah) must be set Sarah's own claim, which rings true, that she was never seriously tempted by the Jacobites, being 'perfectly convinced that a Roman Catholic is not to be trusted with the liberties of England'; and she swore afterwards that she had 'never once repined at the change of the government, no, not in all the time of that long persecution I went through'; she only wished that it had been brought about by someone other than the hated William.[23]

Although her violent personal hostility to William and Mary (like her opposition to Walpole's government later) might have given rise to rumours of disaffection, the only real motive she could ever comprehend for being a Jacobite was self-interest. It was natural, she conceded, for Roman Catholics and those who had lost estates by the Revolution to wish for the return of the exiled King. And from this point of view, whatever intrigues Marlborough's insecurity and frustrated ambition might lead him into, she knew that her own family could have no real stake in a Stuart restoration. Even so, she had to take account of the fact that James might be restored whether she liked it or not, and it is not surprising that she took care to keep up her Jacobite contacts.

Chief among these, of course, was still her sister Frances, but at this time they were entirely preoccupied with a violent personal quarrel. After Tyrconnel's death in 1691 the Irish Protestants had pressed the government to make an example of his widow, who was held to have been a pernicious influence on him during his viceroyalty. As a result Frances was outlawed in Ireland in her own right, and so prevented from claiming her jointure out of her husband's forfeited estate.[24] Then came the further shock of learning that she had been not so much as mentioned in her mother's will. Sarah was sympathetic about the jointure, although in her present circumstances there was little she could do about it; and she tried to soften the other matter by pointing out that what their mother had left, chiefly her Kentish estate, was not of much value. 'Indeed sister,' Lady Tyrconnel replied frigidly, 'I belive there is very few so voide of good nattur that would not think I might expect the same usage your selfe had what letle so ever was left'; and she added, 'all these things might apeare less heavey then at a time [when] som are starveing and others not thought ell in there affairs'. She even hinted that Sarah had been responsible for the unfairness of the will.[25] Sarah was not prepared to let her sister's claim to be starving pass: 'tho I knew there must bee a great change in your fortune, yet having some warning & hearing you returnd all you had into France I have never dreamt of your wanting any thing'. As for their mother's will,

I have noe reason to find fault with [it] because it was certainly intended very kind to me . . . I am very far from saying or thinking you had noe reason to expect a share in what my mother left, but I ded not make my mothers will, & if she had lived a thousand yeares I should never have named the settleing her estate to her. I thought it looked in me soe much like intirest. I never had soe much as a wish but that it might serve her occasions as long as she ded live . . .

And she ended: 'I must own with the same plainnesse you express in yours, I am much more indeferant as to what you think of me sence I had your last leter, then I thought I could ever have been.'[26] This put an end to all communication between the sisters for the next three years.

Mrs Jenyns had not only made Sarah her sole beneficiary, but had stipulated that Marlborough ('tho I love him from my heart') should have no share whatever in the inheritance.[27] Embittered by her long legal battles with her menfolk for control of Agney, she was determined that it should now pass absolutely to her daughter, with no possibility of male interference. Yet as Sarah soon discovered, the will was not in itself sufficient authority for her to possess the estate separately from her husband. Of his own accord, as she relates, Marlborough therefore said he would comply with its provisions, and arranged for the estate to be placed in the hands of trustees (one of whom was Godolphin) for her sole benefit and disposal.[28] It was only one of a succession of such settlements throughout their lives, by which he acknowledged her need to retain her independence even within marriage. But on this occasion, although Sarah probably did not know it, he had a more practical motive as well for increasing her separate fortune. The settlement of Agney was executed on 4 May 1694, the very time at which he sent information to James of the Brest expedition.[29]

Whatever frustration Marlborough might feel at his enforced retirement, the news of the heavy casualties at Steenkirk, Landen, and Brest, which reached the backwater of Holywell from time to time in the gazettes and newsletters, only increased Sarah's thankfulness that her family was for the time being beyond the reach of such dangers. 'The Duke of Marl. & I liv'd very much at St Albans,' she wrote of this interlude many years later,

where we had frequent news of Generals killed in the Wars, for King William had no success in any thing of that sort, & I own as publick spirited as I am, at that time I had rather have had the King of France Master of England, than have had the Duke of Marlborough hazarded in Battles when so many Generals were killed. In this retired way we lived a great while . . . [30]

Indeed, by the end of 1694 it looked as if the Churchills might have excluded themselves from public life permanently by their allegiance to the Princess. Then in December, while Anne was still at Berkeley House and the prospect of a reconciliation apparently as remote as ever, the Queen was taken ill with smallpox. As soon as it became clear that her life was in danger Anne asked to see her. Although she was discouraged from doing so, the King sent a message of thanks and assured her that she would be allowed to visit if the Queen recovered. To one of these messages Lady Derby added a postscript, presenting her duty to the Princess. As Sarah commented with masterly cynicism, 'this civil answer and my Lady Derby's postscript made me conclude more than if the College of Physicians had told it me that the disease was mortal'.[31] The Queen died on 28 December, and on the advice of Sunderland and the Archbishop of Canterbury Anne at once sent William a letter of condolence and asked leave to wait on him.

Sarah was certainly not opposed to the reconciliation in itself. All her references to Sunderland's efforts are approving. Apart from any other consideration, the making up of the quarrel was the only thing that could relieve her of the pressures of the past three years. Indeed it had become obvious to almost everyone that it was high time to put an end to an affair which had become a serious embarrassment to both sides. 'I never heard of any one that opposed the reconcilement but the Earle of Portland,' Sarah added, 'upon which my Lord Sunderland spoke very short to him, as . . . he had a very good talent when he thought people were impertinent.'[32] What she did object to very strongly, however, was the submissive tone of the letter to William which Anne's male advisers had drafted for her. She considered that the Princess had already done enough in the messages she had sent during the Queen's illness, and that the King could not now avoid making up the breach of his own accord. Not only was the Princess his next heir by Act of Parliament, but by right of inheritance her title to the crown was better than his. The unpopular King was therefore bound for his own sake 'to make use of her interest to strengthen his own & to make a court for the wemen'; otherwise, 'everybody who had a mind to shew they did not care for him would certainly do it by making their court to her'. Having been the recipient of Anne's tirades against 'the Dutch abortive' for the past three years, Sarah was also in a better position than the men to appreciate the full insincerity of the letter: 'it was full of expressions that the polliticians make nothing of,' she complained, 'but it was a great trouble to me to have her write what could not be true after such usage.'[33]

As usual, her obsession with sincerity and plain speaking had completely warped her judgement, and of course her opinion was not allowed to prevail on this occasion. William was still King and the issues at stake were worth a few conventional insincerities. As Sarah admitted bitterly, 'I was never the councillour upon such great occasions'. While the *rapprochement* between the King and the Princess was being slowly negotiated, she must also have been uneasily aware that her own position was the chief issue under consideration. Yet left to himself, William had no desire to pursue the quarrel against her, and no further pressure was brought to bear on the Princess to part with her. Once this was settled,

Anne was able to pay a formal visit of condolence to Kensington on 13 January.[34] All this while Marlborough had declared his support for the reconciliation as publicly as possible, realizing that if anything happened to hinder it, he and his wife would be held responsible.[35] Sarah, in her dangerous mood, was kept out of the way altogether. A minor illness of one of the children provided a pretext for her to return to St Albans, and she stayed there until Anne had held her first public Court at Berkeley House on 15 January, coming unobtrusively back to town two days later.[36] Although she continued to keep out of sight during the visits which the King now occasionally made to the Princess, her position was put beyond doubt when William was persuaded to admit Marlborough to kiss hands at the end of March.[37] This was the most Sunderland and Shrewsbury could do for him for the time being. It was to be several more years before the King would trust him with any official appointment.

One of the consequences of the reconciliation was that Anne was no longer excluded from the royal residences. Prompted by Sunderland, the King offered her St James's Palace in exchange for the Cockpit. Although she could not move in until the following winter, there was nothing to prevent her spending the summer at Windsor. Sarah, who had always loved the Castle and its surroundings, was the more willing to go with her because her 8-year-old son Jack had just begun his schooling across the river at Eton. Constantly at loggerheads with the Huguenot tutor whom she had hired to look after him, she wanted to keep a personal watch on his progress.[38] Nor was she unaware of the advantage of educating him in proximity to the little Duke of Gloucester, only two years younger and the eventual heir to the throne. When the Prince and Princess moved their whole household to Windsor in July, Gloucester delightedly took possession of St George's Hall as an ideal place to stage his mock battles, and Lord Churchill was allowed to come over from Eton with a group of friends to take part in a schoolboy version of the siege of Namur, then taking place on the Continent.[39] But the news of its surrender to the King's forces at the end of August produced another disagreement between Sarah and Anne's male advisers. The fulsome letter of congratulation which they drafted for the Princess to send gave Sarah 'more uneasiness than any other instance of her respectfulness' to the King, and she claimed to have been proved right when William 'never returned any answer to it, nor so much as a civil message'.[40]

In December 1695 the Marlboroughs moved into the lodgings in the south-eastern corner of St James's Palace, overlooking the Park, which were to be their London home for the next fifteen years. With the King now visiting St James's regularly, Sunderland persuaded Sarah not to keep avoiding him so ostentatiously. Their first meeting took place one morning when William came to attend chapel at the Palace. Although Sarah took care to stand as far away as she could, 'for fear he, or any body else, shou'd think I came upon any account, but to wait upon the Princess', he went out of his way to show his approval of her presence. William could be courtly when he chose, and the whole episode passed off as well as Sarah's stiff and unforgiving manner would permit.[41]

Although the Princess was now next in line to the throne, she still had no role in government. While Sarah must have watched the rise of the Whigs to power with passionate interest and approval, she therefore continued to live in much the same retired way as before, still spending as much time as she could away from Court. The dullness and unattractiveness of the Princess's other female servants had became a byword, while Prince George found it almost impossible to secure reliable candidates for his senior offices. 'There has been already so many changes to so little purpose', Sarah remarked of one particularly unsatisfactory appointment, '[that] I begin to think it is decreed our family is to be filled with such sort of creatures.'[42] Although none dared quarrel with her openly, she was conscious that her monopoly of favour and influence in this small, enclosed, and ill-assorted society made her the object of much covert envy and criticism. Her assertion that she had given up the practice of selling Court offices was simply not believed; nor did her rather self-righteous bouts of reforming zeal in such matters do anything to reduce the number of her enemies.[43]

Few of the Princess's letters to her for this period survive. Although Mrs Morley and Mrs Freeman now conversed on terms of virtual equality, their friendship was no longer controversial; also, they had less in common than in the past. Anne's monotonous series of pregnancies and stillbirths continued, confining her indoors for months at a time. Lack of exercise, overeating, and frequent attacks of 'gout' combined to make her grotesquely overweight and a semi-invalid while she was still in her thirties.[44] Although Sarah was five years older, her debilitating years of child-bearing were over. With her abundant health and vitality she had the appearance and led the life of a much younger woman ('Indeed you trust too much to your good constitution,' Lady Sunderland admonished her, 'and do not remember . . . that you are past fifteen').[45] It was her growing family who now engrossed most of her attention, and if the accounts she wrote in bitterness after her loss of favour are to be believed (and there must have been at least an element of truth in them), the friendship with Anne had now become a very one-sided affair: 'tho it was extreamly Tedious to be so much where there could be no manner of Conversation, I knew she loved me, & I suffered by fearing I did wrong when I was not with her: for which reason I have gone a thousand times to her, when I had rather have been in a dungeon.'[46] Yet even though there might be less pleasure than ever at Anne's Court, the prospect of advantage was now infinitely greater. The King could not be expected to live long. The Marlboroughs, who had shared the Princess's adversity, had only to bide their time for a few more years to receive their reward. It was during this fallow period that Sarah's intimacy with her mistress enabled Marlborough and Godolphin (the latter shortly to be admitted to the inmost circle as 'Mr Montgomery') to consolidate their position as Anne's confidential advisers in preparation for their coming ministerial roles. Sarah recalled how by this time the Princess 'would not suffer me to live with her but as a friend, or do the least thing without sending me to ask Mr Montgomery's and Mr Freeman's opinion'.[47]

The chief event of the following winter, the discovery of an elaborate Jacobite assassination plot, proved to be a turning-point for the unpopular King, rallying support for him in Parliament and out. Godolphin, as Sarah noted, reacted with 'great horror' to the revelations, which finally convinced him to give up his toying with the Jacobites.[48] One of those arrested, however, was Sir John Fenwick, who tried to extricate himself by producing a confession which cited the former Jacobite intrigues of both Godolphin and Marlborough. They were only saved by the fact that Fenwick had also implicated Shrewsbury and Admiral Russell, the hero of La Hogue. For the sake of these two, the Whigs were prepared to exert all their strength to discredit Fenwick's confession *in toto* and condemn him to death by Act of Attainder. Even so, the affair gave them the opportunity to get rid of Godolphin from the treasury and replace him with their own financial genius, Charles Montagu.

This loss of office drew Godolphin closer than ever to the Marlboroughs. He spent the early summer of 1697 at St Albans, went on with them to Anne's Court at Tunbridge Wells in July, and accompanied them back to St Albans when Anne returned to Windsor in the autumn.[49] It was at this time that a project came to fruition which must have been in the minds of all of them for some years: a match between Godolphin's son Francis, now 18 and just completing his studies at Cambridge, and Lady Henrietta Churchill, who was two or three years younger. Sarah commented that Godolphin's proposal was 'a sufficient proof of friendship because att that time hee might have had his choice of most wemen in England, & our daughter was noe fortune'.[50] In fact she had been worried for some time about the need to dower their large family of daughters well enough to make ambitious matches for them. The Princess now came to their rescue. She was very fond of Henrietta, and Godolphin was by this time second only to the Marlboroughs in her favour. She therefore offered to pay the whole portion of £10,000 herself. Marlborough was delighted and ready to accept the full amount, but Sarah, who knew that Anne was always short of money, demurred. Bearing in mind that their second daughter would soon be marriageable as well, she settled with the Princess that £5,000 should go to Henrietta and £5,000 be reserved for her younger sister when the time came.[51]

As both families gathered in London early in December to witness the fireworks in celebration of the peace of Ryswick and to complete the preparations for the marriage, Marlborough's wilderness years were drawing to an end. The little Duke of Gloucester was now of an age to have an establishment of his own. His governess, Lady Fitzhardinge, would give place to a governor, a post which carried a share in government and a salary of £2,000 a year. The King's candidate was Shrewsbury, but his refusal left the way open for Marlborough, who was of course the Princess's choice.[52] In these auspicious circumstances, the marriage of Henrietta and Francis took place on 28 April 1698, while Sarah (who confessed that she 'never saw any child or friend married in my life that I could hold from dropping tears') looked on and wept copiously.[53] For the time being the young couple, whose settlement was very modest despite the Princess's contribution, were to share her lodgings in St James's Palace, and it was not long before Henrietta also joined her mother as lady of the bedchamber. No harm came from this constant association at first; Sarah insisted that they lived together 'like sisters', and Henrietta's letters to her 'Dear Angell Mama' during any absence were gushingly affectionate.[54] The problems were to come when she grew old enough to claim her independence.

The marriage and the peace also paved the way for a reconciliation with Lady Tyrconnel. 'Your letter made me wet it more then you could have don when a writing,' Frances wrote to Sarah, '. . . and I must againe aferme that in my hole life I never ded love aney thing better then your selfe whatever star rained for thes late yers to make all apeare rong.'[55] In return Sarah asked their uncle, who went over to Paris with Portland's embassy in December, to assure her that 'I shall be content with half as much kindnes as my hart has for her'.[56] Lady Tyrconnel's religion and circumstances remained a bar to any complete return to intimacy between them. She was never quite reconciled to their respective changes in fortune: it was to be some years more before she could bring herself to forgive Marlborough for his part in the Revolution, and she was still capable of writing 'provoking' letters, accusing Sarah of neglecting her interests.[57] Still, there remained a genuine residue of affection between the sisters, and during the next five years Sarah was to devote much time and energy to restoring Lady Tyrconnel to her Irish possessions.

Her sister's situation, which made Sarah sympathetic to the plight of all dispossessed Irish Jacobites, probably contributed to her involvement in a major public scandal which erupted during this same winter. It centred on the Sunderlands' eldest daughter, Lady Clancarty, who in the course of the previous reign had been forced by her parents into a child marriage with a young Irish nobleman of vast estates. The union had never been consummated. Having taken part in the Irish wars on the Jacobite side, Clancarty had been outlawed and, like Frances Tyrconnel, had entered the service of King James at St Germains. Meanwhile his wife continued to live in increasing unhappiness with her parents in England.[58] Then with the peace came the news that the King had granted Clancarty's confiscated estates to the unpopular Portland. Clancarty's mother and a group of her friends, who included Sarah and Godolphin's sister Mrs Boscawen, decided that Sunderland was not doing enough to protect his daughter's interests. Their plan was to encourage Clancarty to come over and consummate his marriage, in the belief that Sunderland would then be bound to get him a pardon and some financial compensation.[59]

Godolphin, in whom Sarah and Mrs Boscawen confided, was thoroughly alarmed at these amateurish intrigues and warned them that 'your kindnesse to my lady Clancartie & Compassion for her Circumstances, is in a fair way of running you into greater inconveniencies than you are perhaps aware of, & of making it wholly impossible for time or better fortune to mend her Condition hereafter'. He urged that on no account should Clancarty attempt to return to England.[60] It was too late. He came over in secret at the end of December 1698, only to be arrested at the instigation of his brother-in-law, Lord Spencer, while in bed with his wife. Sunderland himself publicly disowned his daughter. Sarah joined the many who petitioned the King to deal leniently with Clancarty, and when he was at last pardoned and granted a pension on condition that he lived in exile in neutral territory for the rest of his life, his wife decided that she would rather accompany him than continue her miserable existence in England.[61] But it was only by befriending her children after her death that Sarah was able finally to make some amends for her part in this affair.

Meanwhile the King had delayed settling the Duke of Gloucester's household until he was on the eve of his departure for the Continent in July; and then, because of the government's financial straits, he allowed only a fraction of the sum voted by Parliament. The Princess had barely time to swallow this grievance before another arose over her right to appoint the subordinate members of the household. On being told by Marlborough that Anne had already made her own choice of these, the

King, according to Sarah, 'fell into a great passion, and said she should not be Queen before her time'. While Sarah irresponsibly encouraged the Princess's anger to the full, the more difficult role of mediator fell to her husband, assisted by the King's amenable new favourite, Albemarle. The latter agreed to take a list of the Princess's appointees to Holland and try to get the King to agree to it.[62]

Sarah's anger was not disinterested, for the establishment of Gloucester's household was a further opportunity for her to provide for her family. Her son, to whom Gloucester had taken a liking, was put down as master of the horse, and she also had hopes of slipping in her cousin Jack Hill as a supernumerary groom of the bedchamber. In fact when the King's list was returned, he was found to have altered the Princess's dispositions only in a few minor instances. Lord Churchill had kept his place, and not only did Sarah's plans for Jack Hill succeed, but she also managed to have his younger sister Alice made one of the laundresses;[63] and it was at about this time as well that she finally found a place for the elder Hill sister in the Princess's household.[64] It is not clear precisely when Abigail took up her duties as bedchamberwoman, but it was certainly before Anne came to the throne. Schooled by her family's misfortunes, she quickly proved herself a discreet and conscientious servant, qualities which were in short supply in the Princess's establishment, and it was not long before Anne began to take a particular liking to her.

Sarah's habit of using the royal household to make provision for her dependants was in this case to have the most far-reaching consequences for her own fortunes. Yet at the time the disposal of a set of poor relations seemed of far less moment than the task of settling her second daughter. In June 1698 the Sunderlands' son and heir, Lord Spencer, had been unexpectedly widowed, and before the month was out Lady Sunderland had made the first tentative overtures to Sarah for his remarriage to Lady Anne Churchill. Both politically and dynastically, this was to prove the most significant of her daughters' matches. It was also a flattering measure of how far they had risen in the world. Yet despite the support of Godolphin and his sister, Sarah hesitated before accepting. The Clancarty affair had somewhat soured her feelings for the Sunderlands; she privately told her sister that Spencer's good character made some amends for his parents' vagaries.[65] Nor was she under any illusions as to their motives for seeking the match: 'you are pleased to say you must take a great deale of it to your self and lord Marlborough,' Lady Sunderland wrote in one of her many letters on the subject, 'and that lady Ann can't have much share in it upon so small an acquaintance.'[66]

At 15 the girl already promised to be the most beautiful of the four
very handsome Churchill sisters, but she was also the only one not to
have inherited her mother's robust health, and Spencer was not the
obvious person to make her happy. 'He was tall, of a large make,' Sarah
remembered of this curiously compelling but unattractive figure who
was to play such a large part in her life, 'but [he] had no more genteelness
than a Porter', and his complexion was 'one entire mark' from smallpox.
Although he had an impressive intellect and none of the rakish vices
which had brought his elder brother to a bad end, he was hot-headed and
intemperate. In the heat of one Commons debate he had disgusted his
father by declaring 'that he hoped to live to p-ss upon the House of
Lords'. Even his mother could not deny that he showed too much 'heat
and over earnestness' in politics.[67] Yet as far as Sarah was concerned this
was his main redeeming feature, for Spencer was already making his
mark as one of the leading Whigs in the House of Commons. During the
coming winter she therefore put aside her other misgivings and set
herself to overcome the obstacles to the match.

There was a temporary distraction in February, when Henrietta gave
birth prematurely to a son at St Albans. For the rest of the winter her
mother's whole attention and concern were centred on her and the baby
William ('Willigo'), whose survival remained doubtful for some weeks.[68]
But by April Sarah told Lady Sunderland that she was again 'labouring
like a pack horse' to bring the match about, and that some part of the
difficulty had already been overcome,[69] a reference perhaps to the
consent of the Princess, whose contribution was necessary to complete
the marriage portion. Sarah had apparently secured this without too
much difficulty, despite Spencer's unpalatable political conduct, by
reminding Anne of the debt of gratitude she owed to Sunderland for his
support during her quarrel with the Court. Indeed the Princess, citing
precedents of former monarchs who had dowered the daughters of their
favourites, now promised to provide for the two remaining Churchill
sisters in the same way. Although Marlborough had by this time
established himself as Anne's most trusted adviser, Sarah always insisted,
and probably with justice (the offers were made to her personally), that
this great financial benefit to her family was entirely owing to the
Princess's friendship for her.[70]

In September the two families retired to Althorp to complete the
negotiations. This was always Sarah's ideal country house; 'there was
room enough in it to entertain a King, if one could have so bad a taste as
to like them, or the Company that attends them. And yet it was so
contriv'd that one might live mighty comfortably with a few friends.'[71]
And by the end of their stay the terms of the marriage were agreed. Back

at Windsor for a few days with Anne before settling at St James's for the winter, Sarah had reason to be pleased with the events of the year, although in a letter to her uncle she sounded merely tired and jaded. It was the old problem of reconciling the demands of her personal and public lives. Yet even though she might still complain privately, the future of every member of her family was now so dependent upon the Princess that giving up her position was no longer a serious option. 'I thank God all my family is very well,' she wrote, 'but my own circomstances not very good, being ever in a hurry, which is very disagreeable, but not to be help'd, therefore must be indured.'[72]

Sunderland rightly predicted that the Spencer–Churchill marriage, which took place on 2 January 1700, would 'certainly be turned to politics as every thing is'. This new union between Marlborough, Godolphin, and Sunderland, '*les plus fameux et les plus habiles Politiques d'Angleterre*', was soon public knowledge, and it was assumed that Godolphin's return to the treasury would not be long delayed.[73] Then at the end of July an express brought them all hurrying back to Windsor from another gathering at Althorp. An apparently trivial indisposition of the Duke of Gloucester had put his life in danger within hours, and by the following morning he was dead. Anne clung to Sarah in her grief, refusing to see her other ladies or receive any visits of condolence.[74] Although she still hoped that she might yet produce a healthy child, Sarah, with a mixture of pity and impatience, dismissed this as the wishful thinking it undoubtedly was.[75] The death of the Protestant heir and the indifferent health of both the King and the Princess now made it urgently necessary for Parliament to confirm the succession in the Hanoverian line after Anne's death (the Electress Sophia was both a Protestant and a granddaughter of James I). All through the autumn of 1700 Marlborough and Godolphin therefore worked with Rochester, the leading Tory peer, and with Robert Harley, hitherto the most influential opponent of the Court in the House of Commons, to procure a Parliament with the necessary Tory majority to settle the succession securely.[76]

Gloucester's death also meant that Sarah had to reconsider her son's future, and within a matter of days after the funeral he was packed off, at the early age of 13, to continue his studies under a tutor at Cambridge. Godolphin, who saw him as he passed through London, was impressed by the sensible way in which he took this sudden change in his prospects, reporting to Sarah at Windsor 'without flattery or partiality', that he was 'not only the best natured & most agreeable, but the most forethinking & reasonable creature that one can imagine of his age'.[77] But Sarah was annoyed to learn that Gloucester's other servants were not to expect pensions from the King. This meant that her two Hill cousins, whom she had thought permanently provided for, were back on her hands. She transferred Jack Hill to Prince George's household for the time being, until Marlborough (who always thought him 'good for nothing') was able to find a place for him in the army; and she persuaded the Princess to give Alice Hill a pension, afterwards commuted to a substantial annuity for life—a very handsome compensation for her few months' duty as laundress.[78]

At about the same time her aid was again invoked on behalf of their eldest brother, whose promotion in the customs service required a surety of £2,000 for his good conduct. Always readier to use her influence than to make a financial commitment herself, Sarah referred the young man to his father's relations, the Harleys. Robert Harley, who had formerly refused to do anything for the Hills, could not now help seeing that Sarah would shortly be a person whom it would not be wise to offend, and agreed to the arrangement at once. As she afterwards commented, 'Mr Harly might very well have a mind to give himself a good air to one in my post at that time, if he had not had any view of making the use hee has sence don of Mrs Hill'.[79] Thus it was Sarah herself, in her anxiety to rid herself of responsibility for these poor relations, who created the first bond between Harley and the Hills.

Having watched the Tories 'pulling the government in peices' ever since the Revolution, and having always regarded Rochester as her greatest enemy at Court, Sarah viewed their return to power with the sourest disfavour. Rochester's alliance with Marlborough and Godolphin was sealed with frequent meetings and the occasional social gathering,[80] and it may have been one of these which sparked off her best-known and most spectacular tantrum. The story goes that Marlborough, having 'unadvisedly, considering the lady he had to deal with, invited a guest to his table with whom she was at political enmity', broke the news to her as she was sitting at her dressing-table, combing her hair. When he tried to placate her by admiring the magnificent tresses, she snatched up a pair of scissors, cut them off, and flung them at him. 'Calm enough to provoke a saint', Marlborough said nothing and went away, leaving her to contemplate herself in the glass and reflect as her anger cooled, that for once 'she had done rather a foolish thing'. It was not until many years later, after his death, that she discovered the severed hair 'carefully laid by in a cabinet where he kept whatever he held most precious', and at this point in telling the story 'she regularly fell a crying'.[81]

When the King returned from the Continent in the autumn of 1700, he called a general election, returned Godolphin to the treasury, and made

Rochester Lord Lieutenant of Ireland. Although Marlborough did not get the secretaryship of state for which he had hoped, events in Europe were soon to provide him with a more important role. The childless Carlos II of Spain, ailing for years, at last died in October, rejecting William's painstaking arrangements for the peaceful partition of his huge empire, and leaving it instead wholly to the Duke of Anjou, the 16-year-old grandson of Louis XIV. The French King decided to accept the will in preference to the partition treaty, and in February the following year his army took possession of the Dutch barrier fortresses in the Spanish Netherlands. William's lifetime of work to curb the power of France seemed to have been undone almost overnight.

The new Parliament met in February and performed one of its intended functions in settling the Hanoverian succession. Then by slow and reluctant stages over the next four months, at intervals of attempting to impeach the Whig ministers, the turbulent Tory majority finally voted to send 10,000 men to the aid of the Dutch, and recommended the King to make an alliance with the United Provinces, the Emperor, and other powers for the defence of the liberties of Europe against France. Marlborough's hour had come at last. In June 1701 he was appointed both commander-in-chief of the 10,000 men and plenipotentiary for the negotiation of the treaty.[82] Perhaps only Sarah, for whom the cherished and precarious security of the last few years was now at an end, regretted her husband's restoration to his command. Albemarle, according to her, admitted freely that the King 'had never had any ease since the Duke of Marlborough was out of it, for the officers said that everything he proposed was impracticable, & wou'd do nothing without giving him intollerable trouble'.[83]

When Marlborough embarked with the King in July, Sarah declared her intention of joining him at The Hague as soon as possible. Some observers were uneasy that she should thus leave the field to the Jacobite Lady Sandwich, who had been much in Anne's company since her husband's appointment as master of the horse to Prince George six years before.[84] The early intensity of Anne's feeling for her favourite was perhaps on the wane, weakened by Sarah's unconcealed distaste for Court life and by her preoccupation with her own family. Yet there is no real evidence that Sarah felt or had any reason to feel herself insecure in the Princess's friendship at this stage. She was simply taking the opportunity to show her children something of the world and to have as much of her husband's company as possible before the coming European conflict separated them.

When she went on board the yacht *Henrietta* at Greenwich on 5 September, it was in company with her two younger daughters, their

brother being left behind so as not to disrupt his studies at Cambridge.[85]
At The Hague the States General had placed the Mauritshuis at
Marlborough's disposal, the grandest of their ambassadorial residences,
with its long windows overlooking the waters of the Hofviver in the
heart of the capital. His wife was treated on all sides with great
ceremony, and duly professed herself very sensible of everyone's
civilities. Nevertheless, for her the trip was not to be an outstanding
success. A series of minor ailments aggravated her usual intolerance of
foreign manners and customs, and Marlborough was so often away that
she had to be squired on a shopping and sightseeing jaunt to Amsterdam
by the English Resident, James Dayrolle.[86] Even at Het Loo, William's
palatial hunting lodge in Guelderland, she resisted all attempts to put her
at her ease. When the King asked her how she liked Lady Albemarle's
stilted English and added, 'tell me, & don't flatter her', the challenge to
her sincerity was almost too much: 'I felt my face grow very hot, &
wisht mightily that I might have had the liberty to have ask't him why he
should think I would flatter her, since I had never flatter'd him.'[87] In
such a mood and in such a place she was a liability. By the time they
returned to The Hague in October Marlborough was anxious to get her
back to England as soon as possible, and it is significant that he never
allowed her to accompany him abroad officially again.[88]

When they all at last landed in England at the end of November, it was
to find the country again in the ferment of a general election. The King,
dissatisfied with the conduct of the Tories, had yielded to Sunderland's
persuasions to try the Whigs again. Godolphin at once resigned, and
Marlborough's enemies claimed that only self-interest kept him from
doing the same.[89] In fact there was ample justification for his remaining.
King James had died at St Germains in September and Louis XIV at once
recognized his son as the rightful King of England. William himself was
now plainly a dying man. The broken collar-bone which he suffered at
the end of February 1702 merely hastened his end. On 8 March, with a
major European war about to break out and her right to the throne at
stake, Anne at last succeeded as Queen. Prematurely aged and with no
training in affairs of state, she had never had more need of her friends.

'We Four Must Never Part'
1702–1703

Lᴛʜᴏᴜɢʜ for Sarah the reign of Queen Anne was quickly to prove yet another 'Sceen of Trouble', at first it appeared that all the Marlboroughs' troubles must be over with Anne's accession. At last they reaped the rewards of standing by her through the years of opposition and obscurity. Marlborough was made a Knight of the Garter, appointed captain-general of the forces, and left almost at once for Holland to reassure the Dutch of the Queen's intention of maintaining the Alliance and pursuing the war against France. The two senior bedchamber offices of groom of the stole and mistress of the robes, whose functions Sarah had performed for many years, were now bestowed on her formally, and to these she added the keepership of the privy purse, a low-ranking post usually held by one of the bedchamber-women, but one which was to give her a useful command of the Queen's personal spending money. For the time being, despite rumours of a dukedom, there was no titular increase in rank for the Marlboroughs. Sarah's only concession to her new position was to acquire a page to attend her when she went about in public, and this appointment had been made on impulse, simply because she thought him 'the handsomest Boy that ever I saw in my Life'.[1]

In addition to granting her the three Court offices, the Queen also made Sarah ranger of Windsor Park, a virtual sinecure which was chiefly desirable for the Lodge that went with it. Remembering that when they had ridden by this place in the past Sarah had spoken enviously of it, Anne now took a double pleasure in evicting the loathed Portland and making the gift to her own favourite for life, for 'anything that is of soe much satisfaction as this poor place seems to be to you, I would give my deare Mrs. Freeman for all her days, which I pray God may be many and as truly happy as this world can make you'.[2] Sarah's income from these four offices, amounting to over £6,000 a year, was paid into a goldsmith's account in her own name, and like the rest of her fortune was held quite independently of her husband.[3]

The influence which Sarah commanded in her new position was immediately apparent. A bill restoring Lady Tyrconnel to her rights in her husband's forfeited estate passed both Houses of Parliament within a matter of days of Anne's accession, 'both whigs and tories striving who could favour it most'. 'Thus it is to be the sister of a favourite,' growled its defeated opponents.[4] As mistress of the robes Sarah had a number of subordinate posts directly at her disposal, which she bestowed at once on her own servants.[5] Most of the ladies of the bedchamber also owed their appointments in some degree to her support; Lady Spencer now joined her sister as one of them and Mary was soon to follow. Many requests for pensions and royal bounty likewise came through Sarah. The most striking example of her interest in this respect was the secret grant to Sunderland of a pension of £2,000 a year from the privy purse, an amount which constituted 10 per cent of the Queen's yearly allowance for all her personal expenses. Sarah had persuaded her to make him this gift in recognition of his support when she was Princess,[6] and despite the fact that for some time past he had been on very bad terms with Marlborough and Godolphin because of his intrigues with the Whigs in the last years of William's reign.

Yet this favour and influence had their adverse effects. None of Sarah's Court posts was a sinecure. She was now busy as never before, not only with attendance on the Queen, but in answering, and usually refusing, up to twenty requests a day for places and pensions. This, as she noted, 'her Majesty was pleased [with], because I saved her a good deal of trouble',[7] and certainly the number of rejections was not her fault. The Queen and Prince, who had previously had difficulty in filling their households suitably, were now besieged with applicants, and their financial resources were far from unlimited, especially in the first years of the reign. But together with Sarah's own monopoly of favour and her conspicuous use of it to benefit her family and dependants, the situation aroused resentment. Nor did her manner do her any service; there was too often an edge of impatience verging on open rudeness in her dealings with unsuccessful petitioners. To the mother of a candidate for a maid of honour's post, for example, she wrote that the two qualifications were beauty and a good education; 'the first may be reported, but the other is sometimes fancy, & the Queen will see all that are offer'd, & judg of it her self. Her Majesty has had soe mellancholly a prospect for many years in her drawing room, I don't much wonder that she desires to mend it.'[8]

Having forgone her own pension at the Revolution, Sarah was also particularly disgusted to find that whoever had had a pension in any reign 'within fifty year' expected that it should be continued. 'Till I found it,' she added, 'I could not imagin that people could have so little shame, as to ask mony of a Prince with out personall kindnesse, merrit, or want.'[9] Godolphin's sister-in-law, angered by Sarah's manner of putting off a candidate she had recommended, flounced off with the remark that 'she wished her greatness might do her any good, but she was very sure it would nobody else'.[10] Sarah was well aware of the mingled envy and dislike she attracted. After her years of relative seclusion, she now found herself 'raild at and flatterd from Morning to Night, neither of which was agreeable to me', and knew that 'there were but few Women that would not have poysond me for the Happynesse they thought I enjoyd'.[11]

Although the announcement of Godolphin's appointment as Lord Treasurer was not made until the formal declaration of war against France in May, he and Marlborough at once began to act as the Queen's ministers, mediating between her and the two political parties. The relationship between the Queen, her chief female servant, and the two men was uniquely close. 'Every day makes me more & more sensible of the great Blessing God Almighty has given me in three such Friends as your dear self, Mr Freeman & Mr Montgomery,' Anne wrote at this time, 'a happiness I believe no body in my sphere ever enjoy'd before.'[12] The common bond that linked them was still Sarah. In raising Marlborough to the position which the Queen now confirmed, William had been influenced not only by his obvious abilities, but by his special relationship with Anne. In the course of the two preceding reigns Marlborough had done much to gain her favour in his own right, but the initial advantage which enabled him to do so was that of being Mrs Freeman's husband. Now Sarah's position became an immeasurable asset to him in his dealings with foreign powers as well, by contributing to the sense that he was in the new Queen's complete confidence as well as being her official representative. On the eve of Marlborough's departure for the Continent, a Dutch agent in London remarked that he could scarcely be said to be leaving the Queen because his wife would remain so close to her.[13]

The difficulty was that Sarah was not content simply to use her friendship with the Queen to support the ministers in their posts. She wanted an independent role, and her greatest source of discontent with her new position was that she soon found she had little influence where she most wished to have it: in political matters. The fundamental divergence of opinion between Sarah and the Queen in this respect had been kept in abeyance by their shared opposition to the Court in the two preceding reigns and by William's refusal to allow the Princess any role in government. Now Sarah found that 'the first important step which her Majesty took after her accession . . . was against my wishes and inclination: I mean her throwing herself and her affairs almost entirely into the hands of the Tories'.[14] Although this was something of an exaggeration, Sarah was horrified to see Whigs who had favoured the Revolution and whom she thought much more likely to support the Queen removed to make way for the Tories, who 'for sixteen years had been pulling the government in peices'.[15]

Her own allegiance to Whiggism—what she called 'the honest interest' or, in her more emotional moments, 'the glorious cause of liberty'—had strengthened since the Revolution, although not as a result of any personal ties. 'I had never no engagements to the Whiggs & no obligations to them, but much to the contrary,' she wrote afterwards, 'for they were all violently against me during the breach in the last reigne.'[16] What now fuelled her partisanship was an obsessive fear of France and the Jacobites, deriving partly from such episodes as the assassination plot of 1696 and the conspiratorial talk of her Jacobite friends in William's reign, but chiefly from her lifelong sense of the insecurity of all governments. When the Queen afterwards complained of her favourite's constant campaigning on behalf of the Whigs, Sarah insisted that all she had done 'was in order that wee may bee safe'; it was only under a Whig government that England could be safe from the overweening power of France, and English liberties and property secure from a Jacobite restoration. The ultimate aim of the Tory leaders, Rochester and Nottingham, and of most of their party, she was convinced, was to restore the Prince of Wales,

and since in such a case nobody could bee sure how far a change might bee carry'd when the person deposed had been crown'd I feard the loss of Mrs Morleys life, as well as her three kingdomes, & out of these apprehentions too well grownded, I was perpetually telling her that the whiggs were in her true interest, & that the torrys had one to distroy her . . . [17]

Her specific political aims were not at all profound or sophisticated; asked afterwards what alternative scheme of government she had had in mind at this stage, she could only repeat that she had no scheme 'but to get honest men into the service, and such as would not give us up to France'. But she assumed that the Queen, who for twenty years had consulted her about all her concerns, would now accept her advice in such matters, and she considered herself as well qualified as the ministers to give it, having 'a great deal of experience of the men on both sides, & . . . a certain knowledge of a great many facts, which her majesty could hear from nobody else'.[18]

The Queen was completely unimpressed by these claims to political experience; she remarked prophetically that when Sarah came to know the Whigs better, she would find they were not all they professed to be.[19] Nor did she have any sympathy with Sarah's wholesale condemnation of the Tories, whose support of the Church of England appealed to her own devout Anglicanism and who were certainly much less universally infected with Jacobitism than Sarah assumed. She still loved Sarah (though perhaps less fervently and uncritically than before);[20] but even as Princess she had begun to make a marked distinction between the personal intimacy she looked for from her favourite, and the assistance in public affairs for which she had used her chiefly as a channel of communication with Marlborough and Godolphin. Sarah had performed a very significant role in helping to establish them in her mistress's confidence, but now that Anne was Queen and these two were officially her ministers, she had no need of a mediator with them. Indeed, from the very first Anne made it clear that she was not prepared to accept unpalatable advice about politics from a female servant who had no formal right to give it.

In this situation Sarah was completely out of her depth. The royal friendship, always rather one-sided, appears to have been of little value to her now other than as a means of benefiting her family and wielding political influence. Yet with direct political involvement denied, she was totally unfitted by temperament to exercise the kind of unofficial influence which the Queen's fondness for her might otherwise have permitted. Tact, sensitive persuasion, respect for another person's point of view, were to her simply 'flattery & artifices'. Encouraged by Anne ('dear Mrs Freeman is sincerity itself'), she had continued to pride herself on her 'frank, open temper', but with the passage of years and the growth of over-confidence this had come to manifest itself more and more as a boundless outspokenness, exercised, as another friend remarked, without the slightest distinction of persons 'from the prince downwards'. In fact where crowned heads were concerned, Sarah considered that it was a positive duty 'to speak on all occasions . . . without flattery or dissimulation'.[21]

As soon as the Queen showed signs of resisting her advice, Sarah therefore abandoned the deference which she had always found irksome, and made it clear that in political matters she considered her mistress to be totally incapable of independent judgement: 'ignorant in everything but what the parsons had taught her as a child', misinformed about the Whigs by flatterers at her father's Court, and so unable to see that in supporting the Tories she was being imposed on by knaves and fools.[22] Her persistence in offering this unwanted political advice, and above all her increasing rudeness and ill temper (what she herself called 'a warmth natural to sincerity') when she found that it made no impression, were at the root of all her difficulties with Anne. The Queen, always stubborn in defence of her position and opinions, was shocked at her favourite's lack of regard for either their past friendship or her own new status. She complained afterwards that 'never any friend used another *that was their Equal*' as Sarah had treated her ever since her first coming to the crown.[23] To outsiders the relationship appeared to continue unchanged, but very soon Sarah began to sense a new reserve in the Queen's manner towards her.

She acknowledged afterwards that she never succeeded in influencing the Queen in political matters unless Marlborough and Godolphin also lent their weight to her advice; but she added significantly, 'I followed it very closely with them, as well as with her Majesty'.[24] In this, given her relationship with both men, lay her greatest long-term hope of success. For the next decade, with Marlborough spending only a few weeks of each year in England, he and his wife were to lead essentially separate lives. They were now both middle-aged and grandparents several times over. Yet they were still lovers. Marlborough's letters give abundant evidence of his devotion and absolute emotional dependence on her. At Sarah's insistence he destroyed almost all of her replies, but the few scraps which survive show that his absence only made her more conscious of the bond between them. 'Wherever you are whilst I have life my soul shall follow you my ever dear Ld Marl:,' she wrote in one of these, '& wherever I am I shall only kill the time, wish for night that I may sleep, & hope the next day to hear from you.'[25]

Their friendship with Godolphin had now become so close as to allow their enemies to claim that they lived in a *ménage à trois*, similar to that of their friends the Pulteneys and Henry Guy. In fact Sarah was never tempted to be unfaithful to her husband, not only because she loved him, but because (as she afterwards explained) she was determined to be in no man's power. In any case she was always contemptuous of the assumption that a man and a woman could not be alone together without 'doing whatever can bee thought infamous'.[26] Godolphin was not her lover, but her 'best friend'. His steadiness was to be her mainstay during Marlborough's long absences, and he in turn came to depend on her for comfort and companionship in bearing the immense and reluctantly assumed burden of his office. Her passionate concern with public affairs made her a natural confidante for the anxieties and frustrations which the favourite but unworldly sister, Mrs Boscawen, who had been his close companion after his wife's death, could not fully comprehend. Whenever Sarah was at Court Godolphin visited her daily; 'I scarce ever stir abroad, now you are not in town, but to the Treasury or to Kensington,' he told her forlornly during one of her absences. When she was away he wrote to her every day and fretted at the slightest delay in her replies, 'having no other support in your absence'.[27]

More remarkably, Sarah shared in the ministers' correspondence with each other and, as time went on, even in their correspondence with the Queen. Godolphin not only showed her the letters he received, but often gave her his own to read before they were sent. She came to take this so much for granted that on one occasion, when the secretary of state was about to forward Marlborough's letters to Godolphin at Newmarket, she instructed him to send them to her first so that she could open and read them without delay. Even when Marlborough was in England she claimed the right to open his mail during any temporary absence.[28] This, together with the readiness of the two men to discuss their political difficulties with her, went some way towards satisfying her craving for involvement in public affairs, but it also encouraged her in the confident assumption of a pseudo-ministerial role which was to create increasing difficulties with the Queen.

Yet for all this, Sarah found that her real political influence with the two ministers was strictly limited, at least in the early years of the reign. She could make them acutely distressed, even on occasion positively suicidal, by her political disagreements with them, but she could not single-handedly force them to share her vehement Whiggism. Apart from their own natural Tory sympathies, the realities of what the Queen would accept had to be their most important consideration. Sarah herself was compelled to acknowledge that when Anne first came to the throne, Marlborough and Godolphin would not have had so great a share in her favour and confidence 'if they had not been reckoned in the number of the Tories'.[29]

Marlborough returned from The Hague early in April, but by the end of the month he was preparing to leave again to take command of the army in the field. On 12 May he set out with Sarah for Margate, the nearest port of embarkation for Holland. He was now well into his fifties; his health was not robust and he was going into danger. Constant gnawing anxiety about his safety was to add greatly to Sarah's sense of insecurity in the coming years. At Margate his departure was delayed for a week by contrary winds. Overwrought at their impending parting, she could not keep herself from harping on their political differences. 'This looks to me as if everything were to bee governed by faction and nonsense,' she wrote in answer to a letter from Godolphin which gave her notice of yet more Tory appointments, 'and tis noe matter what look things have in the world, or what men are made use of, if they are but such creatures as will right or wronge bee at the dispose of two or three arbitrary men that are at the head of them'; but she added bitterly, 'I know my opinion is very insignifycant upon most occasions.'[30]

On 20 May the wind turned fair and Sarah parted from her husband at the waterside. From the cliffs above the town she watched the yacht put out to sea, while from the deck Marlborough searched with his 'perspective glass' for a last sight of her. Then he went below to begin a letter to her: 'wee are now out of sight of Margate and . . . I doe at this minute suffer soe much that nothing but being with you againe can recompence itt. If you could be sensable of what I now feel, you would endeavour ever to be easy to mee, and then I should be most happy, for it is you onely that can give mee true content.'[31] Yet it was not protestations of love that Sarah wanted at this moment, but evidence that her political opinions mattered to him. Back in London she immediately sat down to write him a long accusing account of further Tory interference with existing Whig office-holders. From The Hague Marlborough patiently tried to explain the situation to her and begged her again not to let politics affect their personal relations, 'for the quiet of my life depends onely on your kindnes'.[32]

Sarah remained busy and irritable. All through June, while the Queen completed the establishment of her household, the inundation of requests for pensions and places continued. When Marlborough forwarded one from her acquaintance of the previous year, James Dayrolle, she snapped at him for adding to her burden. He hastened to apologize: 'it is not that I am unsensible of the trouble you have, for I doe asure you I aprehend it soe much, that I would be very glad to give the onely time I have to myself to ease you.'[33] Her three remaining children were also claiming her attention. The boy Jack, now 15 and still at Cambridge, continued to promise well, but he was also showing disturbing signs of independence. In June, amid rumours that he was about to be appointed to the Prince's household, he bypassed his mother and wrote directly to his father, suggesting that he was now old enough to join him in the army. Marlborough asked Godolphin what he thought of the idea, adding, 'if you think it will vex Lady Marlborough doe not shoe it'. But it was not easy to keep anything from Sarah. The following month Marlborough sent her a draft of his reply for approval: 'if you doe not like it send mee such a letter as you would have mee write.'[34] It was settled that the boy should remain at Cambridge until the following year, and then go abroad to see the next campaign with his father.

Sarah also had in hand the task of marrying her two younger daughters. In later years she professed to have a horror of tying 'two poor creatures to one another for life at fourteen before either of them know what it is to like or the missery of having reason to dislike what they are bound to'.[35] But the oldest nobility were now anxious to ally themselves with the Queen's favourites, and the flattering prospect temporarily overrode Sarah's distaste for child marriages. By mid-year she had accepted a proposal for the 14-year-old Betty from the young Earl of Bridgwater, and was entertaining several offers for Mary, who had not yet had her thirteenth birthday. The girls themselves remained in seclusion at St Albans while their future was being decided and their mother was in attendance on the Queen at Windsor. It was there, at the beginning of August, in the midst of her usual 'hurry', that Sarah had word that the newly betrothed Betty had been taken ill with symptoms of smallpox. The disease was so universal and its course so unpredictable that the life of any young person who had never contracted it was considered uncertain; a constant worry at the back of Sarah's mind was that her son had not yet come through this danger. She rushed to St Albans 'in a great fright', only to find it a false alarm and the child completely recovered. In her relief she wrote to a friend that she was glad to have made the unnecessary journey, 'for when servants are soe carefull as to aprehend every little thing, & give one notice of it, one thinks ones self very secure tho one is forced to bee often from them'.[36]

She was out of sorts herself at this time, with what was described as a 'fullness of the blood'. Apart from the anxiety and bustle of her situation, she must have been acutely discontented at the results of the general election in July, in which the Tories made decisive gains. Even though she intervened in the Northamptonshire contest on behalf of her son-in-law, Lord Spencer, the one member of the family who was in complete sympathy with her politically, he was not successful.[37] And events in Flanders were also building up to a crisis. In July and again in August Marlborough tried vainly to persuade the Dutch to let him bring the French army to a battle. With extraordinarily bad timing, Sarah chose the first of these occasions to complain that her letters, no doubt full of invective against the Tories, must have gone astray or that he had no time to read them, since he did not appear to be interested in the contents. Marlborough, with a gentle reminder of what was preoccupying him, assured her that 'your letters are soe welcome to mee, that if thay should come in the time I were expecting the enemy to charge mee, I could not forbear reading them'.[38]

Frustrated in his attempts to bring about a battle, he now turned his attention to besieging the French-held fortresses on the Meuse. But there were further delays, and by mid-September even Godolphin had given up hope that he would have any success. Then, in less than a month, Venloo, Stevensweert, Roermond, and Liège all fell in rapid succession to the Allies. By this time the Queen had left Bath, where the Court had spent the late summer, to return to London for the opening of Parliament. But while Anne stayed at Windsor only for a day or two in passing, Sarah, who had been in almost constant attendance since the beginning of the year, remained behind at the Castle for a longer respite before Marlborough returned and the winter season began. It was in the letters which she exchanged with the Queen during this separation that the first clear signs of strain between them can be seen. From Sarah came long accounts of the virtues of the Whigs, and claims that it was only by listening to the 'insinuations of the other party' that the Queen had allowed herself to become prejudiced against them. Anne was still completely unreceptive. 'I know the principles of the Church of England, and I know those of the Whigs,' she replied, 'and it is that and no other reason which makes me think as I do of the last.' She added that it was not she but Sarah herself who was mistaken in her political notions, and begged 'for my poor sake, that you would not show more countenance to those you seem to have so much inclination for than to the Church party'.[39]

During Sarah's stay at Windsor the Queen broached another difficult subject, explaining that she wanted to reward Marlborough for the achievements of the campaign, but was not able to do so financially; therefore, 'I hope you will give me leave, as soon as he comes, to make him a duke'.[40] Sarah's claim that on reading this letter, she was 'for some minutes like one that had received the news of a death of one of her dear friends', was largely affectation. A dukedom for Marlborough had been rumoured since the beginning of the reign, and Godolphin knew in advance what her reaction would be. All the same, there is no reason to doubt the sincerity of her protest that she had personally no desire to be a Duchess. The increased formality was simply an annoyance to her, and the increased rank a matter of indifference: 'when a rule is settled I like as well to follow five hundred as one.' The ladies of the bedchamber already included two Duchesses (of Somerset and Ormonde), whom she took care to treat with due ceremony, 'but as soon as the Queen had made Lord Marlborough a Duke,' she wrote, 'I left off *Graceing them up* for fear they should *Grace me*'. Lady Bathurst received a violently exasperated reply to her well-meant letter of congratulation.[41]

Sarah had originally opposed the promotion on the grounds that it would attract still more envy of their position, and that everyone would say it had been done on her account. Marlborough's success in the field removed the force of these objections, and he himself had no intention of letting his wife persuade him to reject an honour which was necessary to support his position abroad. The real problem was that despite their huge joint salaries, and despite Sarah's earlier claim that only those 'in great want' could reasonably expect a pension from the crown, both of them insisted upon having a grant of public money to support their new rank. When the Queen responded by offering them a pension of £5,000 a year for her life, they were still not satisfied and wanted it settled on their heirs by Parliament. In an unguarded moment later Sarah commented that the offer was 'no such prodigious generosity, considering her long professions, the uncertainty of her life, & what other Princes had don for their servants'.[42] Having supported Anne in her past difficulties, she was now determined to have her reward in full. But as John Evelyn remarked, the settlement was thought 'a bold & unadvised request' from one 'who had besides his owne considerable Estate, above 30000 pounds per Ann in places & Employments, with 50000 pounds at Interest: His Wife also . . . ingrossing all that stirred & was profitable at Court'.[43] When the proposal came before Parliament on 15 December, Tory opposition, led by their old enemy Rochester, ensured that it was rejected.

The next day Anne wrote to Sarah to offer her £2,000 a year from the privy purse, 'besides the grant of the five', as 'something towards making up what has been so maliciously hindered in the Parliament'.[44] Considerable confusion has always surrounded this offer. Sarah, who never mentions the parliamentary events which gave rise to it, always claimed that it had been intended as an addition, not to Marlborough's pension of £5,000, but to the £2,000 a year which she now began to enter in her accounts as her salary as keeper of the privy purse. This was to have a significant sequel, but at the time, with the Bridgwater marriage approaching, what she wanted far more than an increased income for herself was a lump sum for her daughter's dowry. In refusing the £2,000, she therefore added pointedly that she already had enough for herself and only desired the continuance of the Queen's goodness to her children, 'who were & would be marryd, I hoped, into such familys as might be capable of serving her, & of deserving her favour'.[45] It was at this delicate juncture that her son-in-law Sunderland (Spencer had succeeded to the title on his father's death in the autumn) chose to cast doubts on the deserving nature of these marriages by opposing a bill for a settlement on Prince George which Anne had very much at heart. 'Ld Sun: would never do anything against his conscience for any obligation in the world,' his wife explained to her infuriated mother.[46] In spite of this, the Queen did respond to Sarah's reminder by offering a £10,000 contribution to the Bridgwater dowry, but Sarah noted that her manner of doing so was markedly less cordial than on the two earlier occasions.[47]

The violent altercation with Sunderland was a sign of Sarah's frustration and discontent at the end of this first year of Anne's reign. At almost every turn she had come up against the limitations of her influence. Her relations with the Queen and Marlborough were already suffering. Now her anger flared up over a trivial misdemeanour of her son (newly styled Marquess of Blandford), who was also about to be taken out of her reach and control. With the Bridgwater marriage accomplished on 9 February, Marlborough prepared to start his next campaign early. Blandford was kept at Cambridge until the last minute, presumably so that he would be out of his mother's way, but on the day after the wedding Marlborough wrote to tell him that he must be ready to leave for Holland by the end of the month.[48] A week later his parents had the chilling news that he had developed signs of smallpox. Accompanied by two of the royal doctors, Sarah travelled to Cambridge on 17 February, and at once realized that this was no false alarm brought about by the overcarefulness of servants. Blandford had contracted the disease in its most virulent form. By the evening of the following Saturday he was dead.

His parents' lives were laid waste at a stroke. They had lost an only son and heir, not only with every appearance of health and strength, but at the height of his promise as 'one of the finest youths in England for his parts and temper and beauty'. Long after all motives for flattery had ceased, a friend remembered him 'as the most amiable and engaging creature, and endowed with such qualities as promised everything great and good'.[49] Marlborough, who had joined Sarah at their son's bedside the day before he died, took her back to St Albans, where they remained for the next eight days. Sarah refused to receive visits from her daughters or even from the Queen herself. At moments of deepest personal crisis Anne was excluded from the closed circle of friendship. The only company the parents wanted was that of Godolphin, who came up on the Monday and stayed with them for three days. 'The best use of one's best friends is to assist and support one another under the most grievous afflictions,' he had written to Sarah as Blandford was dying; 'this is . . . the greatest occasion of letting the whole world see that God Almighty has blessed you with a Christian patience and fortitude as eminent as the reason and understanding by which you are most justly distinguished from the rest of your sex. God Almighty bless, preserve and comfort you.'[50]

Marlborough talked of retirement, but his presence was now urgently needed on the Continent. Distraught at the prospect of parting, Sarah begged to be taken with him, or at least to be allowed to retire from Court altogether. Godolphin, to whom she appealed for support, knew that Marlborough would never agree, but 'if she had asked mee to fly, in the condition I saw her I would certainly have said I would try to doe it'.[51] The two said their farewells at Greenwich on 4 March, after a pitifully short interval in which to come to terms with their loss. Now

Sarah was terrified that her husband would be taken from her as well. 'There is but one strock of fortune that can be more severe,' she wrote in answer to a letter of condolence, 'and, after naming it, I can say noe more . . . '[52] Her one hope was that she had conceived again before he left, giving some prospect that they might yet have a son to inherit their futile honours. In response to a heartfelt plea from the Queen she came reluctantly back to St James's, instead of going straight to her Lodge in Windsor Park as she had intended.[53] But even there she shunned company, refusing to receive visits of condolence or appear publicly at Court. The boys of Westminster School saw her pacing the cloisters of the Abbey in deep mourning, mingling with the vagrants who came there for shelter. In an age when the loss of a child was a commonplace to be stoically borne, her grief seemed so extravagant that it was reported her head was 'near touched'.[54]

In her letters to Marlborough, she dwelt on the prospect that they would soon be able to retire and live quietly alone together. There was now no trace of the abrasiveness of the previous year. 'If you had not possitively desir'd that I should alwais burn your letters I should have been very glad to have keep[t] your dear letter of the 9th,' he replied to one of them in April,

it was so very kind, & particularly upon the subject of our living quietly togeather, til which happy time coms I am shure I can't be contented . . . I wish I could recall twentie yeares past, I doe asure you, for noe other reason but that I might in probabillity have longer time, and be the better able to convince you how truly sensible I am att this time of your kindness, which is the onely real comfort of my life.[55]

The theme of retirement was such a recurrent one at this time, with Godolphin as well as the Marlboroughs, that the Queen became alarmed and appealed to them collectively not to desert her, 'for what is a crown, when the support of it is gone? . . . we four must never part till death mows us down with his impartial hand.'[56]

The profound shock of Blandford's death affected Sarah physically as well as mentally. 'I beleive there never was a phylosopher in my case,' she wrote to one of her friends; 'Time, one sees by experience, lessens people's greif, when nothing can repare the loss, & some remedy may bee expected for the mind, but health is seldome mended by that, & mine has been out of order a great while.'[57] One symptom was that her menstrual periods had become very irregular, and this in turn cruelly kept alive her hopes of another pregnancy. As each month went past after their parting Marlborough waited anxiously for the reassurance that she had not had 'the troublesome visett' they both dreaded. Most biographers have assumed that she had simply reached menopause, but this is unlikely. She was only 42, and the shock of bereavement was more than enough to account for her unstable state and for her interrupted periods. Since she had borne no children for twelve years there must have been some longer-standing reason for the eventual disappointment of her hopes on this occasion.

With the coming of spring, while the Court was still in London, she found some comfort at Windsor. The ranger's Lodge was a graceful seventeenth-century house, set on high ground not far from the end of the Long Walk, the wide, elm-bordered avenue which ran for two miles from the Castle into the heart of the Great Park. Its immediate surroundings were the elaborate formal gardens, with 'fountaines, cut hedges, and groves pailed in', which Portland had laid out in his capacity as superintendent of the royal gardens. Beyond lay the park itself, with its long vistas, herds of 'pretty deer' grazing up to the gates, and stands of ancient timber, whose guardian and protector Sarah made herself throughout her forty years as ranger. When the Court was not there, she wrote, 'it is of all the Places that ever I was in, the most agreable to me'.[58] She had been so busy during the previous year that she had done little more than formally take possession. It was therefore the one place which had no associations with the past. In mid-May she wrote to Marl-borough that she had no news of the outside world and no business but the pleasant one of furnishing her new house ('if I am good for anything,' she once remarked, 'it is to furnish a House in a useful Manner').[59] The Queen wrote to her with affectionate concern, hoping that 'this fine weather will make you like your Lodg better every day, & . . . invite you often into your Garden when your lameness is gon, which I'me sure will do you more good for the Complaint you sometimes have in your breathing then any thing els'.[60]

Yet all was not well between them. Anne evidently hoped that the bereavement would sweep away their political differences and restore them to their former intimacy. Sarah's response must have been hurtful. She wanted only her husband's company, or, failing that, to be left alone to come to terms with her loss in her own fashion. On 20 May the Court moved to Windsor Castle for the summer, and by the end of the month, in her craving for solitude, she insisted on returning to St James's, ignoring the Queen's protest that 'it must be very stinking and close at this time of year & cannot be wholesome'.[61] And it was not only Anne's sympathy that she rejected. When Lady Bathurst, also in London and concerned about her, offered to accompany her to church, she refused: 'I had spoke to one to carry me to a strange church before I had your offer, which I thank you for ten thousand times, but at that church one shall see a great many people that I know, and if I could I would always do my devotions where I could meet no one of my acquaintance.'[62]

It did not bode well for her relations with the Queen that the one thing capable of distracting her from her personal troubles was her involvement in Whig politics. The first event after the bereavement that roused her to an awareness of outside events had been the news that Anne was about to create a batch of new peers. At the beginning of the reign Sarah had promised her old friend Sir Thomas Felton that whenever this happened she would recommend his Whig son-in-law, John Hervey, for a barony. She now flew into a state of near-hysteria, insisting that if Hervey were not included in the new creation, her word would be dishonoured, and 'I neither would nor could show my face again'. The Queen agreed, and the angry reaction of the other four candidates, all Tories, gave Sarah a few hours' malicious pleasure in the midst of her depression.[63] While they revenged themselves by putting it about that she had been bribed, the ecstatic Hervey sang her praises to his Whig friends as 'one so every way worthy of the favour she possesses, by her incessant vigilance and incorruptible fidelity in all the Queen's interests & . . . by so just and laudable employment of it, wherever the safety & prosperity of England is concernd,' that 'she ought to have been born in the golden age'.[64]

The ministers' increasing difficulties with their Tory colleagues over the conduct of the war also encouraged Sarah's political involvement. With the Dutch generals at odds with Marlborough and with one another, it was already apparent that the promise of the previous campaign in the Low Countries would not be fulfilled. Rochester, discontented at being relegated to the viceroyalty of Ireland, had been forced into resignation during the winter, but several of Sarah's particular bugbears, including the Earls of Nottingham and Jersey, the Duke of Buckingham, and Sir Edward Seymour, remained in the Cabinet, and were now publicly critical of Marlborough's campaign. What he felt in his bitterer moments was to his wife a matter of demonstrable fact, that the Tories were working in favour of France and the Pretender. She constantly urged these opinions in their most exaggerated form on the Queen.

The state of affairs in Scotland gave some grounds for her fears, but neither Marlborough nor the Queen was any more ready than before to accept Sarah's sweeping contention that all the Tories were Jacobites, and still less that the Whigs would be an improvement in their places. Marlborough did not discourage this outlet to her feelings, for 'knowing your heart and soull is soe great a pleasur to mee, that I can't desire you to be discrit in that point'.[65] But the Queen, while also trying to make allowances for Sarah's state of mind, could not help being antagonized anew by her hectoring tone. She tried vainly to put an end to the subject by remarking that 'you are soe fixed in the good opinion you have of some & the ill opinion you have of other people that it is to no manner of purpose to argue anything with you'. But this only exasperated Sarah the more. The spate of political remonstrance continued, mingled with bitter remarks about the Queen's indifference or hostility to her opinions.[66] Personal meetings between them were now apt to end in cold formality or heated argument.

At the same time, by means of such episodes as the Hervey peerage, the Whigs were beginning to recognize Sarah as their greatest friend at Court. She used her confidential knowledge to calm their fears that the Queen had secret intentions to restore the Pretender to the throne; 'which was the more suspected', she wrote afterwards, 'because of the great power that every body knew my brother[-in-law] G[eorge] Churchill had with Mr. Morley [Prince George], who most people beleived a Jacobit in his heart'.[67] She was flattered and excited to find that the Whigs in their turn now came to her with an increasing number and variety of requests for her influence. At first these were still in comparatively minor matters: John Methuen's complaint that Nottingham refused him the title of ambassador for his negotiations with Portugal; Lord Carlisle's grievance when the Board of Ordnance dismissed a protégé of his for being 'unreasonably violent in the Whigg interest'; the claims of one of the Whig Junto's supporters to the governorship of Guernsey.[68] But as time went on her help was to be sought in achieving much more important aims.

The other matter which exercised Sarah while she remained in London throughout June and into July was the conduct of her eldest daughter. The days when she and Henrietta had lived together 'like sisters' were over. Shortly before the beginning of the reign the young Godolphins' family had grown too large to be accommodated in Sarah's lodgings, and they had moved into the Lord Treasurer's house on the south-western corner of St James's Palace. Godolphin was very fond of his daughter-in-law, and under his indulgent regime she had more independence and began to make her own friends, among them Lady Fitzhardinge and Lady Sandwich. But both were now middle-aged women of tarnished reputation and Jacobite leanings, and much as Sarah had once loved them herself, she did not consider them to be fit company for her young daughter. And worst of all Henrietta's new associates in her mother's eyes were a set of literary men, including the playwright William Congreve.[69]

In June Sarah wrote her daughter a long remonstrance on this subject, which she made Godolphin deliver to her while she was in attendance on the Queen at Windsor. There was some ground for Sarah's objections to the company Henrietta was keeping; it was not long before this did begin to attract unfavourable gossip. But the demands she now made went far beyond what a mother could reasonably expect from a married daughter. She even forbade Henrietta to take part in the harmless dances which the Queen regularly gave at Windsor for the young people of her Court. In desperation Henrietta had to beg Sarah to remember that 'she was once of my age herself'. Not surprisingly, her manner became increasingly 'cold and careless', and she soon began to avoid her mother's company as much as possible.[70]

By 6 July, four months and a few days after Marlborough's departure, Sarah at last convinced herself that she really was expecting another child. 'I cannot express how glad I am of the good news you send me of your deare self,' the Queen responded with generous pleasure, 'upon my word since my great misfortune of loosing my dear child, I have not known so much real satisfaction in any thing.'[71] Marlborough, receiving the news amid the frustrations of his campaign, was transported with delight. Now buoyant enough to face company, Sarah moved back to the Lodge, and in a flush of energy called in the builders to begin her adaptations to the house. Within a fortnight she had proof that her announcement had been premature; the pregnancy had simply been a delusion. It was a crushing blow, made worse by the task of breaking the news by letter to her husband and by the long wait for his response. Godolphin, now thoroughly alarmed about her, wrote to warn Marlborough that he thought her very far from well.

'I have received yours of the 23d, which has given mee, as you may easily beleive, a good deal of trouble,' Marlborough replied at once to his wife,

[but] I beg you will be so kind and just to mee, as to believe the truth of my heart, that my greatest concern is for that of your own dear health. It was a great pleasure to mee when I thought that we should be blessed with more children; but as all my happyness centers on living quietly with you, I do conjure you, by all the kindness I have for you, which is as much as ever man had for woman, that you will take the best advise you can for your health, and follow exactly what shall be proscribed [for] you.

Above all he urged her not to be concerned for his disappointment, 'by which you may prejudice more your health, and consequently make mee more unhappy'. He begged Godolphin and the Queen to make sure that she followed the treatment ordered by the doctors, and that she went with them again to Bath, 'for I am very sure to leave her alone will not be good for her health'.[72]

Yet the month Sarah spent with the Court at Bath in September was not a success. She came away still ailing in health and more than ever at odds with the Queen about politics. From all quarters came rumours

that both Tories and Whigs were planning to attack the ministry in the
coming session of Parliament, concentrating on the futility of attempting
to conduct offensive warfare in the Low Countries. The Queen,
distraught at the failing friendship, told Sarah that she expected nothing
but difficulties in the winter, '& your Coldness added to it will make it
insupportable'.[73] Marlborough, always sensitive to criticism of his
conduct, was now convinced that the Whigs were as bad as the Tories,
and talked of resigning his command. Earlier in the year he had urged his
wife to join with him in renouncing parties, adding that he would not
seek the protection of either of them, but 'doe what I think is best for
England, by which I know I shall disoblige both partys'.[74] But Sarah,
who had now found a role to compensate for her personal difficulties,
had no intention of renouncing parties. She still clung to the prospect of
retirement, but when this faded she was to throw herself into the party
battle with more zeal than ever.

'The Detested Names of Whig and Tory'
1704–1705

THE winter was to give Marlborough and his wife little opportunity for the quiet and retirement of which they had written so often during the year. Within a fortnight of the opening of Parliament on 9 November, the high churchmen, led by William Bromley, had introduced their favourite piece of legislation, a bill debarring dissenters from qualifying themselves for public office by 'occasional conformity' to the Anglican communion. By 7 December it had passed the Tory-dominated House of Commons.

While the Queen and both her ministers deplored the divisiveness of the measure, they were not prepared either to condemn it in principle or to alienate the Tories by opposing it openly.[1] But there was no such ambivalence in Sarah's attitude; to her it was simply another ploy of the Tories to enable them to persecute their opponents and bring back the Pretender. In the interval before the bill was carried up to the House of Lords on 14 December she turned on the Queen and Marlborough, berating them furiously for being prepared to make any compromise with the enemies of the government. The Queen, still protesting that she saw 'nothing like persecution in this Bill', appealed to Sarah again in desperation not to let political differences prevent them from living together as they used to do.[2] Marlborough too was now beginning to see the heat and intransigence of his wife's views as a serious threat to their personal happiness. He explained patiently that he could not oppose the bill openly without delivering himself into the hands of their enemy, Rochester, but

to show you that I would doe anything that were not a ruin to the Queen, and an absolut distruction to myself to make you easy at this time, by what has been told mee the bill will certainly be throwen out, unless my Lord Treasurer and I will both speak to pepell and speek in the House, which I doe assure you for myself I will not doe.[3]

With the Empire under threat from the Elector of Bavaria, who had joined himself with France, the affairs of the Allies were also in a state of crisis. Early in January, disgusted at the difficulties of campaigning in the Low Countries, Marlborough spoke to the Imperial envoy for the first time of the possibility of his leading an expedition into Germany.[4] Within a few days he had set out for The Hague to concert operations for the campaign, lamenting to Sarah as he sailed: 'I never goe from you my dearest soull, but I am extreame sensible of my own unhappyness, of not having it in my power of living quietly with you, which is the onely thing that can contribut to the ending of my days happyly.'[5] It was clear that the retirement of which he had written as a virtual certainty at the end of the previous campaign was now to be postponed indefinitely.

Forced to face this, Sarah again began to talk seriously of retiring in her own right. With hindsight it can be seen that her instinct was sound. It would have been better for her to leave the Court at this stage, before her estrangement from the Queen began to affect her husband and Godolphin. On the other hand, her position was now so closely and publicly identified with theirs that her going under any circumstances would have damaged them. In any case her Whig friends, knowing nothing of her difficulties with the Queen and beginning to see her as their greatest champion, would not hear of it. Indeed this was to become their constant response from now on, whenever she showed signs of withdrawing from the party battle. Her closest female friend at this time was Elizabeth Burnet, wife of the garrulous Whig Bishop of Salisbury. An attractive, pious woman, as 'descritt as possible to be having such a husband', she had a fervent interest in politics and many contacts among the Whig MPs and low church clergy, who in turn were not slow to use her friendship with the Queen's favourite as a means of making their sentiments known to the Court. 'I am sensible you would gain quiet & be more happy,' she protested when Sarah talked of retirement, 'but surely now you do more good, & how could the Duke strugle with so many deficulties without your help[?]'[6]

From The Hague Marlborough begged his wife to arrange that they should have a week's respite in the country before he had to return to the Continent and take up his command.[7] If they had been able to have this time alone together, the serious quarrel which flared up between them on the eve of his second departure for Harwich at the beginning of April might have been avoided; but in the event the Duke's business kept them almost constantly in London. Exactly what sparked off the quarrel is not clear. The letters which provide the only evidence are undated, and it is by no means certain that they all relate to the same episode.[8] But politics must have played some part. Goaded by Sunderland and her other Whig friends, Sarah had become more violently critical and suspicious than ever of the ministers' conduct in the course of the winter. At the end of March she attacked Godolphin so furiously for recommending a relation of William Bromley to a Court post that to placate her he was forced to promise that he would never 'speak to the Queen again for anybody as long as I live . . . without telling you first'.[9]

The disappointment of Sarah's hopes of another pregnancy seems also to have aroused a new fear, that her husband was turning away from her to seek the company of younger women. Many years later in her widowhood, she wrote of the love-match between the blind Lord Harcourt and his middle-aged third wife, Lady Walter:

hee said . . . that Eden was fixed in his heart & hee should now never see her grow older. I think she is a very lucky woman for . . . I remember a time that I used to fancy I should have been glad to have put out my own eyes if the Dear Duke of Marlborough would have don the same, that I might never have been tormented with feares of loosing him, but this Lady Walter will bee sure of her lover & see everything herself & I think tis best for most of our sex to have blind husbands.[10]

At Harwich Sarah added to their differences by finding fault with the new will Marlborough had made after the death of their son. In particular she complained that he had not provided sufficiently for the Sunderlands, who now had a growing family and were finding it hard to live within their income. The Duke, who had no reason to favour his son-in-law at this time, told her that she would be able to take care of them out of her personal fortune. Sarah reminded him angrily that the Queen's favour to her had already relieved him of the expensive duty of dowering his daughters, and accused him of trying to interfere in the disposition of her own money.[11] The crowded port was no place for the resolution of private differences, and to force him to pay attention to them she put a paper into his hands at parting, setting out her complaints in the harshest terms. Breaking an earlier promise to join Godolphin and the Court at the Newmarket races, she then went straight from Harwich to St Albans, in a state of violent discontent with herself and all the rest of the world. 'I us'd to run from the Court and shut myself up . . . in one of my Country Hous's quit[e] alone,' she recalled of these interludes,[12] which were both a flight from the havoc created by her destructive moods and an escape from the stresses which brought them on. Taking stock of her conduct in calm and solitude, she soon began to have serious doubts about what she had done, and after a week's brooding on her husband's mood at parting she underwent a complete change of heart. She wrote to him, telling him to destroy the Harwich paper and begging to be allowed to come to him.

Unlike the Queen, Marlborough never let such episodes cause lasting damage to his relations with Sarah. As soon as he received her letter he embraced the reconciliation without question or reproach: 'I doe this minutt love you better and with more tenderness then ever I did before. . . . You have by this kindness preserved my quiet, and I beleive my life, for til I had this letter I have been very indifferent of what should become of myself.' He explained that the expedition into Germany, of which she had known nothing before he left, made it impossible for her to join him, 'but love mee always as I think you now doe, and noe hurt can come to mee'. He urged her to continue sending her letters regularly to him on his long march: 'I have taken the best care I can for them, which you will easily beleive, if you could know my soull, how great a comfort thay are to my very being.'[13]

But it was not until the end of April that Sarah received this comforting reply. In the meantime she stayed on at St Albans, full of foreboding and insecurity at the state of affairs at home and abroad. She was not even substantially cheered by the news that the long-planned dismissals of the two Tory leaders, Seymour and Jersey, had at last been carried out, followed closely by the resignation of Nottingham. The latter was replaced as secretary of state by Robert Harley, on whom the ministers had come to rely for management of the House of Commons, but Sarah's enemies could only account for the choice of such a disagreeable nonentity as the Earl of Kent (universally known as 'Bug') to succeed Jersey as Lord Chamberlain, by claiming that he must have bribed her, either directly or by losing to her substantially at cards.[14]

Godolphin, keeping Sarah informed of these changes by letter, also took the opportunity to reprove her for abusing the Queen's indulgence by staying away from Court for so long. Like the Whigs, he was uneasy at being deprived of the intangible but all-important protection of this personal relationship. When Sarah hinted for the first time that the Queen's attitude to her had changed, he refused to take her seriously, merely remarking that 'a little time will undeceive you in that matter'. In the throes of reconstructing his ministry, and knowing something of the mood in which she had sent Marlborough off on his most important and dangerous enterprise, he came as close to impatience with her at this time as he was capable of:

. . . the security you wish for, you have if you will but think soe. Why should not you beleive mee in this thing as well as in anything else? I know it better than I doe most things, and without any vanity, ten to one better than anybody you talk with. Beleive mee, there has not been one hour since the Revolution, when you have [been] in so much security from France, as at this time.[15]

While Godolphin was glad that Marlborough had undertaken the march into Germany which gave them this security, Sarah continued to be racked with anxiety, both for his personal safety and for the consequences if he failed. He had been forced to keep his destination a secret, knowing that neither the Dutch nor the Tories would have consented in advance to his taking the army so far; and having done so, it was clear that he would be completely at the mercy of his enemies in England and Holland if he did not succeed. On 1 May, finding that he had requested powers to treat with the Elector of Bavaria, Sarah wrote urgently to Godolphin that they should be drawn up so as to 'secure him from any malice of 17 [Nottingham] and some of his creatures, who has had a design to attack both him and you'. 'I know you are apt to think those things are agrevated,' she added, 'but I do beleive it all and think the account very probable.'[16] When she came to town a few days later for the birth of Henrietta's second son, she joined in pressing the Dutch envoy for the reinforcements Marlborough had requested to keep himself from being outnumbered by the French.[17] As he continued his long march east throughout May and June, she noted that his Tory critics still refused to accept the necessity of the expedition, and she probably also heard Sir Edward Seymour's chilling threat that the Commons 'would run him down when he came back, as a pack of hounds do a hare'.[18]

Although the shared anxiety brought no improvement in her relations with the Queen, Sarah continued to take every opportunity of invoking the tangible rewards of royal favour for the benefit of her family. In June she heard that Sunderland's sister, Lady Clancarty, had died after six years of unhappy exile with her husband at Hamburg. Her eldest daughter Charlotte, who had been sent to England to be brought up by her grandmother, had become a great favourite with Sarah, and as soon as she received the news, she immediately secured the Queen's promise that Lady Clancarty's pension would be continued for the children's benefit.[19] Of even greater concern was the dowering of her own youngest daughter. As a small child, Mary's striking likeness to her mother had already been remarked on, and she was now a bewitchingly pretty young girl, as self-confident, quick-witted, and quick-tempered as Sarah at the same age. Her parents had received their first offer of marriage for her when she was only ten years old, and this had been followed by at least half a dozen others, all from leading members of the English or Scottish aristocracy. There were even suggestions from some quarters that she might be a suitable bride for the Pretender, or alternatively for the Hanoverian heir to the throne.[20]

But the proposal most favoured by Sarah had come in the spring of

1703 from Ralph, Earl of Montagu, on behalf of his young son and heir, Lord Monthermer. For the sake of Montagu's wealth and his Whiggism, Sarah was prepared to overlook much else in his extremely dubious public and private life. The chief difficulty about the match was that Mary was only 13, and the boy almost a year younger and childish for his age. While Sarah pretended to be able to discern that Monthermer was the most hopeful of the noblemen's sons at that time, Marlborough had grave doubts about the wisdom of tying his precocious, wayward, and much-loved daughter to this sickly and immature youngster. Nevertheless he left the final decision and all the details of the settlement to Sarah, and when Montagu renewed his proposal in the summer of 1704 she accepted, on condition that the couple should not cohabit until the boy was 16. Mary's marriage portion included the reversion of Montagu's very lucrative mastership of the great wardrobe for his son, the promise of a dukedom, which would soon devolve on the young people, and the sum of £10,000. All of these benefits Sarah owed to the Queen, although Marlborough, as yet not fully aware of the estrangement, was surprised that the £10,000 was not as readily forthcoming as on previous occasions.[21]

By this time the Court had moved to Windsor for the summer. Sarah had become conspicuous by her absence for some months past, but in July there was so much illness among the ladies of the bedchamber that she could not avoid taking her turn in waiting, and the personal contact this brought only confirmed her conviction that the Queen's manner to her had unmistakably changed. In an attempt to stave off further political disputes, Anne would now ply her with 'common questions about the linings of mantoes, & the weather, instead of talking with that intire freedom & confidence that she used to do'.[22] A few days of this treatment were sufficient to wear down Sarah's patience. When Marlborough's aide-de-camp arrived on 10 August after an eight-day ride across Europe, bringing her the famous pencilled note that gave the first news of an overwhelming victory over the French on the Danube, he found her not at Windsor, but in London. Having taken a copy for public dispersal, Sarah sent the messenger on with only a letter of introduction to the Queen.[23] The battle of Blenheim, as the overjoyed Godolphin declared, had delivered the balance of European power into the Queen's hands. Even Sarah's perennial sense of insecurity was temporarily allayed, but the good news did nothing to improve the strained relations between the two women. A week later the Queen was still complaining to Sarah by letter of 'the coldness you have used me with of late', and protesting yet again that there was no real alteration in her own affection.[24]

Outwardly there was still no sign of these difficulties. When Anne attended a thanksgiving service at St Paul's on 7 September, Sarah rode alone with her in the state coach. Even from Marlborough and Godolphin she still took pains to conceal the full extent of the damage, and knowing the periodic quarrels which punctuated all Sarah's close relationships, the Lord Treasurer was still not seriously worried. 'I am very sorry to find Mrs. Morley and Mrs. Freeman cannot yet bring things quite right,' he wrote soothingly when Sarah had left for a visit to the Sunderlands at Althorp early in September; 'I am sure they will doe it at last, and when this case happens betwixt people that love one another soe well, it is not impossible but both may bee a little in the wrong.'[25]

Yet Sarah's most significant response to the victory was not to try to heal her breach with the Queen, but to raise again the question of leaving the Court. Unwell herself, she was also worried by reports of Marlborough's ill health in the weeks following the battle, and continuing to have 'melancholy thoughts' about the loss of their son. Marlborough made it clear once again that he had no intention of immediate retirement: 'if I consider only myself, I agree with you I can never quit the world in a better time; but I have to[o] many obligation[s] to the Queen, to take any resolution, but such as her Service must be first considered.'[26] In spite of their differences, the Queen also refused to hear any talk of resignation. Still hoping to salvage the friendship, and perhaps afraid of Sarah's influence over her husband, she begged her, when she returned from Althorp, to come to the Castle or at least to the Lodge, 'for I can never be easy to have you further off . . . for upon my word I can not live without you, & tho I wish you and Mr Freeman every thing your own harts can desire, you must not think to live out of the world as long as I am in it'.[27]

Sarah did return to the Lodge by mid-September and there, with the exercise of riding out into the park, her health improved. With Sunderland's Whig precepts fresh in her mind (he had told her that France and the Tories would never forgive Marlborough for his victory),[28] her concern with public affairs returned with a vengeance. She was constantly aware that by breaking with the Tories without making any compensating alliance with the Whigs, Marlborough and Godolphin laid their ministry open to the hostility of both parties. Now rumours that the remaining Tories in the Cabinet, the Lord Keeper, Sir Nathan Wright, and the Lord Privy Seal, Buckingham, were caballing with their displaced colleagues to obstruct the government in the coming session of Parliament seemed to confirm her worst fears.[29] In the circumstances, Marlborough's continued insistence that he would not support either party drove her frantic with alarm and frustration. From the Lodge in the last week of September she sent off a series of angry letters, claiming that his refusal to recommend party men to office was only designed to deceive and curry favour with the Queen. She demanded that he write to Godolphin immediately, insisting on the removal of Wright and Buckingham and the replacement of the latter by the Whig Duke of Newcastle.

After the harmony between them since their reconciliation, this attack struck Marlborough as a bolt from the blue. Dreading a repetition of their quarrel, he wrote to Godolphin as she wished ('I can refuse you nothing'); but he remained deeply upset by her opinion of his political conduct. Plunged back for the moment into his mood of the spring, he told her that there was no prospect that they could be happy together in retirement; his only consolation could be 'to leave a good name behind mee, in countrys that have heardly any blessing but that of not knowing the detested nams of Wigg and Torry'.[30] It took nearly two months and a succession of 'kind letters' from Sarah to set matters right between them. Her recommendation of an alliance with the Whigs was certainly quite logical in view of the situation at home and abroad; they were much readier in principle than their opponents to support Marlborough's expensive Continental campaigns. Yet her efforts on their behalf, with the resulting damage to her relations with her husband, might just as well have been spared, for it was by other and more powerful means that the reluctant *rapprochement* between the ministry and the Whigs was being forwarded. The replacement of Buckingham by Newcastle had been considered as far back as the spring, and it is clear that the main influence on Godolphin in that matter was not Sarah but Robert Harley. Marlborough had already assured Godolphin that if he and Harley thought the removal of Buckingham and Wright necessary for the stability of the government, he would make no objection.[31] In spite of this, and of Sarah's outburst, Buckingham and Wright remained where they were for the time being. It was the events of the coming session of Parliament which forced the issue between the ministers and the Whigs.

When the Court moved to London for the opening of Parliament on 24 October, Sarah remained behind at the Lodge awaiting Marlborough's return, which was not expected until December. To the Duke of Montagu she described herself rather bitterly during this interlude as 'a poor country person, who is really so dull as to like this sort of life much better than anything I can propose'.[32] Yet her refusal to come to town owed much more to her continuing difficulties with the Queen than to any real liking for the countryside in winter. One product of this solitude was the first instalment of her memoirs: an account of her part in the Revolution of 1688 and the quarrel between the two Courts in the following reign. At first this was intended simply for the instruction of Elizabeth Burnet. In their allegiance to the Whigs the two women were completely at one, and for this reason Sarah felt that the 'wonderfull partiality' which Mrs Burnet still cherished for William and Mary could no longer be allowed to go unchallenged.[33] What the narrative contained no hint of, however, was Sarah's growing estrangement from Anne, of which her friend still knew nothing at all. 'If I was the Queen I shold be uneasy at your being so long away,' she told Sarah innocently; 'Are you sure you do not consult your quiet too much[?]'[34] As long as Sarah stayed at the Lodge, Mrs Burnet undertook to send her constant accounts of the proceedings in Parliament, quite unaware that in doing so she was providing yet more fuel for political quarrels with the Queen.

Sarah was outraged to learn from this source that almost the first act of the Tory Commons in their address of congratulation for the successes of the year was to couple a lesser naval action under their favourite admiral, Sir George Rooke, with Marlborough's epoch-making victory. She at once complained belligerently to the Queen in terms which assumed her approval of the comparison. 'You know I never looked upon the sea fight as a victory, & I think what has been said upon it, as rediculous as any body can do,' the Queen protested indignantly.[35] On 10 November Sarah had an even more alarming account of Tory preparations to ensure the passage of the Occasional Conformity bill through the House of Lords by tacking it on to the land tax, the principal supply bill for the war. Four days later came an account of the debate in which the bill itself passed the Commons. This brought a fresh onslaught from Sarah against the factiousness of the 'Tackers'. Now thoroughly alienated by her heat and rudeness, the Queen flatly refused to continue their correspondence any longer, 'since everything I say is imputed either to partiality or being imposed upon by knaves and fools'.[36]

Having brought matters to this *impasse*, Sarah at last yielded to the entreaties of her friends to come to town. Godolphin, who had been annoyed at the failure of the Queen's servants in the Commons to prevent the passage of the Occasional Conformity bill, was now confined to his house with a violent cold, and needed Sarah's help to ensure that they did their duty in opposing the Tack.[37] She refused to speak to the Queen face to face on this subject, ostensibly because ''tis not possible to love you & your interest as I doe, & not say a great many things that I know (by sad experience) is uneasy to you, & to noe manner of purpose'. But in her letters she showed no such restraint:

I can't resist saying that I think it a most wonderfull extravagant thing, that it should bee necessary to take pains with your own servants, & the Princes to save Europe & the crown upon your head, I must take the liberty to say it lookes like an infatuation, that one who has sence in all other things, should bee so blinded by the word torry, as not to see what is vissible to all the world besides, as the sun that is now shining & that you will beleive any villian, or any known Jacobitt, if to serve their own ends they doe but call themselves torrys, & other men wiggs, because they oppose them, before those that have given proofs that they would dye every hour in the day to serve you, nay what is yet more, before downright demonsteration in many perticulars.[38]

To Godolphin, who at last realized how serious the rift was and tried to mediate between them, the Queen privately admitted that she had no hope of the friendship's ever being restored to what it was.[39]

A few days later, on 28 November, the proposal for the Tack was thrown out of the Commons. But this was only the first hurdle Marlborough and Godolphin had to face. The Whigs were now determined to take advantage of the government's weak position, either to join with the Tories in overthrowing the ministers, or to exact some concessions for themselves. On 29 November Sarah, accompanying the Queen on her first attendance at the Lords' debates, was witness to what the Tories afterwards described as the 'fatal period' of Godolphin's ministry: the moment when, under attack from both parties, he was seen to be 'discoursing very seriously' with the lords of the Whig Junto, who afterwards diverted the course of the debate. It was understood that under duress he had driven a bargain with them, by which they should be given a greater share in the government in return for their parliamentary support.[40] To Sarah, of course, this was no 'fatal period', but the moment she had been waiting and working for since the beginning of the reign.

The tired victor of Blenheim arrived in England on 14 December to a winter of fêtes and rewards. Schemes for a public monument in London were mooted, but he and his circle feared that this would attract envy, and favoured instead the grant of 'some house and lands belonging to the Crown as a proper mark of distinction to remain in his family for perpetuating the memory of his eminent services'.[41] On 17 January 1705, the Queen proposed the comparatively modest grant of the royal manor of Woodstock, and a bill for the purpose was hastened through both Houses by 5 February. But since the only buildings there were keepers' lodges and the romantic but uninhabitable ruins of the old manor house once frequented by Henry II and Rosamond Clifford, Marlborough then went on to engage the services of the fashionable Whig architect, John Vanbrugh, to build a suitable house on the site, and at some point the Queen let it be understood that she would pay for it. The private residence, to be named after the victory, would thus become the monument which it was not politic to raise more prominently in

London. Yet at this stage nothing whatever was said publicly of her intentions, in Parliament or elsewhere. The grumblings of both Whigs and Tories at the aggrandizement of the Marlborough family, which continued to be audible even in the midst of the victory celebrations, were clearly responsible for this reticence;[42] but together with the extravagance of Vanbrugh's designs as they unfolded during the following months, it was to lay up infinite difficulties for Marlborough and his wife in the years to come.

Since the grant was settled on Sarah for life if she survived her husband, she was sufficiently interested to go with him and his architect to Woodstock at the end of February to decide on the exact site of the house. But they had no sooner arrived than her attention was completely distracted from architectural matters by the news that back in London her eldest daughter had been taken ill with smallpox. Henrietta's relations with her mother had worsened again since the birth of her last child the previous summer. On one occasion Sarah had managed to save the sickly baby's life 'with small common medicines', but when he was taken ill again in the winter, Henrietta turned elsewhere for help. Sarah expected to be consulted about any case of illness in the family, and when the child died in February, plunging the whole family into distress, she made no secret of her opinion that he had been killed by unsuitable remedies.[43] In spite of this, she cut short her visit to Woodstock and travelled back to London 'without sleeping or eating', and until she was satisfied that Henrietta was recovering, never left her bedside, 'but for as much sleep as was absolutely necessary'. Although it was clear from the first that her daughter had the disease in a mild form only and was never in serious danger, Sarah needed to believe that this nursing had saved her life, and as soon as Henrietta began to recover she complained of her ingratitude in not making sufficient acknowledgement. 'Indeed I love you sincerely, and am intierly sensible of your tenderness to mee,' protested poor Henrietta, who was now facing the prospect of permanent disfigurement, 'but with two such afflictions both of them quite fresh, it is impossible for mee to speak or look as at another time.'[44] The illness only served to widen the rift between them.

Having seen his youngest daughter married, the Duke embarked again at Harwich on 30 March 1705, intending to pursue the plans he had laid at the end of the previous campaign for an invasion of France along the Moselle valley. This time his parting with Sarah at the waterside was unmarred by any misunderstandings. Before they left London he had pleased her by transferring a further portion of her personal fortune entirely into her own control. Her investments at this period, made chiefly in the names of male friends and agents, were already substantial, including a mortgage, £4,000 worth of Bank of England stock, and £9,000 lent to the exchequer in anticipation of the land tax revenue.[45] Being willing 'to venture a little in hopes of a great Return', she also began to have the occasional stake in high-risk ventures, foreign and domestic, managed for her by Godolphin and her other City friends.[46] As much a Whig in private as in public affairs, she had come to consider this financial independence to be not merely an indulgence on Marlborough's part, but an essential human right and liberty; without it, she would have been reduced to the level of the dispossessed Continental peasantry, 'who neither Plough nor sow, because they can't call it their own'.[47] Her good humour increased by the prospect of an accommodation with the Whigs (Buckingham had just been forced to resign in favour of Newcastle and the Lord Keeper's dismissal was also imminent), and realizing that a successful campaign was necessary 'to prevent the mallice of the Tackers', she now took one of her short-lived resolutions not to upset or distract her husband with political disputes. Marlborough was delighted to find her 'kinder to me then you have been these many yeares', but still begged her to 'write your mind freely to mee and not beleive that it will vex mee, for I am never uneasy but when I think you have other thoughts of mee, then I would have you have of mee'.[48]

Until this time Sarah's only close associate among the five lords of the Whig Junto had been her son-in-law Sunderland. Now, by means of the Montagu match, she had a personal alliance with another member of this formidable and ambitious group. Charles Montagu, Lord Halifax, was a widower, a highly cultivated and intelligent man, and a cousin of her new in-laws. As unaware as the rest of his colleagues of the true state of her relations with the Queen, he set about assiduously improving their acquaintance and encouraging her political involvement. Years later, when she had turned against him, she was to mock him as 'hideously ugly', with 'no more Breeding than any body that had never seen anything but the Inns of Court, & yet always remarkable to be in Love with all the fine Ladies, by whom he could only be laugh'd at'.[49] But at the time she was entertained by his wit, flattered by the seriousness with which he took her political influence, and quite carried away by his confident predictions of a Whig victory in the coming general election.

'You nor nobody living can wish more for the having a good Parliament then I do,' Marlborough replied cautiously when she wrote to him of the prospect, 'but we may differ in our notions.' While the ministers were now prepared to encourage the Whigs to some extent and discountenance the Tackers entirely, they still hoped to take advantage of the split in the Tory ranks to encourage the moderates; if this strategy succeeded, neither party would be dominant and the Queen would be able to hold the balance of power between them.[50] Marlborough had deliberately left his wife no part to play in dealing with the entrenched Tory interests at their new borough of Woodstock, but St Albans was her home territory. In past years she had paid little attention to the elections there, because Marlborough had placed their interest at the disposal of his Tory brother George, whom she could neither oppose nor bring herself to assist. Now Churchill's fellow member, John Gape, stood revealed not only as a Tory but as a Tacker, and the Court had set up a rival candidate, Henry Killigrew. Although Gape had a strong local interest and the electorate was notoriously large and turbulent, Sarah decided that it was her personal duty to do all she could to unseat him.

As well as instructing her agents to use their influence against him, she therefore went to St Albans herself to canvass the electors in person. Relying far more on her authority as the Queen's favourite than on her local interest, she told them that 'Tackers would be injurious to the Government, and were for the *French* Interest', and that 'it was the Queen's Desire, that no such men should be chose'. Even so, many of the shopkeepers and townspeople stood up to her sturdily, one clergyman even going so far as to bandy words with her, 'pro and con, as to several Points of State'.[51] The contest ended with the mayor, one of Gape's supporters, pronouncing him elected by 236 votes to 233, while the leading Tory newswriter crowed over the defeat of Killigrew and the 'great Lady' who had gone there to assist him.[52]

Halifax condoled with Sarah over 'the foul play' she had met with, and since there were long-standing disputes about the extent of franchise in the borough, he promised that if Killigrew petitioned at the meeting of Parliament, the Whigs would soon 'make Gape and his mayor repent their return'.[53] But the Tories did not wait for the hearing to spread stories of her unwarrantable interference in the election. She tried to take this calmly, 'though I have been a little vexed at some of the things I hear has been reported of me . . . for the spirit of lying runs away with more torrys than ever I had the honour to know'.[54] Marlborough, however, was not at all pleased that his wife had set them both up as targets for the enraged Tories, and warned her that 'if thay can say anything that may vex you or mee thay will do itt, though Killigrew should not petition'.[55]

Sarah stayed on at St Albans for some time after the election, fortifying her Whiggism with such works as Locke's treatise *On Government* and Defoe's satire on the Tackers, *A Journey to the World of the Moon*. When Halifax, himself a patron of literary men, reminded her that Defoe had not only suffered at the hands of Nottingham, but had written verses in praise of Marlborough, she responded by sending him an anonymous present of 100 guineas.[56] It was at this point, she recalled later, that Halifax also began to solicit her for many changes; and not merely in minor offices now, but in Cabinet posts.[57] Although the Whigs had no overall parliamentary majority, they had made substantial gains in the elections, and as a condition of their future support of the government and of Marlborough's operations they now expected a share in ministerial office. Seeing Sarah as the only thoroughgoing Whig in the Queen's inner circle and as a useful channel of communication with the taciturn and unapproachable Lord Treasurer, they lost no time in enlisting her help. The first of their aims was to have Sunderland made secretary of state, and it was to Sarah that Halifax first suggested her son-in-law's appointment to a forthcoming special embassy to Vienna as a preliminary to the higher office. Sarah immediately referred the matter to Godolphin, who managed, though with great difficulty, to secure the Queen's consent.[58]

It was to be the first of many such difficulties with the Queen. She had a great personal regard for her Lord Treasurer, and he had an undoubted right and duty, which Sarah had not, to give her political advice. But as soon as he began to advocate concessions to the Junto, he came up against the same rocklike obstinacy on which Sarah's favour had foundered. Indeed, it was at this point that the full damage Sarah had done by so recklessly sacrificing this favour to her militant Whiggism began to be apparent; for one of the reasons behind the Queen's reluctance to accept Godolphin's advice was her suspicion that in giving it he was allowing himself to be unduly influenced by Sarah. In this Anne certainly did less than justice both to Godolphin's sense of duty and to his political judgement. Sarah had advocated the taking in of the Whigs in season and out since the beginning of the reign, but Godolphin began to do so only when he was convinced by parliamentary pressures that it was unavoidable. Nevertheless, the Queen's suspicions on this score were clearly indicated by the letter she wrote to him in July concerning the appointment of the new Lord Keeper. Knowing that the Whigs had set their sights on this post also, she begged him to find a moderate Tory substitute, and added:

I know my dear unkind friend has so good an opinion of all that party, that to be sure she will use all her endeavour to get you to prevail with me to put one of them into this great post. . . . But I hope in God you will never think that reasonable, for that would be an unexpressible uneasiness and mortification to me.[59]

In spite of this, Godolphin continued all summer to press the claims of the moderate Whig candidate, William Cowper. Sarah knew from her own experience how stubborn Anne could be in such matters. In a well-meant but misguided attempt to spare the ministers the damage of making 'an application so disgreeable to her', she decided to join her efforts to Godolphin's.[60] After her long absences from Court during the previous two summers, she now gave up her retreat at Tunbridge Wells, patched up a reconciliation with the Queen, and agreed to accompany her to Winchester at the end of August. Marlborough and Godolphin were pleased, knowing how much their own credit with the Queen still depended on this friendship, and believing that it would prove 'of great use' in the task of winning her over.[61] If Sarah had confined herself to restoring the relationship on a personal level, all might yet have been well. But she was quite incapable of doing so, and her direct participation in the political issue only irritated the Queen afresh, adding to her worst fears about her favourite's influence on Godolphin.

By the beginning of June, chiefly owing to lack of co-operation from the Allies, Marlborough's cherished plan of attacking France by way of the Moselle valley had been brought to nothing. Sick with disappointment, he marched his army back to assist the Dutch in Flanders. Although his hopes for the campaign were briefly revived by his success in forcing the French lines, he was twice prevented by the Dutch generals from bringing the enemy to what he believed would have been a decisive battle. Sarah's concern for him did not prevent her from breaking her resolution not to add to his difficulties with political disputes. Marlborough was prepared, if pressed, to second Godolphin's efforts on behalf of the Whigs, but he was also well aware of the damage his wife and the Lord Treasurer were doing to their relations with the Queen by this means, and he showed more real sympathy with the strategy favoured by Robert Harley, that the Queen should seek the support of the moderate Tories, even though this was the chief cause of Godolphin's difficulties with her over the Lord Keepership. But when Sarah took her husband to task over this, he only replied wearily: 'when I differ with you it is not that I think those are in the right which you say are always in the wrong, but it is that I would be glad not to enter into the unreasonable reasoning of either party.'[62]

Another source of friction was the building at Woodstock. On 9 June Godolphin had issued a warrant to Vanbrugh on Marlborough's behalf, authorizing him to make the necessary contracts, and twelve days later the first payment of £20,000 was made out of the treasury. But at the same time Godolphin instructed Sir Christopher Wren to provide an independent estimate of the total cost.[63] When he reported back in July with a figure of £100,000, more than twice what Marlborough had originally planned, Sarah was horrified. Even if the estimate were reliable (and it was soon to be far exceeded), the building was clearly an unrealistic gift for the Queen to offer and for Marlborough to accept while the treasury was committed to funding a major war. Under pressure from his wife, the Duke went so far as to write to Godolphin that if they both thought it was 'not a proper time for the Queen to make such an expence, as Lady Marlborough informes me this house will cost, it will be no great uneasiness to me if it be lett alone'. Yet by the end of the month he had instructed Vanbrugh to press ahead with his plans as fast as possible.[64] Godolphin, to whom Sarah appealed to make her husband see reason, agreed with her about the expense and 'unwieldy-ness' of the building, but refused to oppose him in a project so close to his heart.[65] Marlborough is often represented as over-submissive to his masterful wife, and was himself fond of remarking that he could never refuse her anything. Yet nothing demonstrates the limitations of her influence with him in some matters more clearly than the continued slow rise of his baroque palace in the Oxfordshire countryside, in spite of all she could do or say to hinder it.

After her stay at Winchester Sarah went on to Woodstock, and had her worst misgivings confirmed by what she saw there. The house and courtyards alone covered seven acres, with a huge layout of formal gardens in proportion. Even after a summer's work by an army of labourers the walls were only just above ground level, and it was clear that completion would be the work of years. There were also disturbing signs of local hostility during her stay. Lord Abingdon, who had formerly provided a plate for the September race-meeting in the park, was still smarting from his electoral defeat. Now he and the neighbouring gentry boycotted the Woodstock races altogether, and Sarah had only the company she had brought with her ('a parcel of Whiggish, Mobbish people', according to the Oxford Tories) to keep her in countenance.[66]

Back in London at the end of September, the Queen at last gave way over the Lord Keepership. In her later years, stung by what she saw as the ingratitude of the Whigs, Sarah greatly exaggerated her role in this affair, claiming that Cowper owed his appointment solely to her efforts. In the bitterer and more truthful accounts written at the end of Anne's reign, she admitted that her intervention had only succeeded in angering the Queen.[67] Yet at the time the Whigs themselves believed her influence to have been decisive, and the praise and encouragement they now lavished on her would have turned a cooler head than hers. 'I must say one thing in general . . . and that very sincerely, and without the least compliment,' Sunderland wrote from Vienna, 'that if England is saved it is entirely owing to your good intentions, zeal, and pains you have taken for it.'[68] The new Lord Keeper himself begged to be allowed to wait on her to make his acknowledgements in person. Honest enough to find this an embarrassment, Sarah told him that she would not be thanked for anything she had done 'in contributing to bring so valuable a man into that post'. Cowper replied adroitly that even if she would not let him speak, she could not prevent him from thinking as long as he lived.[69] When Parliament met and thanks were again voted to Marlborough for his services, some Whig Members were inclined to believe that his wife was even more deserving of a public tribute; 'Your Grace is admiered & loved more then I know how to express,' Mrs Burnet assured her, '& were it proper would have as publick acknowledgements as any of our most renowned Heroes.'[70]

It was ironic that just when Sarah had damaged her friendship with the Queen beyond repair by her vain attempts to impose her political views, Tories as well as Whigs should have become convinced that 'Queen Zarah' monopolized Anne's favour and exercised an unbounded influence over her; 'for indeed', Bishop Burnet commented, 'she was looked upon by the whole party, as the person who had reconciled the whigs to the queen, from whom she was naturally very averse'.[71] It was unlucky for Sarah that the St Albans election hearing now gave the Tories the opportunity to air their feelings about her in Parliament. The case was heard amid a blaze of publicity in two late sittings of the Committee of Elections and Privileges between 14 and 16 November. It was the first of the disputed elections to be dealt with, and this coupled with Sarah's involvement led both parties to regard it as a trial of strength. To counter Killigrew's claim that his opponents had polled illegal votes, Gape called copious evidence about Sarah's outspoken canvassing. Nervously she mustered 'sensible and credible servants' of her own to testify that she had done nothing improper, and the Whigs rallied to her support by pointing out that such solicitations by local landowners were a commonplace of electioneering.[72]

Thanks to Harley's careful management and the Whigs' determination to use the disputed elections to exclude as many Tackers as possible, Killigrew won his case.[73] But the Tories had not finished with Sarah. When the Committee reported its findings to the House on 24 November, they took the further opportunity to berate her for abusing her privileged position as royal favourite in her canvassing against the Tackers. William Bromley, the disappointed Tory candidate for Speaker, pointed out that Edward III's favourite, Alice Perrers, had been banished for a lesser offence.[74] When Sarah attended the Queen at the House of Lords she had to listen to the same things being said to her face. Having enlarged meaningfully on the first Duke of Buckingham's monopoly of influence with James I, the veteran ministerial critic Lord Haversham looked hard at Sarah and 'farther said he had the Person . . . in his Eye by whom the Queen's Ear was besieg'd'.[75] The true state of affairs between the two women was still one of the best-kept secrets in England.

During the first four years of Anne's reign Sarah had seen the Tory leaders driven one by one from the citadel of power; but in her more honest moments she had to acknowledge that even though she had sacrificed the Queen's favour, strained her relations with her husband, and exposed herself to parliamentary attack to achieve this end, her personal contribution had counted for very little. During the next four years she was to see the attempt at moderation defeated and the reluctant Queen forced to accept four out of the five members of the Whig Junto into her Cabinet. It was in this process that Sarah did at last find a genuine role to play: not by influencing the Queen directly—though she never ceased to try—but by 'following it closely' with Marlborough and Godolphin, acting as their mediator with the Whigs, and keeping them united in pursuit of the Junto's aims. But the cost was that they too soon began to share in her loss of royal favour.

Harley and Abigail
1706–1707

ARLBOROUGH returned from his campaign at the end of December, and left again to resume his command early the following spring. Despite his repeated longings for retirement and his hopes that each successful campaign would bring a lasting peace, there was as yet no foreseeable end for him or Sarah to these agonizing farewells. After the frustrations of the previous campaign he had hoped to lead an expedition to join forces in Italy with Prince Eugene of Savoy, his favourite among the Allied generals. But this project soon proved to be impracticable, and he was again confined to the Low Countries, where he told Sarah that there was no prospect of his being able to do anything 'that shal make a noise'.[1] Then on 16 May came the news of his second great victory over the French, at Ramillies. 'I did not tel my dearest soull in my last the designe I had of ingaging the enemie if possible to a battaile, fearing the concern she has for me might make her uneasy,' he wrote in one of his tenderest letters, 'but I can now give her the satisfaction of letting her know that on Sunday last we fought, and that God Almighty has been pleased to give us a victorie. . . . Pray believe me when I asure you that I love you more then I can expresse.'[2] He had had a narrow escape from death or capture when falling from his horse in the thick of the battle, and his equerry, Colonel Bringfield, had been killed while helping him to remount. Sarah immediately sought out Bringfield's widow and assured her of a pension of £100 a year from the privy purse.[3]

Yet the victory, which resulted in the surrender of the greater part of the Spanish Netherlands to the Allies, gave Sarah little personal satisfaction, for the closeness of Marlborough's escape only emphasized the danger he was in. The stresses of her private and public life were again telling on her health.[4] At last having to relinquish any lingering hope of another child, she still could not shake off memories of her lost son.' Let me be happy with you,' Marlborough comforted her, 'and no doubt the children we have, will give us just reason to be contented.'[5]

But Sarah, in her present state of mind, was not easy for her children to satisfy. The chief culprit this time was not Henrietta, but Mary, who was now living at Montagu House while her young husband accompanied Marlborough on campaign. Not yet 17 and already expecting her first child, she begged her 'dear dear Angell Mama' that 'when you are in town you will let me be very often with you, for that will make me happy'. Yet Sarah was soon complaining that in these visits or even when they met in the street, her daughter did not treat her with the civility of a common acquaintance.[6]

Mary's letters give her own explanation of this behaviour. 'I am prodigiously unfortunate in your always thinking when I doe a wrong thing, that I doe it a purpose to be impertinent,' she protested:

I shou'd think my self the happiest creature in the world, if you wou'd have so much patience with me as always to tell me the moment I have done any thing you don't like, & I shou'd not think I deserved to have a moments happiness if I did ever doe it againe, but I am so unfortunate that you take so many things ill of me without saying what, that it comes att last to make you so angery that then I must owne I doe not know how to behave my self to you, nor what to doe of any kinde.

To Sarah this only made matters worse by implying that she was of 'an unreasonable humour'.[7] In vain Marlborough gently counselled her in her dealings with her daughters, to 'passe by litle faults and consider thay are very young, and that thay can't do other then love you with al their hearts'. But he assured her, when she wrote to forestall any direct appeal from Mary to him, that he would never side with them against her.[8]

The victory at Ramillies and Anne's concern for Sarah's health in the following weeks did something to restore a semblance of friendship between the two women, and there were even some signs of softening over the political issue. The violent and factious conduct of the Tories during the winter session, in particular their attempt to invite Anne's Hanoverian heir to reside in England, had angered the Queen deeply. The Electress Sophia had tried to keep up a correspondence with the groom of the stole since the beginning of the reign, but Sarah, whose friend Ruperta Howe, the wife of the English envoy at Hanover, kept her supplied with a constant stream of critical information about the German Court, privately considered the vivacious and intelligent old lady 'a ridiculous creature', and soon grew impatient with the whole business: 'I can't write or read French, & it was so uneasy to get people to do it for me, & to one of my humour to make letters often to a great person that one never saw, that I got out of the correspondence, I doubt not very civilly.'[9] The Queen shared this personal view of her successor, and the Whigs' opposition to the invitation on her behalf did more than all Sarah's nagging to reconcile her to them. In the indignation of the moment she went so far as to write:

I believe dear Mrs. Freeman and I shall not disagree as we have formerly done, for I am sensible of the services those people have done me that you have a good opinion of, and will countenance them, and am thoroughly convinced of the malice and insolence of them that you have always been speaking against.[10]

Yet neither this professed readiness to 'countenance' the Whigs, nor Anne's unexpected liking for her new Lord Keeper, made her willing to accept any more Whigs into the Cabinet. For at least a year the Junto had nursed the project of having Sunderland appointed secretary of state, imagining that his relationship with the Marlboroughs would help to make him acceptable to her. As soon as the session was over, Godolphin was once again ground between the millstones of the Junto's inexorable demands and the Queen's stubborn resistance. At the end of May he called for Marlborough's support, but the general was clearly reluctant to become involved, and delayed for a month before writing. When he finally did so, Anne replied with a brevity amounting to reproof that although she appreciated Sunderland's zeal for her service, 'you know very well that it is not in my power at this time to comply with what you desire'.[11]

Sarah, Godolphin reported to Marlborough, was 'very uneasy' at this flat refusal.[12] She was convinced that the Queen was not capable of holding out so firmly against her ministers' advice unless she was secretly being encouraged to do so by someone else. In this her instinct, deriving from years of intimacy with Anne, was to be proved sound, although for some time the only influence she could identify was that of George Churchill, exercised indirectly through the Prince. Marlborough disagreed. 'You know that I have often disputes with you concerning 83 [the Queen],' he replied when she told him of her suspicions, 'and by what I have always observed . . . when she thinkes herself in the right, she needs no advice to help her to be very ferm and possative.' When Sarah took him to task for his lukewarm support of Sunderland, he only made his misgivings and the differences between them clearer, but 'I have formerly said so much to you on this subject, and to so litle purpose, that I aught not to have troubled you with all this, knowing very well you rely on other people's judgement in this matter.'[13]

Sarah did not yet tackle the Queen personally about Sunderland's appointment. She knew very well that his relationship to her was far from being the advantage the Whigs imagined; indeed, one of the Queen's chief objections to him was his temperamental likeness to his mother-in-law.[14] But she continued her campaign on behalf of the Whigs in other matters, going so far in July as to reprove the Queen for delays in disposing of Church livings, and for not relying more on Cowper's advice in such matters.[15] This was an issue in which the Queen would brook no interference, and when Sarah came to Windsor for the summer a day or two later, Anne gave her a cold reception.

Sarah could not now help seeing that her support of the Whigs had been personally disastrous for her. At a low ebb both physically and mentally, and resenting their continuing demands on her, she decided to let Sunderland into the secret of her difficulties with the Queen. At the same time she made one of her periodic threats to abandon the Court altogether. Sunderland was sympathetic, but inexorable:

I . . . am sorry to see you are so much in the spleen upon your coming to Windsor; but I hope you will find things mend every day; though I am sure they will never do so if you should take any such resolution as you mention in your letter. For as every thing that is well is entirely owing to you and the pains you have taken . . . I am sure you are too good, and wish too well to the publick to give over doing all you can. I own the return you meet with is very disagreeable [but] I don't doubt but you will overcome all that at last.[16]

Sarah continued discontentedly at the Castle throughout August. By this time the pressure for a decision about Sunderland's appointment had become urgent. Godolphin was convinced that a Whig alliance was essential both for his own political survival and for the support of the war. Even under threat of the Lord Treasurer's resignation, however, the most the Queen would contemplate was an unsatisfactory expedient by which Sunderland would be admitted to the Cabinet without specific responsibility.

When Sarah did at last intervene, it was less for the sake of the Whigs than to help Godolphin, whose difficulties with the Queen she appreciated far better than they. Anne knew that it had been only a matter of time before Sarah became involved, and whenever they were alone together her dread of the subject's being raised was patent. It was the kind of situation that quickly found the limit of Sarah's patience. Towards the end of August she stopped waiting on the Queen altogether, and went off to St Albans, leaving behind what she had to say about Sunderland in writing:

Tho tis easy to see the great change in Your Majesty to me & that I have all the reason in the world to think when I am alone with you tis a great constraint to you, yet having lately received some little markes of kindnesse from you, I can't satisfy myself without waiting upon you, or telling you the reason why I don't do it, which is only for fear of making you uneasy upon this new occation of the secretary [of state] which you will easily beleive I am not Ignorant of, & I must give myself the satisfaction of protesting that my only concern in that matter is for you & and for the trouble which I saw my Lord Treasurer in, for I find he is under a necessity of going out of your servise, which is the greatest mortyfication to him in the world, or to ruin your servise & himself with it.

She insisted that it was purely for political and not for family reasons that she was anxious for Sunderland's appointment, because 'tis certain that your government can't be carried on with a part of the Tories and the Whigs disobliged'; and she concluded, with reference to the suspected influence of George Churchill, by begging that 'Mr and Mrs Morley may see their errors as to this nation before it is too late'.[17] Deeply offended at this last sentence, the Queen sent no reply. It was from Godolphin, passing through St Albans on his way back to Windsor from the Quainton races, that Sarah learnt of her reaction. Flaring up at once at any sign of criticism, she gave him another letter to deliver to the Queen, in which she complained of Anne's 'great indifferency and contempt' in not answering the first. She also made him promise to find out exactly what had given offence.[18]

To Godolphin, the slow disintegration of the friendship between the two women had been as personally harrowing as it was immeasurably damaging in its political consequences. He told Sarah at the end of the year that he would die to have the two of them as they used to be.[19] Although his own relations with the Queen were suffering from the unresolved conflict about Sunderland, he was still willing to try to repair the damage between them. To this end he managed to convince Anne that what Sarah, in her execrable scrawl, had really meant to write in her final sentence was 'notion' rather than 'nation', and that her criticism of the Queen and Prince was therefore much less sweeping and offensive than it had appeared.[20] Five days later, when Sarah was again at Windsor on her way to Woodstock, the Queen wrote her a slightly mollified note ('you had made an *a* instead of an *o* which quite altered the word'), and begged for 'one look' before Sarah continued on her journey.[21]

But to Sarah the dispute had finally brought home the fact that their friendship was at an end. As she remarked bitterly, if Anne had really loved her as she once did, 'she would not have been displeased at the shap of any of my fine leters'.[22] She departed for Woodstock without attempting to see the Queen. Instead she left another letter behind, in which she undid all Godolphin's work by protesting that she could see no essential difference between the two versions of the offending sentence. Then, 'since I am not very like to trouble you again', she proceeded to give a point-by-point reply to a letter which the Queen had just written to the Lord Treasurer, still refusing either to accept Sunderland's appointment or to contemplate parting with Godolphin himself; before Sarah left Windsor he had shown this to her, 'with more concern than I know how to express'.[23]

The Queen was more offended than ever at this latest letter from
Sarah, which, she told Godolphin, 'with a great deal of stiffness and
reservedness in her looks, was *very extraordinary* in her opinion'. And
when he continued to press for Sunderland's appointment, she greatly
distressed him by bursting into 'a passion of weeping', and asking for
time to await a reply to an appeal she had made to Marlborough. The
Duke's lack of enthusiasm for his son-in-law's admission to the Cabinet
had not escaped her notice, and Godolphin wrote anxiously to Sarah that
if Marlborough's response were not firm enough, it would only increase
their present difficulties. In her reply from Woodstock Sarah scolded
him for being moved by the Queen's weeping; but with his experience of
the warmth and sympathy of which she was capable when her feelings
were touched he only replied, 'you are much better natured in effect than
you sometimes appear to bee . . . you would have been so too, if you had
seen the same sight I did.'[24]

In this crisis Godolphin had no help from his closest political
colleagues. Marlborough was reluctant and at a distance. Robert Harley
had always opposed the pretensions of the Whigs and, unknown to the
ministers, was now actually encouraging the Queen in her refusal to take
Sunderland in. Without the co-operation of the Whigs Godolphin
anticipated being 'torn to pieces' in the coming session, and yet could not
reveal to them the full extent of his difficulties with Anne. In his isolation
he had come to rely heavily on Sarah's support and sympathy. Yet it was
now clear that by allowing her to participate in his most confidential
correspondence with the Queen he was only adding to his problems. The
whole episode finally convinced him that, in the task of influencing
Anne, there was 'no room to hope for the least assistance from Mrs.
Freeman'.[25]

What struck Sarah most, however, were Godolphin's doubts about
Marlborough's support. Within a few days of her arrival at Woodstock
she had dashed off five irritable letters to her husband, taxing him again
with his unsatisfactory attitude to the Sunderland affair; 'I see I lye under
the same misfortun I have ever done, of not behaving myself as I aught to
83 [the Queen],' he replied resignedly, and by the same post sent a letter
to the Queen urging her in stronger terms than ever before to agree to
the appointment.[26] Sarah might have become a liability to Godolphin
where Anne was concerned, but from now on she was to be of
considerable help to him (and to the Whigs) in engaging the support of
his recalcitrant colleague.

The other subject which dominated Sarah's splenetic letters from
Woodstock was the state of the building there. What she saw only
confirmed her belief in the impracticality of the whole project. Aware

that delay in payments from the treasury was slowing down the progress of the works, she refused to add to Godolphin's worries by badgering him about it. The most she could do was to tramp about the site in the autumn rain, pointing out 'a great many errors' and insisting upon having them rectified. She left Vanbrugh, who was unused to taking his orders from a woman, thoroughly upset and antagonized, but found an ally in his less flamboyant assistant, Hawksmoor.[27]

The Woodstock races had now been entirely abandoned by the Tory gentry, but Sarah's Whig friends, including Bishop Burnet and his wife, continued to rally round her, and she had High Lodge, with its wide views over the Berkshire downs, fitted up for their accommodation.[28] When the racing company left, a fresh relay of family and friends came to stay with her there, among them the Whig MP, Arthur Maynwaring. A leading member of the Kit-Cat Club and a follower of the Junto, Maynwaring was chiefly known as a witty talker; so much so that Mary, now at a late stage of her pregnancy and temporarily on better terms with her mother, begged Sarah not to expect her at Woodstock until Maynwaring had gone, for 'he is so mallitious that I am sure he will make a thousand disagreeable observations of me'.[29] Yet in her present mood Sarah found Maynwaring's unsparing wit to her liking, and he soon improved his opportunities to make himself one of her closest allies.

Sunderland and Halifax were also expected at High Lodge, but instead, on 17 September, came a letter from Sunderland putting off their visit. He told Sarah with his usual bluntness that the Junto had been consulting about the Queen's offer of a Cabinet post without specific responsibility, and were merely confirmed in their suspicions of the ministers' sincerity. Rather than coming to Woodstock, they were about to have a meeting with Godolphin at which they would deliver the ultimatum 'that this and what other things have been promised must be done, or we and the lord treasurer must have nothing more to do together about business'; and he added, as a further excuse for not visiting her, 'that since it is plain that you are very ill with the queen, purely for acting and speaking honestly and sincerely your mind, nobody knows how far some people might make the queen believe that we were gone only to influence and engage you to be more and more uneasy to her'.[30] Like Godolphin, the Junto now realized that they had misjudged Sarah's personal influence with her mistress; but they still had their uses for her in keeping up their pressure on the ministers.

To Godolphin's despair the Queen continued obstinate, begging him to reconsider the expedient which the Junto had just adamantly rejected. Having joined Sarah at Woodstock, he replied from there on 25 September, and despite her former hint that she would not trouble the

Queen again, Sarah herself could not resist writing once more to support his arguments, adding her suspicion that 'sombody artfull' was helping to bolster the Queen's stubbornness.[31] But she still had not identified the culprit. Just at this time she also sent off a fulsome letter to Robert Harley, thanking him for intercepting the correspondence of some servants whom she suspected of spying. She ended with an apology for troubling him, 'knowing how precious your time is and how well it is employed'.[32] Had she known that it was partly employed in encouraging the Queen's opposition to Sunderland, her tone would have been very different.

Meanwhile she continued her efforts to secure Marlborough's whole-hearted co-operation. To her dramatic accounts of the Junto's threats to 'vex and ruin' the ministers if they were not gratified, she now added 'a great packett' containing copies of all the correspondence which had passed between the Queen, Godolphin, and herself concerning Sunderland. These, Godolphin told Marlborough, she had 'taken more pains to write in her own hand, than any clerk . . . would doe for £100'.[33] The Duke's response was to write once again to the Queen, on 13 October, unequivocally supporting Godolphin.[34] Bringing this about was Sarah's most significant contribution to the affair, but she could not leave matters there. Marlborough had written to her just previously, complaining of his lack of influence with the Queen, and adding that if Godolphin were forced to resign, he could not continue to serve her as a minister. Sarah now sent this letter to Anne as well, along with an extraordinarily presumptuous and offensive covering letter of her own. In it, besides enlarging unrepentantly on her own disinterestedness in being willing to offend the Queen in order to serve her ('what I have done has rarely been seen but upon a stage'), she asked her to 'reflect whether you have never heard that the greatest misfortunes that ever has happened to any of your family, has not been occasioned by having ill advice, and an obstinacy in their tempers'.[35]

Again the Queen complained bitterly to Godolphin, and again he did his best to put Sarah's case:

I went on to tell her that I knew very well all Mrs. Freman's complaints proceeded from having lost Mrs. Morley's kindness unjustly, and her telling her truths which other people would not, to which she sayd, as she has don 40 times, how could she show her any more kindness than she did, when she would never come near her? I sayd she had tryed that severall times and complained it was always the same thing. Upon that she sayd, Mrs. Freeman would grow warm somtimes, and then she herself could not help being warmer than she ought to bee, but that she was always ready to bee easy with Mrs. Freeman.

On the main issue of Sunderland's appointment, Godolphin told Sarah that if Marlborough would only hold firm to what he had written, 'and I doe not doubt he will, I dare say she will doe the thing'.[36] So it proved. The cost was a high one, however, and made higher by Sarah's intervention, for both ministers were now beginning to share markedly in her disfavour.

With the Junto temporarily satisfied by Sunderland's appointment, the parliamentary session of 1706–7 proved the easiest the ministers had yet had to face. Certainly it was a very profitable one for the Marlborough family. In a rare mark of distinction Marlborough's dukedom was made heritable by his daughters, and the House of Commons, more amenable than that of 1702 and with more to reward, now agreed that the pension of £5,000 should also be settled on his heirs in perpetuity. At his request, Sarah was again named as the first of the beneficiaries after his death. This was an unusual provision for a dowager, and one which reflected her view that her services to her family and the Whigs made her an equal partner with her husband; but she also complained that 'nothwithstanding all her everlasting vows of friendship & tendernesse', the Queen showed no concern for her 'poor forsaken Freeman' in this aspect of the settlement.[37] In fact they had now ceased to have any but the most formal contact.

On 31 March 1707, after a week's delay with contrary winds, Sarah again saw her husband embark at Margate; but she had no sooner returned to town than news came of his yacht's being blown back, and for the sake of a few more hours in his company she immediately set out again for the coast. On 2 April they once more said their farewells, and Sarah came back to London.[38] During all her time at Margate she had had no word from the Queen. It was not until five days after her return that Anne sent a conventional note to enquire 'how my dear Mrs Freeman did after the fatiguing Journeys she has had of late'. Jaded and overwrought, Sarah reproached her bitterly for not enquiring sooner, and for showing no awareness that she had just parted from her husband 'perhaps forever, & for her service'. She recalled the similar occasion at the beginning of the reign when hardly a day had passed without a letter. The Queen was completely unmoved. 'As for my not saying anything to you in the Duke of Marlborough's letter,' she replied, 'I did not think it necessary, nor you would not nether at any other time.' She laid the blame for their changed relations squarely on Sarah, although she still left an opening for reconciliation: 'be assured when ever you will be the same to me as you was five year agoe, you shall find me the same tender faithfull Morly.'[39]

Within a week or two Sarah did begin to make an effort to improve matters between them. 'I hope in time you will find the good effects of itt by being able to do good,' Marlborough wrote, acknowledging how essential the relationship still was to the stability of the ministry, 'for otherways all must go to destraction.'[40] But again, Sarah's motive was not to restore the friendship for its own sake, but to assist Godolphin in the latest of his long series of struggles with the Queen over the demands of the Whigs. This time the problem (which had begun to show itself before Marlborough's departure) was Anne's insistence upon appointing her own Tory candidates to the vacant bishoprics of Exeter and Chester. When her decision became public knowledge at the end of May, the Whigs refused to believe that it was not Godolphin's doing, and he had the added difficulty that Robert Harley was not only openly encouraging the Queen to maintain her independence of the Whigs, but that he now had an ally of his own within the royal bedchamber.[41]

Some time in the second week in May, Sarah reported to Marlborough that her cousin Abigail Hill, who had been unobtrusively performing her duties as bedchamberwoman since the end of the previous reign, had begun to speak to the Queen about politics.[42] Isolated in her suburban palace at Kensington and sometimes so crippled with 'the gout' that she could do nothing for herself, Anne had gradually come to depend on Abigail for companionship as well as for her physical comfort. Sarah's estrangement, which meant that she seldom went to Kensington herself, had prevented her from realizing how close this companionship had become.[43] It had been she who created the first bond between Harley and the Hills at the end of William's reign, but this had ceased with the death of Abigail's elder brother some years before. When Harley began to part company with the ministers over the pretensions of the Whigs, and realized at the same time that Abigail had supplanted Sarah as the Queen's favourite servant, it must have been he who took the initiative in renewing the acquaintance. Like Marlborough and Godolphin, he felt the need of a female ally in dealing with the Queen. The extent of Abigail's influence has been questioned by modern historians, and no doubt contemporaries greatly exaggerated it, just as they had exaggerated Sarah's. Yet there can be no question, on the evidence of Abigail's correspondence, that she did aim to use the Queen's favour for political ends, and that she was in collusion with Harley for this purpose. And unlike Sarah, Harley took care to treat his cousin as an equal and a confederate.

All three, Abigail, Harley, and the Queen, were at great pains to conceal their special relationship from Sarah, and for a time they were partially successful. At some point in the spring or early summer of 1707, in Anne's presence, Abigail was privately married to Colonel Samuel Masham, himself once Sarah's protégé (he was a friend of the Fortreys), and now one of the Prince's grooms of the bedchamber. It was a love-match, as Masham's letters make clear, but while his family and Harley's were in the secret, Sarah was not told.[44] She was puzzled and dis-approving when Anne sent for 2,000 guineas from the privy purse as a wedding present (this critical scrutiny of her personal spending was something else the Queen was growing tired of), but had no idea what the money was for.[45] Enlisting Harley's aid to arrange some further favour for Abigail, the Queen stressed that this too must be kept a secret.[46] When the housekeeper of Whitehall Palace was reported killed in Spain at the end of May, Abigail kept up the process of concealment by meekly begging Sarah to obtain the post for her sister Alice, implying that they were still dependent on her favour in all their dealings at Court.[47]

But for the time being, although she continued to be uneasy about Abigail, Sarah had other matters to distract her. All through the spring and early summer she was haunted by the fear of a battle in Flanders, unconvinced by Marlborough's assurances that the caution of the Dutch and the French made it unlikely. One effect of this was a softening of her attitude to Blenheim. 'You know my heart is sett upon the house of Woodstock,' he wrote plaintively in May, 'and you say nothing to mee how it goes on.'[48] Sarah paid a visit to the building in June, and this time, for his sake, she was at pains to restore good relations with the architect, whom she had antagonized by her fault-finding of the previous autumn. Accepting his over-optimistic assurances that one wing of the house would be habitable by the next summer and two more would see the whole finished, she returned to the Court at Windsor early in July, 'so entirely pleas'd', as Vanbrugh wrote to a friend, 'that She tould me, she found She shou'd live to Ask my pardon, for ever haveing Quarrell'd with me'.[49]

Sarah told Mrs Burnet that she intended to stay at Windsor for a good while;[50] for Godolphin's difficulties over the disposal of the bishoprics had now become acute, with the Queen still refusing to accept the Whig candidates, and the Whigs still refusing to believe that he was sincerely trying to persuade her to do so. By the end of the month they were threatening a parliamentary attack on George Churchill and his conduct of the Admiralty under Prince George, in order to force the Queen and her ministers into compliance.[51] Sarah announced her intention of becoming fully involved in this contest. The problem of Harley and the Whigs, she told her husband, could only be solved by an 'intier union' between the two of them and Godolphin for the good of the Queen and England.[52]

There was some reason for her to insist on this 'intier union', for it was clear that the ministers were by no means agreed as to the best means of dealing with Harley's growing influence with the Queen. Marlborough now saw the secretary clearly for what he was: a potential rival as chief minister. But Godolphin, to whom Harley had been a trusted subordinate since the end of the previous reign, was in this respect less clear-sighted. In any case he indicated that he did not want a trial of strength in Marlborough's absence. In reply the Duke urged that he must bring his differences with Harley into the open in the Queen's presence as soon as possible, while to Sarah he wrote that before the next parliamentary session Anne must be forced to choose publicly between Godolphin's and Harley's schemes of government.[53] It is clear, not only that Marlborough foresaw a contest between the Lord Treasurer and the secretary for the Queen's confidence, but that he wanted the matter settled one way or the other before he could become involved in it on his return. Harley's doctrine of moderation had its attractions for him; more importantly, he knew that it greatly appealed to the Queen.

But Sarah, who had now identified the underhand influence on the Queen which she had long suspected, fully shared the Whig view that Harley was dangerous and must be defeated. On 17 July she began her campaign against him and his new ally by seeking a personal interview with the Queen. This took place in a closet within the long gallery at Windsor Castle, and for all the earlier talk of reconciliation it was conducted with little pretence at friendship on either side. Taxed with taking her political notions from Harley and Abigail, the Queen defended both of them, declaring that her ideas were her own and hotly denying that Abigail had any other role than that of a useful servant. When Sarah went on to discuss a letter of advice which she knew the Queen had just received from Marlborough, Anne made it clear once and for all that she would not allow Sarah to involve herself in ministerial matters in this way, as if she had a legitimate official role. In a pointed rebuke, she remarked that she wished nobody 'medled with business more then Mrs Hill'.[54]

Since the personal confrontation had achieved nothing, Sarah continued her campaign by letter. The Queen's anger at the mention of Abigail was impressive enough to make her handle this subject more carefully, but she stuck to her point that her cousin had become the tool of Harley:

sence you say she does not speake to you, I doe beleive she does not derectly medle in anything of that nature, but without knowing it, or intending it, she is one occation of feeding Mrs Morley's passion for the torrys, by taking all occasions to speake well of some of them, & by giving you a prejudice to those that are truly in your interest, for she converses with nobody but those that have an interest or Inclenation to make wrong representations of all things, & all people that would keep you out of the power of your Enemys.[55]

At this point there was a timely revival of the Tory proposal to invite the Electress of Hanover to reside in England, and Sunderland at once seized the opportunity to hint that unless the Queen complied with the Whigs over the Church appointments, they would not consider themselves bound to oppose it as they had formerly done. Sarah promptly conveyed the threat to her mistress,[56] but this time Anne remained unmoved, even by so powerful a lever.

In August, Marlborough wrote directly to the Queen, this time without consulting either Godolphin or Sarah, and tried to force the issue of Harley's influence by insisting explicitly that she must either put her 'business into Mr Harley's hands, or follow Lord Treasurer's measures'.[57] At the same time he wrote to Godolphin, referring to Sarah's information 'that 208 [Harley] and 256 [Abigail]' now had the entire confidence of the Queen, and urging him to tell Anne plainly that if she would not take his advice, he would not be able to carry on the government, 'so that she might have time to take her measures with such as will be able to serve her'. Consulting together, Godolphin and Sarah decided to show this letter to the Queen as well, although they first crossed through the ciphered reference to Abigail, as 'a person not fitt to bee mentioned'.[58] Even so, they both knew that it would make the Queen even more angry with her former favourite, and they were right. In her reply Anne repeated that Harley was not responsible for her attitude to the bishoprics, and complained of Sarah for saying so when she had been so positively assured to the contrary.[59]

Forewarned by Godolphin that Sarah expected him to defend her against the Queen's anger, Marlborough sent his answer to this letter open for his wife's approval before it was delivered. In it he now acknowledged that she had been right as far back as the previous year, in suspecting a rival influence of some kind on Anne: 'I must do her judgment that right, as to say, that she has foreseen some things which I thought would never have happened; I mean concerning the behaviour of some in your service.'[60] Yet he must have been aware that as matters stood between the two women, this could only harden the Queen's heart further against them all. Revealing the full extent of his misgivings at being involved in these destructive struggles to satisfy the ambitions of the Whigs, he now hinted for the first time in one of his letters to Sarah that he would be better off and more capable of doing his duty in a military capacity with his wife and Godolphin out of politics.[61] Sarah showed this letter to the Queen as well, to demonstrate his belief that he no longer had any credit with her, thus incidentally revealing to Anne and to Harley that in some moods Marlborough was prepared to be detached from his wife and Godolphin.[62]

In the meantime, on 26 August, came the news that the Allies had raised the siege of Toulon, the one enterprise which the ministers had counted on to fend off parliamentary criticisms of defeat in Spain and inaction in the Low Countries. From a meeting of the Whig leaders at Althorp came the further information, conveyed in a letter from Lady Sunderland to her mother, that the Junto suspected the ministers of planning to 'bring in the Tories' once more.[63] They threatened to refuse their support in the coming session unless the Queen could be persuaded to give way over the ecclesiastical issue, and they had also decided that Harley must go. Godolphin now went so far as to give Harley an official warning about his conduct, but he still did not offer the Queen the clear choice between Harley's measures and his own which Marlborough had recommended.[64] The responses of both the Queen and Harley separated him even further from the Marlboroughs on this issue. From the secretary came profuse professions of innocence which the Lord Treasurer was apparently ready to accept. The Queen still refused adamantly to be 'Heckter'd or frighted into a compliance' by the Whigs, but she insisted that the only reason she could not give way over the bishoprics was because her word was engaged to her own candidates. She showed some sympathy for Godolphin's difficulties with the Junto, and she absolutely refused to contemplate his resignation: 'if you should put it in practice I realy beleeve it will be my death.' And she added the very significant plea, 'I beg you would not lett this be seen by any body no not by my unkind freind'.[65]

For a time this attempt to separate Godolphin from Sarah appeared to have some effect. She continued her onslaughts against the Tories with more violence than ever, telling the Queen that 'the party you are soe much inclined to are devided madd men, & for the P[rince] of W[ales] who never will nor can support you'. She accused Anne again of making it impossible for Marlborough and Godolphin to serve her while she allowed herself to be secretly governed by Harley and 'some hee is known to Employ' (she still avoided accusing Abigail directly), and predicted that if Harley were allowed to put his own scheme into practice he could not carry on the government for two months.[66] But she did not do so with Godolphin's approval. Afterwards she recalled how at this time he 'would sometimes snap me up, nothwithstanding his good breeding, when I said anything against Mr Harley'.[67] To Marlborough, Godolphin betrayed a similar irritation. He now appeared to accept the Queen's claim that she was not under Harley's influence in the matter of the bishoprics, and insisted that 'there is really no such thing as a scheme or anything like it from anybody else; nor has 42 [the Queen] as yett any thought of taking a scheme, but from Mr. Freeman and Mr. Montgomery'. In answer to Marlborough's repeated advice that he should call Harley's bluff by resigning, he added that he could not 'doe anything soe shamefull as to abandon 42 [the Queen], but upon a joynt measure with Mr. Freeman'.[68] The 'intier union' between the three which Sarah had invoked in the spring was showing signs of strain.

At this point Sarah's suspicions of Abigail Hill gained an added dimension which made her abandon all her earlier circumspection on this subject. Until now her uneasiness about her cousin had been political rather than personal; 'tho I saw she was doing mischeif,' she wrote afterwards, 'I ded not think she could have been such a devil to me.'[69] Samuel Masham had spent the summer with his regiment in Ireland, and with his return imminent the news of his secret marriage to Abigail was gradually allowed to spread by means of gossip. The first rumour reached Sarah's ears about the middle of September. Still unaware that the wedding had taken place, she asked her cousin if it were true that she intended to marry Masham. When Abigail told her that she had actually been married for some months, Sarah could only swallow her annoyance at being kept in the dark for so long, and make the usual compliments. She had no objection to the match itself, and no reason as yet to connect it with what she suspected of Abigail's political meddling. Assuming that the Queen also knew nothing of it, she offered to break the news to her. Abigail tried to put her off the scent by saying that she believed the Queen had already heard of it from the other bedchamberwomen. Seizing on this new grievance, Sarah taxed Anne at their next meeting with not letting her into the secret of her cousin's marriage, and in an unguarded moment the Queen replied 'in a sort of a passion', that she had urged Abigail a hundred times to tell Sarah, and she would not.[70]

The inconsistency between the two responses not only confirmed Sarah's suspicions about her cousin's intimacy with the Queen but also, more important, revealed that Abigail had deliberately tried to mislead her. Sarah at once jumped to the conclusion that she had the worst motives for doing so. By ferreting about and questioning the lower Court servants, she gathered evidence that Abigail had been a favourite for much longer than she had suspected, even as far back as the second year of the reign, when her own difficulties with the Queen had begun to show themselves. She also discovered that Anne had been present at the marriage, and that this was why it had been concealed from her.[71]

She was thus provided with just the explanation she needed for her own loss of favour. Refusing to see that it had been the manner as much as the matter of her political advice which had alienated the Queen, she could attribute Anne's changed attitude to nothing but being told unpalatable Whiggish truths for her own good. She now decided that the Queen would never have turned against her permanently for this reason,

if Abigail had not been at work 'in the dark' all the while, flattering her
Tory prejudices, misrepresenting Sarah's advice, and undermining all
attempts at reconciliation.[72] In short, Sarah now concluded, her cousin's
'ill offices' had been the source of all her difficulties with the Queen.
Convincing herself of this was Sarah's great mistake in dealing with
Abigail Masham. It added a personal bitterness to the political contest,
and led to the 'inveteracy against Masham' which was to turn the
Queen's alienation from her former favourite into aversion and hatred.

For three or four nights after her 'discovery', Sarah went to visit the
Queen, still hoping, as she put it, 'to do some good with her' over the
political issue. She was still so far from regretting the damage she had
done by these tactics, as she told Anne, 'that I think there is nothing in
my whole life that I have soe much reason to bee prowd of'. Each time
she found Abigail waiting to go in to the Queen as she came out.[73] On
these occasions she exchanged silent curtsies with her cousin, but her
looks, Abigail reported to Harley, were 'not to be described by any
mortal but her own self'.[74] Finally, as she was about to set out on her
usual autumn visit to Woodstock, she wrote to Abigail, accusing her of
making 'returns very unsuitable to what I might have expected', and
appointing a meeting between them when she returned to London.[75]

By mid-October they were both back at St James's, but Abigail made
no attempt to keep their appointment. When Sarah reported this to
Marlborough, he again hinted that she should consider abandoning the
contest at Court.[76] But Sarah had no intention of giving way quietly to
her rival. On the eve of the meeting of Parliament she had another
abrasive interview with the Queen, in which she warned of the
impending Whig attacks on George Churchill (who, she implied for
good measure, had an unnatural hold on the Prince's affections), and
complained of Abigail's failure to wait on her. At this, Anne 'pull'd up,
look't very grave,' and answered that she thought Abigail was 'mightily
in the right' to be afraid of the meeting.[77] Sarah then forced Godolphin
to take up the matter. To him the Queen complained bitterly of her
former favourite, both for her violent attacks on Abigail and for speaking
disrespectfully of herself and the Prince.[78] His intervention on these
issues can only have convinced her that there was no hope of
permanently detaching him from Sarah's influence. Yet as a result
Abigail did finally keep her appointment with Sarah. At this last
interview between the cousins before their rivalry divided the political
nation and passed into history, Sarah repeated the theory which she had
now convinced herself was true, that Abigail's 'ill offices' were the real
reason for the Queen's change of heart towards her. Abigail, secure in
the royal favour, made little attempt to defend herself, only remarking

that she was sure the Queen, who had loved Sarah extremely, would always be very kind to her. Then she curtsied and withdrew, leaving her rival for once in her life reduced to stunned silence.[79]

Marlborough returned to England early in November, but this time he could not persuade the Queen to give way. By mid-December, under attack from both Whigs and Tories, the affairs of the government were 'almost at a stand and off the hinges'.[80] Marlborough's prediction that Harley had an alternative scheme in mind proved correct, and it was with his help that a working arrangement involving the moderates of both parties was now worked out.[81] The Duke was much more pleased with this than either his wife or Godolphin. On a visit to Woodstock at Christmas (unaccompanied by Sarah), he kept the valetudinarian Duke of Shrewsbury, a moderate Whig whom the Junto would not accept as a colleague, up until midnight talking about it.[82] Yet by January the ministers had begun to suspect that Harley was working not for them but against them, and that his aim was still to supplant Godolphin as first minister. Sarah gives the clearest account of what they discovered:

There was undeniable proof of his having private meetings with Men of each Party of the Nation, in which his whole aim was to raise a jealousy & uneasiness in both of them, & to whet & exasperate them against the Duke of Marlborough & my Lord Godolphin, by endeavouring to perswade the Whigs that these two Ministers had no other regard to them than to serve their present purposes by them in the Houses of Parliament, and that when that was done they had resolv'd to sacrifice them to the Torys, and then by telling the Torys that the Queen had such a rooted aversion to the Whigs that if it were not for the influence of the Duke of Marlborough & my Lord Godolphin she would not leave a man of them in any Employment.[83]

They also learnt that he had criticized their conduct of the war to the Queen.

To Godolphin this was an unforgivable betrayal, and the greater shock for his earlier reluctance to believe it. He flatly refused to serve any longer with Harley, and declared that the Queen must choose between them. Marlborough, who had long foreseen such a contest, was less surprised. If he had been prepared to continue as general without Godolphin, as the Queen and Harley evidently hoped, as some Whigs believed, and as some of his own letters had seemed to suggest, the Queen would undoubtedly have chosen to retain Harley in preference to the Lord Treasurer.[84] Marlborough's dilemma was acute. On the one hand Godolphin's support at the treasury was indispensable to his conduct of the war; on the other it was clear that he had been largely supplanted by Harley in the Queen's confidence. The Duke's final decision must have been influenced as much by personal as by political factors. He told the Queen that he could live as well with Harley as anyone, but that Godolphin was unpersuadable, and that so many bonds united the two of them that he must support the Lord Treasurer.[85] These bonds included not only their long political alliance, but also their close ties of family and friendship, and particularly their common allegiance to Sarah. Marlborough could not have decided to back Harley in preference to Godolphin without wreaking havoc on his closest personal relationships.

Warned of the impending crisis, Sarah went to the Queen just beforehand, and told her that if Marlborough were forced to resign she must retire too, and asked for a promise that her Court offices would then be divided among her daughters. Evidently she wanted her family, and the Sunderlands in particular, to maintain their position at Court in case of a change of political fortunes. The Queen, who still hoped that Marlborough would agree to continue without Godolphin, gave her good words, telling her that she could not grant the request, but only (according to Sarah),

because she could never consent to part with me as long as she liv'd. . . . At last the whole ended in this that if the Duke of Marlborough could continue in her Majesty's service I should not desire to leave it; but if that prov'd to be impossible I hop'd that she would be pleas'd to grant my request of resigning to my Children, and in that case she promis'd I should do it, and I kiss'd her hand upon that account.[86]

The next day Marlborough wrote to the Queen, telling her that he must resign if she would not part with Harley. Incredibly, the Queen at first showed herself willing to sacrifice both him and Godolphin rather than the secretary. At last the reaction in Cabinet and in Parliament forced her to give way. On 10 February 1708 it was Harley who resigned, taking with him a number of his supporters, including the brilliant young secretary at war, Henry St John, who had been Marlborough's particular protégé since the death of his son. In this crisis Sarah had helped to preserve the union between the two ministers at the time of its greatest stress, and in so doing she had also contributed to a Whig victory at the expense of Harley's political moderation.

'Terrible Battles'
1708–1709

THE publicity surrounding Harley's resignation meant that Sarah's loss of favour, hitherto a secret carefully guarded from all but a few intimates, was now the talk of the coffee-houses. 'I did tell what I discovered to nobody but my Lord Marlborough and my Lord Treasurer,' she wrote of her suspicions of the previous year concerning Abigail Masham, 'and I believe I should always have kept it a secret if I cou'd, but that the Queen soon after made it publick herself, by supporting Mr Harly against my Lord Treasurer & my Lord Marlborough.'[1] It was now common knowledge that in his ministerial intrigues Harley had had an ally among the Queen's bedchamberwomen, 'a great and growing favourite, of much industry and insinuation'. By boasting even after his resignation that he would 'play [her] against anybody', he confirmed all Sarah's claims about Abigail's favour and influence.[2] It was as a result of this, and not merely of Sarah's personal obsession with her rival, that Marlborough and the Whigs became convinced that their problems with the Queen were only half solved as long as the new favourite continued in her post.

Some of the Whigs now told Sarah that Abigail Masham must be removed from Court or that she herself must go, for they could not stay there together, and talked of forcing Abigail's dismissal by means of a parliamentary address. One of the foremost in this scheme was Arthur Maynwaring. The proposal itself made Sarah uneasy, for she knew that it would be seen as a personal attack on the Queen instigated by her to get rid of a rival.[3] Even so, she was not averse from using the threat of it to frighten them both. In the second week of March she and Maynwaring together concocted a long anonymous letter to the Queen, taking her to task for allowing Harley and Abigail ('a little shuffling wretch, whose character is too bad to be describ'd') to come into competition with Marlborough and Godolphin, and threatening the direst consequences if this backstairs route were not completely closed to the ministers' defeated opponents.[4] In the end they thought better of sending it, and for the time nothing more was heard of the address; but the notion remained in Marlborough's mind, and two years later, when the Whigs had a larger majority, it was to be revived with disastrous consequences.

Sarah jokingly dubbed Maynwaring her secretary, and he was quick to adopt the title.[5] The death in December of her lawyer Anthony Guidott, whom she afterwards described (together with Godolphin) as one of the two 'best Friends that ever I had in my Life', had just deprived her of an unobtrusive but important stabilizing influence in her life,[6] and the void was quickly filled by this new and much less wholesome association. Soon Maynwaring became a regular visitor to Sarah's St James's lodgings, and her most assiduous correspondent during any absence. There were two motives behind the immense pains he took to establish himself in her confidence. The first was to encourage her at all costs to restore and maintain her position at Court as the visible guardian of Whig interests there. In this his efforts were to be so unremitting that she came to refer to her gold key of office as 'Maynwaring's key'.[7] In irresistibly flattering terms, he told her that she should now continue at Court not as a favourite, 'but as one more capable of business than any Man, supported by Friends & a strong party in the right interest'; 'the very Air & appearance of such a one about the Queen' would soon defeat all their opponents' schemes.[8] Incitement of this kind, added to Sarah's personal bitterness against her rival, was to complete the destruction of her relations with the Queen.

Maynwaring's second aim was to foster the alliance between the ministers and the Junto which had suffered considerably during the previous year, using Sarah as go-between. Since the defeat of Harley's schemes, he warned her, it was no longer sufficient for Marlborough to remain aloof from parties; 'something more of warmth' towards the Whigs would be required if he was to support his ministry in power.[9] Relations between Sarah and her husband at this time were already very strained, partly over this very issue. Aware that he had damaged his credit with the Queen irreparably by obliging her to part with Harley, the Duke was more unwilling than ever to support the next punishing round of Whig demands for office, which now included the admission of the leading Junto peer, Lord Somers, to the Cabinet as Lord President, and the appointment of Halifax's brother as attorney-general. And again the difficulties between him and his wife may have been personal as well as political. A young dancer named Hester Santlow had just begun to appear regularly on the London stage, and the rumour that she had attracted Marlborough's attention must at some point have become known to Sarah.[10] Even her enemies admitted that she could still outshine most younger women in looks (when Marlborough's reputed mistress was pointed out to one gossip, she commented, 'his Dutchis for all she is many years older . . . yet she is ten timse handsomer'[11]). Even so, Sarah's dread of losing her husband's affection can only have increased with the years. Some of the undated letters concerning her suspicions of an unnamed woman, which have been assumed to relate to their quarrel in 1704, may in fact date from this later period.

These crises at Court and in Sarah's personal life probably had some connection with the unexplained lump sum of £12,000 which she paid herself out of the privy purse on 17 March. The likeliest explanation, as Dr Gregg has suggested, is that this was a back payment of the annual pension of £2,000 which the Queen had offered her in 1702.[12] Ignoring or forgetting the fact that the offer had been intended as compensation for Parliament's refusal to settle the pension of £5,000 and that this omission had since been fully remedied, Sarah still felt herself to have a claim to the extra money. If this was the explanation, however, it certainly did not mark any reconciliation with the Queen. Early in March, after a violent and petty altercation about Abigail's alleged encroachments on her unused lodgings at Kensington, Sarah ceased to visit Anne altogether for several weeks.[13] The following year and again in 1710 she was to remind the Queen of her original refusal of the £2,000, adding that she 'never did mention it again or receive any of it'.[14] Nor were the goldsmith's accounts in which the payment was originally recorded ever presented to the Queen for her inspection. Instead a second set was compiled, in which the £12,000 was fully but silently restored.[15] If Sarah, feeling herself supplanted and ill-used, had been tempted to compensate herself by taking the money without mentioning it to the Queen, she must afterwards have thought better of it. The matter remained in abeyance for three more years.

The attempted Jacobite invasion from Dunkirk, which kept the Court in a state of fluctuating alarm during February and March, also delayed Marlborough's departure for the Continent. But when he did set out on the morning of 29 March, for the first and only time in his long succession of campaigns his wife did not go with him to see him embark.[16] Instead she went off alone to Windsor Lodge, leaving behind a letter for the Queen, in which she reproached her with having shown by her preference for Abigail 'that nothing would be so uneasy as my nearer attendance', and asked to be allowed to resign her offices to her daughters, 'even while my Lord Marlborough continues in your service'. But if Sarah, in her estrangement from her husband, was ready to sever their partnership in this way, the last thing the Queen wanted was a public rupture which would affect Marlborough's position and draw further attention to Abigail Masham. She assured Sarah that 'I can never hearken to that as long as you live,' but added, 'if I should outlive you, your faithfull Morly will remember her promis'.[17]

From her retirement at Windsor Sarah wrote to Marlborough, when she did so at all, in a style that convinced him of her 'resolution of living with that coldness and indifferency for mee, which if it continues must make me the unhappyest man alive'.[18] He had promised Godolphin that he would return for a short time before the campaign opened to help him persuade the Queen to accept the further Whig appointments. But it is clear that he had no serious intention of doing so, and when he sent his excuses in April Sarah's bitterness against him increased. In a clear attempt to withdraw from the political contest altogether, he now told her that he could do no good with the Queen, and that he did not intend to return to England the following winter either, unless she would have it otherwise.[19]

Meanwhile Sarah's Whig friends besought her to return to Court. 'I am sure your absenting yourself for any long time, is doing just what your and all our enemies desire,' Sunderland warned her, and Maynwaring seconded him.[20] Marlborough, who was now as worried about Abigail Masham's influence as any of them, agreed 'that you can't oblige 256 [Mrs Masham] more then by being at a distance with 239 [the Queen]'; but he added, 'I vallu your quiet and happyness so much . . . [that] I would not have you constrain yourself in anything'.[21] When Sarah showed this part of the letter to Maynwaring, he told her to disregard it: 'I should rather have expected that his opinion would have been governed by some high point of wisdom than by such softnesses; and I confess I can see none in discouraging your endeavours, which I think can only do service.'[22]

At the same time there had been a further exchange of letters between Sarah and the Queen, who repeated her old plea that 'it has not bin my fault that we have lived in the manner we have don ever since I came to the Crown', and her old assurance that 'whenever you will be easy with me I will be soe to[o]'.[23] Sarah told Maynwaring that the Queen's expression, 'you wrong Masham and me,' made her sick, and he agreed, comparing it with 'King James the First's usual expression [about the Duke of Buckingham], Steenie and I'. But he argued that since it was absolutely necessary for her to return to Court, she should take advantage of the offer of a reconciliation to do it with the best grace she could.[24] When Sarah did come to town and wait on the Queen in mid-April, her reception was cordial enough to convince Maynwaring that 'your Person is still as agreeable there, as it is everywhere else'.[25] It was even reported that the Queen had reconciled the two rivals for her favour.[26] Sarah herself had no confidence in the reality of all this, but she was cheered by the results of the general election in May, in which the Whigs made substantial gains, and by the ballads and pamphlets against Abigail, Harley, and the Tories which Maynwaring was ready to produce at the slightest hint from herself.[27]

Harley's retirement into the country in the spring also temporarily allayed Sarah's fears about Abigail's political influence. For the time being she believed that there was more danger from George Churchill than from her cousin in this respect.[28] But what pleased her most of all was the letter Marlborough sent to the Queen at the end of April at Godolphin's request, fully supporting the case for Somers' admission to the Cabinet. 'You are so good as to say you will never write of pollatiques that may be disagreable to me if I desire itt,' he wrote at the first signs of her softening; 'You know in friendship and love there must be no constraint, so that I am desirous of knowing what your heart thinkes, and must beg of you the justice to beleive that I am very much concerned when you are uneasy.'[29] Sarah's 'perfect good humour' and frequent attendance at Court during the following weeks reassured the Whigs and made Harley's spies correspondingly uneasy: 'Her Grace is grown the gayest, wanton young thing in the world,' one of them wrote sourly, 'but whether it proceeds from her being restored to favour, or from finding herself in a state above the favour of [the Queen] I cannot tell.'[30] She carried her good humour with her on a brief visit to Woodstock in May, where she not only pronounced herself satisfied with the progress of the building, but even made some attempt to restore friendly relations with her Tory neighbours.[31]

In Flanders there was the prospect of a battle once Marlborough had joined forces with Prince Eugene of Savoy. As one campaign succeeded another, Sarah found these periods of suspense harder and harder to bear. Clearly this was no time to nurse differences with her husband, and Marlborough accepted his restoration to grace, as always, with unquestioning thankfulness: 'I do not say this to flatter you, nor am I at an age of making fond expressions, but upon my word, when you are out of humor, and are disatisfied with me, I had rather dye then live.'[32] In a crucial piece of advice, he told her to concentrate on restoring her personal relationship with Anne and to avoid tackling her directly about politics, 'and that may in length of time enable you to do good to the nation and 42 [the Queen]'.[33] Like the Whigs and even the Queen herself, he was by this time as much concerned with the appearance as with the reality of his wife's favour. For a while Sarah made a real effort to follow his advice and her relations with the Queen continued outwardly good. When the news arrived on 5 July that Marlborough was safe after his third major victory over the French at Oudenarde, there came a letter from 'Mrs Morley' to 'dear dear Mrs Freeman', as warmhearted as any written in the heyday of their friendship.[34]

The difficulty was that Sarah, particularly with Maynwaring as her mentor, was quite incapable of keeping any resolution of self-restraint for long. In his brief note giving her the first news of the victory,

Marlborough had written: 'I do, and you must give thankes to God for his goodnes in protecting and making me the instrument of so much happyness to the Queen and nation, if she will please to make use of itt.'[35] Sarah decided on impulse to do just what he had advised her against: use this last unguarded phrase as the excuse for a fresh attack on the Queen about politics. No sooner had she sent off her note of congratulation, therefore, than the Queen received a long remonstrance in Sarah's most hectoring style, in which she quoted Marlborough's bitter comment and added (as she afterwards paraphrased her own letter),

that it made me melancholly when I reflected that after three such battles wone for your servisse hee aprehended that hee had not much credit with you or that the influence of some ill meaning people might disappoint whatever your most faithfull servants could doe; that I knew your Majesty's answer to this would bee that there were no such people, but everybody knows that impressions must be given by somebody, that the object of the Princes favour [George Churchill] had so sad a charecter in the world that it could not bee supposed to take informations from him; and since you would not indure to have one think you suffered your own faverit to talk to you upon anything of businesse, what account could bee given of your Majestys doing contrary to the advise of soe many of your most considerable subjects and old experienced friends?[36]

The Queen wrote back angrily, denying Marlborough's want of credit with her, and forbidding Sarah to 'mention that person any more who you are pleased to call the object of my favour, for whatever character the malicious world may give her, I do assure you it will never have any weight with me, knowing she does not deserve it'.[37] Ignoring the last prohibition, Sarah at once sent off a reply, pointing out that the Queen had mistaken her reference to Abigail. Anne's only response was to claim sarcastically that she could not answer this letter immediately because she must have 'time to read it over & over againe before I begin to writt, for feare of making any more mistakes'.[38]

All the bad feeling between the two was out in the open once more, and when Sarah joined the Court at Windsor for the summer her fears about her cousin's favour and influence were revived. The Queen had formerly claimed that she regarded Abigail as no more than a useful servant; but now, when taxed about the relationship, she retorted, 'sure I may love whom I please,' and added defiantly that she had friends who would support her against the Whigs.[39] Sarah at once reported this disquieting change of attitude to Marlborough. Although the decision to show his letter to the Queen had embarrassed him considerably, he was as alarmed as Sarah by what the renewed quarrel had brought to light. Sooner or later, he told her grimly, they must have the Queen 'out of the hands of 256 [Mrs Masham], or everything will be labour in vain'.[40]

Even so, he would certainly not have approved of the methods which Sarah, aided and abetted by Maynwaring, now began to take to induce the Queen to abandon her new favourite. It was one thing for the Kit-Cats to compose scurrilous attacks on Abigail, and for Sarah to perform these in private to appreciative audiences of her Whig friends ('I am much improv'd . . . in the two Ballads of the Battle & Abigal, & can sing them most rarely,' she wrote to Lady Cowper in July); Harley and his displaced colleagues were cheering their retirement by composing equally insulting attacks on her.[41] But it was quite another thing for Sarah to send samples of these writings to the Queen herself, accompanied by one of the most insolent letters ever written by a subject to a sovereign, in order to convince her that her reputation was being destroyed by her unnatural passion for her chambermaid:

tho your Majesty was pleased to desire me not to speak any more of her . . . yet I must humbly beg pardon if I cannot obay that command the rather because I remember you said att the same time of all things in this world you valued most your reputation, which I confess surpris'd me very much, that your Majesty should so soon mention that word after having discover'd so great a passion for such a woman, for sure there can bee noe great reputation in a thing so strange & unaccountable, to say noe more of it, nor can I think the having noe inclenation for any but of one's own sex is enough to maintain such a charecter as I wish may still be yours.[42]

On the political issue, even without Harley's immediate presence, the Queen continued as obdurate as ever. For the time being, although Sarah and her friends found it hard to believe, she had broken off all direct communication with him. But Abigail had not, and her letters to him in the code they had settled before he retired to the country, while they show that Sarah was able to keep her somewhat in the background, also make the continuing collusion between the two quite clear. 'My Lady Pye [Sarah] is here still,' Abigail wrote from Windsor on 21 July, '[and] I have not seen my aunt [the Queen] since my duty called me . . . I don't think it any unkindness in my aunt, but because my Lady Pye is here'; and a week later:

I am very much afraid of my aunt's conduct in her affairs, and all [that] will come from her want of a little ready money [courage] for hitherto you know the want of that has made her a most sad figure in the world. I shall be very glad to have your opinion upon things that I may lay it before her.[43]

Vanbrugh summed up the uneasy situation at the end of the month:

Things are in an odd way at Court. Not all the Intrest of Ld Tre[asurer] & Lady Marlb: back'd and press'd warmly by every Man of the Cabinet, can prevail with the Queen to Admit My Lord Sommers into any thing; nor so much as to make an Attorney Generall; She answers little to 'em, but Stands firm against all they say . . . My Lady Marlborough . . . is very much at Court, and mighty well there, but the Q[ueen']s fondness of tother Lady, is not to be express'd.[44]

Sarah had now entirely abandoned Marlborough's advice not to talk to her mistress about politics. On 19 August the two women drove together in apparent harmony to St Paul's to give thanks for Marlborough's victory. But Sarah was upset by the Queen's refusal to wear the jewels she had chosen for the occasion, and while they were actually in the cathedral she could not forbear goading Anne again with Marlborough's lack of credit. When the Queen began to make a heated reply, Sarah told her peremptorily to be quiet in case they should be overheard. The next day she tried to take up the quarrel where they had left off by forwarding another of Marlborough's letters for Anne to read. It was returned with the briefest and coldest of covering notes:

After the commands you gave me on the Thanksgiving day of not answering you, I should not have troubled you with these lines but to return the Duke of Marlborough's letter safe to your hands, and for the same reason do not say anything to that nor to yours which enclosed it.[45]

Early in September Sarah left the Court to make a brief visit to Mrs Burnet at Salisbury. Already ailing in health, the Bishop's wife was to succumb to pneumonia during the following bitter winter, so that this was to be their last unclouded meeting. When Sarah left to return to Windsor, the loss of her vital presence after even a few days of her company left her friend complaining of a sense of dullness and anti-climax 'that I know not how to overcome, I am just like one that has lost the sunshine that makes everything cheerful'.[46] Yet for the Queen Sarah's return to Windsor meant a gathering of storm clouds. In the second week of September they had two 'terrible battles', during which Sarah launched violent attacks on Harley, Abigail, and the Tories.[47] The only benefit was to bring home to her belatedly the wisdom of Marlborough's advice. Until now he had hoped that the relationship between the two women might somehow be usefully maintained. But having watched throughout the year as one disaster followed another in his wife's dealings with the Queen, he now told her with relief that 'the resolution you have taken of neither speaking or writting is so certainly right, that I dare assure you that you will find a good effect of itt in one month'.[48]

Yet while Sarah and her mistress grew ever more estranged, Godolphin's dependence on his colleague's wife since Harley's departure had become noticeably greater, and her influence with Marlborough continued to be of considerable use to him and to the Whigs in their further damaging struggles with the Queen. All this while Sarah was keeping up the pressure on her husband to support the Whig appointments, and her weight added to Godolphin's was more than he could withstand. Almost all the letters of political advice which he sent to the Queen during this year were drafted for him by them; he told his wife plainly that he would never trouble the Queen with his letters, 'but that I can't refuse 38 [Godolphin] and 240 [Lady Marlborough] when thay desire anything of mee'.[49] Harley, who had sources of information in Holland, reported to Abigail that Marlborough had complained to Dutch colleagues about being drawn in this way into the Junto's struggles for office.[50] As a result the Queen became more and more convinced that Sarah was the power behind the ministers; afterwards she complained 'that the Duchess made my Lord Marlborough, and my Lord Godolphin do any thing, and that when my Lord Godolphin was ever so firmly resolved when with her [the Queen] . . . yet when he went to her [Sarah], she impressed him to the Contrary'.[51] This conviction was now turning her completely against them all.

Yet it was in the midst of all these difficulties that Anne made the second of her two substantial grants of property to Sarah. On 31 August a fifty-year crown lease of a plot of ground adjacent to St James's Palace was granted to trustees for her benefit at a nominal rent; although Sarah herself was careful to proclaim that she would not have accepted it, 'but that it was promised her long before the quarrel with Mrs Masham'.[52] On the east side of the Palace, only a few yards from her existing lodgings, it had the same impressive vista south over St James's Park and east along the royal gardens, which then stretched almost as far as Charing Cross. Her plan was to use it as the site for a town house of her own. Declining favour and the talk of resignation during the winter, threatening her with the loss of her only London home, had suddenly made this a pressing matter.

The project meant further differences with Marlborough, who objected that the site was too small for a suitable house, and that the building would cost twice what she had estimated. In a strictly businesslike transaction, which well illustrates the separate nature of their financial arrangements, he at last agreed to contribute £7,000, but only on condition that the house should go along with the dukedom after her death; if she decided to leave it elsewhere, it was to be security for the repayment of the £7,000 to his heirs.[53] But no sooner had Sarah engaged Sir Christopher Wren as her architect (a choice which his rival Vanbrugh took very much to heart) than she began to realize that Marlborough's objections to the site were well founded. While Maynwaring paced out the distances in an attempt to reassure her, other friends put forward expensive proposals for buying up the houses on the northern boundary.[54] It was too late in the year, in any case, to begin building, and the project was allowed to hang fire until Marlborough's return.

But from the army before Lille the Duke wrote that he was 'almost dead' with anxiety and fatigue. For several days in September, with the eyes of all Europe on him, he faced the unthinkable prospect of having to raise the siege. Sarah could only do her best to comfort and sustain him with her letters. He was still hankering after the governor-generalship of the Spanish Netherlands, the prize which the Emperor had dangled before him since 1706, but which he dared not accept because of the objections of the Dutch. The post appealed to him because it was the highest a subject could hold in Europe, because it was worth £60,000 a year, and above all because it would have given him an unassailable refuge above the party battles in England. At first his wife was clearly taken aback; the idea was hardly consistent with his wish for a quiet retirement with her at Blenheim.[55] Yet in the depression which had hung over her since her last futile and destructive battles with the Queen, she was sometimes inclined to welcome the prospect of being out of England. When Maynwaring urged her to look after her health, she told him that she took more care of her life than it was worth, and that the best thing for her present circumstances would be a Jacobite restoration, which would force them all to retire to Marlborough's little principality of Mindelheim in Bavaria, the Emperor's present to him after his victory at Blenheim.[56]

It took a further urgent plea for her help from Godolphin and the Whigs to rouse her from this mood. The Lord Treasurer's relations with the Junto had reached yet another *impasse*, as the Queen still stubbornly refused to make further concessions to 'the five tyrannizing lords'. At a confrontation with Godolphin at Newmarket, they demanded the appointments of Somers and Wharton and the dismissal from the Admiralty of Prince George and George Churchill, and delivered their usual threat, that if this was not immediately done, 'they must lett the world & their friends see they have nothing more to do with the Court'.[57] What was remarkable was the importance both sides attached to Sarah's role in this affair, as the only person in England whose desire to see the Whigs in office was beyond suspicion and who was also on terms of complete confidence and intimacy with the Lord Treasurer. When Somers met her on the road to Windsor at this time, she remembered, 'he did a thing very uncommon upon the sight of me. He stood up in his coach, when the custom was only bowing as one passes by, as if I had been the Great Mogul.'[58] Maynwaring, mediating indefatigably between the ministers and the Junto, entreated her to use her influence to calm the violent and intractable Sunderland, and persuade the Whigs to have patience till Marlborough returned.[59] The Junto wanted her in London, and Godolphin seconded them. Not only her personal support, but her credit with the Whigs had become indispensable to him:

I see so many difficultys coming upon mee from all sides, that unless I would have recourse to you oftner, upon many occasions, than it is possible for mee to have at this distance when the ways grow bad, and the moon fails . . . I am afraid they must needs bee too hard for mee; besides that, I would not willingly make any step, but what is first approved by you.[60]

The Junto's bullying tactics had always been a sore trial of Sarah's loyalty, and as usual her personal sympathies were with Godolphin. She told Maynwaring angrily that they must all have more patience, and berated Sunderland so soundly for his hostility to the Lord Treasurer that he was reported to be ashamed of himself.[61] Yet her political allegiances were still with the Whigs, and at the same time she continued to press Godolphin to achieve all the Junto's aims. 'I assure you my heart is always the same in everything you do not see, as in this which you have the goodnes to take kindly,' he told her when the Queen at last showed signs of giving way, 'and though you think it is my fault that I don't master the difficultys I meet with, yett I feel the contrary every day.'[62]

What finally broke down the Queen's resistance to the Whig appointments and brought Sarah to town at the end of October was the decline of Prince George into mortal illness at Kensington. But after their last bitter altercations, she now found that Anne received her 'like a stranger'. Outwardly her conduct was correct. When the Prince died, she gave the Queen what conventional comfort she could, and supervised her removal to St James's the same day. But her attitude was completely lacking in sympathy or even common humanity. She refused to obey an order to send for Abigail Masham before they left (ostensibly because it would offend the bishops and other courtiers of rank who were not admitted). She was careful to note that Anne ate 'a very good dinner' when she arrived at St James's, and chose to regard her concern for the dignified conveyance of the Prince's huge and unwieldy coffin from Kensington to Westminster as grotesque and absurd.[63] Although she remained in constant attendance at St James's, her aim was not to comfort the Queen, but to keep her rival at bay at this crucial period of the Whig fortunes. Yet she soon noted that Anne would not speak to her freely of anything, 'and I found I could gain no ground; which was not much to be wondered at, for I never came to her but I found Mrs. Masham there, or had been just gone out from her, which at last tired me, and I went to her seldomer'.[64] In fact she would have abandoned the Court altogether if Maynwaring had not warned her that Wharton and Somers now looked upon her as 'the surest support in their offices',

& and if they knew of this little Turn, they wou'd not come so chearfully into 'em, but would really blame you extreamly. For the going once or twice a day, on a sort of visit, how disagreeable so ever, will never be thought so great an Evil as that for it you should avoid doing the greatest Good.[65]

By this time, however, Sarah's greatest concern was not for the Whigs, but for her husband. Despite his ailing health, he had kept his army in the field well into one of the worst winters in memory. On 17 November, with the citadel of Lille at last about to surrender, came the news that he was preparing to cross the Scheldt to give battle to the French in order to forestall an attack on Brussels. For more than a week afterwards there was no certain news of the outcome. Unable to bear company, Sarah fled alone to Windsor Lodge, telling Maynwaring she was so wretched that she wished herself drowned.[66] On 26 November, when her worst fears had been allayed by the news of Marlborough's bloodless success over the French, she came back to Court; but she was still deeply disturbed about reports of his ill health, and wanted to go over to him. This time it was Marlborough who would not hear of it. He intended to fulfil his plan of remaining on the frontier all winter, and he persisted in this despite desperate pleas from Godolphin for his assistance in England. Sarah's first reaction, remembering their differences throughout the year, was to accuse him of not wanting to come back to her. 'Upon my word and honour,' he assured her, 'the only comfortable thoughts I have when I am alone is that after all my trouble I may have some time of living quietly and happyly with you, which can't be if you are in doubt of the esteme and love I have, and ever will have for you . . . For God sake make me happy in believing the truth of my loving you with all my heart and soull.'[67]

His main reason for not returning was to avoid the political turmoil in England. When the House of Commons passed a vote of thanks to the Tory General Webb, he attributed this slight to secret assurances from Harley and Abigail that the Queen would not be displeased at it.[68] Ten days later the Whigs concocted an address of congratulation for the successes of the campaign, in which Prince Eugene's name was coupled with his. This time Sarah herself was so infuriated that Maynwaring had to beg her to be more discreet for fear of damaging relations between the ministers and the Junto still further.[69] In fact by now Sarah was far from satisfied with the Whigs in any respect. Shortly after Somers' appointment as Lord President she had a long, confidential, and unwise talk with him, in which she laid bare the true state of her relations with the Queen. At once his elaborate deference ceased and he applied himself to courting all the Mashams, 'male and female'.[70] Sarah was already aware of the plan to bring Orford into the Admiralty at the earliest opportunity, and she had no objection to this. But Halifax, the one remaining member of the Junto, had already antagonized her by his lack of appreciation of her efforts on his brother's behalf, and now it dawned on her that he also had hopes of displacing Godolphin at the treasury. Sarah found that she had nursed vipers in her bosom. In letter after letter to Marlborough she denounced the 'monstrous designs' of the Junto. Although she still clung to her Whig principles, she assured him that she now entirely agreed with him about the conduct of parties once they were in power, and she proposed coming over to live at Brussels, so that they could both remain out of England until the war was over. Marlborough told her that he could not desert Godolphin completely in this way; but he added, with reference to the first tentative French overtures for peace, 'I hope it will not be long before we may be all three happy.'[71]

Together with most of fashionable London during this bitterly cold winter, Sarah patronized the opera. The lionized Italian *castrato* Nicolini, 'Monsieur Nickolino', as she called him, had been lured to London by her friend Lord Manchester, and she not only attended his performance of the new opera, *Camilla*, but engaged him to sing at a private gathering at her lodgings.[72] But what appealed to her even more was the music performed at St James's Chapel on 17 February, the thanksgiving day for the successes of the campaign, 'much better I believe than has ever been yet heard at any of the Operas'.[73] By this time she was buoyant with the expectation of Marlborough's return after the longest of their separations. Her friend Sir Henry Furnese, one of the City merchants who managed her investments for her, offered her the use of the great house near Dover which he had built from the profits of remitting the pay of Marlborough's army, and Sarah was so impatient for the reunion that she travelled down on 25 February, while Marlborough himself was still on the road to Ostend.[74] His man-of-war was driven further round the coast to Rye, but as soon as he learnt of her whereabouts he left the London road and led his small entourage on a gruelling overnight journey across country to meet her at Canterbury.[75]

The peace negotiations developed so quickly on the Continent that the Duke's stay in London lasted a bare three weeks. But he was back within the month for further consultations, and when he embarked again on 3

May, peace was thought sure. It was with this apparent end to all his troubles in sight that he took the most controversial and ill-advised step of his career. When he had written to Sarah of his longing for retirement after a peace, he meant only retirement from the stresses of ministerial politics, and not a complete resignation of his military appointments. He had been too long 'almost in the place of a King' (in Sarah's unintentionally telling phrase) to contemplate a complete return to private life. Yet in the course of the winter he had become convinced, partly as a result of Sarah's information, that Abigail was in collusion with Harley to turn the Queen against him and so force his resignation. Harley's vitriolic references, in his letters to Abigail and in his private jottings, to Marlborough's 'sordid avarice' and overweening ambition suggest that this was not far wrong, but when the Duke decided that his best means of combating their efforts was to ask the Queen to grant his commission as captain-general for life, he only played further into their hands.[76] Although Anne asked for time to consider and take advice, her disapproval was plain. Marlborough set Lord Chancellor Cowper to work to search for precedents without attracting too much attention, but his response was also discouraging, and gave the Queen the excuse to refuse the request outright by letter.[77] Marlborough had achieved nothing but to arouse her suspicion that he was aiming at an unconstitutional power, and to confirm his own fears about Abigail Masham. Sarah now learnt that Abigail, 'in her nauseous bufooning way', had begun to nickname him King John.[78]

Even so she was happier in the spring and early summer of 1709 than she had been for years past, sharing the general belief that the French would make peace on any terms rather than undergo another campaign. This gave her a fresh incentive to press ahead with her new house. Early in 1709 she was granted a new lease in exchange for the first, to include two more acres of ground from the adjacent royal gardens. Her claim that this second lease had been necessary because of 'a mistake' in the first was deliberately misleading.[79] The additional grant of land from one of the best sites in London, hitherto preserved from building, was actually a much greater favour than the first, and given expressly to provide a larger area for the planned house. Marlborough had always thought the original plot too small; the state of Sarah's relations with the Queen, and the fact that the measuring of the new site began just as he left for the Continent at the end of March, suggest that the Queen had granted it at his request, as a reward for the successes of the campaign.[80]

Wren, now well into his seventies, had been surveyor-general of the royal works for forty years and was the foremost architect of the age. Yet Sarah was not in the least overawed by his colossal reputation. Both the

Duke of Buckingham's house at St James's and the Duke of Shrewsbury's house near Woodstock influenced her choice of design, and she called the two Dukes in to assist at some of her consultations with Wren and his son. But her overriding instructions, which they strictly observed, were that the new house should be 'strong, plain and convenient', and that it 'should not have the least resemblance of anything in that called Blenheim'.[81] On 24 May she laid the foundation stone, and announced that she expected to be a good deal in London during the summer to supervise the work: 'I think I am in the best hands wee have, but their rules does not allways agree with my fancy, & I am forced to bee perpetually on the watch.'[82] With more than a hundred bricklayers and masons on site, the house went up quickly and entirely to her satisfaction. Flattering her to the top of her bent, Maynwaring told her that

Sir Chris Wren had no more hand in designing it than the Bricklayers or Masons; as they are his Instruments, He is yours. . . . Your Grace sits at the head of the work, & directs all the inferiour Ranks of officers, from Mr Wren to those that carry the Morter, who are all alike employ'd onely to finish what you have so well contriv'd.[83]

It was all very gratifying, but it had to be paid for. Within the space of two years Sarah needed £22,000 to secure the lease and fulfil her contracts, and from the evidence of the privy purse accounts there can be no doubt, as Dr Gregg has shown, that she initially obtained the money by borrowing from the Queen's funds. At the beginning of the reign she had lodged these with the same goldsmith, John Coggs, who held her own and her husband's current accounts, and at an early stage she had fallen into the habit of using the Queen's money to supply temporary shortages of her own. She did not ask Anne's permission in advance, and took her own time about repaying these sums. Yet it is clear that she did not regard herself as having done anything untoward; she simply explained that as the goldsmith paid no interest, it made no difference to the Queen whether the surplus funds were in Coggs's hands or her own.[84]

Between August 1708 and January 1710 the privy purse accounts show a total of £21,800 lent to her.[85] The amounts were clearly noted in the accounts as borrowed, and she relied on the fact that Marlborough, who had now agreed to pay for the whole house on its enlarged scale, would eventually provide the money to repay them. Meanwhile the ability to pay cash enabled her to avoid calling in her own interest-bearing investments, and to get speedy work at discount prices. Then in January 1710, before any repayments were made, Coggs went bankrupt.[86] There are no further accounts to show what arrangements Sarah made for the custody of the Queen's money during the last twelve months of her office, or whether her borrowings were repaid at this point or remained to be dealt with later. One can only note her later claim that the building 'cost the Duke of Marlborough betwixt fourty and fifty thousand pound, which the Queen never payd one shilling of, as many people have been told she did'.[87]

Congratulating her in June on the progress of her house, Marlborough begged 'that may not hinder you from pressing forward the building at Bleinheim, for we are not so much master of that as of the other'.[88] Sarah's misgivings about this project were now proving well founded. In his anxiety to have it finished before his favour declined, Marlborough had hurried it on as fast as possible; and in his determination to have it executed in the grandest manner without financial liability to himself, he had let Vanbrugh have a free hand and avoided exercising any control over the expenditure. As a result the building was now seriously in debt, although still far from completion. Sarah was beginning to have renewed doubts about the architect, who was now adding the restoration of the old manor house to his other costly projects, but finding him too forceful a personality and too much in Marlborough's favour to be manageable, she concentrated her efforts instead on the junior officers of the works, who controlled the day-to-day expenditure. In letter after letter she reiterated that all available resources must be applied to the completion of the private apartments in the east wing so that they would be ready to move into the following spring.[89] The tragedy was that the peace negotiations broke up in June without agreement, and there was to be no retirement the following year.

All this while, disgusted with her own treatment and disillusioned with the Junto, Sarah made little attempt even to keep up appearances at Court. The Whigs noted uneasily that she 'never appear'd but when sent for', and that Abigail Masham was 'more and more in esteem'.[90] Bitterly resenting Sarah's behaviour and longing to be rid of her, the Queen now began a deliberate campaign of encroachments on the rights and privileges of her offices: an increased allowance for one of the subordinates in the robes office who had made herself useful to the new favourite; the appointment of 'a crony' of Mrs Masham as bedchamber-woman in opposition to Sarah's candidate. Petty as these were in themselves, they were clearly seen, even by Whigs who realized that Sarah had brought her difficulties on herself, as a deliberate attempt to provoke her resignation.[91] Matters came to a head in July when the Queen ordered Sarah, as groom of the stole, to make the formal presentation of the new bedchamberwoman so that she could take up her duties. In a brief and stormy appearance at Windsor Sarah complied, but afterwards she complained publicly that Anne was treating her with less consideration than her other leading household officers.[92]

The Queen, in a letter more outspoken than any she had yet written to Sarah, retorted that no one thought her ill used but herself, and assured her that she would always be treated with the consideration due to the Duke of Marlborough's wife and her groom of the stole. This was clearly intended to indicate that any special relationship between them was at an end; but it was the retort about her ill usage that particularly stung Sarah, and she now tried for the first time to involve Marlborough directly in this personal quarrel, as she had so often involved Godolphin:

you are pleased to say that nobody thinks me ill used but my self, but your ma[jes]ty is very wrong informed in that matter, & I can assure you my Lord Marlborough thinks so, & if hee has not yet complaind of it to you, it is because hee has so many other things to do that are of more consiquence to the Publick, tho non I have reason to think that are of more concern to himself.[93]

Having written to Marlborough to demand his support, she then yielded to the entreaties of the Whigs so far as to make one more visit to the Queen, before departing on a round of summer visits to Woodstock and Althorp.

Yet when Marlborough's reply came, she found that he not only refused to write to the Queen to complain of her treatment, but advised her not to do so herself: 'it has been always my observation in disputes, especially in that of kindness and friendshipe, that all reproches, though never so reasonable, do serve to no other end but the making the breach wider.'[94] Sarah was far beyond the reach of such common sense. She was bitterly hurt and resentful at his failure to support her, and made no attempt, as she usually did, to conceal this from her friends. 'After it had been said that Nobody thinks so but yourself, it grew very sore that nothing of what you know was writ from Abroad,' Maynwaring wrote discreetly to Lord Coningsby, one of his Whig colleagues, 'but instead of that there were some expressions in a late Letter which shew'd too much unconcern.'[95] Sarah's angry protests reached Marlborough just before he engaged the French at Malplaquet, in what proved to be the bloodiest battle of the war. From Windsor his *aide-de-camp* rode on to Woodstock to bring her the news. She received him with 'unspeakable joy', but the letter from her husband which he brought with him showed how much her reproaches had upset and distracted him in the crucial time before the battle. 'God almighty be praised, it is now in our powers to have what peace wee please, and I may be pretty well assured of never being in another battel,' he ended, 'but that nor nothing in this world can make mee happy if you are not kind.'⁹⁶ She realized that he might have been killed still thinking her unkind.

The carnage of the battle was dreadful to everyone. For several days afterwards Marlborough was prostrated with shock, haunted by the thought of 'so many brave men killed with whome I have lived these eight years, when we thought ourselves sure of a peace'.⁹⁷ A well-intentioned attempt by his secretary to reassure Sarah that the collapse was not serious had the opposite effect. Overcome with remorse and a desperate longing to be with him, she wanted to embark on the next packet-boat to go over to him. In the end she let Godolphin dissuade her, but unable to face the prying eyes at Windsor, she went off to St Albans to calm her nerves and wait for better news.⁹⁸ Even at this stage she seems to have had some inkling that the victory was to prove inconclusive for the all-important achievement of peace. 'I hope you judg right that the French can fight noe more, because that must produce a good peace,' she wrote to Coningsby, 'and without that I am sure my happynesse can't be lasting whatever success may give me for some moments.'⁹⁹

Within a few days she was reassured about Marlborough's health and much mollified by his at last agreeing to write to the Queen to endorse her complaints. A second refusal to grant his commission for life, which he interpreted as confirmation of Abigail Masham's design to force him to resign, had already made him decide to tell the Queen that after the end of the campaign, 'which I hope will put a happy end to this warr', he would 'serve noe more but in Parliament'. Now, at Sarah's insistence, he agreed to give as a further reason for his resignation, 'your Majesty's change from Lady Marlborough to Mrs. Masham, and the severall indignitys Mrs. Masham has made her suffer'. He sent a draft of this letter to Sarah beforehand for her approval, so that at this point, if not before, she must have become aware of his controversial request about the captain-generalcy.¹⁰⁰

Meanwhile, in spite of her grievances against the Whigs, Sarah had rallied yet again to their calls for her help, this time in securing Orford's appointment to the Admiralty. As before, it was her services as an intermediary with Godolphin that they chiefly sought. Sunderland told Somers that he had put the issue 'so home to her, that I cannot but be capable of guessing a little what will be done, by the answer I shall receive'.¹⁰¹ Even so, Maynwaring had first to work very hard to overcome the bad feeling which had existed between the Duchess and the Junto since the previous winter. Somers heard that she had railed against him for assuming that he could 'direct and impose' on Marlborough and Godolphin 'from the first moment he came into business', and complained that when he had tried to speak to her at Windsor, she turned away both times, '& put him out of countenance'. Maynwaring persuaded him to overcome her pique by personally recommending 'the affair of the Admiralty' to her. Halifax and Sunderland joined in, the latter, with his usual outspoken distrust of Godolphin, saying that he had no good expectations from anyone but Sarah, 'who must do the thing at last if it was to be done'.[102] She responded exactly as they wished by urging the appointment on both the ministers.[103]

At the same time Maynwaring renewed his insistence that she should 'remember who is Groom of the Stole' and 'avoid the unwilling censure of friends' by returning to Windsor to perform the formal duties of attendance; 'people have really made me believe that every thing will in a great measure turn upon it, whether Whiggs or Tories shall be uppermost, that is whether the nation will be happy or undone'.[104] Sarah could not hold out against such arguments, and her combativeness was further roused by rumours that the Duchess of Somerset was now working to supplant her as groom of the stole. In mid-September she returned to Windsor, and announced that she was prepared to stay as long as the Queen did, 'to perform all the ceremoniall part'.[105]

Maynwaring and his colleagues had still to be convinced of what Marlborough had known for at least a year: that Sarah could not by this time be in any proximity to the Queen without doing damage which far outweighed any benefit they might derive from her mere presence at Court. It was Abigail Masham's departure for Kensington in September for the birth of her second child that first prompted Sarah to go far beyond 'the ceremoniall part' of her duties, and involve herself once more in a series of disastrous personal confrontations with the Queen. Her initial excuse was that Abigail had again encroached on her lodgings at Kensington. The Queen first angrily denied it and then added in exasperation, 'how cou'd she help using 'em'. At the end of September there was another heated argument over Anne's refusal to give Sarah 'a miserable hole' as an extension of her St James's lodgings.[106]

After a brief journey to London early in October to consult with Hawksmoor about the entrance to her new house (something which was to give her trouble for years to come), Sarah returned to Windsor, this time to tackle the Queen about the much larger issues of Orford's appointment and Abigail's political influence. Although she had long since abandoned all hope of salvaging the personal relationship, she convinced herself that 'the truths I tell her, tho it makes her hate me, makes it more easy for the ministers to govern her'.[107] She was once again completely out of control and in her most destructive mood. On one occasion, having pinned the Queen down in her closet for two hours and harangued her so loudly that the footmen in waiting at the backstairs could overhear her, she emerged triumphantly to tell Maynwaring 'that if the ministers did their parts half so well as she did yesterday we shou'd never more be troubled with Ab[igail] nor with the Tories'.[108] Acutely embarrassed by Sarah's renewed insinuations about her unnatural passion for her bedchamberwoman, Anne had had to turn away from the candle to hide her face. Finally, in a desperate attempt to get rid of her tormentor, she promised a written answer to all Sarah's arguments.

When there was no sign of this after a week, Sarah asked Maynwaring to help her compose a letter of her own, reminding the Queen of her promise. Maynwaring was beginning to be alarmed by the demon he had let loose, but at Sarah's insistence he did join with her in producing a long missive, full of invective against Abigail and reviewing the whole course of events since Harley's dismissal. The only reason the Queen had complied with the Whig appointments, Sarah now claimed, was that 'Abigail and her fools' could not produce a workable alternative scheme of government, and the point to which she returned over and over again was that the Queen had never given her any adequate reason for her loss of favour.[109] No answer came from the Queen for another ten days, but in the meantime, on 25 October, she did send Marlborough a reply to the complaints he had made on his wife's behalf. What had just passed now enabled her to avoid answering these specifically and to turn the blame on Sarah:

I believe nobody was ever so used by a friend as I have been by her ever since my coming to the Crown. I desire nothing but that she will leave off teasing and tormenting me, and behave herself with the decency she ought both to her friend and Queen, and this I hope you will make her do.[110]

The next day she wrote to Sarah in far more specific and devastating terms, telling her once-loved favourite for the first time exactly what she had done to forfeit her position. Sarah could now see herself as the Queen saw her, in all her intolerance, hectoring ill temper, and appalling rudeness. It is significant that she destroyed the original letter, but a paraphrase, partially obliterated but still legible, which she made of the salient passages still survives:

In that [letter] she complains of my inveteracy as she calls it to poor Masham, & says tis very plain I have nothing so much at my heart as the ruin of my cousen, & advises me for my soules sake to lay aside my malice. Next she mentions the misunderstanding that has been between us, for nothing that she knows of but that she could not see with my Eyes & hear with my eares & . . . she says I have been often several months without coming near her & when I have come again looked with all the disdain & ill humour imaginable, & said a great many shocking things, & she adds that it was impossible for me to recover her former kindnesse, but that she would allways behave herself to me as the D: of Marlborough's wife, & as her groom of the stole & she desires me once more not to torment her about Masham.[111]

The Queen would trust her letter to no one but Godolphin to deliver, and it was therefore to him that Sarah, beside herself at 'such language as I never had before', dashed off her first violent response. Considering the Queen's treatment of her, she told him,

I can't think any body but a very worthless wretch for interest would have gon to her oftener then I did, or have looked in any other manner. The word disdaine she makes use of to describ my looks, is an expression as if it came from a man, & mighty rediculous. . . . She takes great care in the leter to tell me tis now impossible that her kindnesse to me can return which is my own opinion, & I need not tell you how little I desire it should. All I have don which she calls tormenting is in order that wee may bee safe, & I own I have some pleasure in making her see she is in the wrong, tho I know she has not worth enough to own it, or religion enough to make any body amends for any wrong nothwith-standing the clutter she keeps about her prayers and my soul. Some people have devotion in their heart, & some in their heads, but she has it noe where. She says her prayers by rote & she beleives by rote . . . I am resolved I will write once more to her whatever resolution Ld Marlborough takes [about his retirement at the end of the campaign], tho I doe solemnly protest I would not have more to doe with her then other ladys for all the treasure upon earth, but I will vex her so much as to convince even her stupid understanding that she has used me ill, & then let her shutt herself up with Mrs Masham . . . [112]

By now, as this tirade clearly indicated, Sarah was wrought up into a state bordering on mania, and her resolution to 'write once more' to the Queen produced not a letter, but a voluminous headlong narrative covering her whole period as royal favourite. The first part consisted entirely of copies of the Queen's early letters to her (the originals, Sarah told Godolphin, 'I am resolved I will not part with whatever course she would take to have them'). Having appealed at length to Anne's religion and conscience, she then promised that if the Queen would read the whole narrative and send word that she was still unconvinced by Sarah's complaints of ill usage, Abigail Masham's name would never be mentioned between them again.[113]

As soon as the Court came from Windsor to St James's at the beginning of November, Sarah moved to Windsor Lodge, keeping at a distance until Marlborough's return. But at this point there was a further difficulty about the Admiralty commission. Orford's appointment had been settled, thanks, so Sunderland, Halifax, and Maynwaring all assured Sarah, to her intervention. Now Sunderland claimed, apparently with some reason, that Godolphin was obstructing the appointment of two of Orford's Whig colleagues and appealed to her again for help, 'for nobody but you can ever bring Lord Treasurer to reason'.[114] Already displeased with Godolphin's shocked and guarded response to her recent exchanges with the Queen, Sarah now wrote accusingly to him, accepting the truth of the Whig charges. To the hard-pressed Lord Treasurer this was the last straw:

whoever has told you that, is either very little informed, or had a mind to doe mee an ill office to you. At any rate though, it seems to mee to bee a very unnecessary pains. So many have been done already and with so much success, that the best office anybody can do mee now is to take mee out of the world.[115]

Yet in the last resort Sarah was the one person Godolphin could not hold out against, and with her help a compromise was at last worked out.[116] It was this affair and Marlborough's return on 8 November that finally brought her up to town. Writing to her a few days later for a large sum from the privy purse (which she then handed over to Abigail Masham to manage), the Queen added: 'I have not yet had leisure to read all your paypers but as soon as I have I will writt you som answer.'[117] For a time Sarah was deluded enough to believe that her narrative would have the effect she intended. She noticed that one day in St James's Chapel the Queen looked at her 'in a very particular & kind manner, which made me conclude for some time that she would have sent to me and desired that all past things might be forgotten'.[118] Maynwaring, incorrigibly mischievous, even went so far as to advise her how she should behave when this happened:

you should then, for the future, live with her like a friend and good acquaintance, always remembering to give yourself high and just airs upon the subject of politics. . . . And then for that noble treasure her heart, I would tell her that since she has given it to so worthy an object as fair-faced Abigail, I would never think of regaining it or of disturbing what is so very well placed. And if you would see her pretty often in this jocose manner (which you could perform rarely if you pleased) I am confident you might so order it, that it would be no great trouble to you, and it would give your friends infinite satisfaction.[119]

But the weeks went by and no answer or message from the Queen ever came. Gradually Sarah had to acknowledge that she had only succeeded in bringing about a complete breakdown in their relations.

11

'Maynwaring's Key'

1710

MARLBOROUGH'S confident expectation that the French losses at Malplaquet would force Louis XIV to give the Allies their own peace terms was quickly disappointed. Back in England the Duke let his Cabinet colleagues dissuade him from his intention to retire, and began almost at once to make plans for his next campaign. At the same time he cemented his shaky alliance with the Whigs by allowing himself to be admitted to the Kit-Cat Club, and by joining in their plans for an exemplary prosecution of the high church demagogue, Dr Henry Sacheverell, in retaliation for his sermonizing against Godolphin and the Whig ministers. At one of these consultations which took place at her lodgings, Sarah was present 'to fill out their tea and wash their cups', and so heard Somers unknowingly seal the ministry's fate by insisting that the prosecution must take place, or 'the Queen would be preached out of the throne and the nation ruined'.[1]

But for the time being, with four out of five of the Junto now in the Cabinet and majorities in both Houses of Parliament, the Whigs were riding high. Basking in the prevailing mood of euphoria and over-confidence, Maynwaring assured Sarah that Harley and the Tories were broken and discouraged, and in Parliament 'things were never likely to go so well and easily since I can remember'. Fulsomely he congratulated her on the alliance between the ministers and 'a strong, industrious, able, well intentioned party, that can never get between them and the Queen'.[2] Yet Sarah recognized the hollowness of all this. Spending the Christmas recess with Marlborough at Woodstock, she was suffering the usual aftermath of her violent moods, and filled with bitterness and foreboding.[3] With her position at Court now virtually untenable and Marlborough already talking of an early departure to the Continent, she was bent on going with him. Uneasily Maynwaring begged her yet again, for the sake of the Whigs, not to abandon the Court. He even clung to the hope that Marlborough might be able to effect a reconciliation with the Queen: 'I cannot but think that [he] has brought about a great many more difficult things than this in his life.'[4]

Yet only a few days after their return to town there was a crisis which revealed Marlborough's relations with the Queen to be in no better state than his wife's. On 10 January Sarah's Whig friend Lord Essex died, and on the secret advice of Harley the Queen at once instructed Marlborough to give his vacant regiment to Abigail Masham's brother, the 'good for nothing' boy whom Sarah had clothed, educated, and started on his military career. To the general this appeared as a deliberate attempt to undermine his authority in the army and the latest step in Abigail's systematic campaign to force his resignation. When the Queen refused to listen to his arguments, his impulse was to offer her an immediate choice between Abigail's services and his own. Although his Cabinet colleagues managed to dissuade him, they were otherwise divided as to the best means of dealing with his grievance.[5] On the following Sunday, with a council due in the evening, Marlborough took his wife off to Windsor Lodge, telling them that he would stay there 'till I see what part everybody will take'. But he departed urging that 'now is the time or never for getting rid of . . . Mrs M[asham]'.[6] In his absence the more hot-headed of the Whigs took the hint, and began to canvass support for a parliamentary address to remove Abigail from Court.

It has generally been assumed that in this ill-advised attempt to force the Queen to part with her favourite bedchamberwoman, Marlborough was chiefly influenced by the vengeful passions of his wife.[7] In fact all the evidence is to the contrary. By this time he had become even more obsessed than she was with Abigail Masham's influence. The loss of royal favour on which he depended to maintain his credit abroad had warped his judgement and profoundly demoralized him. Just before the crisis arose, he complained of 'a sinking and lowness of his spirits that he knows not what to think of'.[8] Reproaching the Queen afterwards for her treatment of him at this time, Sarah admitted that 'if it had been necessary to make Lord Marl disatisfyd with such usage I should certainly have endeavourd it, but there was no room for that, & hee came from your majesty to me with tears in his Eyes, which was a very unusuall thing in him'.[9] Embittered as she was against Abigail, Sarah still had great misgivings about the project for a parliamentary address. She knew from her own experience in the previous reign how tenacious the Queen could be in such matters. Well before the confrontation over the Essex regiment she had told both Maynwaring and Coningsby that 'she thought it unreasonable to ask the Whigs to press her [Abigail's] remove when she was soe insignificant', and that it would turn the Queen so completely against them all, 'and particularly the Freemans, that there would be no living with her after it, with any satisfaction'.[10]

For once it was Marlborough's judgement that was at fault, and not his wife's. His first mistake had been in attempting to combat Abigail's influence by repeatedly asking the Queen to make him captain-general for life, for it was this more than anything else which had convinced her of the need to curb his power in the army. He was doubly misguided in hoping to defeat the rival influence at Court at this late stage by demanding the removal of a bedchamberwoman; Abigail had already done her work in helping Harley to re-establish his contacts with the Queen, who now had the independent support of other malcontents and would-be ministers, most notably the Dukes of Shrewsbury and Somerset. Marlborough's third error was in threatening resignation over this issue without first making sure that his Cabinet colleagues were prepared to support him.

Godolphin and the more moderate Whig ministers were appalled at the possible consequences of the crisis, both at home and abroad. When the Queen, alarmed at the threat to Abigail and under pressure from them, showed signs of giving way over the nominal issue of the regiment, they urged Marlborough to come to town without pressing the 'monstrous competition' between himself and a bedchamberwoman any further. Sarah, realizing that the damage had been done, was vehemently opposed to his doing so:

. . . if she [Abigail] wanted new arguments to govern the queen, she cannot fail of showing her that as soon as the parliament is up, or an ill peace made, that she might remember how near she was being forced by this ministry, and that she cannot be safe till she has got rid of them all. . . . I am sure if he does [come to town], I shall wish he had never proceeded in this manner, but have gone to council in a cold formal way, never to the queen alone, and declared to all the world how he was used, and that he served till the war was ended, only because he did not think it reasonable to let a chamber-maid disappoint all he had done.[11]

But her main reason for opposing Marlborough's return was a personal one. If nothing else, the crisis offered the prospect of a relief from the separations and anxiety which she had now endured for eight years in succession. 'I was very glad when hee took a resolution to goe into the country,' she wrote afterwards, '& I wish'd from my soul that hee might never bee perswaded to head the Army again . . . I think I had reather have the king of France rule here, then have him in another battle.' When Marlborough did give way and returned to London on 23 January, she was almost as distraught as when he had agreed to command the army again after the death of their son.[12] Meanwhile the Queen's efforts to rally the support of the Tories in Parliament had convinced the Whigs that the project for an address against the new favourite was impracticable. The dispute about the disposal of the regiment was superficially patched up, but as Sarah had foreseen, the attempt to remove Abigail Masham marked the beginning of the end for the Whig ministry.

Marlborough was now determined to leave for The Hague as soon as possible, and for several weeks Sarah persisted in her intention of going with him. Unable to bear the thought of remaining any longer at Court 'with such ill usage & mortifications as I was to expect', she wanted him to persuade the Queen to let her resign her places to her daughters according to the earlier promise. Marlborough was in a dilemma. He did not want his wife to do anything that would expose the precariousness of his own position; yet it was clearer than ever that she could not be trusted in any proximity to the Queen. He persuaded her that she must retain her Court offices for yet another year, but promised to do all he could to make it easy for her.[13] At his request the Queen therefore agreed to keep up appearances by letting Sarah retain her posts for the time being without requiring her attendance at Court. In return Marlborough assured her that Sarah would not renew her letter-writing campaign, or press for the execution of the promise about her daughters. In fact the Queen had long ago assured Abigail Masham (who duly reported it to Harley) that she would never appoint Lady Sunderland groom of the stole.[14] It was common talk that whenever she was free to part with Sarah, the Duchess of Somerset would succeed to this post, and already Abigail herself was carrying out the day-to-day duties of keeper of the privy purse. But Marlborough, whose main aim was to keep Sarah quiet in his absence, let her assume that the promise would eventually be performed 'when he came back or in a proper time'. Sarah immediately demonstrated how incapable she was of any forbearance towards the Queen. On the eve of Marlborough's departure for Harwich on 19 February, she again raised the subject. Anne's irritable reply, 'I thought I shou'd have been troubled no more with it,' finally made it clear to her that there was no prospect of the promise's ever being fulfilled.[15]

After seeing Marlborough leave again for the Continent, Sarah had intended to go straight into the country; but the Whigs had more use than ever for her influence with Godolphin. While Marlborough was still at Harwich there came a panicky plea from Sunderland to send her back to town as soon as he had embarked,

to keep Lord Treasurer up to do what is right; for without her I know we shall all sink. . . . Besides the danger to the whole, none of our heads are safe, if we can't get the better of what I am convinced Mrs. Morley designs; and if lord treasurer can but be persuaded to act like a man, I am sure our union and strength is too great to be hurt.[16]

Having returned to London, Sarah herself was tempted to stay to witness Sacheverell's trial, which began at Westminster Hall on 27 February, although at first she was more preoccupied with the conduct of the Duchess of Somerset than with the proceedings themselves. On the first day she reminded the Queen that when she was present incognito at long public functions it was usual for the ladies in waiting to be allowed to sit. Yet when the Duchess of Somerset came into waiting the next day, she persisted in standing. Her intention, Sarah was convinced, 'was to make the Queen observe that I had done something that was impertinent & that nobody understood so well as herself, what was the right behaviour for a groom of the stole'. She insisted upon seeing the Queen privately to have the matter out. The snappish and dismissive answer she received would normally have made her flare up in anger, but she controlled herself: 'we were alone, & I was resolved to keep my temper til my Lord Marlborough came home.'[17]

At the trial itself, Sarah was at first too much edified by the elaborate parade of Revolution principles which the prosecuting Whigs produced to realize the harm they were doing themselves. The light punishment meted out to Sacheverell, and above all the spontaneous outbursts of high church feeling from the mob, soon brought home the truth. As Lord Cowper's sister-in-law commented bitterly, 'a Church ministry we now want and shall have, as soon as Johny [Marlborough] can decently be thrown aside'.[18] The atmosphere of imminent political crisis which hung over the Court in the days after the trial made Sarah in no hurry to go into the country, and while she lingered in London her resolution to keep her temper with the Queen gave way in one last disastrous episode. At the beginning of April she asked for another private interview, this time to clear herself of reports that she had spoken disrespectfully of the Queen to her friends. Determined to avoid another personal confrontation, Anne told her to put what she had to say in writing, and promised that this time it would be answered without delay.[19] Sarah replied that the subject was too delicate to be committed to paper. When the Queen tried to take refuge at Kensington, she followed, making it clear that she intended to stay until she was given a hearing.

Very reluctantly Anne admitted her, but only to repeat that she must put what she had to say in writing. When Sarah ignored her and began to pour out her torrent of self-justification, the Queen tried to leave the room. Sarah followed her to the door to prevent her. She was now beside herself and weeping hysterically, and the Queen had no choice but to hear her out. For once the tirade did not concern Abigail Masham. Almost Sarah's first words were to assure Anne that 'that person is not, that I know of, at all concerned in the account that I would give you'. It was the Duke and Duchess of Somerset whom she held chiefly responsible for spreading the current stories about her. 'She used to entertain her confidents with telling them what a praying, godly idiot the queen was,' one of her enemies reported, 'and was wise enough to think they would keep such a secret for her.'[20] Sarah's comments (in her letters to Godolphin and Maynwaring, for example) on the Queen's 'stupid understanding' and hypocrisy in religious matters are a clear enough indication that these stories had some basis in fact. Yet she now claimed that she was no more capable of speaking disrespectfully of the Queen than of killing her own children, and on the political issue, fortified by the Sacheverell trial, she was more impenitent than ever: 'what I had offended her in was, because I knew it was for her service and security; and it was what she had heard a good deal of in Westminster Hall, and I could never repent of anything of that nature.' She then demanded to know what other tales the Queen had been told, so that she could refute these as well. Anne seized on her initial assurance that what she had to say would require no answer. To all Sarah's pleas, she therefore repeated over and over again: 'you desired no answer and I shall give you none.' At last Sarah gave way, telling her that 'she would suffer in this world or the next for so much inhumanity'; to which Anne made her famous reply, 'that would be to herself'.[21]

Lingering alone in the gallery to compose herself, Sarah had time to reflect on what had passed. Hitherto appearances had been kept up between them in public, but now she feared that if they should come face to face in company, Anne would 'affront her publicly' by refusing to speak to her. She went back to the Queen, who assured her that 'she never did that in her life to any';[22] in the event she made sure that they were never to see each other again in public or in private. The following day Sarah left town for Windsor Lodge, where she was to remain for the next two months, brooding over what she had done and clinging to the hope that peace would resolve her difficulties.

On 13 April the Queen appointed the Duke of Shrewsbury Lord Chamberlain. Although he was a moderate Whig, he had allied himself with Harley against the ministers and the Junto, and since the appointment had been made without consultation, it was clear evidence of the Queen's ultimate intention to rid herself, under Harley's guidance, of the ministry which had now entirely lost her confidence. Disturbed as the Whigs were, they could not resign, as Maynwaring explained to Sarah, 'because a new Parliament wou'd be the Consequence of that, which wou'd be dangerous to choose whilst the Nation is in such a Ferment'.[23] Isolated for the time being within a Cabinet of his political enemies, Shrewsbury hinted that nothing prevented his allying himself with them but the breach between Sarah and the Queen, and added that Anne herself would have no thought of going over to the Tories if it were not for her fear of a renewed parliamentary attack on Abigail Masham. Grasping at these straws, Sarah's Whig friends clamoured once more for her to come to town, or at least write to the Queen, to give her satisfaction on this point.[24]

At the same time the more violent advocates of ministerial change were pressing the Queen to dismiss Sarah altogether as a means of inducing Godolphin to quit his post. Alarmed and not yet prepared to part with her prime minister, the Queen briefly gave encouragement to a plan to persuade Sarah 'to make her submissions'.[25] The task of mediation was delegated to one of the royal doctors, Sir David Hamilton. Godolphin made no overt objection, but refused to become personally involved. He believed that Sarah was safe enough until Marlborough returned, provided she kept quiet, and after the Kensington episode his overriding aim was to keep the two women completely apart. He knew that their relationship had passed far beyond the reach of such mediation, and that Sarah was quite incapable of making the necessary submissions. He told the Whigs who urged it on him that they did not know her.

Maynwaring, who had never forgiven Godolphin for his obstruction of the address against Abigail Masham in the winter, saw to it that this comment came to Sarah's ears.[26] In her present mood his insinuations fell on fertile ground, and greatly to Godolphin's distress, she now reproached him with making 'ill returns' for her 'long continued kindness and friendship'.[27] Just how little he deserved this accusation of disloyalty he was shortly to prove. By the middle of May the Queen herself had abandoned the reconciliation scheme, and instead was trying to save the Lord Treasurer by making one last effort to detach him altogether from Sarah. But when Hamilton put this to him, Godolphin refused without hesitation. He could not break with Sarah without also breaking with Marlborough, to whose support his whole administration was dedicated. And whatever the outcome of the present crisis, he also knew that his public career was drawing to an end, and the whole of his private life was bound up with theirs. He told Hamilton that he would do anything else for the Queen, but 'it was impossible their Relation being so near, and their Circumstances so united, for him to break off from the Duchess'.[28]

He knew that he had probably sealed his fate. On the same day he wrote to Marlborough, in a remarkable acknowledgement of their political dependence on Sarah's relationship with the Queen:

'tis hardly imaginable how farr 13 [Somerset]'s malice and inveteracy has wrought up 42 [the Queen]'s displeasure to 240 [Lady Marlborough], and to all those who will not forsake her. And if it were not for the prejudice which this brings upon Mr. Freeman and 38 [Godolphin], they could easily overcome all other difficultyes.[29]

Although Godolphin kept up the pretence that Somerset's mischief-making had turned the Queen against Sarah, he must have known perfectly well that her own intemperate behaviour was chiefly to blame. Yet even as he faced the full extent of the damage she had done by squandering the Queen's friendship, he remained endlessly patient and forbearing, refusing to be provoked by her suspicions and reproaches, and writing long letters to try to make her comprehend the methods he was using to eke out the life of his ministry.[30] Sarah probably never knew of his reply to Hamilton's proposal, but she retained sufficient balance not to let Maynwaring's malice and the stresses of the moment destroy the friendship of a lifetime. At the end of the month she wrote to Marlborough that whatever suspicions the Whigs had of Godolphin, she had no doubt that he was in their true interest. Marlborough agreed: 'it is impossible for him to be other then our friend.'[31]

It was what the crisis revealed about the fundamental weakness and self-delusion of the Whigs that most disgusted Sarah. Indeed, her political insight at this time was far sharper and more prescient than theirs. When Maynwaring argued that the ministerial changes had come about only because Abigail Masham and the Duchess of Somerset had encouraged Harley's schemes in the hope of succeeding to her posts, she brushed aside these simplistic explanations impatiently. She also saw with absolute clarity that in the present political ferment there was no hope of saving the ministry by an alliance with Shrewsbury: 'I take it for granted either hee & the jacobitts will get the better or the other interest will run him down, there is now no middle way.' As for the Whigs themselves:

what a melancholy reflection it is . . . that now their fate depends upon gaining a man, that t'other day they would have flown over the top of the house if any body had proposed his coming into employment. Either their bottom is not strong, or else we apprehend shadows; if the first, I think they have been very much to blame to 38 and 39 [Godolphin and Marlborough], if the last, they must yield to 28 [Shrewsbury] just come into the service.

She pointed out that if Shrewsbury's desire for an accommodation was genuine, there was no need for any disclaimer to the Queen from her about the attack on Abigail: 'let him joyn heartily with 89 [the Whigs] & give her what asurances they please; I suppose she will not imagin that like Duke Trinkolow I can make a rebellion by my self.'[32]

After her last experience at Kensington Sarah steadfastly refused to have any further contact with the Queen, either in person or in writing.

Although she was still incapable of accepting any responsibility for the damage she had done, she now acknowledged that she had been deluded in seeing herself as 'one more capable of business than any Man'. To Lady Cowper, who joined in urging her to return to Court, she wrote:

I am sure you wish the same thing that I shall ever doe, which is that those men may have the chief influence att court that will make a right use of it . . . in things of that nature tis a simple [i.e. silly] thing for a woman to imagin she can doe any good, & yet I am sure there was a time, that I did servise to those that are in the honest interest & I hope you will beleive that I would go as far as my feet would carry me to bee of the least use towards procuring our safty, & to make the government strong for which my Lord Marlborough has so often ventured his life but . . . sence that ill woman has gaind upon the Queen, how is it possible that I can doe any good, or strugle now the Duke and Dutchess of Somerset make it their whole businesse (& are with the Queen half the day) to doe me ill offices, only in order for her to bee groom of the stool.[33]

When Maynwaring, Robert Walpole, and James Craggs continued to pester her on this subject she became so angry that Marlborough, who depended on them for much of his political information, had to beg her 'not [to] take anything of this so ill as to have disputes and coldness with them'.[34] Even so, both he and Godolphin urged her to keep her resolution of having no further dealings with the Queen. 'They know what they wish, and what would doe them good, if they could have it,' Godolphin told her, 'but they don't know how little a matter will serve your enemy's to hurt you.'[35]

What finally made Sarah abandon her resolution not to write to the Queen was the threatened dismissal of Sunderland; for Maynwaring and his friends still maintained that the only means of staving off this blow was for her to give the assurance that no further attempt would be made against Abigail. Sooner than be accused of not doing everything in her power to save her son-in-law, she gave in. Maynwaring, cock-a-hoop at this victory, then set about persuading Godolphin to prepare the Queen for the receipt of her letter. Much against his better judgement the Lord Treasurer agreed, but when he broached the subject of the address Anne cut him short, telling him that she looked on it 'as entirely out of all Question now'. Godolphin reported back to Maynwaring that this was no better than he had expected, and added pointedly that if those who were now most anxious to disclaim the address against Abigail had been prepared to do so earlier the whole crisis might have been averted.[36]

In the meantime Sarah had come to town, armed with a long letter for the Queen. Despite Godolphin's unpromising reception, this was sent on 7 June, and everything about it was calculated to confirm the Queen's hostility. Having denied any personal involvement in past or future attacks on Abigail, Sarah went on to berate her mistress for 'going into a scheme with a collection of the worst people in the world', and to hint that if she continued with her design to discard the Whigs, Abigail would be liable to attack in the next session of Parliament. She could not resist repeating her complaints about her own treatment ('you might have don what you would in other matters without using me ill, which is what I have most reason to complain of'), and she reminded the Queen again of the hundreds of her letters full of protestations of eternal friendship which she still had in her possession.[37]

After a lull of several days, while Sunderland's fate continued to hang over him, the Queen's reply, drafted for her by Harley, arrived:

Having had asurances from your self & the Duke of Marlborough just before he went into Holland that you would never speake to me of Politicks, nor mention Mashams name again, I was very much surprised att receiving a long letter upon both, but I shall trouble you with a very short answer, looking upon it as a continuation of the ill usage I have so often met with which shews me what I am to expect for the future.

In a postscript she requested the return of all her letters, 'it being impossible they can now be agreeable to you'.[38] In reply Sarah refused outright to surrender the letters, but she did go so far as to beg the Queen 'upon her knees' to defer Sunderland's dismissal until after a peace had been made.[39] In fact the blow fell on the very day this letter was sent.

It was now quite clear that the dismissals of Godolphin and Sarah herself must follow: the only questions were when and in what manner. After the Queen had taken personal offence at a chance remark of her tired and embittered Lord Treasurer at a Cabinet council early in July, Harley urged her to seize the excuse to 'get quit' of him. A letter of dismissal was drafted at this point, although its dispatch was delayed for over a month while Harley continued to work on the Queen.[40] At last, on 8 August, it was delivered to Godolphin's house by a groom from the royal stables, and the treasury was put into commission with Harley as chancellor of the exchequer. The Queen had a bad conscience about this shabby method of parting with her Lord Treasurer; but Sarah had become so obsessed with the justification of her own conduct that she was able to extract some comfort from the charge that Godolphin had treated the Queen disrespectfully, 'because tis just the same that was said of her by 42 [the Queen] and their flatterers & and she now hopes it was without cause'.[41]

The Queen needed no urging from Harley to part with Sarah. Only two factors stayed her hand. The major one was the need to retain Marlborough's services at least until the end of the campaign; for he made it clear that if his wife were to be dismissed while he was at the head of the army he would immediately resign. Godolphin, acknowledging that Sarah's removal was now inevitable, assured the Queen through Hamilton that if she would let her keep her offices until the end of the campaign, 'then she might act in it as she pleased'.[42] After this it was a matter of inducing Sarah to stay quiet in the country for the rest of the year, to avoid giving the Queen any excuse to remove her prematurely.

Yet Sarah remained in town for the greater part of the summer. At first she had the excuse of awaiting Lady Sunderland's lying-in. But by the end of July the baby (a girl called Diana who was to become Sarah's favourite grandchild) had safely arrived, and still she showed no signs of going. Her passive and fatalistic mood of the spring had quite vanished. The criticisms of her conduct now beginning to find their way into the government press made it obvious that when the time came she would be not merely dismissed, but publicly disgraced,[43] and she became convinced that if she could not prevent the blow altogether, she could defer and soften it by means of the Queen's letters which she still had in her possession. At about the time of Sunderland's dismissal she had begun to compile what she called her 'History of Mrs Morley': a full account of her relations with the Queen, to be illustrated by letters of the previous reign in which Anne had made the most vehement protestations never to part with her, and making much of the unfulfilled promise to let her daughters succeed her.[44] Early in July Sir David Hamilton told the Queen of Sarah's threat to publish a justification of her conduct, 'and in it would be contayn'd what would reflect upon her Majestys Piety, such as breaches of Promise and Asseverations'. The only way to guard against this, Hamilton warned, was 'by not provoking her in the Method of dismissing her'. Far from deterring the Queen, these threats only made her more determined to be rid of Sarah.[45] Yet she was seriously worried by them, and for the time being, despite hints in the press of her imminent dismissal, Sarah kept her posts.

It was the end of August before she finally went into the country, thus putting herself out of Maynwaring's sphere of influence. He complained that as long as she remained there he was able to see little of her, while Godolphin, 'who has nothing else to do now, will never be an inch from her whilst he lives'.[46] Throughout August and September, with the remaining Whig ministers preparing to resign, her mood was still aggressively confident. Whether they had a new Parliament or the old one, she was convinced that 'wee shall get the better of all the busy knaves & fools'.[47] The readiness of the new ministers to leave her in her places and continue the payments for Blenheim only confirmed her suspicion that they felt themselves insecure. Never very confident of

Marlborough's Whiggism, her main fear now was that he would be too ready to accommodate himself with them and so hinder her hopes of revenge:

it is plain to me they are yet afraid of my Lord Marlborough, & would manage him if they can till they get more strength, and they would prevent my Lord Godolphin & Lord Marlborough from being in the Interest of the Whigs, which is a new argument of their being so if that had been wanted. Therefore I hope they will all join to treat them like Conspirators & wretches that have endeavour'd to destroy all the fruits of their labours for so many Years.[48]

About to depart in September for the Whig electioneering conclave at Althorp, with the dissolution of Parliament now certain, she was still optimistic: 'those that are least sanguin think there will be more whiggs than there has been torys a great while & the torys divided, which with the weight of 50 [the Elector of Hanover] who is quite right will certainly ruin this new scheem.'[49] The results of the general election in October, with its huge Tory majority, were a rude awakening from these dreams.

Forbidden by Marlborough to set foot in St Albans while the poll was being taken, Sarah's main contribution to the Whig election campaign was to endanger the success of his candidates at Woodstock. Alarmed at the mounting debt on Blenheim, and fearing that the promise of payment was being used to 'ensnare' her husband into co-operating with the new ministers, she wrote just beforehand to put a complete stop to the works. She then proceeded to harry the clerk of the works unmercifully to produce a detailed account of all the money owing. Vanbrugh, already engaged in negotiations with the new treasury commissioners, was infuriated anew at her interference and appealed to Marlborough. Meanwhile the officials on the spot worked frantically to prevent the army of unpaid workmen from jeopardizing both the building and the success of the election. To Godolphin Marlborough sent off a plea, if he were anywhere within a day's journey, to go and restrain Sarah from doing any further damage. Sulkily she complied, but her suspicions that her husband had been 'ensnared' by this means smouldered on.[50]

The surge of high church feeling that brought the Tories back to power at first knocked all the fight out of her: 'in my life I never heard of such madness as at London & every where about the Church, which I daresay not one of the old Ministry had the least thought of hurting.' She had to acknowledge that 'the spirit of the Nation appears to be Torism', with all this implied to her of universal crypto-Jacobitism: 'I really think the nation was never so near being ruined, I can't see how 'tis possible for us to escape.'[51] Beginning to see exile as a real prospect, she confessed to Maynwaring that her philosophy would be lost if she were forced to live out of England.[52] She stayed in the country, first at St Albans and then at Windsor Lodge, awaiting Marlborough's return and the outcome of his negotiations with the new ministry, which would also determine her own fate.

Once the Queen had agreed to let Sarah keep her Court offices until Marlborough returned, Hamilton advised her to let nothing more be heard of the 'History of Mrs Morley'. It was Swift's *Examiner* of 23 November which made Sarah break silence and renew her threats of publication; for this journal, set up by Henry St John (now reinstated as Harley's secretary of state), was acknowledged to be the chief ministerial organ of the press. In his famous squib Swift forestalled accusations of ingratitude against the new ministry for their treatment of Marlborough and his family by itemizing and valuing the enormous rewards the Duke had received; and at the end he slipped in a paragraph about a certain 'lady's woman' who had appropriated £22 of her mistress's allowance of £26 for her own use. The allusion to Sarah as keeper of the privy purse was unmistakable; £26,000 was the Queen's annual allowance for her personal expenditure and £22,000 was almost exactly the amount Sarah had borrowed to finance Marlborough House.

This did not prevent Sarah from exploding with indignation to Hamilton, in a letter which was clearly intended to be read to the Queen:

... to bee printed & cryd about the country for a common cheat, & pickpockit is too much for human nature to bear, when it is so much in my power to publish other papers of a very different kind, I doe not mean those that are full of professions of endless kindnesse & friendship, & of dreadfull Imprecations if ever it was otherwise, but those in which Mrs Morley had acknowledged my care & frugality in her servise, those in which she has pressed me to accept of Advantages which I have refused . . . [53]

Although Sarah had specifically excluded the letters of friendship, the Queen at once took alarm about them, and ordered Hamilton to send an urgent message to her, begging her not to carry out her threat. Still with a view to deferring her dismissal, Sarah told Hamilton that she would not attempt publication while she was in the Queen's service, but that sooner or later she must defend herself against the *Examiner*'s accusations.[54]

The other matter which made the Queen uneasy was Sarah's possible influence over her husband in the matter of his command. Marlborough was now isolated in a ministry of his opponents, who were already taking summary measures to curtail his power. Yet both sides were under great pressure from the Allies to bury their political differences for the time being, so that he could remain at the head of the army for one more campaign. If he were prevented from doing so, Godolphin warned the Queen, the Alliance would simply fall to pieces before peace could be made.[55] The days when Sarah had confidently predicted that her husband would be 'too big' for the new ministers were over; 'some times I think by the discourse of him that they think it of too much consiquence to put him out after such success's,' she noted at the end of October, 'but they print millions of lyes in case it happens to quiet those that would not like it, but I believe what they wish most is that hee would act with them till he has lost every friend that hee has, & then they may bee at liberty to hang him.' In an attempt to guard against this, she assured her friends that Marlborough would be ready to 'stand & fall by the Whig interest'.[56] What the ministers and the Queen now feared was that she would persuade him to resign altogether and go into opposition with his former colleagues. Having complained to Hamilton of the *Examiner*'s attacks on the Duke at a time when even his enemies acknowledged the need for him to continue as general, Sarah added, 'but how impracticable that is I need not say after such barbarous and inhuman returns of all kinds as hee has met with'. His remaining in the service, she repeated, was 'the thing in the world I desire he shou'd not do'. In great agitation, the Queen begged Hamilton to persuade Sarah not to 'inflame' her husband.[57]

Sarah herself lingered on at Windsor Lodge, waiting for the return of the Duke, who was delayed at The Hague by business and contrary winds. But from Mrs Boscawen she now learned that Godolphin, harassed by the attacks of the Tory House of Commons on his administration, was badly in want of her comfort and support.[58] With the Queen about to come out of mourning after her two years of widowhood, Hamilton also advised her to return to Court to order the necessary new clothes. On 12 December she did so, only to find that the Queen would not see her even in the routine business of her office.[59] Ostentatiously Sarah had apartments prepared at Montagu House, as a sign that she and her husband both shortly expected to leave their St James's lodgings.[60]

Yet in matters of this kind Sarah's influence over her husband was always less than was generally supposed. Marlborough knew that the Allies and most of his former colleagues still wanted him to retain his command. At The Hague it had been put to him by one of the new ministers' go-betweens that 'he would be no sooner at home than he would be led into the rage and revenge of some about him'. 'You mean my wife and those I must live with,' Marlborough had replied calmly, and declared his intention 'of sticking to her Majesty's service as long as even his greatest enemies should think it possible or practicable for him'. At his audience with the Queen on 29 December he gave the same assurances.[61] Tired out and 'terribly mortified' as he was, he remained tenacious of power. What the few hours with Sarah in the coach on the road to London had chiefly convinced him of was the need to have her 'made Easy', which, as he confided to Hamilton, 'he hopd by her having more Patience, and the Queen more Goodness might be done'.[62] Having acquiesced in the dismissals of his political colleagues and his most loyal officers, he still hoped to avert the final ordeal of his wife's removal.

It was a vain hope from the first. When Maynwaring broached the subject with Harley, the minister would only remark cryptically that this was 'the rock which all woud break upon, if care were not taken to avoid it'. But at his first meeting with Marlborough on 10 January Harley made it clear that Sarah's removal must be the basis of any agreement between them.[63] The Duke and his wife at once declared that the ministers, not daring to dismiss him outright, were trying to force his resignation by this means.[64] In fact the ministers were able to disclaim all responsibility for the refusal to give way about Sarah. Marlborough was told that 'if every one of them should go down on their knees to the Queen to ask it of her, she has conceiv'd such a prejudice against her that they would not be able to prevail'.[65] The most the Queen would agree to was to part with Sarah quietly, preserving the appearance of a voluntary resignation. Those who were most anxious for Marlborough to keep his command wanted Sarah to take immediate advantage of this concession, but she refused, saying that it would only confirm all the accusations against her in the ministerial press.[66]

Nevertheless, as the pressures built up in the second week of January she had to change her attitude to both Marlborough's position and her own. By now she realized that most of the former Whig ministers, her City friends, and the foreign envoys were as anxious as the Queen for Marlborough to stay in office. She was even more impressed by the threat of what was in store for him from the ministers if he did not:

many people thought that if the Duke of Marlborough quited the servise they would immediately proclaim him an enemy to the queen & kingdom after having had great advantages from the government, & give their reasons in print all over the countrys that it was because hee could not bee protecter, & his wife bee permitted to use the queen disrespectfully.[67]

But the most urgent consideration was a personal one. The conflicting pressures on this most sensitive of issues had reduced Marlborough to a pitiable state of mind and body. 'I never saw any body in my life under so much trouble as the Duke of Marl: was,' Sarah wrote afterwards. She became convinced that he 'cannot live six months, if there is not some end put to his sufferings on my account'.[68] In an interview with the Hanoverian envoy on 14 January she at last agreed to do whatever was necessary about her own offices to enable Marlborough to keep his.[69]

For the moment, however, this was still not resignation. Shrewsbury and Hamilton, both in the Queen's confidence and both with some sympathy for Marlborough's plight, encouraged him to believe that the Queen might yet respond to a personal appeal from him.[70] Wanting to satisfy Sarah, and afraid of the effects of her removal on his credit abroad, Marlborough decided to make this last effort to save her. At his request she wrote a simple letter of apology to the Queen, for once avoiding all recriminations and self-vindication, and promising to do nothing further to offend for the future. On 17 January Marlborough carried it in person to the Queen.[71]

The advice he had been given proved to be quite misguided. The Queen refused even to consider keeping Sarah in her places. When all his arguments had failed, Marlborough at last agreed to try to persuade her to resign, telling the Queen that 'if in a fortnight he could not accomplish it, she might do what she thought best'.[72] Irritated at these delaying tactics, Anne insisted upon having Sarah's gold key of office delivered to her within three days. The next day, when Marlborough tried to protest that the regiments of his dismissed officers were being disposed of without consulting him, the Queen replied that she could discuss no further business with him until he had brought the key. When he returned and told Sarah, she made him take it at once;[73] 'one who was very intimate in the family' added that what she had actually done was throw it 'into the middle of the room, and bid him take it up, and carry it to whom he pleased'.[74] On the evening of 18 January Marlborough delivered the key into the Queen's hands, thereby bringing the long relationship, which had brought him so much benefit and done him so much harm, finally to an end.

Paper Wars
1711–1712

HAVING given up her posts, Sarah's next task was to submit her final privy purse and robes accounts. In making up the former she was persuaded 'by her friends' to lay claim to the complete back payment, now amounting to £18,000, of the £2,000 a year which the Queen had offered her in 1702. Bent on exacting compensation for her dismissal, she persisted in ignoring the fact that the disappointment concerning the pension of £5,000 which had prompted the offer had long since been remedied. If the loans for the building of Marlborough House had not yet been repaid, she may also have hoped to set the £18,000 off against these. An unnamed friend (perhaps Hamilton) was sent to ask the Queen if she would still consent to the grant. When he did so, as Sarah recorded,

she looked uneasy & was so poor sperited or simple as to try to put it off with saying, why she had two thousand pounds salary out of the privey purse. That's true madam, replyed the person, but if your majesty considers this leter it is an addition which you were pleased to desire her to take as a reward for her faithfull servise. At which she looked out of countenance, & as if she had much rather not have allowed it, but upon reading her leter consented to it, & I write the coppy of her own leter in the accounts she sign'd & charged under it the summ of £18,000.

What she in fact wrote was not a copy, but a careful paraphrase of the letter, omitting the sentences which made the real origin of the Queen's offer clear.[1] Since Sarah had also drawn on the privy purse to pay outstanding debts to tradesmen from the robes, Harley was able to annoy her in return by refusing to discharge her robes accounts from the exchequer until she had first repaid the Queen out of her own pocket.[2] 'I apprehend that you will think I was in the Wrong to put her in Mind of the £18,000,' Sarah wrote to an acquaintance years later, 'as I did myself, I confess it.'[3]

It was probably the thought of what Sarah might do with the other letters in her possession that made the Queen give in to this quite unjustifiable demand.[4] Even so, her fears of publication were not realized. Since one condition of Marlborough's retaining his command was that he should put a stop to 'the rage and fury of his wife' in this as in other respects, any attempt on Sarah's part to carry out her threat of publication would immediately have made his position untenable.[5] In any case this project had already achieved its immediate aim as far as she was concerned. Considering what had gone before, her dismissal was a remarkably quiet affair. Swift, clearly acting on ministerial orders, avoided all mention of it in the *Examiner*, allowing the Whigs to keep up the pretence that Marlborough had made a voluntary resignation of his wife's offices. Hamilton was in no doubt that the threat of publishing the Queen's letters was chiefly responsible for this forbearance.[6]

But it was one thing to restrain Sarah from publication, and quite another to put a stop altogether to her 'rage and fury' against the Queen. Lord Cowper, visiting the Marlboroughs just after Sarah's dismissal, found the exhausted Duke in bed with a great deal of company in the room and his wife sitting at the bedside, 'railing in a most extravagant manner against the queen'. Marlborough told his shocked visitor 'that he must not mind what she said, for she was used to talk at that rate when she was in a passion, which was a thing she was very apt to fall into, and there was no way to help it'.[7] As far as Sarah was concerned, her plans for the 'History of Mrs Morley' had merely been postponed. In February she told Lady Cowper that the whole story of her relations with the Queen would be put 'in a true light, if not before after my Death', and added:

I have a hundred Letters under her own hand in which she says she is satisfied that all I said to her, was from the real concern I had for her Good, which I think will look very well in this extraordinary History, where it will appear she did all manner of Injustice to me, & put me away, without any manner of reason.[8]

As a collaborator she turned to Bishop Burnet, who was interested in the tale of her relations with the Queen for its bearing on his own history of the reign. All through the spring and summer of 1711 she corresponded with him, answering his questions and sending him copies of the various narratives which she had put together during the previous year. Although she was not at all satisfied with his finished text, this was to be only the first of several such attempts.[9]

After the humiliations of the winter, Marlborough was anxious to get out of England at the earliest opportunity, but before he left he established working relations with the new ministers for the conduct of the campaign. Although their mutual distrust remained, they undertook that his troops should be paid regularly and even that funds would be forthcoming for Blenheim. They also made it clear that they had two powerful weapons to use against him if he refused his co-operation. One was the ministerial press; Marlborough had already shown himself to be particularly sensitive to Swift's attacks in the *Examiner*. The other, much more serious, was the threat of parliamentary enquiries into his financial administration. Since at least 1708 Harley (who was shortly to be made Lord Treasurer and raised to the peerage as Earl of Oxford) had had in mind a deduction of 2½ per cent from the pay of England's quota of foreign troops as a matter on which Marlborough might be called to account by Parliament. The moment the Duke did anything to forfeit the protection of the Court, St John now warned, 'such scenes will open, as no victories can varnish over'.[10]

As in so many other political matters, Sarah was profoundly at odds with her husband about his alliance with the new ministers, and this conflict was to have its effect on the closing stages of his career. For all her apparent submission to the pressures for his retaining his command, she was not really reconciled to his doing so, nor to the idea that her own treatment did not justify his resignation; 'I confess I thought using his wife so ill was as great an affront as any,' she remarked after his departure, 'but could not be sure I was not too partial in that matter.'[11] Acutely conscious of the vulnerability of his position, Marlborough begged her not to do or say anything in his absence that would provoke the Queen or the ministers, 'since whilest I am in the Service I am in their power, especially by the villanous way of printing, which stabes me to the heart'. At the same time he assured her 'that I know them so perfectly well, that I shall always be upon my gard'.[12]

Yet Sarah, who never conciliated an enemy in her life, did not consider the *Examiner*'s attacks to be sufficient reason to truckle to his masters: 'I had rather they should write so as long as the world endures, than only to say that common thing my self that I am an humble servant to any of these ministers who deserve to be hanged.' Her only response to Marlborough's heartfelt plea for her discretion was to redouble her abuse of them in the hope that what she said and wrote would be brought to their notice.[13] As far as she was concerned, the best means of dealing with the *Examiner* was to encourage the two Whig journals, the *Medley* and the *Observator*, to reply in kind. Having visited Godolphin's old lodgings in Windsor Castle at the end of April, she told Lady Cowper that the shabby furnishings made her reflect on his lack of concern for the rewards of public life, and 'I would have writ an Observator, or a Medley upon it if I had been able'. A few days later, when an issue of the *Observator* did come out on this topic, she took particular care to bring it to the notice of her friends.[14]

The *Medley* had been set up by Maynwaring during the previous autumn for the express purpose of combating the *Examiner*, and despite his failing health, he continued his editorial supervision of the journal and of most other important Whig propaganda throughout the first half of 1711. In this there can be no doubt that he worked closely with Sarah and the opposition leaders. His favourite ploy at this time was to try to undermine Oxford's credit with the Tories by taunting them with his unfulfilled promises of calling the Whig ministers to account for financial irregularities. 'These men did not want to be put in mind to punish the late ministers if they coud,' he told Sarah, 'but since there is nothing against them, & it is impossible to punish them as it certainly is, I think it very right that the Publick shoud know all this.'[15] This dangerous over-optimism now communicated itself to her. When James Craggs hinted that Marlborough was in the ministers' power, not just by means of the press, but from the more serious activities of the Tory commissioners of public accounts, she would not take him seriously,

first because I think hee talkd as if hee had been very carefull to manage the Publick mony, & cautious not to sign any thing that might hurt him self, & next because I think if these wicked infamous sett of men could have ruind my lord Marlborough they would have don it long agoe, not only to have Justifyd themselves to the world, but to put it out of his power for ever to revenge the wounds they have given him, which I hope he will never forget . . . but I still pray, & hope hee will not bee used by them, but waite for the first opertunity to joyn with those that will bring these wreatchs to Justice.[16]

Continuing to suspect that Marlborough had been lured into co-operating with the ministers by assurances of payment for Blenheim, she issued dark warnings to one of her spies on the site that Oxford's promises of payment could not be relied on, and asked to be kept informed of 'all the mad things' Vanbrugh might attempt now that he had escaped from her control.[17]

As Marlborough had feared, his wife's removal from Court and the knowledge that he no longer had the confidence of the Queen or her new ministry had robbed him of much of his former prestige and authority abroad. During the first weeks of the campaign he remained inactive, complaining that 'the dayly Vexations I meet with, dose not only break my sperit but also my Constitution'.[18] Sarah's concern for him only increased her hostility to the ministers: 'I never am so Melancholly as when I think of him, & what a terrible thing it must be to him to see all the pains he has taken with the hazard of his Life so often, so disapointed & mangled by a company of wretched Knaves & Fools.'[19] By mid-year, as Marlborough had foreseen, her attitude was beginning to affect his relations with his new colleagues. When he and others on his behalf appealed for the support which would restore his authority, and referred to the continued goading of the *Examiner* as his 'greatest grievance', the ministers hinted that his inaction was deliberate, and retorted that he could not complain of the press when the *Medley* and *Observator* were 'patronised and promoted' by his nearest relations. Oxford (as Maynwaring reported back to Sarah) added that he himself was 'called rogue every day in print, and knew the man that did it'—a pointed reference to Maynwaring himself—'yet he should live fairly with him'.[20] An issue of the *Examiner* which came out a few days later gave a clear indication of the ministers' suspicions about Sarah's continuing influence over her husband. The description of her as 'Fulvia' was not unflattering ('though pass'd her Meridian, her Bloom was succeeded by so graceful an Air, that Youth could scarcely make her more desirable'); but she was represented as constantly plotting with her party against 'Agrippa' (Oxford), and advising her husband, the general 'Anthony', to undertake no action during the campaign, since military success would only help to support 'Agrippa' in power.[21]

Oxford now tried to drive a further wedge between Marlborough and his wife by blaming Sarah's provocative behaviour for putting at risk the continued payments for Blenheim. When she moved out of their St James's lodgings, she had deliberately left her furniture and servants behind, relishing the opportunity for a further confrontation with the Queen. In May Marlborough ordered her to vacate the lodgings completely. But when Sarah complained that Mrs Cowper, one of the Queen's bedchamberwomen and 'an humble attendant upon Mrs Masham', still occupied an apartment in the courtyard of Marlborough House which she needed to store their goods, the Queen sent a message that it was not convenient for her remove Mrs Cowper, and that Sarah could rent storage space elsewhere for ten shillings a week. Sarah retaliated by stripping her lodgings of all their fittings, discarding the keys, and declaring that the Queen might buy others for ten shillings. When Oxford presented Anne with a warrant for Blenheim in July she refused to sign, 'saying, that she would not build a house for one that had pulled down and gutted hers . . . and had lately sent a message by Mrs. Cowper that she had reason to be angry at'. Oxford assured Marlborough blandly that he would do his best to overcome the difficulty, but Sarah did not need Maynwaring to tell her that 'nothing is more malicious, or more villainously meant, than this turn about Blenheim, to make 39 [Marlborough] believe that 240 [Lady Marlborough] is the cause of that not being done, which, of all things, he desired to have done'.[22]

Cut off from reliable communication with Marlborough by letter, Sarah sent over Dr Samuel Garth as her personal emissary in July, to report on his health and give him her view of the ministers' designs.[23] In fact he was not as deluded by their offers of an accommodation as she assumed. He told a Dutch colleague at this time that he knew very well they were only waiting for an opportunity to destroy him,[24] but this simply made him more determined to dissociate himself from his wife's opposition activities. From now on he employed one of his secretaries, Henry Watkins, a Tory of whom Sarah was deeply suspicious, to draft his letters to the ministers and improve relations between them.[25] 'He utterly denies his giving any manner of encouragement to the Medley,' Watkins reported, 'and when I spoke last to him on that subject I almost put him into a passion, and he concluded my argument with saying: "I wish the devil had the Medley and the Examiner together."'[26] His reaction to the complaints of his inaction was to seek a closer alliance with Oxford for the conduct of the campaign; in return, he promised 'to be with him as he was with Lord G[odolphin]'.[27]

The ministers in their turn gave him good words. The cessation of the *Examiner*, about to be suspended in any case, was represented as a concession to his feelings and a sign of restored good relations.[28] Oxford then sealed the alliance by making a merit of overcoming the Queen's resistance to signing the warrant for Blenheim. Marlborough now bestirred himself to action, and in a brilliant and bloodless manœuvre passed the French lines and laid siege to the fortress of Bouchain. Sarah was profoundly disturbed by all of this. When the news of his success reached London, she told her Whig friends that she would be able to take no pleasure in it, 'if he pulls off his Hat to such a scandalous set of Men as is now at Court'.[29]

From St James's she had first moved into the apartments which had been prepared for her at Montagu House. Work on her own house, which had gone on so prosperously during the first year, was now at a complete standstill while she wrangled with Wren and his son about the rising costs. Persuading herself that 'the poor old man' had been cheated in his contracts and that she could make better ones with tradesmen of her own choosing, she decided to sack him altogether.[30] Inevitably political animus played a part in all this. To the Whigs, Wren junior was 'a sad little knave', while Sir Christopher was said to have more interest with Oxford than anyone except Mrs Masham.[31] It was no time for a good Whig to have architectural business in such hands. But within a few weeks Sarah had left Montagu House to take up makeshift quarters in the damp and inconvenient outbuildings of Marlborough House. The attempt to live under the same roof with the daughter who was now a Duchess as well and more wayward than ever had not been a success. 'So lately at Montagu House,' Sarah reproached Mary after they had separated, 'when I have not had a thought of any thing but to be kind & easy to you, you have answerd me so as I was ashamed it should bee heard.'[32] She remained in town until the end of June, supervising her new workmen and measuring for fittings and furniture, so that the new house would be ready to live in by the winter. But in the midst of these preparations she also found time to have Holywell refurbished, and there at the beginning of July she embarked on a three months' season of 'magnificent housekeeping' which was to make the old house a summer headquarters for at least one faction of the divided Whig opposition.[33]

Sarah's relations with the Junto, and with Somers and Halifax in particular, had now completely broken down. While she denounced them for their treacherous intrigues with Harley, they blamed her openly for ruining their cause by her mismanagement of the Queen's favour—a charge that was certainly not without foundation, although it scarcely became the Whigs, who had used her and egged her on for as long as it suited their purposes, to make it. Sarah, seeing herself as a martyr to their cause, was outraged at their ingratitude. Since even Sunderland now gave her a wide berth, the Holywell group was confined to Godolphin and his son, Maynwaring, the Craggses senior and junior, Robert Walpole, and the Cowpers nearby at Cole Green.[34] Maynwaring, already mustering recruits for his winter campaign to 'scribble down' the ministry, kept up their morale by composing verse and prose squibs against their opponents.[35] But what they were all waiting for was news of the new ministry's secret peace negotiations with France, of which rumours had been circulating since the spring. By the beginning of September it was known that Matthew Prior had returned from a two months' mission to Paris, and that the peace terms only waited the approval of Parliament. Sarah, like all the Whigs, dreaded 'a peace of Mr Prior's making, which I hope even this Parliament would prevent',[36] and when the news of Marlborough's success at Bouchain came a few days later, Maynwaring was quick to point out to her that this would be of great advantage to them in their opposition to the ministry's schemes.[37]

Within the week he had seen through the press an anonymous pamphlet called *Bouchain: in a Dialogue between the Medley and the Examiner*, which was the opening shot in this campaign. As well as celebrating Marlborough's success, it threatened the ministers with a parliamentary enquiry into their 'underhand Trinketting with France' without the consultation of the Allies, and argued that after the military achievements of the year, a peace on lesser terms than the Whigs had formerly insisted on could not be justified. Since the pamphlet claimed to have been written on the information of someone who knew Marlborough personally, it was effectively a challenge to the ministers on his behalf.[38]

St John at once took notice of this, and saw that a warning was delivered to him.[39] After weeks of forbearance, the ministerial journalists began to renew their baiting of the general, belittling the achievements of the campaign and claiming that his opposition to the peace could only come from a self-interested desire to prolong the war.

Yet when Sarah sent a copy of *Bouchain* to Marlborough, together with the first ministerial reply, his reaction showed that she and her circle had delivered this challenge without his knowledge and in disregard, if not in positive sabotage, of his attempts to conciliate the ministers. He told her that they 'should never apear in print', and at once sent messages to Oxford and St John, dissociating himself completely from 'the writings and discourses of such as pretend, either out of friendship to me, or by my encouragement, to promote the continuance of the war'.[40] To Sarah he wrote of the peace as inevitable and of retirement, if necessary out of England.[41]

At the beginning of October Sarah's guests left for London to prepare for the parliamentary opposition to the peace, but they continued to keep her well abreast of their activities. By 3 October, only a week after the secret peace preliminaries had been signed at Windsor and ten days before their details were released illicitly in the Whig press, she was fully informed of their contents, which confirmed that the new ministry had abandoned the Whig aim of 'No peace without Spain'. At first she was pessimistic about the opposition's chances of success. She knew that Maynwaring was directing a full-scale press campaign, in which, in spite of Marlborough's protests, the general's success was still put forward as the principal argument against agreeing to peace on the terms now proposed. Yet much as she enjoyed the Whig ballads and pamphlets, she had her fears that 'they won't do more than vex',[42] and in this she was to be proved right. For the time being the Whigs appeared to have the best of the debate, but St John was merely holding his fire. Secretly he had set Swift to work on a devastating reply.

Shortly after this Sarah came up to London herself, 'call'd to a very pleasant work, the furnishing of my new house'. On the night of 23 October she slept in the main building for the first time, and 'was so delighted that I thought there should have been some extraordinary Ceremony, as a Sack posset or throwing the Stocking'. What she now learnt of the objections of some Tories to the peace terms made her more optimistic: 'they & the honest people together may have such a strength when the P[arliament] meets as to make the King of France hearken to reason'.[43] Encouraging this alliance was to be the basis of the Whig opposition strategy, and Sarah at once set to work to make her contribution to it. In the three weeks before Marlborough's return on 17

November, she got Marlborough House ready to hold assemblies for both Whigs and Tories on a scale that would rival those of the chief ministerial hostess, the Duchess of Shrewsbury.[44]

But Marlborough's participation was an essential part of this strategy, as both sides knew, and Sarah was still very worried about his ambivalent attitude. When he went to pay his respects to the Queen at Hampton Court on his return, she told her friends that she hoped he would not stay at Court long, 'since I am sure there is nobody there that is not his Ennemy, whatever they may tell him'. When he came back to St James's, she mustered a Whig conclave to persuade him to join with them.[45] These consultations, together with the hope of an alliance with the Tory moderates and the Elector of Hanover's declaration against the peace, persuaded Marlborough that they had a prospect of successfully opposing the ministry. Within a few days of his return, Maynwaring was rejoicing that he 'never had so much spirit nor behaved himself so rightly'.[46] Sarah's aim of joining her husband publicly with the Whig opposition had at last been achieved. Yet it was only now that the damage she and her friends had done by trying to involve him prematurely became apparent. If Marlborough had been allowed to pursue his policy of secrecy and conciliation unhampered by his wife's public caballing against the government and by the activities of her journalistic friends, the ministers would have been less well prepared than they were to receive his opposition when it came. As it was, the commissioners of public accounts, whose investigations Sarah had discounted, had their charges ready: Marlborough was accused of taking bribes from the army bread contractors and of appropriating the $2\frac{1}{2}$ per cent deduction from the pay of the foreign troops for his own use.

Then on 27 November Swift published his long withheld reply to the Whig opponents of the peace. *The Conduct of the Allies*, written to St John's instructions, represented the whole war as a gigantic conspiracy between Marlborough and the Allies to secure profits for themselves at England's expense. As it circulated widely in London and the counties in the following weeks, the pamphlet simultaneously completed the destruction of Marlborough's credibility as an opponent of the peace and prepared the Commons to accept the commissioners' charges against him. At the very end of the year the Queen secured the government a majority for the peace terms at a stroke by creating a batch of a dozen Tory peers (among them Abigail Masham's husband). At the same time, using the pretext of the commissioners' findings, she dismissed Marlborough from all his posts. On 24 January 1712 the gratuity which he had received from the army bread contractors was voted illegal and unwarrantable and the deduction from the pay of foreign troops public money and to be accounted for; and the threat of further action was left hanging over him to discourage his further opposition.[47]

In the meantime Prince Eugene had landed in England as the Emperor's envoy, on a belated and unsuccessful mission to persuade the government to reconsider the peace terms. Ignoring hints that he would do well to keep out of Marlborough's company, 'he came immediately to Marlborough House,' as Sarah remembered, '& told the Duke of Marlborough all the Particulars, where he dined often'.[48] Such coalitions between the discontented foreign envoys and the Whigs made the Court uneasy, and rumours of plots abounded. When the Marlboroughs announced their intention of holding a ball for the Prince on the Queen's birthday, printed papers were hawked about the streets, representing it as 'a sort of vying with the Court', and hinting at darker matters; in Sarah's words,

that it was a Plot cover'd with the name of a Ball, & that the Queen was not safe at St James's & tis certain that there were orders given to increase the Guards, & to have them ready horsed. Whether these inventions are only to delude the poor people . . . or to bring a Mob upon us to pull down our House I can't be sure, but tis certain there never were upon Earth such a set of Brutal ignorant Knaves.

The ball was put off, but Sarah sent word that she would be at home to any visitors who cared to come; the guests would see her little granddaughter dance, 'which I believe may be done without any Danger to the State'.[49]

From now on, for months to come, Marlborough's life was to be made wretched by these 'dayly & almost hourly scandals of grub-street Pamphletts', which Sarah, resilient herself, would not let him ignore: 'it really gives me no trouble because tis so infamous a proceeding that I think it does my lord Mortimer [i.e. Oxford] more hurt than the Duke of Marlborough with all people that know what a principle is.'[50] But Swift's attack on her as the dishonest lady's woman still rankled. Since their connection with the Court was now entirely severed, she at last felt free to make a public reply, and with Maynwaring's help a justification of her conduct as mistress of the robes and keeper of the privy purse was put together.[51] Since female authorship was widely regarded as at worst disreputable and at best derisory, she remained uneasy about publishing it in the first person,[52] but in the end the problem was solved by abandoning the project altogether. One of the friends to whom she showed Maynwaring's manuscript was Robert Walpole, who had been confined to the Tower for the duration of the parliamentary session in order to deprive the Whigs of their most able debater in the Commons. Tactfully but firmly he advised Sarah not to draw the fire of the government's ruthlessly expert journalists by any such publication, and much against her own inclination she allowed herself to be dissuaded.[53] Ill health probably made her further disinclined to put up a fight at this time. She was suffering from erisypelas or 'St Anthony's fire', a subcutaneous infection of the skin which was to become recurrent in her old age. 'My Face is as bad today as ever, & I must think of nothing but my dark room,' she told Lady Cowper, '& it returns so often that it makes me melancholy.'[54]

The Marlboroughs had always intended that Godolphin should share their retirement, and having registered their protests in the House of Lords against the peace negotiations and the conduct of the campaign under the Duke of Ormonde, the two men retired with Sarah into the country in July. At Blenheim the works were at a standstill by the Queen's order ('let them keep their heap of stones', Godolphin said), but at St Albans Marlborough pitched his campaigning tent on the bowling green to entertain their friends, who were amused to see that the greatest general of the age could not always command his wife. One of them noticed him reprimand Sarah for sitting rather than kneeling at family prayers, 'but she obeyed not'.[55] Early in August they learnt that Matthew Prior and 'a popish priest' had gone to Paris with the embassy of Henry St John (now raised to the peerage as Viscount Bolingbroke): 'very good attendants to settle a Peace for England,' Sarah commented sarcastically.[56]

On a brief visit in August to his racing stud in Wiltshire, Godolphin filled his letters to Sarah with anything he thought would please or cheer her, from a visit to his sister-in-law, who 'has one of the prettiest little places that ever was seen', to 'a new riding equipage . . . which I believe you will find more easy and convenient than your hatt'.[57] She kept these affectionate jottings because they were to be the last. He had no sooner returned to St Albans early in September than he was taken ill with one of his recurrent attacks of stone in the kidneys. This time, though Sarah nursed him devotedly and raged at the impotence of the doctors, he did not recover. After a few days she wrote to the Cowpers that there was very little hope of his life, '& after saying that, you will not wonder that I can write no more'.[58] There was time for his colleagues to gather and say their farewells; in later years it was to be remembered that on his deathbed Godolphin had recommended Robert Walpole to Sarah's friendship. Then in the early hours of the morning of 15 September he died, leaving both the Marlboroughs desolate. The friendship which had withstood the stresses of more than thirty years of public life was broken at a time when they had never had more need of it. 'Hee was certainly the truest friend to me & all my family that ever was, & the best man that ever lived,' Sarah wrote in heartfelt tribute to Bishop Burnet.[59] Among the ropes of pearls and heaps of diamonds in her jewel box she kept a little crystal locket containing a scrap of Godolphin's hair.[60]

Marlborough now put into action a plan which had probably been decided on some time before: to leave England for the Continent before Parliament met. Using Maynwaring as a go-between, he applied to Oxford for a pass to travel through the Low Countries and Germany, in order to settle in Italy. Glad to be rid of him, the Lord Treasurer overcame the resistance of Bolingbroke and the French, although this was better founded than any of them knew. Marlborough chose to represent himself as a broken man, seeking only to put himself out of reach of the Queen's displeasure and the persecution of his enemies. In reality he was still the ministry's most active and dangerous opponent, and never more so than when he was at large in Europe. His other object in going abroad was no less than to persuade the Allies to mount an armed invasion of England, in order to overthrow the ministry and prevent the Jacobite restoration which was believed by the Whigs to be the likeliest outcome of the peace.[61]

In the interval between the issuing of the pass and Marlborough's departure at the end of November, Maynwaring, who had been ailing for months, died. In his final weeks there had been a coolness with Sarah. Having turned the younger James Craggs out of Holywell for trying to rape one of her servants, she now held him responsible for two violently abusive anonymous letters which she had just received ('. . . you have quarrelled with all your friends by turns,' one of them ran, 'your Children & Servants start at your name, your husband dares not say his soull is his owne before you least it should anger you . . . ').[62] Any attempt by Maynwaring to take his friend's part would have been enough to turn Sarah's anger on him. But she relented at the last, and it was 'to his Glory', his biographer Oldmixon wrote, 'that the greatest Lady in England wept often by the side of his Death Bed'.[63]

Having seen one successful invasion against popery in her lifetime, and regarding Oxford and Bolingbroke as infinitely more ill-intentioned than James II, Sarah was full of zest at the prospect of having 'justice' done on them by the same means. Since it would not be safe for her to remain a hostage in England in case the scheme failed, it was settled that she should join her husband as soon as she could. But she had always been reluctant to fix a day even for moving from one of her houses to another, and this time she could not be sure that she would ever see England again. She had to make a new will and ensure that her fortune would be properly looked after in her absence. Of this, £27,000 was left in the hands of Lord Cowper, and further investments were held by

William Clayton, an exchequer official whose wife had taken the place of Mrs Burnet as one of her closest friends, and by Robert Jennens, who had married Anthony Guidott's niece.[64] Then there was her packing to be done: over 120 parcels, containing vast quantities of household linen and clothing.[65]

When she was at last ready to go, it was hinted that the ministers might try to put difficulties in her way. In alarm she turned to Cowper, who assured her that there was nothing they could legally do to keep her from joining her husband. This tempted her to leave the country without asking for the usual passport. Then the recollection of what Marlborough was engaged in made her think better of it: 'it might give them a handle for some new lye, that I was run away with some Whig Plot.' Nor, on reflection, was she really worried about being kept in England, 'knowing very well that there is a desire both in Dame Dobson & Nab [Anne and Abigail] to have me out of their Neighbourhood'.[66] When she applied to the secretary of state for a pass in January 1713, one was immediately supplied.[67]

Sarah's departure from London was marred by petty disagreements with Henrietta and Mary about the farewell treats she devised for their children,[68] but there remained a large enough party of family and friends to accompany her as far as Dover to see her set sail. 'God knows how all this madnesse & infamy will end, but if it is punish'd as it ought to bee I am sure there must bee a great many hanged,' she commented grimly as she embarked: 'I really long as much to bee out of this horrid countrey as I used to doe to come into it.'[69]

A Sort of Banishment
1713–1714

FROM Dover Sarah had a quick but extremely uncomfortable passage to Ostend. Obstructiveness by the port officials meant that she had to travel by the smallest and most primitive of the packet boats: 'I wanted many conveniences that are usual & was forc'd to have the door of the place where I lay open in the night when violent sickness had put me into a great sweat, for a little air to keep me alive, tho' the sea was perpetually dashing in upon me.'[1] But from the moment she landed the most ceremonious treatment was accorded her by everyone for her husband's sake. She was gratified, partly because it showed their affection for him, but still more because it indicated 'what People must think Abroad of this Ministry and Parliament'.[2] She travelled on to Maestricht where Marlborough was waiting to take her to Aix-la-Chapelle.

Already it was apparent that he would not be able to persuade the Allies to engage in any violent attempt against the ministry. The Elector of Hanover, while prepared to make contingency plans for putting the army into Marlborough's hands in the event of the Queen's death, steadfastly refused to intervene directly in English politics during her lifetime.[3] Since the Queen, although declining in health, was in no immediate danger, Sarah despaired: 'I have had no hopes a great while but in one thing . . . & I much doubt whether it will happen in time. I can see no human means that can defend us from an Arbitrary Government in a little while.'[4] They lingered at Aix-la-Chapelle until April, waiting for the weather to allow them to continue their journey into Germany.

As Marlborough had anticipated, Sarah found Aix, with its poverty, scarcity of provisions, and total absence of 'conveniences' in its domestic arrangements, thoroughly disagreeable. Even so, with her capacity for involving herself in the passing moment, she remained reasonably cheerful. 'If our Ennimies do prevail to our utter ruin, I think I had best go into a Monastery,' she told Lady Cowper: 'Here are several in this Town, and tis all the Entertainment I have to visit the Nuns & the

Churches. I supp'd with about twenty of them t'other night but twas a very slight one, nothing but brown bread and butter . . . [and] they were as fond of me as if I had not been a Heritick.' Worldling that she was, she even felt a passing envy for the tranquillity of their lives: 'I do believe those that are in these houses with their own Inclinations are the most fortunate people in the world; for I don't see what can happen to trouble such as think of nothing but Heaven.' Protestant though she was, she was also prepared to acknowledge that they had their uses, 'providing in a decent way for Women of Quality that have little or no fortunes, and teaching young people in the nature of a school'. All her disapproval was reserved for the monastic foundations for men, 'who have in some places three parts in four of all the Land in the country, & think of nothing but imposing upon the miserable people to get more'.[5]

Towards the end of April the Marlboroughs set out for Frankfurt in a blizzard, travelling at a snail's pace with their great train of coaches and servants. In spite of the discomfort Sarah was ravished by the snow-capped Rhineland scenery, and particularly by the castle of the Elector of Trier at Coblenz on the confluence of the Rhine and Moselle, 'a place for Jupiter to live in', with 'several different Prospects the most extraordinary and agreeable that ever I saw'. They were now retracing Marlborough's steps on his most famous campaign:

& that part of the journey gave me occation for many melancholly reflections, the whole Army having march'd over all those difficult places in order to overcome France, which succeed[ed] so well as to make the French faction in England very angry, who notwithstanding all the wonderfull successes (with the help of Abigail's ministry) have thrown away all the blood & treasure that it cost & given our trad[e] at last to the King of France.[6]

Eventually they arrived at Frankfurt and settled at one of the best houses in the town. By this time the novelty of travelling was beginning to pall for Sarah. Now further from England than she had ever been in her life, and knowing that they had failed in the prime object of their journey, she felt the bleak truth that they were no better than 'a sort of banishd People in a strang Country'. She conceded from what she had seen that Frankfurt might be 'the best Town one can bee in Abroad; but indeed one must have sufferd a good deal to make one find any Ease and Satisfaction by being here'.[7] Even when she was driven distracted with toothache, she did not dare to trust herself to the local surgeons, and had to devise a remedy of her own to relieve the pain.[8] The weather was still bitterly cold, and the only form of heating they had was stoves, 'which is intolerable and makes my Head so uneasy that I can't bear it'. In her practical and energetic way she started to have a chimney built, so that she could make the open fires she was used to. 'That looks as if we were to stay here a long while,' she wrote to James Craggs senior,

but I can see no reason for it, when ever we can get a better hous, let it bee where it will, for what has the D. of Marl: to manage now wherever he is if they can settle French government & 11 [the Pretender] . . . & if the people of England ever sees the abuses that have been put upon them, *the nearer he is to help them the beter for both*.[9]

The Court of Hanover agreed with her. Indeed they had been reluctant to see him go so far from England in the first place. But Marlborough had no intention of settling in Germany or Italy, as he had led the ministers to believe. His object was to use Frankfurt as a base from which to take possession in person of his little principality of Mindelheim, and conduct negotiations with the Emperor and Prince Eugene for armed assistance in the event of an attempt to restore the Pretender. These were successful up to a point, the Emperor sending messages by the Prince that he was ready to make the utmost efforts to support the Hanoverian succession.[10] The Princes of the Empire came to wait on them as if they were exiled royalty. Sarah was particularly taken with the Elector of Mainz: 'his shap is, like my own, a little of the fatest, but in my Life I never saw a Face that expressed so much Opennesse, Honesty, Sense, and good Nature.' She watched from their windows as the Imperial troops marched past, and saw them pay the same respects to Marlborough as when he had been general: 'it gave me melancholly Reflections, and made me weep; but at the same Time I was so animated that I wishd I had been a Man that I might have ventured my Life a thousand Times in the glorious Cause of Liberty . . .'[11]

Yet by the time Marlborough left at the end of May for a fortnight's visit to Mindelheim, 150 miles away, Sarah had had her fill of ceremonies and was not interested enough to go with him. 'I am alone in this place, where I have no pleasure but the fresh air,' she wrote to the Cowpers while he was away, '& yet I do protest I would not change my condition with any of my enemys that have don so much mischief to their country'; even so, 'if I could have my wish, it should be only to be at any of my own houses in security, that I might sometimes see my Children & enjoy the agreeable conversation of a few friends, that is the Life I ever preferr'd before Power or Riches or Honour, nay sometimes I think it is to be desir'd before Health.'[12] Although Marlborough's meetings with Prince Eugene were to keep them in Germany for some weeks longer, as soon as he returned from Mindelheim they began to make plans to move back to the Low Countries, to be at hand in case of a crisis.

Meanwhile Sarah's correspondents kept her constantly informed of the proceedings in Parliament. Like all the Whigs, she was worried by

the Queen's declaration of her friendship to the House of Hanover—
'the most impudent thing that ever I saw or heard in my life'—regarding
it as a deliberate attempt to conceal the ministry's real designs from the
majority of the nation who were still in favour of a Protestant succession.
Yet the terms of the treaty of Utrecht, when they appeared in print, gave
her some hope even while they outraged her. All her expectations were
centred on the general election that was due in the autumn:

I hope it will not bee so difficult a thing for an honest man to bee chose as wee
had reason to apprehend, for now that the cheats & abuses of the ministers are so
plainly seen in this scandalous peace, they must certainly resent it unless one can
imagin the whole nation will sell themselves to France, which I can't be sure they
will not, tho tis as foolish as the Indians that sell their gold for beads & bells.[13]

In her passionate concern for the coming struggle, she again wished
herself a man and able to play an active role: not as a soldier now, but as
an MP: 'I am confydent I should have been the greatest Hero that ever
was known in the Parliament Hous if I had been so happy as to have
been a Man.' But she consoled herself with the thought that 'tho a
Woman I did all I could to prevent the Mischiefs that are coming upon
my Country, and having nothing to reproach myself with, nor nothing
in my Power that can doe any good, I am as quiet and contented as any
Phylosopher ever was'.[14]

   In fact Sarah had more of a role to play than this suggests. Her
correspondence with her friends in England was a real service to her
husband, keeping them in touch with their Whig allies and providing a
constant flow of political information, some of which was significant
enough to be passed on to Hanover. Apart from her immediate family,
her regular correspondents included Godolphin's nephew Hugh Boscawen,
now an influential Cornish MP, and Sir Gilbert Heathcote, the governor
of the Bank of England.[15] Writing to them was also a much-needed
outlet for her own feelings. The risk that her abuse of the ministers
would fall into the wrong hands did not worry her. As she remarked, her
opinion of them 'would be no great discovery', and 'they can't hang me
while I am on this side the Watter'.[16]

   But her repeated insistence that she had no responsibility for the evils
that had come upon them does not suggest an entirely clear conscience.
In fact, as she well knew, some of the Whigs had already begun to accuse
her of contributing to their downfall, and in July she had a guest whose
presence brought her brooding on this subject into the open. When her
son-in-law Montagu, who was travelling on the Continent, came to
Frankfurt to pay his respects, he brought with him the Tory MP,
Archibald Hutcheson. A staunch supporter of the Protestant succession,
Hutcheson was much solicited by the Whigs as a recruit to their

parliamentary alliance against the Court, and when Marlborough invited
him to consider their house his own during his stay, Sarah therefore put
herself out to be agreeable to him.[17] In her isolation any English
conversation was a boon to her, and the fact that Hutcheson was going
on to Hanover, where her conduct during her last years at Court was not
highly thought of by the old Electress, prompted her to put down some
'memorandums' on the subject for his instruction. In this, her third such
apologia since her dismissal, she used the only assistant she had to hand,
her chaplain Whadcock Priest.[18] Having brought him with her from
England so that the household should never want Protestant worship in
its wanderings through Catholic countries, she had quickly found him an
excellent choice: 'truely honest, and modest' as well as 'really what a
Man should bee as to Religion, perfectly good and just in all Things,
without imposing Superstition and Nonsense'.[19] He now proved equally
valuable as a collaborator, managing to reduce her chaotic stream of
recollection to an orderly narrative, without sacrificing the overriding
sense of her own personality. The work was still in progress when the
household packed up once more to return to the Low Countries at the
end of August.

Before they left, they had the disheartening news that the general
election was likely to produce a Parliament at least as strongly Tory as
the last. Nevertheless Sarah was relieved to be going; 'like sick People I
am glad of any Change, though this Place was better than Aix-la-
Chapelle.'[20] Marlborough's former quartermaster-general, Cadogan, on
his way to England to stand for election at Woodstock, had taken a
house for them at Antwerp, and this time, as she reported to Mrs
Boscawen,

wee came allmost 250 miles in Elleven days, with more ease then can bee
imagind by those that have seen these countrys, but all people wherever wee goe
endeavour to make us as easy as they can, & we have been much obliged to the
church; upon the road wee had no place to lye at one night but at a cloister, &
the Abbey of Tongelo has lent us the best house in this town.

Again she was gratified by the attention, but 'tho one is pleased with
such people, & wish's to return their goodnesse to us, I must own I
allways wish upon such occasions, that one could rather live some where
& not be known'. What prompted this comment were the ceremonies of
welcome prepared for them at Antwerp. These lasted eight hours and
included a French play which she had to sit through although she did not
understand a word of it; 'it was a most heavy day to me.'[21]

By now she realized that there was no immediate prospect of a return
to England. All their friends still thought it necessary for Marlborough
to remain abroad, 'for the same reasons that determined him to go'. In

England, his former chaplain Dr Hare warned her, his life 'would be too much exposed to villainous attempts, when it was most wanted', and he begged her not to think of coming without him, for 'notwithstanding the fatigues he has undergone, he has but a tender constitution; and upon that account, besides a thousand other reasons, can very ill be without your Grace'.[22] Sarah gave herself up to the task of settling them all into their new home, an occupation which never failed to give her satisfaction, in whatever circumstances it was undertaken. By hiring the house next door for additional space, and with the help of 'the very usefull & tolarable' furniture lent them by the Abbey, she had soon made 'as many conveniences as wee want, which is a thing they know nothing of abroad'. Once they were all comfortable, she told Mrs Boscawen, 'I believe I shall like this place much better then Frankford, for here is not so much company, & very good provissions; tis the finest old town I beleive in the world, but grown poor & ruind for want of trade, which will bee soon the decay of England.'[23] Another advantage Antwerp had over Frankfurt was that letters from England took only a few days to reach them. They could now feel themselves in much closer touch with events at home.

At intervals of leisure Sarah continued with her narrative, declaring to all and sundry, as one of the ministers' informants reported in a passable imitation of her invective, that 'that Thing (meaning the Queen) had treated her so barbarously that she would write her secret history, and the miscreants about her (which is the name she gives the Ministry) had no quarters to hope for but from the Pretender'.[24] Sarah knew better than anyone alive that the Queen had no personal inclination to restore her half-brother to the throne, and she also accepted as plain matter of fact what many of the Jacobites in England found hard to realize: that the Pretender, like his father, 'would loose three Crowns' rather than turn Protestant.[25] But this did not allay her fears of a Stuart restoration, and the outcome of the elections at first plunged her into despair:

I give every Thing for lost since I have had an Account that wee have, if it bee possible, a worse Sett of Men for three Year in the new Parliament than there was in the last; and they were chose in such a Manner as shews there is no Law, Sense, or Honesty left in that unhappy Country . . . Tis past a Doubt what is intended, and the Question is only whether this Parliament will bring him in, or, if they wont, whether the King of France, with the P[rince] of W[ales]'s Party, are not able to doe it by force.[26]

Marlborough, who was conducting one of his long series of precautionary and self-serving negotiations with the exiled Court, was sufficiently alarmed to offer to change his place of residence to the south of France in return for protection against parliamentary prosecution. But he withdrew his offer when the immediate danger passed, and the Jacobite court itself had no illusions about his sincerity.[27] And whatever lay in store for them, courting the Pretender, except to gather intelligence of his plans, was never an option for Sarah: 'after what the D. of M. has don, & even poor me, for the sake of vertue & liberty, for all the treasure upon earth I would not have him change his side.'[28]

Still relying on the alliance between the Whigs and the Hanoverian Tories, she soon began cautiously to hope that 'the Case is not so desperat as to bee past Recovery, if People that have Sense, and Fortunes would but consider what is truely their own Interest'.[29] In England there were rumours that they intended to return in the spring, but Sarah told the friends who sounded her out that this was not a serious prospect until the outcome of the situation in England could be more clearly seen.[30] She was undecided as to what to do with her money, whether to risk leaving it in England where she might not have access to it in case of a change of dynasty, or to have it transferred abroad; but in the end she took the first option: 'I can't fancy Securitys here, where one knows nor understands Nobody.'[31] Finding that she had brought so many goods with her that she needed little money herself, she gave away a good deal in charity. The desperate and widespread poverty of the Continent shocked her, and relieving this she thought 'the best way of employing what one can spair, allways taking Care not to depend upon any Body one's self'.[32] But she begged those in charge of her investments in England to husband them well, 'that if 38 [herself] should be so unfortunate as not to see her other friends again, she may not want the support of 50 [money]'.[33]

She was cheered to learn of the ministers' panic when the Queen was taken ill in December, seeing it as evidence that they were not yet far enough advanced in their preparations to bring in the Pretender, 'but to be sure they will quicken their measures now'.[34] As she waited for the beginning of the session, she now made no attempt to conceal her homesickness; her 'very Being' depended 'upon a right Resolution taken in this Hous of P[arliament], for without that it will bee in vain to think of living in England'. As it was postponed beyond the beginning of the new year, her fears grew that the plans for a Jacobite coup were proceeding apace, and that it would soon be too late for Parliament to save them:

tho I know one shall bear whatever one can't help, I pray most heartily that I may not be tryd any further, for tis quite another Thing to hear that one is never to see England nor one's Children again . . . then it is to leave a disagreeable Court when one knows one has not deserved ill Treatment, and only to make a Sort of Pilgrimage for a little while, hoping to see Justice don upon some of one's Enemys.[35]

When Parliament did meet, it was soon clear that there was little prospect of aid from that quarter. Sarah's greatest scorn was reserved for the proceedings of 16 April, at which an address of thanks was voted for the peace: 'to save their dear honour, they have voted, what every body knows, (that has sense enough to feed themselves) what they believe, and know to be every word false.' As for the Queen's assurances of her unwavering support of the Hanoverian succession, 'to shew how far the goodnesse of Her Majesty extends, & the desire She hath to make all people easie, I have very good reason to believe, that She hath given all the assurances that can be desired, of her kind intentions to her friends [the Jacobite Court] at Barleduc'.[36] Sarah's hopes were now pinned on the opposition plan to persuade the Elector of Hanover to send his son to reside in England, and on the probability that the Queen would die before the ministers could bring their schemes to fruition: 'it is next to impossible that one with such a Complication of Distempers can continue long.' The only comfort was that 'wee can't bee much longer in uncertainty'.[37]

Yet the Queen lingered on, and it was soon apparent that the Elector would never agree to send his son, or take any other decisive action, as long as she lived. 'To tell you the truth,' Sarah wrote to James Craggs in her anxiety and frustration, '. . . it looks to me as if hee would accept of 59 [England] only if hee can have it without Hazard or trouble, which is what one can hardly expect will be the case.' She concluded that there was now no hope but by a change of the ministry, a prospect of which the open feud between Oxford and Bolingbroke gave some hopes: 'this makes me think that 42 [Marlborough] may be of more use in 59 [England] then any where else.'[38] Marlborough agreed, 'saying the Queen was younger and more likely to live than he, & he wou'd injoy the rest of his Life with his Children & friends'.[39] By April they began to make their first definite plans for returning to England as soon as Parliament rose. The decision was hastened by a series of family crises in England. Early in 1714 their two Godolphin grandchildren, Willigo and Harriet, developed smallpox, a disease which Sarah trusted no one but herself to nurse successfully.[40] Although both of them recovered, Lady Bridgwater, who was stricken with the same illness in March, did not. The loss of one daughter with no possibility of seeing her before she died was followed by the news that Lady Sunderland, weakened by a difficult pregnancy, was also seriously ill. The shock of her sister's death had brought on a miscarriage, and for weeks her life was in danger. Concern for her temporarily drove all politics out of Sarah's head. She simply longed to be back in England before any other calamity befell her family.[41]

Using Lady Bridgwater's death as the occasion, Marlborough sounded out the Queen's attitude to his return (although he avoided asking permission, since this would imply that he 'had been guilty of somthing that made it necessary'). At the same time he responded to the overtures of Oxford, who was seeking an alliance with the Whigs to strengthen his position at Court.[42] It was then a matter of passing the time until the end of the session. As at Aix, Sarah's chief entertainment came from the continuous cycle of religious processions and shows; 'a Folly for allmost every day of the year', as she put it. But she was shocked out of her usual contemptuous tolerance for such 'buffoonery and Tricks' by a play representing the life of Christ, put on twice a week by the tradesmen of the town, with music between the acts, 'just as it is in any play hous'. It was 'much the most monstrous thing that I have seen sence I was abroad, which is saying a great deal,' she told Mrs Clayton; 'I would not see it again unless I were draged to it.'[43]

As the weather grew warmer they were able to take exercise out of doors, and found even chance acquaintances eager to offer them the freedom of their gardens. Yet in this as in every other matter, Sarah was struck by the inconvenience of arrangements abroad in comparison with those in England. Instead of the gravel paths for which English gardens were famous, there was only sand. This got into her shoes and was so irritating that she liked the roads or the fields better, 'where the D. of Marl. and I go constantly every Day in the Afternoon, and stop the Coach and go out wherever wee see a Place that looks hard and clean'. In this way they regularly walked two miles every day, 'which does me a great deal of good'.[44]

In their hunger for English faces and voices, they kept open house for any young traveller of good birth and acceptable political views who happened to be passing through Antwerp. One of these was George Bubb, returning from a tour of Italy. Sarah, who had heard of the Italian practice of caricature, asked him to recommend an artist who could make her a picture of Abigail Masham, 'covered with running sores and ulcers, that I may send it to the Queen to give her a right idea of her new favourite'.[45] It was at this time also that Lord Stanhope (the future Earl of Chesterfield) first impressed her with his 'good Sense, Wit and Breeding'. She and Marlborough grew so fond of his company that they kept him with them 'from morning to night' all the time he stayed in Antwerp.[46] The next to enjoy this somewhat overwhelming hospitality were the 19-year-old Lord Lonsdale and his handsome younger brother Anthony, both 'wonderfull honest & good young men'. When the latter fell ill with smallpox, Sarah banished his doctor and nursed him as carefully as if he had been her own son. 'Without laughing,' she told

Jennens, 'I do believe I am better than any Physician even in England, because I have been very well instructed, and I leave out all the knavish part of the Profession.' She was delighted when the boy came through the disease with his good looks unimpaired.[47]

Another guest whom she virtually adopted at this time was the Earl of Essex, a boy of the same age as her son when he died, whose impudent high spirits were a relief from the gloom which descended on her whenever she contemplated the situation in England. He formed a mock confederacy with Marlborough's page for the assassination of the Queen, took the visiting Dutch ambassador to task for mismanaging the peace, threatened to beat a chance acquaintance who had not heard of the battle of Ramillies, and offered himself as a future husband for Lady Harriet Godolphin. After his reluctant departure on his travels in March he continued to correspond with Sarah in the same strain, addressing her as 'dear Mama' and signing himself 'your dutyfull son', ignoring the protests of his older companion that his letters were 'not write respectfull enough'.[48]

In Germany this companion, a young Irishman called Samuel Molyneux, separated from Essex and went on alone to Hanover as the Marlboroughs' confidential agent. The information he sent back to Sarah helped to bring about Oxford's downfall; for he was at Hanover when harsh letters arrived from the Queen and the Lord Treasurer, declaring that the former would always refuse her consent to the Electoral Prince's residence in England, whatever the consequences might be. When printed copies of these letters, which completely undermined Oxford's professed position as the champion of Hanover, were circulated in London early in July, the rumour was that Sarah had come upon them when rifling through her husband's papers and communicated them to her Whig friends in England without his permission. In fact it was to Sarah that Molyneux first sent copies of the letters, at the Electress's express request and with the strong hint that the Electoral Court would be glad to have them distributed in England.[49]

Oxford, now locked in mortal combat with Bolingbroke, believed that his rival had connived at this strategy, and in mid-July Bolingbroke did evidently open negotiations with Marlborough on his own account, promising him his old posts in return for an alliance to support the Hanoverian succession.[50] In fact the Pretender's explicit refusal to abandon his religion had long since made a restoration scheme impracticable for either minister,[51] but Sarah was still determined to fear the worst and of the two she preferred Bolingbroke to Oxford, being convinced that the latter 'will do the business more surely than that violent wretch Ld B', for 'tho he is as wicked as any man living, I don't believe he has so many talents to do mischief as the Sorcerer [Oxford] has'. She therefore hoped that Oxford would be the first to fall.[52] But she rightly had no confidence that Marlborough was genuinely welcome to either of the ministers, whose negotiations with him had been forced on them by their mutual hostility, by the precariousness of the Queen's life, and by his determination to return with or without their co-operation. In June she warned Craggs that his decision should not be made known until Parliament rose, in case official steps were taken to prevent it.[53] Many years later she was asked to comment on the persistent story that the Queen herself, worn out and disgusted by the feuding of her ministers, had turned back to Marlborough in her last weeks, inviting him to return to the government. If she knew anything of this, she carried the secret to her grave. Those who spread the story, she remarked, did 'not mention what we did to compass this great favour . . . I can only answer that I never heard one word of it before'.[54]

Keeping to his intention of returning to England as soon as Parliament was up, Marlborough set out with Sarah for Ostend on 16/27 July. The Hanoverian envoy Bothmer, who understandably needed reassuring about the negotiations with Oxford and Bolingbroke, was surprised that he did not wait for the outcome of the contest between them, now nearing its climax, and he attributed this to the 'impetuosity of the dutchess'.[55] In her letters Sarah does not sound very impetuous. Describing their leisurely journey to Ostend to Mrs Clayton, she added that she would rather stay at the port itself for several more days than come without a wind that was favourable enough to get them over in the daytime, 'because it is intolerable to goe to bed in those boats'.[56] Evidently she dreaded a repetition of her outward voyage.

She had her wish that Oxford should fall first. On 27 July the Queen at last dismissed him, and the next day the Marlboroughs, who probably had advance notice of the event, embarked. Just what Sarah had wished to avoid then happened. Their boat was struck by a storm that kept them at sea for four nights and three days, during which she could not take off her clothes or get any rest. Even so, in the midst of the danger and discomfort, she was impressed by the conduct of the ship's captain, who was not only skilful, but 'managed every thing with as much calmnesse & temper as if hee had been design'd for a devine'.[57] While they were still being buffeted at sea, events in England were coming to a head, and being dealt with just as calmly and efficiently. On 30 July the Queen was taken mortally ill; by the morning of 1 August she was dead, and the Treasurer's staff in the Duke of Shrewsbury's hands. A messenger came on board to give the Marlboroughs the news as their battered little boat approached Dover harbour.[58] The same afternoon the Elector of Hanover was peacefully proclaimed George I.

The Hanoverians
1714–1716

'My Lord Duke, I hope your troubles are now all over', was the new King's greeting to Marlborough when he landed in England himself six weeks later; but for Sarah the Hanoverian era had even before this begun to produce its own fresh crop of difficulties. Circumstances had deprived the Duke of the opportunity to return to England as the saviour of the Protestant succession. Now they learnt, while they were still on the road to London, that he and Sunderland had been excluded from the list of Lords Justices, appointed to carry on the government until the King's arrival. In their places, Sarah noted in disgust, room had been found for the odious Duke of Kent, 'and such sort of people'.[1] The Hanoverians had always distrusted Sunderland's extremism, and although they were glad to have Marlborough on their side in case of any attempt by the Pretender, the accusations of overweening ambition had done their work. Except in an emergency they were not prepared to trust him with any power, civil or military, in the King's absence. To demonstrate to the Germans the magnitude and popularity of the figure they had slighted, Marlborough allowed the City to give his cavalcade a ceremonial entry into London. 'He is not pleased . . . that there is any man but the King higher than him in this country,' the Hanoverian envoy noted after their first meeting.[2]

For Sarah their homecoming was further spoilt by an immediate breakdown in her relations with her youngest daughter. She was already resentful that Mary had responded to her reproaches while they were abroad by writing to her father, 'to endeavour to do me ill offices in a rude manner'. Although the Montagus came to meet them as they entered London and afterwards dined at Marlborough House, Sarah complained that Mary 'never said one single word to me the whole time I was there, but look'd with a scornfull air, as if she had a mind to express that she came there to see her Father & not me'. She was even more shocked when Mary's young husband, hitherto a great favourite of hers, stoutly took his wife's part: 'I wetted a Pocket handkerchief without making the least Impression upon him.'[3] The Marlboroughs remained in

London only long enough for the Duke to take the oaths in Parliament before leaving to visit Lady Sunderland at Bath. On the round trip they were able to take in all the country houses which Sarah had so longed for in her exile. In the last week of August she finally came to rest at St Albans, 'more tird than [in] any of my Travels', and perhaps for the first time in her life (she was now fifty-four) beginning to feel her age. Even so, and despite her public and private grievances, she was thankful: 'you can't bee sensible of the happynesse I feel in returning to my own children & hous's,' she wrote to a friend, 'which I think I may now injoy with safty & quietnesse.'[4]

They returned to London in time for the King's arrival on 17 September. Even at the height of her frustration with his cautious conduct as Elector, Sarah had been sure that he would make a good King, perhaps the best England had ever had.[5] When she met him in person this good opinion was confirmed. George I was always her favourite monarch, although admittedly this was not saying very much. 'Tho' he was not very *bright* nor wou'd have made any great figure in History,' she wrote later, after she had fallen out with the Court, he was 'a good natur'd man, & if he had had good ministers would have made the nation happy.'[6] She also took care to pay her compliments to his two female favourites, his illegitimate half-sister, the Baroness von Kielmansegg, and his mistress, the Countess von der Schulenburg, 'which is certainly right to do,' she told Lady Cowper, 'tho' most of our Country are so ill bred as not to think of it'.[7]

Superficially her relations with the lively and intelligent Princess of Wales, who spoke English fluently, were even more cordial. When Caroline first came to England, Sarah recalled, 'she sent me a message, as obliging as if I had been her equal, to know how I did, & added that she long'd of all things to see me'. But when Sarah waited on her, she was taken aback:

her face [was] frightfull, her eyes very small & green like a Cat & her shape yet worse, & she was dress'd in so ridiculous a manner that the first time I saw her, I was amazed, & she put me in mind of Drolls I had seen at Bartholomew Fair when I was a girl, where the Women used to stand in Ballcanies dressed up with the air of a Princess, with a great deal of Friz'd hair, & very much powder'd.

The Princess wanted to consult her about precedents for Court ceremonial, and here at once they were on contentious ground. For Sarah decided that the formalities observed by Anne when she was a Princess would be the most suitable rules to go by, and Caroline was equally determined that as Princess of Wales at a Court where there was no reigning Queen (George I had divorced his wife years before), she should follow the rules of Queen Mary. Sarah was irritated that 'a little

German Princess . . . that some people call'd Madam Anspach' should give herself such airs. Although she found the Princess entertaining and was half won over by her friendliness, the two outspoken and self-willed women could never be long in each other's company without one or the other giving some cause for offence. Sarah was particularly annoyed that Caroline expected her to join in finding fault with Queen Anne: 'I cou'd not answer her as freely on that subject as my inclination was to do, but I defended my dead mistress.' Indeed, against this outsider, she was even prepared to defend Abigail Masham, when the Princess accused her of having made away with some of Queen Anne's jewels. Sarah, who had often arranged them for Anne to wear, was able to certify that none were missing: 'in this manner I justify'd Lady Masham, who I believed never rob'd any body but me.'[8]

There was no such ambivalence in her feelings for the Prince of Wales, whom she cordially detested from the start for his vanity and boorishness. One incident, which took place in the Princess's dressing-room, provided her with a favourite anecdote:

one of the little Princesses had been severely whipt, & was crying extreamly. I knelt down to the Child & caressing her [said], my dear little Princess, why would you not send to me in this misfortune for I would have done all I could to save you, to which the Princess [of Wales] answered, Children must be whipt, & I had much rather make her cry now, then that she should make me cry when she is a Woman. His Royal Highness came into the Conversation & said he believed the reason the English people were such strange Creatures was, that they had not been whipt, & this was before a whole Room full of English People. I made no reply, tho' I had a strong Inclination to have said, that I believed His Royal Highness had been often whipt, or he could not have been so very *polite*.[9]

A further source of friction with the Hanoverians was the Marlboroughs' attempt to restore their family to the monopoly of Court favour which they had at first enjoyed under Anne. In the end the Duke's insistence on pressing the claims of all his relations to office earned him a rebuke from the King.[10] Having made it clear to the Princess that the Duchess of Montagu's acceptance of the post of lady of the bedchamber was none of her doing, Sarah added in her pique,

that I hoped she would believe it was not for want of all the duty and respect imaginable, that none of my family had offered themselves to her Royal Highness, but the King not having given all the men employment, tho' they had great merit in having been always for his Majesty's interest, I did think it reasonable that her Royal Highness should oblige other families in letting them have the honour to wait upon her.[11]

Yet as far as Sarah was concerned, the ambition to return to public life

did not extend to herself and her husband. Marlborough had been
restored to the post of general, which he now agreed to execute without a
salary; but he was by no means content with this nominal compensation
and, in competition with Halifax and Townshend, aimed at ministerial
status. Apart from his desire to see his public accounts safely passed, his
old habits of power died hard. To out-distance his rivals, he even cast
eyes on his wife's old post of groom of the stole, which in the end the
King was to leave unfilled.[12] Sarah, who was at pains to scotch rumours
that she wanted to return to Court herself, did all she could to dissuade
him:

I said every body that liked the revolution and the security of the law had a great
esteem for him; that he had a greater fortune than he wanted; and that a man
who had had such success, with such an estate, would be of more use to any
court than they could be of to him: that I would live civilly with them, if they
were so to me, but would never put it into the power of any king to use me
ill.[13]

Of his two rivals, Halifax, for many years a favourite of the
Hanoverian Court, had received an earldom and at last achieved his
ambition of succeeding to the treasury. Yet Marlborough was able to
ensure that the supreme power eluded him.[14] 'My Lord Halifax and the
rest of the great men dined with me at Marlborough House the same day
they had done these great things for him,' Sarah remembered. 'He hardly
spoke a word the whole dinner time, looked full of rage, and as if he
could have killed everybody at table; and the reason of that behaviour
was that they did not give him the white staff, instead of making him the
first commissioner of the Treasury.' She had now completely turned
against him: 'if I should say all I know of his falsnesse, & ill principles,
Ambition & vanity it would fill a volum.'[15] Halifax was able to take his
revenge by making as many difficulties as Oxford in passing Sarah's
robes accounts and by turning a deaf ear to her solicitations about the
salary and taxes at Windsor Park, which until now she had been able to
pay herself without difficulty from the privy purse.[16] He was also
foremost in reviving the Whig complaints of her conduct in the previous
reign: 'they railed at me everywhere,' she remembered, 'and said that I
had ruined them, and were as violent as the Tories had been.'[17] Her
invaluable chaplain Priest had just died, but with the help of the low
church controversialist, Benjamin Hoadly, who had become a close
friend, she set about compiling a fresh defence of her conduct, according
to which Harley and Abigail had taken advantage of the Queen's passion
for the Church to undermine the Marlboroughs in her favour. When
Hoadly was made Bishop of Bangor a few months later, she claimed that
it was entirely owing to her recommendation.[18]

Although the King's inner ministry in the first winter of his reign appeared to have reduced itself to Townshend, Marlborough, and the two Hanoverians, Bothmer and Bernsdorff,[19] Townshend was clearly seen to have established himself as the principal English member. Declining in health and reputation and not in the complete confidence of the King, Marlborough was a doubtful match for the ambitious younger Whigs on whom the mantle of the Junto had now fallen. 'The Duke of Marlborough . . . in his old age was making the same figure at court that he did when he first came into it,' Lady Mary Wortley Montagu observed: 'I mean, bowing and smiling in the antechamber while Townshend was in the closet.'[20] The latter had succeeded to the post which Sunderland regarded as rightfully his, that of principal secretary of state, and for all her misgivings about her husband's return to public life, Sarah was by no means pleased to see him and her son-in-law so unceremoniously supplanted by the overbearing secretary, 'our present governour', as she sourly termed him.[21] If Marlborough had any real power, it was still a secret from her, she remarked in December 1714, and by February she knew 'by a thousand other things that hee is not a minister'.[22]

One sign of this had been his inability to protect Sunderland from the prospect of viceregal exile in Ireland, which his frail wife particularly dreaded.[23] It was true that there had been a distance between Sunderland and his wife's family since the fall of the Whig ministry in 1710. Apart from political differences, there was his taste for 'low women', and shortly there were to be public accusations of homosexuality as well.[24] Yet in order to maintain the family interest, as well for Lady Sunderland's sake, the appointment had to be opposed, and in the course of the first year of the reign, Marlborough did manage to gain some ground against his chief rival. When death removed another of the old Junto members, Lord Wharton, from the post of Lord Privy Seal in April 1715, Sarah assured her daughter that if they would have patience it would not be long before a place should be found for Sunderland in England.[25]

For the time being, however, her dislike of Townshend did not extend to his genial brother-in-law and junior partner, Robert Walpole. Remembering Godolphin's fondness for him and finding him ready enough to sympathize with her grievances against Halifax, she continued to regard him as her friend, even to the point of defending him against Sunderland's resentment. But she had also become tactlessly fond of joking about 'the beggary she first knew him in', when he was little better than a clerk to Marlborough, attending him 'with a bag of writings, like Mr Cardonnel'.[26] Walpole, knowing that there was no longer any need for him to defer to Marlborough's Duchess, bided his time. When Halifax died, allowing him to succeed as chancellor of the exchequer in the autumn of 1715, she found him no readier to grant her requests than his predecessor, and she was soon complaining that 'I have not succeeded in any one thing these two years which in Justice could not bee refused to an enemy'.[27]

Apart from politics, Sarah's chief preoccupation in the first winter of the Hanoverian era was to launch her eldest granddaughter into society. With her parents' consent, Lady Harriet came to live at Marlborough House, on the understanding that her grandparents would be responsible for finding a suitable match and providing her with a dowry. Small, plain, and self-effacing, like all the Godolphins, Harriet wanted decking out in elaborate clothing and jewellery to make her noticed, and Sarah employed Marlborough's old colleague Lord Stair, now ambassador in Paris, to procure the latest fashions for her.[28] The match she had in her sights was the young Earl of Clare (soon to be created Duke of Newcastle). But when he, delicately hinting at Harriet's want of physical attractions and his own encumbered estates, demanded a dowry of £40,000, Sarah was insulted: 'Lady Harriote is not a Cittyson, nor a Monster, & I never heard of such a fortune in any other case.' The negotiations, in which Vanbrugh had acted as go-between, were abruptly broken off.[29]

In the spring of 1715 Sarah suffered her first serious illness for many years, becoming 'so bad that Sir Samuel Garth would have let me blood twice in one day and I kept my chamber a great many'.[30] Her sickroom now became the scene of a violent quarrel with her eldest daughter. Henrietta's relations with her mother had worsened noticeably since the death of Godolphin, who had helped to keep the peace between them. She herself was later to write of 'a Godolphin and a Marlboroughs different way of feeling'.[31] As a mature woman, she found Sarah's attempts to revive the extravagant emotionalism of her adolescence distasteful. When her mother hugged her '& wept over Her, begging Her still to love me', Henrietta's only response was a frozen and embarrassed silence and 'a little squeeze with her hand'.[32] Mary had the same difficulty, warning Sarah by letter that 'I am the most awkward reserv'd creature in the world, [and] as sensible as I am of your goodness, I shall be unable when I see you to return you those thanks which you will ever deserve from me'.[33] Their mother, who could only be persuaded that her children sufficiently returned her affection and care if they made her constant professions of love and gratitude, was deeply hurt.

As the days of her illness went by, her anger at Henrietta's cool and infrequent visits mounted. One day when she was convalescent,

Henrietta appeared in her bedchamber in company with a common acquaintance. In answer to his polite enquiries about her health, Sarah remarked pointedly that she was much better and that she was glad of it, 'for it would ease my Lady Godolphin of the trouble of either coming or sending to see how I did'. All Henrietta's resentment at her mother's carping now poured out. She reminded her that she had not always been a model of attentiveness to her own mother, and accused her of being so unreasonable and demanding that she was sometimes dissatisfied with the ever-dutiful Lady Sunderland and even with Marlborough himself. These were matters which Sarah could never bear to have touched on. Flying into what she admitted was 'a very great Passion', she told her daughter 'that she had lost all shame, & that the Company she had kept had corrupted all her morals'. Afterwards she tried to keep the quarrel from Marlborough, who was always made miserable by such episodes, only to find that Henrietta had already appealed to him of her own accord. With his intervention and that of Henrietta's husband, whom Sarah reduced to tears by her emotional demands for his support, the quarrel was patched up. But the long letters of recrimination which she could not refrain from writing in answer to Henrietta's stiff attempts at apology ensured that the reconciliation could never be more than superficial.[34]

In the summer Sarah went to take the waters at Epsom to complete her recovery. Marlborough, left alone in London where the Whigs were taking their parliamentary revenge against Queen Anne's last ministry, missed her sadly. Sunderland was no substitute for Godolphin as an ally, and for all the difficulties she caused him, Sarah was now closer to him than anyone on earth. 'I do with all my heart wish the aire and Watters may do you good,' he wrote to her, 'but if you have any Consideration for me, you will some times think of my being alone, both before I go to bed, and when I weak [wake] in the morning, and that there are many things of which I can open my heart to nobody but your self.'[35] It is unlikely, however, that he fully opened his heart to her about one important matter which occupied him during this summer: the prospect, which in Scotland soon became a reality, of a large-scale Jacobite rising. Even while he supervised the government's military preparations, he kept up his past policy of reinsurance by sending the Pretender a contribution of £4,000 towards his attempt.[36]

Considering how great a terror a Jacobite restoration had been to her in the past, Sarah's reaction to this new alarm was remarkably cool. Those who claimed that the whole affair was a Whig trick to justify the persecution of the Tories exasperated her, but Louis XIV, an ogre to her since childhood, was now dead, and she was fortified by Stair's assurances that the invasion would have no support from France. Parading her inside knowledge, she told her friends that she was not at liberty to reveal all the details she knew, but 'I hear that there is even in Scotland more men for this government then for the P[retender] so that without the assistance of France I don't find that there is any reason to apprehend, & I hope in a little time wee shall have a good prospect of quiet'.[37] Her calculations of her own fortune at this time show that she was now worth well over £100,000 in her own right, of which the bulk was invested in government funds and South Sea stock. She was so confident of the supression of the rising that she did not even consider it necessary to sell the latter for fear of a fall in the market, and while her husband remitted funds to the Pretender, she lent a further £6,000 of her own money to help finance the government's operations.[38]

Nor did she let the Jacobite threat spoil her cheerful occupation of preparing furniture for Blenheim.[39] By this time the treasury had agreed, at least in principle, to pay the debt incurred before the Queen stopped the works there in 1712, and Marlborough, realizing that he could expect no more than this, was preparing to complete the building at his own expense; it was a just punishment, his wife told him unsympathetically, for letting the extravagant Vanbrugh have the management of it.[40] During much of the autumn and winter of 1715 she remained at Windsor Lodge, disregarding his pleas for her company in London. When the news came in mid-November of the defeat of the Jacobites at Prestonpans by General Wills, she merely remarked that 'such a Resolution as his at the Beginning of these Troubles in all Probability would have set us at Ease long agoe'.[41]

Quite apart from his ambivalent attitude, Marlborough had not been fit to go on campaign in person. The combined stresses of the rising and his attempt to regain ministerial power hastened his physical decay, and by the winter he was incapacitated with violent headaches and giddiness. It needed only one more blow to bring about the final collapse, and in the early spring of 1716 this came with the death of his favourite daughter. Lady Sunderland, constantly ailing in health, had been taken ill with pleurisy, but the immediate cause of her death appears to have been septicaemia, following a careless blood-letting. Sarah vented her grief in the manner her family had increasingly come to dread, by raging against the doctors with a violence that was not far short of temporary dementia. In this case her chief victim was Dr Mead, who 'did as certainly murder my Dear lady Sunderland as if hee had shot her thro' the head'.[42] She could only console herself by offering to take charge of her daughter's youngest girl, Diana, now a 'pritty talking child' of five years old. Her plan was to set up a nursery at St Albans for her and her Bridgwater cousin, Lady Anne Egerton, and be there herself as much as she could. But it was now Marlborough who needed most of her attention: he 'will be running up and down to several places this summer, where one can't carry children; and I don't think his health so good as to trust him by himself'.[43] In fact he had been left broken and inconsolable by the death of the one child who was able to live peaceably with her mother, and as he came downstairs at Holywell on 28 May, he was felled by a massive stroke. He lay unconscious for three days, and it was a fortnight before he was pronounced out of danger.[44] 'From morning to night & from night to morning' for a further month, Sarah watched and nursed him at St Albans, until he was well enough in mid-July to go to Bath to convalesce.

The six weeks he spent there produced only a partial recovery. 'He certainly looks better then hee has don this many yeares,' Sarah reported to James Craggs; but the stroke had affected both his speech and his emotional control. In company he refused to say a word, and the slightest agitation of mind reduced him to tears. 'His spirits are still low,' she added anxiously in September, '& I can't say that hee is so able to talk upon any thing as he was before hee was sick . . . as he is, he must have nothing to vex him but to please and entertain him as much as possible.'[45] Yet as far as she was concerned, there could be no pleasure or entertainment at Bath, which she found worse than any Continental town for 'Stinks and Dirt'. When she saw the extrovert Duchess of Shrewsbury 'as well pleased in a great Crowd of Strangers as the common People are with a Bull-baiting or a Mountebank', she was inclined to be envious: 'I am only sorry that I can't find pleasure as others doe, for in this world those that have most have little enough.'[46] She occupied herself with supervising her husband's treatment, a task which in his present condition called for all her ingenuity and patience, and with losing her money at cards; for all her years of practice, she was always a poor card-player, constantly distracting herself with talking and then having to ask 'what is trumps'; she admitted, 'I can't mind what I am doing enough to have much hopes of winning.'

Marlborough had been struck down just as the plans he had made with his son-in-law for ousting Townshend were coming to fruition. When the King left to spend the summer at Hanover, Sunderland prepared to follow him to continue the work of undermining his opponents in person. There were those who believed that Sarah had now succeeded as head of the family interest, bribing her son-in-law to do her political bidding. 'The Schemers', as Lady Cowper called them, now flocked to Bath, for though the Duke could not advise, he could lend his Name and Purse, both which the Duchess governed (a Pleasure to her, who loved Power even more than the Duke). Lord Sunderland came for Instructions twice or thrice before he went away, and Nothing was talked of at Bath but the great Things that were to be done when the King came over . . . and 'tis no Wonder Sunderland was so devoted to her, since he was so well paid for it; for since this Illness she got the Duke to alter his Will, and take Everything from my Lady Godolphin he could hinder her of, and leave the Bulk of his Estate to Sunderland and his Children.[47]

Sarah had certainly been fully informed from the first about the scheme for getting rid of Townshend, and despite her fears that a Whig schism would restore the Tories to power (and so raise the spectre of sending them on their travels to Antwerp again), she was glad of the prospect.[48] She was also present at the meeting at Bath on 3 August, when Sunderland and Cadogan came to take their leave of Marlborough before setting out for the Continent, and well aware of the purpose of Sunderland's journey; the King, he wrote to her from Hanover, 'is in every respect as Ld Marlborough could wish, & I flatter my self that my being here, will be of some use to what your Grace, & all honest people wish'.[49] Yet although Sunderland continued to treat her with deference and undoubtedly had expectations that she would provide for his younger children, there was no truth in Lady Cowper's story that she had made him the Marlborough heir. In fact he was now embarked on an independent political career, and Sarah had reservations about both him and his partner Cadogan which would not be kept to herself for much longer.

It was while Marlborough was ill at St Albans that she first began to have suspicions about Cadogan's custody of the funds, amounting to £40,000 or £50,000, which he had managed on their behalf while they were on the Continent. She believed that having invested the money in Holland at 3 per cent, he had re-lent the securities to the Emperor at more than double the interest for his own profit. The more he prevaricated, the more convinced she became that he hoped to keep the money until Marlborough died, and then succeed to his military posts as well. With the help of James Craggs and Marlborough's old paymaster, Benjamin Swete, she managed to have the securities transferred to safe hands in Holland without revealing her suspicions to her husband; '& if my Lord C: should suspect me not to bee so inosent in that matter, as I have appeard to bee, I can bear that with patience provided I can bee of any use in securing what is so considerable to the D: of M:'.[50]

The other great matter which devolved on her as a result of Marlborough's illness was the completion of Blenheim, and this was a change which did not promise at all well for Vanbrugh. Although the architect protested truthfully that he had never done anything without the Duke's authority, and although Sarah admitted that Marlborough would never supervise the expenditure on Blenheim properly even when he was well, she now blamed Vanbrugh for everything she disapproved of about the building. While they were at Bath she repeatedly questioned both his estimates for the cost of finishing and his contracts with the workmen; she also complained, with more justice, that while the house was still uninhabitable, he continued to divert resources to his favourite projects of the Grand Bridge and the repair of the old manor house. A youth spent in the Restoration Court had left her with little sympathy for the illicit loves of royalty and she could see no point in perpetuating the memory of Henry II and Rosamond Clifford. Yet she noted grimly that friends who came via Blenheim to visit Marlborough at Bath could hardly keep from laughing when they talked of the work that was in progress on these ruins. As for the bridge, Vanbrugh's expensive solution to the problem of spanning the marshy chasm before the main front of the house, it was the kind of project that only royalty could afford to embark on, '& they have so seldome any understanding, & so much mony in their power, that I think tis no great matter how they are used'. Declaring that it could never be finished 'without a Land Tax from the Parliament', she got Marlborough to sign an order putting a stop to it, 'tho I don't tell him a tenth part of the maddnesse of it, for fear of vexing him'.[51]

When they arrived at Woodstock from Bath on 3 October they were able to see for themselves. Even Sarah now quailed before the magnitude of the task ahead of her. After four years of neglect the site was 'a chaos that turn's one's brains but to think of it'. Finishing appeared 'so terrible an Undertaking' that only Marlborough's passion for the place, greater now than ever, could persuade her to take it on.[52] For the first week of their visit Vanbrugh was with them, and there was a good deal of plain speaking about the future conduct of the building. Left to herself, Sarah would undoubtedly have sacked him at this stage, with as little ceremony as she had once dismissed Wren; but again she had Marlborough's feelings to consider. 'I have no mind to fall out with Sir John,' she told Craggs,

& much less to vex the D: of Marl: at a time when his health is so bad. At the same time I think I owe it to him & to my family to prevent, if I can, having a great estate thrown away in levilling of hills, filling up pricipices & making bridges in the air, for no reason that I, or any body else can see, but to have it said here after that Sir John Vanbrugh did that thing which never was don before.

Although she transferred as much control of the building as she could to her 'Oracle', the cabinet-maker James Moore, she therefore had no intention when Vanbrugh left for London in mid-October of parting with him altogether. The following day she wrote to Craggs confidently of 'the union between Sir John & me'.[53]

It was a union that barely lasted the month. At Bath she had had the opportunity to reopen the Newcastle marriage negotiations through the politically neutral channel of the Duke's agent, Peter Walter, thus by-passing Vanbrugh and his awkward connection with Townshend and Walpole.[54] But Marlborough was now making difficulties about providing even the reduced dowry of £20,000. To Sarah, in her stress and frustration, the architect suddenly seemed to be the source of all her troubles. The only way she could relieve her feelings was to send after him one of her notorious recriminatory narratives, beginning, as Vanbrugh described it,

from the time this Building was first ordered by the Queen, And concluding upon the Whole, That I had brought the Duke of Marlb: into this Unhappy difficulty Either to leave the thing Unfinishd, And by Consequence, useless to him and his Posterity; or by finishing it, to distress his Fortune, And deprive his Grandchildren of the Provision he inclin'd to make for them.

Vanbrugh was already stung by his exclusion from the marriage negotiations, in which he had acted with genuine goodwill towards both sides. Exploding with wrath and indignation, he now declared that he would have nothing further to do with Blenheim unless Marlborough recovered so far as to shield him 'from such intolerable Treatment'.[55] Sarah never fully appreciated the impact of her personality on other people, and it was an indication of her surprise and embarrassment that she said not a word of this to her husband. It was left to him to enquire plaintively the following year why it was that he had heard nothing from his architect since his last visit to Woodstock.[56]

Meanwhile work on the building had stopped for the year, and the Duke and his wife amused themselves by riding and driving about the park in the fine autumn weather. They had the grandchildren with them, and as a treat the keepers herded all the deer together for them to see. To Sarah, always soft-hearted in such matters, 'it was a very pritty sight, but they were in stoney ground and apprehended I believe that we came to destroy them so I beged that they might be put at liberty'.[57] Then without warning on 9 November, just as she had pronounced him 'so prodigiously mended, that I am not in the least doubt of his perfect recovery', Marlborough suffered another stroke. Within ten days he was up and at least as well as before, but friends saw that Sarah was noticeably 'more staggerd & less sanguin than usual . . . upon seeing a return of that cruell disease which she hoped was mastered'.[58] In her

1. THE MARLBOROUGH FAMILY. Sarah, Countess of Marlborough, with her husband and five children (from the left: Elizabeth, Mary, Henrietta, Anne, and John), painted about 1697. Sarah's disputes with the painter perhaps account for her rather sour expression.

2. MISTRESS AND SERVANT. Anne as Princess (*left*), with her son, William, Duke of Gloucester. The damaged engraving (*right*) purports to show Anne's favourite bedchamberwoman and Sarah's self-effacing rival, Abigail Masham, of whom no fully authenticated portrait is known.

3. THE MINISTERS. John Churchill, 1st Duke of Marlborough (*left*) and Sidney, 1st Earl of Godolphin (*right*). Both portraits were painted about 1705, after the triumph of the Blenheim campaign.

4. ST JAMES'S. St James's Palace in the early eighteenth century, flanked to the west by Godolphin House (on the corner next to Green Park) and to the east by Marlborough House.

5. WHIG ASSOCIATES. Arthur Maynwaring (*left*), Whig pamphleteer, MP, and Sarah's self-appointed political mentor under Queen Anne, and their one-time ally, Sir Robert Walpole (*right*), who afterwards became prime minister and Sarah's arch-enemy.

6. SONS-IN-LAW. Charles Spencer, 3rd Earl of Sunderland (*left*), at first Sarah's favourite son-in-law, became her bitter enemy when he rose to power in his own right under George I. Francis, 2nd Earl of Godolphin (*right*), remained her long-suffering fellow trustee of the family wealth throughout her widowhood.

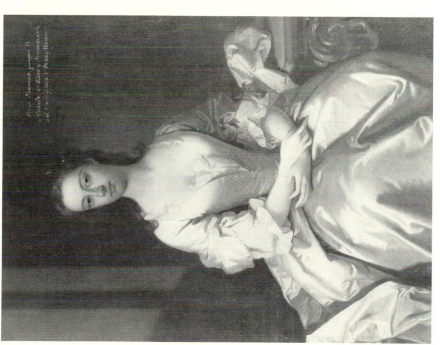

7. GRANDCHILDREN. Diana, Duchess of Bedford (*left*) and Charles Spencer, 3rd Duke of Marlborough (*right*), two of the children of Sarah's favourite daughter, Lady Sunderland. The early death of the one and the spendthrift habits of the other embittered their grandmother's last years.

A Perspective View of the Lodge & Stables in Windsor Great Park.

A North West View of Blenheim House and Park in the County of Oxford, with Woodstock in the Distance. | *Vüe Septentrionelle du Côté de l'Ouest de la Maison et du Parc de Blenheim, dans le Conté d'Oxford, ayant le Village de Woodstock à quelque Distance.*

8. HOUSES. Windsor Lodge (*top*) and Blenheim (*bottom*). The former, granted to Sarah for life by Queen Anne, became her favourite house. The latter, which she never liked, was completed by her in memory of her husband.

panic she first sent for his daughters from London, then countermanded
her orders, then repeated them.

Mary, with whom she had been on better terms since Lady
Sunderland's death, was ill herself and unable to travel, so it was a
reluctant Henrietta who came alone. Accepting the gossip that her
mother was trying to turn her father against her, she had made an
unsuccessful attempt to have a letter delivered to him secretly in advance
by one of his servants. Sarah was mortally offended with both of them:

I am sure there never was a servant in the House that was not a direct fool, but
must see, that to have saved the Duke of Marlborough's life I would have laid
down my own, [and] . . . it was barbarous usage in a daughter to do anything
that could shew any body she thought I would not deliver a letter of Hers to her
Father.

Nevertheless she staged a pantomime reconciliation with Henrietta, who
'look'd as if she would kill me'. 'I hope I shall be forgiven this piece of
dissimulation,' Sarah added,

because I really think it is the only one that ever I was Mistress of doing in my
life. Nor could I have done this upon any consideration, but the fear of making
the Duke of Marlborough uneasy at that time. When we return'd to London we
went on in the usual manner, Dogged rudeness, & I trying to hide it.[59]

The renewed quarrel also spoiled her relations with Henrietta's
daughter. Marlborough at last yielded to his wife's pleas to provide the
£20,000, and the Newcastle marriage took place at Marlborough House
on 2 April 1717. Yet in visits afterwards the new Duchess would not say
one word more than she could avoid. The further Sarah displayed her
hurt feelings, the more reserved and taciturn Harriet became, until at last
they ceased to have any contact at all. 'I believe', Sarah added, 'her
Mother contributed a great deal towards making her live with me in this
manner.'[60] Indeed, from now on the whole Godolphin clan, whom she
had always liked and respected, closed ranks against her.

Sunderland's Ministry
1717–1720

T HE threatened split in the Whig ranks quickly followed the King's return from Hanover in the winter. Townshend, dismissed as secretary of state, was soon followed into opposition by Walpole and the rest of their supporters. In April 1717 a new administration was formed under the triumvirate of Sunderland, Stanhope, and Cadogan. The effects of this schism were aggravated by the ambitions of the Prince and Princess of Wales. Sarah had been privy for some time to the discontent of the junior Court:

> The Princess had a notion that the Prince should govern & then she was sure it would be right because she would govern him . . . in order to bring about that scheme she gave King George 1st a most horrid Character, & said such things of him to me when alone as frighted me to hear, but when she saw I wou'd not enter into it, I was troubled no more with such sort of Conversations.

With the Princess's favourite, Mrs Clayton, who also sounded her out, Sarah was more plain-spoken, telling her how ill-advised it was for the Prince and Princess to risk damaging the Hanoverian interest 'by fighting against a King in Possession, & a Father'. She noted that this former friend and protégée, whom she was already beginning to see as the new Abigail Masham, quickly cooled towards her, and that the Prince and his servants in Parliament joined with the dispossessed Whigs in opposing the government on every issue, 'right or wrong'.[1]

In this first winter of his illness Marlborough was seen little outside Marlborough House. Although he was still able to judge very well of anything that was said to him, Sarah reported, in company he seldom said anything, 'which I take to proceed from Lowness of Spirits & perhaps some apprehensions of his late distemper'.[2] Neither the air of Blackheath nor the waters of Tunbridge Wells, where he spent the spring and summer of 1717, were to produce any great improvement. At the King's insistence he retained his military offices.[3] His presence was still needed to give weight to Sunderland's narrowly based ministry and forestall the incipient rivalry between Stanhope and Cadogan about the succession to his command. The day-to-day work of administering the army was to be carried out by Cadogan and the younger Craggs, as secretary at war, on his behalf.

Sarah was now her husband's chief intermediary with the outside world. She examined all his mail in advance as a matter of course, 'taking any thing out that hee would bee peevish to see', and reading the rest to him herself. Since Marlborough was seldom able to do more than sign his name, she drafted letters on his behalf, and on controversial matters (such as the Cadogan affair) was quite ready to carry on correspondence in his name without his knowledge. She also kept a sharp eye out to intercept visitors who might try to see him alone for purposes of which she disapproved. It was not impossible to elude her vigilance, as she herself admitted. Marlborough was sometimes well enough to go out without her on official business; Vanbrugh was able to make his peace in the summer on one such occasion. Servants could be bribed to deliver letters secretly or admit visitors contrary to her orders. It was some time before Sarah identified the valet who was chiefly responsible for these lapses and found a pretext to get rid of him.[4]

No doubt much of this protectiveness was necessary. She claimed that even when Marlborough appeared well, 'he had such sudden Illnesses, and took so many things, that he was not safe without some Body that was us'd to Him: Nor was He ever quite easy if I was not within Call'.[5] It was by this unremitting care that she now repaid him for his years of love and forbearance to her. Nevertheless there was an element of truth in the taunt that she exaggerated both his invalidism and her protective role because it suited her to keep control of his affairs. For the first time in her life she could feel that her elusive and devious husband had no secrets from her and no allies she did not approve of. Certainly, given her capacity for harbouring suspicions and grievances and her contempt for the arts of the 'pollitician', her mediation was to make the declining stages of his career more difficult and controversial than they would otherwise have been.

These difficulties were not long in coming. The opposition made their first serious onslaught against the ministry early in June 1717, with a parliamentary attack on Cadogan for his alleged embezzlement of transport money at the time of the Jacobite rising. The threat was beaten off, but only by the narrow margin of ten votes. Sarah had very mixed feelings. 'I am as glad as any body of the success in the hous of commons,' she told Sunderland, 'because I am satisfyd of the ill designs of the Prince & Princesse, & the difficultys it would have brought upon all that wish well to the king had they prevaild.' Yet she could not keep from hinting that Cadogan 'deserved to bee severly censured upon more accounts then one relateing to mony if it could have been don with out hurting those that mean to carry on the government honestly', and she also insisted in Marlborough's name that his friend General Lumley, who had voted with the opposition, should be spared the dismissal which the King now intended as a punishment. Sunderland grudgingly agreed to do his best for Lumley, although he pointed out that the attack on Cadogan 'was butt a leading one to others, that were settled by the new faction against the whole administration & indeed against the King himself'.[6]

In July Sarah had another brush with Cadogan over the bestowal of an ensign's commission in the Guards on a young favourite of hers, Humphrey Fish. She had taken this boy into her household as a page during the previous reign, and he had quickly proved himself 'a very valuable youth'. But no sooner was he old enough to enter the army under Marlborough's patronage than she found Cadogan repeatedly putting him aside in favour of more politically useful candidates. He did not give way until Sarah 'spoake of it with more freedome then a man in power cares to hear', and he made it clear 'at the same time that hee allowd the D: of Marl: this great feavour in his own Regiment [that] hee was inraged at me for not being put off another year or two'.[7] In fact, as the first year of Marlborough's illness went by, Sarah became convinced that Cadogan and Craggs (whom she still blamed for the anonymous letter of 1712) were systematically taking advantage of his weakened state to slight or exploit him as they chose. They wanted him to support them in the House of Lords and to act as the figurehead for military ceremonial: 'to go into Hide Parke', she noted on one occasion during this baking summer, '& to sett upon a horse long enough to have killd some in health in such hott weather'; at the same time they were using him as a screen for their own corrupt practices in the army, and letting him solicit in vain on behalf of deserving officers, 'as if hee were a Country Gentleman only & not the General'. By the autumn she was declaring that no ministry of which Cadogan was a member could last long, and threatening to call a consultation of Marlborough's friends to consider the best means for him to resign his employments without showing disrespect to the King.[8]

For the time being, however, these differences were concealed from the outside world, and some still clung to the belief that Sarah was the real power behind Sunderland's ministry. Oxford's friends, for example, were convinced that it was she who chiefly pressed on his impeachment in the summer of 1717; and they were certainly right in claiming that she was 'almost distracted' with fury when, by the connivance of the opposition, Oxford was freed without trial.[9] As for Marlborough, vindictively bent on the punishment of his old enemy, 'when he saw the House of Lords intent on discharging Lord Oxford, [he] wept like a child. His Duchess and some others were forced to take him out of the House.'[10]

But once Sarah had turned against Sunderland himself, as she did in the autumn of 1717, her real feelings about his ministry could no longer remain a secret. Sunderland was now a widower of eighteen months, and finding his situation 'very uneasy to him'. The news that greeted the Marlboroughs when they returned from Tunbridge to Windsor Lodge in September was that he planned to remarry. With his whole fortune settled on the children of previous marriages, he had been forced to choose a comparatively humble bride, and the young woman, Judith Tichborne, was described by Sarah, with some exaggeration on all counts, as a girl of 15, 'without a shilling and without a name'. She at once conjured up a scene in which, after Sunderland's death (he was only in his early forties), his heir, her grandson Lord Spencer, would have a third of his inheritance 'torn away' for a life 'as young at least as his own', and the four younger children, Anne, Charles, John, and Diana, would be beggars dependent on an impoverished elder brother or a cruel stepmother.[11]

Sarah certainly had a duty to look after the interests of her grandchildren, whose mother, as she pointed out, had been an advantageous match for Sunderland. But what made her interference quite unwarrantable was the ferocious and indiscriminate criticism of Sunderland and his intended bride that went with it. The fact that Judith Tichborne's character was unblemished did not deter her: 'God knows what she may be even as to that, when she is put upon a foot so different from any thing that she has been used to.' As for Sunderland, she had now convinced herself that he was chiefly to blame for her daughter's death: 'if she had been the wife of any man in the world but my Lord Sunderland she had been now living which had been happy for her poor children & for me.' His abrasive conduct in the previous reign, 'not only to me but to the D: of Marl: & the late Earl of Godolphin & in short his best friends' was another (and fairer) part of the indictment. Although she admitted that he had been 'honest to the Publick' until now, 'how can he continue so, when his Occasions for money are so much increased by a Wife, & another Brood of Children[?]'[12] This at least was to prove an uncannily shrewd prophecy in the light of Sunderland's conduct during the South Sea crisis.

What Sunderland himself clearly hoped for, not unreasonably, was that the Marlboroughs would provide for his younger children, and to this end he had to bear patiently with his mother-in-law. But Sarah was determined not to absolve him from his responsibilities in this way. Fond as she had become of little Diana, she even threatened to send her back to her father if he did not satisfy her demands. Sunderland offered to put £700 a year into trustees' hands for the children's maintenance. Sarah, who had suggested much more 'in order to get something', objected to the amount and the security. When he refused to give way, she could only relieve her frustration by spreading her opinion of him about publicly: 'I know hee is master of himself, but I am as free as hee is, & I can see no reason why I should take a banter for a settlement'; at least those who had thought him her political puppet would now see that she did not govern him, and that he was 'a very obstinate creature'.[13]

At this point also, the hostility between the two Courts came to an open rupture. At the christening of one of the royal children in November the Prince of Wales flew into a rage and publicly insulted the Duke of Newcastle, who had been nominated as a godparent against his will. The King at once took the opportunity to punish him for his parliamentary opposition by expelling him from St James's altogether. Despite her strained relations with the ministers, Sarah ostentatiously took the side of the Court in this quarrel. When the reclusive King, for the first time in his reign, began to hold regular drawing-room gatherings to prevent his son from stealing the limelight, she attended even when Marlborough was not well enough to go with her. The King, no doubt warned of her discontent, went out of his way to be welcoming; he 'never waited to come round the circle but when she appeard he crost derectly to her, & tho neither spoke the others Language with the help of the Lord of the bedchamber & the great earnestness & animation in the Dutchesses way of speaking, a conversation was carry[ed] on'.[14] Meanwhile the Prince and Princess set up a rival court at Leicester House, where they and their supporters, as Sarah noted, 'us'd all their skill to ridicule the King & give him a very bad Character, [and] on the other side the King's ministers described the Prince in a true light, so that between both sides the generality of the World were pretty well inform'd, of what they were to expect'.[15]

In the spring of 1718 Sunderland took over the treasury from Stanhope, who retired to the more congenial post of secretary of state for the north, with Craggs junior as his colleague for the south. Sarah was now at odds, more or less, with every member of the government. Her quarrel with Cadogan was out in the open. When he persistently refused to co-operate with her in transferring the disputed funds back to England, she lost patience and threatened him with legal proceedings. He in turn declared that the real reason for his refusal to hand over the money was that he knew she was trying to get it for herself.[16] Admittedly she had had nothing in particular until now against Stanhope. Indeed, when soliciting her salary as ranger of Windsor Park from him before he left the treasury, she went out of her way to tell his wife that 'without the support of his reputation in the world our present ministry would make but a melancholly figure'.[17] But her repeated inability to get her business at Windsor settled had become such a grievance that she even talked of selling her favourite Lodge, because 'it is never like I find to give me anything but trouble',[18] and when Stanhope left the treasury without satisfying her, she began to turn against him also. Even when Sunderland at last persuaded the King to reinstate the salary in the summer of 1718, she continued to take every occasion of complaining about the ministers and their lack of consideration for past services. 'Lord Marlborough lingers out,' Craggs junior commented at this time; 'he has a lady who exposes and uses his name very frequently. I love him well enough to wish it were over; he is a melancholy memento.' There is no doubt that he was speaking for all his colleagues.[19]

The Marlboroughs went early to Tunbridge Wells in 1718, so that the Duke could have the benefit of a whole season of taking the waters. But he was no sooner there than he suffered another serious relapse. Although he recovered sufficiently to be moved back to London in May, he was for some weeks assumed to be dying. 'There was no body beleiv'd he could get through it,' Sarah wrote, '& I was my self so fearfull that he wou'd not, that I cou'd not speak for weeping.' Yet he recovered again, so as to be at least no worse than before, and at the end of May they retired to the peace of Windsor Lodge. There he walked, took the air in his coach, and played at ninepins. 'Your father is with constant watching & Care generally pretty easy to himself,' Sarah reported to the Duchess of Montagu, 'but I fear there is very little hope that he will ever be as he has been.'[20] Yet for all her battles and anxieties, her own energy continued unabated. Every evening she played romping games and danced impromptu country dances with the grandchildren, the servants, and whatever company was to hand, explaining to wondering spectators that the exercise was good for her and gave her 'longer breath'. 'The Lord have mercy upon us now,' Henrietta sighed when she heard this.[21]

It was now a matter of urgency to get Blenheim finished so that the Duke could see it before he died. There was no question of Vanbrugh's reinstatement; Marlborough no longer had the strength or the will to protect him from Sarah. At Woodstock she and James Moore were now in complete charge, and the injustice with which the architect was undoubtedly treated should not be allowed to obscure their achievement.

In two summers the great house, which had been a shell in 1716, was ready to live in. Even Vanbrugh was unwillingly impressed, though in his eyes the finishing was 'in no good or gracefull manner'.[22] Sarah, with an invalid husband and a large family of grandchildren to provide for, had, as she admitted, been more concerned with convenience than with splendour or architectural principles:

I have only taken away passages to make conveniences, of which there is yet enough to content any Etalian builder, but Sir John's Inclenation was to have the whole principle floor with vast great rooms & walks all around them like a church, which made it quite impossible to live in the hous, unless one could have liked to have made such an expense for the sake of showing the place to strangers, & to have lived ones self in the cellar, or to have gon up as many steps to bed, as roomes of 22 foot high, at least require.[23]

Since it was too late in the year to move in, they contented themselves with a brief stay at High Lodge in September to view the progress. They had a lean time of it—Sarah complained of the self-indulgent Oxford clergy for engrossing all the local provisions—but she found everything that she expected had been performed: 'Mr Moore is a meracle of a man.'[24]

Back at Windsor Lodge at the end of September, Sarah was alarmed by the news that the Duchess of Newcastle was dying at Claremont. Finding herself more concerned than she expected to be, she ignored strong hints that her presence was not wanted, got into her carriage, and was at Claremont in less than two hours. There she had her low opinion of the medical profession confirmed, for the Duchess, a lifelong hypochondriac, was plainly in no danger. Even so, she found herself excluded from the sickroom, where her enemy Dr Mead was in charge. After sitting for some time with the embarrassed Duke of Newcastle in an antechamber, she had no choice but to take her leave, concealing her dudgeon as best she could. 'I am sure you have often heard of my Passions and Resentments,' she wrote to a friend, 'but I fancy you will think that I governed them upon this Occasion, if I have such Things, as well as wise People doe.'[25]

It was a time of illnesses and deathbeds. In London the following January, it was the turn of Sir Samuel Garth. Although Sarah had little more faith in him than in the rest of his profession—'his manner of treating even himself is odd'—she had always loved him for his wit, his humanity, and his beneficent good nature. She helped to nurse him herself, and was at his bedside when he died.[26] At the end of the month Lady Bridgwater's only son, Lord Brackley, fell victim at Eton to the same disease which had killed his mother. Convinced that she could have saved him if she had been given the chance, Sarah made Sunderland promise that when his two schoolboy sons came to pass through the same ordeal, she would be allowed complete control of their treatment. Sunderland, afraid of the infection for his young wife, agreed with what Sarah thought to be callous readiness. When the elder boy, Charles, developed the symptoms in May 1719, she rushed with relays of chairmen to his school in Hampstead and carried him to Marlborough House, where she nursed him 'with as true an affection, as if he had been my only son'. It took a serious illness to arouse such feeling towards Charles. Even when he was a child she noticed a reserve and an obstinacy in his temperament, and a strong physical resemblance to his father, which did not bode well for her future relations with him. His younger brother Johnny, with his open impulsive nature and his likeness to his mother, was much more appealing to her.[27]

But it was the Godolphin and Sunderland heirs, Lord Rialton ('Willigo') and Robert, Lord Spencer, who were her chief favourites, even though her bad relations with their parents kept them at a distance and the former was giving cause for concern on other counts. He had been educated entirely at home by a tutor, Nicholas Mann, whose chief claim to the post was that he had once been a companion of the first Marquess of Blandford at Cambridge. Too late, everyone realized that the absence of other influences was turning a boy of charm and promise, the heir of two great families, into a weak and aimless young man with no sense of his position or responsibilities. Failing to persuade him to settle down and marry, his father decided to send him abroad under the supervision of Lord Spencer's governor.[28] Early in June Sarah was reduced to floods of tears when he came to Windsor Lodge to take his leave: 'I felt so much at parting & after he was gon, more then ever I ded upon any such occation.' She packed a box of her most tried and trusted medicines for him to take with him, and secretly remitted money to him when he overran his allowance and did not dare to apply to his parents. For a time at least, his letters, in an ominously weak and childish hand for a young man of twenty, kept her in touch with his doings.[29] Soon she had persuaded Marlborough to add a codicil to his will, making Rialton (and after him Spencer) financially independent from the time of his death.[30] She was never without some means of detaching the grand-children from their parents and bringing them under her own control.

Examples of Sarah's quarrelsomeness are legion; her life was littered with discarded intimacies. Yet it is fair to note that she was almost equally ready to convert old enmities into new friendships as her political allegiances shifted. Although she continued to pay her duty to the Hanoverians, her age as well as her hostility to the ministers meant that she was now more at home with members of the 'old Court', including some who had formerly been her greatest foes. Her main winter recreation was to play at ombre, at which her constant companions were the old Duke of Buckingham, Lady Burlington, and Lady Orkney.[31] Lady Burlington was smooth-tongued, tactful, and (despite a coolness at the end of Anne's reign) impossible even for Sarah to quarrel with for long. Lady Orkney, the former Betty Villiers and titular mistress of William III, was a more surprising companion; but Sarah now found that 'notwithstanding her first step into the world, [she] has a good understanding, & has breed up her children very well'.[32] There was also the Earl of Nottingham, who had won her over so completely by his opposition to the treaty of Utrecht and by his stately cordiality since that she obliterated as many of her earlier criticisms of him as she could find in her narratives of Queen Anne's reign. His son Lord Finch, also a great favourite, reported to him that 'she does not think there are in this whole poor Island two so honest men as your Lordship & I'.[33]

At Blackheath Sarah had made the acquaintance of Lady Cairnes and her Huguenot relation Marie La Vie, which soon ripened into a close friendship with their whole cosmopolitan circle. She would invite them to dine at Marlborough House in company with the witty Lady Mary Wortley Montagu, newly returned from her husband's embassy at Constantinople, and Lady Darlington (Madame Kielmansegg, raised to the British peerage). The latter, Lady Mary wrote, 'had a greater vivacity in conversation than ever I knew in a German of either sex. She loved reading, and had a taste of all polite learning.'[34] Another friend of the same kind was Sarah's neighbour at Windsor, a former maid of honour to Queen Anne who had remained unmarried, Jane Kingdom. Sarah's attitude to such women, far more widely read and disciplined of mind than herself, was always ambivalent. Their conversation, even while it fascinated her, could easily make her feel gauche and inferior, particularly when she was outnumbered by them. Whenever this happened she took refuge in a bitter, self-depreciating philistinism ('I am no scholar nor a wit, I thank God'), which did less than justice to her genuine hunger for self-improvement. When she invited Lady Darlington, Miss La Vie, and Lady Mary to Marlborough House 'to be in the clouds together', Lady Cairnes, lively but unintellectual, was always asked as well, 'to talk common sense with her'.[35] Much more restful were the kind of friends once described by Swift as 'middling folks, whom one may govern as one pleases, and who will think it an honor and happiness to attend us, to talk and be silent, to laugh or look grave just as they are directed'. The Jennenses were of this kind, as was Dean Barzillai Jones, an Irish clergyman who acted as Marlborough's domestic chaplain and constant whist partner while they were in the country. With his inexhaustible fund of anecdotes, he was one of the few people who could rouse the silent Duke from his chronic depression.

Now, in the summer of 1719, Blenheim was waiting to receive them, and it was only Marlborough's precarious state of health that held them back. Sarah suspected that the real reason for the caution of the medical men was her insistence on having one of them in attendance at Woodstock—'I can't sleep fifty mile from London, if one of the best surgeons does not lye in the hous'—and 'therefore they will defer our going as long as they can to attend to their other business'.[36] It was not until 10 August that Marlborough was permitted to set out. 'His head is always clear,' Sarah reported to Stair in Paris, 'and sometimes I flatter myself that he may quite recover; but my fears of him are more and greater than my hopes.'[37] Their chief guests at this historic house-warming were Bishop Hoadly and his friend Dr Samuel Clarke, their parish priest at St James's. Richard Steele, hoping to make himself Marlborough's official biographer, was invited as well, and there was a large gathering of young people. The Jennenses brought their adolescent son. Mary Cairnes was a constant companion of the young Spencers. Lady Anne Spencer, whose marriage Sarah now had in hand, came to join her younger sister, along with Lady Charlotte Maccarty, daughter of Sunderland's unhappy and long-dead sister, Lady Clancarty. The Sunderlands had always refused to take 'giddy-headed Lady Charlotte' into their house,[38] leaving Sarah to befriend her and her turbulent brother, Lord Muskerry. Her kindness to these dispossessed young people was in the long term to prove more rewarding than all her services to her own family.

As a celebration the young people got up a performance of Dryden's tragedy of Anthony and Cleopatra, *All for Love, or The World well Lost*, staged in what the disgraced Vanbrugh had long ago described as Sarah's 'favourite bow-window-room'. The leading role was taken by Humphrey Fish, now a captain in the army, but still an invaluable member of the household. Lady Charlotte played Cleopatra. Decked out in the family jewels and the velvets and brocades which were waiting to be made into window-curtains, the players put on two glittering performances. Hoadly composed a prologue in honour of the occasion, while Sarah, noticing that Fish and Lady Charlotte were growing too ardent ('I doubt Fish is flesh,' Steele whispered to Hoadly during one scene), went through the play and 'scratched out some of the most amorous speeches'. Marlborough was delighted, and in the pleasure of at last inhabiting Blenheim, passed the whole summer without a relapse.[39]

Since Sarah was now too old to take riding exercise, the Earl of

Nottingham introduced her to a new kind of horsedrawn 'chair', and she had one made just large enough to seat Marlborough and herself, so that they could drive easily about the park. The sight of the young people 'distracted with pleasures', neglecting their studies to ride about and play from morning till night, delighted her.[40] She was always happiest with the young, on whom she could lavish her capricious affection, controlling and indulging them at will. When Charles Evelyn, Mrs Boscawen's young grandson, paid her a visit that winter at Marlborough House, she 'held him in her arms and said that if she had such a boy he should never goe to school but run about, read plays and do whatever he had a mind to'. Yet it was noticed that when she held a masquerade that same winter to celebrate Lady Anne Egerton's birthday, and invited forty young people, the Duchess of Montagu's two daughters, Lady Mary and Lady Isabella, were conspicuous by their absence.[41] By this time Henrietta had completely hardened her heart against her mother, and Mary had taken her sister's part.

In order to avoid seeing Sarah alone, they would come to Marlborough House only at the hours of company; and what outraged her most was that they made no attempt to conceal the quarrel, going up to their father 'without taking any notice of me, as if they had a pleasure in shewing everybody that they insulted me'. 'I am sure I have lost some hundreds at deep play', she added, 'by not knowing one card from another as soon as they made their entry into my room, because from the minute I see them I know what they will do, let who will bee by to observe what I would willingly hide.' Years later Mary Cairnes confirmed the truth of this: 'I have seen such behaviour from them to her that young as I was it has shock'd me. . . . The Dutchess us'd to say she had made them all such fine ladies that it had turned their heads.' There was real pathos in her situation at this time, much though she had brought it on herself. She still loved her daughters, 'notwithstanding their terrible usage . . . enough to have dyed to have saved their lives & to have made them hapy', and 'a thousand times upon such occasions when my heart has been ready to break, and the company all gone, I have gone up to the poor Duke of Marlborough with a chearfull face, hoping he might not observe always such cruelties, and talk'd of other things as if I felt nothing'.[42] His health was still a constant source of anxiety to her. During this winter he would sometimes seem to be much improved, able to do the honours at his granddaughter's masquerade and talk freely to those he was at ease with. At others, visitors would find him huddled 'in a dark corner of the roome by the Chimney', not 'speaking a word or taking any notice of what was doing'.[43]

By this time, largely owing to her care of the Spencer children, Sarah's relations with Sunderland had somewhat improved. Now her marriage plans for his elder daughter rekindled their antagonism once more and ushered in the last phase of their relations. After some difficulty in finding a suitable match, Sarah, with the guidance of the elder Craggs, pitched upon William Bateman, the wealthy son of a director of the South Sea Company. Financially the match was an impressive one and yet another example of Sarah's acumen; 'she is a notable Grandmother,' one of the Harleys commented admiringly when it became public knowledge. Although the patrician Sunderland was by no means happy about Bateman (of whom the King was to remark that he could make him a peer but not a gentleman), he acquiesced, glad to have his plain-faced daughter disposed of and evidently assuming that Marlborough would provide the whole marriage portion of £10,000, just as he had provided the Duchess of Newcastle's.[44] But Sarah was again bent on seeing that Sunderland did not evade his responsibilities to his children. The most she would do was persuade Marlborough to give Lady Anne her legacy of £5,000 in advance as a contribution to her dowry. She then set about forcing the reluctant Sunderland to provide the balance by selling the South Sea stock in which her daughter's marriage portion had been invested. Parting with South Sea stock at this time was the last thing Sunderland wanted to do. While Sarah fumed and hectored, his trustees held out, delaying the marriage settlement until well into the spring of 1720. 'At last,' she noted, 'as Craggs and he knew when the Stock would sell best, it was sold for more than it was bought at'; for by this time the South Sea boom was well into its stride.[45]

The South Sea Company had its origins in Oxford's attempt in 1711 to find an alternative to the Whig-dominated Bank of England for government borrowing. Because of this, Sarah, for all her 'great trading in stocks and companies', at first refused to have any truck with it. But after 1714 the Company was publicly converted to the Hanoverian interest, and by 1717 she had over £30,000 of her own fortune invested in it.[46] Then in the winter of 1719–20, the Company put forward a scheme to take over much of the burden of the National Debt, by encouraging the government's long-term creditors to exchange their securities for South Sea stock. It was a project which depended for its success on the stock's being promoted to an artificial height. 'Old Craggs', as Sarah noted, 'was the chief Manager of that Project, for he govern'd the Earl of Sunderland entirely who had the Cheif power with George I.'[47] Several members of the government, including Sunderland, were bribed with free grants of rapidly appreciating new stock to secure their compliance in the dubious methods by which the scheme was promoted.[48] For a time, until the late summer of 1720, the directors of the Company had all the success they could wish. The market soared and there was a public rush to subscribe.

The Marlboroughs took no part in this mad scramble for instant paper fortunes. The rival directors of the Bank, Nathaniel Gould (Lady Cairnes's brother) and Sir Gilbert Heathcote, were their personal friends. In any case Sarah herself had enough insight to realize at an early stage that the boom could not be sustained, and that the real purpose of the scheme was to 'put power into such hands, that no body doubts considers their private interest more then paying debts or publick good'.[49] In late May and early June, shortly before the stock reached its peak, she sold all her existing holdings, and persuaded Marlborough to do the same, making them a profit of £100,000.[50] She then resisted all invitations to buy new stock, or to subscribe any of their government securities into the Company: 'I am certain such an estate as the Duke of Marl: & I have upon those funds cannot be sold for ready mony, & if one should take securitys upon bargains made, if any shock should come to that stock how will such securitys be made good where so many people are deept in it[?]'[51] It was yet another instance, she could claim with justice afterwards, of the benefit which had accrued to her family by her management. Yet her refusal to let their wealth be used to promote the scheme made enemies of several who until now had been her most confidential friends and advisers, including Robert Jennens and Craggs himself. When the latter tried to get access to Marlborough privately to coax him to reinvest, she intercepted the messenger, persuaded her husband not to agree, and took the further precaution of asking the trustees who managed his money to do nothing without consulting her first. The baulked Craggs could only revenge himself by declaring that Marlborough would have been well long ago if it had not suited Sarah better to have him an invalid in order to keep control of his affairs.[52]

She was certainly not alone in realizing the riskiness and essential crookery of the scheme. A friend whom she tried to dissuade from investing while the stock was still rising agreed that it would bring ruin to the country in the end, 'but every body now agrees . . . that it will rise still a great deall higher, & tho nobody liks the thing yet [they] are willing to get by it since estates are got by it'.[53] The advantage which the Marlboroughs, who were now worth well over a million pounds between them, had over most of their contemporaries was simply that they could afford to stand aloof and indulge themselves in the luxury of not helping the ministry's henchmen. 'I do not think it is so much the D: of Marl's businesse to stock job or to assist these governors, as it is to keep his principle safe with what ever interest is to be had in the plain common way,' Sarah could declare loftily; '. . . I had reather chuse to keep what we have as long as wee can without assisting them in the least thing tho one could have an advantage by it, which is insignificant to the D: of Marl:.'[54]

These opinions did not keep her from lending money, mostly on good land security, to other speculators (the princely Duke of Chandos among them), or from badgering Sunderland for subscriptions in Marlborough's name for needy friends and relations. But in making her ungracious demands for 'this thing which is called a favour', she continued to harp on the change in Sunderland's attitude to her.[55] The fact was that both the Marlboroughs were now thoroughly disaffected from their son-in-law's administration. In the spring of 1720 Walpole and Townshend had used their parliamentary strength to force their way back into the ministry. 'The King's Ministers were tir'd out with the trouble & opposition the Princes Governors gave them, [and] they [Walpole and his supporters] were tired too of fighting so many Battles, & having no Employments except those that had inconsiderable salarys from being the Princes servants,' as Sarah put it with cynical accuracy, '. . . upon which a treaty was proposed to reconcile the two Courts.' Soon they all met at Court, '& before every body hug'd and Kiss'd one another, who just before had in all Conversations made it their business to ridicule one another, & likewise the whole Royal family'.[56]

Sunderland no longer had so great a need of his father-in-law's presence, particularly as it meant continued dealings with Sarah. Yet when rumours began to circulate that he was planning to divide Marlborough's posts between Cadogan and Stanhope, the Duke himself was by no means as ready as before to give them up.[57] At this time the real improvement in his condition which Sarah had looked for so long was unmistakable. The ministers heard that when he and Sarah visited the Prince of Wales at Richmond in July, the Duke, formerly so silent in public, had 'expressed himself with bitterness, saying that, although he did not expect to recover his health and strength to the degree he formerly enjoyed it, he found himself well enough to make those people's heart ache who had been waiting for his spoils'. He declared himself ashamed to be one of the Lords Justices during the King's absence in Hanover when the Prince was excluded, and said that he would go to no more of their meetings. Reporting all this to Stanhope, Craggs junior still saw Sarah's influence at work: 'you'l understand this matter better, when you reflect on the abusive language which my lady duchess bestows every day most plentifully upon us.'[58]

Sarah was at first charmed by their reception at Richmond: 'the princess was so very kind to the Duke of Marlborough and to poor me, and had so many agreeable ways of expressing it, that I really love her . . .

I am sure if others are treated as we were, they will never want a full court of the best sort of people that this country affords.'[59] Yet as far as she was concerned, any inclination to transfer their allegiance to the heir to the throne was quickly nipped in the bud when she learnt that the Princess had been spreading gossip about her quarrels with her daughters: 'I am so true a Britain [sic] that I have a mind never to goe more to that great lady, & to give the reason for it,' she told Mrs Boscawen, 'for tho I must own to a friend like you that I have great reason to bee desatisfyd with my childrens behaviour to my self, yet I still remember that they are my children.'[60]

By this time they had retired again to Blenheim for the summer, where Sarah was delighted at the continued improvement in Marlborough's health. She was now able to flatter herself that he would soon be as well as any man of his age could expect to be, and she could feel with justice that this owed much to her careful nursing: 'I am sure if he had been left to doctors & to the care of servants hee had been gon long agoe, but I have the satisfaction of knowing that never any king was so watchd and attended, which has preserved his life.'[61] Their complement of guests this time included the opposition MP, Grey Neville, whose singing delighted her. Young Lord Carnarvon, heir to the Duke of Chandos and the splendours of Cannons, also came over from Oxford to be scrutinized as a possible match for Lady Anne Egerton, and in his honour Sarah got up 'a sort of ball with a scraping fiddle', which kept him late into the evening.[62]

Marlborough was so content at Blenheim that they delayed their usual autumn journey to Windsor Lodge until mid-October. By this time, as Sarah had foreseen, the South Sea Bubble had burst and the government was facing a major crisis. She was sorry for the innocent victims of the crash, but 'I don't pitty those that have lost only imaginary gains which they could not enjoy without the ruin of others'.[63] Her main wish now was to see Craggs and the directors of the Company punished, and back in London she lost no time in canvassing all the MPs of her acquaintance, arguing that 'there was no way of recovering the Credit of the Nation, but for the Parliament to do as much Justice as they could'.[64] It was Grey Neville who now led the demands for an enquiry into the ministers' involvement in the affair. Not content with this, Sarah took it upon herself early in December to have a long talk with Cadogan's *aide-de-camp*, 'endeavouring to persuade him that it was most for his [Cadogan's] Interest to join with the Duke of Marlborough who was of my mind in all that Proceeding'. Given the state of her relations with Cadogan and the ministers' resentment at her use of her husband's name, this was incredibly ill-advised. Cadogan went straight to Sunderland and Stanhope and told them of the extent of her canvassing.[65]

During the previous four years Sunderland had endured much at the hands of his mother-in-law. Now in a state of extreme tension at the impending parliamentary enquiry, he came to the end of his forbearance with her. Summoning Marlborough alone to his house in Piccadilly, he threatened retaliation if the Duke would not keep her under control. Among other things, he hinted at dubious financial transactions in the name of Sir Henry Furnese, who had conducted many of Sarah's investments in the later years of Queen Anne's reign, and accused her of sending money to assist the last unsuccessful invasion project of the Pretender; 'and at that part of the discourse He held up his hand in a great fury, and added that the King could prove it'. Sarah had heard something of this story before, but in relation to Marlborough rather than herself: 'it was certainly whisper'd about with a design only to make people easy when they resolv'd to satisfy my Lord Stanhope in putting out the Duke of Marlborough to make him General.'[66] The accusation as far as she was concerned was laughable (although a Jacobite agent, typically hopeful and ill-informed, had reported after a rumour of Marlborough's death in 1716, 'I would not despair of the Duchess who is worth £500,000 at least'[67]). But for Marlborough it came uncomfortably close to the truth. It seems likely, in fact, that Sunderland, who was now courting the Jacobites for precautionary reasons, did have information from this source about his father-in-law's remittances to the Pretender in 1715. The Duke came home 'half dead' with alarm and shock, and told Sarah what had passed.

A cold-shouldering at two successive drawing-rooms convinced her that Sunderland's talk of the King's displeasure had not been idle, and her letters of self-justification brought only haughty and non-committal replies, in what she knew to be 'my Lord Sunderland's stile'. While the town buzzed with the story, Sarah relieved her indignation by showing the correspondence about in all company. It was little consolation to her that Sunderland's ministry barely survived the winter. To her disgust Walpole was able to save him from the wrath of Parliament, though at the price of his resignation from the treasury. Both the elder Craggs and Stanhope succumbed in different ways to the stress of the parliamentary battles, the former by an overdose of laudanum, the latter by a stroke. It was only the accident of Stanhope's death on 5 February 1721 that forestalled Marlborough's dismissal, and prevented the complete severing of their connection with the Court. As for Sarah, 'from that hour she detested courts & courtiers. She said the King had done too much if she was innocent & too little if she was guilty, but she defy'd him.'[68]

Defying the Court
1721–1722

IT was all very well for Sarah to set the Court at defiance, but the rupture could not have been worse timed with regard to the other matter which demanded her attention at this time: the impending legal proceedings over the debt incurred at Blenheim before the Queen stopped the works there in 1712. Although the government had theoretically accepted responsibility for this in 1715, only about a third of the money had ever been paid.[1] Having applied first to the treasury and then to Marlborough himself in vain for the remainder, the Strongs, the master masons who were the most substantial of the contractors concerned, had begun proceedings against the Duke personally in the Court of Exchequer in 1718. At the time Sarah had paid little attention, thinking that 'nothing was so improbable as for such a design to succeed after so many publick acts of the queens in this building & so many Acts of Parliament'.[2] When Sunderland, at the height of the South Sea boom, had issued a further instalment of the debt, with the promise of more to come, she refused to take advantage of this to postpone the trial.[3] Even as the hearing approached, she was far more concerned at the outcome of the South Sea investigations, telling their counsel Sir Thomas Pengelly, who was also a member of the parliamentary committee of enquiry, 'I think I could submit to the losing our Cause if your endeavours could put this miserable Countrey upon a better foot'.[4]

Meanwhile their chief opponent had emerged not as the Strongs, but as their fellow defendant, Vanbrugh. The cause turned on the interpretation of Godolphin's warrant to the architect in 1705, which had authorized him in Marlborough's name to make contracts with the workmen. Although the document contained no mention of the Queen's intention to pay for Blenheim, Marlborough argued that Godolphin had issued it not as his agent, but on the Queen's behalf in his capacity as Lord Treasurer. If this disclaimer were accepted, Vanbrugh lay open to legal action from all the Blenheim creditors for making contracts in the Duke's name without sufficient authority. Already embittered by his quarrel with Sarah, he was alarmed and indignant at thus being 'thrown among the workmen, to be torn to peices', and exerted himself to the utmost on the Strongs' behalf. And in his depositions on their side he took particular care to bring Sarah's conduct into the evidence, claiming that in her instructions to the workmen in 1710 she had implicitly accepted liability for any debt which the crown would not pay.[5]

It was this evidence of Vanbrugh's which made Sarah decide, on the eve of the hearing, to take the conduct of the case into her own hands. In fact, in her instructions to counsel she was far more concerned to justify her dealings with the architect than with the main point at issue, and she wanted them to present the whole case accordingly, 'for one is tired to tell ones own storey'.[6] Her disputes with the lawyers on this subject cannot have helped the conduct of the case. After a three-day hearing in the Court of Exchequer in February 1721, the judges decreed that Marlborough was bound personally by Godolphin's warrant (which predated any public act of the Queen or Parliament concerning Blenheim) and must pay what remained of the Strongs' debt.[7] Whether this legalistic view would have prevailed if Marlborough had possessed the influence he once had, and if his wife had not just had a public quarrel with the Court, is another matter.

Sarah was very much discomfited that they had to defend themselves by disclaiming Godolphin's warrant, and assured his son that she would rather pay every penny of the debt than cast a slur on his memory: 'I need not tell you to what degree I valued him when living, nor how I allmost worship his memory since his death.'[8] But the likeliest explanation to her mind was that both the warrant and the decree had been obtained by the trickery and corruption of her two current scapegoats, Vanbrugh and 'Old Craggs'. On 20 March, therefore, she lodged an appeal with the House of Lords, ignoring the warning of her friend Lord Carlisle that the Lords would be unlikely to overrule the judges on a point of law concerning Marlborough's liability for the debt, even though 'in strickness & according to the promise of the Crown he ought not to pay it'. His advice was to accept the judgement and petition the treasury to recover the money afterwards, but what he was really trying to make clear to her as tactfully as he could was that, having alienated Sunderland and separated herself from her family interest in the government, she could not expect any favour from the Lords.[9]

But for Sarah an appeal to the treasury was now out of the question, since it meant 'soliciting & beging' from her bitterest enemies.[10] With the Lords' hearing provisionally fixed for the end of April, she began to circulate a long manuscript statement of the case as she saw it to all the peers who could be expected to attend. Realizing that political considerations were bound to influence the vote, she pinned her greatest hopes on those who seemed likeliest to oppose the Court on principle, whatever the issue. The two former Lord Chancellors, the Tory Harcourt and the opposition Whig Cowper, responded with disconcerting coolness, but from the Jacobite Tories, including their leader Bishop Atterbury, she was pleased to find that she had 'more civill returns after they had the case then I expected'.[11] And to her delight the Earl of Nottingham, whose particular brand of cranky integrity and old-fashioned rhetoric could still command respect, told one of the Exchequer judges that he wondered how they could make such a decree contrary to law and common sense, and promised her that he would speak in Marlborough's favour in the Lords until something was said that he could not answer.[12]

By the end of April, with the hearing now put forward to May, Sarah had some reason to feel encouraged by the results of her canvassing. The contractors, Vanbrugh noted, were correspondingly low-spirited, 'from the fear they are under, that She and her Family, will at least be Able to keep a great many Lords away, who wou'd not Vote for her if they were in the House'.[13] But Sarah knew very well that she was by no means sure even of the neutrality of her family. Newcastle was a particular friend of Vanbrugh and Godolphin was his relation by marriage, and both were supporters of the government. And the all-important influence would of course be that of Sunderland. Although he had surrendered the treasury to Walpole, he was still first minister in the King's estimation and dominated the House of Lords. It was quite impossible for Sarah to approach him personally after what had passed. For this she had to rely on Godolphin, a man of scrupulous personal integrity, whose main desire was for a quiet life. Because the case turned on the validity of his father's warrant, she was prepared to excuse him from voting himself, but she appealed to him at least to 'help to influence some about the Court from acting either openly or privately against the D: of M: in this affair, which if they do not, I have a great deal of reason from the civil returns I have had from many lords to whom I have sent the case, to promise myself success'.[14] But Godolphin was an unlikely person to overbear the implacable Sunderland, and even without the quarrel the ministers now had infinitely more pressing claims to deal with than the Blenheim debt. By the beginning of May Sarah's earlier optimism began to evaporate:

I have too much reason to apprehend that my Ld Harcourt will make use of all His Art to confirm this unjust decree, & that my Ld Sunderland has acted Under hand as Vile a part to the Duke of Marlborough as ever he did to me, and my Lord Townshend is Certainly influenced by Sir John, so that we are to expect all the mischief that can proceed from such men as are interested and low enough to give themselves up to the Court.[15]

Her greatest hope of overturning the exchequer decree had always lain in an appeal to the spirit rather than the letter of the documents on which the case turned; whatever the wording of the warrant, it had clearly never been the intention of the Queen or Godolphin to make Marlborough pay for Blenheim. Instead Sarah again chose to confuse the issue by using her canvassing to continue her vendetta against Vanbrugh. Unhampered by the professional judgement of the lawyers, the author of her case (who was probably Bishop Hoadly) gave in fully to her insistence that the architect be presented as the true villain of the piece.[16] Since Vanbrugh had been theatrical entrepreneur, dining companion, and architectural consultant to the Whig aristocracy for more than twenty years, this could only add to the number of her enemies. In defiance of the standing rule of the House he rushed his reply into print on the eve of the hearing, and despite the clear signs of its hasty composition, *Sir John Vanbrugh's Justification of what he depos'd in the Dutchess of Marlborough's late Tryal* showed how unwise Sarah had been to choose her scapegoat from among the foremost wits of the age. Of the case itself he remarked, 'I . . . find so much honest Language in it, fair stating of Facts, and right sound Reasoning from them, that one would almost swear it had been writ by a Woman.' He also strongly hinted that the Marlboroughs were lying when they denied all knowledge of the methods used to fund the building:

Will any one believe, that in so many quiet, fire side, evening Conferences, as happen'd between those two great Lords and her Grace; the manner and method of receiving in, and laying out, those Hundreds of Thousands of Pounds, should never be part of the Amusement? Sure there's some great forgetfullness in this matter.

He conceded that the Queen and Godolphin had never intended to make Marlborough responsible for paying for Blenheim; but the debt which was in dispute, he pointed out, had come about because the Marlboroughs had knowingly pressed ahead with the building faster than money was issued from the treasury to pay for it.[17]

Shortly before the appeal was due to be heard on 8 May, Sarah's troubles were increased by an acute attack of stone in the kidneys, which confined her to bed for several days. With the help of laudanum she managed to attend the hearing, 'to be within call, in case any accident happen'd, That the Duke of Marlborough shou'd not be well', but she came home in a state of collapse, and for several hours afterwards was in pain as severe as any she remembered in childbirth. Friends noticed how shaken she was by the illness, and Marlborough, who had become totally dependent on her, was devastated. This was an appeal to which she always rallied; weary as she was of her 'wretched life', she told one of her friends, 'as long as I can contribute to make the poor Duke of Marlborough easy, I would live upon any conditions'.[18]

At this hearing the proceedings had been postponed on a legal technicality, evidently arranged between Harcourt and Cowper in order to give the Marlboroughs a chance to save face by dropping the case. But Sarah was determined to see it through to the end.[19] After much consideration she decided that it would not be wise to let Marlborough testify personally in the House that he had never been consulted about Vanbrugh's warrant: 'tho tis certain hee can speak very well & easyly some times, hee is often too much Effected upon any thing that gives him trouble, or pleasure, & when hee is so it is very melancholly to see.'[20] The death of one of Nottingham's daughters on 23 May, the first day of the full hearing, meant that he could not attend, so that in the end the only speaker on Marlborough's side was Lord Peterborough, his eccentric and superannuated former military rival, whose support Sarah had not sought and which she would gladly have done without. The vote against them, forty-three to twenty-five, made it clear how far she had isolated herself and her husband by her quarrels with their family and the Court. 'Almost all the Lords of weight', including most of the leading office-holders, were on the other side, and the abstentions included three out of the four Marlborough sons-in-law.[21] Refusing to acknowledge Godolphin's genuine scruples, Sarah blamed Walpole for his lack of support.[22] But the decisive influence was undoubtedly that of Sunderland. At this juncture he was capable not just of mustering the Court against them, but of dispersing most of the other opposition support for which Sarah had hoped. The hearing coincided with the negotiations by which he temporarily secured the parliamentary co-operation of the Tories and Jacobites, and Harcourt and Cowper, whom she had found so unaccountably cold, were also being spoken of as candidates for ministerial appointment in a new mixed administration that was rumoured to follow the South Sea crisis.[23] Atterbury attended the first day of the hearing but not the second, and few of the others who had initially raised her hopes in the end supported her. 'To please his new Friends,' Sarah noted,

and to save Mony for the Crown, which had been given to pay the Debts, [Lord Sunderland] acted against the Duke of Marlborough with all the Violence of his Temper, with great Art got several People, that I had inform'd well of the Matter, to vote in this scandalous Case. Which was, to say that Lord Treasurer Godolphin acted for the Duke of Marlborough, and not for the Crown. . . . I was in the House when the Cause was heard and my Lord Sunderland would not vote for the Duke of Marlborough; but stood sometimes under the Throne and at others behind the Canopy, Coming out to People, and talking in a mad and silly Way, that he wish'd he had been at Liberty to vote against Him.[24]

The Blenheim appeal case was a sorry end to Marlborough's public life, marking the final point in the decline of his reputation and influence in the Hanoverian era. In the long view he was paying the price for his own attitude to Blenheim, which Sarah had once rightly described as both his passion and his greatest weakness. The Lords might well feel that enough unregulated public money had been poured into this bottomless pit. In the shorter term, however, both the political crisis of 1720 and his wife's readiness to make powerful enemies were undoubtedly much to blame. Sarah would never learn that she would always find herself at a disadvantage in quarrelling with the Court. 'As fond as I was once of England,' she commented bitterly, 'I begin to wish my self now at Antwerp or in Greenland.'[25]

Instead they made the best of their retreat to Windsor Lodge. There Marlborough's health continued to improve, and in the presence of witnesses he was able to execute the last of the settlements which guaranteed his wife her independent fortune.[26] But still Sarah could not relax. Although the exchequer decree had been confirmed beyond further appeal, she was still not prepared to knuckle under and pay the Blenheim debt. In fact she had always been convinced, probably with some foundation, that there would have been no debt in the first place if it had not been for the excessive prices and the malpractices of the workmen and officials: 'I am confydent sence the world was made there never was so many fowle practices as has been in this building excepting in the S: Sea.' Encouraged by Lord Chancellor Parker's support in the appeal, she now set in motion a vast Chancery suit against all the Blenheim workmen, to expose these 'fowle practices' and so prevent them from following the Strongs' example.[27]

This was no sooner done than she found Walpole proposing to pay off the civil list debts by a deduction of sixpence in the pound from all pensions and salaries. Spoiling for another fight with the Court, and determined that Marlborough's grant of £5,000 a year should not be 'put upon the same foot of Pensions that are given to Men for Betraying the Libertys of their Country', she wrote to demand its exemption: 'tho' it was as inconsiderable as Mr. Hambden's Groat for which he went to Prison . . . there is the same reason for it, for when an Act is broak in a Trifle, They may carry it as far as they Please.' But no such favours were to be extended to opponents of the Court, and when Godolphin reminded Sarah in August not to overlook the presentation of the miniature French standard which was the annual quitrent for Woodstock, she hastened to comply, 'least Mr Walpole shou'd make the Omiting it a handle to take away the rest of the Pension'.[28]

As a bitter afterthought she added, 'it wou'd have been Luckey for me if he had been ingenious enough to have taken away the House before the Duke of Marlborough took it upon him in 1716'. They were about to make their usual summer pilgrimage to Blenheim, and for Sarah this meant a further exhausting round in her struggle to tame 'that wild unmercifull hous'. This time she embarked on the greatest challenge of all, the completion of Vanbrugh's Grand Bridge and causeway. For years she had poured scorn and abuse on this whole project, as 'the maddest thing that ever was thought of'. Now, surveying the chaos of half-finished earthworks and masonry before their front door, she realized that she would have to do something about it. ''Tis what I never intended to do,' she added defensively,

but I think it would be very wrong (after so much mony has been paid for this building both by the queen & the D: of Marl: himself) to let a place just before the great front of such a hous lye in so ruinous a condition over which we must pass to go into the Parke, & sence we must have a way of some sort or other, upon a thorow examination into every thing I am convinced that what I am doing will bee best, & will cost less then to pull the whole thing down & begin quite another design.

Marlborough's favourite military engineer, John Armstrong, was put in charge and promised a usable bridge by the following summer, and now that Sarah felt herself completely in control, the project for the first time began to kindle her imagination. It was a taxing business, however, even for her apparently inexhaustible energy. 'I was up this morning soon after six,' she added, 'tis now night & I am quite tired.'[29] At 61, she was beginning to feel an ominous weakness in her legs and hands.

But no sooner did she have the house and park in hand than the borough of Woodstock threatened to slip out of her control. In September 1721 she was reported (by her old enemies, the Oxford Tories) to have wept with rage at her loss of the mayoral election; 'but I take it to be a mistake,' one of them commented cruelly, 'for she is too masculine to cry, ever since another in the family has been too subject to it.'[30] At a parliamentary by-election in October, with the help of money and 'great mismanagement on the other side', she did succeed in getting her candidate home, but at the general election early the following year the local Tories were better organized, and both her candidates were thrown out. She could only revenge herself by ignoring a petition of the townspeople against some aspect of the building works, for 'no Body in that Town has Merrit enough to put me to any inconvenience upon Their account'.[31]

Adopting a more realistic strategy at St Albans, she managed here to get William Clayton elected in alliance with the Tory candidate. At long last her rooted distrust of the Tories, already weakened by her succession of quarrels with the Whig leadership, was giving way. 'As to party business,' she assured Godolphin, 'I have non of that warmth that you have seen in me, for I have been long convinced that there is very few men on either side that really is concerned for anything but their own present interest.'[32] The strength of government influence meant that those who were resolved, as Sarah now was, 'to distress the court', could no longer afford the luxury of keeping up old party hostilities. Even so, her new strategy brought her some curious allies. Among them was Thomas Gape, son of the Tacker she had opposed so strenuously in Anne's reign, 'who, with his drawn sword, begun the riot on the election day, and caused the music to play "The King shall enjoy his own again"'.[33] Such associates, together with Sunderland's accusations, began to give Sarah the reputation among willing believers, of being 'a thorough profest Jacobite'.[34]

Another distasteful expedient on such occasions was wholesale bribery, but when the mayor of St Albans grew uneasy at the methods he was required to use, Sarah sent him word that 'it would be a Tory parliament, which, with her interest, would bring him off'.[35] The prediction proved wildly over-optimistic. Despite the financial crisis, the rivalry between Sunderland and Walpole, and the combined efforts of their opponents, the results of the general election gave her little to hope for. Yet her reaction to the Atterbury plot later in the year shows how wide of the mark was the belief that she had turned into a Jacobite. When her friend Lady Lechmere scoffed at the government revelations and complained about the suspension of the Habeas Corpus Act, she earned herself a lecture on the imprudence of opposing the ministers just because they were in power.[36] Sarah admitted that the alternatives were unsatisfactory: 'to have the pretender or bee secured against him, by giving more power to men that have shewn upon so many occasions that they have neither understanding nor any sort of Justice in their nature'. Yet she still felt that it would be 'an Infatuation for people to think they should bee better by bringing in popery which would fix our slavery for ever'.[37]

At Blenheim in the autumn of 1721 Sarah had told a friend that she was not looking forward to coming to town for the winter; for in London it was impossible to conceal or ignore their estrangement from their family. Henrietta and Mary still visited their father, but in the same manner as before, and all Sarah's efforts to hide the true situation had not been able to keep him from becoming aware of it. Now better than at any time since his first illness, he tried tentatively to establish independent contact with his daughters by going alone one day to Montagu House. In return Mary offered to invite Sunderland and Henrietta there to meet him without Sarah present. But to Sarah herself this was a blatant attempt by Mary 'to get her father from me', and she insisted that he could not accept any invitation from which she was excluded. An appeal from Marlborough to his daughter only brought complaints that Sarah had 'done things that were not done by any mother, kind or unkind'. To reconcile these two proud women, who would not agree to bury their differences even in their common love for him, was now beyond his strength. When he read Mary's letter, he sadly remarked that there was no more to be done.[38]

This was to be the last opportunity for any such reconciliation. In April 1722, apparently in the prime of life and with a long political career still ahead of him, Sunderland was struck down by acute illness and died within a few days. His brother-in-law, Daniel Pulteney, and his chief political ally, Lord Carteret, at once sent for the heir who was still travelling in Europe, and sealed up Sunderland's papers to await his arrival. As soon as she heard of this, Sarah insisted on having Marlborough's seal added. In fact she had no official business to do so, since Sunderland had appointed his two brothers-in-law, Godolphin and Pulteney, as executors and guardians of his children; and her intervention caused great alarm within the ministry.

Her main motive seems to have been to keep a check on Pulteney, whom she suspected of intending to provide for Sunderland's widow at the expense of her own grandchildren. Yet there was much in Sunderland's recent activities that was controversial, and the ministers, with the Atterbury plot about to be exposed, were more concerned at what his papers might reveal of his recent negotiations with the Jacobites. The next day, with Pulteney's connivance, they broke open all the seals and carried off what documents they thought relevant. Sarah was beside herself with impotent fury. She recognized Sunderland's Jacobite activities for what they were—simply a means of fencing against his political rivals—and she was convinced that if the papers had been left undisturbed, they would have shown him, in the panic of the South Sea crisis, using his own money to bribe Parliament. She also suspected Pulteney of having removed evidence that he had intended to alter his will before he died. As it was, the only will that came to light had been made when Sunderland expected great gains from the South Sea, and the residue remaining for his eldest son when the large legacies were paid would leave him with only his bare paternal estate.[39]

The young man of twenty who landed at Dover in May to take up his inheritance was an object of general interest and approval. Mary Cairnes was completely dazzled: 'he was what Shakspear makes Lady Piercy say of her Lord: ". . . the Glass, the Picture & the Book, in which the Youth of England dresst themselves".' Sarah, whose standards of masculine beauty were very exacting, thought that he could not strictly be called handsome, but he had teeth 'as white as pearl, and that, having good eyes, makes him look very well'.[40] For some time, apparently on the orders of their parents, both he and his cousin Rialton had ceased to write to her. In fact the latter, formerly her chief favourite, had got rid of his governor and was lingering about the Pretender's court at Rome, while a satirical pamphlet concerning his Jacobite sympathies was cried about the London streets to the acute embarrassment of his whole family.[41] Sarah now took young Lord Sunderland, who had inherited his mother's charm as well as her looks, into his place. She was ready to dote on him even before their meeting: 'I hope I shall find in you all the comforts I have lost in your Dear mother whos picture you were once, & as I beleive from what you write that you will act like a son I shall have all the pleasure in the world in making you mine.'[42]

But the price of this favour was unquestioning obedience. The rightful place for this young man was clearly at Court, and it was rumoured even before he landed that a gentleman of the bedchamber's place would be offered him, with the promise of a Garter to follow. Sarah had no intention of letting Walpole or Carteret snatch this glittering prize from her. She sent a message to Dover asking him to come straight to her at Windsor Lodge, and warning him to be on his guard against the ministers when he saw them,

who I know will court you very much in order to deceive you, & make you as they have don many noble men a tool of theirs to carry on their durty work for mean pentions & the hopes of preferment as they call it in some place that you are above accepting upon such termes as you must have it upon, & . . . I don't doubt but you will consult with your surest friends before you accept of any thing, & consider that you have somthing more valuable to depend upon then the promises of ministers . . . whos measures have ruined the nation & who are detested by the generality of this country.[43]

At the Lodge she explained that if he refused the bedchamber place she would make him an allowance of £1,000 a year in lieu of the salary, pay his younger brothers the rent of Sunderland House (which was settled on them) so that he could live there until they grew up, and make him the principal heir of her own fortune; so long, that is, as his political conduct continued to satisfy her. She told him, in refusing the ministers, to lay the fault on her, 'saying, "I was his Grandmother, that he was already oblig'd to me, and might have more Obligations".'[44] It was once remarked that 'all the Stanhopes and Spencers are taught to look on a Walpole as one they are to hate by inheritance'.[45] Sunderland chose to make the best he could of this, as of the rest of his inheritance, and took his grandmother's money.

'I thank God your Grandfather is better every year,' Sarah had written to Sunderland while he was on his way home. Yet she knew more clearly than anyone how precarious Marlborough's health was. As a youth Sunderland's likeness to his mother had been so striking that for some months after her death Marlborough could scarcely bear to see him.[46] Perhaps the agitation of the reunion now proved too much. In the early hours of 12 June doctors set out from London and Oxford in answer to an urgent summons from the Lodge. It was soon clear to Sarah that the blow she had managed to fend off for six years was now about to fall. Sunderland and his brothers and sister were there. Jane Kingdom was also in unobtrusive attendance. These presences were some comfort. But on 15 June there were other and far less welcome actors in the 'dreadfull scene' at the Lodge. Sarah tells the story in the starkest and most moving of all her narratives:

The afternoon before their Father died when I had no hopes of his recovery, I was mightily surpriz'd and troubled at what I did not expect, that the Dss of Montagu, & my Lady Godolphin were without . . . I am sure it is impossible for any tongue to express what I felt at that time; but I believe any body that ever lov'd another so tenderly as I did the Duke of Marlborough may have some feeling of what it was to have one's children come in, in those last hours; who I knew did not come to comfort me, but like enemies . . .

For Sarah this was the last and most terrible of many partings. Time was short, and constraint or intrusion were intolerable. The doctors could do no more, and she wanted only to be alone with her husband in his last hours, while he was still conscious and able to understand what she said. Yet his daughters, one of them his heir, could not be excluded:

. . . at that time I thought my soul was tearing from my body, and that I could not say many things (which otherwise I would have done) before them, yet I would not refuse them to come in, for fear I should repent of it . . . but I beg'd of them that they would not stay long in the room, because I could not come in while they were there being in so much affliction . . . They staid a great while (as I thought) and not being able to be out of the room longer from Him, I went in though they were there, & kneel'd down by Him: They rose up when I came in, & made Curtsys but did not speak to me, and after some time I called for prayers: when they were over I ask'd the Duke of Marlb: if He heard them well, and He answer'd, Yes, & He had join'd in them.

When it was dark he was carried from the drawing-room to his bedchamber and put to bed. Sarah sent the young grandchildren away, but still the daughters, with the Duchess of Newcastle, remained in the room. Sarah tried to get rid of them by saying that she needed privacy to lie down and rest. If she had appealed to them personally instead of sending messages across the room by Jane Kingdom and the servants some human feeling might have been preserved. But their relations had degenerated too far:

She [the Duchess of Montagu] answer'd, Will our being here hinder Her from lying down? Then I sent Grace [her maid] to Her again, to ask her If she had such an affliction & was in my condition, Whether she would like to have me with Her? She said, No. But did not go out until I sent to her a third time, and then they all three went out of the room, and the Dss of Newcastle went quite away, but the others staid in the Drawing room & Hall till four in the morning.

This was the hour when Marlborough died. At about two o'clock, leaving his bedside for a moment to fetch a cordial, Sarah noticed Jane Kingdom still sitting in a window seat at the end of the room. Unable in this extremity to bear any presence, however sympathetic, she appealed to her, 'that if she would do any thing for me as long as she liv'd that she would go out & go to bed'. Mrs Kingdom went out, but waited in the next room and came in to her again 'after the terrible stroke was given', to give her what comfort she could.[47]

For nearly a month afterwards, while arrangements were made for the lying in state at Marlborough House, Sarah kept to her bed, exhausted in body and mind. The long strain of watching and nursing was over, and the blow was no easier to bear for being so long expected. Acquaintances who came to offer condolences were not turned away, 'but I had been much more easy if I had seen Nobody'.[48] Only one visit stood out in her memory. This was when Sir Gilbert Heathcote and Sir Nathaniel Gould came out to Windsor in a hired coach to pay their respects. She felt a special gratitude to these hard-bitten City merchants, who did not normally trouble themselves with such rituals; it was 'very polite in men of business'.[49]

It was the middle of July before she began to take the reins into her hands once more, roused by the gossip which reached her from London concerning the events at the Lodge while Marlborough lay dying. Henrietta and Mary were spreading stories of being turned away from their father's deathbed and of hearing Sarah and Jane Kingdom talking and laughing together after they had left the room. Sarah realized that she could not show her face again unless she did something to contradict this gossip. Her answer was to compose a long narrative of her relations with the daughters and the Duchess of Newcastle, detailing every misdemeanour they had committed since they were children. This document, which became notorious in the family as the Green Book, she forced on her embarrassed friends for comment and sympathy.[50] Only Mrs Boscawen dared to hint at what it really revealed about the causes of the daughters' inexplicable alienation. Having paid the tribute to Sarah's maternal tenderness which was expected of all readers of the Green Book, she added mildly: 'the laying their faults before them soe early & offering good advice, I take to be one great instance of it, tho perhaps in this case it proved the greatest offence, if one may be permitted to judge by the event.'[51]

Then there was the funeral to organize. Since Marlborough's ultimate resting place, the chapel at Blenheim, was not ready, there was to be a temporary interment at Westminster Abbey, preceded by a full state funeral: in spite of everything, the Hanoverians were prepared to put past difficulties down to Sarah's influence and pay this tribute to him as a national hero. Sarah herself supervised operations from Windsor Lodge, and found much to worry and disturb her, particularly in the current state of her relations with the government. In the first place there was the traditional ceremony of including seventy-two Chelsea pensioners in the procession, one for each year of Marlborough's age, 'for I suppose them to be miserable spectacles from their wounds in the war & I am doubtfull whether the wicked enemies to the poor Duke of Marlborough might not say something disagreeable upon that'.[52] Then the French ambassador, now (to Sarah's great unease) the envoy of a friendly power, complained about the funeral medal she had commissioned, which represented Marlborough as the scourge of France. The new Duchess, in defiance of the etiquette governing female relations on such occasions, persisted in attending the rehearsals of Buononcini's anthem ('The cedar is fallen') as if she were a common sightseer.[53] And as a final embarrassment, Dean Jones, whose company Sarah had endured for seven years for Marlborough's sake, took it upon himself to suggest that the King should pay all the funeral charges. Although she thought that 'while the poor Duke of Marlborough was living it was a shame to the King, & to the ministers that they showed no more consideration for him', yet she could see, with all London talking of the riches revealed by his will, how it would appear if there were any attempt to 'lay an expence upon the publick only to save mony to a family that has so much'.[54]

At last, on 9 August, the whole vexed and solemn business came to a climax. At midday the Duke's black-draped funeral car with its eight horses left Marlborough House, the suit of armour on the coffin looking 'as if he were lying armed himself' and adding 'a great deal to the solemnity'. All through the long summer afternoon the procession of horse and foot guards, Chelsea pensioners, heralds, and mourners wound through packed streets to the Abbey 'in the best order of anything (of the kind) that has been seen this many years'. As the artillery salute thundered in St James's Park, Atterbury 'said dust to dust, and shut up that last scene of pompous vanity'.[55] Marlborough was gone, but the tasks he had left his widow would occupy her for the rest of her life.

Head of the Family

1722–1725

THE suspicions of Henrietta and her circle that Sarah had persuaded Marlborough to cancel the settlement on his eldest daughter were proved groundless as soon as the will was read. Even so, the new Duchess of Marlborough received her great inheritance ungraciously enough, objecting to the size of her mother's jointure, and still more to the fact that Sarah was left with greater control over the estate than the heirs themselves.[1] Sarah's position under the will was certainly an unusual one. Instead of retiring to the position of dowager, she was now virtually head of the family. Blenheim and Marlborough House remained hers for life, and she had a power to dispose of the latter as she chose. She was also the chief of seven trustees whom Marlborough had appointed to invest his wealth in land and government funds. Henrietta herself had no power over the estate (although her husband was another of the trustees), but could only receive what income remained after the payment of the other charges. Of these the largest was Sarah's immense jointure of £20,000 a year.[2]

Sarah certainly relished her dominant position. It annoyed her that she had to concede status to her daughter even in the formal matter of title. She maintained (quite wrongly) that Henrietta had no right to begin signing herself 'Marlborough', without the normal female usage of an initial. She also objected to having to instruct her friends to address her as 'Dowager Duchess', to prevent her letters being delivered to Godolphin House by mistake.[3] Yet the provisions of the will were not, as Henrietta resentfully maintained, of Sarah's dictating. Marlborough had always told his wife that her settlement would be exceptional, to let 'the world see the kindness and estime I have for you',[4] and the great increase in it given by his last will was in explicit acknowledgement of her care of him in his final illness. Sarah herself took care to point out that her own part in making and preserving his fortune was a further justification. In any case, £5,000 of the £20,000 represented the pension which had been settled on her by Parliament in 1707; Marlborough had given her a rent charge in lieu of this when she told him that she 'hated to make low Court'sies to Ministers and solicit for any thing'.[5] The manor of Woodstock had also been settled on her by Act of Parliament before Henrietta's succession to the title was foreseen. The grant of land for Marlborough House had been made to her personally by Queen Anne. And as Sarah pointed out to Godolphin, it had always been Marlborough's intention, in order to preserve his estate, that whoever inherited it should do so only as a tenant for life, with no independent power to dispose of it.[6]

Sarah lost no time in consolidating her position by drawing as many of the grandchildren as possible into her orbit. Yet it was ironic that the one provision in Marlborough's will which certainly was of her making, the independent settlement on Henrietta's son, now Marquess of Blandford, seemed to have failed in its object of detaching him from his parents. Evidently acting on his mother's orders, he sent his grandmother no message of any kind after Marlborough's death. Her two Montagu granddaughters were also kept out of her reach. But the Spencer grandchildren were now well and truly under her control. Her adoption of Diana had been ratified by Sunderland's will, and shortly after his death she offered to take charge of the two younger boys as well. Their guardians, only too glad to have this burden taken off their hands, readily agreed. It did not take her long to decide that the arrangements made by their father for their education were unsatisfactory. Within a month of Marlborough's death she removed them from Eton to Windsor Lodge and, influenced by her reading of Locke, decided to have them educated under her eye by a private tutor.[7]

Finding one whom she was prepared to take into her household, however, was another matter. Her refusal, after her experience with Dean Jones, to consider another clergyman narrowed the field considerably. So did her insistence that skill in mathematics must be the main qualification. 'I wish very much at this time, it were in my Power for once, to make a man on Purpose,' wrote Dr Clarke patiently, after several candidates had been put forward and rejected: 'Your Grace (I am sure) will believe I would not spare any Pains in forming him. But we must be content to take the World as we find it.'[8] This was something Sarah was never content to do; but just as they had begun to despair, the paragon was unexpectedly found in the person of a young man called James Stephens. The son of a clergyman but untainted by the cloth himself, reliable, honest, discreet, and brilliant at mathematics, he was to prove an invaluable addition to the household in one capacity or another until his death more than thirty-five years later.

Until now, with her father's consent, Lady Anne Egerton had

continued to share the nursery with her Spencer cousins. Then in August 1722 the Duke of Bridgwater, who had just remarried, sent for her home on a visit. Already nursing a grievance against him for his refusal to co-operate in the Chandos match, Sarah was instantly suspicious that he was trying to gain control of his daughter's legacy from her grandfather, or even to go to law for a larger share. She made the girl write to say that she was not well, and that her grandmother's 'melancholy condition' made her unwilling to part with her. Bristling with scepticism, Bridgwater himself appeared at the Lodge early the next morning, and found that Sarah's melancholy condition had not affected her tenacity. After an ominous interview in which he grew 'pretty warm in his complexion', he was at last forced to concede a postponement of the visit for a day or two.[9] As soon as he was out of the house Sarah sought legal advice—and was frustrated to learn that a father had an absolute right to resume custody of his daughter whenever he chose. It was no consolation that Lady Anne was duly returned to her within the week with a polite note of acknowledgement for the visit. Her sense of being in complete control of the child's destiny had been destroyed.[10] From now on Diana, younger and more docile, whose role as her adopted daughter was uncontested, became markedly her favourite.

Sarah's restless spirit next took her to Blenheim to see what remained to be done there. Hawksmoor's refusal to become involved in the legal proceedings about the debt was final confirmation to her that he was 'as much honester as hee is more able than Sir John', and she accepted the offer of his services in the finishing.[11] The party she took with her included Lord Sunderland, his cousin Lady Charlotte and her new husband Mr West, the heir of Lord De La Warr; the latter advantageous match, it was generally acknowledged, would never have come about if Lady Charlotte had not been so obviously under Sarah's protection. Yet even in this cheerful company, she found that she had come to Blenheim too soon. While she could be busy during the day all was well, but in the evenings depression set in. The works they had decided on, she told Lady Cairnes, would 'soon make this place finer then ever any body imagind it would bee, but I am more melancholly here then any where else when I reflect where hee is now for whom it was built'.[12] Sweet-natured and attentive as Lord Sunderland was, she also felt a hollowness in their relations:

hee is as easy with me as I can desire, & I beleive wee shall allways live so with one another, but I can't say that the love I have for him is like what I had for my own children. However I must bee contented & make the best of those comforts which I have left, & I do beleive that whole branch and La: Ann Egerton will be good to me, not only because I hope they are so in their natures, but most of them will want me, & my fortune is in my own power.[13]

In her determination to control these affectionate and well-disposed young people, and bind them to her as she had failed to bind her daughters, she could never let them forget the financial hold she had over them.

From Blenheim she travelled on via Althorp to St Albans, where she found the gardens which had been Marlborough's pride and personal creation in danger of being swamped by a waterworks project, set up by a servant of her electoral rival, Lord Grimston. Although she suspected a plot in revenge for his defeat at the general election, the Blenheim appeal made her wary for the time being of further litigation: 'if I can buy grownd to prevent this mischief I shall chuse to give two hundred years purchase . . . reather than begin a lawsuit which tis probable will end like Sir Johns from the injustice of our governors.'[14] From Holywell she returned to the Lodge in November, and announced that she intended to stay there all winter with no company but that of the younger grandchildren.[15] One reason for this was to avoid the unwanted attentions of her old acquaintance, Lord Coningsby. Of late years his behaviour, always eccentric, had become positively deranged. On a visit to Blenheim in the summer he had embarrassed the whole household with the oddity of his talk, and now he was besieging her with passionate love letters, begging when she came to London, 'to be allowed to wait on you and throw myself at your dearest feet'.[16]

In any case the hostility of her daughters and their friends meant that Marlborough House had few attractions for her. With her usual compulsion to find a scapegoat, she had convinced herself that Jane Kingdom's manner of delivering her messages at Marlborough's death-bed must have been entirely responsible for the offence they had taken, and this additional quarrel deprived her of the only congenial adult companionship within reach of the Lodge.[17] Brooding on the whole business, she sank further into depression, telling herself and her friends 'that whoever has been once so happy as I have been, & have nothing left but mony which from my humour I don't want much of, deserves to be pitty'd'. To keep herself occupied, she set going alterations to the Lodge and its gardens, and when the weather brought these to a halt at the end of November, she asked Mrs Jennens to send her a consignment of furnishing fabrics: 'I can make them up by Christmasse, having Nothing to do but to amuse myself with such Things.'[18] Yet these reclusive moods, although genuine enough, seldom lasted long. A few days later came a letter which reminded her that there was another important aspect of her duty as head of the family which she had not yet come to terms with, and brought her smartly back to London and the world of affairs.

Marlborough had died worth just over a million pounds. Of this

almost half was invested in short-term loans to the exchequer, advanced
on the annual revenue of the land and malt tax.[19] In his lifetime Sarah had
no say, at least officially, in the disposal of his money, but now the male
trustees needed her consent to continue the loans. On 3 December
Godolphin wrote to say that they were about to make the usual
agreement with the treasury. Although the rate of interest, he admitted,
would be lower than in previous years, at least the principal would be
secure and no part of it would be long unproductive. Instantly suspicious
of any dealings with Walpole and enjoying her deciding role, Sarah
announced that she would come to London immediately to satisfy
herself that the proposal would answer the intentions of Marlborough's
will. She suddenly remembered that priority had been given to purchases
of land, to be made with her approbation; only the residue was to be
invested in public funds.[20]

In the end, after a chilly interview with Walpole, she did give her
grudging consent to the continuation of the loans for the time being, but
helping him in any way was painful, and she never ceased to regard her
acceptance of the lowered interest rate (from 5 to 3 per cent) as a signal
example of altruism and public spirit. To Godolphin she emphasized that
this must be only a temporary arrangement, and that they should lose no
time in putting the money more profitably into land.[21] Apart from their
duty to carry out the terms of the will, real estate seemed the only safe
investment while 'we have such a cloud as the vast summ of paper mony
that hangs over our heads, & I fear will break some time or other'.[22]

In other respects she found the Trust in a highly unsatisfactory state.
Besides herself, it consisted of the three sons-in-law, her friend John
Hanbury, and two of Marlborough's former men of business, William
Clayton and William Guidott, the latter the nephew and successor of her
faithful Anthony. Hanbury, the least active, was the only one who had
her complete confidence. Finding both Clayton and Guidott noticeably
less deferential to her than they had been in the Duke's lifetime, she
began to harbour suspicions about their honesty.[23] Of the sons-in-law,
Godolphin, although bound to take an active role for his wife's sake, was
hurtfully cold and formal. In fact it surprised only Sarah that her
relations with him suffered from her unbridled hostility to his wife and
daughter. Again it was Mrs Boscawen, one of the few human beings
privileged to tell Sarah unpalatable truths, who asked her if she seriously
expected him to put duty to her before loyalty to his wife: 'if your Grace
will pleas to reflect & lay all things togeather I believe you will find this a
difficult case, wherein some failings may be allowable.'[24]

But at least Godolphin's frigid courtesy was preferable to the outright
hostility of the Dukes of Bridgwater and Montagu. As soon as Sarah set

going the process of confirming the will, they announced their intention of contesting the whole settlement, with a view to having Marlborough's wealth divided equally among all his daughters. In great panic and distress Sarah summoned her lawyers, who tried to comfort her by pointing out that if they succeeded she would be better off, by becoming entitled to a third of all the personal estate herself. Sarah protested indignantly that she did not want any more money, 'and would not for any Consideration suffer the Duke's Intention to be defeated, and his Estate torn in Pieces'. She insisted on attending the meeting of the counsel on both sides personally. After they had sat up until two in the morning examining all the documents, it became clear that the only consequence of setting aside the last will would be to bring the similar one of 1712, still uncancelled, into force. The two Dukes gave way, Bridgwater with a particularly bad grace, and refused to take any active part in the Trust.[25]

This was one reason for his decision to remove his daughter once and for all from Sarah's custody. Another was that they were in competition for the most eligible Whig match in England: Bridgwater's young brother-in-law, the Duke of Bedford. Bridgwater, who wanted this match for his daughter, knew that as long as Sarah had a choice she would try to obtain him for her favourite, Diana.[26] In June 1723 he sent for Lady Anne home with all her belongings. Sarah again made the girl write to say that she was not well and could not bear to leave her grandmother. This brought Bridgwater storming into Marlborough House late one night, with a footman's greatcoat flung over his shoulders 'and the air of being quite mad'. Put off till the next morning, he arrived so early that they were all in bed and sent a message in to Sarah, 'that if Lady Anne was sick, it was she that had made her so', and he would wait no longer. While his daughter was hastily got ready, he prowled about in the hall 'with the most ill natur'd Countenance that ever was seen in any humane Creature', making sure that she was not spirited away without his knowledge. The moment she was dressed, he bore her off in hysterics in his coach.[27]

Yet if Sarah's fellow trustees were more of a hindrance than a help, she was not without support from other quarters. Lord Bristol (the former Lord Hervey), an old friend whose loyalty had survived his wife's squabbles with her and her daughters, and Lord Harborough, an agreeable nonentity and a constant member of her card parties, were now talked of as the great rivals for her favour.[28] Sarah herself, who was becoming fond of governmental metaphors to describe her personal relations, preferred to think of such male friends and advisers as her 'councellours', and she soon had a new and far more unexpected addition to their number. The Duke of Somerset, one of the richest and certainly the proudest of the Whig magnates, had been her acquaintance for nearly forty years. For most of that time she had not had a good word to say for him, and after his temporary alliance with Harley in 1710 the invective she heaped on this 'nauseous creature who is yet more a knave then a fool' had passed all bounds. When a reconciliation was urged on her for political reasons in 1714, she absolutely refused it.[29] Yet as far as Somerset was concerned, it was a very one-sided enmity. In Marlborough's helpless last years he had sympathized with his treatment at the hands of the ministry, and after his death the warmth of the younger Duke's condolences completely won Sarah over. He offered his services as pall-bearer at the funeral and came from his summer retirement at Petworth expressly for the purpose.[30] When his wife died a few months later Sarah asked his sister-in-law, Lady Ann Harvey, to pass on her condolences in return, 'which I assure you are very sencere, for the goodnesse hee expressed upon the Dear Duke of Marlborough's subject has forever bound mee to bee his constant well-wisher & most faithfull humble servant'.[31]

Even now, on the verge of old age, Sarah was still beautiful, with 'most expressive eyes, and the finest fair hair imaginable'.[32] In the summer of 1723 she met Somerset again at Lady Ann's house, and a few days later she received a letter from him, containing a passionate declaration of love and a proposal of marriage. The myth, originating with Horace Walpole, that she haughtily refused him the heart and hand that had belonged to Marlborough has long since been exploded. She professed herself honoured and flattered by his proposal, but told him that 'if I know anything of my self I would not marry the Emperor of the world, tho I were but thirty years old'.[33] Sarah always wrote of marriage in terms of a yoke or a putting on of bonds. Although Somerset offered to renounce her property (swearing he only wanted possession of her 'charming person'), she could not expect a second husband to be as indulgent as Marlborough had been. For her, remarriage could only mean loss of independence, and this, as she confided to the discreet Lady Burlington, was her chief reason for rejecting this most eligible of matches.[34] Nevertheless she begged Somerset, in what was certainly not just a matter of polite form, that he would continue to be her friend, and when he asked to be allowed to visit her at times when he would not 'bee interrupted from farther laying open the very Bottome of my Heart', she did not refuse him.[35]

In mid-August Sarah set out on her annual visit to Blenheim, in company with Hawksmoor and Lady Burlington's son. Young Lord Burlington, whom she must have known since he was a child, was now the leader of the neo-Palladian school of architecture, but when they came to Blenheim, she was rather reassured than otherwise to find him 'very much inclined to dislike everything' there; it confirmed her opinion of Vanbrugh. She was also pleased to find her latest project for a lake and cascade to the east of the house well advanced. The sight of the Grand Bridge towering over its narrow marshy stream had brought unkind quips from Marlborough's enemies ('The arch the height of his ambition shows | The stream an emblem of his bounty flows'). Now the lake would be in scale with the bridge, Sarah explained to Somerset, and make it appear necessary, 'that was the subject of every body's rediculedbefore'.[36]

Hawksmoor reminded her of the need to put up a suitable inscription concerning the occasion of building Blenheim, and after what had passed in the House of Lords, she decided that she could not do better than quote directly from the Acts of Parliament by which the grant had been bestowed. In suggesting that these should form part of an obelisk, Burlington gave her the first notion for what was to become the Column of Victory. At first Sarah toyed with the idea of placing it on the site of the old manor house (now finally demolished): 'that would please Sir John best, because it would give an opportunity of mentioning that King whose scenes of love he was so much pleas'd with.' But pleasing Sir John was no longer a good reason for doing anything, and 'if there were obelisks to bee made of what all our kings have don of that sort, the countreys would bee stuffed with very odd things'. The site she finally fixed on was the Grand Avenue on the north axis of the house; but then there was the further problem of who should compile the inscription. In employing any kind of expert from a lawyer to an architect Sarah had long been accustomed to command the best, and the best in such matters, as someone (probably Burlington) reminded her, was the Tory poet, Alexander Pope. The difficulty, as she delicately put it to Somerset, was that 'his notions are so different from ours as to liberty'.[37] The Duke promised to sound Pope out on her behalf.

She poured out all these doings to Somerset in the confidence that he would take 'some share in everything that gives me either satisfaction or trouble'. After the long strain of Marlborough's illness and the bitterness of the rupture with her daughters, his warmth and sympathy were a comfort. Yet she also made it clear to him that her overriding commitment was still to her dead husband, and that the tasks Marlborough had left her in themselves made it impossible for her to remarry: 'there is no doubt such offers would tempt any person that were at liberty to accept of them, but my case is in many things different from other wemens.'[38] Seeing her obvious desire that he should not withdraw altogether, Somerset took her to mean that he had simply made his proposal too soon after the deaths of their respective partners, and he settled down to court her a little longer.

In September she moved on to take the waters at Bristol. For a time the informality of the unfashionable resort pleased and relaxed her. Stories of her daily journey down the jolting track to the waters, with her still magnificent hair eclipsed under a 'dowd' (an informal kind of cap) and carrying a large bag of silver to distribute to the poor, circulated for months afterwards. But the novelty soon palled, and Beau Nash, the celebrated master of ceremonies, and her other acquaintances at Bath soon lured her back to join them.[39] From there she wrote again to Somerset, asking him to meet her at Blenheim, 'to help me in undertakings that are so much above my capasity that I want the assistance of all my friends who have any good tast in Building'. But since their frequent meetings in London had become common talk, she begged him this time to bring a chaperone.[40] To the fascination of the gossips, Somerset sped to Blenheim at her call and stayed there with her for five days.[41]

When they both returned to London in October, he continued to be a charming and attentive suitor. Presents ('trifling fairings', as he called them) showered upon her: the best orange flower water, delicacies for the table, a set of ivory manicure instruments, a portrait of Rosamond Clifford. He squired her to and from the law courts, interviewed lawyers, estate surveyors, and poets on her behalf, and was a constant attendant at her card table in the evenings. But when he went so far as to send a draft marriage settlement in which he renounced all claim to her wealth, she returned it at once and for some time treated him with 'a greater Reservedness than ordinary'.[42] Much as she enjoyed the courtship while it could be treated as a light-hearted pretence, with Somerset playing the role of obsequious 'councellour' to her exacting 'souvereign', she did not need the Oxford gossips to tell her that this state of affairs would not last long once they were married. When, inevitably, the matter of Somerset's dealings with Harley was raised, these two arrogant and opinionated people had a glimpse of the pitfalls of committing themselves to a closer relationship. The Duke was so clearly offended by her criticisms that she hastened to smooth things over: 'I do really beleive you were drawn into every thing that was wrong by the artifices of a great many very skillfull men, & that was helpd by a lady [his wife] that I acknowledge I should not have named, who had passions of her own to gratify . . . but there is no occasion to talk of these things.' When Somerset complained that she was merely holding the subject in reserve, 'ready to bee Revived and Repeated, as occasions might happen', she denied it vehemently; 'I think by your leter that all is not yet right, & I shall bee mighty fearfull of saying any more on these subjects, because I wish never to make you uneasy but to have your friendship as long as I live.'[43] Such self-restraint was a measure of how much the relationship meant to her. The difference was only a temporary one, and the Duke was soon courting her as ardently as ever.

This dalliance was all very well, but it distracted Sarah's attention from what she felt were her chief duties. 'I have a great deal of businesse that I have neglected too much & allmost every day produces some new trouble,' she told Somerset at the end of December.[44] The two components of this trouble were land and litigation. Now quite convinced that Walpole was taking advantage of the Trust in the matter of interest rates, she was more determined than ever to carry out Marlborough's wishes about the purchase of estates. Godolphin patiently pointed out that given the huge amounts of money they had to dispose of, they had little choice but to take what terms Walpole was prepared to give; they could not buy or sell stocks in sufficient quantities without affecting the market to their own disadvantage. Mortgages could provide only a tiny outlet, and suitable estates were not easy to come by.[45]

His views might have prevailed if Sarah's first flush of enthusiasm for land had not coincided with the auctioning off of the South Sea directors' confiscated estates. In bidding for these she could have the combined satisfaction of carrying out Marlborough's wishes and helping to deprive the miscreant directors of their ill-gotten spoils for the benefit of the public. Godolphin gave a cautious agreement in principle, but insisted that their bidding must be fixed at a level which would give them at least a 3 per cent return on their capital. Since many of the estates fetched inflated prices, this immediately caused difficulties. Sarah argued that if they wanted to invest seriously in land they must take 'a resolution of not being out bid'. She noted bitterly that Godolphin answered her long, urgent remonstrances on these subjects with brief notes, asking for yet more exchequer tallies and bills to be taken from the strong box at Marlborough House 'to lend at three per cent to Mr Walpole'.[46]

But while she chafed under these constraints in Trust matters, she was a free agent in her own affairs. Those estates which she could not persuade Godolphin to acquire, she would buy herself. By the winter of 1724, after intensive consultations with surveyors and lawyers, she had successfully bid for five modestly priced South Sea properties for the Trust and six more in Oxfordshire, Surrey, Huntingdonshire, and Warwickshire, at considerably higher prices, for herself. Of the latter, the first and most expensive was Sir Theodore Janssen's estate at Wimbledon, which cost her almost £25,000. Janssen had demolished the

great Tudor house overlooking the Surrey downs, formerly owned by
the Cecils and the Earl of Danby, and the South Sea crisis had come upon
him before he had had time to replace it. Even so, the property was still a
bargain because of the value of the timber on it. But years later, when
Sarah's enthusiasm for land had dwindled, she admitted that the other
two Surrey estates, Chilworth (£22,020) and Crowhurst (£13,620), had
been 'very dear bought'.[47]

She was also in conflict with Godolphin over the multiplying Trust
lawsuits. Although in some moods she was prepared to admit that 'not
being cheated at all . . . would give one a great deal more trouble than
anything is worth', she still felt that it was an essential part of her duty as
trustee to do all she could to keep Marlborough's great fortune from
being eroded by fraud or maladministration.[48] In the first place there was
her continuing battle with the Strongs over the Blenheim debt. By
February 1724, despite Godolphin's objections, she was planning
another appeal to the House of Lords over the extent of their claims. As
a result the matter was referred back for further consideration to the
Court of Exchequer, but the really cheering aspect of the case was the
support she again received from the Lord Chancellor Macclesfield.[49]
This promised well for the hearing of the great Chancery suit which she
had begun in 1721 against all the Blenheim creditors. On 9 June 1724
Macclesfield did indeed go on to delight her even more by decreeing that
the workmen must give a full statement of work done and payment
received and refund any surplus; that the surveyor-general, Samuel
Travers, must account for the £220,000 of public money which had
passed through his hands; and, best of all, that Vanbrugh (cursing loudly
at being 'forc'd into Chancery by that B. B. B. B. Old B. the Dutchess of
Marlb:') had no right to payment from Marlborough's estate for any
work done before 1712.[50] But what pleased her most was the speech in
praise of Marlborough with which Macclesfield prefaced the decree:
'there is a great addition in the manner even of doing strict justice, & the
picture he made of the Duke of Marl & his actions is what I shall
remember with all gratitude to him as long as I live.'[51] In her joy at this
victory Sarah did not yet realize the error she had made in placing herself
at the mercy of the slow-grinding mills of Chancery. She would not
always be able to rely on a sympathetic Lord Chancellor, and her
troubles with the Blenheim officials, far from being over, were just
beginning.

No sooner had this decree been pronounced than she embarrassed
Godolphin further by beginning proceedings against their fellow trustee,
William Guidott. When the solicitor was at last prevailed on to submit
full accounts of his investments on Marlborough's behalf, she discovered,

among other irregularities, evidence of large amounts of mortgage interest received and not credited. At once she filed a bill against him in Chancery to recover the money.[52] This was to prove another long-drawn-out affair. Guidott, who was an MP, first used his parliamentary privilege to delay putting in his answer. But when he finally did so Sarah found that he had justified himself by claiming that Marlborough had paid him no allowance for his services, and she launched herself with characteristic obsessiveness into the task of running him into the ground:

I am harrass'd to Death, having risen every day for a great while, by Candle Light to take care that no Witness should be neglected to be sent for in order to prove that never any man was so much trusted as Mr Guidott was, or that abused a trust so much, but I shall certainly prove him to be the worst man that ever appear'd in Westminster Hall.[53]

Somerset continued to escort her to and from these hearings at Westminster, and in the evenings was her favourite partner at ombre: 'lett that alliance bee Repeated soe often in this & in other things,' he wrote hopefully, 'untill it becomes soe sacred & Holy an alliance [as] to make us perfectly Happy in each other.' Sarah continued to encourage him as far as she could without positively misleading him. Although she could not make him as happy as he desired to be, she told him, yet she had kinder thoughts of him than of any other man. 'I need not in return use many wordes,' he replied, 'because you doe already know what I have from my Heart & soul most sincerely declared, that you are the woman, the very woman, the onely woman I doe love, I doe value, I doe adore the most.'[54]

Second only to Somerset in her esteem by this time was another former enemy, her Oxfordshire neighbour, the blind Lord Harcourt. While the Oxford clergy were scandalized by the fact that he began his courtship of his third wife when his second was only a few weeks dead, Sarah was charmed by his romantic ardour: 'I think she is a very lucky woman for I never remember her handsom & lord Harcourt is the most agreeable man in conversation that ever I knew.'[55] Lady Burlington commented teasingly that she did not think Sarah's resolution of not remarrying safe until Harcourt had chosen someone else.[56] He paid the inevitable penalty for winning her over by being overwhelmed with copies of all her legal papers for his unofficial opinion, but in return she gave him unlimited permission to call for venison from Woodstock Park. There was much socializing between Blenheim and Cockthrop during Sarah's usual late summer visit to Woodstock in 1724, and she presented the new Lady Harcourt with a set of japan toiletries which had belonged to Queen Anne.[57]

The company of her circle of young people also continued to be a great solace. Lady De La Warr (the former Lady Charlotte West), who had long been almost an honorary grandchild, was always 'good & very kind' to her.[58] Lady Anne Egerton was gone, and the unsatisfactory Charles Spencer had been packed off to finish his education at an academy in Geneva, but her two favourites, John and Diana, remained in her immediate care. This lively and attractive pair, whom she had brought safely through the perils of smallpox, were now of an age to be real companions to her, and her letters were soon full of the sayings and doings of 'Dye and Johnney'. Diana in particular, like her mother and grandfather before her, had mastered the gentle art of managing Sarah. At 13, her grandmother declared, she already had 'more sence than any body that I know of my sex'.[59]

Pretty, sweet-tempered, and an heiress, the girl had already begun to attract suitors. One of them was Somerset's grandson, Master Wyndham. Lady Orkney put forward her great-nephew Lord Weymouth. Another was young Lord Shaftesbury, whose mother, Sarah told Somerset, 'makes me think of myself and Dye for if she is speaking and her son begins to say anything, she leaves off to hear him, & seems to think that all the company should give attention to him'. To all these eligible offers Sarah could politely reply that the young people were not yet old enough to give their informed consent.[60] She was certainly in no hurry to lose Diana, but the real reason for her delaying tactics was that her sights were set much higher. Bridgwater's plans for his daughter's marriage to the Duke of Bedford had been thwarted. Bedford's mother, who came from a family of City merchants, refused to fall in with an aristocratic marriage of convenience between her 15-year-old son and a girl who was some years older. Instead she had reached a private understanding with Sarah that when the time was ripe, the boy should be bestowed on Diana.[61]

By this time there were promising signs that the Marlborough heir might also be returning to the fold. In the spring of 1724 a brief letter came from Blandford, telling Sarah that he would shortly be coming back to settle in England.[62] A few months before (and twenty years after the birth of her last child) his mother had given birth to a daughter, Mary, who was generally assumed to have been fathered by William Congreve. With the long-suffering Godolphin prepared to be complaisant, Henrietta and her friends brazened it out, but Blandford was not pleased. Sarah herself had reason enough to be worried by this unexpected new grandchild. Since Marlborough's titles were heritable by his female as well as his male heirs, it was not impossible that 'Moll Congreve', as she dubbed the baby, would one day be Duchess of

Marlborough in her own right. Indeed, if the child had been a boy it would have taken precedence over the Spencers. As it was, there were still four grandsons in the way of this dreadful contingency, and at least the affair had the effect of weakening Henrietta's influence over her son.

Sarah, much as she loved Blandford and wished to retain her hold over him, had a good deal to forgive. The only communication she had had from him since Marlborough's death had been a graceless note nine months after the event, giving her directions how to pay the independent income which she had procured for him.[63] Nor did he now make any apology for his neglect. Reports of her displeasure left him unmoved; he only commented that it would be 'troublesome and fruitless' to keep up a correspondence with her.[64] She did not reproach him directly, but a frank letter to Nicholas Mann, who had been sent out by Godolphin to disengage his son from his Jacobite companions, brought another brief note from Blandford in July, this time professing 'a perfect sense' of her goodness to him.[65] This was sufficient for Sarah, and she took him again to her heart.

There was much for her to do. The Marlborough heir must not be allowed to lie under suspicion of Jacobitism, and to her friends she passed on Mann's over-optimistic assurances that Blandford had never been seriously attracted by the exiled Court or by Roman Catholicism: 'nobody laughs more at the pop[e], & all that sort of stuff then hee does, & if hee were not so well settled in his religion as I beleive him to bee, his great estate would secure him to the present government.'[66] Arrangements would have to be made on his return for him to be called to the House of Lords by writ. He must be encouraged to think of marrying, and in the meantime he must have somewhere suitable to live. She investigated several town houses. Better still would be an apartment under her eye in Marlborough House, which she now promised to leave to him when she died, bypassing his mother, 'for what is in my power shall not be filled with poets, Jades & fidlers'.[67]

In Paris in the spring of 1725 Blandford's path briefly crossed that of John Spencer, passing through on his way to join his brother at Geneva, and as 'happy and brisk as a bird out of a Cage' to be free of his grandmother's surveillance.[68] This meant that she had also lost the services of her most trusted servant, Humphrey Fish, whom she sent with him as governor. But if she had to bear the absence of two of her favourites, she was about to gain a substitute, though it came about through the disappointment of her hopes in another direction. In the summer of 1724 the widowed Duchess of Bedford had died. Smartly the Duke of Bridgwater secured the guardianship of his 16-year-old brother-in-law, and made the match between him and Lady Anne Egerton which his mother had refused to consent to in her lifetime. They only waited for Parliament to open so that the marriage settlement could be ratified.

Sarah did not see fit to betray that she had been outmanœuvred. Only her friend Lady Burlington, who knew the truth, privately commiserated with her.[69] She even reproached Lady Anne for keeping the affair a secret, and had a rude message in return from Bridgwater that he had commanded his daughter to hold no communication with her whatsoever.[70] This did not deter Sarah. With the help of Lord Harcourt, who agreed that Bridgwater had to be carefully watched lest he take advantage of the young couple, she busied herself soliciting all the peers of her acquaintance about the marriage settlement; and she claimed the credit when they agreed to a jointure of £3,000 for her granddaughter, in return for the £20,000 which was due to her by her mother's marriage settlement and her grandfather's will.[71]

She soon had her reward. In April 1725, ten days before the wedding, Bedford himself wrote to tell her of his secret plan to run away with his bride to Woburn as soon as they were married. She gave him her hearty approval, and afterwards, to Bridgwater's fury, there was an open exchange of visits between St Albans and Woburn.[72] The more Sarah saw of the young Duke, the more impressed she was. 'Nobody upon earth ever governd me, nor ever shall,' she told him when he complained to her of Bridgwater's dictatorial ways; '. . . I beleive your dear Grace is of the same temper & I love you much the better for it.'[73] Having imbibed the old Whiggism of his family to the full, he had a precocious detestation of Walpole and all his works which added to her delight in him. Among other things, they were agreed in despising the new Order of the Bath. When Walpole tried to lure Bedford and Sunderland with the promise of it, Sarah sent a haughty message that the only Order either of them recognized was that of the Garter.[74] When Bedford came to town at the end of the month to apply to Chancery to change his guardian, Sarah begged him to treat Marlborough House as his own. There he temporarily turned Diana out of her place as 'secretary of state', and Sarah was soon declaring him to be 'the best Servant and Minister that ever I had' and 'a perfect Miracle of his Age'. On reflection she considered that 'Providence designs to make me amends for some of my past Sufferings by the Goodnesse and Kindnesse of this young Man, for I am told by severall of my Friends that hee says hee loves mee of all Things; and I am sure that I will preserve it by doing every Thing that I can to serve him'.[75] When he asked her to furnish Southampton House in Bloomsbury, ready for him and his wife to move into in the winter, this congenial task kept her in London, ferreting about in attics, sale-rooms, and auction houses, until well into the summer.[76] At 65 both her energy and her 'Perpetuall hurry of business' continued unabated.

At last she was free, in the best of health and spirits, to leave for Blenheim, where the end of her labours was now in sight. The lake, cascade, and bridge she found almost complete, 'and as beautifull as can bee imagin'd'; when everything was quite finished, she decided, 'it will certainly bee a wonderfull fine Place, and I believe will be liked by every Body, and I am glad it will bee so, because it was the dear Duke of Marlborough's Passion to have it don'.[77] She filled the attic storey with her friends. The Hanburys and Lord Harborough came with her. The Harcourts visited from Cockthrop. Sunderland, still supreme in her favour, though skilfully evading her attempts to marry him off, joined her from Althorp, and of course there were the young Bedfords and Diana. In this congenial mixture of old and young company, basking in the sense of having done her duty, Sarah was happier during this Indian summer at Blenheim than she remembered being on any earlier visit.[78]

The Queen and Sir Robert
1726–1730

Y<small>ET</small> Sarah's Indian summer was soon on the wane. For all her undiminished energy, she was facing not only old age but progressive disability. In the second winter of her widowhood she had had a severe attack of 'gout', which left her unable to walk without help for several weeks.[1] 'Gout', a vague contemporary term for any kind of painful inflammatory condition, seems in her case to have been some form of rheumatism or arthritis, aggravated by winter weather and perhaps also by scurvy, a deficiency disease which was endemic at all levels of eighteenth-century society. These winter illnesses now became a regular occurrence. Her depression and irritability while they lasted were made worse by enforced contact with the medical profession. In the winter of 1724–5 she told Blandford that she must expect to die 'a little sooner or later',

as ones friends will have it, by the assistance of Doctors. When I am well enough to reason, I think it very indifferent when this happens, and yet there is something in nature that contradicts reason, and makes one start at pain and then one takes nautious medicines in hopes they may keep one longer in the world which I have been a long time very weary of & if I could have walked out of it, I am confident I should have gone many years agoe.[2]

The warm weather invariably restored her at first, and she would boast of being able to travel from Blenheim to London in a day without being tired. Yet each fit lasted longer than the one before, and left her limbs weaker. The next winter the ill effects continued well into the following summer. By this time she had also decided that Somerset's courtship, enjoyable though it was, had been allowed to go on long enough. Unable to ignore the signs that 'the old subject of love' was no longer welcome, he finally bowed out of the life of his 'tyrant but yet charming souvereign' in the autumn of 1725, and the following winter consoled himself by marrying one of the many daughters of the Earl of Nottingham. With a cordial exchange of congratulations and acknowledgement, his relations with Sarah declined into a friendly formality.[3]

Meanwhile her arrangements for Blandford's return proved to have been completely thrown away; indeed, they deterred him. From Paris Lady Anne Bateman reported that he did not 'make a figure' there suitable to his rank. Mann told Sarah that he had no ambition to make a figure in England either, and no desire whatever to be called up to the House of Lords.[4] Sarah's long weekly letters of advice and affection put his companion in mind 'of some animal that stifles her young with too much fondling'.[5] As Mann predicted, Blandford's replies soon petered out altogether. Clearly he had given up any thought of returning to England in the foreseeable future. And the news of his two Spencer cousins was no more satisfactory. The only use of their being abroad, Sarah considered, was to make them fluent in French, to 'keep them out of harms way while they are so young that they can't keep the best company in England, and to make them see that nothing is so agreeable as England take it alltogether'. The Swiss academy she intended 'to have been but in the nature of Oxford'. Yet instead of keeping them at their studies, the proprietor was letting them waste their time and run up extravagant bills. She was horrified to find that they were getting through more money than she and Marlborough had spent while they were abroad with their huge entourage in 1713. It had all grown past a jest, she told Humphrey Fish, as she took them out of the academy and put them entirely into his charge.[6]

Fish had grown from a valuable youth into a very impressive young man, fit for better tasks than the thankless one he was now performing. Those who encountered the party were far more struck by him than by his two unremarkable young charges.[7] His letters to Sarah, in a firm, characterful hand, were respectful without being obsequious, and he was not afraid to stand up to her when her demands and prohibitions became unreasonable. She repaid him with a frankness and confidence far greater than those normally bestowed by aristocratic employers on their children's governors. All her hopes that her grandsons would at last turn out well were now pinned on him. She made it clear that if they would not follow her instructions in living economically and applying themselves to 'useful learning', she would leave them to depend solely on the £500 a year which they had inherited from their father: a terrifying prospect for these two spendthrift young men.

Her hopes of comfort from the Duke of Bedford had also been quickly disappointed. The outcome of his marriage confirmed her worst misgivings about such teenage matches. The couple proved to be sexually incompatible. Within a few weeks he had abandoned his bride at Woburn, declaring that he would let his estate pass to his brother 'rather than go through the filthy drudgery of getting an heir to it'. 'This comes of living till sixteen without a competent knowledge either of practical or speculative anatomy,' commented Lady Mary Wortley Montagu, who evidently blamed his mother's insistence on bringing him up in the unnatural suburban seclusion of Streatham.[8] The boy whom Sarah had found so promising seized what consolations were nearest to hand. At the great house-warming ball at Southampton House in February 1726, it was noticed that he 'did the honours very well, particularly what related to drinking'. He was soon to be seen at assemblies with Lord Sunderland (as compulsive a gambler as his father and grandfather) and Lord Essex (another of Sarah's adolescent favourites gone to the bad), 'playing pretty deep'.[9]

Sarah joined the anxious group of adult relations who vainly tried to bring about a reconciliation. She found it hard to blame Bedford, who continued to be affectionate to her; his gambling and drinking, she thought, might not have been so bad, 'if he had not had a great Aversion to his Wife'. Yet when she encouraged him to confide in her, he was too embarrassed to do so. 'I that was a Grandmother did not know the secrets between them,' she wrote sadly afterwards. She could only advise her granddaughter that considering his youth and 'great foundation of sense', matters might improve if she bided her time and tried not to displease him.[10] In the meantime the example of Bedford and Sunderland made her adamant that the two young Spencers should never gamble. If she heard that they disobeyed her, she told Fish, she would never give them a shilling, 'living or dying'.[11] The disaster of the Bedford marriage was one reason for Sarah to delay her plans for marrying Diana. Another, even more disturbing one was that the girl had developed scrofula, a disfiguring tubercular condition of the glands in her neck. Sarah sought a cure far and wide, and in the meantime Diana's companionship helped to redeem the sudden bleakness which had descended on her personal life.

Another consolation was her perennial fascination with politics. By the mid-1720s, having got rid of the last of Sunderland's henchmen, Cadogan into retirement and Carteret to Ireland, Walpole was in his heyday. To Sarah, as to all the opposition Whigs, his monolithic power, his readiness to ally the country with France, and his cynically effective methods of parliamentary management were a perversion of Whig principles, as much of a threat to the constitution in their way as the would-be absolutism of the Stuarts, and a great deal worse than the Tory policies he had once opposed. Yet she was still locked in an uneasy financial alliance with him. Every winter, with her reluctant and argumentative consent, Godolphin renewed the agreement for lending the Trust money to the exchequer in anticipation of the land and malt tax revenue.[12] The rate of interest remained at 3 per cent. Since her first agreement to lend in the winter of 1722–3 had coincided with the reduction from 5 per cent, Sarah now convinced herself that she alone had enabled Walpole to bring this about, and that it would have been impossible for him to have made 'so much as an appearance of sinking the public debt' if it had not been for the Trust money.[13]

These, like many of Sarah's claims, were part truth and part wild exaggeration. The easy availability of the huge fund of Marlborough money for short-term borrowing was undoubtedly very useful to Walpole, particularly in his first years at the treasury. Yet he disliked being dependent on her assistance as much as she resented having to give it, and very soon he was able to demonstrate that the Trust had at least as much need of him as he of the Trust. 'The public credit is now in so flourishing a condition,' he wrote to Townshend in 1723, 'that upon some difficulties the duchess of Marlborough had a mind to make in that loan, I could have had £200,000 in land tallies . . . and I think it is plain we shall have the whole supply of next year at 3 per cent even without the Marlborough money.'[14] In February 1726 Godolphin agreed that in return for an immediate supply of £100,000 which Walpole needed, the Trust would be allowed to re-lend its remaining capital to the exchequer as it became due for repayment on the previous year's loan. The first, Walpole acknowledged, was a favour to the government; but giving the Trust money preference in the second, he maintained, was a favour to the Trust, since the exchequer might have had the funds elsewhere at the same or lower rates.[15] To Sarah, this was plain confirmation that he was playing the Bank and the Trust off against one another, in order to keep the interest rates low.

In fact, of course, it was not only the Trust money, but the stable financial climate of Walpole's creation, together with the continuing peace in Europe, which had made the lowering of the interest rate possible. As a friend pointed out when Sarah grumbled, 'money must needs become a mere drugg, if not lent to the Government, if a Peace can be continued a few years longer'.[16] Accustomed to the wartime rates of Godolphin's administration and unwilling to allow Walpole any virtues, Sarah could never be brought to acknowledge this. In 1727, when war with Spain over Gibraltar was imminent, the government interest rate rose to 4 per cent, and this made her a little more ready to give her consent to Godolphin's agreements with the treasury.[17] Although she continued to take every opportunity of buying land, she admitted that progress was slow, and at heart she realized the truth of his claim that there was nowhere else to invest so large a sum of money safely.

The fact was that in all her dealings with Walpole, Sarah was living in the past. Still unable to forget that he had once been her husband's clerk, she was ready to bridle at any change in his demeanour to her now that he was prime minister. For the sake of Godolphin and the Trust money, Walpole was ready to do her some favours: to grant her the reversion of some old houses in Pall Mall so that she could widen the entrance to Marlborough House,[18] and even (much against his better judgement) to relieve her of the taxes on Windsor Park. Yet she continued to nurse every grievance against him, real or imagined, from his grudging attitude over the taxes to his failure to exempt her from the general prohibition against driving coaches through St James's Park. Her conviction (not entirely unfounded) that the Hanoverians and the Whigs owed everything to Marlborough, together with the memory of Godolphin's long years at the treasury, when all her requests had been granted informally, nurtured her natural arrogance. Walpole complained that she refused 'to submit to the usual forms of doing business'; she made demands where she should have asked favours or submitted formal petitions, and took offence if they were not instantly complied with.[19] She was well aware that the ill will was mutual. When the Spencers offered to send her a present of the latest fashions from Paris, she warned them to do so privately, 'for I hate solicitation; and I know Sir Robert, notwithstanding all his former obligations to me & my Family, would give me all the Trouble he could, if I had but a Pound of Tea seiz'd at the Custom House'.[20]

In the autumn of 1726 Marlborough's old chaplain and Walpole's lifelong friend, Francis Hare, took it upon himself to mediate between them. When this proved useless, he went bravely back to first causes. In a classic remonstrance, which many must have wished but none except Queen Anne had ever yet dared to make to Sarah, he took her to task for 'ill-grounded suspicions, violent passions, and a boundless liberty of expressing resentments of persons without distinction from the Prince downwards, and that in the most public manner, and before servants'. He added that she could only do herself harm by quarrelling with the Court, and pointed out that 'if people were at liberty to vent in all places all the ill they thought true of others, it would destroy society, & there would be no living in the world'. Sarah, still priding herself invincibly on her sincerity, was quite unmoved; 'if all the good wishes that I have made for this government (not to mention some services) can't make the ministers treat me with common decency, I don't see why I should deny myself the pleasure of speaking my mind upon any occasion.'[21]

Although she had not been to Court since her snubbing at the time of the South Sea crisis, she still occasionally visited the Prince and Princess of Wales at Richmond. On the surface her relations with the Princess

were still all smiles and graciousness, and little Prince William, the future
Duke of Cumberland, was a particular favourite. In the summer of 1726,
to mark the finishing of Blenheim, she invited them all to visit;[22] but this
was taken and probably intended as a compliment only, and never acted
upon. In private Sarah held the Princess guilty of the same fault as
Walpole: that of not granting every favour the moment it was asked. In
June 1727 George I died, and Caroline became Queen. But when
Humphrey Fish asked Sarah to use her influence to get him a place at
Court, the grievances came pouring out:

The Person that you think I have some pretensions to ask a favour of, 'tis true
has made monstrous professions to me and I am sure I have deserved as
much as any body can do upon the subject that she has the benifitt of [the
Hanoverian succession], and never did any thing to give the least occation for
her not to make good those professions, but the truth is, that she never means
any thing that she says, but she loves to talk and thinks that every body will be
pleas'd with words, and even in a thing that was a trifle [the right to drive
through the Park] . . . since she could have done it herself, tho' she has been put
in mind of it, she has not granted what she said was so reasonable.[23]

Their first encounter at the beginning of the reign confirmed the ill
feeling on both sides. The Queen, having summoned Sarah to consult
about precedents, went on to talk of George II's first speech to his
Council, which had been drafted for him by Walpole. Sarah was already
cynical about this—it was 'a very good one, as all Kings make, tho' I
don't know of any of those professions that have been kept'—and when
Caroline put a hand confidentially on her shoulder and said, 'I assure
you, my dear Duchess, that the King made every word of this speech
himself,' she could hardly keep a straight face between amusement and
outrage; that she, the wife and companion of chief ministers, should be
supposed not to know how royal speeches were produced: 'this might
have been a proper discourse to any body that came from the Indies, but
nothing could be more ridiculous than to say it to me.' Her feelings must
have been plain enough, for when she next came to ask a favour, she
complained that Caroline made her wait for four hours in an outer room,
'when she might have dispatch'd me civilly in two minutes'.[24]

Sarah's feuds with her family were still an inexhaustible source of
amusement to the Queen, and there was no lack of mischief-makers to
relay unguarded talk to and fro. On the eve of the coronation Sarah
received the following anonymous letter:

Her M[ajesty] said that at present you was mighty gracious to her, she did not
know how long it would last, but you said you would walk at her coronation
tho' you went upon crutches, but she feared that wou'd be dangerous to you as
you might happen to walk by the young D[uchess] of Marl: who she thought

cou'd never resist the temptation of tripping up one of your crutches, & so went on talking of the way you was with your family, & seemed to think it was as much your fault as theirs . . . I beleive it was being peevish that you did not chuse rather to make her the compliment of lending her your dimants for the Coronation then of wearing them your self.[25]

This was enough to make Sarah, blazing with the coveted diamonds, quite determined to take her place in procession with the other Duchesses. The radiance which had enthralled Marlborough and Queen Anne and brought elderly peers to kneel at her feet was still potent. Even though she had to help herself along with a stick, it was noticed that she managed to make 'a better figure than many of her juniors'. When they all came to a halt for a time, she rested her feet by commandeering a drum and seating herself on it in all her finery, amid the cheers of the crowd and the soldiers.[26] Yet once the formal homage was over, she made no attempt to conceal her real feelings for the new monarchs, and shortly afterwards she received another letter from her anonymous informant:

she [the Queen] says now, that the time is come which she expected, for that you raile publickly at her as much as you cou'd do at the most insignificant person, but she does not wonder at it, for you have been so much used to be Q[ueen], that it is impossible you shou'd like an other, she believes it would have been the same thing if she had done all the unreasonable things which you desired of her, she says that you would have her provide for half your family, tho' you have more money than she has, and won't do the least thing for any of them your self.[27]

The one great benefit Sarah expected from the new reign was that Walpole's power would come to an end, since George II was known to detest him and his two closest associates, Townshend and Newcastle. Yet before long, with the aid of the Queen and his own indispensable mastery of Parliament and the treasury, the minister was as firmly in the saddle as ever. The only consolation was that the last months of George I's reign had seen the growth of the first effective parliamentary opposition to Walpole, headed by his former colleague, William Pulteney. Sarah, who had fought so hard to get the Whigs into power under Queen Anne, was becoming firmly convinced that opposition was 'of great use and necessary against all ministers' (except, she added inevitably, 'the Duke of Marlborough and the late Lord Godolphin, who, without partiality, I am sure, never meant anything but the good and security of England').[28] From now on she followed each winter's proceedings in the House of Commons avidly, and soon her letters began to read like abstracts of Pulteney's speeches, with their complaints of mismanagement, heavy taxes, increased civil list debts, the hire of expensive Hessian mercenaries, and wars used as a pretext to get money voted for other purposes. The ministers, she noted with relish in the last session of George I, had been 'miserably expos'd lately in the Debates . . . & Sir R. W. had things said to him that never were before heard of in publick, & of his Corruption; which made him lose, what he us'd to value himself upon, his Temper: For they say, he foam'd at the mouth'.[29]

Pulteney, whose family had long been Sarah's friends, lost no time in recruiting her to his party. He knew that politics still fascinated her, that she dearly loved to feel herself of consequence to men at the centre of affairs, and that she would go to any lengths to see Walpole worsted. 'You have Friends, you have Credit, you have Talents, you have Power, & you have spirits stil to do an infinite deal of service, if you will please to exert them,' he told her flatteringly.[30] What he meant was that she had money, electoral influence, and grandsons of parliamentary age who must vote as she directed them or be disinherited. At a time when the opposition had to count every vote against Walpole, her command of at least two, and possibly all four, parliamentary seats at Woodstock and St Albans, as well as her influence over Sunderland's conduct in the House of Lords, was in itself reason enough for Pulteney to take trouble over her. In fact her whole system of education for the young Spencers was designed to fit them to be his disciples as well. This was what lay behind her bullying insistence that they concentrate on 'useful learning' —French, history, and above all accounts—and not waste their time on dilettante studies such as architecture, music, painting, and medals. It was expertise in public accounts, above all else, which made Pulteney able to meet and match Walpole in debate. 'If a young Man would make his Fortune in this Country he must make himself useful, & consequently some time or other, such a one as may be fear'd by Ministers,' she told them; 'Otherwise, there is nothing to be got here, but by such vile means as I would not receive Life upon.'[31]

Although the death of the old King meant a general election two years sooner than it would otherwise have been due, Sarah was not wholly unprepared. As early as 1725 she had begun to improve her interest at Woodstock. She visited Oxford in search of models for Marlborough's tomb at Blenheim, behaved graciously, and patronized local tradesmen. A little coterie of university clergy, who had once not had a good word to say for her (nor she for them), now attended her wherever she went, cringing to her, a more inveterate opponent noted, as if they had been her footmen. She took advantage of a quarrel between her old enemy Lord Abingdon and the Oxford freemen to strengthen her interest, and began to lay plans for packing the Woodstock Common Council with her own nominees.[32] It was Charles Spencer who was to be the beneficiary of all this. 'One would think so modest a proposal from the heirs of Blenheim should not meet with any opposition,' she wrote, remembering her past difficulties with this stubborn little borough, 'but reason does not always govern in this world: however, I must try, for it would be shameful that one of the Duke of Marlborough's family should not be chosen in that town.'[33] The fact that Spencer was still a few months under age when the general election was called prematurely was in her eyes no reason to change her plans. It was only when her opponents found out and challenged her that she hastily nominated Blandford, still abroad and totally indifferent to the whole matter, in his place. She had originally intended to put him up for St Albans, to keep that seat in the family until John Spencer was of age. But even before her enforced change of plan at Woodstock, she decided against it. A scheme for dividing the borough by agreement with Grimston was defeated by another strong local interest. She decided that it was not worth an expensive contest to have a grandson elected who could not be bothered to come to England to cast his vote against Walpole.[34] Her parliamentary ambitions for both the Spencers would have to be postponed, although only for the time being.

In the meantime Pulteney continued to cultivate her assiduously, using the two projects closest to her heart at this time: her legal proceedings against Guidott and the embellishing of Blenheim. The Guidott lawsuit had not gone at all as she had hoped. While he had delayed putting in his answer, the Lord Chancellor Macclesfield fell from power, charged with corruption and unpitied by his ministerial colleagues. For the sake of 'the Justice which hee ded in so hansome a way to the Dear Duke of Marlborough's memory', Sarah helped him with bail. Although she acknowledged that 'nothing wants reformation more then the courts of law', she maintained that he had been guilty of nothing that had not been practised even by that 'feaverit of the wiggs', Lord Somers. Besides, as she pointed out, few members of Walpole's Parliament were in a position to point the finger in such matters:

tis well known that if a member in either hous has a place or a pention if hee does not vote black is white contrary to the design of Parliaments hee shall bee turnd out the next day, & receive no more pention, now I would fain know if that is not the most dangerous & worst sort of corruption.[35]

The real problem was that Macclesfield's successor, Lord King, was no friend to her or the Trust, and very much one to Guidott, who had travelled the northern circuit with him as Lord Chief Justice. When the cause came before him in November 1726, even though the discrepancies in the solicitor's accounts were undeniable and £5,000 ordered to be repaid, King refused to decree that there had been any intentional fraud in the case. At first Sarah was tempted to let the matter rest: 'it is not a trifling sum that has been recover'd: And it is a very great Advantage to me, to be eas'd of that part of my Trouble.'[36] Yet she could not bear to be gainsaid, even by a Lord Chancellor. Before the year was out, she had a long narrative of the case as she saw it printed and circulated as 'an appeal to the World' against King's decree. One copy was sent to the Lord Chancellor himself, while she prepared to appeal yet again to the House of Lords to have him overruled.[37] It was in mustering support for this among the opposition peers that Pulteney helped her. Lord Chesterfield and Lord Lonsdale, whom he introduced to her in this connection, were both old acquaintances to whom she was kindly disposed; indeed Chesterfield, as Lord Steward, now became her 'Friend at Court'.[38] But a few months later Pulteney achieved the much more remarkable feat of reconciling her with his chief partner in opposition, Lord Bolingbroke, now restored to his English estates (though not to his seat in the House of Lords) after his panic flight into the Pretender's service in 1715. In spite of the lack of a parliamentary base, however, he was making a brilliant contribution to the campaign against Walpole by his writings for the chief opposition journal, the *Craftsman*. Now, at Pulteney's instigation, he turned these talents to another literary project: the inscription for the obelisk at Blenheim.

This project had been hanging fire since 1723. Despite pressure from the Duke of Somerset, Pope had excused himself from the uncongenial task,[39] and nothing was produced by anyone else that found favour. Since the only purpose of the obelisk in Sarah's view had been to house the inscription, Hawksmoor's designs were shelved. It was not until the autumn of 1726 that Godolphin introduced her to another Palladian, Lord Herbert, who revived her interest in the matter.[40] In the winter of 1727–8, while Herbert drew up his plans, there was a renewed effort to get the inscription ready. It was a huge task. The Acts of Parliament had to be edited to remove unnecessary verbiage, and a summary of Marlborough's conduct during the whole war composed as an introduction. The groundwork was done by Macclesfield, and William Townesend did his part by making suggestions for enhancing the text by variations in the lettering which Sarah thought 'very Poetical for a mason'.[41] Yet the result left her still unsatisfied.

It was at this point that Pulteney and Bolingbroke rescued her. In the summer of 1728 Pulteney took charge of all the unfinished drafts and delivered them to his colleague. When the result was sent back to Sarah, she instantly recognized the account of the campaigns as 'the finest Thing that 'twas possible for any Man to write'. Its spare incisive prose appealed to her more than the most elaborate verse panegyric, and she saw how skilfully Bolingbroke had contrived to answer the only objections that had ever been made to Marlborough's conduct of the war 'without arguing, which would have been absurd in a Thing of this Kind'. She could never read it without weeping, 'which I take to be one sign that it is good'. Pulteney joined her at Blenheim in August, where they had the whole inscription set up on boards to make sure that it would fit on the faces of the pedestal.[42]

There appears to have been no personal contact between Sarah and Bolingbroke, that 'violent wretch' whose pardon she had opposed because he had 'forfeited all pretensions to any one single vertue'.[43] It was Pulteney who conveyed the inscription to and fro to have minor alterations made.[44] But he assured her that it had been written not only by an able hand but with a good heart, and her acceptance of the services of this old enemy was not so surprising as it seems. Bolingbroke, for all their political differences, had always hero-worshipped Marlborough, and his present opposition to Walpole would have been more than enough to redeem him in Sarah's eyes, even without this. When another friend remarked that the inscription made him reflect on those 'that for their own By-ends, & Love of Power & private Gain', had made Marlborough's successes of little use, she took this as a reference, not to Oxford and Bolingbroke, but to Walpole and Townshend. A Whig and a Tory, she considered, 'if they have Sense & Honesty mean the same thing'. It was not the Tories who were now her enemies, but the Court Whigs who 'had no ground to stand on, but what the Duke of Marlborough gave them', and had used it to betray their former principles.[45]

In December 1727 Charles Spencer came of age and immediately set out for home. Although he went through the formality of asking his grandmother's permission to do so, Fish made it clear to her as tactfully as he could that Charles now considered himself his own master.[46] Her first act when he set foot in England in February 1728 was to suggest to Godolphin that Blandford should now vacate Woodstock in his favour. Whereas the absent Marquess could be of no use in Parliament, his cousin, taught like the rest of his family to hate a Walpole by inheritance, was eager to cast his vote with the opposition.[47] But Godolphin refused to co-operate in turning out his son, and in other respects Sarah was not pleased with Charles Spencer. His resemblance to his father had increased with maturity, and he seemed to have derived little benefit from his years abroad. The most she could say for him was that he seemed well-behaved, '& they say hee has sence, but hee has nothing at least before me that is entertaining, tho you know my manner does not constrain any body'. She refused to give him any additional income, and by mutual consent they parted, Charles going to live with his elder brother. She could only keep a disapproving eye on him from a distance, noting that, as she had expected, he was 'much too expensive for a younger brother'.[48]

Her hopes were now fixed on John Spencer, who was to stay abroad for some time longer with Humphrey Fish: 'I am sure [I] wish him better, & love him more, than any body that is now in the World.' Fish's somewhat rose-coloured reports convinced her that Johnny was at last applying himself to his studies and turning into the 'considerable man' who would be capable of fulfilling all her ambitions.[49] Then in the summer of 1728 the two moved to Dijon, where they both fell ill of the endemic 'malignant fever'. While John Spencer eventually recovered, his governor, the better man of the two, did not. Sarah, to her credit, felt his death deeply: it 'struck me & troubled me more than I thought anything could possibly have done, but the Loss of some of my dearest Relations'. She had planned to make him Marlborough's official biographer (Steele, in his perennial improvidence, having disgraced himself irrevocably by pawning the papers she had lent him); now she had no hope of finding another reliable candidate in her lifetime.[50] She hung his picture among the great gallery of aristocratic portraits at Blenheim, and sent John Spencer an urgent summons home as soon as he was fit to travel: 'no words can express how dear you are to me, and I shall be in torture till I see you, therefore pray let it be as soon as you can come with safety.' He arrived in November, and in her relief and pleasure at seeing him again after more than three years he seemed to fulfil all her expectations.[51] She settled him under her eye in the little apartment in the courtyard of Marlborough House which had once lodged Queen Anne's bedchamber-women. Ultimately her plan was to get him the title Lord Churchill, which she claimed to know a way of obtaining, 'tho' I am incapable of ever being a Courtier my self', and 'by this, I thought I shou'd make one of the Dear Duke of Marlborough's Grand-sons represent Him in the World by his Name, supported with my own Estate'.[52] Events were soon to concentrate her ambitions still more exclusively on the two Spencers.

It had been in the summer of 1727, just as Sarah finished settling her elections, that the first rumour reached her of Blandford's being 'in danger of marrying a very low & odd woman'.[53] Having put his family off guard by sending Nicholas Mann to England to enquire about a suitable match, he had gone to Utrecht to pay his addresses to a burgermaster's daughter, whose family he had met in Paris. The following summer the worst was confirmed when he crossed the

Channel to tell his father formally of his intentions. Godolphin was even more horrified than Sarah, but thanks to her insistence on making her grandson entirely independent of his parents, there was nothing he could do to prevent the match. Blandford, coming only as far as Rochester, made no attempt to see his grandmother, but the following week he broke the news to her by letter. He spoke of the young woman's beauty and good birth, and added, rubbing salt in the wound, that 'if the fortune be not so very large, surely it is a point not worth thinking of one minute in my case, whom your Grace has been so Kind, as to make easy that way'.[54]

Sarah laboured long and hard over her reply, on which she pinned all her hopes of forestalling the match. It was an appeal more in sorrow than in anger, for she still had a fondness for him which no amount of neglect or weakness could remove. 'I do protest that I never was so much afflicted at any thing that has ever happened to me as I am at what you have written except the Death of the Dear Duke of Marlborough, & my only son,' she began pathetically; '. . . You have ownd several times that your hapy circumstances is owing intirely to me, & therefore I hope you will not return this by breaking my heart which it will certainly do to see the Duke of Marlborough's heir marryd to a burger masters daughter.' She begged him to come to England, '& see the world a little more, before you dispose of your self in so sad a mannor'.[55] The appeal had no effect and the marriage went ahead. The only lesson she could draw was that she had made Blandford too independent too soon. She would take care not to make the same mistake with his Spencer cousins. But as Sarah once remarked, 'the heart is a long time a-breaking', and hers was certainly not broken in the sense she predicted by her grandson's misalliance. The interest aroused by the Prince of Wales, newly arrived from Hanover at the beginning of 1729, made her continue to frequent the Court, and at a card party in January her spirits, the languishing Lady Bristol reported, 'were beyond anything I ever saw for the whole time, tho she was forced to be carried to the table in a chair, & fixd there before the King & Queen came'. Afterwards she had company to supper, and stayed up till three in the morning; 'I own I envy her constitution more than her money.'[56] Yet these moods often presaged an equally violent reaction. By the end of January Sarah was at death's door with her old combination of 'gout' and stone in the kidneys, and a succession of relapses kept her in danger for weeks. It was not until mid-March that she was well enough to give her consent to the next round of exchequer loans, and in April her limbs were still so weak that she could not stand.[57]

From now on, for all but a few weeks in the summer, she became a total cripple, having to be carried about in a chair and lifted in and out of her coach with a mechanical hoist. The disability also began to affect her hands, a major aggravation 'because I am us'd to do every thing for myself'.[58] Her handwriting deteriorated and she resorted more and more to dictation for her letters. Her greatest comfort during her illness had come from Lord Sunderland. She found that he had 'as much Compassion in his nature as his Mother had, which is saying a great deal for that Sex'.[59] Her greatest worry when she thought she might be dying had been that her will was now completely out of date, and as soon as she was well enough, she set about making new settlements. Although Sunderland was to be her chief heir, her property was now ample enough for her to provide generously for his two brothers as well, so long at least as their conduct continued to satisfy her. Between 1724 and 1729 she had acquired six more estates, including Cippenham (confiscated from Robert Knight, the South Sea cashier) in her favourite countryside near Windsor, which she proudly called 'the finest Farm in England'. And as well as parcelling out these lands in her will, she now decided, with the assistance of Lord Herbert, to build a mansion of her own on the great terrace at Wimbledon to replace that demolished by Janssen. While Holywell was of little use except as 'a quiet inn' for any member of the family who happened to be travelling north and Windsor Lodge would revert to the crown in due course, the new house would remain permanently in the family to endow her heirs in a fitting style.[60]

Yet even while this will was being drawn up, it was brought to nought. Sunderland, however well he concealed it, must have felt the burden of his grandmother's domineering affection as much as his cousin Blandford. As soon as the worst of her illness was over he took himself off to Paris with a group of friends to pass his time out of her reach. There in September 1729 he came down with a fever. Having long been accustomed to supervise any illness in her family, Sarah did not let the distance and her own disability deter her on this occasion. At the first news that he was in danger she dispatched a consignment of medicines by express and set out from Windsor Lodge to follow them. But she got no further than Brentford when she was met by the news that he was dead, literally bled to death, as the accounts of his companions made clear, by the French doctors in their efforts to bring down his fever. It was the cruellest of blows, she told Lady Mary Wortley Montagu, 'to have one droop so untimely from the only branch that I can ever hope to receive any comfort from, in my own family'.[61]

There was nothing for it but to try once more what comfort Blandford could supply. When he wrote just before Sunderland's death to enquire after her health, she let his letter go unanswered. But when she received another such overture in the winter, she seized the chance to bring him again into the family circle. In February 1730 she sent a long, reasonable, and not unkindly reply, reminding him of his long neglect, but adding, 'I still love you too well to reproach you: Therefore I desire only to look forward, & to forget all that is past.' She had tried to dissuade him from his marriage, she admitted, 'but when it was done, I was desirous to make the best of it. And I sincerely wish you may be always happy . . . And I think you may be so, & make such a Figure as you ought to do, if you please.' She reminded him that he was heir to one of the greatest fortunes in England, 'and then think how odd it must appear to all People to have such a Man live, as you do, at Utrecht, from all your Relations, or Friends that are of Value'.[62]

Blandford replied that he now wanted to return to England, but because of his mother's 'long ill conduct' (Henrietta had just made herself conspicuous again by her mourning for Congreve's death), he could have nothing to do with her, and his father opposed his return on such terms. This put Sarah into a quandary. She could hardly disapprove of his attitude to his mother; on the other hand, 'it would be wrong in you to take any notice of the wonderfull behaviour in her when your father seems to know nothing of it'. She told him that he must go through the formality of asking to wait on his mother, who (she had taken care to find out) would almost certainly refuse to see him. 'Madam,' Blandford replied,

I fear I did not sufficiently explain my self . . . with regard to the Circumstance of seeing my Mother; which I have so determind a Resolution not to do that if My Father persists that I should see Her, as the condition of my living well with him, I should (notwithstanding the Honour I ever had for him) think myself acquitted from the Obligation of seeing either of them.

Sarah took this flat rejection of her advice without a murmur, only remarking that she was pleased to find herself able to write on such a sensitive subject coolly and without prejudice.[63] Secretly she could not help being gratified that he had now turned to her in preference to both his parents.

Blandford at last arrived in England in June 1730, after more than ten years' absence, bringing his new wife with him. She was tall and fair and not unattractive, but certainly no great lady. Afterwards Sarah wrote rather cruelly that 'if any body saw her by Chance, they would be ready to ask her to shew them what Lace she had to sell'.[64] Yet at the time she made a surprisingly good impression on the whole family. It was Blandford over whom heads were shaken. While no one could deny that he had inherited his share of the legendary 'sense, good-nature and honesty' of the Godolphins, his years of aimless wandering about the Continent had turned him into a self-indulgent eccentric, rapidly descending into chronic drunkenness and quite incapable of taking up his natural position in the society of his own country.[65] His closest friends were still Jacobites, and he had apparently been secretly received into the Roman Catholic church before he left the Continent. The exiled Court, obliged to clutch at such straws and noting Sarah's contempt for 'the present Electoral Family', even hoped that he might be a means of drawing her in with her fabulous wealth to support them.[66] Of this there was not the slightest prospect. Yet she alone appeared blind to Blandford's failings, or accepted them with amazing tolerance. It was enough that he was now in England to add his vote to the opposition, and that he continued 'mighty kind' to her. In the winter he invited her and a large family party to dinner and then kept them all waiting for two hours without excuse. When he appeared, she merely called to him 'in all the good humour in the world, oh my Ld, I conclude you have been in the house of commons'. Blandford, while the other guests held their breath, admitted that he had not; 'then says she, I wish I was nearer to you, that I might beat you'. He merely remarked that he was very glad she was not nearer, and the incident subsided, Sarah giving no sign that she thought 'anything wrong or odd in him'.[67]

Parliament was never far from Sarah's thoughts by this time. She continued to follow the opposition's issues with consuming interest, wishing as in the anxious last months of Queen Anne's reign that she was a man and able to take part in the debates herself. 'I woud not wish your sex such a Loss,' one of her friends told her, 'but I do wish there were ten men in the House of Lords of your Graces Genius & Spirit, I am sure many affairs woud be better conducted for the Publick: However tho Your Grace cannot enact, you can obtain some things to be enacted by your Influence, where you see occasion.'[68] Having spent her whole life in the company of men of ability in public affairs, Sarah must have realized by now that the grandsons through whom she sought to act vicariously in politics would never be of the calibre of their fathers and grandfathers; but she could only do her best with the rather unpromising material to hand. A by-election at St Albans early in 1730 would have been the perfect opportunity to add John Spencer to the ranks of Walpole's opponents, if her indiscreet criticism of Grimston had not deprived her of his support.[69] While she waited for another opportunity to occur, she turned her attention to the marriages of her remaining Spencer grandchildren, determined that these at least, unlike Blandford's, should be entirely of her own making.

Dividing the Family
1730–1733

I F the grandchildren were now old enough to figure in Sarah's political and dynastic ambitions, they were also old enough to want their independence, and they could not have it while the old lady remained alive, guarding the huge mountain of family wealth and using the threat of disinheritance to quell any sign of rebellion or dissent. 'All your family wish for your death,' Sarah's anonymous informant had told her at the time of the coronation, 'because that is the only time they hope to have any thing but orders and directions from you.' This informant was probably none other than her eldest Spencer grandchild, Lady Bateman.[1]

Lady Bateman's brother Charles had succeeded to Sunderland's title and to his place as Sarah's chief heir, but only for a brief period to his favour with her. He had never submitted readily to her control, and within a month of his brother's death she was stipulating that her new will should be drawn up on paper rather than parchment, 'for if the present Lord Sunderland or others greatly concern'd in this Will should behave ill or marry without my Approbation, I will certainly alter it'.[2] In fact the chief influence on the new Lord Sunderland was not his grandmother, but his elder sister. Lady Bateman had grown into a clever, plain-faced woman with a taste for management and intrigue, and Sarah had alienated her without being fully aware of it by well-meant but insensitive harping on her husband's obvious lack of affection for her. 'Perhaps I might judge wrong in that matter from the Difference of the Duke of Marlborough's Behaviour to me, even before Company,' she conceded when the humiliated Lady Bateman protested she had nothing to complain of, '. . . you know I don't think it a sign of Love what some of our Friends do before People. But He, upon all occasions, shew'd all the Regard & Tenderness imaginable.'[3] Tied to her morose homosexual husband, Lady Bateman's closest relationships continued to be with her brothers and sister. If Sarah is to be believed, she had even made herself useful in procuring mistresses, not just for Charles but for the

impeccable Robert: 'indeed I have often reproach'd them in my own
Mind, that they would make use of a Sister for such an Employment.'[4]
Since Sarah, for all her bouts of ill health, showed no sign of releasing her
grip on the family by dying, Lady Bateman, a far stronger character than
any of her brothers, decided to issue a challenge to her in her lifetime.
Once Charles had inherited the Sunderland title, she set herself, as Sarah
put it with a characteristic political metaphor, to become his 'premier
Minister'.

Among those who recognized this role was the Duchess of Montagu.
For some time there had been hints that a reconciliation between Sarah
and her youngest daughter would not be an impossibility. During her
mother's illness in the winter of 1728–9 Mary had enquired after her
several times. Now she made overtures through Lady Bateman for a
match between her younger daughter and the new Lord Sunderland.
Sarah, having refused to respond on the first occasion, was perhaps
having second thoughts. She claimed that if the Duchess of Montagu had
proposed the match and a reconciliation to her at the same time, 'in a
Months Time I should have been as fond of it as she could have been'.
Instead she was infuriated to find that Lady Bateman, fearing to lose her
hold over her brother, had found some means to discourage the proposal
without consulting her.[5] It was only a matter of time before this
managing role brought her into open conflict with the grandmother who
would brook no rivals in her control of the family.

The meantime Sarah hastened the overdue business of finding a match
for Diana, so that Lady Bateman should at least have no opportunity of
interfering in this. When she made her appearance at Tunbridge Wells in
the summer of 1730, looking very well, it was noticed, in spite of her
disability, and managing to enliven the dull resort by her mere presence,
her main purpose was to give Diana an informal opportunity to meet a
prospective suitor.[6] A fortune of £50,000 was more than enough, when
joined with the girl's looks and rank, to make her the best match in
England, and Sarah declared her to be 'a treasure in herself besides what I
shall give her'. Yet she claimed that worldly motives would not be
allowed to influence the choice: 'I had much rather Marry her to a Man
that she lik'd with a moderate Fortune.' For all this, the person she
invited to meet Diana at Tunbridge, the Irish Lord Justice William
Conolly, had nothing much to recommend him but the immense fortune
he had just inherited from an uncle. Diana had no intention of letting
herself be sold to a nobody, and told her grandmother that she did not
like him.[7]

Having launched this great prize in the marriage market, Sarah had to
be very vigilant, especially as there were signs that Diana too was

beginning to chafe under her control. The girl's closest friend at this time was Lady Rich, whom, as the daughter of Edward Griffith by his second marriage, Sarah had until now been prepared to recognize as a relation of sorts. But when she found the friendship beginning to attract unfavourable gossip, she told her granddaughter that when they returned to London Lady Rich would have to be civilly dropped. Diana managed to warn her friend by letter, but the reply was unluckily delivered to her in her grandmother's presence. Demanding to see it, Sarah dashed off a brutal answer which she forced Diana to copy out and send in her own name.[8] Soon there was talk at the Wells that Diana was planning to make a bid for freedom by eloping with an army officer, Thomas Bludworth.[9] Forewarned by an anonymous letter, Sarah had just time to whisk her away to the seclusion of Windsor Lodge, where they remained for the next four months.

It must have been during this interlude that the attempted match between Diana and the Prince of Wales took place, if indeed it occurred at all. Horace Walpole, the only authority for the story, tells how the Prince, being kept short of money by his parents, was tempted by Sarah's offer of her granddaughter, accompanied by a fortune of £100,000; how a date for their secret wedding at the Lodge had actually been set when Sir Robert Walpole found out and managed to prevent it, and so 'the Secret was buried in silence'.[10] A dowry of £100,000 was certainly well within Sarah's capacity; nor was it the first time that a child of hers had been mentioned as a possible match for royalty. She was not afraid to couple her granddaughter's name, hypothetically at least, with that of the Prince. Telling Mrs Boscawen of Diana's rejection of Conolly, she added, in what was perhaps just a figure of speech, 'I wou'd not dispose of her to His Royal Highness the Prince of Wales nor to any King in the World, if she did not like it.'[11] Walpole's story may have had its origin in some such remark. Yet there was just enough unusual coming and going between the Lodge and the Castle in the autumn of 1730 to give some credibility to the tale. Lord Hervey, in attendance at Windsor in September, reported that the Batemans had become very friendly with the Prince, and that 'Old Marlborough is come to the Lodge, and lets Lady Di. sometimes be of the party'. Although Hervey added mysteriously 'thereby hangs a tale', he did not elaborate. Nor did the Duchess of Newcastle, when she told her aunt that she dared not write all the particulars she could tell her of the gossip concerning Diana's marriage.[12]

Yet Hervey's account suggests that if anyone was behind the match, it was the intriguing Lady Bateman rather than her grandmother. And what effectively disproves the story as far as Sarah was concerned is the evidence of her unprecedentedly cordial relations at this time with the King and Queen. Early in September, at a stag-hunt for the royal family in Windsor Park, according to Hervey,

the first thing that presented it-self . . . was her Grace of Marlborough, flying in an easterly Wind & an open Chaise, her Hands in Flannel & her Shoulders in Embroidery; & what was in her Heart I know not, but out of her Mouth flow'd nothing but Oyl & Honey. Many Douceurs pass'd between her, the King, the Queen, & Sir Robert; & after what has happen'd I don't think it at all impossible but the next News I send you may be that she has danced all night at Court of the Birth Day.[13]

Shortly afterwards Sarah waited on the Queen, 'which I should not have thought of,' she told Somerset, 'so very weak & lame as I am. But . . . she was so gracious as to press me to come to the Castle in such a manner that I thought it was less ill manners to trouble her than to refuse.'[14] Back in town in the New Year, one of her first engagements was to join the King and Queen at their gaming table on Twelfth Night, a privilege which cost her over £500 in stakes. At 70, she was still astonishingly untouched by the years. 'She really look'd as well, & as young as she has done these ten years, & much better than most people there,' the Duchess of Newcastle reported, adding in even greater wonder that she also seemed 'in great good humour with their Majestys'.[15] One practical explanation of this was that Sarah was hoping to forward Jane Kingdom's claims to a pension from the Court. In fact this friendship was now so far restored that she had appointed Mrs Kingdom Diana's companion and chaperone in case she herself died before her grand-daughter married: an arrangement probably designed to keep the girl from falling entirely into her sister's hands.[16] When the pension was granted, Sarah declared that the King and Queen had obliged her so much that she thought she ought at least to hold her tongue about them, '& since it will have that effect,' the Duchess of Newcastle added, 'if I were they, I should think it money mightily well employ'd'.

Whatever thoughts Sarah might or might not have had of the Prince of Wales, they were certainly over by the winter, when she began actively to seek a match for Diana among the nobility. The girl had come to town looking 'as handsome as an angell' and with the scrofulous scars on her neck completely healed (Sarah's bank account reveals that she paid the fabulous fee of £190 to the surgeon who wrought the cure).[17] On 5 February her grandmother gave her a ball at Marlborough House to mark her public emergence into the marriage market. The Duchess of Newcastle noted that she was still kept under the strictest surveillance, but 'I really believe the Dss of Marlborough is satisfied about her for they say she is, if possible, fonder of her than ever'.[18]

Within days, Sarah was deep in negotiations with the Duke of Dorset for his son and heir, Lord Middlesex, but she drove too hard a bargain in return for her £50,000 and Dorset soon bowed out.[19] Perhaps a rival proposal from Lord Chesterfield might have tempted her, if it had not dawned on her just beforehand that the match which Bridgwater had cheated her of was again within her grasp. Although the Duke of Bedford had patched up a reconciliation with his wife in public, they had never cohabited, and he was now far in decline with consumption. The younger brother, exactly Diana's age, on whom he had devolved the duty of getting an heir, was just returned from his travels. In April 1731 Sarah asked Bedford to use his influence in favour of the match. Since heiresses were not normally thrown away on younger brothers, this must have been a plain declaration to the Duke that he was not expected to live more than a few months. Even so, he warmly promised his help.[20] Lord John Russell, short, plump, and plain in his dress and manner, was not a romantic figure, but this time there were no complaints from Diana that she did not like her suitor's person. As for Sarah, she was so delighted with him that she was ready to declare him 'a tall man'.[21] Pointedly refraining from discussing her plans with Sunderland and Lady Bateman even after they were common knowledge, she took the young couple off to Blenheim to keep them out of the way of interference until the business was quite settled.[22]

They had only just arrived, however, when the news came that Blandford was dangerously ill at Oxford. In the twelve months he had been in England he had drifted apart from his wife, who remained childless, and further under the influence of his hard-drinking Jacobite companions. In the summer of 1731 he was staying at Balliol, to attend the annual meeting of the Tory 'High Borlase' club. There on 24 August, after a night of drunken feasting, he collapsed in delirium and died within twenty-four hours. His wife arrived just beforehand and Sarah just afterwards with Diana in her wake, carrying a heavy basket which was supposed by the bystanders to contain some of the legendary Marlborough gold. More probably it held the medicines which Sarah had brought in the hope of taking Blandford's treatment into her own hands and saving him. She stayed for two hours, dividing her time between Lady Blandford, whom she overwhelmed with sympathetic attention, and the doctors, whom she cross-questioned suspiciously about their treatment. At length she was convinced that Blandford's drink-sodden constitution had made the case hopeless. Casting about for some other scapegoat, she pitched on the tutor who had attended both the first Lord Blandford and the grandson she had taken into his place. 'I hope the [devil] is now picking that man's bones who taught him to drink,' she muttered, '. . . his name was Man[n], and he first deprived me of my son.'[23]

Blandford's mother, applauded by the hangers-on at Godolphin House, declared that she felt nothing but indifference at the news, 'and that anybody who had any regard to *Papa's* memory must be glad that the Duke of Marlborough was now not in danger of being represented in the next generation by one who must have brought any name he bore into contempt'.[24] Sarah, who had so obstinately loved Blandford and declared at Oxford that she would have given half her estate to save him, now claimed him from his indifferent mother and wife, and dealt with him as befitted the Marlborough heir. The chapel at Blenheim, the last of her works there, was almost complete; 'decent, substantial and very plain', without any of the 'Wonderful Figures and Whirligigs' she so disapproved of, it awaited only the installation of Rysbrack's glorious monument. Hastily she had it put in order and consecrated. On the evening of 4 September Blandford was interred there privately, the first of the family to rest in the vault where she would one day be laid with Marlborough.[25]

The shock put only a temporary damp on her spirits, which now soared to one of their ominous manic peaks. She nominated John Spencer in Blandford's place at Woodstock, and after a few days broke the news of Diana's match officially to Sunderland and Lady Bateman. 'She is as coquet as if she was eighteen, and as rampant as if she were drunk,' Lord Hervey commented; 'I expect to hear soon of her listing some strapping lusty Granadeer in her service or her taking some young Actor off the Stage; if her Spirits hold out much longer it is impossible her Virtue should.'[26] Sarah admitted to Lady Mary Wortley Montagu that she felt as if Diana's marriage had given her a new lease of life:

I propose to myself more satisfaction than I thought there had been in store for me. I believe that you have heard me say that I desired to die when I had disposed well of her; but I desire that you would not put me in mind of it, for I find now I have a mind to live till I have married my Torrismond, which name I have given long to John Spencer.[27]

Before she turned her attention to her Torrismond, however, she had the less congenial task of seeing Sunderland properly disposed of. With Blandford dead, she was acutely aware that only the two unmarried Spencer brothers stood in the way of the dukedom's devolving on Henrietta's daughters, and therefore (since the Duchess of Newcastle was sickly and childless) descending to 'Moll Congreve's' line.[28] Sunderland was now heir to the Marlborough title when Henrietta should die; it was vital that he should marry suitably without delay and beget sons. Yet whenever the subject was raised he prevaricated, saying that he could not like any woman for more than a few months. After Blandford's death he installed the mistress of the moment in his household and lavished his increased income on extravagant hunting equipages and alterations to the house and stables at Althorp.[29]

What Sunderland chose to do with his paternal estate would normally have been none of Sarah's business, except that by the terms of Marlborough's will (terms which she herself had devised) he was bound to convey Althorp to his younger brother when he inherited the dukedom. Sarah was angry with him for wasting his money and spoiling a house which she regarded as only held in trust for John Spencer and his children. What was worse, in her view, the alterations were being conducted by 'that infamous fellow' Roger Morris, whom she was about to sack from her own building schemes at Wimbledon for persistently ignoring her instructions. Yet when she tried to remonstrate with Sunderland, Lady Bateman opposed her and even talked of his overriding the will and giving his brother an equivalent for Althorp in money when the time came.[30] This heresy confirmed her worst suspicions of an evil influence at work in the family.

As for Sunderland, having succeeded to his cousin's independent income, he frankly rejoiced that he would 'be no longer obliged to manage that unloving, capricious, extravagant old Fury of a Grandmother', and boasted in his cups that he intended 'to kick her A— & bid her kiss his own'.[31] Sarah could not help seeing a marked change in his manner, but decided to keep up appearances in public. By the spring of 1732 she heard that he had parted with his mistress, and was therefore more receptive to the idea of a wife. During one of his infrequent visits to Marlborough House she told him that she 'was glad to hear he had not so great an Aversion to Marriage as he formerly had; for our Family wanted posterity very much', that the woman she had in mind for him would be well bred and healthy, 'and for money, twas no matter whether she had any thing or nothing'. To this Sunderland, already deep in marriage negotiations of which she knew nothing, only replied 'with a stiff air and disagreeable voice, "I won't marry without telling you"'.[32]

When he came in a day or two to fulfil this promise, she was ill in bed and refused to see him. Afterwards she even claimed to have been dying. Sunderland, no doubt relieved to be spared a personal interview, sent in the message that he had decided to marry one of the daughters of Lord Trevor and was to complete the legal formalities the next day. To Sarah the match itself was bad enough. The girl was the granddaughter of one of twelve humble Tory peers created by Queen Anne in 1711 to ensure the passage of the peace of Utrecht through the House of Lords. But what made her volcanic with rage (it was Lord Hervey who dubbed her 'Mount Aetna') was the realization that the whole business had been deliberately concealed from her, and still more that it was entirely of Lady Bateman's devising.

Elizabeth Trevor's father and Lord Bateman were first cousins, and it was to the Bateman home at Totteridge that Sunderland was going to finalize the arrangements. Lady Bateman, Sarah now claimed, realizing that Sunderland was inclined to marry, saw that 'it would be best for her to find out some body bred very low as Mrs Trevor was, that she might continue in the Post of her Brother's Premier Minister and govern all his Affairs'.[33]

Beside herself at this 'monstrous Usage of a most tender Grand-mother', Sarah abandoned all pretence to be dying, sat up in bed, and called for pen and paper. Out poured all her long memory could supply of the sins and shortcomings of the Trevors for three generations, ranging from the seduction of Mary Trevor (the girl's great-aunt) by Thomas Thynne of Longleat in 1678 and the dubious origin of the family title to the 'mean ordinary Look' and bad teeth of the girl herself. Sarah added that she had just spent two hours altering her will, taking from Sunderland everything that was in her power to withhold. It only irked her that this did not amount to more than her own property and the lease of Marlborough House; if she could, she would have stripped him of his grandfather's estate as well.[34] Sunderland must have enjoyed writing his reply:

I receiv'd Your Grace's extraordinary Letter last Night, & I own my Discerning won't let me see any Reason in what your Grace is pleas'd to say against my Marrying; unless Invectives are to be look'd on as Arguments. I shan't endeavour to convince Your Grace, that it is a Match of my own seeking & not of my overbearing sister's (as you are pleas'd to call her) because in the Passion Your Grace must be, when you wrote such a Letter, all Arguments would be of very little use. As for your putting me out of your Will, it is some Time since I neither expected or desir'd to be in it. I have nothing more to add but to assure Your Grace, that this is the last time I shall ever Trouble you by Letter or Conversation. I am your Grace's Grandson, Sunderland.[35]

But Sarah managed to have the last word: 'You end that you are my Grandson: Which is indeed a very Melancholy Truth; but very lucky for You. For all the World except yourself is Sensible, that had you not been my Grandson You wou'd have been in as bad a Condition as you deserve to be.'[36]

Her next task was to see that the rest of the family knew where their duty lay. John Spencer received a peremptory summons to her bedside. Confined to his house under treatment for venereal disease, he at first tried to stave off the ordeal by protesting that he was too ashamed to be seen in public. When she insisted, he arrived in such a state of nerves and weakness that he could scarcely walk across the room. She read him Sunderland's 'Foolish, Brutal and Ungrateful Letter' and then showed him a list of the lands which she had taken from his brother to settle on him. Nobody, she added, could imagine that she would give him so great an estate, unless he would behave in all respects as if he were her son. Spencer refused to take the hint. He undertook not to marry himself without her consent, but she could not get him 'so much as in a look' to find fault with his brother's conduct. A few days later he sealed his fate by going to Totteridge to attend the wedding, there to be assured by Bateman that he deserved a statue of gold for his magnanimity.[37] Yet enjoyable as it was to set the autocratic old woman at defiance, Spencer was soon having second thoughts. When he tried to visit her as usual on his return to London, she ordered him out of the house. He too was entirely disinherited.

'She has actually burnt her will; the courage of the old Fury at above seventy, for it will take up some time to make another,' the Duke of St Albans commented half-admiringly. Henrietta declared that she had always thought her mother mad and now was quite convinced of it.[38] Sarah was very far from being mad, but in the grip of one of her towering, extravagant rages, she was capable of behaving as if she was. It fuelled this mood still further to learn that Lady Bateman had unsuccessfully tried to persuade Diana to attend the wedding as well, 'which could be for no other Reason, but to make Her appear to the World as black as herself. Who is certainly the worst Woman that ever I knew in my Life.' As a demonstration of this she blackened the face of Lady Bateman's portrait at Marlborough House, declared that her outside was now as black as her inside, and left it hanging in its place for all to see.[39] Having demanded the support of her friends, she was mortally offended when Jane Kingdom sent her a patronizing reply, treating her conduct as the childish tantrum it was.[40]

Sarah had every intention of living to make good her new settlement. The question was, with Diana married and all the grandsons either dead or disinherited, who should now be the beneficiary of her wealth? It was out of this difficulty that the idea for the Marlborough almshouses at St Albans was born. Sarah was often approached by destitute veterans of Marlborough's campaigns or their surviving families, and did what she could to relieve them by piecemeal charity. Now she decided to create a permanent endowment for their benefit. Without waiting for her anger to cool, she dashed off a letter to the attorney-general, Sir Philip Yorke, asking his advice on how to proceed.[41] This done, she carried out her plan of travelling north to Scarborough to take the waters. One of her first stops on the road was at Woburn, to pay a visit to the delinquent Duke of Bedford, still just managing to hold his own in the battle with mortal illness. His last resort was to travel to Lisbon in the autumn in the hope that a warm climate would prolong his life; but Sarah found her granddaughter distraught at his insistence that she must go with him because his gambling debts were so great that he could not afford to maintain two households.

In her concern for this unhappy young couple, Sarah became a different person from the disinheriting fury of a few weeks before. As always the young Duke's presence wrought its charm over her. He welcomed her warmly and said 'a thousand pretty things', she reported to Diana, 'and it was impossible to see him in such a condition without being touched with some melancholy to think that a man who might have been so happy and have made so great a figure . . . should in so few years time bring himself into so sad a condition in all respects'. She noticed that he hated to have his illness taken notice of, and in the gallery at Woburn, as she stumped indefatigably from picture to picture between her crutches, she pretended more weakness than she felt in order to give him constant opportunities to sit down and rest. She solved the difficulty over his wife by offering to collect her on the way back from Scarborough and take her to live at Marlborough House while he was away, the one expedient they were both prepared to accept.[42] Then, with parting injunctions to the Duke not to be taken in by architects in the repair of Woburn, she pursued her journey into Yorkshire.

At Kimbolton she found another grandchild in need of her protection. Isabella, Duchess of Manchester, the elder Montagu daughter, had fallen out with her mother for much the same reason that Mary had fallen out with Sarah. They were three generations with 'the same fury temper and the same fairy face'. Isabella's was another unhappy marriage, made by her father in the absence of sons to preserve the shared family name; but Sarah noted approvingly that in spite of her marital troubles and her parents' refusal to help her, she had managed to preserve her reputation, 'when she was like a Bird out of a Cage, and knew nothing of the World'. Admittedly there was the drawback that she had 'an unfortunate Temper, which she cannot help. And tho she is sometimes extremely agreeable in Conversation, that Humour comes upon her like a fit of a Fever, and she will snap any body up in a strange manner.' For the time being, however, in her need to fill the void left by the Spencer quarrel, Sarah was prepared to overlook these outbursts and take the young Duchess under her wing.[43]

At York, a comparison of the ancient Gothic cathedral with the new assembly rooms built by Lord Burlington completed her disenchantment with the Palladians. In fact she was not in a mood to make the best of anything. Moving on to Scarborough, she immediately pronounced it to be the worst place she had ever seen in England. The wells were inaccessible and lacking in even the most basic amenities. The primitive communal latrines amused the frivolous Duchess of Manchester, Sarah told Diana, but 'I came home as fast as I could for fear of being forced into that assembly'. She resolved to go out as little as possible, but her lodgings, supposedly the envy of the place, were dirty, cramped, and plagued with the noise of passing coaches and the howling of packs of hounds kept for the sport of the visiting gentry. The human company made her no amends. With the exception of Lord Chesterfield and his sister, there was nobody 'that one would not choose rather to be deaf and dumb than to be with them'. When visitors did come she played cards to avoid having to talk to them.[44] In the free and easy milieu of the spa this unsociability was resented, and her neighbours looked forward to her going: 'she neither liked nor was liked.'[45]

Sarah had now travelled the length and breadth of England in search of waters which would cure her scurvy and restore the use of her limbs. For a brief time she cherished the hope that Scarborough would be of real benefit and so repay her trouble and discomfort. When after a few weeks her 'gout' returned, her disillusion with this and all similar places was complete. She told Diana that she would no longer expect miracles, but 'submit to my two crutches and live in my own house, as long or as little a time as God pleases'.[46] By the end of August she was on her way home.

As she had driven away from Marlborough House on her journey north, she noticed a calash standing before John Spencer's door, waiting to take him into Hampshire for the summer. Both Sunderland and the Russells owned or leased properties in the county, and it was not long before the young people all joined forces there. Sarah had no objection to Diana's continuing to see her brothers; there was no reason, as she put it, to apprehend 'any deep plot from them'. But she had her spies everywhere, and when she learnt—not from Diana herself—that Lady Bateman had joined the party, she began to grow uneasy. At first she told herself that it did not matter, 'since she cannot now marry Lady Russell, nor do her any great Mischief'. Yet as the intimacy continued after their return from the country to a point where they 'almost liv'd together', she began to grow alarmed and suspicious, for 'no body can be sure what further Mischiefs such a Creature as Lady Bateman may effect'.[47]

For the moment, however, she brooded and held her peace. Diana, to the delight of the dying Duke of Bedford as well as her husband, was expecting her first child and must have nothing to disturb her. All through the summer Sarah had been on tenterhooks, thinking of the escapades a group of heedless young people might indulge in, and remembering her own miscarriage from follies she had committed when she was very young. Diana herself grew nervous as her confinement approached and begged her grandmother, who had been the only mother she had known since her earliest childhood, to be with her when the time came. Sarah, whose tenderness was always most aroused when those she loved faced danger or suffering, assured her that 'I will do in that matter, as you would have me, and it is not easy to believe how much I would give to save you from any pain, if that were in my power'.[48]

Early in November came the news that the Duke of Bedford had died at Corunna. The glittering inheritance which Sarah had planned for her granddaughter was now hers. But there could not be even a muted rejoicing, for just beforehand Diana had been thrown out of a chaise she was driving and gone into premature labour. Her son was born alive but died shortly afterwards. Sarah tried to conceal the loss from her until she had recovered from the first shock of the accident.[49] But her hatred of Lady Bateman was now as strong as her love for Diana, and she could scarcely wait for the girl's full recovery before delivering her long-withheld ultimatum. A draft letter which she suppressed suggests that she had at first considered effacing herself altogether from the situation: 'sence I can never make myself hapy, I will make you easy . . . for I find my soul so fastend to you that I shall ever wish your good & safty.' But the letter actually sent was much more uncompromising: if Diana continued to see Lady Bateman, she must break off all but the outward appearance of association with her grandmother. If, on the other hand, she wanted them to continue as they were:

you must be very plain with Lady Bateman—for there is no acting in a thing of this kind by halves or by trimming—in letting her know that you can have no commerce with her . . . that all people that are either good or reasonable are and must be sensible that there is no precedent of such a treatment to a grandmother that for thirty years has been labouring to assist and serve the whole family, and has done it with great success; and that you cannot live with any quiet or ease if you do anything that is grievous to me.[50]

Diana, for all her constant professions of love and gratitude, was not entirely submissive; one of her first acts after her marriage had been to renew her intimacy with Lady Rich.[51] But in the end she did give the required undertaking, and by the next post came a vitriolic anonymous letter for Sarah:

I know your Grace is mad, but if you ever have an interval do but consider what you are doing now in a family that you pretend to espouse, instead of making them considerable by being united which is of more consiquence then all your ill gotten money, you are indeavoring to bring them in to as many quarels as you have your self, brothers & sisters & all you woud have quarel, I think there is now of those that are in your power, but the Duke of Bedford & the Dutchess of Manchester that you have not made infamous by quitting Lady Bateman's friendship only because you have taken a fancy against her. Is it not enough for you to exercise your pretty temper your self & for some atonement to your family, intaile your money without your wickedness, & dye as soon as you can.[52]

Having secured Diana, Sarah turned her attention to John Spencer, with whom she used even more summary tactics. Relations and friends had been marshalled to intercede for him while she was still at Scarborough, and at her return Spencer himself sent a message asking to see her. She was obdurate: 'I cannot think of you as I did: Nor can there ever be any more Conversation between us.' At the end of November she ordered him out of his apartment in the precincts of Marlborough House. At this Spencer capitulated entirely, having to confess that he was confined by the same treatment he had undergone in the summer. He professed the utmost gratitude for all his obligations to her, begged her forgiveness, and promised never to see the Batemans again. Sarah was half softened and half disgusted. She agreed to see him when he had recovered, but 'I desire you not to believe that I am so very weak as to take Promises for a Certainty; for there must be a great deal of Time to shew the Truth of that'.[53]

Having brought him to heel, there was another matter which she had to address without delay. Lady Bateman's activities threatened not only her personal control of the family, but her direction of its political affairs as well. John Spencer's fall from grace had apparently ended his hopes of being elected by his grandmother's interest at Woodstock or St Albans. Now she learnt of an alternative scheme to put him up for Hampshire at the next general election, using Sunderland's and Bedford's interest. Displeased as she still was with Spencer, she was not prepared to relinquish control of the one grandson she had left who was still a commoner, particularly as the Hampshire election could not succeed without the assistance of the Court Whigs. In trenchant letters to him and Diana she made it clear that the plan must go no further. Spencer's rightful place was at Woodstock, where 'He is sure to succeed. And in a handsome way, as my Son and Heir. . . . [and] if the Court shou'd ever be in the Right (which I very much wish they may, tho' I beleive they never will) He may then Vote according to his Honour and Conscience without Suspicion or Reproach.'[54] Thankful for this hint that she did intend to restore him as her chief heir, Spencer hastened to assure her that he would not think of Hampshire as long as she would let him stand for Woodstock.[55]

If anything was needed to confirm Sarah in her suspicions of Lady Bateman's political machinations, it was the interest taken at Court in the reconciliation with Spencer. Within a few days she was describing to Diana how the King had approached an acquaintance of hers in the drawing-room and asked for details of the affair; after which he went over to Lady Bateman and 'honoured her a great while with his conversation':

this, with a great many other things that I know, makes me see plainly, that she is a great favourite at Court, and that must be from the hopes the ministers have of dividing a family, who, if they were wise would be strong enough to make any ministry afraid of disobliging them. But they certainly think, that by her means they shall get my Lord Sunderland. And I believe they will.[56]

John Spencer's escapades indicated that it was high time for him to be suitably married, but Sarah's first discovery when she began to look into his affairs in preparation was that, contrary to her advice, he had lent his brother several thousands of pounds. Immediately she began to badger Sunderland to repay the money, or at least to give some negotiable security for it.[57] It also rankled with her to the point of obsession that in a weak moment after Blandford's death she had given him the fabulous diamond-hilted sword which the Emperor had bestowed on his grandfather. The more she brooded, the more she became convinced that if she did not get this heirloom back into her custody, Lady Bateman would pick out the diamonds and replace them with paste.[58] Lord Winchilsea (the former Lord Finch) was pressed into service as a mediator.

The painfully polite and submissive notes with which Sunderland answered her long, accusing letters on these matters plainly indicated that he had begun to regret the complete break with her. He returned the sword with a message which concluded that he was her most obedient humble servant and 'I wish I might be allowed to say, Dutyfull Grandson'. Sarah was unimpressed, attributing the graceful turn of phrase to Winchilsea. It annoyed her that Sunderland refused to settle the debt to his brother as she wished, by conveying the family house in Piccadilly to him. Instead, he cleverly countered this by telling her that he would readily do it if she would leave him Marlborough House.[59] The negotiations between them dragged on into the summer. 'The weather is so hot that I am almost kill'd,' she wrote to Diana, 'And I can't go out of Town until I have settled the whole affair between your two Brothers.' When at last it was done, she added that she was glad she would never have any occasion to see Sunderland again.[60]

Having once turned against him, Sarah had convinced herself that he was a worse life than his 52-year-old aunt, and so would probably never live to inherit his grandfather's title. When the first rumours of Henrietta's declining health reached her in the summer of 1733, she therefore refused to take them seriously.[61] By September, however, it was quite clear that Henrietta was dying. Sarah sent a message, 'that notwithstanding all that was past she woud come and see her if she likd it'. But Henrietta's feeling for her mother had long since turned irrevocably to aversion, and even in such circumstances there was a hint of the inevitable recriminations in store. She sent back the cold reply that 'she was not in a condition to see any body'.[62] On 27 October at Windsor Lodge, Sarah had the news that she was dead.

She found herself unexpectedly overwhelmed with wretchedness. Her love for her daughter, though overlaid with years of pride and injury, was still alive. She brooded over the unclouded period of Henrietta's adolescence, before she had been 'flattered and practised upon by the most vile people upon earth', and spent hours scrawling passages from the Books of Job and Ecclesiastes into her commonplace book with her crippled hand. 'I can't say I am quite living, nor am I quite dead,' she wrote in answer to Diana's anxious enquiries, '. . . But I can say with Job that my eyes are dim with sorrow, and my nerves are as shadows, and indeed I think my circumstances is more like his than anybody's that I have heard of or read of.'[63] While she was sunk in this depression and self-pity, a letter arrived from the grandson who now, contrary to all her predictions, bore the title Duke of Marlborough. In it he owned himself deservedly under her displeasure, and begged leave 'to do what I own I ought to have done before, that is . . . to wait of you sincerely to ask Pardon for what I have done'.[64] He was fortunate that it reached her at a time when she was having to face the consequences of nursing grievances against her closest family. Her response was uncharacteristically subdued:

I am as much pleased, as I can be with any Thing, to read such a Letter as I have received from you. But it is for your Sake. For as to myself, I am so humbled and worn out with continual Afflictions and Disappointments, that I can never more be sensible of any Joy. And as I expect none, I grow fond of entertaining my self with my own Melancholy; and nothing is so desagreeable to me, as what goes about to divert my Mind from it. This is a sort of Nonsense, that one must feel, before one can understand. But I grow so well acquainted with this desmal kind of Ease, that I shall not go to London, till something calls me that I cannot avoid . . . But when I must go, I shall be as glad as I can be to see you, who was always your affectionate Grand-mother.[65]

The young Duke had powerful reasons of self-interest for wishing to make up with her. Under the terms of his grandfather's will, if he did not convey the Sunderland estate to his brother within three months he would forfeit his right to the Marlborough wealth, and his affairs were already in such a parlous state that he could not hope to make the transfer without his grandmother's help. Nevertheless his submission had every appearance of being spontaneous and whole-hearted. Not waiting until she chose to come to London, he appeared on the doorstep of Windsor Lodge two days later and took the old lady by storm. 'It is not easy for me to describe without lessening it, the goodness of his behaviour in every respect,' Sarah told Diana. 'All that he said was so extremely good natured, and with good sense. And I do really believe, he is very sincere.' She had the grace to acknowledge in return that she had been 'too angry' about his marriage, 'and for that I have asked him to forgive me with tears'. She promised to receive his wife when she came to London, conceding that as she seemed to suit him, 'I think he will be happier than if he had married one that in appearance had been more proper for him'.[66]

Her gloom vanished completely. Not only had she successfully beaten off a challenge to her control of the family and seen it reunited under her leadership, but she now had an heir to the Marlborough title from what had always been (saving Lady Bateman's presence) her favourite branch of it. As she wrote to Diana, 'I have now a prospect for the future of enjoying a great deal of happiness from the three children of your most beloved mother'.[67] But this prospect, like so many others in Sarah's life, was soon to resolve itself into yet another scene of trouble.

'Warm in Opposition'
1733–1735

'THERE is even a flying report that secret orders are given for Lady Bateman's picture to be whitewashed,' Lord Hervey wrote, as the news spread that the Marlborough family had healed its divisions, 'But this wants confirmation.'[1] Indeed it could not have been further from the truth. The state of affairs which Sarah found when she arrived in London in mid-November only confirmed the utter blackness of the Batemans in her eyes. She now regretted the diversion of £50,000 of her fortune into the building of almshouses; but if the report were true that John Spencer and his brother were still consorting with 'that Machiavel' Lady Bateman, she remarked ominously, it might possibly contrive more business for her of the same kind. From time to time the same suspicion even cast a shadow over her relations with Diana.[2]

Sarah was determined that the conveyance of the Sunderland estate to John Spencer should be watertight, leaving no pretext for other claimants to the Marlborough property (the Batemans in particular) to challenge it. The problem was that Sunderland had encumbered his paternal inheritance with debts and a large settlement on his wife, and the transfer could not be made until these were cleared off and a new jointure on the Marlborough estate substituted. Sarah was horrified at what he was now obliged to disclose of the state of his affairs. His wife's portion was less than he had been led to believe and most of it not payable until after her father's death. On his behalf she approached Lord Trevor and the Bishop of St David's, one of the trustees of the settlement, ostensibly to try to persuade them to disgorge some of the dowry to help him out of his difficulties. Really she just wanted to have the pleasure of letting them know what she thought of them. Lord Trevor, whom she described as something between a fool and a madman, managed to evade her by remaining in the country, but for the Bishop, whom she ran to earth in his London house, there was no escape. She left him outraged by a rudeness 'greater, I think, than I had ever before met with in my life' and determined never to repeat the experience: 'if she comes again to my house I'll not see her, and if she sends for me I will excuse myself from going.'[3]

In fact, since the clause in the will which was causing all the difficulty was of Sarah's devising, it was only fitting that she should have to find a way out. Early in December she declared that she would make both the brothers happy by using her own money to clear the Sunderland estate. Yet it was not her way to perform any business quietly. At first she pretended to doubt whether she could afford it, what with the fall of the stocks caused by the rumours of a Continental war, and the amount which 'Lady Bateman's Plott' had caused her to squander on almshouses. Then one of her lawyers raised the more sinister difficulty that the transfer of the new Duchess's jointure to the Marlborough estate could only be effected by giving it precedence over her own. This was an 'extravagant insolence' which Sarah positively refused to countenance.[4] By this time, with the onset of winter and the strain and bustle of the whole affair, she had succumbed to an acute attack of illness. Confined helpless to her bed, with the time allowed for the transfer fast running out, she told Diana that it was all too much for her: 'how lucky wou'd it have been for me if I had Dy'd before your Grandfather.' Yet even illness could not get the better of her for long. This was the supreme moment of her trusteeship, with the fulfilment of Marlborough's will depending entirely on her. 'Tho she at some times seems to be low spirited,' James Stephens reported to Diana, 'yet when she is employed about any thing that engages her attention, she can talk with as much vigour as ever I remember her.'[5] At last an expedient was found to meet the difficulty over the jointure, and the lawyers were ordered to put the conveyance in hand with all speed. The two young men, mere puppets in these dynastic arrangements, could only watch from a safe distance and make their acknowledgements as best they could.[6]

While this was going on the Bedfords remained at Woburn, consulting with their neighbour Lord Carteret about the coming general election. Carteret had a family of daughters whom Sarah had for some time had in mind as possible matches for her grandsons, and although two had been disposed of, Diana reported that the third was now marriageable and seemed pretty and sensible. The two men also wanted her permission to set up John Spencer as Knight of the Shire for Bedfordshire.[7] Sarah had followed Carteret's career with interest, from the time of his alliance with Sunderland to his banishment to Ireland by Walpole and his recent decision to throw in his lot with the 'patriot' opposition, recognizing that his brilliance made him the likeliest successor as chief minister if Walpole fell. She had her reservations about him; she had not forgotten his part in the seizure of Sunderland's papers in 1722. Yet she admitted that 'tis better to have Patriots that have been Courtiers, than to have none at all'. She gave Diana permission to propose the match for John Spencer, and in order to forward it, agreed to let Bedford and Carteret dispose of him electorally as they pleased.[8]

Under Diana's guidance the marriage negotiations went ahead quickly and cordially—rather too much so for Sarah, who as soon as she began to recover felt that matters had been taken out of her hands. Nevertheless she was pleased. Although the dowry was small, she believed that Carteret would be just the influence the wayward brothers needed to guide their political careers.[9] In January both families gathered in London. The young lady found favour not only with the easy-going bridegroom, but with his far more exacting grandmother, who hurried the lawyers on irritably, 'for when a Match is determin'd to be, it is disagreeable & awkward to continue formal visits longer than is absolutely necessary'. Although still ailing in health, she took the details of the settlement into her own hands. She would contribute £5,000, but she would not be tied down by having Spencer specifically named as her heir. The pin money was to be no more than £200 a year, to be raised to £400 on any increase of his fortune, 'without saying what. . . . there is more danger of his giving her more than he can afford than less'.[10] John Spencer and Georgiana Carteret, laden with the jewels Sarah had given her, were married on 14 February 1734. Her Torrismond had been safely disposed of at last.

The political significance of the match was not lost on the Court. When the Spencers and the Carterets attended the drawing-room a few days later, expecting the customary congratulations, they were snubbed by the King and Queen.[11] Bedford and Marlborough both joined 'the Liberty or Rumpsteak Club', made up of peers who had met with the same treatment on account of their opposition (one of them had suggested the name by complaining that the King had 'turned his rump to him' in the drawing-room). Others included Lords Winchilsea, Chesterfield, Marchmont, and Stair, all Sarah's regular visitors and correspondents.[12] She herself, although not officially a member, had a kind of legendary ancestral status for the whole group. 'Tell me no more of Youth,' a verse from *The Toasts of the Rump Steak Club* ran,

> this glass shall boast
> An old immortal, undecaying Toast!
> In the quick Lustre of whose piercing Eye
> Still shine the beauteous Sparks of Liberty:
> Whose Spirit undepress'd by Fourscore Years
> Except for England's Safety, knows no Fears;
> From whom a Race of Toasts and Patriots came,
> England shall pledge me, when I Marlb'rough name.[13]

The Excise crisis of the previous year had given the patriots their most hopeful prospect yet of bringing Walpole down. A preliminary to his Excise scheme (essentially the replacement of the tax on property by a tax on consumption) had been the reintroduction of the salt tax in 1732, and Sarah's attitude to this had been complicated as usual by the continuing dependence of the Trust on government borrowing. When Godolphin asked her to consider lending on this fund, she hesitated long before giving her reluctant consent, 'for it is a Thing I dislike extremely'.[14] With the full-blown Excise scheme, a major political issue, there could be no such compromise. Under Pulteney's guidance, she put his clerk (and her own relation), John Merrill, up at the by-election at St Albans on the death of Thomas Gape, amid a blaze of anti-Excise publicity.[15] As Walpole was about to move his scheme to Parliament in March 1733, Westminster had been crammed with merchants lobbying against it. Among them was a deputation of Sarah's Surrey neighbours, who waited on her at Marlborough House to beseech her to use her influence with the members of both Houses to have the Excise defeated. She shared the triumph of the opposition when Walpole was forced to drop the scheme (and was gratified to be told by the Surrey merchants that 'we owe to your Grace's influence that this Bill big with mischiefs to our Trade and Libertys was thrown out of the House of Commons');[16] and she also shared their frustration and outrage when he quickly recovered his majorities and defeated their attempts to instigate enquiries into fraud and corruption. In the government revenge that followed a number of rebellious lords, including her friends Marchmont, Stair, and Chesterfield, were dismissed from their offices.

Although the Excise had been defeated, it remained the central issue in the general election of 1734. Its opponents had certainly exaggerated Sarah's direct influence on the parliamentary battle, but her electoral interest, increased by her many estate purchases, was now of real significance to the opposition. Paying only lip-service to the view that 'my simple sex are not allowed to be judges in such matters', she had launched her campaign as soon as the session was over, by circulating copies of the relevant division lists: 'I think all Countries should know who voted for Excise & against enquiring into Things to come at the Truth in order to do Justice.' When Diana protested that the election was still nearly a year away, Sarah pointed out that Walpole himself had begun his electioneering early and those who wished to defeat him must not be behindhand, 'for a corrupt Parliament is all he has to support his unjustifiable proceedings, and a good one is all we have to save us from slavery'.[17] In August she dispatched letters to her agents and tenants. Her message was the same to all: her support would go to 'those men who have . . . not in former Parliaments given their votes to keep themselves in their employments', and her policy was still that all strands of the opposition, including the Jacobites, should unite 'without distinction of that odious thing, Party'.[18] No doubt it was this attitude which led the Pretender himself to make a remarkable appeal to her for support:

You will not be surprized at my writing to you on this important occasion, when you consider that few or none of your sex may have it so much in their power as you to contribute to the success of my Cause, especially by your influence over so many noble Persons whose conduct will I hope entitle them to particular marks of my favour hereafter.[19]

By this time Sarah had certainly abandoned all pretence at cordiality for the Hanoverians. At her last attendance at Court she had gone out of her way to be rude to the King, 'giving him to understand he was too much of a German'. Civil messages from the Queen after Henrietta's death did not soften her in the least: 'all these things are to make fine weather with as many people as they can in order to make people contribute, who have any substance, to their own undoing.'[20] Yet the assumption that her opposition to the government indicated Jacobite sympathies was as usual completely misplaced. 'I am sure there is no Person living that wishes more sincerely than I do the Prosperity of this present Government according to the Act of Settlement,' she wrote in one of her electioneering letters, 'And you may the easier believe this Profession, because it is so much for the Interest of my Family to have it supported.'[21] While Diana and her husband found it distasteful that impeccable Whigs such as the Russells should have to hobnob with crypto-Jacobites, for Sarah, with her overriding aim of getting rid of Walpole, the argument of political expediency was sufficient:

considering the vast power that ministers have by disposing of places, honours and money I can't see how it is possible to keep them within just bounds, but by the help of some that have not thoroughly the principles that one wishes, and some of them may assist those that wish what is for the true interest of England, without being able to effect their own designs.[22]

But with the Carteret marriage safely accomplished and the general election approaching, Sarah began to have second thoughts about giving up John Spencer to his in-laws in Bedfordshire. Her ecstatic delight in the Duke of Bedford had quickly cooled. With little of his brother's charm, he had infinitely more strength of character, and from the first moment of his inheritance he had set himself to restore the family fortunes and interest. Self-assured and independent beyond his years, he was not prepared to submit himself totally to the control of his male peers, much less to his wife's grandmother. And if his readiness to make electoral pacts with government Whigs in preference to Tories was a cause for concern with his whole party,[23] for Sarah it was a personal affront to her principles. Walter Plumer, her Hertfordshire neighbour and a leading opposition MP, had joined Pulteney as one of her electoral mentors by this time, but his tempting plan to use John Spencer to capture the Court stronghold of Westminster foundered because Bedford had promised his interest to the government candidate.[24] Now Sarah discovered that the Duke had taken Spencer from her for the Bedfordshire election only to join him with another inveterate government supporter, Sir Rowland Alston. If two suitable opposition Whigs could not have been found, she wrote crossly to Diana, it would have been much better for Bedford to assist the sitting member Charles Leigh, who was a respectable Tory. Alston's vote and Spencer's would now cancel each other out, 'which is doing no good as to the public. And I have no notion of contributing to have an ill man chosen, without any benefit from it.'[25]

She decided that it was time for her to resume control of her grandson. While Spencer was actually on the road to Bedfordshire to prepare for his election, she sent him a peremptory message to go to Woodstock to secure his position there first, 'which place I always thought most natural for him to stand for'. Only when he had done so did she allow him to put in an appearance in Bedfordshire. Even then she made it clear that she would much rather he had gone to St Albans, as she had originally intended, to support her other candidates.[26] Spencer was elected at both Woodstock and Bedfordshire, and in due course he would have to choose which seat to retain. At St Albans, Walter Plumer managed to save the day for her by finding a substitute candidate and using her money to win over the powerful dissenting interest.[27] But it was Marlborough's conduct that pleased her most. The news that he had placed all his interest in Hampshire at the disposal of the government's opponents showed her that he was 'made in some parts like his old Grandmother'. She was so delighted that she felt strong enough to have lifted him up and kissed him.[28]

The general election of 1734 was the high-point of Sarah's participation in opposition politics. Courted, flattered, and consulted by their leaders, both peers and commoners, and even by the Pretender himself, she enjoyed a greater sense of power and importance than she had felt for years. So committed did she become to the task of adding to the numbers against Walpole that no personal considerations could stand against it. The ultimate proof of this came when she heard that Lord Masham intended to put up his son as a candidate for Windsor; 'if he had,' she told Diana, 'I do really believe my Interest, with the assistance of your two Brothers, would have carried it. And to shew what a publick Spirit I have, the unparalleled Ingratitude of the Father & Mother would not have hinder'd me from exerting myself to get one Vote for the Publick.'[29]

Yet once the contest was over, the reckoning came. Her friends Stair and Marchmont were no longer among the representative Scottish peers in the House of Lords, and in spite of his long and distinguished service, Stair was even dismissed from his regiment and so lost his chief means of livelihood. To show her sympathy in a practical way, Sarah made him the first of a series of annual loans of £1,000 to enable him to improve his estates, destroying the bond afterwards so that no claim could ever be made on him.[30] But it cheered her to be told that although the government would still have a majority in the House of Commons, the opposition was sure of at least two hundred votes, 'a Number sufficient to make Sir Robert very uneasy'. Now that her active electoral role was over, she could do no more than urge her male associates to fight on until 'Time or Chance' increased their number. 'If I was a man, I am sure I would fight on to the last moment . . . ' she wrote to Stair; 'This sounds very courageous in one of my sex, but I certainly have as much resolution to pursue anything that is right as yourself.'[31]

Yet as the excitement of the election died down, she sank into depression and irritability. She could no longer hobble about on crutches, nor even raise herself from a chair without help, and she was driven distracted with itching from scurvy. She was also more burdened than ever with vexatious business. After the family quarrel she had temporarily washed her hands of the Trust, and Godolphin had conducted business peaceably through James Stephens, who was doing invaluable service as its secretary and accountant. But he no longer had the same reason to take an active part as before his wife's death, and Sarah soon resumed control. It was a change that did not augur well for the grandson who was now, in theory at least, the chief beneficiary of the Trust. Although Marlborough's political conduct had delighted her, in financial matters their relations quickly became very strained. At the time he inherited the dukedom he was already, as far as she could calculate, nearly £30,000 in debt, and spending more in a year than his grandfather at the height of his power: 'I suppose those that got by him persuaded him there could never be any End, whatever he did, of the Marlborough Estate.'[32] The reality, as she tried to bring home to him, was very different. His grandfather's capital was certainly very great, but the income had been much reduced by the lowering of government interest rates, by the fall in the stock market, and above all, she had to admit, by the investment of so much of it in land.

By this time her estate buying, both for herself and the Trust, had tailed away.[33] It had not taken her long to discover that land was a great deal more complicated and expensive to administer than loans to the government. As the proprietress of a far-flung and disparate series of holdings, most of which she could never visit herself, she was largely dependent on the services of bailiffs and stewards, a class of men with their own intricate methods of accounting, of whom she was always inclined to be suspicious. Even the chief steward Charles Hodges, her servant for more than thirty years and a byword for integrity, she set down in the end as 'a very bad man', on the grounds that when he died suddenly she had found among his papers the draft of a letter to Godolphin finding fault with some aspect of her management of the Trust.[34] Now she was becoming more and more convinced that his successor, Thomas Norgate, was 'a very great rogue'. It made matters much worse that she had no sooner established herself and the Trust as major landowners than the country was plunged into a serious agricultural depression. Proprietors all over England were finding it hard to get rents from their existing tenants or to engage new ones without undertaking costly repairs and improvements.[35]

Sarah's difficulties with her estate at Crowhurst on the borders of Kent and Surrey were a case study of all the problems she faced as a landowner. She had bought it at the time of the South Sea confiscations for 'a very extravagant Price', on the assurance that it was the best land in the area. Yet in the first seven years of her ownership, through 'so many Abuses, that ''tis hardly credible, as bad as the World is', she had received almost nothing from it. Her first bailiff had absconded without collecting any rents. Another was in prison for failing to pay the arrears over. A third told her that he was unable to let much of the land, which therefore produced 'nothing but Bills for Repairs and Management of the Ground'. In desperation she turned to a Dorking lawyer, who 'seem'd to me to be a fine Gentleman and talk'd so well that I believ'd him for a long time'; but in the end he did nothing but put her off 'with ridiculous unaccountable Letters now and then'.[36] Her claim that she was an easy landlady seems to have been justified enough. With her lifelong horror of debtors' prisons, she always refused to take extreme measures against any tenant who fell into arrears, 'if he has done honestly, & is only unfortunate',[37] and matters did improve somewhat as far as Crowhurst was concerned when she at last managed to find an efficient steward. But arrears of rent from the other estates built up throughout the 1730s. Her 'vast labour' in trying to secure her own and the Trust's money by putting it into land seemed to have been largely unproductive.

Then there were the lawsuits which she had undertaken to save the Trust fortune, and which had only served to deplete it further, dragging on year after year and costing more in legal fees than could possibly be made good if they were successful. Even Sarah, with her zest for litigation, could see that this was simply 'throwing good Mony after bad'. From bitter experience she knew that lawsuits involving people of their social and political consequence would usually be decided in favour of those that had 'the best Interest at Court'; this was another disadvantage of being in opposition.[38] But when she asked Godolphin to speak to Walpole about Lord Chancellor King's obvious prejudice against the Trust, he was reluctant to do so. Having prided herself for years on being 'a great lawyer', she was at first tempted to take on the task of reforming the judiciary single-handed, until Godolphin reminded her that even Oliver Cromwell, at the height of his power, had tried and failed at this task. The only realistic solution, they were agreed, was to settle the existing suits as fast as they could.[39] Yet when King was replaced as Chancellor by Talbot in 1734, this only grew more difficult. Although his father had been Sarah's friend and his brother her page (albeit a ne'er-do-well who had had to be dismissed for pawning plate), Talbot at once outraged her by decreeing that one of the more substantial Blenheim contractors, whose case came before him in May, should be paid his debt with interest and costs. This effectively reversed Macclesfield's decree of 1724 in the Trust's favour, and invited all the other creditors to renew their claims.[40]

The greater part of the income which remained from the Trust after all the legal costs and administrative expenses were deducted was taken up by the huge jointures charged on the estate, which those of Godolphin and Lady Blandford, now added to Sarah's, brought to nearly £30,000 a year. Marlborough was entitled only to what remained after they had been paid. As Sarah, whose annuity was by far the largest, was well aware, 'it is necessary for me to dye to support the Duke of Marlborough'.[41] This she still showed no sign of doing (although it is fair to note that she did lend him money and forgo her right to her jointure payments for some time in order to give him first call on the income).[42] While she lived, he did not even have the right to live at Blenheim, which he talked of wistfully as the finest place in England. Sarah, who never intended to live there herself and had reports that it was growing shabby with neglect, toyed from time to time with the idea of handing it over to him. Although this would have been a sensible as well as a generous gesture, in the end she was never satisfied enough with him to make it. Even the lodge in Windsor home park, which he begged from her after Henrietta's death, using the persuasive Pulteney as a go-between, she would only reluctantly lend him on condition that he made no expensive alterations.[43]

At first he made a real effort to retrench, but within a few months he was backsliding. Sarah's long, well-intentioned, and laboriously compiled letters concerning his affairs brought only two or three lines of scrawl in reply. The young Duke in fact was a hopeless and incurable squanderer, already largely dependent on moneylenders to maintain his style of living. As his friend Lord Hervey admitted, he would have exceeded his income if it had been fifty times greater than it was.[44] Diana said what she could in her brother's favour, and Sarah agreed that he had many good qualities: 'I can only wish that he may alter in things that are to his prejudice, but I fear nature is too strong for my wishes to have any effect. And that great as his fortune is, he will never be easy in money matters.' Since John Spencer's wife was expecting her first child, her care of the Trust was now as much for future holders of the title as for the present one. Some day, she hoped, Marlborough would have a worthy heir.[45]

Towards midsummer Sarah was able to go to Windsor Lodge, where she was cheered to find that for all his earlier escapades, Johnny seemed to be settling down well as a husband. His young wife adored him, 'though he is always dressed like a keeper or a farmer', and was going on well with her pregnancy.[46] But within the month, she was back in London. The thought haunted her that if she could not find some means of defeating the Lord Chancellor's decree, every tradesman who had ever been employed at Blenheim would be encouraged to try what he could get by the same means: 'I can see no End of it, as long as there is any Knave in this fruitful Land of such Creatures.'[47] She was also on an errand of mercy. Lady De La Warr, dangerously ill and neglected by her husband, was asking to see her. As usual this relationship brought her nothing but satisfaction. 'I am glad I did come to town,' she reported to Diana after her first visit, 'because in my life I never saw anybody express such joy as she did to see me and I am sure it was real.' It was the more gratifying that Lady De La Warr, having no faith in doctors, was prepared to submit entirely to her advice. Sarah visited her constantly, although it meant being carried up a flight of stairs 'not much better than a ladder' until she was out of danger.[48]

Yet her own health showed no improvement. Still with no more use of her limbs 'than a child bound up in swaddling clothes', she was soon tired out, not only with her legal problems, but with the business of finishing Wimbledon. The house, an austere Palladian structure in grey brick, was almost finished, although not entirely to her satisfaction. She had long since got rid of Lord Herbert ('often mad and always very odd') and the idiosyncratic Roger Morris, although not without an inevitable dispute about the size of the latter's bill; it was her house, she told him at parting, and whatever he thought of her taste ('to have things plain and clean from a piece of wainscott to a lady's face') she was old enough to know what she liked. In fact she had now done with architects altogether. In their place at Wimbledon she appointed a salaried clerk of the works, who could at least be relied on to do as he was told, 'which no architect will', she told Diana, 'though you pay for it'.[49]

Nevertheless, the main problem about Wimbledon was of her own making. Presumably on account of her disability, she had instructed Herbert to make the main entrance accessible without a flight of stairs—'I won't go up steps'. His solution was to dig a moat-like depression, spanned by a bridges, for the house to stand in, so that the principal floor was exactly at ground level. Now that she saw it finished she was disconcerted; the house 'looked as if it was making a Curtsie'. Even so, the pleasurable task of furnishing awaited her, and Charles Bridgman, whom she liked and trusted, was beginning to lay out the gardens, taking full advantage of the high ground and long views. When it was finished, she told Diana, 'it will be a delightful place to my taste'.[50]

After a brief visit there she returned to the Lodge, where she was more at ease than anywhere else, but 'as for pleasure I must never expect any thing like that'. Diana tried to cheer her by inviting herself on a visit, 'to be in your house for a day or two, just in that same delightfull manner as when I was your own Dye'.[51] But the solitude afterwards only made Sarah worry more, both about public affairs (in this case about Walpole's failure to defend England from the growing power of France) and about her grandson's position. As the accounts were made up, the arrears of rent incurred while Henrietta had held the title, and now due to her husband, were proving so great that if priority were given to their payment, Sarah calculated that it would be several years before the new Duke could receive any income at all. Unable to accept that this was partly due to economic conditions beyond anyone's control, she searched as usual for a scapegoat, and found one in the chief steward, Thomas Norgate, who had once been Godolphin's servant: 'most of those low sort of men that have raised themselves by receiving peoples mony I have very seldom found honest.' Yet Godolphin, scrupulously so himself, believed Norgate to be no worse than others of his type, and he warned her that if she got rid of him from the Trust she would be lucky to find anyone better.[52]

When she summoned Norgate to Marlborough House, he managed to evade her questions by pretending to have been taken suddenly ill with colic, and she hesitated to begin legal proceedings against him, fearing another affair like the Blenheim suit, 'without any hope of a conclusion'.[53]

But when Godolphin suggested that they at least obtain a legal opinion as to whether he or Marlborough had prior claim to the Trust estate revenue, she convinced herself that Norgate was responsible for his doubts, and declared that it was unfair to make Marlborough suffer for arrears which had come about through the roguery of Godolphin's agent. Even when he gave way over the legal issue, she continued to accuse him of having a greater regard 'for one that has been robbing you for so many years' than for herself, and raked up the old reproach of his coldness to her after Marlborough's death. The correspondence ended with her sending him a great packet of documents, in which, as he described it,

besides taking the pains of writing a very long letter with your own hand, and of dictating & writing some observations on Mr Norgate's accounts, Your Grace has been pleas'd to send me in a servant's hand a most severe, not to say cruel recapitulation of the faults of every one of my family, whether living or dead. Many of them I had never before heard of, none of them had I been able to prevent, tho from the beginning I endeavour'd it all I could; and, for such of them as can properly be call'd my own, your Grace had, for a great while now past, given me all the reason in the world to hope & believe they had been both forgiven and forgot.

Godolphin was a retiring and sensitive man who had suffered much at the hands of his wife and her mother. Unable to bear the situation any longer, he offered to resign as trustee.[54] Marlborough, in whose name Sarah had wrought this havoc, was at first grateful for her efforts; but as she plunged deeper into the one-sided quarrel with Godolphin, he became embarrassed with the whole affair, and she was soon complaining to Diana that he did not make her a proper return for her pains.[55]

On a compensating impulse, when she heard that John Spencer was passing through Maidenhead on his way to London, she decided to go to meet him there unannounced, 'like a lover'. Predictably she found him taken up with a group of friends of his own age and her presence obviously unwelcome. She returned to the Lodge and solitude: 'let one drudge as much as one will for the Good of ones Family, there will be many that will be glad to be rid of one.' Diana tried to coax her to London to consult with the doctors about her health and to cheer herself with amusements such as the opera, but she refused; no doctor could do her any good and she was too disabled to enjoy any of the pleasures of London life. Any company but Diana's would be 'tiresome or vexatious: & even you, as long as I know you are well & happy, I can be contented not to see you'.[56]

With the first session of the new Parliament approaching, William Pulteney joined his own persuasions to Diana's. He wanted Sarah at hand so that her friends could apply to her for assistance, 'which is often highly necessary on many Publick Occasions'. Sunk in the depression that followed her worst quarrels, Sarah replied that she would spend what little life was left to her entirely in the country and never see London again. Pulteney wooed her out of this mood in his most seductive style:

Believe me, Madam, no one living is of more consequence than you are; you have Friends, you have Credit, you have Talents, you have Power, & you have spirits stil to do an infinite deal of service, if you will please to exert them, & why you should lock your self up I cannot concieve: a little Bustling in the business of the World will give you a new flow of spirits & methinks if it be true that Sir Robert designs to attack you at Woodstock, that spur should animate you to bid him, and not only him, but every body else defiance . . . [57]

He was referring to John Spencer's impending choice between Bedford-shire and Woodstock. Since there would normally have been no comparison between a county seat and a small borough, it was assumed that Spencer would resign the latter, and Walpole now had designs on this opposition stronghold whenever he should do so. But Sarah snappishly rejected any suggestion that it would be 'a Diminution' in this case for her grandson to opt for Woodstock. She wanted Bedford to patch matters up with the Tory Charles Leigh and release Spencer to stay at 'his own borough'.[58] The Duke resisted; he was on bad terms with Leigh, and Sarah had given her word to let Spencer be chosen for Bedfordshire. Having appealed to her friends among the opposition leaders to persuade him to give way, she was angered to find that the young Duke and his interest were more important to them than her family pride. Yet even when they used the almost irresistible argument that if she refused the contest, it would look as if she was 'afraid of Sir Robert', she would not be moved: 'tho I would have been glad to have gone thro any Trouble (which is a good deal to a woman loaded with many Difficulties & very ill Health) yet I cannot be perswaded that there is any Sense or Honour in giving up what my Grand-son is in Possession of very rightly for I know not what.'[59]

If Spencer himself had gone against her while she was in this mood, he would again have risked losing his inheritance. He gave in, and Bedford had to find another candidate (not Leigh) to take his place. But he did so with a very bad grace,[60] and the whole affair was an embarrassment both to Sarah's family and to the leaders of the opposition, who began to see why Queen Anne's Whigs had at last found her more of a liability than an asset. This quarrel spoiled some of her pleasure in the birth of a son to the Spencers in December 1734, 'a very strong lusty child' who ensured that there would be at least one male heir in the next generation. It was disappointing that the baby took so much after the Carterets in looks; but, as Sarah told Diana, 'if he makes a good man and is healthy I do not much care whom he is like'.[61]

By now she had abandoned her solitude at Windsor and come to town, and the issue which most absorbed her attention during this first session of the new Parliament was the intended petition of the representative Scottish peers against the methods used by the government electioneers in Scotland. She told Diana that she would rather be present in the House of Lords when it was debated than go to the opera.[62] Both sides mustered their forces to the last man. Within the secret councils of the patriots, however, there was serious division. Carteret refused to give the petition his full support, ostensibly on the grounds that there was insufficient evidence of government corruption, but in reality because he did not relish taking second place to Chesterfield, 'the Commander-in-Chief of this Scottish brigade', and was never without a view of his own eventual return to the ministry.[63]

Sarah, whose relations with Carteret were already strained by the Bedfordshire election dispute, had nothing but contempt for his trimming and half measures. Whatever her shortcomings in other matters, she was still of use to the opposition leaders for her unrivalled ability to bring the Duke of Somerset up from his retirement at Petworth for crucial divisions. On this occasion she wrote to her old lover at length, 'because I cannot be sure that upon such a subject most People [Carteret for example] will not be more Cautious than I shall be in writing to your Grace'. Perhaps the long detail of her argument about the constitutional significance of the Scots' petition had been suggested to her by Chesterfield, but the conclusion was all her own. Authoritative, articulate, and passionately sincere, the letter gives some clue as to why Walpole's opponents not only put up with, but still went out of their way to cultivate this cantankerous and indomitable old woman. 'For my own Part,' she ended,

I am very indifferent who is Minister, I am sure I have nothing to ask; nor can I expect to be long in this World. But as long as I must live in it, I do solemnly protest, I would do every thing in my Power to prevent any one Man's having Power to Lord it over all the rest of his Fellow Subjects, though it were my own Son that were Premier Minister. For I have not near so much Desire to put Sir Robert's Reign to an End, as I have to recover our Constitution. And if we cannot do that I think 'tis no Matter who governs.

Somerset put aside his winter course of physic and came at her bidding.[64]

But the result of this, as of other cherished opposition measures, was disappointment. Walpole seemed to be entrenched for another seven years, and a personal episode soon confirmed Sarah's disillusion with her political allies. Because of the agricultural depression, the lands settled on Blandford's widow as her jointure no longer produced their former value in rents and for some time she had been campaigning to have them augmented. Sarah, who was still fond of her, blamed the influence of her sister, and when Lady Blandford remarried in the summer of 1734, she was pleased. Sir William Wyndham, the bridegroom, was a man she knew and liked, both as the Duke of Somerset's son-in-law and as Pulteney's Tory ally in the House of Commons. She sent him a message of congratulation, 'which I thought was right, having known him so long', and he returned it with a personal visit. 'He is an extreme agreeable Man,' she reported to Diana, 'and there can be no doubt that a Man of so much good sense will take care that his Wife shall not be governed by her Sister.'[65] The word went round that 'old Marlborough' had declared that 'if Sir William had courted her some time ago, she would have had him herself'.[66]

For Wyndham, however, Lady Blandford's jointure was a major part of her attraction. In February 1735 he began Chancery proceedings to try to force the Trust to increase the settlement of land. Sarah, with some justification, was outraged; the original settlement had been made in good faith and was already more generous than Lady Blandford's fortune had warranted. What was the point of working to overthrow Walpole if such men were to be put in his place? Wyndham's suit, she told John Spencer, was

very foolish, scandalous and without any foundation of Reason, Law, Equity or Justice. And yet he is now one of the great Patriots. Which makes me reflect on what is very melancholy and of more Consequence. Because I see there is very little Difference between Men when they come into Power . . . they generally think only of themselves, without any Regard either to Principle or Honour.[67]

The one good consequence was that shared disgust at the whole business helped to draw her and Godolphin together again.

Sarah remained in London well into the summer of 1735 in her usual 'hurry of business'. Although her disability was as severe as ever, the discontent of the previous year had miraculously vanished and she was full of energy and spirits. Two of her grandchildren at least now gave her complete satisfaction. Diana was dubbed 'Cordelia', 'which I think is the name of King Lear's good child, and therefore a proper title for you, who have been always good to me'.[68] John Spencer, now safely installed at Woodstock, was 'dear Johnny', and the recipient of long letters by nearly every post. In return he was invited, for the first time since the quarrel over his brother's marriage, to return to the same childhood informality and address her as 'dear Grandmama': 'I mortally hate

Madam & your Grace which I call Bug-Words.' 'Little Johnny', the hope of the next generation, was flourishing, and Mrs Spencer was already expecting another child. They invited Sarah to pay them a visit at Althorp. She refused, unable to face Roger Morris's desecration of what she had always regarded as the perfect country house; 'but I was pleased with your kind expression in wishing that I might.'[69] She made a new will, entirely reinstating Spencer as her heir, with the exceptions of Wimbledon which she settled on Diana, Marlborough House, which was to go with the title, and the endowment for her almshouses at St Albans, now being handsomely finished under the direction of Francis Smith of Warwick. Recollecting that she was the last of her father's line, she planned, if the Spencers should have a second son, to give him the Christian name Jenyns and make him heir to her parental estate.[70]

But there was no such harmony in her dealings with the Duke of Marlborough and his family. Part of the difficulty was that his wife, unlike Lady Blandford in similar circumstances, had notably failed to win her over: 'extremely ill-bred, simple and pert' was Sarah's verdict after two years of trying to make the best of the match. Marlborough himself continued as unsatisfactory and unbusinesslike as ever, even though she was labouring for his benefit 'Hours every Day to bring the Estate out of that miserable Condition in which Mr Norgate left it'. Floundering, in spite of all she could do, ever deeper into debt, he came to dread her inevitable scolding and disapproval. When he came to Marlborough House to sign new leases for the Trust farms, his 'icy cold' manner hurt and offended her; all she could do was 'Drudge on' and conceal her disapproval from the world.[71] Summoned away from his country pursuits again in July to settle his answer to the Wyndham suit, he mistook the day and inconvenienced everyone: 'I said no more upon it then that he was very young & I wishd that I were so to[o], tho that is not quite true, for I only wish to be able to walk & to help my self, & live without any great pain.'[72]

At 75 no one could have lived less in the past. During the spring and summer of 1735 there was a constant stream of visitors at Marlborough House, and they did not consist merely of lawyers and stewards and the staid dowagers who made up her evening quadrille parties. While the opposition leaders were growing tired and discouraged, and either falling by the wayside or yearning for the security of office, this inexhaustible old woman, who had seen more governments come and go than any of them, was already beginning to draw into her circle the younger generation, the 'cubs' of the opposition who had not yet had time to become disillusioned with her (nor she with them). Lord Marchmont might be relegated to his Scottish estates, but his twin sons, Lord

Polwarth and Alexander Hume Campbell, were now MPs. Polwarth, 'a very valuable young man, and very agreeable', immediately succeeded to his father's place in her esteem, and when she asked him to bring along his brother to be introduced, she liked him equally well.[73]

Then there was her young cousin, George Lyttelton. Their kinship (through her Temple grandmother) did not prevent her from despising his father, Sir Thomas, as a slave of Walpole: 'twas for that reason I imagine, he has an employment he can know nothing of'.[74] Nor did George Lyttelton's talent for writing verse much impress her, especially when he presented her with a poem 'On Liberty' which contained no tribute to Marlborough. But he was establishing himself, under the tutelage of Cobham and Chesterfield, as a favourite of the Prince of Wales and a promising spokesman for the opposition in the Commons, and this was the basis of the 'great friendship' which she now began to profess for him.[75] Two independent-minded law officers, the Lord Chief Justice Hardwicke (the former Sir Philip Yorke), 'the most valuable man of that profession', and the Master of the Rolls, Sir Joseph Jekyll, whom Walpole cordially detested, also became her regular visitors and consultants in her law affairs.

Her letters to her grandchildren were crammed with the Court and political gossip which she gleaned from these associates, and she continued to follow the progress of the Continental war from which Walpole had kept England aloof with gloomy relish, finding the situation 'much worse I think, than ever I knew it in my long Life. And how we shall get any Security is past my finding out'; 'Spain and France have a vast Army that will soon be able to give what Laws they please to us.' When that happened, 'we must bid farewell to Althorp, Blenheim, and to all Property, and to conclude, be intire Slaves'. She was now making almost daily visits to see the furniture put up at Wimbledon and consult with Bridgman about the gardens; 'but I have this allay, that I fear soon after it is done some of the dependants of France will have the possession of it.'[76]

A much nearer allay was in store. Since the loss of Diana's son two years before there had been another miscarriage 'for want of Care', and at this second disappointment Bedford became 'a good deal peevish'. His efforts to restore his family's position would be pointless if he had no heir.[77] The desire to bear a child now dominated Diana's life, and Sarah tried to reassure her that 'when you have succeeded in having one child there will be no reason to fear that you will not have many'.[78] By the spring of 1735, having apparently recovered from a long bout of ill health, Diana believed herself to be pregnant again, but after some weeks she reported to her grandmother from Woburn that what she assumed to be normal morning sickness had become almost continuous. Early in August Sarah set out from St Albans to see for herself. There to her shock and horror she found the girl emaciated and with 'Death in her Face', still clinging to the hope of her pregnancy and confined indoors in the sweltering heat by Bedford's resident doctor, for fear of bringing on another miscarriage. Sarah's relations with the Duke had become so strained that she knew he would not listen to her opinion, and she hurried back to London to seek expert advice in secret.[79] Pausing at St Albans, where her children and grandchildren had been brought up, she was overwhelmed with misery. An affectionate note of thanks for her visit arrived from Diana, from whom she had concealed the full extent of her fears:

[and] tho I think it ought to make my heart joyful, the Tears drop down so fast that I cannot see to write. . . . Tho this Place is convenient & suits well enough with my Inclination, who never was fond of magnificent things, yet tis so dismal to me to have left you ill at Woburn to be here alone in a Place that makes me reflect upon many Scenes of Happiness, none of which can ever return, that I cannot bear to stay.[80]

Diana promised that she would now take the air as much as possible and asked to borrow Marlborough's old campaigning tent for the purpose. To indulge her, Sarah dispatched the rat-gnawed relic at once: 'I wish it may be of any use and please you, but I think the chief value of it is, to think that it was your dear Grandfather's tent, when he did such wonderful things to secure the nation from being enslaved by the French king.' All the tenderness she was now capable of was centred on Diana: 'while I am in these apprehensions I could wish not to think of you. But that is impossible, for whoever is with me or whatever I am obliged to do, my dear Cordelia is always in my mind.'[81]

Even so, she did allow her attention to be distracted momentarily from her granddaughter's condition when Marlborough reported from Windsor that the Duke of St Albans was claiming the right to drive through the park in his coach. The Duke was an old enemy, whose claim as constable of the Castle to be her superior as ranger, was an unfailing source of provocation. When she had tried to stop him taking game from the park, he retaliated by calling her 'such names . . . as I never yet saw written'.[82] Now she appealed at length to the Duke of Newcastle, reminding him that no one had ever claimed the right to drive through the park but the royal family and the ranger, and 'of the truth of this, I am sorry to say it, I am a witness for full fifty years'. Newcastle at once put the matter beyond argument by telling her that the Queen granted it to the Duke of St Albans not as a right, but as a personal favour. Sarah had still not learnt that she would always come off worst in a dispute with royalty.

She consoled herself by sending an argumentative reply; not that she expected it to do any good, 'but I had a mind to vex them which I think this leter will do, tho they are all such Idiots'.[83]

On medical advice Diana was now about to come to London, and Sarah, who had been planning a visit to Blenheim, put it off in order to meet her there. What she saw at Bedford House revived her worst fears. Diana was now far gone in 'a consumption', a term then given to any wasting disease, and the doctors could do nothing for her. It is not clear whether the pregnancy had always been a delusion, or whether it had simply aggravated an existing condition; but the threat of death to those she loved always drove Sarah frantic with impotent rage and pain, and she now claimed that Bedford and his doctor, who 'pass'd all his time in eating, drinking, sleeping and going a Hunting with His Grace', had wilfully encouraged her granddaughter to misinterpret her symptoms until it was too late to give her proper treatment. She tried to take charge of the case herself, on the grounds that 'I must have more experience than any body about her', and to have James Stephens (now an Oxford D.Med.) called in to consult. Her conduct at family deathbeds had become notorious, and Bedford excluded her.[84]

While Diana lived, Sarah had to swallow her sense of outrage for fear of being shut out of the house altogether. But as she 'sat silently in outward rooms, bathed in tears', she watched Bedford narrowly and persuaded herself that he was only pretending to be grieved: 'he din'd with at least half a dozen People every day when she was in great Extremity, talk'd a great deal upon any ridiculous Subject, and often made Speeches like a Philosopher, how he would behave when she was Dead. This seem'd strange to me, having often observ'd there is nothing so silent as true Grief.'[85] When Diana died on 27 September, Sarah could contain herself no longer and told him that he had murdered her for want of common care. Bedford was so shocked that he fainted. Soon she was demanding the return of the jewels she had given to Diana at her wedding, the tent which had just been sent to Woburn, and anything else she could think of to harass him. Bedford reminded her that she had said she would never ask for the jewels back until she danced at Court. 'By God, then I will dance at Court tomorrow,' Sarah replied. 'The Duchess of Marlborough behaved like herself,' Lord Hervey commented; 'that is, not merely unreasonably and tiresomely, but madly and brutally.'[86]

She could no longer find comfort, as after her son's death, in haunting the cloisters of Westminster Abbey or mingling with the congregation in strange churches. But when a visitor to Marlborough House almost stumbled over her as she lay prostrate on the floor in a darkened room, she explained 'that she was praying, and that she lay thus upon the ground, being too wicked to kneel'.[87]

The Patriots' Prophetess
1736–1741

'AT my age I cannot expect to continue long,' Sarah told Marchmont in the winter following Diana's death, 'nor have I anything now left to make me desirous of it.'[1] Yet she had been writing in these terms for a dozen years past, and while young people in their twenties and thirties dropped about her one by one, their grandmother, disabled as she was and weary of life as she professed to be, seemed destined to go on forever. Even so it was to be an increasingly bleak existence, largely passed (as Lady Mary Wortley Montagu put it), 'in paddling with her will, and contriving schemes of plaguing some, and extracting praise from others, to no purpose, eternally disappointed, and eternally fretting'.[2] Certainly her relations with the grandsons offered no compensation for the loss of Diana. Within the month, the savage mood which had reduced the sturdy Duke of Bedford to a state of collapse was turned on Marlborough.

From the newspapers Sarah learnt that the Duke, contrary to all his promises to her, was making expensive alterations at Windsor. On the way to her own Lodge she stopped in the home park and asked a servant to show her what was going on. There she saw that Marlborough had embarked on an immense new garden layout, with serpentine rivers, mounds, and summer houses, and this even though he could not meet his ordinary expenses without running further into debt. By her own account she reasoned with him 'with all the Calmness and kindness imaginable'; but afterwards she brought a team of men from London to destroy everything he had done, 'pulled up the trees, and cut and hacked everything she came near'.[3] In the winter Marlborough came to her of his own accord with a proposal for committing part of the Trust income to the payment of his debts. Still angry with him over this affair and claiming (probably with truth) that he was not being honest about the full extent of his owings, she refused to help him.[4] This was the turning-point in their relations. The Duke of Bedford now stepped in and offered to arrange a further loan, so that Marlborough could 'go to law and torment the old dowager', with a view to breaking her hold on the family wealth.[5] Indeed, all three young men now joined forces against her in one way or another; soon John Spencer's drunken escapades in Bedford's company were the talk of the town.[6]

It was Sarah's passion for politics, rather than any personal relationship, that was to be her chief consolation for the remaining years of her life. Yet even the political situation did not seem to promise much for the time being, and the fact was, although she did not fully realize it as yet, that by outliving two of her grandsons and then pursuing her quarrels with Marlborough and Bedford to the point of open rupture, she had greatly reduced her significance to the chiefs of both sides. Pulteney and Bolingbroke, in any case, had grown weary of the burden of leadership. Wyndham let his suit drag on, refusing either to abandon it or to bring it to court, and Carteret also kept his distance. Only Chesterfield, Lyttelton, and the Hume Campbells remained in favour. 'When the Parliament meets, to be sure there is sufficient ground for very good speeches,' Sarah wrote to Marchmont, 'but I believe they will signify very little, for there is no honour, conscience or even common sense, in the generality of mankind.'[7] It was disheartening to the opposition that a European peace had saved Walpole from their attacks on his conduct of foreign affairs. Even Sarah had to concede that the 'intire Destruction' of England which she had felt to be imminent in the summer might not happen at once; yet 'no thinking Man can beleive that a Peace forc'd upon the Emperor from his Misfortunes, and which gives more strength to France by an Encrease of Troops, Mony, and Power can continue long for the Quiet of England, tho' it makes Sir Robert easy at present'.[8]

Although she continued to resent the dependence of the Trust on Walpole's agreement to let them lend as much of their surplus capital as possible to the exchequer, the agricultural depression left them with few alternative methods of investment, and in February 1736 she asked Godolphin to make the usual arrangement. But her own and her grandsons' role in the opposition had left its mark, and this time it was Walpole who 'grumbled pretty much',

and said He could not but think it a little hard that, in preference to others who gave him fair quarter, He should be press'd to accommodate the affairs of those who omitted no opportunity of thwarting & opposing him to the utmost of their power, not sparing to mingle it with all the personall ill will that could be . . .

Sarah's first impulse was to send him a long narrative of all her complaints against him, from the time he had shown too much consideration for Abigail Masham in 1710 to his refusal to let her fill up Henrietta's life in the grant of Windsor Park. But when Godolphin pointed out that this would lose them all chance of the loan, it was a measure of her discouragement that she wearily gave in: 'if I had any Power, I beleive I should have shewn it; or any Wit, under such Provocations. But I have neither, and leave it intirely to you.'[9]

With great reluctance Walpole did finally agree to accept a loan of £150,000 from the Trust, but probably only because he knew that he would soon have a favour to ask of Sarah on the Queen's behalf. For shortly afterwards he approached Godolphin with two proposals: Caroline wanted to make a road over common land belonging to the manor of Wimbledon and also to acquire two acres of copyhold ground for enclosure within her garden at Richmond. The first, Godolphin reminded Sarah, was a request which no landowner would refuse to a neighbour. Yet Sarah, having just learnt that the Queen had been talking publicly in the drawing-room of the late Duke 'in the most foolish and indecent manner that ever any body did', was very much tempted to do so. She only gave in when she reflected that it would be awkward to explain to everyone why she was being unco-operative. She contented herself with stipulating that the Queen should give £300 to the poor of the parish: 'a great deal more than 'twas worth', as she admitted, but 'I hook'd Her in so she could not refuse it'.

The request concerning the copyhold, however, she absolutely declined, on the grounds that the admission of a wealthy tenant would endanger the rest of the manor. Caroline made no attempt to conceal her fury, declaring (in what had become a favourite Hanoverian jibe at the Marlboroughs' overweening ambition) that the real cause of Sarah's 'Spite and Perverseness' was her disappointment at not being mistress of St James's Palace herself. She talked of legal proceedings and remarked, more ominously, that she was surprised at Sarah's readiness to offend the Court after she had repeatedly forfeited all the property she held from the crown, if there was any inclination to take advantage of it. In fact there was nothing the Queen or anyone else could do to force Sarah's compliance over the copyhold, and the matter was dropped for the present; but it was not the last she was to hear of it.[10]

In July 1736 Sarah moved as usual to Windsor Lodge. Although Wimbledon was now furnished and waiting for her, its associations with Diana made it too painful a retreat and she let it stand empty. At Windsor she remained for the next eight months, seeing very few people but her own servants.[11] Yet she was not unhappy—Marchmont and Stair both commented on her good spirits—and she busied herself with reading and sorting through her papers.[12] Although much correspondence went into the fire, she could not bring herself to destroy Marlborough's letters or her own accounts of her relations with Queen Anne, of which Hoadly's was still the most definitive version. But she realized that even this now needed complete rewriting. Her attitude to nearly all the chief characters had been modified with the years: Sunderland and Walpole had done more damage to the nation than Oxford and Bolingbroke, Mrs Clayton had been more mischievous than Abigail, and above all Queen Caroline made her realize how many virtues Queen Anne had possessed. Yet Hoadly was shy of her since her quarrel with the Queen, and Voltaire, of whom she had had hopes during his visit to England in the late 1720s, had proved too critical of her own conduct to be a suitable collaborator.[13] She decided that the only thing was to leave the original to her executors 'to doe what they Judg best with, for it is not fitt that I should ever make it Publick'.[14]

She spent much time reading. The *Craftsman,* suffering from Bolingbroke's departure abroad, no longer satisfied her, but she found ample compensation in *Gulliver's Travels,* which delighted her so much that she was ready to forgive Swift for all his past attacks on her and her husband. She also had the company of her three dogs, all with 'Gratitude, Wit, and good Sense, Things very rare to be found in this Country'. The one pleasure she longed for was to be able to walk about her gardens and park; 'but alas! that is not permitted: For I am generally wrapped up in Flannell, and wheel'd up and down my Rooms in a Chair.'[15] Her greatest satisfaction came from her correspondence with Stair, who took this way of repaying her for her continued financial assistance. The long, belligerent, one-sided, but well-informed accounts of politics and affairs at Court which she dictated to him at least once a month, and two or three times a week while Parliament was sitting, gave her back some sense of real involvement in the affairs of the opposition.[16] Nor was this entirely unfounded, for Stair's colleagues in the south were happy to leave the task of keeping him informed to her, since she could write more frankly than they dared to, 'and surely', as Marchmont acknowledged, 'did it with vastly more spirit'.[17] When no acquaintance was going north who could deliver her letters privately, she cheerfully dispatched her diatribes against the royal family and Walpole by the ordinary post, telling Stair that it could do him no harm because they had ruined him already, 'and I think they cannot hang me for writing the Truth, and I had rather be hang'd than do any thing that could merit their Favour'.[18]

It was not until February 1737 that she reappeared in London, drawn by the opening of Parliament and by the usual round of business on her grandsons' behalf, which this time included the purchase of a town house in Grosvenor Street for John Spencer and his family. The main news, which she relayed immediately to Stair, was that the King was worse in health than the Court was prepared to admit publicly; and at first this raised her hopes. Since the previous year, through her friendship with

Lyttelton, she had been in personal contact with the Prince of Wales, and had liked what she saw and heard.[19] Now on the worst of terms with his parents, he was looked to by the opposition as their head. On 22 February Pulteney moved a settlement of £100,000 on the Prince, and although the government managed to defeat it, the minority vote was as high as 204, the same ominous number which had persuaded Walpole to drop the Excise bill. 'A great many charming Truths were said on that side; no Justice or common sense was expressed on the other,' Sarah reported to Stair. In view of the King's state of health, she predicted that even Walpole's majority would soon 'grow very weary of voting to starve the next Heir to the Crown'. 'You know I am never very sanguine,' she concluded, '& for a long time could not imagine which way the Liberties of England could be saved: But I really do think now that there is a little glimmering of Day-light.'[20]

The chink through which it had come soon closed. The King showed no signs of dying and such issues did not arise every day. As the session progressed, Sarah's disillusion with the conduct of the opposition returned in full force: 'tho' I naturally love Patriots, I cannot find any good Reason for what they have done.'[21] A case in point was their attitude to the government policy which still gave her the greatest alarm, namely, the failure to defend England from the power of France and therefore from the prospect of a Jacobite restoration: 'it is impossible for any body with Common Sense to beleive that France won't endeavour to put one upon this Throne, that will be govern'd by them, as soon as they think it safe to attempt it.' If this happened, she feared that, so unpopular had the Hanoverians made themselves, most people might not easily be able to decide 'which was the easiest Servitude, under France, or Germany', and she asked Stair to keep her letters on this subject, 'to see if I have been a true Prophetess or not'. Yet when she poured out these forebodings to her opposition acquaintances in London, she could get nothing more from them than that 'they hope it won't be as I imagine. And that, if France attempted Us, it would unite everybody in England.' It was a complacency that exasperated her beyond bearing.[22]

In her conviction of the truth of her prophecies, she now began drastically to alter the balance of her investments. Within a matter of weeks in the spring of 1737 she had sold her remaining South Sea holdings in order to increase her Bank stock from £64,000 to £104,000.[23] Having been loyal to the Bank from its first foundation, she still felt that she would be in safer hands there than anywhere else, although she admitted that if the ruin she foretold did come about, Bank stock would be as much affected as anything else, and in that case she might live to see an end of all income from the public funds.[24]

It was with this eventuality in mind that she also began to buy land again on a grand scale, laying out more than £150,000 over the next eighteen months, chiefly in the rich agricultural counties of Northamptonshire and Bedfordshire where she already had extensive holdings. In her present mood the high prices and continuing difficulty of getting rents were no longer a deterrent. Although she used up all her reserves of capital and greatly reduced her short-term income by this means, she consoled herself that if the worst happened at least she would not starve, 'having bought Land enough to produce Beef and Mutton at very dear Rates'.[25] Accordingly she went on to stock her estates to capacity, having her own definite and idiosyncratic tastes in this as in everything else. Stair was instructed to send cattle 'of the small sort' from Scotland, for 'I can't endure the large Beef, that one can buy in any of the Markets here'. John Spencer had to send into Wales for her sheep for the same reason. She did not care if they arrived lean, 'as I can keep them a good Table in several of my Places'.[26]

The Queen and Walpole now found ways of revenging themselves for Sarah's outspoken opposition and her refusal to co-operate over the Wimbledon copyhold. The first step was the cancellation of her annual allowance of £500 a year as ranger of Windsor Park, the issue which had embittered her relations with the Court since the first arrival of George I. Realizing that there was no possibility of going to law to recover it, she decided to react with bravado, claiming that it was an honour to be 'put upon the Foot of those that have lost their Places for being honest'.[27] A much more serious matter was the message she received from Walpole, that in future he would take no Trust money at all on the exchequer loans. There was no alternative, as Godolphin pointed out, but to put as much of this capital as they could into Bank stock and landed estates without delay.[28]

At the end of July Sarah went out of town to spend the summer at Wimbledon, her first substantial stay there since the house had been completed. The cutting off of the Windsor allowance had spoilt her pleasure in this favourite retreat. It was while she was there that the quarrel between the Prince of Wales and his parents came to a head. On 31 July the Prince hurried his wife away to St James's while she was actually in labour, rather than have her give birth under his parents' roof at Hampton Court. Had the child been a boy instead of 'a little rat of a girl' (as the Queen described her granddaughter), there would certainly have been accusations of trickery. As it was, the King sent a message expelling the Prince and his family from St James's. On the Prince's orders, Lyttelton sent Sarah his version of the affair, which she in turn reported to Stair.[29] Joining the many opposition peers who waited on the

Prince at Kew, she even offered him the use of Marlborough House as a temporary London home.[30] When he chose the nearby Norfolk House instead, she returned to London herself at the end of October. As she admitted to Stair, it was much earlier than her usual time, but after all her trouble Wimbledon had completely failed to fulfil her expectations. It had proved too damp and unhealthy for long-term residence, 'and Consequently I have thrown away a vast sum of Mony upon it to little purpose'.[31]

She was now sure that only 'an Accident of Deaths' could save England; either the death of the Queen, from whose favour Walpole was believed to derive all his power, or of the King himself, since this would allow his son to succeed, 'the only Person that I know we can expect any good from . . . but I much apprehend that all his good Intentions will come too late to save us from Destruction'.[32] As she waited impatiently for the opening of Parliament, one of these 'accidents' occurred. On 9 November the Queen was taken ill of the effects of rupture, which she had concealed for many years for fear of losing her power over the King. After lingering in agony for twelve days, while Sarah dispassionately described the stages of her decline to Stair, she died on 20 November. As it was now no treason to say it, Sarah wrote,

I freely own that I am glad she is dead. For to get Mony . . . and to support Sir Robert in all his Arbitrary Injustice, [she has] brought this Nation upon the very Brink of Ruin, and has endangered the Succession of her own Family by raising so high a Dissatisfaction in the whole Nation, as there is to them all, and by giving so much Power to France, whenever they think fit to make Use of it . . .

She was convinced that, left to himself, the King would 'hear Reason, when any one dares to speak it', and that 'in time England might flourish again'.[33] In fact Walpole proved more than equal to maintaining himself in power without the Queen. By February the following year Sarah had to acknowledge in despair that 'he governs this Country more absolutely, and with more Ease, than he did in Queen Caroline's time'.[34]

Nauseated by the panegyrics that came out to the dead Queen's virtues, Sarah decided to produce her own antidote. The last of her ornaments for Blenheim was a marble statue of Queen Anne by Rysbrack, which she set up during this year in the bow-window room. Her change of heart about her former mistress was now complete: 'her kindness to me was real. And what happened afterwards was compassed by the contrivance of such as are in power now.'[35] As raw material for an inscription she composed her own long eulogistic character of the Queen, but having given it to several of 'the best Authors' to adapt and polish, she was never quite satisfied with the result. In the end she had only a brief formal inscription put on the base of the statue, while her own character, just as she had composed and signed it, was published in the press. 'Tho' I make no observations upon it, no body can read it without reflecting upon the Difference of the Proceedings in Queen Anne's reign & the present,' she admitted to Stair, yet 'if saying the Truth of Queen Anne offended Worshipers of Queen Caroline, that must be her fault, & not mine.'[36]

The conduct of the patriots and the Prince of Wales completed Sarah's disenchantment with affairs after the Queen's death. To Stair's eager and optimistic questioning, all she could say was that 'I believe you have not a right notion of 3 [the Prince] for I don't find that either Friends or Enemys think of that Figure, as you seem to do. His right notions come from the opinion of others and are liable to change.'[37] As for the patriots, it now dawned on her inescapably that they had been more remarkable for the maverick brilliance of some of their leaders than for any unity of purpose or consistency in action. The real need was for 'men of substance' from both parties to unite, 'but I don't see the least appearance of their trying my Scheme'. Although she could still command the attendance of opposition members in her evening circle at Marlborough House, and was avid for details of debates, the heady days of the Excise crisis and the 1734 Election were long over and she felt impotent and excluded from their counsels:

It is no surprize to me, that I should know so little of what is doing, or design'd. For what does it signify to tell any thing to an old Woman? Who can be of no Manner of Use: Tho' I have been apply'd to, on many Particulars formerly, upon Elections, and when some seem'd to be more warm in Opposition than at present. . . . I said yesterday to a Considerable Man, that I did not know but that it might be prudent in War to avoid a Battle, if they were sure to lose it, But if I were a Man, I would fight Vigorously every Battle in Parliament, tho I was sure to be beaten. They Answer'd me, that it was very right to do so. At the same time I don't see any thing that looks like a Preparation for it.[38]

In fact the main reason no one told her anything of opposition schemes was that there was nothing to tell. Marchmont, after vain attempts to promote consistent plans of conduct, fell into despair and talked of going back to Scotland, looking 'as several others do, upon the opposition as at an end'.[39] The only slight optimism Sarah felt arose from the complaints of the merchants which came before the Commons in March concerning their treatment at the hands of Spain: 'I think there is some little Chance if we have a War. But without it, we must be worse and worse every Year.'[40]

In the meantime she followed her own maxim and fought what battles she could. Early in 1738, Lord Vere Beauclerk, one of the MPs for Windsor, had to seek re-election after his appointment as Lord of the Admiralty. As a brother of the Duke of St Albans, he was one of the 'family of idiots' whose presence in Windsor Park was still a constant provocation to her. Although St Albans was Lord Lieutenant of the county and the King looked on Windsor as his own borough, Sarah had never ceased to dream of establishing her electoral influence there, and with Marlborough's help she now succeeded so far in the by-election as to get a double return. But this meant that the matter would be decided in the House of Commons, and therefore the battle was as good as lost. After three days' hearing, Lord Vere was declared re-elected by a majority of eighty votes.[41] Yet this was nothing compared with the bombshell which was about to fall within her own family: an event which even Sarah, amid all her other forebodings, had not thought to anticipate, although it was not entirely unpredictable.

Until now, however unsatisfactory Marlborough's management might be in his private affairs, she had been able to find no fault with his political conduct. When, three days after the election hearing, she was told that he had just accepted the colonelcy of a West India regiment, she was incredulous, until later the same day the Duke himself confirmed it in one of his brief scrawls.[42] Sarah tried to limit the damage by persuading him to reserve the right of voting as he chose. But luring him away from the opposition had been Walpole's main objective, and within a few days Marlborough had changed sides and was supporting the Court in the House of Lords. The minister was triumphant, declaring to the Commons: 'you see I know the way how to get every body I have a Mind to.'[43]

Sarah chiefly blamed the influence of the Duke's friend Henry Fox ('the Fox that stole my Goose', as she wittily called him), and of Lady Bateman, 'the vilest Woman I ever knew in my Life; and deserves to be burnt'. The latter, she was sure, had been promised a place at Court in return for her brother's defection, 'and she imagin'd she should be a sort of Madam Mant[enon] and govern all'. In this she was probably right; but what she did not add was that she herself had unwittingly paved the way by persuading the Prince of Wales not to take Lady Bateman into his wife's household, on the grounds that she would be a dangerous influence in the family.[44] Nevertheless, there was certainly more to Marlborough's acceptance of the regiment than family pressure and a desire to follow in his grandfather's footsteps. When Sarah had refused to help him clear his debts two years before, he had fallen into the rapacious hands of the lawyer Matthew Lamb, who had lent him money on extortionate terms in anticipation of her death. Once Walpole had declined to take any more Trust money in exchequer loans, so stopping his most reliable source of income, Marlborough's situation must have become desperate; just before he accepted the regiment, Sarah had pointed out to him with some relish that for the coming year the estate would produce less than it had ever done, 'from the vast sum that has lain so long dead: And a great deal more will be so very soon'.[45] The regiment and the post of lord of the bedchamber which was soon added to it provided Marlborough with a much-needed augmentation of his income, but there can be no doubt that larger financial bargaining entered into the matter as well. Within the month Walpole had agreed to renew the cycle of Trust loans to the exchequer, beginning with £200,000, a larger sum than Godolphin had been able to persuade him to accept for some years past.[46] Sarah had reason enough to be exasperated by her grandson's improvidence, but if she had given him the help he asked for from family funds, he might not have fallen so easy a victim to Walpole.

She took two steps as a result of his defection. The first and most inevitable was to cancel her existing will, in which she had given him 'more than any body could have expected': namely Marlborough House and the lodge in Windsor home park.[47] In fact she not only cancelled the latter bequest, but turned the Duke and his family out of the house that same summer and bestowed it on John Spencer. It was this spiteful act which caused the greatest ill feeling, not least because Marlborough had no other country home to go to. He resisted eviction until the last moment, and then removed or destroyed everything he had added to the house and gardens, even to 'some inconsiderable Boards to feed Fowl upon'. Sarah was reported to have had her revenge by making a puppet-show, 'with waxen figures representing the Trevors tearing up the Shrubs, and the Duchess carrying off the chicken-coop under her arm'.[48]

At least John Spencer's reaction to his brother's desertion had been gratifying. When the news broke in the House of Commons, Sarah told Stair, he 'burst into Tears, and run away immediately to Windsor Lodge, saying he was so much asham'd, that he could not stand it'.[49] Yet for all this, she could not help fearing that he might be persuaded to do the same thing. In her new will she therefore added a clause debarring him and his son from inheriting one penny of her wealth if they ever accepted any post or pension from the government. She was determined, even from beyond the grave, to ensure that no minister would ever be able to buy the allegiance of her heirs, although the cost would be to exclude them from any role in public life except a parliamentary one. Her only regret was that she had not thought of the idea earlier and recommended it to her friends: it 'would have been of great Use to the Nation, if People of great Estates had taken the same Method'.[50]

Her second step was to file a bill in Chancery in June 1738, asking the Court to take over the guardianship of the Trust. Her own great age and estrangement from her grandson were the ostensible reasons, but her real motive was to preserve the 1st Duke's settlement from any attempt against it at the instigation of Matthew Lamb. In fact this simply gave him and his client the opportunity they had been waiting for. When Marlborough's answer to her bill was filed in November, she found that he had not only appealed to have the Trust properties taken out of her hands and put into his own control, but for good measure had accused her of cheating him of the full income to which he was entitled, by not allowing him at least a 3½ per cent return on his grandfather's whole estate. It was a claim, as Sarah pointed out indignantly, which made no allowance for the payment of the various legacies and jointures, or for the expenses of the lawsuits and investment in land.[51] She set about assembling the required evidence of her management of the Trust in a fighting spirit, in order to 'make it plain to all the World, that there never was any Trust so Carefully, & honestly perform'd: Nor ever any Man so ungrateful, and so foolish, as the Duke of Marlborough has been, in Impeaching me for doing the contrary'.[52]

What made this challenge all the more threatening in Sarah's eyes was that in January 1739, after almost seven years of marriage, the young Duchess of Marlborough at last gave birth to a son. Sarah had long feared that if ever her grandson should have a son of legal age to join with him in breaking the entail, he would try to do 'the most infamous Thing any Man can do': that is, set aside his grandfather's settlement and sell the estates to pay his debts. Now this prospect was a step nearer reality. The fact that she, even with her phenomenal longevity, could not possibly live to see it happen did not comfort her. Her desire to control her family, as in the case of John Spencer, extended far beyond the limits of her own life. When her grandson called at Marlborough House and triumphantly told her porter to tell 'the Dowager Duchess of Marlborough' (a style she resented as much as ever) that his wife had been brought to bed of a son, she flared up in irrational fury: 'this was extreme ridiculous and stupid, to call me Dowager Dutchess to my own servant: Which look'd as if he apprehended otherwise that my Porter might go to the other Dutchess to tell her she was brought to bed.' She was well aware of how much he longed to be rid of her, and although her health was much as usual she sent back the message, 'that to complete his joy she was very ill'.[53]

Yet the glacial slowness of the Court of Chancery meant that she could expect no immediate resolution of this dispute with her grandson, and in the meantime the terms of the Convention, by which the government hoped to settle the grievances of the merchants against Spain, gave the opposition a real chance of bringing Walpole down. By February 1739 their optimism had communicated itself even to their gloomiest prophetess, whose passion for the parliamentary battle seemed only to have increased with age. But she had been disappointed so often that she found it hard to hope: 'the City is certainly in a great Flame, and so are all the Countrys. And yet when they call for the Question I still fear.' Her informants kept her supplied with daily and almost hourly accounts of the proceedings in the House of Lords, which in mounting excitement she relayed to Stair: who was present and absent, who spoke and how they voted in the preliminary divisions. 'All that I write I am sure is true,' she ended one account breathlessly, 'and I really do think it begins to be Day-light.'[54]

The vital division when it came on 1 March was the bitterest of disappointments. After nine hours' debate the motion to thank the King for the terms of the Convention was carried by ninety-five votes to the opposition's seventy-four. Sarah sent Stair the division list with her own pungent commentary, according to which the government's slender majority had been composed of 'Bishops, Pensioners, Place-men and Idiots': Lord Salisbury was 'a mad Man, who drives stage Coaches'; Lord Fitzwalter had been 'once on the Country side, since gained by a Title'; Lord De La Warr had 'Great Employments' and was 'a most worthless Wretch'; Lord Warwick had 'not a shilling to live upon but his pension from the Court'; Lord Trevor, her grandson's father-in-law, had been 'Got by the D[uke] of M[arlborough] a Fool. He made a Bonfire for his having a West-India Regiment.' And Marlborough's place in this list was the most painful of all to record, although she still would not acknowledge the main motive for it: 'No body can give a Reason for his Vote, having such an Estate.'[55]

She had no expectation of a better result in the House of Commons, 'for I think there is no reasonable Hope that there should be a Majority in five hundred & fifty odd Members who are composed of the same sort of Men, some of which want even Cloaths'.[56] Of course she was right: Walpole carried it there on 8 March by 260 votes to 232. All the opposition could think of to do by way of protest was to abandon Parliament in a body for the rest of the session. It was true that the dwindling government majorities did not bode well for Walpole, but for the moment there seemed no way of dislodging him while he and the King lived. At first Sarah took some comfort from being told that the minister looked ill and dejected, but even this faint hope vanished when she heard that he had acquired a young mistress, 'which looks as if he was in very good Spirits'.[57] In fact Walpole, for all his multiplying infirmities, colossal bulk, and beleaguered situation, seemed almost as indestructible as herself. Coming out of the City, where she had been on an estate-buying errand, she met him in his chariot. What ironic civilities may have passed between this pair of old friends and adversaries are not recorded, but Sarah commented with a touch of admiration, 'I was surpriz'd to see him: For I really think he look'd handsome and very well.'[58]

During her summer retreat to Wimbledon some of the more restless opposition spirits, such as the Scots MP, James Erskine, tried to use her influence to stir things up in preparation for the coming session, but she had been disappointed too often, and this time she would have none of it.[59] In October, much against Walpole's judgement, war was declared against Spain, but even this remedy, of which Sarah had once had some hope, did not alter her conviction of England's inevitable ruin. As the meeting of Parliament approached she consulted with her opposition friends, and found that none of them thought any good could be done.[60] Soon the government's supporters were congratulating themselves that so quiet a session had never been known. Sarah's correspondence with Stair dwindled, because, as she explained, she had nothing but melancholy accounts to give him.[61]

The winter of 1739-40 was one of the coldest in living memory, and for Sarah this meant constant pain from inflamed joints. Yet even in her eightieth year, she knew her time was not yet. 'I am almost always ill,' she wrote to Stair with as much stoicism as she could muster, ' . . . [and] I can never be better, but must submit to live as long as my Constitution will hold out, tho when I recover any Illness, 'tis only soon after to bear more Pain.'[62] It was her old friend Marchmont who now predeceased her, lamenting to the last that the divisions among the opposition were destroying them. Sarah at once wrote with grace and tact to his son and successor to offer him an advance on the legacy bestowed in her will, 'since I believe upon this sad occasion you may want money immediately'.[63]

The pity of it was that she had no such generosity to spare for her own family; for just at this time Marlborough was making overtures for a reconciliation and being remorselessly rejected, even though he had chosen a promising mediator in his cousin, Lord Clancarty (the former Lord Muskerry, whose father had died at Hamburg in 1734 after more than thirty years of exile). Clancarty, it must be said, was one of Sarah's more inexplicable favourites. After a youth spent in drunken brawling (he had lost an eye in one such episode), a post had been found for him in the navy, as the best way of providing for a peer with a 'rough temper' and no estate; but he never abandoned his rakish manners, or the

Jacobitism of his family, or the hope of one day reclaiming his father's forfeited estates. Even his sister admitted that 'his Judgement is not his brightest side'.[64] Yet he must also have possessed something of her charm and the grace of spontaneous gratitude, for to Sarah, in spite of all his weaknesses, he remained 'a very honest Man'. As soon as John Spencer had a town house of his own, she gave Clancarty the little apartment in the courtyard of Marlborough House to live in, and from the early 1730s onwards paid him an annuity of £400 in lieu of the pension which the Hanoverians had taken away.[65] In May 1740 he came to her with a message from Marlborough, begging to be admitted to pay his duty.

But the young Duke's Court and military appointments, instead of helping him out of his difficulties, had drawn him into ever greater extravagance, and with their lawsuit impending, she was in no mood to be indulgent with him. She sent back the harsh message by Clancarty that after all that had happened, she must have more evidence than words of his repentance.[66] The only use she made of his approach was to badger him for the repayment of the long-standing debt to his brother. This brought her a plaintive note from Marlborough, 'such a one as one might have expected from a cook-maid', hoping she would not insist upon repayment immediately, 'because I am really just now more in want of money than I ever have or perhaps ever shall be again'. When she persisted and threatened him with another lawsuit, he replied more ominously that she must do as she thought fit, but 'as for the reflections the world will make on it, I really think every thing consider'd that they won't fall on me'.[67]

Sarah began to put two and two together. She had long suspected that the brothers were privately on better terms than they chose to appear to her; now she heard that Marlborough was claiming to have acted as surety for John Spencer in his borrowing. Turning to Spencer himself, she reminded him that in the past she had always tried to avoid making him uneasy by prying into his personal finances. But now, under pressure, he did admit that he had recently borrowed £5,000 to clear his other debts.[68] In fact, although he lived in dread of her finding out, he had begun as early as the spring of 1738 to borrow huge sums from moneylenders, repayable at double the money in the event of her death.[69] Sarah's autocratic methods and the indefinite deferment of his inheritance had long since destroyed any affection or sense of duty Johnny might have felt for her. When she had likened herself at one family gathering to the root of a great tree with 'all her branches flourishing about her', Spencer muttered that the branches would flourish more when the root was underground. It was now common knowledge that he was as anxious as his brother to be rid of the old woman.[70]

Perhaps Sarah was not yet prepared to realize this, but she had long ago written to Diana that Johnny, for all his attractive qualities, wanted 'a great deal to get through this world in the manner that I wish he should do'.[71] Although the threat of disinheritance had kept him firm to the opposition, she could now see clearly enough that he would never be the patriot hero she had once hoped for. In the House of Commons young men of his age, George Lyttelton and William Pitt (grandson of her old friend Lady Grandison), were making names for themselves by their oratory, but Spencer remained no more than a make-weight for the opposition and never spoke in debates.[72] His private life was even less satisfactory. The honeymoon period of his marriage was over and no more children followed after the boy and girl born in the first years. With his health already in decline from his various excesses (which included an addiction to chewing tobacco), his nervous creditors were beginning to ask themselves whether he could manage to outlive his grandmother. The apothecary who attended them both spoke of Sarah as a very good old life, and Spencer as a very bad young one.[73] Gossips might smile at her severity towards the Duke of Marlborough, when his brother, with much the same failings, 'kept a fast hold of the old lady's favour all the while, and in her eyes could do nothing wrong'.[74] But Sarah was not blind to John Spencer's failings; as in Blandford's case, she simply did not choose to notice them.

In any case the suit concerning her management of the Trust was at last about to come before Lord Chancellor Hardwicke in Westminster Hall, and what happened to her own fortune was nothing to her compared with this central purpose of her widowhood. She attended the hearing on 20 June 1740 in person, and did not at all like what she heard. It was true that no fault was found with her administration of the Trust; although sometimes wrong-headed, it had been conspicuously honest and conscientious, and Hardwicke decreed that her approval would still be necessary for future transactions. Nevertheless, he made as many concessions to her grandson as he could without actually contravening the provisions of the will. While the title had been held by a woman, Sarah's position might be allowed to go unchallenged, but the spectacle of a Duke of well over thirty and in desperate financial straits being kept out of the bulk of his inheritance indefinitely by a notoriously domineering grandmother was bound to arouse uneasiness in such a society. As Sarah herself admitted, it was natural for people to think that what had been left to her 'was too much to settle on a Woman, when there was a Title, when they don't know the Inducements to it'. She was also inclined, probably rightly, to suspect Walpole's further influence at work in her grandson's favour.[75] By Hardwicke's decree, he became entitled in his own right to the income from the lands which his grandfather had acquired before his death, and to the pension of £5,000 a year which Sarah had long ago renounced for an equivalent rent charge; this amounted to about £9,000 a year in all.[76]

In practical terms this meant that there would be less to pay her and the other annuitants who, according to the will, had first call on the income. Convinced that her counsel was 'tir'd out, and not puting the Case in a true Light', Sarah decided that it was time for her to take over. 'Just as the Hammer was going to strike', she put him aside and with an assumption of longevity which would have been laughable in any but so indestructible a matriarch, asked Hardwicke what would happen if her grandson predeceased her and her jointure was in arrears. Then there was the question of Marlborough's right to the diamond-hilted sword: 'that sword *my* lord would have carried to the gates of Paris,' she declared; 'Am I to live to see the diamonds picked out one by one and lodged at the pawnbroker's?' Word went round that the Duchess of Marlborough had again 'amused the world by pleading her own cause in the Court of Chancery'.[77]

From Sarah's point of view there was an even more sinister item in Hardwicke's decree. Marlborough's will, among its other complex provisions, contained a clause designed to prevent any collusion between a father and son for the purpose of breaking the entail. With this in view, he had empowered his trustees to resettle the entail on the birth of each successive heir, so that none would ever have more than a life interest. But what seemed to Sarah to be further proof of her husband's wisdom and far-sightedness was actually a controversial legal expedient as yet untested by the Courts, and the young Duke's lawyers now challenged it, claiming that as an attempt to create a perpetuity it was illegal. To Sarah this was plain confirmation of her prediction that he was only waiting for an opportunity to disperse the estate which his grandfather had so carefully amassed.[78] It was the political implications of this that filled her with the greatest horror. A succession of poverty-stricken Dukes of Marlborough would continue to be easy prey for Walpole and his like. She therefore argued passionately for the entail to be upheld, at least for one more generation, 'which if it is not done will certainly bring the present Duke of Marlborough's children with that great Title to be a Pensioner for votes in Parliament'.[79] Since Hardwicke left his ruling on the matter in suspense while he took further advice, she could not be sure what further inroads might not be made into the settlement.

Yet for all these worries and frustrations, her energy and spirits still showed no sign of flagging. One of her occupations during this summer of her eighty-first year was to buy and furnish another town house, this time for the newly widowed Duchess of Manchester. Cheerfully singing ballads as she worked, she was able to congratulate herself on being still 'the best upholsterer in England'.[80] In the evenings she held regular musical supper parties at Marlborough House which lasted until two or three in the morning, or went out with her friends to eat cheese-cake and 'hear fine Musick' at Marylebone Gardens.[81] It was not until the end of the summer that she got away briefly to Wimbledon, where her main purpose was to improve an important new acquaintance: that of Alexander Pope at his Twickenham villa.

Sarah was to remark that she had now lived so long that she had very few friends left who were of much value.[82] It was certainly true that her longevity and quarrelsomeness combined had cost her a good many close relationships. Yet she was never without the capacity, even in extreme old age, of making new friendships; and still on occasion, as in this case, out of old enmities. There had apparently been no direct contact between the Duchess and the poet since her unsuccessful attempt to persuade him to produce an inscription for the Column of Victory in 1723. Indeed, in the course of the following decade a number of hostile references to Marlborough and his widow, including a cruelly mocking portrait of the Duke in his last years, appeared in Pope's letters and verses. Nevertheless, both this and an equally bitter companion portrait of Sarah remained unpublished.[83] By the latter half of the 1730s the two had many friends in common, and it was now clear from their shared opposition to Walpole that their 'notions as to liberty' were not so very different after all. Then in 1738 Sarah made another direct approach, perhaps initially in her search for authors to help with the inscription for Queen Anne's statue. Again the response was unpromising. To the frail and sophisticated poet she seemed to have all the demanding energy, unpredictable moods, and undeveloped intelligence of an adolescent, and the prospect of their acquaintance at first had little charm. 'The Duchess of Marlborow makes great Court to me,' he told Swift, 'but I am too Old for her, Mind & body.'[84] Yet for the sake of his witty conversation, as well as to keep him on her side, she continued to pursue the reluctant poet, until he finally gave in and let her send her coach to bring him to Wimbledon, protesting all the while that 'Your Grace will find me, upon farther Acquaintance, really not worth all this Trouble.'[85]

Even at Wimbledon Sarah's round of business never ceased. With a general election due the following year, she had innumerable letters to write to her stewards and bailiffs, 'to engage as many as they can, besides tenants, to vote against pensioners and placemen, in order to save, if

possible, the last stake'.[86] Meanwhile she devoured accounts of affairs
abroad with as much gloomy fascination as ever, dwelling on the plight
of the patriots' hero, Admiral Edward Vernon, surrounded by French
and Spanish ships in the West Indies; on the unaccountable delay in
sending Sir John Norris to intercept the Spanish fleet; on the rumours of
invasion and the lack of experienced officers to defend England against
it; on the huge expenses of the civil list and the growth of the army, 'not
designed for the establishing of the Liberties of our Country', but only
to give commissions in return for votes in Parliament.[87] In fact by the
autumn the sense of impending crisis had driven all electioneering
strategies from her mind; 'as the case now stands, this Parliament will
determine the matter one way or the other', and in spite of all past
disappointments her hopes rose again:

Sure Sir Robert has judged as ill in making the City of London angry with him,
as in any thing. And since when good Members attended we got the better of the
Excise Bill & the Convention, in spite of all their Corruption, I think it is not
unreasonable to hope that a great deal of Good may be done at a time that there
is hardly a Creature that walks the Street that does not see the sad Condition the
Nation is in.

Still more energetic and belligerent at fourscore than most of her
male associates, she tried to incite the Lord Mayor and aldermen to
celebrate Vernon's birthday publicly with venison of her providing. And
having sent one MP a sheaf of opposition papers and ballads, she added
that she hoped he would not stay in the country to read them, 'for Men
that have Sense & Honour can do a great deal of Service even before it
comes to voting'.[88]

The result of all this was yet another disappointment. The failure of
the attack on Walpole in both Houses on 13 February 1741 seemed only
to fix him more firmly in power, ending in an orgy of mutual
recrimination among the Tories and opposition Whigs. Sarah was again
brought face to face with the fundamental disunion of the opposition;
and while they wrangled Walpole was 'in reality King, and will be so as
long as he lives . . . and as long as there is any money in the nation, I
think he will not part with his power nor trust to a new ministry'.[89]
There was nothing for it but to see what improvement the general
election could produce. Although she no longer had the role of seven
years before, her electoral influence still made it worthwhile for the
opposition leaders to take trouble over her. Pulteney continued to attend
her evening parties, but she no longer trusted him with the direction of
her affairs. Instead she found herself courted by a new ally, Sir John
Hynde Cotton, who had replaced Wyndham as one of the Tory leaders
in the Commons. Although he was reputed a Jacobite, Sarah thought

(and Stair agreed with her) that he had 'too great an estate and too much sense really to be for a Popish government', and she had no qualms about accepting his help.[90]

At Woodstock John Spencer and his Tory partner James Dawkins were again her candidates and were returned unopposed. It was St Albans that gave her trouble. Encouraged by Cotton and Walter Plumer, she again attempted the difficult task of returning both members, but this time she found the opposition of Grimston and the corporation too strong for her. The town had had no great benefit from the almshouses and Sarah herself had not set foot in it since her brief visit in 1735. When her agents told her of the corporation's attitude, 'her Graceless' (as the anti-Marlborough faction dubbed her) 'thumped her cane to the ground in a rage saying they knew not what they did'. She declared that she would never see St Albans again, or trouble herself further about it.[91] Expensive election contests, which she had once relished, now seemed as futile as everything else: 'if by giving a hundred thousand pounds immediately I could save my country I should think it better laid out then in any other way, but one single vote can be of no consiquence but to make people merry upon my subject, & vex me out of the little life that I have left.'[92]

Her growing sense of being out of things was confirmed. In August she moved again to Wimbledon, and from there wrote rather sourly to Hardwicke, who had apologized for not having waited on her in London:

as I am quite alone in this place, I am better pleas'd than I have been a great while, for I see nobody. And at London one is always in dread of seeing those one never wishes to see, or in expectation of seeing some few that are generally better employ'd than to come. Hopes, I think, seldom come [to] anything. And upon the whole I think my situation is not an ill one. I cannot be disappointed when I have no hope. And I fear nothing in the world but the French.[93]

Her chief consolation was now in the company of Pope and his friend Nathaniel Hooke, a fellow Roman Catholic whom Sarah's friends had introduced to her in the spring of 1741 as a suitable person to help with the long-deferred project of publishing her memoirs. His works of classical history had brought him more reputation than financial reward, and as far as they were concerned it was an act of charity to a needy literary man. 'I have brought Mr. Hooke and her together, and having done that will leave the rest to them,' Chesterfield told Marchmont, 'not caring to meddle myself in an affair, which I am sure, will not turn out at last to her satisfaction, though I hope, and believe, it will be to his advantage.'[94]

Having at last secured an able and willing collaborator, Sarah decided that the account of her conduct at Court should be only one aspect of his task. The charge that she had not dealt fairly by her grandson, although not upheld by the court, still rankled, and she also wanted Hooke to compile a justification of her conduct as trustee: 'the present Duke of Marlborough makes it as necessary for me to defend my self against this Calumny, as 'tis against the Rage of the two different Parties'.[95] While Hooke settled to his work, Pope sent her pineapples from his garden and received venison in return. The two men came to see her and she returned the visit to view Pope's famous grotto; and when the poet departed to pay visits elsewhere, he left Hooke behind at Twickenham, 'whose Company you own you like, & who I know likes yours, to such a degree that I doubt whether he can be Impartial enough to be your Historian'.[96]

Meanwhile the first session of the new Parliament was approaching, and with it, at long last, Walpole's nemesis. After the elections Sarah was convinced that if only men of estates could agree to tell the King that a complete change of 'Men & Measures' was essential, 'the Business would be done in three Hours'.[97] But for a time, even though Walpole's end was so near, it seemed that she might not live to see it. At the end of November she was taken ill with an acute attack of erisypelas, and for several weeks her life hung in the balance. Refusing to have anything further to do with doctors and their tormenting, inflexible methods—'I won't be blistered and I won't die', she shouted at one of them as he made his retreat—she managed to pull herself through in the end with the help of an apothecary, and so disappoint Walpole's supporters yet again of their 'eager Expectation of her Death'.[98] Meanwhile on 16 December the opposition had won their first victory in gaining control of the Committee of Elections, and from then on the minister's days were numbered. Perhaps the news helped Sarah's recovery, for by 20 January she was able to dictate a short letter to Stair, rejoicing with him at 'how well things go in the House of Commons', where her opposition friends assured her that Walpole could not escape being punished. 'My spirits are low,' she ended, 'and I can say no more but I think I shall get over this Illness.' By the following month she was able to confirm that she was out of danger, and 'tho my Age and Infirmitys make life of no Value, yet 'tis good not to be in great pain'.[99]

But in the end she could not fully rejoice at Walpole's resignation. Instead of the promised punishment, he was removed to the House of Lords, and from the beginning it was clear that this was not to be the complete change of men and measures she looked for. The Earl of Wilmington, an ageing nonentity, had replaced Walpole at the treasury by his agreement. Newcastle remained where he was, and was joined by

Carteret as secretary of state. It was a bad sign to Sarah that neither Chesterfield nor Gower (the Tory leader in the Lords) was to be included in the ministry. The only good news was that Stair was to be sent for from Scotland, 'for they wanted such men as your Lordship'.[100]

It was in the midst of this political upheaval that *An Account of the Conduct of the Dowager Duchess of Marlborough* at last saw the light of day. Hooke's first briefings at Sarah's bedside led to stories that she had dictated the whole work to him, talking for six hours together without notes, 'in the most lively as well as the most connected manner'.[101] Certainly she had an endless fund of anecdotes which she could 'tumble out' to order on any occasion, but it was her existing manuscript accounts that had been his chief source, and in comparison with these the published text now appears excessively dull and discreet. The suppression of much of the personal detail about Queen Anne, together with Sarah's overriding determination to prove that she had saved the Queen £100,000 by her economical management as mistress of the robes meant (as a disappointed Horace Walpole put it) that the *Conduct* was 'rather the annals of a wardrobe than a reign'.[102] Even so it made something of a stir at the time, and a number of answers were published. Sarah dismissed them all with arrogant indifference: 'I have done what I had great pleasure in, vindicated myself by incontestable proofs from the vile aspersions that had been thrown upon me by the rage of parties . . . and I do not care what fools or mad people say of me, which will always be a great majority.'[103] The accomplishment of this task, together with Walpole's fall, not only contributed to her recovery but wrought one of her astonishing rejuvenations. Old Lord Bristol, having spent two hours by her bedside in March, told a friend that he had never seen her look better, 'nay I think I may say so well, these seven years'.[104]

In addition to the main work, Hooke had prepared a 47-page 'postscript' concerning her dispute with her grandson; but at the last minute, when this was actually in print, Sarah retained enough sense not to parade the family quarrel any further for the amusement of the world, and withdrew it from publication.[105] Hooke's friends rallied round to make sure that he was well rewarded for his work, and there was a payment, apparently of some thousands of pounds, which was sufficient to give him security for life.[106] Yet as far as Sarah was concerned, this was a retainer as well as a recognition of past services. She had found it very useful to have a resident literary man, and she was to keep Hooke by her for much of the following year, invoking his help in whatever projects she had to hand.

'An Old Woman is a Very Insignificant Thing'
1742–1744

IN the spring of 1742 Sarah was better in health and spirits than at any time since Diana's death. Yet any hope she might have had that the Duchess of Manchester would become another Diana to comfort her last years was quickly disappointed. Installed in her new house in Dover Street, Isabella was soon discovering that the price of accepting her grandmother's help was to submit her opinions, conduct, and friendships entirely to her approval. And Sarah was soon noticing that among the young Duchess's regular visitors were some of her own worst enemies, including the Herveys, Henry Fox, and Lady Bateman. But when she delivered the usual ultimatum, Isabella only retorted that she could not tell her friends not to come to her because it might prevent her grandmother from leaving her twopence halfpenny. They continued in a state of uneasy truce, until one day Sarah tried to have the last word in some argument by quoting a favourite passage from Shakespeare, in which Brutus forgives Cassius for the 'rash humour' he had inherited from his mother. This she thought 'a very kind, Civil and gentle Reproach from a Grand-mother', but it was too much for the Duchess of Manchester, who replied, 'I had my ill humours from my Mother and she had hers from you'. Sarah, still unable to confront this simple truth, made her granddaughter a frigid bow and told her not to give herself the trouble of making any more visits. They never saw each other again.[1]

Yet it may well have been this episode which at last prompted Sarah to a long overdue reconsideration of her relations with Isabella's mother. The Duchess of Montagu was now old enough and objective enough, even if Sarah was not, to see that the only real barrier between them was too great a similarity of temperament. But when she had made overtures for a reconciliation two years before through a well-meaning acquaintance, Mrs Hammond, Sarah's response had been as unpromising as ever; she had excerpts from the Green Book copied out to send to her daughter, so that 'she should not continue in her notion that she had done nothing wrong'. This brought a stiff and formal letter back from Mary, protesting that she was 'very much mortify'd' by what she had read, and adding, 'I am extreamly sorry that I have offended your Grace, I humbly ask your pardon.' Mrs Hammond urged that for a woman of the Duchess of Montagu's spirit and pride this was saying a good deal. Sarah retorted that ''twas no more than if she had trod by Chance on my Toe'. Mary then sent a warmer and more heartfelt letter, professing 'both shame & sorrow for all that was past', and begging to be forgiven. Sarah grudgingly admitted that this letter was a good one, and she could no longer withhold the formal forgiveness her daughter asked for, but she would not agree to a meeting:

tho I believe her Wit entertaining, I can read that out of any Book. And am Content with the very few Friends I keep Company with, when I am out of Pain. And at my Age, tis impossible to love any body with Passion, as I did her a great while, but I own that has been long burnt out. And I have now nothing to do but be as quiet as I can.[2]

When the Duchess of Montagu enquired after her again during her recent winter illness, Sarah's only response had been to reproach her with the cautiousness of this earlier attempt. She still refused outright to see her.[3] Yet when Mary herself was taken ill in May, not long after Sarah's break with the Duchess of Manchester, it was the elder woman who now took the initiative. A stiff little message arrived at Montagu House, containing the recipe for one of her own favourite remedies. It was the most she was now capable of as a signal that she might at last be prepared to let bygones be bygones. Mary, to her credit, seized the opportunity with both hands:

I hope you won't think I take too much liberty in writing to you, as it comes from the fullness of my heart upon your great goodness to me. . . . I hope [if] it is only to compleat your own work, that now you have made me well you will make me happy, & give me leave to wait upon you to thank you, & to ask your pardon upon my knees for ever having offended you, & to assure you that I am with the greatest affection & tenderness your Graces most obliged & most obedient dutifull daughter.[4]

Incredibly Sarah still refused to give in. She thought it unfair that Mary should expect to wipe out thirty years of her suffering by a simple apology, and still felt that there had not been reproaches enough; or perhaps she simply wanted to stave off the ordeal of their meeting. There are several surviving drafts of her reply, and the one actually sent shows clear signs of adaptation by a more sophisticated literary hand, very probably that of Hooke.[5] 'Dear Madam,' Mary wrote back in one last effort to reach her, 'give me leave to say no more than that my faults came from my head, not my heart, & that I have been so far from not having loved you for thirty years, that I have not been so many days without knowing that I loved you.' Finally Sarah had to capitulate. The last item in their correspondence is a note from Mary, making an appointment to come to Marlborough House that evening.[6]

What passed at the meeting is not known. It is likely, as Sarah had predicted, that there was constraint on both sides. Nevertheless the breach had been healed, and it was never to be reopened. One sign of this was her direction that nothing relating to Mary from the Green Book should be preserved after her death.[7] It was only the disorganized state of her papers (method, as she once remarked, was something she knew nothing of) and her executors' preoccupation with their larger tasks that prevented her wishes from being carried out. In her last will, made only a few weeks before her death, she left her daughter a significant legacy; not money, of which she had no need, but a set of miniature portraits of her father and two sisters, Lady Sunderland and Lady Bridgwater. Symbolically she was restoring Mary to the family circle.

As usual Sarah remained at Marlborough House well into the summer of 1742, occupied with business, and in particular with the last stage of her interminable Chancery suit against the Blenheim creditors. Much to Hardwicke's amusement she still insisted upon attending the hearings in person, even though it meant being at Westminster Hall by seven in the morning.[8] Three years before he had delighted her by deciding the cause of the gardener, Tilleman Bobart, in her favour, and this had seemed to augur well for the other outstanding suit, that of the former surveyor-general, Samuel Travers, which, as she confided to Hardwicke's wife, was

a thousand times worse than Bobart's, and infinitely more ridiculous. And therefore I think it will give my Lord Chancelor very little trouble, which I am glad of; because I do pity extremely what he suffers in hearing so much repetition, which I take the liberty to call nonsense, on the side of those that are in the wrong.[9]

'I know they can never get any thing,' she added as she began energetically to collect evidence against Travers' executors, 'but . . . I hate a Rogue of all things upon earth.'[10] As long as she had a rogue to pursue, her life could never be lacking in zest.

Even though her friendship with Hardwicke and his wife had since virtually ceased, she was still supremely confident. The outcome of the hearing on 31 July was therefore a profound shock. Instead of vindicating all her proceedings concerning Blenheim, as she had intended, his decree that Travers' executors should be free to revive their suit against her made them all seem futile.[11] Since 'that most infamous Cause' could be 'sent back after one & twenty years, contrary to Justice & common sense, against plain Proofs & the strongest Law', she announced then and there that she would have nothing further to do with the Trust. She wrote to Godolphin, requiring him to take the principal direction on himself, because she was too old to carry the burden of it any longer.[12]

Godolphin was now in his sixties, more reclusive than ever and ailing in health himself. He knew perfectly well that Sarah's determination to be rid of the Trust was not the result of age or sudden incapacity, but of pique and frustration at her defeat in Chancery, and the humiliating sense it had given her 'that an old Woman is a very insignificant thing'. He had no desire to take over the conduct of lawsuits which but for her would never have been begun, and must have anticipated that as long as she was alive she would make difficulties about any Trust proceedings which she did not initiate herself. He urged her, tactfully and politely at first, to think again.[13] But when she continued to press him, in long letters which again bear signs of being drafted by Hooke, he told her plainly that in the event of her death or real incapacity he would take over from her, but as things were he did not think it incumbent on him to do so. His passive obstinacy turned all her anger against him. After twenty years of vigorous management, she now made the breathtaking assertion that she did not believe a woman could be a principal trustee. When he continued unmoved, she flew into one of her ungovernable tempers, berating him with his coldness to her over twenty years and accusing him of being the cause of all the problems of the Trust, up to and including the Travers fiasco.[14] Godolphin could only preserve a dignified silence. Although they were occasionally to exchange brief formal messages about Trust business, this was the effective end of their association. The sad thing was that Sarah's protestations that she had always loved and respected him, both for his own sake and for his likeness to his father, were quite true.

In the overwhelming desire to separate herself from other human beings which always followed her most catastrophic rages, Sarah took refuge at Windsor Lodge. There she calmed herself with reading the philosophers—Socrates was her current favourite—and with the company of her two little great-grandchildren, another John and Diana Spencer, who were sent over to visit her from the lodge in the home park:

They are both of 'em charming, and they talk enough. And I find they are mighty fond of coming to me. For I play at Drafts with 'em and they both beat me shamefully. . . . I heard they have been told I intended to give them a Present. Upon which they press'd Grace mightily to know what it was? And after she acquainted me with their curiosity I ask'd 'em if they would have a Kiss or Gold and they both cry'd out very eagerly Mony.[15]

The older and more difficult she became, the greater attraction the very young had for her, since they at least were unlikely to challenge her dominance. And there was still one granddaughter, the youngest, with whom she had not quarrelled. Incredible as it may seem, 'Moll Congreve' now moved into the place left vacant by Diana and the Duchess of Manchester. Henrietta's daughter had grown into a young woman of great beauty and charm, doted on by her family and knowing nothing of the rumours about her irregular parentage. While she still lived at home Sarah had no contact with her, but in the summer of 1740, at the age of 16, she was married to the Duke of Leeds. Sarah seems first to have taken up with the couple as a result of her lawsuit with Marlborough, in which they gave her their support.[16] She also thoroughly approved of the young Duke's political views, and by the time she had fled to Windsor Lodge in the autumn of 1742 they were exchanging long weekly letters. Finding them in financial difficulties, she helped them out with a present of £3,000.[17] Perhaps at bottom they had much the same motive for being nice to her as the little Spencers: 'Mony'. But after the break with Godolphin, the relationship brought her comfort, giving her back a last tenuous link with the line of her beloved Lord Treasurer.

Apart from this, her servants were now her greatest source of consolation. Admittedly she did have a violent falling-out at this time with her steward, Chris Loft, who paid the inevitable penalty of being denounced as the greatest villain on earth when she claimed to have found irregularities in his accounts. But she had nothing but good words for the rest of her household; her housekeeper, butler, coachman, porter, and chairmen were all the best she had ever known of their kind.[18] Her head chambermaid, Grace Ridley, had grown up, married, and been widowed in the household, and her daughter now lived there with her. In her will Sarah was to repay these two for their years of care and companionship by leaving them not merely comfortable but wealthy.

It was the first time since the withdrawal of her allowance five years previously that she had felt free to stay at Windsor. A petition to the new Treasury Lords in June 1742 concerning the unauthorized felling of trees ('I never cut down a Tree so long as it will bear a Leaf where I have power') had had a favourable hearing, giving her hopes that her other grievances about the place might at last receive attention.[19] Yet for all Wilmington's courtesy, she knew that he was only a caretaker at the treasury, and that the real power in forming the new administration lay with Carteret and Pulteney, now Earl of Bath. She believed it only a matter of time before the latter replaced Wilmington, and her contempt for these two betrayers of patriot aspirations knew no bounds. Stair had accepted the posts of commander-in-chief and ambassador at The Hague and she now heard of his doings only by report. But when he briefly renewed their correspondence in the winter to forward a letter from a woman she had known in the days of her exile, her bitterness poured out:

Your Lordship seems to think I am not pleas'd with the Men in places, being of Opinion that they can't be honest. I do confess that I was a little suspicious as to some of them . . . I thought you was made Use of, as a Man of Reputation, to carry on the Farce of the Great things that were to be done for England. And I own I am so stupid as not to see yet that any Measures are taken for the Security or Advantage of it, either by the Change of measures as to our Laws, or Men. 'Tis plain the Dutch won't trust us, and I don't wonder at 'em. Nor do I beleive one word of the very bad Condition the French are in.[20]

Yet although public affairs still fascinated her, her sense of 'insignificance' in all such matters was now confirmed beyond doubt. The overnight visit which Chesterfield, Marchmont, and Pope paid her at the Lodge in September was too brief to be satisfying.[21] The poet, exhausted by her volubility, was apt to fall asleep in his chair as she talked, while Marchmont and Chesterfield had heard her predictions of England's ruin and her complaints about the Court Whigs too many times to pay them much attention. The fact was that by this time the great age of adversarial politics, which so profoundly appealed to Sarah's temperament, and in which she had found a variety of roles to play, had begun to give way to a period of more subtle combinations among the men who sat at Westminster; and in this new political world, although it continued to rivet her attention, she could have no real place.

Having once conversed on equal terms with Queens and first ministers, she was reduced to keeping up her chief correspondence with humbler men on the fringes of public life: with Erasmus Lewis, once under-secretary to Robert Harley, and Richard Glover, a minor author and West India merchant who kept her supplied with news of Admiral Vernon's actions.[22] Vernon was now her great hero. In the autumn of 1742 she not only commissioned a bust of him by Rysbrack and persuaded Pope to produce an inscription, but had it mounted to match those of Marlborough and Godolphin at Wimbledon, thus raising him to her personal pantheon of disinterested saviours of their country.[23] But once this tribute had been paid, she marked the bitter acceptance of her position as an 'insignificant' old woman by remaining at Windsor Lodge all winter, something she had not done since Diana's death. When Lyttelton tried to rouse her to take a hand in a St Albans by-election in

January 1743 she would do no more than give nominal support to his candidate: 'I am as Unalterable as he is, and his friend, Mr Pitt. But while there is so great a Majority in the House of Commons, as will from Corruption and Folly give up all that is Valuable to a Triumvirate Government, what can a poor Woman of 80 do that signifies any thing?'[24]

The one affair which did secretly make her wish that she was in town was the hearing at the end of January 1743 of the Chancery cause concerning Lady Blandford's jointure. Although she kept up the pretence of having abdicated the position of principal trustee, anything to do with the Trust concerned her as much as ever, and she commissioned a shorthand writer to take down the proceedings for her benefit. The barrister on Lady Blandford's side was another brilliant young Scot, William Murray, the future Earl of Mansfield, whose advice Sarah had tried to take herself on occasion. One night, returning late to his chambers after supper, he had found them almost blocked up with her equipage of footmen and pages, and Sarah herself planted disapprovingly in his consulting chair; 'instead of making an apology, she thus addressed him: "Young man, if you mean to rise in the world, you must not sup out." ' Murray, already rising in the world without her help, had refused the huge retainer she offered.[25] In fact he was about to be captured by the government, as the one speaker whose eloquence could match that of Pitt and Lyttelton in the Commons, and this endeared him even less to Sarah. She was completely unimpressed by his arguments on Lady Blandford's behalf ('this I suppose is what great men call Eloquence'), and the result was final confirmation that she no longer had any interest with the Lord Chancellor. Contrary to all the assurances of her lawyers, he came down on Lady Blandford's side, decreeing that the Trust should make good, with arrears, the shortfall in the value of her rents.[26]

The one person whose relations with her benefited from this affair was Marlborough. Only a few days before the trial, urged on by John Spencer and his opposition friends, she had refused her consent to the continued lending of Trust money to the exchequer, on the grounds that the new government was using false information to draw lenders in, and therefore would have no scruple about stopping payments in the event of a crisis.[27] But after the hearing Marlborough pointed out in desperation that the decree in Lady Blandford's favour would reduce his income still further, and that if the ruin Sarah foresaw should come about, the money would be no safer lying in the Bank than lent to the government. Moved by his professions of sorrow for all his faults and follies, she gave way and the treasury accepted £104,000 of the Trust money.[28]

Having once given in, she now had a complete change of heart. Since her great burst of estate buying in the late 1730s, she had again become disillusioned with land. Her solicitor, James Waller, having grown rich in her service, was spending more time at his new country house than in minding her affairs. She also had to suffer the indignity of being sued, and beaten, in Chancery by a 'land jobber', 'a very low, ordinary Man, that carrys about Particulars of Estates', who had claimed a larger fee for his role in one of her purchases than she chose to pay him.[29] She conceded that land 'can't run away', but the continuing difficulty of getting rents was now aggravated by the doubling of the land tax from two shillings to four shillings in the pound. Land, she concluded,

is the Troublesomest thing in the World to have to do with. And I believe when we are undone 'twill be all alike whatever one's Fortune is in. Therefore when I have any Mony, I had rather avoid the Troubles of Land, & have it where I can easily get at it, that I may give it away when I see the storm near, & disappoint the Government from taking it away.[30]

In fact, for all her determination to fear the worst of government policies, her common sense must have told her that this undoing was much more remote than she predicted, and for the moment she certainly did not consider the storm near enough to give any of her money away to her deeply indebted grandsons. Instead, lending her surplus capital on the security of the land tax, for all her former forebodings, seemed suddenly 'safe and easy, at least for a year or two'. In March 1743 she applied to the treasury to lend her own money as well as the Trust's. But Wilmington was now in decline, and the chancellor of the exchequer, Sandys, was one of the turncoat patriots whom she had too loudly criticized. He now had his revenge by telling her rudely that they would not accept any of her money if he could help it. This 'new affront from our great and wise governors' confirmed her alienation from the world.[31]

Her usual winter ailments aggravated her peevish mood, and Hooke's company began to pall. Since she now made no attempt to conceal her agnostic religious views, in his eyes she seemed very unprepared for death. Following some over-earnest attempt on his part to force his orthodoxy on her, she grew irritated with him and packed him off for good.[32] She could not even be bothered with Pope's company, when he begged her to admit her poet 'to bring his Ode along with him on the first of January'. He rallied her with a display of mock hurt feelings, half teasing and half flattering:

What a Girl you are?—I have a mind to be reveng'd of you, and will attribute it to your own finding yourself to want those Qualities, which are necessary to keep a Conquest, when you have made one, & are only the Effects of Years &

Wisdome.—Well, if you think so ill of yourself, leave me off. I could indeed have endured all your Weaknesses & Infirmities, but this.[33]

Marchmont in his turn tried to capture her interest with an account of proceedings in the House of Lords, but with no more success. It was natural, she conceded, for young men to be optimistic; but as far as she was concerned, even if the opposition could succeed in Parliament, the changes after Walpole's fall, 'when the patriots joined with the Court', showed that the country would never be the better for it. It was only in response to his enquiry after her health that she could rise above this petulant mood, and reply with dignity and courage:

I think, I am no present danger of death; and when it does come, I hope I shall bear it patiently, though I own I am not arrived at so much philosophy as not to think torturing pain an evil; that is the only thing that I now dread, for death is unavoidable; and I cannot find that anybody has yet demonstrated whether it is a good thing, or a bad one.

Evidently fearing that her difference with Hooke might have prejudiced Pope against her, she added, 'if you talk to Mr. Pope of me, endeavor to keep him my friend, for I do firmly believe the immortality of the soul, as much as he does, though I am not learned enough to have found out what it is'.[34]

Marchmont and Pope together made one last effort to coax her out of her depression with a joint letter, full of playful affection, calling her their 'Oracle in the Woods', an 'Errant Sibyl', who insisted upon giving her answers in writing rather than by word of mouth. As for her bodily ailments, since her letter made it clear that they had not affected her mind, 'we cannot help flattering ourselves, that we may be admitted to converse with a Soul that is certainly immortal if any Soul be so; & that the body out of which it talks at this rate is yet in tennantable repair, & fitt to enjoy any reasonable conversation'. As the head of their school of philosophy, they begged her to send for them so that they could sit at her feet and confirm themselves in their beliefs.[35]

Sarah was completely won over by this *jeu d'esprit*, which, as she told Marchmont, gave her more pleasure than a visit, since it could be enjoyed 'without the disppointment when Mr. Pope falls asleep, nor the dread of your taking leave when you were weary'. Much more cheerful now, she went on to embroider the theme of immortality in her own fashion. Her servants, being 'very careful' of her, had just persuaded her to have the chimney of her bedchamber at the Lodge swept. This gave her the thought that the souls of kings and first ministers when they died might go into chimney-sweeps' bodies, but with the punishment of remembering their former grandeur. Even so, the condition of one of the sweeps, a ragged little climbing-boy (a member of that huge underclass whose lot, as she acknowledged, would be unaffected by any change of government), touched her heart, and she sent a servant with him to Windsor to buy him some new clothes. She still would not let Pope and Marchmont come to her, but she assured them that as soon as she had fixed a day for coming to London, 'I will give my two scholars notice of it, whom I had rather see than anybody there'.[36]

Against all the odds her friendship with Pope endured, although each had reason enough to be wary of the other. Sarah knew that among the poet's unpublished verses was a satirical sketch of the archetypal termagant, 'Atossa', which in its early form had been a composite portrait of herself and the Duchess of Buckingham (another eccentric old dowager, an illegitimate daughter of James II by Katherine Sedley, with whom Sarah still occasionally crossed swords). Although Pope had since adapted it, and apparently even dared to interpret it to her, as entirely a portrait of the rival Duchess, the revised version still bore an unmistakable likeness to herself, and she did not want it published in any form.[37] The story, current after their deaths, that she gave him a large sum to suppress it is probably a crude version of what passed between them on this delicate issue; but there was talk of her buying him a town house or of leaving him a legacy in her own lifetime. In the winter of 1741–2 there were three large withdrawals from her bank account (of £3,000, £1,500 and £4,000 respectively), the only ones in the long sequence between 1725 and 1744 whose purpose is not clearly specified. One of them almost certainly represents the payment to Hooke; one of the others may well have been for Pope's benefit.[38]

Pope, in his turn, had ample evidence of how precarious his favour was, as one by one his friends followed each other out of grace. Hooke's fate was a mild one compared with some. Only a year or two before, Lord Cornbury had been so much in Sarah's favour that she had included him in her will. Then in 1742 a violent dispute had blown up between them about the annual allowance of venison to which the Trust was entitled for an estate bordering on Cornbury's preserve of Wychwood Forest. Sarah complained bitterly at having to pay the keepers' fees on these occasions, and to build her boundary walls 'as high as the Tower of Babel' in order to keep Cornbury's deer from straying. It ended with her dumping a deer carcass in the courtyard of his London home, with the message ('I value myself more upon sincerity than anything else') that in future he could keep his deer and maintain the walls himself.[39]

Then there was her violent revulsion against Pope's friend William Murray, who had not only successfully turned counsel for Lady

Blandford, but had then supposedly tried to alter the decree further in her favour after Hardwicke had delivered it. Sarah told Marchmont that after this she would never have anything further to do with him; 'and if I were a judge, I would punish any man that attempted it; for I think it is as bad as forgery.'[40] Pope took due note. Generous and entertaining as she could be when she was pleased and deferred to, any disagreement might suddenly flare into violent antagonism. When Marchmont told him in the summer of 1743 that Sarah wanted to see him to talk over the political consequences of Wilmington's death, Pope replied that he 'could listen to her with the same Veneration, & Belief in all her doctrines, as the Disciples of Socrates gave to the words of their Master, or he himself to his Daemon (for I think she too has a Devil, whom in civility we will call a Genius)'.[41]

Yet for all this, it is clear that a real sympathy and affection did grow up between them, aroused on Sarah's part by the poet's extreme physical frailty, and on his by the bleak situation of this destructive dreadnought of an old woman with her fabulous wealth and unquenchable passions, who feared nothing on earth but torturing pain and the French. The two letters published in a nineteenth-century life of Selina, Countess of Huntingdon, which purport to show that in her last years Sarah turned against 'that crooked perverse little wretch at Twickenham', and came under the influence of his saintly Methodist neighbour, are quite unlike her usual style and are almost certainly later fabrications designed to enhance Lady Huntingdon's reputation.[42] Pope's own letters tell a different story. In the last, written during his final illness in February 1744, he admitted that he had tried to hide the seriousness of his condition from her, 'for I really think you feel too much Concern for those you think your Friends'. But he promised, 'the first 2 or 3 days, that I feel my Life return, I will pass a part of it at your Bedside,' and 'in the meantime I beg God to make Our Condition supportable to us both'.[43]

In the end it was not the Earl of Bath who replaced Wilmington at the treasury in August 1743, but the Duke of Newcastle's brother, Henry Pelham. For the first time in the Hanoverian era, public affairs seemed to Sarah really to have taken a turn for the better. Pelham was universally acknowledged to be an honest man. She had been afraid of Bath's appointment because she thought it the worst thing that could happen; whereas in choosing Pelham, 'I think they have done the best thing that they could now do . . . For he has a great stake: And I find every body that I know likes him.'[44] Better, as far as she was concerned, was to follow. At the end of the campaign of 1743 Stair resigned as commander-in-chief in protest at the King's preference for his Hanoverian generals, and a number of British officers, including Marlborough, followed him out in sympathy. Sarah was delighted, not only because 'I wish that no body that bears the Name of Marlborough should do a wrong thing', but because she now thought it unlikely that the Lord Chancellor would favour him in allowing him to break his grandfather's entail.[45] When the Duke of St Albans tried to enlist Marlborough's support for an election, she sent him the triumphant message that her grandson might be a fool, but 'he should not be everybody's fool'.[46]

Yet she was still not softened enough towards him to give him any financial help, when he approached her again through Clancarty in the winter. He was now so much in debt that almost all his income was taken up with interest payments to his creditors. He had an opportunity to reduce this interest, but only on condition that he would make over the entire surplus receipts of the Trust 'to these Harpys' as security. The project needed Sarah's consent, and she refused to give it, on the grounds that it would put her in the power of his moneylenders if there were any failure of Trust revenue. Instead she advised him to retrench his expenses and devote the savings to paying his debts, and he would then 'make a better figure then he had ever done with the vast sums he had thrown away'.[47] Although she had lost her last chance of dying at peace with the grandson who bore the name of Marlborough, she was probably right by this time to refuse to help him. The Duke, whose debts now ran into hundreds of thousands of pounds, had long since lost all touch with reality in managing his affairs; nor could there be any real sincerity in his professions to her. Not long before, he had written to his wife of Sarah's spitefulness in living so long, and of the building he would begin at Blenheim as soon as her death relieved him of his financial problems.[48] In fact, as Sarah had known for some time, his situation was well past any such simple remedy.

Yet even after all that had passed, she still expected him to acknowledge her as head of the family, and to take no step without consulting her. When the Jacobite invasion from France which she had so long predicted seemed about to become a reality in February 1744, he went to the King and offered his service. But she complained that he had not said 'the least word of it to Her, tho' he must know upon the apprehending of an invasion, she must have thought it right to have done every thing for the defence of his Countrey'.[49] For all her Jacobite friends and political associates, she never ceased to equate a Stuart restoration with ruin to herself and England, and in the spring of 1744, having apparently renounced estate buying for good, she hastily put £40,000 more of her fortune into the safety of land.

The following year was to see this Jacobite threat more seriously revived, but 'one great happiness there is in death,' Sarah had once written to Stair, 'that one shall never hear any more of anything they do in this world'. By this time it was clear that her grandsons and their creditors would not have much longer to wait. James Stephens, observing her from day to day with an experienced medical eye, noticed that her seemingly inexhaustible strength of constitution was at last beginning to fail.[50] She was aware of it herself, and in a favourite phrase, began 'packing up to be gone'. In this task it was a great help to her that for the first time in thirty years the treasury was in sympathetic hands. In December 1743 Pelham sent her a courteous message, inviting her to lend on the land tax revenue.[51] Still smarting from Sandys's insult, she first had to have her say about this, even at the risk of alienating yet another ministry: 'I am always sincere,' she began inevitably, 'and, for aught I know, some people may think me too much so.' Yet in the end she advanced not only £300,000 on behalf of the Trust, but £123,000 on her own account, the largest amount she had ever lent.[52] When she followed this with one of her interminable accounts of her grievances about Windsor Park, Pelham remained patient, replying that he had always thought the suspension of the allowance wrong and would try to have it restored. He then referred her to the treasury secretary, John Scrope, for her day-to-day business.[53]

In Scrope, who was at least as ancient, almost as rich, and at times as cantankerous as herself, she found not merely a helpful official but a friend. When she signed herself, 'though I am insignificant, your friend and humble servant', he ventured to tease her gently in the manner of Pulteney and Pope; it showed that 'even the Great Dutchess of Marlborough is not always exempt from the Vapours' that she could ever imagine herself insignificant. She sent him her picture and encouraged him to visit, though 'I know . . . my own Infirmity of keeping you longer than you have time to spare'. With his help she renewed the lease for Marlborough House for a further fifty years. She had always wanted to observe her husband's wishes that the house should go with the title, and she now decided that it should go to every heir except the present Duke, who would sell or mortgage it if he should ever have it in his power. She knew that it was of no use to leave him any of her own fortune either, since he would only squander it and 'come at last to the Treasury for a Pention for his Vote'; but she confided to Scrope her plan to leave his children legacies on condition that they would not co-operate in breaking their great-grandfather's settlement.[54]

By following her husband's example and leaving her own fortune entirely in the hands of trustees, she was able to protect it from the worst consequences of John Spencer's makeshift post-obit bargains. It was clear in any case that he would not long outlive her, and her main concern was for the great-grandson who would be her eventual heir. She had no intention of leaving him to be brought up by the Carterets. Through Clancarty (increasingly her mediator with both grandsons) she instructed Spencer to appoint trustees to direct his education, and chose three out of the four of these herself: James Stephens, William Pitt, and Chesterfield.[55] She also left large bequests (£10,000 and £20,000 apiece) to Pitt and Chesterfield, the commoner and peer whom she would most have liked Spencer to resemble. Her new will was made quickly and signed on 11 August 1744. She felt that she had done all she could to preserve and bestow the family fortune as her husband would have wished.

This business kept her in London all summer, and in any case she was not strong enough now to bear the journey to one of her country houses. Although her time was fast running out, she had one more important matter to deal with. 'I am entered into new Business, which entertains me extreamly,' she wrote to Scrope on 13 September, 'tying up great Bundles of papers to enable two very able Historians to write the Duke of Marlborough's History . . . [and] I am satisfied that what will be proved to be true will make it the most Charming History that has ever been writ in any Countrey.'[56] Her two historians were Richard Glover and David Mallet, the latter recommended to her by his countryman the Duke of Montrose, a patriot colleague of Marchmont and Stair. Realizing that she could never live to see so long a work finished, she had James Stephens take down her recollections for their instruction. These narratives of events which she remembered 'as well as if it had happened but yesterday' were the last things she produced.[57] Although she was now in constant pain, she had the letters of Marlborough and Godolphin read to her, and this impressive and intimate record of their long partnership confirmed her belief that 'never any two Men Deserved so well from their Countrey'.[58]

Yet even with this excuse to dwell on the past, the battles of the moment kept tugging her attention back to the present. Every episode suggested a current parallel: if Marlborough had been like the present patriots, he would have satisfied his ambition by helping James II to establish popery in England; Queen Anne's Tories, however reprehensible, fell 'very short of the great Performances . . . of my Lord Carteret and his Partner my Lord Bath'; from the manner of Marlborough's and Godolphin's dismissals, 'one would think that my Lord Sandys had been at the head of the councill upon these Occasions'.[59] In this sense, old as she was, she never really outlived her time.

Sarah's last letter to Mallet was dated 6 October 1744. Her final illness was now gaining fast on her. Two years before she had had the strength to overcome an attack, and even now, after three or four days of acute illness, she seemed about to rally; then she sank again. Stephens and Clancarty consulted together, and decided to send for John Spencer from Bath. The scapegrace Johnny arrived just in time to say his farewells. When she died on the morning of 18 October, it was with this small group at her bedside.[60] Although Clancarty was perhaps the only one who was really sorry to see her go, there was incredulity, as the news spread, that so apparently inextinguishable a life should at last have been snuffed out; dying, as the Duchess of Montagu remarked, was not in her mother's style.[61] She went into the unknown not hoping or fearing very much; only trusting, in spite of everything, that the sincerity on which she had so long prided herself would be her saving grace if any were needed. 'Whenever the stroke comes,' she had written to Scrope, 'I only pray that it may not be very painfull, knowing that every body must Dye, and I think what ever the next world is, it must be better then this at least to those that never did Deceive any Mortall.'[62]

On 30 October, according to the instructions in her will, Marlborough's body was taken up from Westminster Abbey and sent on its last journey out of London. The next day Sarah's unobtrusive procession followed from Marlborough House. Two days later they were laid together in the vault beneath the chapel at Blenheim, 'as was always intended'.

Epilogue

SARAH died possessed of twenty-seven estates in twelve counties, with a capital value of more than £400,000 and an annual rent roll, after outgoings, in excess of £17,000 a year: all of them, except her parental lands of Sandridge and Agney, of her own acquiring. In addition, she had well over £250,000 in capital, chiefly invested in Bank of England stock or lent to the exchequer on the security of the land tax, and there was a further £12,100 in annuities. It was a fortune which must easily have made her the richest woman in her own right in England.[1] The bulk of it passed to John Spencer. Yet when his creditors closed in after her death, he had to explain that he had no ready money to dispose of; the trustees were applying all the income for the time being to the payment of debts and legacies. In fact in the twenty months he survived his grandmother, he received little benefit from his great inheritance.[2] When he died in June 1746, his 11-year-old son became probably the wealthiest schoolboy in the land.

Marlborough's debts were so great by the time of Sarah's death that, as she had predicted, the extra income released by this means was no more relief to him than 'a drop of water put into the sea'. In December 1744 his affairs had to be placed in the hands of trustees for the payment of his creditors.[3] He died in 1758, just before his son came of age. In due course the 4th Duke applied to the Court of Chancery, and the Trust, over which Sarah had presided so long and so autocratically, and which had served its purpose, was finally dissolved.[4]

Of the houses Sarah had built or inhabited, Blenheim passed immediately into her grandson's possession and is still fulfilling its function of commemorating the 1st Duke's victory today. Marlborough House apparently stood empty until the 4th Duke could inherit it in 1758. Its solitary inhabitant was James Stephens, who lived on in the apartment Sarah had given him, pursuing his indefatigable labours as trustee until he died, still in harness, in 1759.[5] After John Spencer's death the Lodge at Windsor which had been Sarah's favourite house passed to the Duke of Cumberland. Holywell remained empty until her great-grandson's widow chose it as her dower house in 1783. She lived there intermittently during the thirty years of her widowhood, passing her time in charitable works and the supervision of the Marlborough almshouses. Wimbledon also stayed in the Spencer family until its complete destruction by fire in 1785.

The biography which Sarah had planned in her last weeks was never written. Glover soon renounced the task, and it was not until seven years after Sarah's death that James Stephens found time amid his other labours to sort and hand over to Mallet the mass of papers which were to be his chief source material.[6] But to digest these was quite beyond Mallet's powers and when he died in 1765 it was found that he had scarcely written a line. Assuming that the archive would come back to them as Sarah's heirs, the Spencers promised unrestricted access to the historian and philosopher, David Hume, who hoped to find in it evidence of Marlborough's Jacobite intrigues. Sarah's surviving executor and Hume's countryman, Lord Marchmont, was suspicious of his motives and obtained a legal opinion which established that the papers were part of Marlborough's estate, and therefore should go to his heirs and not to Sarah's.[7] They remained at Blenheim for the next 200 years, before being acquired by the nation in 1973.

In stipulating that her heirs must accept no post or pension from the government, Sarah had not debarred them from receiving a peerage. Shortly after he came of age, John Spencer the younger wrote to the Duke of Newcastle to point out that he had always supported the government in Parliament, and that since he was unable to accept office, he could not receive any favour from the King except a title. He was duly created Viscount and (in 1765) Earl Spencer.[8] But two more generations were to pass before Sarah had a descendant, who, 'if the dead could know what the living are doing', would have seemed to her to justify all her labours for her family. In John Charles, Viscount Althorp, one of the guiding spirits of the Reform Bill and 'the very best leader of the House of Commons that any party ever had', Sarah's desire to found a great and politically responsible family, endowed with her own fortune, was finally realized.[9]

APPENDIX I
The Marlborough Family Tree

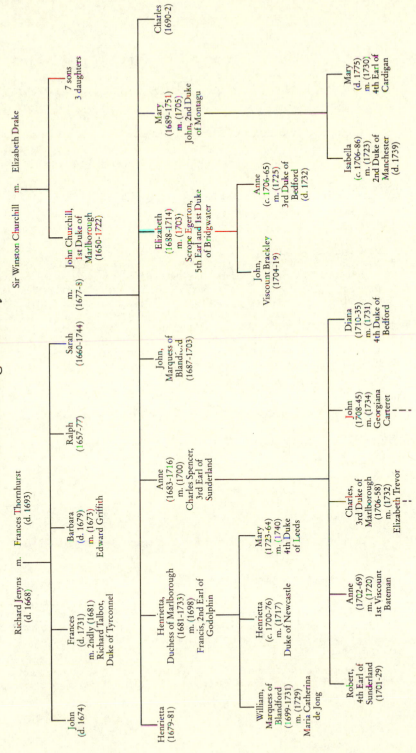

The Estates of Sarah, Duchess of Marlborough

Estate	County	Former owner	Date of purchase	Price, £	Net rent, 1744 £
Sandridge	Herts				1,400
Agney	Kent				720
Wimbledon	Surrey	Janssen (SS)	Apr. 1723	24,950	843
Coldnorton, Whitchurch, and Goring	Oxon	Hawes (SS)	May 1723	7,750	276
Hailweston	Hunts	Astell (SS)	Nov. 1723	15,010	599
Chilworth	Surrey	Houlditch (SS)	Nov. 1723	22,020	902
Crowhurst	Surrey	Gibbon (SS)	Jan. 1724	13,620	[463 in 1736]
Sindlesham	Berks	Jones	Jan. 1724	8,000	437
May Farm	Oxon	Bisshop	Nov. 1725	6,540	250
Marsten Jabet	Warwicks	Surman (SS)	May 1726	6,755	[292 in 1736]
Holm	Beds	Meres	Jul. 1727	15,442	666
Cippenham	Bucks	Knight (SS)	Jun. 1728	13,920	447
Stantonbury	Bucks	Wittewronge	Jul. 1728	20,714	685
Dunton and Kimble	Bucks	Hamden	Nov. 1730	29,605	1,273
Castlethorp	Bucks	Tyrrell	Apr. 1731	15,000	580
Strixton	Northants	Wiseman	Apr. 1736	17,734	682
Potton	Beds	Bromsall	May 1736	3,531	162
Bozeat	Northants	Wiseman	Aug. 1737	13,631	539
Marsten	Beds	Snagg	Dec. 1737	20,445	838
Brampton	Northants	Norwich	May 1738	37,000	1,400
St Thomas	Staffs	Fauconberg	Aug. 1738	29,000	1,114
Shillingford	Berks	Packer	Aug. 1738	48,000	1,450
Steventon	Beds	Floyer	Feb. 1739	2,550	105
North Creak (mortgage foreclosure)	Norfolk	Armiger	Apr. 1740	16,650	649
Balking	Berks	Bedford	Mar. 1744	2,300	100
Steene	Northants	Crewe	May 1744	20,200	723
Theddingworth	Northants	Cave	May 1744	18,000	676

Sources: Annotated auction particulars of South Sea (SS) officials' estates (Bodleian F1,5,6 Med); Close Rolls (PRO C54); Sarah, Duchess of Marlborough's account in Bank of England Private Drawing Office Ledgers; lists and valuations of her estates (BL Althorp Papers D17 and D22).

These estates are distinct from those acquired for the 1st Duke of Marlborough's Trust estate, for which (to 1738) see the Chancery suit, *1st Duke's trustees v. 3rd Duke*, pp. 10–12 (Althorp Papers D39).

NOTES

ABBREVIATIONS AND SHORT TITLES OF FREQUENTLY CITED WORKS

BIHR   *Bulletin of the Institute of Historical Research*

BL   British Library

Brown   *The Letters and Diplomatic Instructions of Queen Anne*, ed. B. Curtis Brown (1935)

Burnet   *Bishop Burnet's History of his own Time*, ed. M. J. R[outh] (6 vols., Oxford, 1833)

Churchill   W. S. Churchill, *Marlborough: His Life and Times* (2 vols., 1947)

Coxe   W. Coxe, *Memoirs of the Duke of Marlborough* (Bohn edn., 3 vols., 1847)

CSPD   Public Record Office, *Calendar of State Papers Domestic*

CTB   Public Record Office, *Calendar of Treasury Books*

Delany   *The Autobiography and Correspondence of Mary Granville, Mrs Delany*, ed. Lady Llandover, 1st and 2nd ser. (6 vols., 1861–2)

EHR   *English Historical Review*

Graham   *Annals and Correspondence of the Viscount and 1st and 2nd Earls of Stair*, ed. J. M. Graham (2 vols., Edinburgh, 1875)

Hamilton   *The Diary of Sir David Hamilton 1710–1714*, ed. P. Roberts (Oxford, 1975)

Hervey   *Lord Hervey and his Friends*, ed. Lord Ilchester (1950)

HLQ   *Huntington Library Quarterly*

HMC   Historical Manuscripts Commission

JSAHR   *Journal of the Society of Army Historical Research*

LG   *Letters of a Grandmother 1732–1735*, ed. G. Scott Thomson (1942)

Luttrell   Narcissus Luttrell, *A Brief Historical Relation of State Affairs* (6 vols., Oxford, 1857)

Memoirs   *Memoirs of Sarah, Duchess of Marlborough*, ed. W. King (1930)

MGC   *The Marlborough–Godolphin Correspondence 1701–1711*, ed. H. L. Snyder (3 vols., Oxford, 1975)

ML   *Letters of Sarah, Duchess of Marlborough . . . at Madresfield Court* (1875)

Montagu   *The Letters and Works of Lady Mary Wortley Montagu*, ed. Lord Wharncliffe (2nd edn., 3 vols., 1837).

PC   *Private Correspondence of Sarah, Duchess of Marlborough* (2 vols., 1838)

PRO   Public Record Office

RO   Record office

Rose   *A Selection from the Papers of the Earls of Marchmont*, ed. Sir G. H. Rose (3 vols., 1831).

SM   Sarah, Duchess of Marlborough

Thibaudeau   *Catalogue of the Collection . . . of Alfred Morrison*, ed. A. W. Thibaudeau, 1st ser. (6 vols., 1883–92) and 2nd ser. (6 vols., 1882–93)

Thomson	K. Thomson, *Memoirs of Sarah, Duchess of Marlborough* (2 vols., 1839)
UL	University Library
Vanbrugh	*The Complete Works of Sir John Vanbrugh*, ed. B. Dobrée and G. Webb (4 vols., 1928)
VCH	Victoria County History
Wolseley	Viscount Wolseley, *The Life of John Churchill, Duke of Marlborough* (2 vols., 1894)

Introduction

1. *ML* 43: SM to Robert Jennens, 27 Oct./7 Nov. [1713].
2. BL Add. MS 61447, fo. 2: SM to John Spencer, 29 June 1732.
3. *ML* 37, 41: SM to Jennens, [4/15] June [1713], 5/16 May [1714]
4. *PC* ii. 27: Francis Hare to SM, 1 Dec. 1710; Churchill, i 992: narrative comp. for SM by Bishop Burnet, [1711]; Thibaudeau, 1st ser. iv. 154: SM to Mary Godolphin, 3 Nov. 1718.
5. HMC, *8th Report*, pt 2, 110: SM to Duke of Manchester, 24 Aug. [1733].
6. A. L. Rowse, *The Later Churchills*, Penguin edn. (1971), 14.
7. *ML* 37: SM to Jennens, 5/16 May [1714].
8. BL Add. MS 61469, fo. 63: SM's instructions to counsel, 14 June 1723.
9. BL Add. MS 61454, fo. 122: Edward Griffith to SM, 4 Oct. 1694.
10. *LG* 96: SM to Duchess of Bedford, Oct. 1733.
11. Thibaudeau, 1st ser. iv. 153: SM to Godolphin, 2 July [1719].
12. BL Add. MS 61454, fo. 187: SM to Lady Rich, 7 Sept. 1730; Add. MS 61351, fo. 232: SM to Lord Stanhope, 11 Dec. 1720.
13. *Memoirs*, 303
14. Bodleian Library, Add. MS A. 191, fo. 5: SM to Burnet, 25 Sept. 1712.
15. Burnet, vi. 33, Dartmouth's note; BL Add. MS 61453, fo. 176: Lady Tyrconnel to SM, 23 Dec. [1704].
16. Bedford Office: SM to Duke of Bedford, 5 May 1725.
17. Devon RO Seymour MSS L18, 24/16: SM to Duke of Somerset, 7 July 1724.
18. Ibid. 23/26: 30 Aug. 1723; *ML* 72: SM to Jennens, [4/15] July 1713.

Chapter 1

1. BL Add. MS 61440, fo. 123: SM to Blandford, 2 Oct. 1728; I. Butler, *Rule of Three* (1967), 18; *PC* ii. 112: SM to Bishop Burnet [1711].
2. D. Green, *Sarah, Duchess of Marlborough* (1967), 24.
3. H. C. Andrews, 'Notes on the Rowlett and Jennings Families', *Miscellanea Genealogica et Heraldica*, 5th ser. 8 (1932–4), 88–107.
4. *CSPD 1638–9*, 27: Jenyns to Council of State, 23 Sept. 1638; *Memoirs*, 125.
5. BL Add. MS 61452: Jenyns pedigree, 1639; *CSPD 1638–9*, 78: Ralph Pollard to Council, 27 Oct. 1638.
6. J. A. Temple, *Temple Memoirs* (1925), 47; H. L. L. Denny, *Memorials of an Ancient House* (Edinburgh, 1913), 215–16.
7. PRO C6/170/61.
8. PRO *Calendar of Proceedings of the Committee for Advance of Money*, 191.
9. PRO C10/36/122; C6/109/87; HMC, *7th Report*, 8; *Commons' Journals*, v. 459.

10. P. W. Sergeant, *Little Jennings and Fighting Dick Talbot* (1913), i. 6.

11. M. F. Keeler, *The Long Parliament* (Philadelphia, 1954), 23; History of Parliament, *The House of Commons 1660–1690*, ed. B. D. Henning (1983), ii. 649.

12. BL Add. MS 61421, fo. 73^v: narrative by SM, 1704.

13. *CSPD 1650*, 540; PRO C2/I and J 29/33; C6/109/87; C5/506/78.

14. C. J. Simmons, 'Churchill Court and Manor', *Somersetshire Archaeological Society Proceedings*, 30 (1885), 33–9; P. N. Dawe, 'The Dorset Churchills', *Notes and Queries for Somerset and Dorset*, 27 (1958), 185–91; HMC, *Bath MSS*, ii. 174: Sir W. Churchill to J. Gibbon, 22 June 1686.

15. PRO C10/52/117; PRO *Calendar of Proceedings of the Committee for Advance of Money*, 3051.

16. PRO C5/506/78, 79.

17. W. Brigg (ed.), *The Parish Registers of St Albans Abbey 1558–1689* (Harpenden, 1897), 86–90, 93, 230–1; BL Althorp Papers D55: notes by James Stephens in the suit *Spencer v. Janssen*, c.1750.

18. J. E. Cussans, *History of Hertfordshire* (1870–81), iii. pt 2, 222, first mentions Water End in this connection.

19. VCH, *Hertfordshire*, ii. 434; BL Althorp Papers P3: plan of Sandridge, 1726.

20. Wolseley, i. 153–4; the Middle Ward corresponded with the Abbey parish (see VCH, *Hertfordshire*, ii. 469).

21. Sir H. Chauncy, *The Historical Antiquities of Hertfordshire* (1700), opp. 428: plan of St Albans by John Oliver, bef. 1686; Herts RO Inventory A25/3792.

22. PRO C5/506/78, 79; National Register of Archives Report 8510 (Jenyns MSS): indentures, June 1663; C. H. Hartmann, *The King's Friend* (1950), 130; Sergeant, *Little Jennings*, i. 58–9.

23. A. Hamilton, *Memoirs of Count Grammont*, ed. Sir W. Scott (1896), 265–8, 329–30, 337–8.

24. Sergeant, *Little Jennings*, i. 201–5.

25. PRO C5/506/78, 79, 81.

26. Bodleian Library, Lister MS 4, fo. 95: Lady Lister to Martin Lister, 4 Nov. 1667 (for the second marriage of Mrs Jenyns's mother to Sir Martin Lister, see Denny, *Memorials*, 215).

27. Ibid. fo. 91: 20 Nov. 1667.

28. PRO PROB 11/418/12: will of Frances Jenyns, 1692.

29. G. S. Steinman, *Althorp Memoirs* (n.p., 1869), 51.

30. Herts RO Manorial Records 40910, 40917; PRO C5/506/78, 79, 81, 84; National Register of Archives Report 8510 (Jenyns MSS): indenture, 10 Apr. 1671.

31. PRO C10/471/84; C8/228/41; C5/506/81.

32. Yale UL Osborn Collection: SM to Alexander Hume Campbell, 26 Sept. 1741; BL Stowe MS 751, fo. 110: SM to James Craggs snr., 25 June/6 July [1714] ('having suffered for more then fifty year for my sencerity').

33. Denny, *Memorials*, 221: Mrs Jenyns to Lister, 30 May 1667.

34. C. H. Ashdown, 'The Accounts of St Albans Grammar School', *Home Counties Magazine*, 6 (1904), 57; BL Add. MS 61422, fo. 194^v: narrative by SM; B.L. Add. MS 61458, fo. 98: Mrs Burnet's character of SM.

35. Montagu, i. 77.

36. BL Add. MS 61466, fo. 164: Lady Blayney to Duchess of Marlborough, 25 Feb. 1772.

Chapter 2: 1673–1678

1. *LG* 147: SM to Duchess of Bedford, 21 Oct. 1734.
2. BL Add. MS 54225, fo. 150: SM to Mary Godolphin [Nov. 1718]; Add. MS 61464, fo. 17: SM to Hare [1710].
3. W. D. Christie (ed.), *Letters Addressed . . . to Sir Joseph Williamson*, Camden Society, new ser. 8 (1875), ii. 27: from N. Armorer, 2 Oct. 1673.
4. BL Add. MS 61467, fo. 206: SM to Scrope, 22 Sept. 1744; E. Chamberlayne, *Angliae Notitia* (1676), 205.
5. BL Add. MS 61453, fo. 41: SM to Lady Hamilton [1675].
6. Churchill, i. 993: narrative comp. for SM by Burnet [1711].
7. BL Add. MS 61474, fo. 1; cf. Green, *Sarah*, 25, where SM's endorsement, 'Mrs Fortry', is misread as 'Mistress Loughry'.
8. BL Add. MS 47012 B, fo. 13: SM to Mrs Southwell, 5 Sept. 1736.
9. BL Add. MS 61474, fo. 114: note by SM; Add. MS 61421, fos. 75ᵛ–6: narrative by SM, 1704.
10. B. Bathurst (ed.), *Letters of Two Queens* (1924), 64: Mary to Frances Apsley, c.1675.
11. E. Boswell, *The Restoration Court Stage* (Cambridge, Mass., 1932), 170–226.
12. BL Add. MS 61421, fo. 111: narrative by SM, 1704.
13. *Diary of Mary, Countess Cowper*, ed. S. Cowper (1865), 196–7: SM to Lady Cowper, 3 Sept. 1716.
14. *The Diary of John Evelyn*, ed. E. de Beer (Oxford, 1959), 744.
15. Devon RO Seymour MSS L18, 23/34: SM to Somerset, 30 Oct. 1723.
16. PRO C6/170/61.
17. A. W. Thibaudeau (ed.), *The Bulstrode Papers*, (1897), 303, 313; J. H. Wilson, *Court Wits of the Restoration* (Princeton, 1948), 30.
18. Thibaudeau, *Bulstrode Papers*, 311; *The Works of John Sheffield . . . Duke of Buckingham* (1726), ii. 22; Bathurst, *Letters of Two Queens*, 37–8 (the title 'Mrs' was given to unmarried as well as married women at this period).
19. Rose, ii. 267–8: SM to Marchmont, 3 Mar. 1742[/3].
20. BL Add. MS 61458, fo. 98: character of SM by Mrs Burnet.
21. BL Add. MS 61474, fo. 4.
22. Green, *Sarah*, 37; National Library of Wales, *Calendar of Wynn (of Gwydir) Papers 1515–1690* (Aberystwyth, 1926), 415–22.
23. Hamilton, *Grammont*, 268.
24. BL Add. MS 61464, fo. 84: Hare to SM, 24 Sept. 1726; Add. MS 9199, fo. 125: character by Henry Etough; Hamilton, *Grammont*, 374.
25. Churchill, i. 48.
26. Ibid. i. 60; *Tangier at High Tide: The Journal of John Luke*, ed. H. Andrews (Geneva, 1958), 201; BL Add. MS 63057 B, fo. 1: Burnet's 'History', [late 1690s].
27. BL Add. MS 21948, fo. 381: Churchill to Duke of Richmond, 25 Oct. 1672.
28. Churchill, i. 998: SM's 'Instructions to the Historians' [1744]; 'Feversham's Account of the Battle of Entzheim—1674', *JSAHR* 1 (1921), 35–43; BL Add. MS 51337, fo. 209: Sir W. Churchill to G. Strangways, 29 Dec. 1674; *CSPD 1673–5*, 479.
29. Thibaudeau, *Bulstrode Papers*, 308, 311; *Notes and Queries*, 193 (1948), 293: Duchess of York to Lady Bellasis, 19 July 1675.
30. *CSPD 1675–6*, 25; H. Forneron, *Louise de Kéroualle, Duchesse de Portsmouth* (Paris, 1886), 131.

31. Wolseley, i. 175.
32. BL Add. MS 61427, fos. 27, 22; cf. Churchill, i. 125, 121.
33. G. M. Trevelyan, *England under Queen Anne*, Fontana edn. (1965), ii. 23; BL Add. MS 61458, fo. 98: character of SM by Mrs Burnet.
34. BL Add. MS 61427, fos. 60, 45; cf. Churchill, i. 110–11.
35. Forneron, *Louise de Kéroualle*, 121–2: Courtin to Louvois, 14/24 Sept. 1676 (transl.).
36. Ministère des Relations Extérieures, Paris, CPA 120C, fo. 206: Courtin to Louvois, 6/16 Nov. 1676; Forneron, *Louise de Kéroualle* 130–1; Churchill, i. 114: Courtin to Louvois, 19/29 Nov. 1676.
37. Forneron, *Louise de Kéroualle*, 131: Courtin to Louvois, 27 Nov./7 Dec. 1676.
38. V. de Sola Pinto, *Sir Charles Sedley* (1920), 132–7.
39. Forneron, *Louise de Kéroualle*, 131: Courtin to Louvois, 27 Nov./7 Dec. 1676.
40. HMC, *Rutland MSS*, ii. 32, 34: Lady Chaworth to Lord Roos, 23 Nov., 25 Dec. 1676; BL Add. MS 61475, fo. 47: anon. letter to SM, 7 Nov. 1712.
41. BL Add. MS 61427, fos. 21, 59; cf. Churchill, i. 122, 124.
42. BL Add. MS 61427, fos. 30, 12; cf. Churchill, i. 121, 123, 126.
43. W. D. Cooper (ed.), *Savile Correspondence*, Camden Society, 71 (1858) 49: Savile to Halifax, 8 May 1677; Churchill, i. 998: SM's 'Instructions' [1744].
44. *CSPD 1677–8*, 60, 200, 236; R. Clark, *Anthony Hamilton* (1921), 63–5.
45. BL Add. MS 18730, fo. 29: Lord Anglesey's diary, 27 Sept. 1677; Devon RO Seymour MSS L18, 30/4: SM to Somerset, 11 Sept. 1730.
46. HMC, *Bath MSS*, ii. 174: Churchill to Gibbon, 22 June 1686.
47. Herts RO Manorial Records 40933, 40938–40939.
48. BL Add. MS 61427, fos. 35, 36, 38; cf. Churchill, i. 127–8.
49. HMC, *Rutland MSS*, ii. 42: Lady Chaworth to Lord Roos, 22 Nov. 1677; BL Add. MS 18958, fo. 3: Duke of York's household establishment, 1677–8.
50. BL Add. MS 61422, fo. 35: narrative by SM, 1709.
51. Churchill, i. 998: SM's 'Instructions' [1744]; HMC, *Dartmouth MSS*, i. 56: Churchill to Legge, 5 Jan. 1681.
52. BL Add. MS 18958, fos. 3, 13: Duke of York's establishment, 1677–8.
53. Churchill, i. 60–2; BL Add. MS 47128, fo. 50: character of Marlborough by Lord Egmont.
54. BL Add. MS 61348, fos. 3–18ᵛ: receipts, May–Nov. 1677.
55. BL Add. MS 18958, fo. 13: Duke of York's establishment, 1677–8; Add. MS 61421, fo. 106ᵛ: narrative by SM, 1704.
56. Wolseley, i. 195.
57. J. H. Jesse, *Memoirs of the Court of England during the Reign of the Stuarts* (1840), iv. 311–12; BL Add. MS 61446, fo. 15: SM to Marlborough, 3 May 1732; HMC, *Rutland MSS*, ii. 49–50: Lady Chaworth to Lord Roos, 16 Apr. 1678.
58. *CSPD 1678*, 134.
59. Wolseley, i. 199.
60. BL Add. MS 18958, fo. 7: Duke of York's establishment, 1677–8. The earliest reference to Sarah by her married name is in Herts RO Manorial Records 40935: transfer of the Sandridge mortgage, 15 June 1678.
61. BL Add. MS 61427, fo. 71ᵛ. This letter, postmarked 5 July and important for dating the Churchills' marriage, is misdated Mar. 1678 in Wolseley, i. 202–3.
62. BL Add. MS 61427, fos. 73, 79, 81: Churchill to SM, 20 July and n.d. [1678]; Wolseley, i. 212.

63. Ibid. i. 213; Longleat, Coventry MSS 31: Bulstrode to Coventry, 17/27 Sept., 4/14 Oct. 1678.

Chapter 3: 1679–1684

1. BL Althorp Papers D14: SM to Mallet [Oct. 1744].
2. PRO SP 77/52, fos. 151, 154: Bulstrode's dispatches, 12/22, 19/29 May 1679.
3. CSPD 1679, 351; Longleat, Coventry MSS 31: Bulstrode to Coventry, 19/29 Aug. 1679.
4. Churchill, i. 992: narrative comp. for SM by Burnet [1711].
5. Bathurst, Letters of Two Queens, 109: Anne to Frances Bathurst, 22 Sept. 1679.
6. BL Add. MS 61421, fo. 107: narrative by SM, 1704.
7. Churchill, i. 140–2: Longford to Arran, 6 Sept. 1679; Wolseley, i. 221; Longleat, Coventry MSS 31: Bulstrode to Coventry, 19/29 Sept.–25 Sept./6 Oct. 1679.
8. Burnet, ii. 245.
9. Sir T. Lever, Godolphin (1952), 17–43; BL Add. MS 15889, fos. 33–8: Lady Sunderland to Evelyn, Mar.–June 1679.
10. BL Add. MS 61427, fo. 87: Churchill to SM [Nov. 1679]; cf. Churchill, i. 146.
11. BL Add. MS 61427, fos. 93, 95, 101: Churchill to SM, 3, 13, 24 Jan. 1679/80; cf. Wolseley, i. 235–6.
12. Quoted in J. P. Kenyon, Robert Spencer, Earl of Sunderland (1958), 58.
13. Wolseley, i. 231; The Correspondence of Henry Hyde, Earl of Clarendon, ed. S. W. Singer (1828), i. 51: York to Clarendon, 14 Dec. [1680].
14. J. S. Clarke, The Life of James the Second, (1816), i. 659–87.
15. CSPD 1680–1, 322; Westminster Public Libraries, Burial Register of St Martin-in-the-Fields, 2 July 1681.
16. PRO 31/3/149, fos. 80, 99: Barrillon's dispatches, 21/31 July, 8/18 Aug. 1681; Westminster Public Libraries, Baptismal Register of St Martin-in-the-Fields, 29 July 1681.
17. HMC, Dartmouth MSS, i. 67–8: Churchill to Legge, 12 Sept. 1681.
18. Christ Church, Evelyn MSS: diary of Sir John Evelyn, 6 July 1723.
19. Viscount Dillon (ed.), 'Some Familiar Letters . . .', Archaeologia, 58 (1902), 161: York to Lady Lichfield, 26 Nov. [1681].
20. BL Add. MS 61464, fo. 17: SM to Hare [1710].
21. Thibaudeau, 1st ser. iv. 154: SM to Mary Godolphin, 3 Nov. 1718.
22. Sir J. Lauder, Historical Notices of Scotish Affairs, Bannatyne Club, 87 (1848), 331–3.
23. Churchill, i. 154.
24. P. M. Cowburn, 'Christopher Gunman and the Wreck of the Gloucester', Mariner's Mirror, 42 (1956), 114–26; Churchill, i. 158.
25. BL Add. MS 61427, fo. 114: Churchill to SM [1682].
26. BL Add. MS 61346, fo. 51: receipts for repairs, 25 Nov. 1682.
27. PRO 31/3/153, fo. 72: Barrillon's dispatch, 9/19 Nov. 1682.
28. BL Add. MS 18958, fo. 7: Duke of York's establishment, 1677–8; H. J. Coleridge, St Mary's Convent, Micklegate Bar, York (1887), 133–4; H. Foley, Records of the English Province of the Society of Jesus (1877–83), v. 750.
29. BL Add. MS 61426, fos. 172–4: narrative comp. for SM by Bishop Hoadly, 1715.
30. Burnet, ii. 91, Dartmouth's note.
31. Newberry Library, Case MS E5 M3827: C. Dumare to Esther Masham, 2 Dec. 1703, 12 Nov. 1704; BL Add. MS 61426, fo. 173: narrative comp. for SM by

Hoadly, 1715; Add. MS 61474, fos. 77, 98, 161–4: Mary Cornwallis to SM [1703?]–1708.

32. *The Tangier Papers of Samuel Pepys*, ed. E. Chappell, Navy Records Society, 73 (1935), 311.

33. BL Add. MS 61442, fo. 87: Lady Sunderland to SM, 10 Sept. [1684?].

34. BL Add. MS 61427, fo. 115: Churchill to SM [Mar. 1683].

35. BL Add. MS 61421, fo. 111: narrative by SM, 1704.

36. Wolseley, i. 199.

37. BL Add. MS 61423, fo. 1: SM to Hamilton, 16 June 1710.

38. BL Add. MS 61421, fo. 111: narrative by SM, 1704; Huntington Library, RB 284482: narrative by SM interleaved in Sir A. Alison, *Life of John, Duke of Marlborough* (1852), i, aft. 24.

39. BL Add. MS 61423, fo. 160: narrative comp. for SM by Burnet [1711].

40. BL Add. MS 61414, fo. 3: Anne to SM [1683].

41. *PC* ii. 65: SM to [Burnet?], 23 Apr. 1711.

42. *Memoirs*, 10.

43. Green, *Sarah*, 64; BL Add. MS 61414, fo. 15: Anne to SM [1683–4].

44. Brown, 12: Anne to SM, 20 Sept. 1684.

45. *PC* ii. 65–6: SM to [Burnet?], 23 Apr. 1711; BL Add. MS 61426, fo. 6: narrative comp. for SM by Hoadly, 1715; *Memoirs*, 255.

46. HMC, *7th Report*, 363: T. Deane to Lord Preston, 29 Feb. 1683.

47. BL Add. MS 61427, fo. 117: Churchill to SM [July 1684]; cf. Wolseley, i. 256.

48. BL Add. MS 61346, fos. 107–8: receipts, 15 Jan. 1684/5.

49. Child's Bank, Ledger for 1681–7, fo. 98; *CTB 1681–5*, 1480.

50. BL Stowe MS 751, fo. 126: SM to Craggs, 6 Aug. [1716]; Churchill, i. 995: narrative comp. for SM by Burnet [1711].

51. Chauncy, *Antiquities of Hertfordshire*, 470; Herts RO Manorial Records 40938–40939.

52. Herts RO Manorial Records 40952–40956; Northants RO Althorp Papers, EP Herts, Box 195: valuations of Sandridge and Holywell, 1684; BL Add. MS 61363, fo. 5: Lady Hamilton's agreement, 2 June 1684.

53. F. Harris, 'Holywell House, St Albans', *Architectural History*, 28 (1985), 32–6.

54. *LG* 30: SM to Duchess of Bedford, 24 June 1732.

55. Dillon, 'Some Familiar Letters . . .', 187: York to Lady Lichfield, 28 Oct. [1684].

Chapter 4: 1685–1688

1. BL Althorp Papers D14: SM to Mallet [Oct. 1744].

2. BL Add. MS 61423, fo. 160^v: narrative comp. for SM by Burnet [1711]; Add. MS 61463, fo. 122: SM to Mrs Clayton, 20/31 Mar. 1714; Rose, ii. 31: SM to Marchmont, 15 June 1734.

3. J. Miller, *James II* (1989), 120–1.

4. BL Add. MS 61421, fo. 110^v: narrative by SM, 1704.

5. Burnet, iii. 282.

6. Wolseley, i. 304: Churchill to SM, 30 June 1685.

7. BL Stowe MS 751, fo. 129: SM to Craggs, 1 Sept. 1716.

8. BL Add. MS 61442, fos. 95–7: Lady Sunderland to SM [July 1685]; Add. MS 61414, fo. 21: Anne to SM [7 July 1685].

9. Wolseley, i. 341: Churchill to SM, 9 July 1685.

10. BL Add. MS 61414, fos. 36, 41: Anne to SM [July 1685].

11. Ibid. fo. 44: [July 1685].
12. BL Add. MS 61425, fo. 61: narrative comp. for SM by Priest, 1713.
13. PRO 31/3/160, fo. 163; 170, fo. 26; 174: dispatches of Barrillon and Bonrepos, 19/29 Oct. 1685, 25 May/4 June, 5/15 Dec. 1687.
14. BL Add. MS 61442, fo. 102: Lady Sunderland to SM, 21 Sept [1685].
15. PRO 31/3/160, fo. 163: Barrillon's dispatch, 19/29 Oct. 1685.
16. BL Add. MS 61442, fos. 111–12: Lady Sunderland to SM [1686].
17. Brown, 18: Anne to Mary, 10 Aug. [1687].
18. BL Add. MS 61414, fos. 80, 98: Anne to SM [summer 1686].
19. BL Add. MS 61442, fos. 111–12: Lady Sunderland to SM [1686].
20. BL Add. MS 61414, fo. 102: Anne to SM [July–Aug. 1686].
21. *PC* ii. 114–15: SM to Burnet [1711].
22. BL Add. MS 61414, fo. 68: Anne to SM [summer 1686].
23. Ibid. fo. 72: Anne to SM, 1 Apr. [1686].
24. *LG* 172: SM to Duchess of Bedford, 25 Aug. 1735.
25. Brown, 19: Anne to Mary, 26 Nov. 1686.
26. *Memoirs*, 11–12.
27. BL Add. MS 61414, fos. 74–7: Mary to SM, 28 May, 14 June [1686].
28. BL Add. MS 61421, fo. 111: narrative by SM, 1704.
29. BL Add. MS 61414, fo. 104: Anne to SM [Aug. 1686].
30. Brown, 20: Anne to Mary, 29 Dec. 1686.
31. Constantijn van Huygens, *Journaal . . . 1673–1678*, Werken van het Historisch Genootschap gevestigd te Utrecht, new ser. 32 (1881), 247; S. Baxter, *William III* (1966), 150; *Supplement to Burnet's History of my own Time*, ed. H. C. Foxcroft (Oxford, 1902), 291.
32. Wolseley, i. 196; W. H. Black (ed.), *Catalogue of the Ashmole Manuscripts* (Oxford, 1845), no. 436.14.
33. Brown, 20–1: Anne to Mary, 29 Dec. 1686.
34. E. Gregg, *Queen Anne* (1980), 46–7; Brown, 26: Anne to Mary, 13 Mar. 1687; Sir J. Dalrymple, *Memoirs of Great Britain and Ireland* (Edinburgh, 1771–88), ii. pt 2, 190–1: Churchill to Prince of Orange, 17 May 1687.
35. PRO 31/3/170, fo. 26; 174: Bonrepos's dispatches, 25 May/4 June and [Dec.] 1687.
36. Brown, 17: Anne to Mary, 10 Aug. [1687].
37. Clarendon, *Correspondence*, ii. 153; Brown, 34–5: Anne to Mary, 14, 20 Mar. 1688.
38. PRO 31/3/174: Barrillon's dispatch, 5/15 Dec. 1687.
39. BL Add. MS 61421, fo. 107: narrative by SM, 1704.
40. Herts RO Manorial Records 40960–40961.
41. PRO 31/3/175: Barrillon's dispatch, 16/26 Jan. 1688.
42. Wolseley, i. 196.
43. Baxter, *William III*, 231–2.
44. *Memoirs of Thomas, Earl of Ailesbury*, [ed. W. E. Buckley], Roxburghe Club (1890), i. 174; Clarke, *Life of James the Second*, ii. 197; Gregg, *Queen Anne*, 56–8.
45. BL Add. MS 61421, fo. 71: narrative by SM; Herts RO Panshanger MSS F228, p. 108: SM to Lady Cowper, 8 Nov. [1710].
46. Burnet, *Supplement*, 291.
47. BL Add. MS 61421, fo. 71; *Memoirs*, 15.
48. BL Add. MS 61421, fo. 145^v; Butler, *Rule of Three*, 94; Herts RO Manorial Records 40963–40964.

49. Brown, 44: Anne to Prince of Orange, 18 Nov. 1688.

50. D. H. Hosford, 'Bishop Compton and the Revolution of 1688', *Journal of Ecclesiastical History*, 23 (1972), 209–18.

51. BL Add. MS 61421, fos. 5–6: narrative by SM, 1704.

52. Burnet, *Supplement*, 530; Dr Williams's Library, Roger Morrice's 'Entring Books', ii. 327.

53. Clarke, *Life of James the Second*, ii. 222–4; *The Autobiography of Sir John Bramston*, Camden Society, 32 (1845), 336.

54. HMC, *7th Report*, 418: Middleton to Preston, 25 Nov. 1688, 7 p.m.

55. Ibid. 25 Nov. 1688, 7 a.m.; Dr Williams's Library, Roger Morrice's 'Entring Books', ii. 327.

56. BL Add. MS 61421, fo. 6: narrative by SM, 1704.

57. Luttrell, i. 479; M. Haile, *Queen Mary of Modena* (1905), 213.

58. BL Add. MS 61421, fos. 5–6.

59. Clarendon, *Correspondence*, ii. 214, 216.

60. HMC, *Dartmouth MSS*, i. 214–15: Pepys to Dartmouth, 26 Nov. 1688; Luttrell, i. 479; *The Works of John Sheffield . . . Duke of Buckingham*, 3rd edn. (1740), ii. 70.

61. BL Add. MS 61421, fo. 6.

62. Burnet, iii. 335; *HMC, Dartmouth MSS*, i. 214–15: Pepys to Dartmouth, 26 Nov. 1688; HMC, *7th Report*, 418: Middleton to Preston, 25 Nov. 1688, 7 p.m.; BL Add. MS 34487, fo. 40: newsletter, 28 Nov. 1688.

63. *Memoirs*, 14.

64. BL Add. MS 36707, fo. 49: newsletter, 27 Nov. [1688].

65. N. Japikse (ed.), *Correspondentie van Willem III en van Hans Willem Bentinck*, i. pt 2 (The Hague, 1928), 630.

66. BL Add. MS 61421, fo. 5; *Memoirs*, 14.

67. D. H. Hosford, *Nottingham, Nobles and the North* (Hamden, Conn., 1976), 103.

68. *Memoirs*, 13; BL Sloane MS 3929, fo. 113: newsletter, 1 Dec. 1688; E. M. Thompson (ed.), *Correspondence of the Family of Hatton*, Camden Society, new ser. 23 (1878), ii. 118–19: J. Horton to Lord Hatton, 2 Dec. 1688; Ailesbury, *Memoirs*, i. 191.

69. Clarke, *Life of James II*, ii. 226; Burnet, iii. 335, Dartmouth's note.

70. Dr Williams's Library, Roger Morrice's 'Entring Books', ii. 369; *Memoirs*, 13.

71. *An Apology for the Life of Mr Colley Cibber*, 2nd edn. (1740), 58–9.

72. HMC, *9th Report*, pt 2, 460: Prince of Orange to Compton, 5 Dec. 1688; *Letters of Philip, Earl of Chesterfield* (1829), 335: to Halifax, 16 Dec. 1688.

73. G. A. Ellis (ed.), *The Ellis Correspondence* (1829), ii. 368–9: newsletter, 19 Dec. 1688; BL Add. MS 34487, fo. 48: newsletter, 18 Dec. 1688.

74. Chesterfield, *Letters*, 335.

75. BL Add. MS 61479, fo. 54: notes by SM [1720s].

Chapter 5: 1689–1692

1. H. C. Foxcroft, *The Life and Letters of Sir George Savile, 1st Marquis of Halifax* (1898), ii. 202.

2. Dr Williams's Library, Roger Morrice's 'Entring Books', ii. 450–1.

3. BL Add. MS 61421, fo. 145^v: narrative by SM; Churchill, i. 999: SM's 'Instructions' [1744]; *Memoirs*, 15.

4. *Memoirs*, 16.

5. Ibid. 16–17. (italics added)
6. L. G. Schwoerer, *The Declaration of Rights 1689* (Baltimore, 1981), 220.
7. James Macpherson, *Original Papers . . . from the Restoration to the Accession of the House of Hanover* (1775), i. 284–5.
8. *Memoirs*, 19; Burnet, iii. 406–7.
9. *Memoirs*, 18.
10. *Commons Journals*, x. 225, 258.
11. Wolseley, i. 196.
12. *Memoirs*, 22.
13. *Memoirs*, 14, 26; Buckingham, *Works*, 3rd edn., ii. 87.
14. BL Add. MS 61421, fo. 11: narrative by SM, 1704.
15. *Commons Journals*, x. 310.
16. *Memoirs of Mary, Queen of England 1689–1693*, ed. R. Doebner (Leipzig, 1886), 17–18.
17. *Memoirs*, 24.
18. *Commons Journals*, x. 312; Mary II, *Memoirs*, 17; *Memoirs*, 24–5.
19. Mary II, *Memoirs*, 24–7.
20. BL Add. MS 61414, fos. 147–9: Anne to SM [1691], with SM's notes.
21. Mary II, *Memoirs*, 30; Dalrymple, *Memoirs*, ii. pt 3, 125: Mary to William, 22 Aug. 1690.
22. BL Add. MS 51511, fo. 15: Halifax's notebook; Add. MS 61421, fo. 16^v: narrative by SM, 1704.
23. HMC, *Finch MSS*, ii. 360; A. Browning, *Thomas Osborne, Earl of Danby* (Glasgow, 1944–51), ii. 180–2: Nottingham and Danby to William, 15 July 1690.
24. Dalrymple, *Memoirs*, ii. pt 3, 128: Mary to William, 26 Aug. 1690.
25. Butler, *Rule of Three*, 94: SM's will, 18 Aug. 1690.
26. *Memoirs*, 15.
27. BL Althorp Papers D13: inventories of SM's books [1690s].
28. BL Add. MS 61456, fo. 4: Lady Scarborough to SM [Oct. 1690].
29. BL Add. MS 61414, fo. 145: Anne to SM [1691?].
30. Wolseley, ii. 160: Marlborough to SM, 27 Aug. 1690.
31. Clarke, *Life of James the Second*, ii. 446.
32. BL Add. MS 61422, fos. 128–9: narrative by SM.
33. Ailesbury, *Memoirs*, ii. 280.
34. Clarke, *Life of James the Second*, ii. 449.
35. BL Add. MS 61422, fo. 194: narrative by SM.
36. PRO PROB 11/311/65 and 11/370/110: wills of Lady (Alice) Jenyns and Ralph Jenyns; Steinman, *Althorp Memoirs*, 58–9.
37. *Memoirs*, 125.
38. BL Add. MS 61422, fo. 194: narrative by SM.
39. C. H. Ashdown, 'The Accounts of St Albans Grammar School', *Home Counties Magazine*, 7 (1905), 269.
40. BL Add. MS 61422, fo. 195: narrative by SM; *Memoirs*, 126.
41. *Memoirs*, 28–9; Mary II, *Memoirs*, 38.
42. BL Add. MS 61118, fo. 21: note by SM.
43. BL Add. MS 51511, fo. 15^v: Halifax's notebook; Add. MS 61456, fo. 4: Lady Scarborough to SM [Oct. 1690]; Kent Archives Office, Stanhope MSS O59/1: Yard to Stanhope [c. 10 Sept. 1690], 9 June 1691; Lever, *Godolphin*, 82–3, 297.
44. BL Add. MS 61414, fo. 115: note by SM.
45. *MGC* 151: Godolphin to SM, 18 Feb. 1703.

46. HMC, *8th Report*, pt 1, 562: newsletter to Dijkvelt, 14/24 July 1691; BL Add. MS 61418, fo. 22: notes by SM.

47. Green, *Sarah*, 40: SM to Mrs Jenyns [Sept. 1691].

48. BL Add. MS 61474, fo. 14: Lady Fitzhardinge to SM [20 Jan. 1692].

49. BL Add. MS 61456, fo. 10: Lady Scarborough to SM [Aug. 1691].

50. BL Add. MS 61414, fo. 115: notes by SM.

51. *Memoirs*, 26.

52. Ibid. 27.

53. Child's Bank, Ledger for 1688–1732, fos. 66–7.

54. Ailesbury, *Memoirs*, ii. 245 (in fact a son and four daughters).

55. L. von Ranke, *A History of England* (Oxford, 1875), vi. 178: Bonnet's dispatch, 26 Jan./5 Feb. 1692.

56. Gregg, *Queen Anne*, 81–2.

57. *Memoirs*, 11.

58. BL Add. MS 61414, fos. 133, 169: Anne to SM [?22 June 1691, 27 Apr. 1692].

59. Churchill, i. 344–5; Kent Archives Office, Stanhope MSS O59/1: Yard to Stanhope, 2 Feb. 1692; Ranke, *History of England*, vi. 177–8; Burnet, iv. 161–2; BL Add. MS 29578, fo. 290: Lyttelton to Hatton, 2 Feb. 1692.

60. [Daniel Defoe], *A Short Narrative of the Life of . . . John, Duke of Marlborough* (1711), 8–9; BL Add. MS 61453, fos. 46, 48.

61. BL Add. MS 61474, fos. 14, 114: notes by SM; Add. MS 61414, fo. 169: Anne to SM [27 Apr. 1692].

62. BL Add. MS 61421, fo. 141^v; Add MS 61423, fo. 161: narratives by SM; *Memoirs*, 30.

63. *Memoirs*, 30–1; Huntington Library, RB 284482: narrative by SM interleaved in Alison's *Life of Marlborough*, i, aft. 24.

64. Kent Archives Office, Stanhope MSS O59/1: Yard to Stanhope, 16 Feb. 1692; *Memoirs*, 31–4, 39–40.

65. BL Add. MS 61414, fo. 155: Anne to SM [5 Feb. 1692].

66. *Memoirs*, 30; BL Add. MS 61421, fo. 27^v: narrative by SM, 1704.

67. *Memoirs*, 51, 53; BL Add. MS 61414, fo. 167: Anne to SM [Feb. 1692].

68. *Memoirs*, 59: Anne to SM [early 1692].

69. Luttrell, ii. 360, 385; Baron de Grovestins, *Histoire des luttes . . . entre les puissances maritimes et la France* (Paris, 1851–4), vi. 314: L'Hermitage's dispatch, 23 Feb./4 Mar. 1692; BL Add. MS 61414, fos. 163, 176: Anne to SM [23, 26 Feb. 1692]; Constantijn van Huygens, *Journaal . . . 1688–1696*, Werken van het Historisch Genootschap gevestigd te Utrecht, new ser. 25 (1877), 57.

70. *Memoirs*, 60–1.

71. BL Add. MS 61414, fo. 179: Anne to SM [Apr.–May 1692].

72. Grovestins, *Histoire des luttes*, vi. 314; BL Add. MS 61421, fo. 41^v: narrative by SM, 1704.

73. *Memoirs*, 58–9: Anne to SM [early 1692].

74. BL Add. MS 61421, fo. 27: narrative by SM, 1704.

75. *Memoirs*, 49–51.

76. HMC, *Finch MSS*, iv. 100: Nottingham to Blathwayt, 26 Apr. 1692.

77. Brown, 55: Anne to SM [5 May 1692].

78. T. Howell (comp.), *State Trials*, xii. 1053–4, 1072–5, 1165; HMC, *Finch MSS*, iv. 230–1: Nottingham to Portland, 14 June 1692.

79. Howell, *State Trials*, xii. 1174; HMC, *Finch MSS*, iv. 127: Nottingham to E. Russell, 7 May 1692; *CSPD 1691–2*, 270.

80. Thompson, *Hatton Correspondence*, ii. 176: Lyttelton to Hatton, 10 May 1692.

81. *CSPD 1691–2*, 278; Grovestins, *Histoire des luttes*, vi. 328.

82. *Memoirs*, 45: Anne to SM [11 May 1692].

83. BL Add. MS 61421, fos. 26–7; narrative by SM, 1704; Grovestins, *Histoire des luttes*, vi. 328.

84. *CSPD 1691–2*, 296; *Memoirs*, 62.

85. Thomas Sprat, Bishop of Rochester, *A Relation of the Late Wicked Contrivance of . . . Robert Young* (1692–3), pt 2, 45; Foxcroft, *Halifax*, ii. 152; Luttrell, ii. 470.

86. *Memoirs*, 47–8: Anne to SM [8 June 1692].

87. HMC, *Finch MSS*, iv. 217: Nottingham to Portland, 10 June 1692.

88. *Memoirs*, 45–6; BL Add. MSS 61414, fo. 215; 61415, fo. 5: Anne to SM [10, 14 June 1692]; Luttrell, ii. 525, 536.

89. HMC, *Finch MSS*, iv. 452: Kingston to Nottingham, 11 or 12 Sept. 1692; *Memoirs*, 68–70; Grovestins, *Histoire des luttes*, vi. 359–60: L'Hermitage's dispatch, 16/26 Sept. 1692.

90. Luttrell, ii. 594; BL Add. MS 34096, fo. 194: newsletter, 25 Oct. 1692; Add. MS 61455, fo. 4: Lady Bathurst to SM, 20 Oct. [1692].

91. BL Add. MS 61415, fo. 34: Anne to SM [Jan. 1693].

92. BL Add. MS 61423, fo. 166: narrative comp. for SM by Burnet [1711].

93. BL Add. MS 61454, fo. 111: Griffith to SM [May 1693].

Chapter 6: 1693–1701

1. Bedford Office: SM to Bedford, 5 May 1725.

2. BL Add. MS 61453, fo. 124: Lady Tyrconnel to SM, 5 Apr. [1699].

3. BL Add. MS 61454, fo. 111: Griffith to SM [May 1693].

4. BL Add. MS 61442, fo. 116: Lady Sunderland to SM, 1 May 1693.

5. BL Add. MS 61451, fo. 158: narrative by SM.

6. *Memoirs*, 78.

7. Devon RO Seymour MSS L18, 23/28: SM to Somerset, 3 Oct. 1723; Churchill, i. 995: narrative comp. for SM by Burnet [1711].

8. Harris, 'Holywell House', 34–5.

9. Yale UL Osborn Collection: SM to Stair, 3 Mar. 1736[/7]; BL Add. MS 61455, fo. 178: Lady Sandwich to SM [c.1694]; Add. MS 61442, fo. 148: Lady Sunderland to SM, 15 Aug. [1699?].

10. Yale UL Osborn Collection: SM to Charles Middleton, 6 May [*temp*. Anne]; Devon RO Seymour MSS L18, 24/14: SM to Somerset [4 June 1724]; *MGC* 83, 176: Marlborough to SM, 6/17 July 1702, 23 Apr./4 May 1703.

11. BL Althorp Papers D49: SM to Spencer, 8 Sept. 1738; Lever, *Godolphin*, 107; BL Add. MS 61455, fo. 166: Lady Howard to SM, mid–1690s.

12. BL Add. MS 61415, fos. 51–79, 81: Anne to SM [summer 1693].

13. Ibid. fo. 74: [?Aug. 1693].

14. BL Add. MS 61455, fo. 18: Lady Bathurst to SM, 24 Aug. [1693].

15. BL Add. MS 61454, fo. 115: Griffith to SM, 9 Nov. 1693; Add. MS 61455, fo. 124: Jane Middleton to SM [1693].

16. Clarke, *Life of James the Second*, ii. 519, 522–3; *Private and Original Correspondence of Charles Talbot, Duke of Shrewsbury*, ed. W. Coxe (1821), 54: to William, 17 July 1693.

17. E. M. Lloyd, 'Marlborough and the Brest Expedition', *EHR* 9 (1894), 130–2; J. Childs, *The British Army of William III* (Manchester, 1987), 222–36.

18. Shrewsbury, *Correspondence*, 46–7, 53: to William and reply, 22 June, 5/15 July 1694.

19. BL Add. MS 61474, fos. 61–4, 183: Anne Merryweather to SM, 3 July 1703; Susanna Counter to Judith Forster (SM's maid), 8 July 1709; Bank of England Archives: SM to the cashiers, 21 Mar. 1726, 3 Aug. 1743.

20. BL Add. MS 61421, fo. 44: narrative by SM, 1704.

21. BL Add. MS 61455, fo. 185: Elizabeth Higgons to SM [autumn 1694].

22. Ailesbury, *Memoirs*, ii. 280; Macpherson, *Original Papers*, i. 285; HMC, *Finch MSS*, iv. 452: Kingston to Nottingham, 11 or 12 Sept. 1692.

23. *Memoirs*, 15.

24. J. G. Simms, *The Williamite Confiscations in Ireland* (1956), 31, 131.

25. BL Add. MS 61453, fos. 64–6: Lady Tyrconnel to SM, 22 Apr./2 May [1694].

26. Ibid. fos. 70–3: SM to Lady Tyrconnel [May 1694].

27. Steinman, *Althorp Memoirs*, 51.

28. Bedford Office: SM to Bedford, 5 May 1725.

29. BL Althorp Papers D38: schedule of SM's papers, fo. 189.

30. Longleat, Portland MSS, Misc. Box 2: extracts from a narrative by SM.

31. *Memoirs*, 74–5.

32. BL Add. MS 61421, fo. 62: narrative by SM, 1704.

33. *Memoirs*, 77; BL Add. MS 61415, fo. 109: note by SM.

34. BL Add. MS 17677 PP, fo. 113: L'Hermitage's dispatch, 4/14 Jan. 1695.

35. Ibid. fo. 119: 11/21 Jan. 1695.

36. BL Add. MS 61433, fos. 25–9: Godolphin to SM [11, 12, 15 Jan. 1695].

37. BL Add. MS 17677 PP, fo. 209: L'Hermitage's dispatch, 29 Mar./8 Apr. 1695.

38. BL Add. MS 61455, fos. 30, 60–8: Lady Bathurst to SM 15 June [1695] and n.d.

39. Jenkin Lewis, *Queen Anne's Son*, ed. W. J. Loftie (1881), 81.

40. *Memoirs*, 79–80.

41. BL Add. MS 61421, fo. 67: narrative by SM, 1704.

42. HMC, *Bathurst MSS*, 6: SM to Lady Bathurst [1690s].

43. Ibid. 7; Gregg, *Queen Anne*, 109–10.

44. BL Add. MS 17677 SS, fo. 360: L'Hermitage's dispatch, 6/16 Sept. 1698; Add. MS 30000 D, fo. 241: Bonnet's dispatch, 30 July/10 Aug. 1700.

45. BL Add. MS 61442, fo. 147: Lady Sunderland to SM, 1 Aug. [1698?].

46. BL Add. MS 61422, fo. 111^v: narrative by SM.

47. Thibaudeau, 1st ser. iv. 153: SM to Mary Godolphin, 3 Nov. 1718.

48. BL Add. MS 61118, fo. 21^v: note by SM.

49. James Vernon, *Letters Illustrative of the Reign of William III*, ed. G. P. R. James (1841), i. 293–4: to Shrewsbury, 26 June 1697; Christ Church, Evelyn MSS: Godolphin to Mrs Boscawen, 25 July, 14 Sept. 1697.

50. BL Add. MS 61418, fo. 22: SM to Anne, 29 Oct. 1709.

51. *Memoirs*, 202; BL Add. MS 61415, fo. 131: note by SM.

52. Vernon, *Letters*, i. 444: to Shrewsbury, 21 Dec. 1697.

53. BL Add. MS 61415, fo. 146: Anne to SM, 28 Apr. [1698].

54. BL Add. Ch. 13594: marriage settlement, 1698; BL Add. MS 61451, fo. 73^v: narrative by SM, 1722; Lever, *Godolphin*, 111.

55. BL Add. MS 61453, fo. 74: Lady Tyrconnel to SM, 27 Dec. [1697].

56. Bodleian Library, Lister MS 4, fo. 3: SM to Lister [Dec. 1697–Jan. 1698].

57. BL Add. MS 61453, fo. 176: Lady Tyrconnel to SM, 23 Dec. [1704]; Yale UL Osborn Collection: SM to Coningsby, 13, 16 Nov. [*temp*. Anne].

58. Kenyon, *Sunderland*, 102–3.

59. BL Add. MS 61474, fo. 24: SM to Lady Westmorland, 28 Oct. [1698].

60. Christ Church, Evelyn MSS: Godolphin to Mrs Boscawen, 7 [Nov. 1697].
61. Kenyon, *Sunderland*, 301–3; BL Add. MS 61442, fo. 125: Lady Sunderland to SM, 3 March [1698].
62. *Memoirs*, 82–3.
63. BL Add. MS 61421, fo. 67: narrative by SM, 1704; *CSPD 1697*, 343–4; *Memoirs*, 127.
64. *Memoirs*, 126; BL Add. MS 61415, fo. 32: Anne to SM [early 1690s].
65. BL Add. MS 61453, fo. 148: Lady Tyrconnel to SM, 8 Nov. [1699].
66. BL Add. MS 61442, fo. 160: Lady Sunderland to SM, 20 Oct. [1698?].
67. Longleat, Portland MSS, Misc. Box 2: extracts from a narrative by SM; Hervey, 290: SM to Henry Fox, 23 Nov. 1732; BL Add. MS 61442, fo. 145: Lady Sunderland to SM, 12 June [1699].
68. BL Add. MS 15948, fo. 31: Godolphin to Mrs Boscawen, 7 Feb. 1699; Add. MS 61442, fo. 139: Lady Sunderland to SM, 25 Feb. [1699].
69. Ibid. fo. 140: 16 Apr. [1699].
70. *Memoirs*, 202; BL Add. MS 61451, fo. 158: narrative by SM.
71. Butler, *Rule of Three*, 320: SM to Spencer, 31 May 1732.
72. Bodleian Library, Lister MS 4, fo. 8: SM to Lister, 16 Oct. [1699].
73. Shrewsbury, *Correspondence*, 592: Sunderland to Shrewsbury, 26 Sept. 1699; BL Add. MS 30000 C, fo. 178: Bonnet's dispatch, 5/15 Sept. 1699.
74. BL Add. MS 17677 UU, fo. 292: L'Hermitage's dispatch, 13/24 Aug. 1700.
75. BL Add. MS 61442, fo. 167: Lady Sunderland to SM, 25 Sept. [1700].
76. Kenyon, *Sunderland*, 318–19.
77. BL Add. MS 61433, fo. 49: Godolphin to SM, 13 [Aug. 1700].
78. BL Add. MS 61422, fos. 195–7: narrative by SM.
79. Ibid. fo. 194^v. For the kinship between Harley and the Hills, see Steinman, *Althorp Memoirs*, 58–9.
80. HMC, *Portland MSS*, iii. 626, 633: Guy to Harley, 5 Sept., 15 Oct. 1700.
81. BL Althorp Papers L19: catalogue of paintings, ii, no. 228; Montagu, i. 78.
82. H. Horwitz, *Parliament, Policy, and Politics in the Reign of William III* (Manchester, 1977), 277–94.
83. Longleat, Portland MSS, Misc. Box 2: extracts from a narrative by SM.
84. BL Add. MS 30000 E, fo. 339: Bonnet's dispatch, 5/16 Sept. 1701.
85. BL Add. MS 7078, fo. 37: newsletter, 5 Sept. 1701.
86. *MGC* 39: Marlborough to Godolphin, 17/28 Oct. 1701; BL Stowe MS 243, fos. 123–5: Stanhope's dispatches, 9/20–17/28 Sept. 1701.
87. BL Add. MS 61421, fo. 68: narrative by SM, 1704.
88. *MGC* 37: Marlborough to Godolphin, 3/14 Oct. 1701.
89. Ibid. 48.

Chapter 7: 1702–1703

1. Bedford Office: SM to Duchess of Bedford (64), 1 Nov. 1733.
2. *MGC* 66–7: Anne to SM, 19 May 1702.
3. Hove Public Library, Wolseley MSS M1/112/1: SM's account with Coggs, 1708–9.
4. Simms, *Williamite Confiscations*, 132; Kent Archives Office C7/26: SM to Stanhope, 24 July 1702.
5. *Memoirs*, 93.
6. BL Add. MS 61420, fo. 75: privy purse accounts, 30 June, 31 Oct. 1702

(payments to Sunderland's chaplain, Charles Trimnell); Add. MS 61451, fo. 158: narrative by SM.

7. BL Add. MS 61441, fo. 88: SM to Elizabeth Godolphin, 2 May 1702; *PC* ii. 114: SM to Burnet [1711].

8. BL Add. MS 33388, fo. 158: SM to Lady Oglethorpe, 22 Apr. [1703].

9. BL Add. MS 61421, fo. 52: narrative by SM, 1704.

10. BL Add. MS 61441, fo. 88: SM to Elizabeth Godolphin, 2 May 1702.

11. *ML* 72: SM to Jennens, 4/15 July 1713.

12. BL Add. MS 61416, fo. 73: Anne to SM [?31 May 1702].

13. *De Briefwisseling van Anthonie Heinsius 1702–1720*, ed. A. J. Veenendal (The Hague, 1976–), i. 17: L'Hermitage's dispatch, 10/21 Mar. 1702.

14. *Memoirs*, 86.

15. BL Add. MS 61421, fo. 69: narrative by SM, 1704.

16. BL Add. MS 61423, fo. 166: narrative comp. for SM by Burnet [1711].

17. BL Add. MS 61418, fo. 29: SM to Anne, 29 Oct. 1709.

18. *PC* ii. 110–11: SM to Burnet [1711]; BL Add. MS 61423, fo. 66: SM to Hamilton, 22 Dec. 1710.

19. BL Add. MS 61416, fo. 95: Anne to SM [?16 June 1703].

20. The claim in Horace Walpole's *Reminiscences*, ed. P. Toynbee (Oxford, 1924), 134, that Sarah knew she had lost Anne's affection even before she became Queen, though an exaggeration, probably contains a grain of truth.

21. *PC* ii. 455: Hare to SM, 26 Aug. 1726; Churchill, i. 992: narrative comp. for SM by Burnet [1711].

22. *Memoirs*, 255; *PC* i. 85: SM to Anne [1707?].

23. BL Add. MS 61434, fo. 94: SM to [Godolphin, 27 Oct. 1709], quoting a letter from Anne (italics added); Brown, 286: Anne to Marlborough, 25 Oct. 1709.

24. *PC* ii. 111: SM to Burnet [1711].

25. Churchill, i. opp. 130.

26. Lord Fitzmaurice, *The Life of William, Earl of Shelburne*, 2nd edn. (1912), i. 20; BL Stowe MS 751, fo. 102: SM to Craggs, 12/23 June 1714.

27. *MGC* 129, 1139: Godolphin to SM, 16 Oct. 1702, 25 Oct. 1708.

28. Longleat, Portland MSS, iii, fo. 207: SM to Harley [1704–1707]; Herts RO Panshanger MSS F63, fo. 72: SM to Lady Cowper [Jan. 1715].

29. *Memoirs*, 88.

30. *MGC* 61: SM to Godolphin, 19 May 1702.

31. Ibid. 67: Marlborough to SM, 20/31 May 1702.

32. Ibid. 69: 29 May/9 June 1702.

33. Ibid. 86: 12/23 July 1702.

34. Ibid. 78, 93: Marlborough to Godolphin and SM, 25 June/6 July, 23 July/3 Aug. 1702.

35. Devon RO Seymour MSS L18, 23/38: SM to Somerset, 23 Dec. 1723.

36. BL Egerton MS 1695, fo. 8: SM to Lady Longueville, 3 Aug. [1702].

37. E. G. Forrester, *Northamptonshire Elections and Electioneering 1695–1832* (1941), 27.

38. *MGC* 101–2: Marlborough to SM, 10/21 Aug. 1702.

39. Brown, 98–9: Anne to SM, 24 Oct. 1702.

40. Ibid. 97: 22 Oct. 1702.

41. BL Add. MS 61416, fo. 18: notes by SM; Longleat, Portland MSS, Misc. Box 1: extracts from a narrative by SM; HMC, *Bathurst MSS*, 9: SM to Lady Bathurst [Dec. 1702].

42. BL Add. MS 61424, fo. 114: narrative by SM.
43. Evelyn, *Diary*, 1092.
44. Brown, 103: Anne to SM, 16 Dec. 1702.
45. BL Add. MS 61424, fos. 114–15: narrative by SM.
46. BL Add. MS 61442, fos. 5–6: Lady Sunderland to SM, [Jan. 1703].
47. Brown, 115: Anne to SM [Feb. 1703]; BL Add. MS 61418, fo. 25ᵛ: SM to Anne, 29 Oct. 1709.
48. Green, *Sarah*, 89; Cambridge UL Houghton (Cholmondeley) MSS 289: Blandford to Horace Walpole, 11 Feb. 1703.
49. Kent Archives Office, Stanhope MSS C7/21: Katherine Philips to Stanhope, 23 Feb. 1703; BL Add. MS 9199, fo. 117: Etough's notes of conversations with Horace Walpole.
50. BL Add. MS 61416, fo. 50: Anne to SM [22 Feb. 1703]; Add. MS 61395, fos. 34ᵛ, 38: Cardonnel to Marlborough, 23, 25 Feb. 1703; *MGC* 151: Godolphin to SM, 18 Feb. 1703.
51. Ibid. 152: Godolphin to Marlborough, 26 Feb. 1703.
52. HMC, *Atholl MSS*, 60: SM to [Tullibardine?], 17 Mar. 1703.
53. BL Add. MS 61416, fo. 55: Anne to SM [?3 Mar. 1703].
54. Delany, 2nd ser. iii. 167; HMC, *Portland MSS*, iv. 59: Lady Pye to Abigail Harley, 14 Apr. 1703.
55. *MGC* 170: Marlborough to SM, 20 Apr./1 May 1703.
56. Brown, 125: Anne to SM [22 May 1703].
57. BL Egerton MS 1695, fo. 1: SM to Lady Longueville, 3 May 1703.
58. H. Hudson, *Cumberland Lodge* (Chichester, 1989), 51–5, 60.
59. *MGC* 191: Marlborough to SM, 24 May/4 June 1703; BL Add. MS 47012 B, fo. 13: SM to Mrs Southwell, 5 Sept. 1736.
60. BL Althorp Papers D13: Anne to SM, 12 May [1703].
61. BL Add. MS 61416, fo. 104: Anne to SM, 2[9?] June [1703].
62. HMC, *Bathurst MSS*, 8: SM to Lady Bathurst, 12 June [1703].
63. *Memoirs*, 210–12; BL Add. MS 61424, fo. 9ᵛ: narrative by SM.
64. *Letter-books of John Hervey, 1st Earl of Bristol*, [ed. S. A. H. Hervey] (Wells, 1894), i. 206: to Sir R. Cocks, 8 July 1704.
65. *MGC* 219: Marlborough to SM, 8/19 July 1703.
66. BL Add. MS 61416, fos. 91, 95, 97, 111; Brown, 126: Anne to SM, 14, [16?], 18 June, 5 July, 25 Aug. 1703.
67. BL Add. MS 61418, fo. 29: SM to Anne, 29 Oct. 1709.
68. BL Add. MS 61416, fo. 122: Anne to SM, 9 July [1703]; *MGC* 194–5; BL Add. MS 61655, fo. 33: SM to Sunderland, 11 Sept. [1703].
69. Lever, *Godolphin*, 148–52.
70. BL Add. MS 61416, fo. 104: Anne to SM, 2[9?] June [1703]; Lever, *Godolphin*, 152.
71. BL Add. MS 61416, fo. 122: Anne to SM, 9 July [1703].
72. *MGC* 229–30, 234: Marlborough to SM and Godolphin, 2/13, 5/16, 12/23 Aug. 1703.
73. BL Add. MS 61416, fo. 139: Anne to SM [16 Oct. 1703].
74. *MGC* 183, 240: Marlborough to SM, 13/24 May, 29 Aug./9 Sept. 1703.

Chapter 8: 1704–1705

1. H. L. Snyder, 'The Defeat of the Occasional Conformity Bill and the Tack', *BIHR* 41 (1968), 172–6.

2. Brown, 129: Anne to SM [10 Dec. 1703].
3. *MGC* 259: Marlborough to SM [?10 Dec. 1703].
4. D. Francis, 'Marlborough's March to the Danube', *JSAHR* 50 (1972), 86–7.
5. *MGC* 260: Marlborough to SM, 18/29 Jan. 1704.
6. BL Add. MS 61458, fo. 8: Mrs Burnet to SM [Feb. 1704].
7. *MGC* 266: Marlborough to SM, 28 Jan./8 Feb. 1704.
8. Ibid. 272–4. One letter printed here as no. 279 (BL Add. MS 61427, fo. 28) dates from before their marriage; see also pp. 142–3 above.
9. *MGC* 271: Godolphin to SM, 27 March 1704.
10. BL Add. MS 61466, fo. 118: SM to Lady Cairnes, 27 Aug. [1724].
11. BL Add. MS 61428, fo. 26: Marlborough to SM [11/22 Apr. 1704]; this is a fuller copy of the letter than that in *MGC* 276.
12. *ML* 36: SM to Jennens, 5/16 May [1714].
13. *MGC* 287: Marlborough to SM, 24 Apr./5 May 1704.
14. G. S. Holmes, *British Politics in the Age of Anne* (1967), 211.
15. *MGC* 285, 288: Godolphin to SM, 24, 26 April 1704.
16. Ibid. 293: SM to Godolphin, 1 May 1704.
17. Heinsius, *Briefwisseling*, iii. 105, 169: Vrijbergen's dispatches, 21 Mar./1 Apr., 19/30 May 1704.
18. *MGC* 357: Marlborough to SM, 14/25 Aug. 1704; Trevelyan, *England under Queen Anne*, i. 366.
19. BL Add. MS 61443, fo. 169: SM to Clancarty [June 1704]; *MGC* 332: Marlborough to SM, 25 June/4 July 1704.
20. Luttrell, iv. 560; Macpherson, *Original Papers*, i. 687–8; BL Add. MS 61463, fo. 116: SM to Mrs Clayton [early 1714].
21. BL Add. MS 61451, fos. 56, 123: narrative by SM; *MGC* 178, 336: Marlborough to SM, 5/16 May 1703, 2/13 July 1704.
22. HMC, *Buccleuch MSS (Montagu House)*, i. 352: SM to Duke of Montagu, 23 July [1704]; BL Add. MS 61423, fo. 67: SM to Hamilton, 22 Dec. 1710.
23. BL Add. MS 61416, fo. 168: Anne to SM, 10 Aug. [1704].
24. Ibid. fo. 172: 18 Aug. [1704].
25. *MGC* 366: Godolphin to SM, 1 Sept. 1704.
26. Ibid. 373: Marlborough to SM, 15/26 Sept. 1704.
27. BL Add. MS 61416, fo. 176: Anne to SM, 21 Aug. [1704].
28. BL Add. MS 61443, fo. 1: Sunderland to SM [14 Aug. 1704].
29. *MGC* 390–1: SM to Godolphin, 19 Oct. 1704.
30. Ibid. 384–5, 393: Marlborough to SM, 9/20 Oct., 23 Oct./3 Nov. 1704.
31. HMC, *Portland MSS*, ii. 184–8: Harley to Newcastle, Apr.–Dec.1704; *MGC* 334–5, 373: Marlborough to Godolphin and SM, 2/13 July, 15/26 Sept. 1704.
32. HMC, *Buccleuch MSS (Montagu House)*, i. 353: SM to Montagu, 18 Nov. [1704].
33. BL Add. MS 61421, fo. 1: narrative by SM, 13 Nov. 1704.
34. BL Add. MS 61458, fo. 33: Mrs Burnet to SM [19 Nov. 1704].
35. *Commons Journals*, xiv. 392: 25 Oct. 1704; BL Add. MS 61416, fo. 192: Anne to SM [31 Oct. 1704] (misdated 10 Nov. 1702 in *MGC* 148).
36. BL Add. MS 61416, fo. 195; Brown, 100: SM to Anne, 20 Nov. 1704, and reply, 21 Nov. [1704].
37. Snyder, 'Defeat of the Occasional Conformity Bill', 181–3.
38. BL Add. MS 61416, fo. 201: SM to Anne [25 Nov. 1704].
39. Gregg, *Queen Anne*, 193.

40. Burnet, v. 225–6, Dartmouth's note.
41. BL Add. MS 17677 AAA, fos. 62, 82: L'Hermitage's dispatches, 12/23, 19/30 Jan. 1705; Heinsius, *Briefwisseling*, iv. 39: Vrijbergen's dispatch, 12/23 Jan. 1705; HMC, *Bath MSS*, i. 63: Godolphin to Harley [Jan. 1705] (misdated [Sept. 1704] by editor).
42. Abel Boyer, *The History of Queen Anne* (1735), 177.
43. BL Add. MS 17677 AAA, fo. 152: L'Hermitage's dispatch, 20 Feb./2 Mar. 1705; Add. MS 61451, fo. 74: narrative by SM.
44. BL Add. MS 61451, f. 74; Add. MS 61432, fo. 95: Henrietta to SM [early 1705].
45. BL Add. MS 61472, fo. 176: deed of settlement, 18 Mar. 1705.
46. *ML* 34–5, 76: SM to Jennens, 5/14 May [1714], 26 Sept./7 Oct. 1713; BL Add. MS 61417, fo. 112: SM to Anne [?Feb. 1708]; Herts RO Panshanger MSS F79: Cowper's list of SM's investments, 24 Dec. 1712.
47. BL Add. MS 61447, fo. 135: SM to Lady Bateman, 14 June 1727.
48. *MGC* 419, 422, 426: Marlborough to SM, 13/24, 19/30 Apr., 23 Apr./4 May 1705.
49. BL Althorp Papers D14: SM to Mallet [Sept. 1744].
50. *MGC* 423: Marlborough to SM, 19/30 Apr. 1705.
51. *Commons Journals*, xv. 38; W. A. Speck, *Tory and Whig: The Struggle in the Constituencies* (1970), 58.
52. HMC, *Portland MSS*, iv. 188: Dyer's newsletter, 10 May 1705.
53. BL Add. MS 61458, fo. 158: Halifax to SM [?10 May 1705].
54. HMC, *Buccleuch MSS (Montagu House)*, i. 354: SM to Montagu, 21 May [1705].
55. *MGC* 468: Marlborough to SM, 26 July/6 Aug. 1705.
56. BL Add. MS 61458, fo. 58: Mrs Burnet to SM, 14 June 1705; ibid. fo. 162: note by SM; H. L. Snyder, 'Daniel Defoe, the Duchess of Marlborough, and the *Advice to the Electors of Great Britain*', *HLQ* 29 (1965–6), 57.
57. BL Althorp Papers D14: SM to Mallet [Sept. 1744].
58. BL Add. MS 61458, fos. 163–5: Halifax to SM, 15, 22 May 1705; Brown, 165: Anne to Godolphin, [23 May 1705].
59. Ibid. 172: Anne to Godolphin, 11 July 1705.
60. *Memoirs*, 258.
61. *MGC* 483: Marlborough to SM, 22 Aug./2 Sept. 1705.
62. *MGC* 466–7, 476: Marlborough to Godolphin and SM, 16/27 July, 23 July/3 Aug., 26 July/6 Aug., 13/24 Aug. 1705.
63. D. Green, *Blenheim Palace* (1951), 43, 50, 300; *CTB 1705–6*, 313, 356.
64. *MGC* 461: Marlborough to Godolphin, 12/23 July 1705; *The Letters and Dispatches of John Churchill, First Duke of Marlborough*, ed. Sir G. Murray (1845), ii. 207: to Vanbrugh, 27 July/7 Aug. 1705.
65. *MGC* 495: Godolphin to SM, 13 Sept. 1705.
66. *Remarks and Collections of Thomas Hearne*, ed. C. E. Doble, Oxford Historical Society (1885–1921), i. 287.
67. *Memoirs*, 104, 258; BL Add. MS 61423, fo. 66: SM to Hamilton, 22 Dec. 1710.
68. *PC* i. 12: Sunderland to SM, 8/19 Sept. 1705.
69. BL Add. MS 61464, fo. 151: SM to Bishop Blackburne, 20 May 1721; *The Private Diary of William, First Earl Cowper*, ed. E. C. Hawtrey, Roxburghe Club (1833), 4.
70. BL Add. MS 61458, fo. 49: Mrs Burnet to SM [?1 Dec. 1705].
71. Burnet, v. 230.

72. *Commons Journals*, xv. 37–8; Longleat, Portland MSS, iii, fo. 213: SM to Harley [Nov. 1705]; Burnet, v. 230.
73. W. A. Speck, '"The Most Corrupt Council in Christendom": Decisions on Controverted Elections 1702–1742', in C. Jones (ed.), *Party Management in Parliament 1660–1784* (Leicester, 1984), 108–9.
74. Burnet, v. 230; BL Add. MS 61474, fo. 132: note by SM.
75. Hearne, *Remarks and Collections*, i. 102.

Chapter 9: 1706–1707

1. *MGC* 537: Marlborough to SM, 4/15 May 1706.
2. Ibid. 546: 13/24 May 1706.
3. Luttrell, vi. 49; BL Egerton MS 2678, fos. 8–9: privy purse accounts, 21 Jan., 26 Mar. 1707.
4. Luttrell, vi. 58.
5. *MGC* 591: Marlborough to SM, 17/28 June 1706.
6. BL Add. MS 61450, fo. 14: Mary to SM [Jan. 1706]; Add. MS 61451, fo. 56ᵛ: narrative by SM.
7. BL Add. MS 61450, fos. 33, 43: Mary to SM [June 1706].
8. *MGC* 537, 596: Marlborough to SM, 4/15 May, 20 June/1 July 1706.
9. BL Add. MS 61458, fos. 107–14: Ruperta Howe to SM, 1706; Thomson, i. 464: SM to Anne, 7 Aug. 1707; BL Add. MS 61423, fo. 55: SM to Hamilton, 10 Dec. 1710.
10. Brown, 177: Anne to SM [?Dec. 1705].
11. *MGC* 563: Godolphin to Marlborough, 26 May 1706; HMC, *8th Report*, pt 1, 43: Anne to Marlborough, 9 July [1706].
12. *MGC* 632: Godolphin to Marlborough, 23 July 1706.
13. Ibid. 638: Marlborough to SM, 29 July/9 Aug. 1706.
14. Brown, 197: Anne to Godolphin, 30 Aug. 1706.
15. HMC, *8th Report*, pt. 1, 53; Brown, 211: Anne to SM, 5 July, 17 July [1706].
16. *PC* i. 14–15: Sunderland to SM [20 July 1706].
17. BL Add. MS 61417, fo. 19: SM to Anne [27 Aug. 1706]; cf. Coxe, ii. 13.
18. BL Add. MS 61417, fo. 22: SM to Anne, 30 Aug. [1706]; cf. Coxe, ii. 13–14.
19. *MGC* 684: Godolphin to SM, 9 Nov. [1706] (misdated 17 Sept. by editor; cf. ibid. 733 and n. 36 below).
20. Ibid. 661: 1 Sept. 1706.
21. Coxe, ii. 15: Anne to SM [6 Sept. 1706].
22. BL Add. MS 61417, fo. 32ᵛ: note by SM.
23. *Memoirs*, 116–20: SM to Anne [6 Sept. 1706].
24. *MGC* 670–1, 679: Godolphin to SM, 7, 14 Sept. 1706.
25. Ibid. 675: Godolphin to Marlborough, 10 Sept. 1706.
26. Ibid. 695: Marlborough to SM, 26 Sept/7 Oct. 1706; Coxe, ii. 8: Marlborough to Anne, same date.
27. *MGC* 694–5: Godolphin to Marlborough, 25 Sept. 1706; Marlborough to SM, 26 Sept./7 Oct. 1706.
28. Hearne, *Remarks and Collections*, i. 287; Green, *Blenheim Palace*, 80.
29. *MGC* 676, 678; BL Add. 61450, fo. 13: Mary to SM [Sept. 1706].
30. Coxe, ii. 4–5: Sunderland to SM, 17 Sept. 1706.
31. Ibid. 11–12: Godolphin to Anne, 25 Sept 1706; BL Add. MS 61417, fo. 50: SM to Anne [26 Sept. 1706].

32. HMC, *Bath MSS*, i. 102: SM to Harley, 18 Sept. 1706.

33. *MGC* 696, 700: Godolphin to Marlborough, 28 Sept. 1706; Marlborough to SM, 30 Sept./11 Oct. 1706.

34. Coxe, ii. 16–17: Marlborough to Anne, 13/24 Oct. 1706.

35. *MGC* 705: Marlborough to SM, 7/18 Oct. 1706; *PC* i. 51–4: SM to Anne, 20 Oct. 1706.

36. *MGC* 683–4, 733: Godolphin to SM, 9 Nov. [1706] (1st sheet misdated 17 Sept. by editor; 2nd sheet incorrectly printed as part of a letter of 9 Nov. [1704]; cf. BL Add. MS 61434, fos. 11–14, 50–3).

37. Longleat, Portland MSS, iii, fo. 86: Marlborough to Harley [10 Jan. 1707]; BL Add. MSS 61417, fo. 60; 61418, fo. 28ᵛ: SM to Anne [Jan. 1707], 29 Oct. 1709.

38. *MGC* 737–45.

39. BL Althorp Papers D13: Anne to SM [7 Apr. 1707], with SM's note.

40. *MGC* 772: Marlborough to SM, 8/19 May 1707.

41. G. V. Bennett, 'Robert Harley, the Godolphin Ministry, and the Bishoprics Crisis of 1707', *EHR* 82 (1967), 735–7.

42. *MGC* 790: Marlborough to SM, 22 May/2 June 1707.

43. BL Add. MS 61422, fo. 23; Add. MS 61425, fo. 120: narratives by SM.

44. Newberry Library, Case MS E5 M3827, pp. 283, 296: C. Dumare and Samuel Masham to Esther Masham, 1 July, 4 Oct. 1707; HMC, *Portland MSS*, iv. 406: Lady Pye to Abigail Harley, 12 May 1707.

45. Gregg, *Queen Anne*, 237; *MGC* 829: Marlborough to SM, 23 June/4 July 1707; George Lockhart, *The Lockhart Papers*, ed. A. Aufrere (1817), i. 316.

46. Longleat, Portland MSS, iii: Anne to Harley, 'Thursday' [1707].

47. BL Add. MS 61454, fo. 198: Abigail Hill to SM [June 1707].

48. *MGC* 777: Marlborough to SM, 12/23 May 1707.

49. Vanbrugh, iv. 14: to Manchester, 18 July 1707.

50. BL Add. MS 61458, fo. 63: Mrs Burnet to SM [June 1707].

51. *MGC* 834: Godolphin to Marlborough, 27 June 1707.

52. Ibid. 845: Marlborough to SM, 10/21 July 1707.

53. Ibid. 811, 824, 837: Godolphin to Marlborough, 8 June 1707; Marlborough to Godolphin and SM, 16/27 June, 30 June/11 July 1707.

54. BL Add. MS 61417, fos. 73, 75, 81: Anne to SM [17 July 1707]; SM to Anne, 18, [21] July 1707.

55. Ibid. fo. 76: SM to Anne, 18 July 1707.

56. Thomson, i. 464: SM to Anne, 7 Aug. 1707.

57. Brown, 230: Anne to Marlborough [25 Aug. 1707].

58. BL Add. MS 61110, fo. 102: Marlborough to Godolphin, 18/29 Aug. 1707 (the crossed-out reference to Abigail is not included in the letter as printed in *MGC* 886); *MGC* 890: Godolphin to Marlborough, 25 Aug. 1707 (where the 'person not fitt to bee mentioned' is wrongly identified as Harley).

59. Brown, 231: Anne to Marlborough [25 Aug. 1707].

60. *MGC* 891: Godolphin to Marlborough, 25 Aug. 1707; Coxe, ii. 159–60: Marlborough to Anne, 4/15 Sept. 1707.

61. *MGC* 997: Marlborough to SM, 8/19 Sept. 1707.

62. BL Add. MS 61417, fo. 96: SM to Anne, 14 Sept. 1707.

63. *MGC* 904–5: Marlborough to SM, 4/15 Sept. 1707.

64. Bennett, 'Robert Harley', 739–41.

65 BL Add. MS 52540 L, fo. 48: Anne to Godolphin, 12 Sept. 1707.

66. BL Add. MS 61417, fos. 96, 105: SM to Anne, 17 Sept., 29 Oct. 1707.

67. Christ Church, Evelyn MSS: SM to Lady Evelyn, 17 Oct. 1736.
68. *MGC* 931–2: Godolphin to Marlborough, 7 Oct. 1707.
69. BL Add. MS 61417, fo. 94: note by SM.
70. BL Add. MS 61422, fos. 6, 9ᵛ: narrative by SM.
71. BL Add. MSS 61416, fo. 131; 61417, fo. 94: notes by SM.
72. BL Add. MS 61418, fos. 30–2: SM to Anne, 29 Oct. 1709.
73. BL Add. MS 61425, fo. 121: narrative comp. for SM by Priest, 1713; Add. MS 61417, fo. 101: SM to Anne, 29 Oct. [1707].
74. HMC, *Portland MSS*, iv. 454: Abigail Masham to Harley, 29 Sept. 1707.
75. *Memoirs*, 132–4: SM to Abigail Masham, 23, [24] Sept. 1707.
76. *MGC* 940: Marlborough to SM, 28 Oct./8 Nov. 1707.
77. BL Add. MS 61422, fo. 5: narrative by SM.
78. BL Add. MS 61425, fo. 122: narrative comp. for SM by Priest, 1713; Add. MS 61417, fo. 101: SM to Anne, 29 Oct. [1707].
79. BL Add. MS 61425, fo. 122.
80. BL Add. MS 61399, fo. 36ᵛ: Cardonnel to Lumley, 12 Dec. 1707.
81. Bennett, 'Robert Harley', 743–6.
82. Cowper, *Diary*, 43; BL Add. MS 57862, fo. 69: Coningsby to Marlborough [Jan. 1711].
83. BL Add. MS 61425, fo. 123: narrative comp. for SM by Priest, 1713; cf. H. L. Snyder, 'Godolphin and Harley: A Study of their Partnership in Politics', *HLQ* 30 (1966–7), 269–70.
84. G. S. Holmes and W. A. Speck, 'The Fall of Harley in 1708 Reconsidered', *EHR* 80 (1965), 677–8, 687–94.
85. B. W. Hill, *Robert Harley* (New Haven, 1988), 241: De Beyries' dispatch, 17/28 Feb. 1708.
86. BL Add. MS 61425, fo. 124: narrative comp. for SM by Priest, 1713.

Chapter 10: 1708–1709

1. BL Add. MS 61422, fo. 8: narrative by SM.
2. *The Correspondence of Jonathan Swift*, ed. H. Williams (Oxford, 1963), i. 69: to King, 12 Feb. 1708; 7th Duke of Manchester (ed.), *Court and Society from Elizabeth to Anne* (1864), ii. 281: Addison to Manchester, 13 Feb. 1708; *PC* i. 113: Maynwaring to SM [7 Apr. 1708].
3. BL Add. MS 61418, fo. 88: SM to Anne, 7 June 1710.
4. BL Add. MS 61417, fos. 123–6: drafts to Anne by SM and Maynwaring, 13 Mar. 1707/8.
5. BL Add. MS 61459, fo. 10: Maynwaring to SM [early 1708].
6. Luttrell, vi. 248; *ML* 34: SM to Jennens, 5/16 May [1714]; BL Add. MS 62569, fo. 138: Jennens to SM, 12 Dec. 1714.
7. J. J. Cartwright (ed.), *The Wentworth Papers* (1883), 105–6: Wentworth to Raby, 30 Jan. 1710.
8. BL Add. MS 61461, fo. 30: Maynwaring to SM [Apr.–May 1710].
9. *PC* i. 103: Maynwaring to SM, 6 Apr. 1708.
10. S. J. Cohen, 'Hester Santlow', *Bulletin of New York Public Library*, 64 (1960), 96, 101. There was also gossip at this time about Marlborough's supposed attempt to marry an illegitimate daughter to one of his officers, Francis Palmes, with a dowry of £10,000 (BL Add. MS 70632: endorsement on verses, 'Prisca's Advice to Novinda', 1707); but this daughter is otherwise unidentified, and I

am indebted to David Hayton of the History of Parliament for information that Palmes apparently never married.

11. Cartwright, *Wentworth Papers*, 127: Lady Wentworth to Raby, 27 Aug. 1710.

12. Gregg, *Queen Anne*, 272–3.

13. Heinsius, *Briefwisseling*, vii. 210, 232: L'Hermitage's dispatches, 30 Mar./10 Apr., 9/20 Apr. 1708.

14. BL Add. MS 61418, fo. 28: SM to Anne, 29 Oct. 1709; Add. MS 61423, fo. 17: SM to Hamilton, 28 Nov. 1710.

15. Hove Public Library, Wolseley MSS M1/112/3: privy purse accounts, 17 Mar. 1707/8; cf. BL Add MS 61420, fo. 83, where there is no entry for 17 Mar. and the total credit is £12,000 more. For the postdating of the latter set, see the entry for 12 Dec. 1707 (f. 81), where a minor error noted in the earlier set under 12 Dec. 1707 and 24 Jan. 1708 has been corrected. Gregg, *Queen Anne*, 272–3, 329, relying on the earlier set, suggests that Sarah took the money at this point, as well as claiming it again in 1711.

16. *MGC* 943; BL Add. MS 61399, fo. 121ᵛ: Cardonnel's letter-book, 31 Mar. 1708.

17. BL Add. MS 61417, fos. 130–3: SM to Anne and reply, 31 Mar. 1708.

18. *MGC* 951: Marlborough to SM, 9/20 Apr. 1708.

19. Ibid. 961–2, 966: 22 Apr./3 May, 25 Apr./6 May 1708.

20. Coxe, ii. 210: Sunderland to SM, 6 Apr. 1708; *PC* i. 104–6: Maynwaring to SM, 9 Apr. 1708.

21. BL Add. MS 61429, fo. 190: Marlborough to SM, 25 Apr./6 May 1708 (printed inaccurately in *MGC*, 965–6).

22. *PC* i. 393: Maynwaring to SM [13 May 1708].

23. BL Add. MS 61417, fo. 135: Anne to SM [10 Apr. 1708].

24. *PC* i. 111: Maynwaring to SM [7 Apr. 1708].

25. BL Add. MS 61459, fo. 32: Maynwaring to SM [22 Apr. 1708].

26. *The Correspondence of Sir James Clavering*, ed. H. T. Dickinson, Surtees Society, 178 (1967), 4: Ann to Sir J. Clavering, 29 May 1708.

27. Snyder, 'Daniel Defoe, the Duchess of Marlborough, and the *Advice to the Electors of Great Britain*', 60–2; F. H. Ellis (ed.), *Poems on Affairs of State 1704–14* (New Haven, 1975), 306–21.

28. *MGC* 976: Marlborough to SM, 6/17 May 1708.

29. Ibid. 981–2: 13/24 May 1708.

30. HMC, *Portland MSS*, iv. 489: Lewis to Harley, 18 May 1708.

31. *MGC* 996: Marlborough to SM, 27 May/7 June 1708.

32. Ibid. 991: 24 May/4 June 1708.

33. Ibid. 1014, 1032: [?17/28 June], 8/19 July 1708.

34. BL Althorp Papers D13: Anne to SM, 'Munday night' [5 July 1708] (postmarked 6 July).

35. *MGC* 1024–5: Marlborough to SM, 1/12 July 1708.

36. Green, *Sarah*, 313: SM to Anne, 7 July [1708], paraphrasing her own letter of 5 July, which does not survive.

37. BL Add. MS 61417, fo. 145: Anne to SM [6 July 1708]; cf. Brown, 229 (wrongly dated 16 Sept. 1707 by Gregg, *Queen Anne*, 250).

38. BL Add. MS 61417, fo. 151: Anne to SM [7 July 1708].

39. *PC* i. 255–6: Maynwaring to SM [July 1708].

40. *MGC* 1049: Marlborough to SM, 22 July/2 Aug. 1708.

41. Herts RO Panshanger MSS F228, p. 27: SM to Lady Cowper, 18 July 1708; BL

Add. MS 70333/22 and 25: 'Queries' in Harley's hand, 14 May, 31 Mar. 1708; J. A. Downie, *Robert Harley and the Press* (Cambridge, 1979), 106-10.

42. Green, *Sarah*, 318-21: SM to Anne, 26 July 1708.
43. HMC, *Portland MSS*, iv. 495, 499: Abigail Masham to Harley, 21, 27 July 1708; for the code, dated 14 May 1708, see BL Add. MS 70290/1.
44. Vanbrugh, iv. 25: to Manchester, 27 July 1708.
45. *Memoirs*, 156-7: Anne to SM, with reply [21, 22 Aug. 1708].
46. BL Add. MS 61458, fo. 83: Mrs Burnet to SM [4 Sept. 1708].
47. BL Add. MS 61459, fo. 101ᵛ: Maynwaring to SM [?11 Sept. 1708]; Coxe, ii. 295: 'Heads of the Conversation with Mrs. Morley', 9 Sept. 1708.
48. *MGC* 1107: Marlborough to SM, 20 Sept./1 Oct. 1708.
49. Ibid. 1073: Marlborough to SM, 12/23 Aug. 1708.
50. Longleat, Portland MSS, x, fo. 56: Harley to Abigail Masham, 16 Oct. 1708.
51. Hamilton, 9.
52. *CTB 1708*, 379-80; HMC, *Portland MSS*, iv. 509: Lewis to Harley, 22 Oct. 1708.
53. *MGC* 1003, 1016-17, 1118: Marlborough to SM [3/14] June, 20 June/1 July, 28 Sept./9 Oct. 1708.
54. BL Add. MS 61459, fos. 90-1: Maynwaring to SM [7 Sept. 1708].
55. *MGC* 1101: Marlborough to SM, 13/24 Sept. 1708; on this subject, see R. Geikie and I. A. Montgomery, *The Dutch Barrier 1705-1719* (Cambridge, 1930), 13-143 *passim*.
56. BL Add. MS 61459, fos. 113-15: Maynwaring to SM [Sept.-Oct. 1708].
57. Trevelyan, *England under Queen Anne*, ii. 443: Sunderland to Newcastle, 19 Oct. 1708.
58. BL Althorp Papers D14: SM to Mallet, 24 Sept. 1744.
59. BL Add. MS 61459, fos. 119, 122: Maynwaring to SM, 18, [19] Oct. [1708].
60. *MGC* 1132: Godolphin to SM, 17 Oct. 1708.
61. *PC* i. 284: Maynwaring to SM, [23 Oct. 1708].
62. *MGC* 1142: Godolphin to SM, 26 Oct. 1708.
63. Coxe, ii. 360-1; *PC* i. 412-16: narrative by SM.
64. *PC* i. 415-16.
65. BL Add. MS 61459, fo. 142: Maynwaring to SM [?4 Nov. 1708].
66. Ibid. fo. 147 [23 Nov. 1708].
67. *MGC* 1172, 1207-8: Marlborough to SM, 9/20 Dec. 1708; 24 Jan./4 Feb. 1709.
68. Ibid. 1183, 1185: 20/31 Dec., 23 Dec./3 Jan. 1708/9.
69. *PC* i. 215-16: Maynwaring to SM [27 Dec. 1708].
70. BL Add. MS 61134, fos. 229, 232: notes by SM; BL Trumbull Papers, Misc. liii: Johnstone to Trumbull, 3 Jan. 1709.
71. BL Add. MS 61458, fos. 126-7, 170: notes by SM; *MGC* 1207-8, 1210: Marlborough to SM, 24 Jan./4 Feb., 27 Jan./7 Feb. 1709.
72. Cartwright, *Wentworth Papers*, 166: Lady Wentworth to Raby, 10 Dec. 1708; Herts RO Panshanger MSS F63, fo. 70: SM to Lady Cowper [1 Jan. 1709].
73. Herts RO Panshanger MSS F228, pp. 26-7: SM to Lady Cowper, 17 Feb. 1708/9.
74. BL Add. MS 61459, fos. 163-5: Maynwaring to SM [26 Feb. 1709]; Herts RO Panshanger MSS F79: Cowper's list of SM's investments, 24 Dec. 1712.
75 Thibaudeau, 2nd ser. ii. 75: Cardonnel to Watkins, 1 Mar. 1709; *MGC*, 1231-2: Marlborough to SM, 27 Feb. 1709.
76. *MGC*, 1207: Marlborough to SM, 24 Jan./4 Feb. 1709; Longleat, Portland MSS, x, fo. 56: Harley to Abigail Masham, 16 Oct. 1708; BL Add. MS 70331/1:

'Plaine English', 24 Aug. 1708; H. L. Snyder, 'The Duke of Marlborough's Request of his Captain-Generalcy for Life', *JSAHR* 45 (1967), 73: Marlborough to Anne, 29 Sept./10 Oct. 1709.

77. Churchill, ii. 639–40.

78. BL Add. MS 61423, fo. 44: SM to Hamilton [Dec. 1710].

79. *CTB 1709*, 172, 183, 191–2; BL Add. Ch. 76137: ground plan distinguishing the two grants, 1744; Thomson, i. 474.

80. HMC, *Portland MSS*, iv. 522: Abigail Harley to her aunt, 29 Mar. 1709.

81. Cartwright, *Wentworth Papers*, 89: Wentworth to Raby, 7 June 1709; *MGC* 1136: Marlborough to SM, 21 Oct./1 Nov. 1708; BL Add. MS 61422, fo. 129: narrative by SM; Green, *Blenheim Palace*, 106.

82. Herts RO Panshanger MSS F63, fo. 57: SM to Lady Cowper [summer 1709].

83. BL Add. MS 61459, fo. 28: Maynwaring to SM [summer 1709].

84. BL Add. MS 61472, fo. 21: SM to Coggs, 12 Oct. [1702]; Egerton MS 2678, fo. 10: privy purse accounts, 14 June 1707; Add. MS 61417, fo. 112: SM to Anne [?Feb. 1708].

85. Gregg, *Queen Anne*, 279, citing Wolseley MSS M1/112/3, 4, 5.

86. Luttrell, vi. 535.

87. BL Add. MS 61425, fo. 99: narrative comp. for SM by Priest, 1713.

88. *MGC* 1269: Marlborough to SM, 29 May/9 June 1709.

89. Bodleian Library, Top. Oxon. c.218, fos. 38–9, 51: SM to Bobart, June–July 1709.

90. Clavering, *Correspondence*, 32: Ann to Sir J. Clavering, 2 June 1709.

91. Heinsius, *Briefwisseling*, ix. 73: L'Hermitage's dispatch, 8/19 July 1709; Clavering, *Correspondence*, 21–2, 40: 9 Dec. 1708, 3 Sept. 1709; *CTB 1709*, 89, 181; BL Add. MSS 61417, fo. 186; 61418, fo. 16: notes by SM.

92. BL Add. MS 61417, fo. 181: Anne to SM [27 July 1709]; Add. MS 61459, fo. 184: Maynwaring to SM [?8 Aug. 1709].

93. BL Add. MS 61417, fo. 187: SM to Anne, 6 Aug. 1709.

94. *MGC* 1336, 1345: Marlborough to SM, 8/19, 15/26 Aug. 1709.

95. BL Add. MS 57861, fo. 121: Maynwaring to Coningsby, 20 Aug. 1709.

96. BL Add. MS 61313, fo. 189: Metcalf Grahme to Marlborough [Sept. 1709]; *MGC* 1359: Marlborough to SM, 31 Aug./11 Sept. 1709.

97. *MGC* 1381: 22 Sept./3 Oct. 1709.

98. Ibid. 1368, 1372: Cardonnel to SM, 5/16 Sept. 1709; Godolphin to Marlborough, 12 Sept. 1709; BL Add. MS 61460, fo. 27: Maynwaring to SM [11 Sept. 1709].

99. Yale UL Osborn Collection: SM to Coningsby, 17 Sept [1709].

100. *MGC* 1370, 1389: Marlborough to SM, 8/19 Sept., 29 Sept./10 Oct. 1709; Snyder, 'Duke of Marlborough's Request', 73: Marlborough to Anne, 29 Sept./10 Oct. 1709.

101. Lord Hardwicke (ed.), *Miscellaneous State Papers from 1501 to 1726* (1778), ii. 480: Sunderland to Somers, 8 Aug. 1709.

102. BL Add. MSS 61460, fos. 24–5; 61459, fo. 178: Maynwaring to SM [?8 Sept. 1709] [summer 1709].

103. *MGC* 1383, 1397: Marlborough to SM, 22 Sept./3 Oct., 10/21 Oct. 1709.

104. BL Add. MSS 61459, fos. 179–80; 61460, fo. 15: Maynwaring to SM [Aug. 1709].

105. Yale UL Osborn Collection, SM to Coningsby, 17 Sept. [1709].

106. BL Add. MS 61422, fos. 25–6, 38: narratives by SM.

107. BL Add. MS 61460, fo. 100: SM to Maynwaring, 3 Nov. 1709.
108. Burnet, v. 454, Dartmouth's note; BL Add. MS 61460, fos. 74–5: , Maynwaring to SM [7–14 Oct. 1709].
109. Ibid. fos. 9, 93–4: Maynwaring to SM [Oct. 1709]; Add. MS 61418, fos. 1–8: SM to Anne, 16 Oct. 1709.
110. Brown, 285–6: Anne to Marlborough, 25 Oct. 1709.
111. BL Add. MS 61423, fos. 65–6: SM to Hamilton, 22 Dec. 1710, quoting Anne's letter of 26 Oct. 1709.
112. BL Add. MS 61434, fo. 93: SM to [Godolphin, 27 Oct. 1709] (see Brown, 286: Anne to SM [27 Oct. 1707], for Godolphin's delivery of the letter of 26 Oct.).
113. BL Add. MS 61418, fos. 20–32: SM to Anne, 29 Oct. 1709.
114. BL Add. MS 61460, fo. 75: Maynwaring to SM [?14 Oct. 1709]; H. L. Snyder, 'Queen Anne versus the Junto', *HLQ* 35 (1971–2), 333–6.
115. *MGC* 1405–6: Godolphin to SM, 5 Nov. 1709.
116. Snyder, 'Queen Anne versus the Junto', 336–8.
117. BL Add. MS 61418, fo. 68: Anne to SM [?14 Nov. 1709].
118. Ibid. fo. 70: note by SM.
119. *PC* i. 268–9: Maynwaring to SM [Nov. 1709].

Chapter 11: 1710

1. *Memoirs*, 260.
2. *PC* i. 158–9, 263, 270: Maynwaring to SM [Nov.–Dec. 1709].
3. BL Add. MS 61460, fo. 136: SM to Maynwaring, 27 Dec. [1709].
4. *PC* ii. 63–4: Maynwaring to SM [30 Dec. 1709].
5. Coxe, iii. 6–8.
6. J. H. Jesse, *Memoirs of the Court of England from the Revolution in 1688 to the Death of George II* (1843), i. 395–6: Marlborough to Coningsby, 'Wednesday night' [18 Jan. 1710] (misdated 16 Jan. 1711).
7. Thomas, Lord Coningsby, 'Account of the State of Political Parties', *Archaeologia*, 38 (1860), 9–11; G. S. Holmes, *The Trial of Doctor Sacheverell* (1973), 114; Gregg, *Queen Anne*, 302.
8. BL Trumbull Papers, Misc. liii: Johnstone to Trumbull, 23 Dec. 1709.
9. BL Add. MS 61418, fo. 135: SM to Anne [June 1710].
10. BL Add. MS 57862, fo. 47: Coningsby to Marlborough [Jan. 1710]; *PC* i. 269: Maynwaring to SM [Nov. 1709].
11. Coxe, iii. 14–15: SM to Maynwaring [19 Jan. 1710].
12. BL Add. MS 61418, fo. 135: SM to Anne [June 1710].
13. BL Add. MS 61422, fos. 58ᵛ–9: narrative by SM.
14. HMC, *Portland MSS*, iv. 526: Abigail Masham to Harley, 14 Sept. 1709.
15. BL Add. MS 61422, fo. 59: narrative by SM.
16. Coxe, iii. 31: Sunderland to Marlborough, 21 Feb. 1710.
17. BL Add. MS 61422, fo. 63: narrative by SM.
18. Clavering, *Correspondence*, 74: Ann to Sir J. Clavering, 23 Mar. 1710.
19. Brown, 301–2: Anne to SM, 3, 6 Apr. 1710.
20. Burnet, v. 454, Dartmouth's note.
21. *PC* i. 295–9: narrative by SM, 1710; BL Add. MS 61425, fos. 129–32: narrative comp. for SM by Priest, 1713.
22. BL Add. MS 61425, fo. 132ᵛ; Hamilton, 28.
23. BL Add. MS 61460, fo. 200: Maynwaring to SM [15 Apr. 1710].

24. Ibid. fos. 27–8: [Apr.–May 1710].
25. Hamilton, 7–8; BL Add. MS 61460, fo. 204: Maynwaring to SM [17 Apr. 1710].
26. BL Add. MS 61460, fo. 29: Maynwaring to SM [30 Apr. 1710].
27. *MGC* 1477: Godolphin to SM, 29 Apr. 1710.
28. Hamilton, 9.
29. *MGC* 1497: Godolphin to Marlborough, 16 May 1710.
30. Ibid. 1511–13: Godolphin to SM, 1 June 1710.
31. Ibid. 1521, 1531: Marlborough to SM, 8/19, 15/26 June 1710.
32. BL Add. MSS 61460, fo. 212; 61461, fos. 24, 30: SM to Maynwaring [c.18, 28 Apr. 1710]; Maynwaring to SM [Apr.–May 1710].
33. Herts RO Panshanger MSS F63, fos. 158–9: SM to Lady Cowper, 14 May [1710].
34. *MGC* 1492, 1499: Marlborough to SM, 11/22, 18/29 May 1710.
35. *MGC* 1501: Godolphin to SM, 19 May 1710.
36. BL Add. MS 57682, fos. 58–60: Coningsby to Marlborough, 7 June 1710.
37. BL Add. MS 61418, fos. 88–92: SM to Anne, 7 June 1710.
38. Ibid. fo. 106: Anne to SM, 12 June 1710.
39. Ibid. fos. 108–23: SM to Anne, 13 June 1710.
40. Hill, *Robert Harley*, 128; BL Lansdowne MS 885, fos. 24–5: 'An Account of the Earl of Oxford by his Brother'.
41. Yale UL Osborn Collection: SM to Coningsby, 12 Aug. 1710.
42. Hamilton, 13.
43. Heinsius, *Briefwisseling*, x. 562: L'Hermitage's dispatch, 11/22 July 1710.
44. F. Harris, 'Accounts of the Conduct of Sarah, Duchess of Marlborough', *British Library Journal*, 8 (1982), 12–13.
45. Hamilton, 12, 28.
46. BL Add. MS 57861, fo. 154: Maynwaring to Coningsby, 14 Oct. 1710.
47. Yale UL Osborn Collection: SM to Coningsby, 22 Aug. 1710.
48. Herts RO Panshanger MSS F228, p. 37: SM to Lady Cowper, 31 Aug. 1710.
49. Yale UL Osborn Collection: SM to Coningsby, 14 Sept. [1710].
50. Vanbrugh, iv. 48–50: to Marlborough, 3, 10 Oct. 1710; Churchill, ii. 763: Travers to Marlborough, 8 Oct. 1710; *MGC* 1645–6, 1650: Marlborough to Godolphin and SM, 14/25 Oct. 1710; SM to Godolphin, 17 Oct. 1710.
51. Herts RO Panshanger MSS F228, pp. 58, 69, 76: SM to Lady Cowper, 13, [15], [?31] Oct. 1710.
52. BL Add. MS 61461, fo. 97: SM to Maynwaring [late 1710].
53. BL Add. MS 61423, fos. 16–17: SM to Hamilton, 23 Nov. 1710.
54. Hamilton, 20; BL Add. 61423, fos. 34–5: SM to Hamilton, 6 Dec. 1710.
55. Trevelyan, *England under Queen Anne*, iii. 352: Godolphin to [Seafield], to be shown to the Queen, 17 Dec. 1710.
56. BL Add. MS 61461, fo. 97: SM to Maynwaring [late 1710]; Add. MS 61464, fo. 20: SM to [Hare, 31 Oct. 1710]; Herts RO Panshanger MSS F63, fo. 66: SM to Cowper, 18 Oct. [1710].
57. BL Add. MS 61423, fos. 15, 52; Herts RO Panshanger MSS F207: SM to Hamilton, 28 Nov., 10 Dec., [c.13 Dec.] 1710; Hamilton, 21.
58. BL Add. MS 61441, fo. 104: Mrs Boscawen to SM, 7 Dec. [1710].
59. BL Add. MS 61423, fo. 86: note by SM.
60. Luttrell, vi. 668.
61. HMC, *Portland MSS*, iv. 635: Drummond to Harley, 29 Nov./9 Dec. 1710; Hamilton, 23.

62. Hamilton, 23.
63. BL Add. MS 61422, fo. 115: narrative by SM; Hamilton, 26; Thibaudeau, 2nd ser. ii. 83: Cardonnel to Watkins, 12 Jan. 1711.
64. O. Klopp, *Der Fall des Hauses Stuart* (Vienna, 1875–88), xiii. 24: Hoffman's dispatch, 12/23 Jan. 1711; Hamilton, 26.
65. Huntington Library, Stowe MSS 57, iv. 259: Brydges to Drummond, 16 Jan. 1711.
66. Thibaudeau, 2nd ser. ii. 83: Cardonnel to Watkins, 5 Jan. 1711; BL Add. MS 61423, fos. 79–80: SM to Hamilton [Jan. 1711].
67. BL Add. MS 61461, fo. 104: Maynwaring to SM [Jan. 1711]; Add. MS 61422, fo. 126: narrative by SM.
68. BL Add. MS 61422, fo. 121ᵛ: narrative by SM; Coxe, iii. 175–6: SM to Anne [17 Jan. 1711].
69. R. Pauli, *Aufsätze zur Englischen Geschichte*, new ser. (Leipzig, 1869–83), ii. 354.
70. BL Add. MS 61422, fo. 156: narrative by SM; Hamilton, 27.
71. Coxe, iii. 175–6: SM to Anne [17 Jan. 1711].
72. Hamilton, 29.
73. BL Add. MS 61422, fos. 119–20, 140: narratives by SM; *Letters and Correspondence . . . by the . . . Lord Visc. Bolingbroke*, ed. G. Parke (1798), i. 76, 79: to Drummond, 19, 23 Jan. 1711.
74. Burnet, vi. 33, Dartmouth's note.

Chapter 12: 1711–1712

1. BL Add. MS 61424, fos. 114–15: narrative by SM.
2. BL Add. MS 61420, fos. 102–3: SM to Treasury [1715–17].
3. BL Add. MS 61467, fo. 207: SM to Scrope, 22 Sept. 1744.
4. Gregg, *Queen Anne*, 328–9.
5. Bolingbroke, *Correspondence*, i. 25–7: to Drummond, 28 Nov. 1710.
6. Hamilton, p. xliv.
7. Burnet, vi. 34, Dartmouth's note.
8. Herts RO Panshanger MSS F228, p. 76: SM to Lady Cowper, 11 Mar. [1711].
9. Harris, 'Accounts of the Conduct', 14–16.
10. BL Add. MS 70331/1: Harley's 'Plaine English' (24 Aug. 1708), p. 21 (for the huge sums received by Marlborough from this deduction see his personal account with the army paymaster in BL Add. MS 61406); Bolingbroke, *Correspondence*, i. 81: to Drummond, 23 Jan. 1711.
11. BL Add. MS 61422, fo. 120: narrative by SM.
12. *MGC* 1662: Marlborough to SM, 5/16 Apr. 1711.
13. BL Stowe MS 751, fos. 5, 50: SM to Craggs, 20 July [1711], 2/13 June [1714].
14. Herts RO Panshanger MSS F223, p. 82: SM to Lady Cowper, 5 May 1711.
15. J[ohn] O[ldmixon], *The Life . . . of Arthur Maynwaring* (1715), 192–230; BL Add. MS 57861, fo. 162: Maynwaring to Coningsby, 5 June 1711; Add. MS 61461, fo. 137: Maynwaring to SM [June–July 1711].
16. BL Stowe MS 751, fos. 7–8: SM to Craggs, 28 July 1711.
17. Bodleian Library, Top. Oxon. c.218, fos. 55–6: SM to Bobart, 17 Apr., 7 Sept. 1711.
18. Churchill College, Erle–Drax MSS 2/40, fo. 74: Marlborough to Thomas Erle, 30 May/10 June 1711.
19. Herts RO Panshanger MSS F228, p. 85: SM to Lady Cowper, 23 June [1711].

20. HMC, *Portland MSS*, v. 24: Drummond to Oxford, 26 June/7 July 1711; *PC* ii. 77–8: Maynwaring to SM, [8] July 1711.

21. *Examiner*, 51 (12–19 July 1711).

22. BL Add. MS 61422, fos. 167–70; Thomson, ii. 514–19: narratives by SM, 1711; *PC* ii. 77–8: Maynwaring to SM, [8] July 1711.

23. HMC, *Portland MSS*, v. 56–7: Watkins to Drummond, 19/30 July 1711.

24. Sicco van Goslinga, *Mémoires relatifs à la Guerre de Succession de 1706–1709 et 1711* (Leeuwarden, 1857), 146–7; this undermines the thesis put forward by Michael Foot in *The Pen and the Sword* (1957), that Marlborough was duped by Oxford and St John.

25. BL Add. MS 61125, fo. 124ᵛ: note by SM on a letter drafted by Watkins.

26. HMC, *Portland MSS*, v. 50: Watkins to Drummond, 15/26 July 1711.

27. Rose, ii. 77–9: Stair to Marchmont, 10 Dec. 1736; HMC, *Portland MSS*, v. 43: Stair to Lord Mar, 12/23 July 1711.

28. BL Add. MS 61164, fo. 201: Craggs to Marlborough, 17 Aug. 1711; Add. MS 33273, fo. 98: Sutton to Watkins, 31 July 1711.

29. Herts RO Panshanger MSS F228, p. 90: SM to Lady Cowper [29 July 1711].

30. Green, *Blenheim Palace*, 106.

31. BL Add. MS 61461, fo. 125; *PC* ii. 67: Maynwaring to SM [9, 10 May 1711].

32. BL Add. MS 61450, fo. 77: SM to Duchess of Montagu, 12 May [1711].

33. HMC, *10th Report*, pt. 1, 144: Watkins to Drummond, 23 Aug./3 Sept. 1711.

34. Herts RO Panshanger MSS F228, p. 86: SM to Lady Cowper, 23 June [1711]; ibid. F63, fo. 136: SM to Cowper, 26 Feb. [1717]; Yale UL Osborn Collection: SM to Coningsby, 14 Sept. 1710; BL Althorp Papers D14: SM to Mallet, 24 Sept. 1744; BL Add. MS 61451, fo. 155: narrative by SM.

35. Oldmixon, *Maynwaring*, 331–8; Herts RO Panshanger MSS F228, p. 94: SM to Lady Cowper, 23 Aug. 1711.

36. Herts RO Panshanger MSS F228, p. 100: SM to Lady Cowper, 14 Sept. 1711.

37. BL Add. MS 61461, fo. 145: Maynwaring to SM [Aug.–Sept. 1711].

38. BL Trumbull Papers Add. 136: Bridges to Trumbull, 28 Sept. 1711; *Bouchain* (1711), 38–42. The author, who is still not known for certain, was generally assumed to be Marlborough's chaplain, Francis Hare, although he denied it (BL Add. MS 22201, fo. 1); for Maynwaring's part, see Oldmixon, *Maynwaring*, 324.

39. Bolingbroke, *Correspondence*, i. 365: to Harrison, 21 Sept. 1711.

40. *MGC* 1682: Marlborough to SM, 8/19 Oct. 1711; Coxe, iii. 255, 260–1: Marlborough to Oxford, 8/19 Oct. 1711; Bolingbroke, *Correspondence*, i. 413: to Anne, 17 Oct. 1711.

41. *MGC* 1684: Marlborough to SM, 11/22 Oct. 1711.

42. Herts RO Panshanger MSS F228, pp. 101–4: SM to Lady Cowper, 1, 3 Oct. [1711].

43. Ibid. pp. 104–5: 3, 24 Oct. 1711.

44. Cartwright, *Wentworth Papers*, 208: Lady to Lord Strafford, 15 Nov. 1711; BL Trumbull Papers Add. 136: Bridges to Trumbull, 5 Dec. 1711.

45. Herts RO Panshanger MSS F228, p. 79: SM to Cowper [18 Nov. 1711].

46. BL Add. MS 57861, fo. 170: Maynwaring to Coningsby, 27 Nov. 1711.

47. Foot, *Pen and the Sword*, 291–354.

48. BL Add. MS 61479, fo. 25: narrative by SM.

49. Cartwright, *Wentworth Papers*, 248: Wentworth to Strafford, 12 'Jan.' [Feb.] 1712; Herts RO Panshanger MSS F228, pp. 78–9: SM to Lady Cowper [8 Feb. 1712].

50. BL Add. MS 33225, fo. 116: Hare to Watkins, 11 Apr. 1712; Add. MS 28057, fo. 385: SM to Godolphin [3 Apr. 1712].
51. Harris, 'Accounts of the Conduct', 17–20.
52. Herts RO Panshanger MSS F228, p. 79: SM to Lady Cowper [12 Feb. 1712].
53. BL Add. MS 61424, fos. 82ᵛ, 100: notes by SM.
54. Herts RO Panshanger MSS F228, p. 33: SM to Lady Cowper [1712].
55. Lady Verney (ed.), *Verney Letters of the Eighteenth Century* (1930), i. 338: W. Vickers to Lord Fermanagh, 19 Aug. 1712.
56. Herts RO Panshanger MSS F228, p. 135: SM to Lady Cowper, 8 Aug. [1712].
57. Lever, *Godolphin*, 250–1; BL Add. MS 61434, fos. 158–61: Godolphin to SM [18–22 Aug. 1712].
58. BL Add. MS 61441, fos. 113, 117: Mrs Boscawen to SM, 11, [13?] Sept. [1712]; Herts RO Panshanger MSS F228, p. 137: SM to Lady Cowper [Sept. 1712].
59. Bodleian Library, Add. MS A. 191, fo. 5: SM to Burnet, 25 Sept. 1712.
60. Thomson, i. 472: inventory of SM's jewels.
61. E. Gregg, 'Marlborough in Exile 1712–1714', *Historical Journal*, 15 (1972), 594–9.
62. BL Add. MS 61475, fos. 47–53: anon. letter to SM, 7 Nov. 1712; Add. MS 61451, fo. 111: narrative by SM. This did not outwardly affect her relations with Craggs snr., who continued to be her close confidant.
63. Oldmixon, *Maynwaring*, 343.
64. Herts RO Panshanger MSS F73 and F79: Cowper's notes of SM's investments, 1712–15; *ML*, 47–8.
65. Green, *Sarah*, 183.
66. Herts RO Panshanger MSS F228, pp. 139–41: SM to Cowper [Jan. 1713].
67. PRO SP 44/113: Dartmouth to SM, 30 Jan. 1713.
68. BL Add. MS 61451, fo. 75: narrative by SM; Add. MS 61450, fo. 180: SM to Duchess of Montagu, 5 Jan. 1742.
69. Yale UL Osborn Collection: SM to Coningsby, 9 Jan. 1712[/3].

Chapter 13: 1713–1714

1. Herts RO Panshanger MSS F228, p. 152: SM to Lady Cowper, 6/17 Feb. 1713.
2. *ML* 26: SM to Jennens, 12/23 Feb. 1712[/13].
3. Gregg, 'Marlborough in Exile', 599–602.
4. Herts RO Panshanger MSS F228, pp. 155–6: SM to Lady Cowper, 29 Mar./9 Apr. [1713].
5. Ibid. pp. 156–7.
6. BL Add. MS 61475, fo. 65: SM to Kneller, 23 Apr./4 May [1713]; Yale UL Osborn Collection: SM to Coningsby, 28 May/8 June [1713].
7. *ML* 72, 99: SM to Jennens, [4/15] July, 21 Apr./2 May [1713].
8. BL Add. MS 61445, fo. 67: SM to Spencer, 7 July 1728.
9. BL Stowe MS 751, fo. 29: SM to Craggs, 21 Apr./2 May [1713] (italicized passage in cipher, decoded by Craggs).
10. Gregg, 'Marlborough in Exile', 602–3.
11. *ML* 32–3: SM to Jennens, 14/25 May 1713.
12. Herts RO Panshanger MSS F63, fo. 92: SM to Lady Cowper, 26 May/6 June [1713].
13. Yale UL Osborn Collection: SM to Coningsby, 28 May/8 June [1713]; BL Stowe MS 751, fo. 62: SM to Craggs, 14/25 June [1713].

14. *ML* 37, 41: SM to Jennens, [4/15] June [1713], 5/16 May [1714].
15. BL Add. MS 61475, fos. 63–4: list of SM's correspondents, [1713].
16. Herts RO Panshanger MSS F63, fo. 93: SM to Lady Cowper, 6/17 June [1713]; *ML* 51: SM to Jennens, 21 Feb./4 Mar. [1714].
17. Huntington Library, HM 44710, fo. 147: Hutcheson to Kreienberg, 2/13 Aug. 1713.
18. Harris, 'Accounts of the Conduct', 21–2.
19. *ML* 35–6: SM to Jennens, 5/16 May [1714].
20. Ibid. 73: SM to Jennens, 30 Aug./10 Sept. 1713.
21. Christ Church, Evelyn MSS: SM to Mrs Boscawen, 15/26 Sept. [1713].
22. *PC* ii. 94–6: Hare to SM, 20 Oct. 1713.
23. Christ Church, Evelyn MSS: SM to Mrs Boscawen, 15/26 Sept. [1713].
24. HMC, *Portland MSS*, v. 338: Drummond to Oxford, 18/29 Sept. 1713.
25. *ML* 60: SM to Jennens, 14/25 Jan. [1714].
26 Ibid. 75–6: 26 Sept./7 Oct. 1713.
27. Gregg, 'Marlborough in Exile', 604–7.
28. BL Add. MS 61463, fo. 116: SM to Mrs Clayton [early 1714].
29. *ML* 44: SM to Jennens, 27 Oct./7 Nov. [1713].
30. Herts RO Panshanger MSS F63, fo. 167: SM to Lady Cowper, 13/24 Feb. [1714].
31. *ML* 43: SM to Jennens, 27 Oct./7 Nov. [1713].
32. Ibid. 68: [4/15] July 1713.
33. BL Add. MS 61463, fo. 116: SM to Mrs Clayton [early 1714].
34. Christ Church, Evelyn MSS: SM to Mrs Boscawen, 17/28 Jan. 1713[/14].
35. BL Add. MS 62569, fo. 77; *ML* 53: SM to Jennens, 5/16 Dec. [1713], 14/25 Feb. [1714].
36. J. M. Kemble (ed.), *State Papers and Correspondence Illustrative of the . . . State of Europe from the Revolution to the Accession of the House of Hanover* (1857), 499–500: SM to Count Bonneval, 10/21 May 1714.
37. *ML* 58: SM to Jennens, 22 Jan./2 Feb. [1714]; Herts RO Panshanger MSS F63, fo. 167: SM to Lady Cowper, 13/24 Feb. [1714].
38. BL Stowe MS 751, fo. 49: SM to Craggs, 2/13 June [1714].
39. Longleat, Portland MSS, Misc. Box 2: extracts from a narrative by SM.
40. Christ Church, Evelyn MSS: SM to Mrs Boscawen, 14/25 Feb. 1713[/14].
41. BL Add. MS 61442, fo. 58: Lady Sunderland to SM, 26 Apr. [1714]; Stowe MS 751, fo. 29: SM to Craggs, 16/27 [June? 1714]; Stowe MS 227, fo. 222: Bothmer to Robethon, 16/27 July 1714.
42. Gregg, 'Marlborough in Exile', 612–15; BL Stowe MS 751, fo. 92: SM to Craggs, 12/23 May 1714.
43. BL Add. MS 61463, fo. 123: SM to Mrs Clayton [Mar. 1714].
44. *ML* 36–7: SM to Jennens, 5/16 May [1714]; BL Add. MS 61463, fo. 136: SM to Mrs Clayton, 13/24 June [1714].
45. Fitzmaurice, *Shelburne*, i. 99.
46. *ML* 97: SM to Jennens, 7/18 May 1714; *The Letters of Philip Dormer Stanhope, 4th Earl of Chesterfield*, ed. B. Dobrée (1932), ii. 10: to Berkeley, 29 May 1714.
47. BL Stowe MS 751, fo. 102: SM to Craggs, 12/23 June 1714; *ML* 107–9: SM to Jennens, 21 June/2 July 1714.
48. *ML*, 60–1: SM to Jennens, 14/25 Jan. [1714]; BL Add. MS 61465, fos. 1–3: Essex to SM, 8/19 Mar., 22 Mar./2 Apr. 1714.
49. Gregg, 'Marlborough in Exile', 613–14; Cartwright, *Wentworth Papers*, 402:

newsletter to Strafford, July 1714; HMC, *Portland MSS*, v. 662: 'Memoirs of the Harley Family'; Coxe, iii. 357–61: Molyneux to SM, May–June 1714.
50. Gregg, 'Marlborough in Exile', 614.
51. J. H. and M. Sheenan, 'The Protestant Succession in English Politics, April 1713–September 1715', in R. Hatton and J. S. Bromley (eds.), *William III and Louis XIV* (Liverpool, 1968), 258–9.
52. Herts RO Panshanger MSS F228, pp. 161–2: SM to Lady Cowper, 18/29 June [1714].
53. BL Stowe MS 751, fo. 108: SM to Craggs, 23 June/4 July [1714].
54. *PC* ii. 481: SM to Thomas Cooke, 6 Apr. 1742.
55. Macpherson, *Original Papers*, ii. 636: Bothmer to Robethon, 16/27 July 1714.
56. BL Add. MS 61463, fo. 137: SM to Mrs Clayton, 14/25 July [1714].
57. Christ Church, Evelyn MSS: SM to Mrs Boscawen, 23 Nov. [1714].
58. Coxe, iii. 374.

Chapter 14: 1714–1716

1. Longleat, Portland MSS, Misc. Box 2: extracts from a narrative by SM. Summaries of this narrative, which she called 'Queen Caroline's History', are in BL Add. MS 61418, fos. 222–6, but the original is now unlocated; these extracts are by Margaret, Duchess of Portland.
2. Macpherson, *Original Papers*, ii. 640: Bothmer to Bernsdorff, 6/17 Aug. 1714.
3. BL Add. MS 61451, fo. 57: narrative by SM.
4. *ML* 112–13: SM to Jennens, 10, 23 Aug. 1714; Yale UL Osborn Collection: SM to Coningsby, 15 Aug. [1714].
5. BL Stowe MS 751, fo. 110: SM to Craggs, 25 June/6 July [1714].
6. Longleat, Portland MSS, Misc. Box 2: extracts from a narrative by SM.
7. Herts RO Panshanger MSS F230, p. 12: SM to Lady Cowper [Sept. 1714].
8. Longleat, Portland MSS, Misc. Box 1: extracts from a narrative by SM.
9. Ibid.; cf. Montagu, i. 79.
10. J. M. Beattie, *The English Court in the Reign of George I* (Cambridge, 1967), 158–9.
11. *PC* ii. 105–6: SM to Mrs Clayton, [Oct.] 1714.
12. Montagu, i. 125; Beattie, *English Court*, 56.
13. Coxe, iii. 376.
14. BL Trumbull Papers, lii: Bateman to Trumbull, 7 Jan. 1715; E. Gregg, *The Protestant Succession in International Politics* (New York, 1986), 264.
15. *Memoirs*, 265; Herts RO Panshanger MSS F63, fo. 72: SM to Lady Cowper [early 1715].
16. BL Add. MS 61420, fos. 102–3: SM to Treasury [1715–17].
17. *Memoirs*, 5, 265–6.
18. Harris, 'Accounts of the Conduct', 23–7.
19. W. Michael, *England under George I: The Beginnings of the Hanoverian Dynasty* (1936), 374: Bonnet's dispatch, 24 Dec./4 Jan. 1714/15.
20. Montagu, i. 110–11.
21. BL Stowe MS 751, fo. 122: SM to Craggs, 28 July [1716].
22. *ML* 117: SM to Jennens, 13 Dec. 1714; Christ Church, Evelyn MSS: SM to Mrs Boscawen, 25 Feb. 1715.
23. HMC, *Buccleuch MSS (Montagu House)*, i. 361: Lady Sunderland to Duchess of Montagu [late 1714].

24. Longleat, Portland MSS, Misc. Box 2: extracts from a narrative by SM; Hearne, *Remarks and Collections*, vi. 236.

25. BL Add. MS 61442, fo. 64: Lady Sunderland to SM [12 Apr. 1715].

26. *PC* ii. 469: SM to Hare [Aug. 1726]; Montagu, i. 111; *Memoirs*, 268.

27. BL Stowe MS 751, fos. 123–4: SM to Craggs, 28 July [1716].

28. Graham, i. 292–3: SM to Stair, 22 Feb. 1715.

29. BL Add. MS 61451, fo. 77: narrative by SM; Add. MS 61353, fo. 217: SM to Vanbrugh [8 Nov. 1716].

30. BL Add. MS 61451, fo. 86^v.

31. Christ Church, Evelyn MSS: Lady Godolphin to Lady Evelyn, 9 July [1718].

32. BL Add. MS 61451, fo. 85^v.

33. BL Add. MS 61450, fo. 85: Duchess of Montagu to SM [Apr. 1716].

34. BL Add. MSS 61451, fos. 86–90.

35. BL Add. MS 61431, fo. 201: Marlborough to SM [summer 1715].

36. HMC, *Stuart MSS*, i. 407: Pretender to Bolingbroke, 28 Aug. 1715; Gregg, 'Marlborough in Exile', 617.

37. BL Add. MS 62570, fos. 13–17: SM to Jennens, 13, 17 Sept. [1715].

38. BL Add. MS 61472, fo. 189: SM's 'Account of my Money', 15 Sept. 1715; Add. MS 61466, fo. 185: narrative by Lady Blayney (Coxe, iii. 387, incorrectly cites this as stating that Marlborough lent the money); Cowper, *Diary of Mary*, 184: SM to Lady Cowper, 1 Oct. 1715.

39. *ML* 121: SM to Jennens, 2 Sept. 1715.

40. F. Harris, 'Parliament and Blenheim Palace', *Parliamentary History*, 8 (1989), 45–6; BL Add. MS 38056, fo. 3: SM to Pengelly, 30 Nov. 1720.

41. BL Add. MS 61431, fos. 203–8: Marlborough to SM [Sept.–Oct. 1715]; *ML* 122: SM to Jennens, 15 Nov. 1715.

42. Bristol, *Letter-books*, ii. 18–20: Lady to Lord Bristol, 8, 10 Apr. 1716; BL Add. MS 32679, fo. 33: SM to Newcastle [24 Sept. 1717].

43. Coxe, iii. 397: SM to Sunderland, 13 May 1716.

44. Huntington Library, Stowe MSS 57, xiv. 11–12, 71–2, 89–90: Brydges to Bladen and Hammond, 17 Apr., 31 May, 12 June 1716.

45. BL Stowe MS 751, fos. 122, 158: SM to Craggs, 28 July, 24 Sept. [1716].

46. Herts RO Panshanger MSS F63, fos. 162–3: SM to Lady Cowper, 3 Sept. 1716.

47. Cowper, *Diary of Mary*, 122–3.

48. BL Stowe MS 751, fos. 122–3, 130: SM to Craggs, 28 July, 1 Sept. [1716].

49. BL Add. MS 61352, fo. 67: narrative by SM; Add. MS 61443, fos. 62–3: Sunderland to SM, 20/31 Oct. 1716.

50. BL Stowe MS 751, fos. 131–3, 166–7, 174: SM to Craggs, 3, 29 Sept., 1, 5 Oct. 1716; Add. MS 61352, fos. 61–70: narrative by SM.

51. Vanbrugh, iv. 68–81: to SM, June–Oct. 1716; Green, *Blenheim Palace*, 170, 303–4; Thomson, ii. 532–3; BL Stowe MS 751, fos. 140, 145–6: SM to Craggs, 7, 13 Sept. 1716.

52. Coxe, iii. 415: SM to Mrs Clayton [Oct. 1716]; *ML* 166: SM to Mrs Jennens, 21 Aug. 1725.

53. BL Stowe MS 751, fos. 153, 175, 185: SM to Craggs [20 Sept.], 9, 14 Oct. 1716; Green, *Blenheim Palace*, 141–3.

54. BL Add. MS 61451, fos. 77–8, narrative by SM; Stowe MS 751, fo. 172: SM to Craggs, 5 Oct. 1716; Vanbrugh, iv. 83–4: to SM, 6 Nov. 1716.

55. Vanbrugh, iv. 90, 85: to [Carlisle], [1717]; to SM, 8 Nov. 1716.

56. Ibid. iv. 89: to [Carlisle], [1717].

57. BL Stowe MS 751, fo. 191: SM to Craggs, 7 Nov. [1716].
58. BL Add. MS 61463, fo. 154: SM to Mrs Clayton [Oct.–Nov. 1716]; Christ Church, Evelyn MSS: Mrs Boscawen to Lady Evelyn, 13 Nov. 1716.
59. BL Add. MS 61451, fos. 91–2: narrative by SM.
60. Ibid. fos. 79–80, 89.

Chapter 15: 1717–1720

1. Longleat, Portland MSS, Misc. Box 1: extracts from a narrative by SM.
2. BL Add. MS 61351, fo. 18: SM to Cadogan, 17 Dec. 1716.
3. Coxe, iii. 399.
4. BL Stowe MS 751, fos. 129, 133, 189, 212: SM to Craggs, 1, 3 Sept., 6 Oct., 5 Nov. 1716; Add. MS 61451, fo. 60^v: narrative by SM.
5. BL Add. MS 61451, fo. 115^v.
6. BL Add. MS 61443, fos. 65–7: SM to Sunderland, with reply, 9 June 1717.
7. BL Add. MS 32679, fo. 50: SM to Newcastle, 1 Nov. [1717].
8. Ibid. fos. 49–51; Add. MS 61441, fo. 30: note by SM.
9. Swift, *Correspondence*, ii. 273: Lewis to Swift, 2 July 1717; HMC, *Portland MSS*, v. 668: 'Memoirs of the Harley Family'.
10. HMC, *Beaufort MSS*, 97: Somerset to Lady A. Coventry, 2 July 1717.
11. BL Add. MS 61443, fos. 73–8: Bishop Trimnell to SM, with reply, 15, [18] Sept. [1717].
12. Ibid.; Add. MS 61441, fo. 26: SM to Newcastle, 16 Oct. 1717.
13. BL Add. MS 61443, fos. 104–5: Sunderland to SM, 14, 25 Oct. 1717; Add. MS 32679, fos. 39, 42: SM to Newcastle, 13, 15 Oct. 1717; HMC, *Portland MSS*, v. 534: newsletter, 7 Nov. 1717.
14. R. Hatton, *George I* (1978), 206–8; Beattie, *English Court*, 272–4; BL Add. MS 61466, fo. 185: narrative by Lady Blayney.
15. Longleat, Portland MSS, Misc. Box 1: extracts from a narrative by SM.
16. BL Add. MS 61351, fo. 50: SM to Cadogan, 24 Apr. 1718; Add. MS 61352, fo. 53: narrative by SM.
17. BL Add. MS 61471, fo. 11: SM to Lady Stanhope, 9 Nov. 1717.
18. BL Stowe MS 751, fo. 124: SM to Craggs, 28 July [1716].
19. Graham, ii. 363: Craggs jr. to Stair, 11 May 1718.
20. BL Add. MS 61450, fos. 129–31: SM to Duchess of Montagu, 24 July 1718.
21. Christ Church, Evelyn MSS: Mrs Boscawen and Lady Godolphin to Lady Evelyn, 8, 9 July [1718].
22. Ibid.: SM to Mrs Boscawen, 7 Sept. 1718; Vanbrugh, iv. 112: to Tonson, 1 July 1719.
23. Christ Church, Evelyn MSS: SM to Mrs Boscawen, 27 Aug. 1719.
24. Yale UL Osborn Collection: SM to Coningsby, 'Saturday morning' [Sept. 1718]; Christ Church, Evelyn MSS: SM to Mrs Boscawen, 20 Sept. 1718.
25. Thibaudeau, 1st ser. iv. 153: SM to Mary Godolphin [27 Sept. 1718]; *ML* 129–31: SM to Jennens, 29 Sept. [1718].
26. BL Stowe MS 751, fo. 161: SM to Craggs, 26 Sept. [1716]; Christ Church, Evelyn MSS: Mrs Boscawen to Lady Evelyn, 20 Jan. 1719.
27. Hervey, 290: SM to Henry Fox, 23 Nov. 1732; BL Add. MS 61451, fo. 147: narrative by SM; *LG* 51–2: SM to Duchess of Bedford, 21 July 1732; BL Add. MS 61445, fos. 35, 39: SM to Fish, 25 Mar., 12 Apr. 1728.
28. Christ Church, Evelyn MSS: Elizabeth Godolphin to Lady Evelyn, 29 Oct. 1716; Sir John to Lady Evelyn, 20 Jan. 1719.

29. Ibid.: SM to Mrs Boscawen, 6 June 1719; BL Add. MS 61440, fo. 24: Rialton to SM, 9/20 Jan. 1720.

30. BL G.14844: *An Account of the Conduct of the Dowager Duchess of Marlborough* (1742), 'Postscript', 16–18.

31. BL Add. MS 61466, fo. 185ᵛ: narrative by Lady Blayney.

32. Devon RO Seymour MSS L18, 23/28: SM to Somerset, 3 Oct. 1723.

33. *Sotheby's Catalogue*, 5–10 April 1869, lot 675: SM to Mary Godolphin, 6 Nov. 1718; Leics RO Finch MSS, Bundle 27: Finch to Nottingham, 20 Dec. 1720.

34. Montagu, i. 114.

35. BL Add. MS 61466, fo. 164: Lady Blayney to Duchess of Marlborough, 25 Feb. 1772.

36. Yale UL Osborn Collection: SM to Coningsby, 25 July 1719; [R. Heathcote] (ed.), *Sylva, or the Wood* (1786), 243: SM to Samuel Clarke, [4 July 1719].

37. Graham, ii. 135–6: SM to Stair, 9 'Nov.' [Aug.] 1719.

38. BL Add. MS 61443, fo. 62: Sunderland to SM, 20 Oct. 1716.

39. Coxe, iii. 417–19; [J. Duncombe] (ed.), *Letters by Several Eminent Persons . . . including the Correspondence of John Hughes* (1773), i. 292 (episode misdated 1718).

40. Leics RO Finch MSS, Bundle 26: SM to Nottingham, 6 July [1719]; Yale UL Osborn Collection: SM to Coningsby, 3, 11 July 1719.

41. Christ Church, Evelyn MSS: Mrs Boscawen to Lady Evelyn, 19 Jan 1720; Lady Medows to Lady Evelyn, 22 Dec.1719; SM to Mrs Boscawen, 11 Oct. 1720.

42. BL Add. MS 61451, fo. 60; Add. MS 61478, fo. 154: narratives by SM; Christ Church, Evelyn MSS: SM to Mrs Boscawen, 11 Oct. 1720; BL Add. MS 61466, fo. 177: Lady Blayney to Cuninghame, 24 Oct. 1777.

43. Christ Church, Evelyn MSS: Lady Medows to Lady Evelyn, 22 Dec.1719; diary of Sir John Evelyn, 17 March 1720.

44. BL Add. MS 61447, fo. 14: narrative by SM; Add. MS 70148: Abigail Pye to Abigail Harley, 21 Apr. 1720; BL Add. MS 61443, fo. 118: Sunderland to SM, 2 July 1719.

45. BL Add. MS 61451, fos. 159–60; Add. MS 61471, fos. 73–4: narratives by SM; Add. MS 61655, fo. 47: SM to Sunderland, 14 Feb. 1720.

46. Herts RO Panshanger MSS F63, fo. 165: SM to Cowper [Dec. 1712]; BL Add. MS 61472, fo. 194: SM's 'Account of my Mony', 4 July 1717.

47. Longleat, Portland MSS, Misc. Box 1: extracts from a narrative by SM.

48. J. Carswell, *The South Sea Bubble* (1960), 114–15.

49. BL Add. MS 61456, fo. 169: Lady Pembroke to SM [summer 1720].

50. Carswell, *South Sea Bubble*, 154–5; Coxe, iii. 403; BL Add. MS 61471, fo. 84: note by SM.

51. BL Add. MS 61463, fos. 165–6: SM to Mrs Clayton, 12 Aug. [1720].

52. Ibid. fo. 159: SM to Clayton [summer 1720]; Christ Church, Evelyn MSS: SM to Mrs Boscawen, 11 Oct. 1720.

53. BL Add. MS 61456, fo. 169: Lady Pembroke to SM [summer 1720].

54. BL Add. MS 61463, fo. 159: SM to Clayton [summer 1720].

55. Huntington Library, Stowe MSS 57, xvii. 195: Chandos to SM, 29 Sept. 1720; Christ Church, Evelyn MSS: diary of Sir John Evelyn, 3 Mar. 1720; BL Add. MS 61456, fos. 156–69: Lady Pembroke to SM [1720]; Add. MS 61655, fos. 51–8; Add. MS 61443, fos. 128–40: letters between SM and Sunderland, June–Aug. 1720.

56. Longleat, Portland MSS, Misc. Box 1: extracts from a narrative by SM.

57. BL Add. MS 61443, fo. 140: Sunderland to SM, 8 Aug. 1720; History of Parliament, *The House of Commons 1715–1754*, ed. R. Sedgwick (1970), i. 30.
58. Lord Stanhope, *History of England . . . 1713–1783*, 3rd edn. (1853), i. appendix, p. xciii; W. Coxe, *Memoirs of . . . Sir Robert Walpole* (1798), ii. 189: Craggs jr. to Stanhope, 15, 19 July 1720.
59. Coxe, iii. 420: SM to Mrs Clayton, 9 July 1720.
60. Christ Church, Evelyn MSS: SM to Mrs Boscawen, 11 Oct. 1720.
61. Ibid.
62. Ibid.: 28 Aug. 1720; BL Add. MS 61463, fos. 161, 163: SM to Mrs Clayton, 9 July [Sept. 1720].
63. Christ Church, Evelyn MSS: SM to Mrs Boscawen, 11 Oct. 1720.
64. BL Add. MS 61418, fo. 206: narrative by SM.
65. BL Add. MS 61451, fo. 95: narrative by SM.
66. Ibid.; BL Add. MS 61418, fos. 206, 210ᵛ: narratives by SM; Add. MS 61463, fos. 175–6: SM to Mrs Clayton, [Dec. 1720].
67. HMC, *Stuart MSS*, iii. 251: J. Menzies to C. Kinnaird, 13 Nov. 1716.
68. BL Add. MS 61466, fos. 185–6; Add. MS 61418, fo. 207: narratives by Lady Blayney and SM.

Chapter 16: 1721–1722

1. *CTB 1714–15*, 292, 344, 737.
2. BL Add. MS 61464, fo. 102: SM to Blackburne, 18 Apr. 1721.
3. BL Add. MS 61655, fos. 66–7: SM to Sunderland, 12 Aug. 1720; Add. MS 61443, fos. 145–6: Sunderland to SM, 16 Aug. 1720; Leics RO Finch MSS DG7, Box 4969, Bundle Law 51, No. 9: 'Memorandums' by SM [1721].
4. BL Add. MS 38056, fo. 7: SM to Pengelly, 16 Feb. 1721.
5. Vanbrugh, iv. 191–2; BL Add. MS 38056, fo. 103: Vanbrugh's deposition, 1720.
6. BL Add. MS 38056, fo. 68: SM's instructions to counsel, Feb. 1721.
7. BL Add. MS 61356, fo. 93: SM to the Lords, Apr. 1721.
8. BL Add. MS 61436, f 10: SM to Godolphin, 26 Apr. 1721.
9. BL Add. MS 61465, fo. 40: Carlisle to SM, 5 Mar. [1721].
10. BL Add. MS 61464, fos. 130, 142: SM to Blackburne, 5, 16 May 1721.
11. BL Add. MS 61464, fos. 123, 128, 138: SM to Blackburne, 3, 4, 12 May 1721; Huntington Library, Stowe MSS 57, xviii. 232–3: Chandos to Harcourt, 11 Apr. 1721; BL Add. MS 61463, fo. 18: Chandos to SM, 1 May 1721; Add. MS 61475, fo. 177: Atterbury to SM [?21 Apr. 1721].
12. Leics RO Finch MSS DG7, Box 4969, Bundle Law 51, No. 15: SM to Nottingham, 13 Apr. 1721; BL Add. MS 61464, fos. 123, 145: SM to Blackburne, 3, 16 May 1721.
13. Vanbrugh, iv. 133: to Carlisle, 22 Apr. 1721.
14. BL Add. MS 61436, fos. 10–12: SM to Godolphin, 26 Apr. 1721.
15. Herts RO Panshanger MSS F63, fo. 154: SM to Cowper, 6 May 1721.
16. BL Add. 61356, fos. 95–102; Harris, 'Parliament and Blenheim Palace', 50–1.
17. In the BL copy (115. k. 23) the references to SM in the title and text have been obliterated and therefore do not appear in Vanbrugh, iv. 177–92, which was reprinted from it.
18. BL Add. MS 61464, fos. 124, 132, 134: SM to Blackburne, 3, 7, 9 May 1721; Add. MS 61466, fo. 97: Lady Cairnes to SM [?9 May 1721].

19. *Lords Journals*, xxi. 513; BL Add. MS 61464, fos. 134, 138, 140: SM to Blackburne, 9, 12 May 1721; Vanbrugh, iv. 134: to Carlisle, 25 May 1721.

20. BL Add. MS 61464, fos. 122, 134: SM to Blackburne, 3, 9 May 1721.

21. Vanbrugh, iv. 134: to Carlisle, 25 May 1721; BL Add. MS 61465, fo. 53: Lady Lechmere to SM, 2 Sept. 1721.

22. BL Add. MS 61464, fos. 148, 157: SM to Blackburne, 7, 26 May 1721; Add. MS 61463, fo. 185: SM to Mrs Clayton, 9 Oct. 1722.

23. G. V. Bennett, *The Tory Crisis in Church and State* (Oxford, 1975), 226–9; HMC, *Portland MSS*, v. 616: Harley to Oxford, 18 Feb. 1721.

24. BL Add. MS 61451, fo. 155: narrative by SM.

25. Herts RO Panshanger MSS F63, fo. 152: SM to Cowper, 6 May 1721.

26. Mrs Clayton's account of the settlement, sold at Bloomsbury Book Auctions, 25 Oct. 1990, lot 157.

27. BL Add. MS 61464, fo. 104: SM to Blackburne, 28 Apr. 1721; Green, *Blenheim Palace*, 152.

28. BL Add. MS 54225, fos. 143–4: SM to [Godolphin], 2 Aug. 1721.

29. BL Add. MS 61466, fos. 99–100, 102: SM to Lady Cairnes, 29 Sept. [1721].

30. BL Egerton MS 2540, fo. 187: Clarke to Nicholas, 19 Sept. 1721.

31. HMC, *Portland MSS*, vii. 305, 318: Stratford to Harley, 29 Oct. 1721, 23 Mar. 1722; *Transactions of the Birmingham and Midland Institute, Archaeological Section*, xii (1884–5), 9: SM to Townesend, 17 Oct. 1722.

32. Thibaudeau, 1st ser. iv. 155: SM to Godolphin [18 July 1719].

33. HMC, *Verulam MSS*, 117–19: case of Grimston and Lomax [1722].

34. Vanbrugh, iv. 149: to Carlisle, 19 July 1722.

35. HMC, *Verulam MSS*, 117–19.

36. BL Add. MS 61465, fos. 102–4: Lady Lechmere to SM, 15, 17 Oct. 1722.

37. BL Add. MS 61463, fo. 185: SM to Mrs Clayton, 9 Oct. 1722.

38. BL Add. MS 61451, fos. 97–9: narrative by SM; Churchill, ii. 1034–5: letters between Marlborough and Duchess of Montagu, 1, 2 Jan. 1721[/2].

39. BL Add. MS 61443, fos. 151–3: narratives by SM, 1722.

40. HMC, *10th Report*, pt. 4, 345: Johnston to Grahme, 26 May 1722; BL Add. MS 61466, fo. 165: Lady Blayney to Duchess of Marlborough, 25 Feb. 1772; Rowse, *Later Churchills*, 13.

41. Lord March, *A Duke and his Friends* (1911), i. 55: Duchess to 2nd Duke of Richmond, 6 Dec. 1721.

42. BL Add. MS 61444, fo. 9: SM to Sunderland [May 1722].

43. Ibid. fos. 9–10.

44. BL Add. MS 61451, fo. 159: narrative by SM.

45. Coxe, *Walpole*, iii. 312: Hervey to Walpole, 23 Dec. 1735.

46. Christ Church, Evelyn MSS: Mrs Boscawen to Lady Evelyn, 13 Oct. 1716.

47. BL Add. MS 61451, fos. 99–102: narrative by SM; cf. Churchill, ii. 1037, and Butler, *Rule of Three*, 301–2.

48. *ML* 137: SM to Mrs Jennens [July 1722].

49. *Memoirs*, 266.

50. BL Add. MS 61451, fos. 1–106.

51. BL Add. MS 61441, fo. 143: Mrs Boscawen to SM, 1 Sept. [1722].

52. Pierpont Morgan Library: SM to Clarke [July 1722].

53. BL Add. MS 61466, fos. 179, 183: Lady Blayney to Cuninghame, 24 Oct. 1772, 21 May 1778; Bristol, *Letter-books*, ii. 217, 219: Lord to Lady Bristol, 8, 13 Aug. 1722.

54. Christ Church, Evelyn MSS: SM to Mrs Boscawen, 10, 11 Sept. 1722.
55. H. S. Hughes, *The Gentle Hertford* (New York, 1940), 70; J. Sutherland, *Background to Queen Anne* (1939), 212–22.

Chapter 17: 1722–1725

1. BL Add. MS 61436, fo. 119: SM to Godolphin [Nov. 1724]; Add. MS 61451, fo. 173: narrative by SM.
2. BL Althorp Papers D9: Marlborough's will, 19 March 1721[/2].
3. BL Add. MS 61451, fos. 102–3: narrative by SM.
4. *MGC* 176: Marlborough to SM, 23 Apr./4 May 1703.
5. BL Add. MS 61446, fo. 120: SM to Marlborough, 19 Sept. 1734.
6. BL Add. MS 61436, fo. 119: SM to Godolphin [Nov. 1724].
7. BL Add. MS 61451, fo. 147: narrative by SM; Add. MS 61465, fo. 108: Lady Lechmere to SM, 30 Oct. 1722.
8. BL Add. MS 61476, fo. 10: Clarke to SM, 24 July 1722.
9. BL Add. MS 61449, fos. 21–3: Bridgwater to Lady A. Egerton [19 Aug. 1722], with SM's reply; Add. MS 61466, fo. 173: SM to Lady Cairnes, 21 Aug. 1722.
10. BL Add. MS 61466, fos. 10, 139: Jane Guidott to SM, 10 Aug. 1722; Diana Spencer to Marie La Vie, 16 Sept. 1722.
11. Leics RO Finch MSS DG7, Box 4969, Bundle Law 51, No. 11: notes by SM, 1721; Green, *Blenheim Palace*, 309–10: Hawksmoor to SM, 17 Apr. 1722.
12. BL Add. MS 61466, fo. 108: SM to Lady Cairnes, 29 Sept. 1722.
13. Ibid. fo. 107.
14. BL Add. MS 61463, fo. 184: SM to Mrs Clayton, 9 Oct. 1722.
15. BL Add. MS 61466, fo. 111: SM to Lady Cairnes, 16 Oct. 1722.
16. BL Add. 61466, fo. 108: SM to Lady Cairnes, 29 Sept. 1722; Add. MS 61463, fo. 67: Coningsby to SM, 10 Dec. 1722.
17. BL Add. MS 61466, fos. 67–70: narrative by SM, 24 Oct. 1722.
18. *ML* 146; BL Add. MS 61466, fo. 15: SM to Mrs Jennens, 25, 29 Nov. 1722.
19. BL Althorp Papers D39: valuation of Marlborough's estate, in *1st Duke's Trustees* v. *3rd Duke*, 5 June 1738; P. G. M. Dickson, *The Financial Revolution in England* (1967), 432.
20. BL Add. MS 61436, fos. 22–3: Godolphin to SM, with reply, 3, 4 Dec. 1722.
21. Ibid. fos. 40–1: 23, 30 April 1723.
22. Devon RO Seymour MSS L18, 23/7: SM to Somerset [22 July 1723].
23. BL Add. MS 61476, fos. 40, 46: Kellum to SM [early 1723]; SM to Clarke, 12 May 1723.
24. BL Add. MS 61441, fo. 145: Mrs Boscawen to SM, 5 Sept. [1722].
25. BL Add. MS 61451, fo. 173: narrative by SM.
26. BL Add. MS 61466, fos. 180–1: Lady Blayney to Cuninghame, 24 Oct. 1777.
27. BL Add. MS 61449, fos. 37–9; Add. MS 61451, fo. 131: narratives by SM; Green, *Sarah*, 238–9.
28. Bristol, *Letter-books*, ii. 269, 276, 316, 330: letters between Lord and Lady Bristol, 24 Apr., 1 May, 30 June, 16 Sept. 1723; BL Add. MS 61457, fos. 135–74: letters between SM and the same, 1711–19.
29. BL Stowe MS 751, fo. 19: SM to Craggs, 10/21 June [1713]; Cowper, *Diary of Mary*, 184: SM to Lady Cowper, 1 Oct. 1715.
30. Leics RO Finch MSS, Bundle 27: Lady to Lord Nottingham, 28 July 1722.
31. Devon RO Seymour MSS L18, 22/1: SM to Lady A. Harvey, 26 Nov. 1722.

32. Montagu, i. 77.
33. Butler, *Rule of Three*, 304–5.
34. BL Add. MS 61456, fo. 97: Lady Burlington to SM, 14 Oct. 1723.
35. BL Add. MS 61457, fo. 23: Somerset to SM, 2 Aug. 1723.
36. Devon RO Seymour MSS L18, 23/24, 23/27: SM to Somerset, 20 Aug., 20 Sept. 1723. The lines were by the Oxford clergyman, Dr Abel Evans.
37. BL Add. MS 61457, fos. 27–30: SM to Somerset, 20 Aug. 1723 (draft partly in Fish's hand).
38. Devon RO Seymour MSS L18, 23/24, 23/26: SM to Somerset, 20, 30 Aug. 1723.
39. Ibid. 23/28: SM to Somerset, 3 Oct. 1723; BL Add. MS 61466, fo. 190: Hanbury to SM, 5 Nov. [1723]; Bristol, *Letter-books*, ii. 329–35: Lady to Lord Bristol, 14, 16, 18, 21 Sept. 1723.
40. Devon RO Seymour MSS L18, 23/30: SM to Somerset, 11 Oct. [1723];
41. HMC *Portland MSS*, vii. 366: Stratford to Oxford, 16 Oct. 1723; BL Egerton MS 2540, fo. 223: Clarke to Nicholas, 20 Oct. 1723.
42. BL Add. MS 61457, fos. 61, 66: Somerset to SM, 1, 16 Dec. 1723.
43. Devon RO Seymour MSS L18, 23/4, 24/25: SM to Somerset, 2, [4] Jan. 1723[/4]; BL Add. MS 61457, fo. 82: Somerset to SM, 2 Jan. 1723[/4].
44. Devon RO Seymour MSS L18, 23/42: SM to Somerset [28 Dec. 1723].
45. BL Add. MS 61436, fo. 123: Godolphin to SM, 18 Nov. 1724.
46. Ibid. fos. 94–5, 97: 15, 21 Mar. 1724.
47. BL Add. MS 61471, fo. 90^v: list of Trust estates, 1723–4; Christ Church, Evelyn MSS: diary of Sir John Evelyn, 9 June 1722 (for Wimbledon); BL Althorp Papers D17: SM's lists of her estates.
48. *LG* 67: SM to Duchess of Bedford, 30 Aug. 1732.
49. BL Add. MS 38056, fos. 112–13; *Lords Journals*, xxii. 270; Devon RO Seymour MSS L18, 24/7: SM to Somerset, 1 Mar. 1724; BL Stowe MS 750, fo. 412: Somerset to Macclesfield, 1 Mar. 1724.
50. BL Add. MS 61356, fos. 159–70: Chancery decree, 9 June 1724; Vanbrugh, iv. 170: to Tonson, 25 Oct. 1725.
51. Devon RO Seymour MSS L18, 24/11: SM to Somerset, 10 June [1724].
52. BL Add. MS 38056, fos. 16–17: SM to Pengelly, 25, 28 June 1724.
53. *ML*, 150–1: SM to Jennens, 17 July 1725; BL Add. MS 29549, fo. 126: SM to Winchilsea, 16 Nov. 1725.
54. BL Add. MS 61457, fos. 97, 103: Somerset to SM, 25 Feb., 3 May 1724.
55. HMC, *Portland MSS*, vii. 380: Stratford to Oxford, 1 July 1724; BL Add. MS 61466, fo. 118: SM to Lady Cairnes, 27 Aug. [1724].
56. BL Add. MS 61456, fo. 101: Lady Burlington to SM, 3 Sept. [1724].
57. BL Add. MS 61469, fos. 68–82: letters between SM and Harcourt, 1724; HMC, *Portland MSS*, vii. 384, 386: Stratford to Oxford, 1, 17 Oct. 1724.
58. BL Add. MS 61466, fo. 124: SM to Lady Cairnes, 5 Sept. 1724.
59. Devon RO Seymour MSS L18, 23/30: SM to Somerset, 11 Oct. [1723].
60. Ibid. 23/2, 24/25: SM to Somerset, 7 Feb. [4 Jan. 1724].
61. BL Add. MS 61451, fo. 131: narrative by SM.
62. BL Add. MS 61440, fos. 43, 46: Blandford and Mann to SM, 8/19, 9/20 May 1724.
63. Ibid. fo. 38: Blandford to SM, 8/19 Apr. 1723.
64. Christ Church, Evelyn MSS: Mann to Mrs Boscawen, 3/14 Mar. 1724.
65. BL Add. MS 61440, fos. 47–9, 54, 74: SM to Blandford and Mann, 25, 26 May 1724; Blandford to SM, 29 July/9 Aug. 1724.

66. BL Add. MS 61466, fos. 122–3: SM to Lady Cairnes, 5 Sept. 1724.
67. Christ Church, Evelyn MSS: SM to Mrs Boscawen, 'Thursday evening' [Jan.–Feb. 1725].
68. Ibid.: Mann to Mrs Boscawen, 4/15 June 1725.
69. BL Add. MS 61456, fo. 102: Lady Burlington to SM, 3 Sept. [1724].
70. BL Add. MS 61449, fo. 49: SM to Lady A. Egerton, 25 Dec. 1724.
71. BL Add. MS 61469, fo. 85: Harcourt to SM, 4 Mar. 1725; Add. MS 61451, fo. 132: narrative by SM.
72. BL Add. MS 61449, fos. 51–7: Bedford to SM, 12, 27 Apr. 1725.
73. Bedford Office: SM to Bedford, 5 May 1725.
74. BL Add. MS 61449, fos. 60–2, 72: Bedford to SM, [May 1725]; March, *A Duke and his Friends*, i. 141.
75. *ML* 152–3: SM to Jennens, 25 July 1725.
76. BL Add. MS 61449, fos. 64, 72, 74: Bedford to SM, 13 May, 10 June, 4 July 1725.
77. *ML* 166: SM to Mrs Jennens, 21 Aug. 1725.
78. E. W. Harcourt (ed.), *Harcourt Papers* (Oxford, [1880–1905]), ii. 194–5: Elizabeth Harcourt to Evelyn, 18 Sept. 1725; BL Egerton MS 2540, fo. 461: Clarke to Nicholas, 30 Sept. 1725; Add. MS 61457, fo. 109: Somerset to SM, 5 Oct. 1725.

Chapter 18: 1726–1730

1. Devon RO Seymour MSS L18, 23/44: SM to Somerset, 10 Dec. 1723.
2. BL Add. MS 61440, fo. 69: SM to Blandford, 10 Jan. 1724[/5].
3. BL Add. MS 61457, fos. 108, 111–13: Somerset to SM, 29 July 1725, 5 Feb. 1726, with reply.
4. BL Add. MS 61447, fo. 129: Lady A. Bateman to SM, 2/13 June 1724; Add. MS 61440, fo. 64: Mann to SM, 12/23 Sept. 1724.
5. Christ Church, Evelyn MSS: Mann to Mrs Boscawen, 9/20 March 1725.
6. BL Add. MSS 61444, fos. 97, 137; 61445, fo. 33: SM to Fish, 1 Feb., 26 June 1727, 29 Feb. 1728; Rowse, *Later Churchills*, 8–13.
7. HMC, *Ailesbury MSS*, 232: Ailesbury to Bruce, 26 Nov. 1727.
8. Montagu, ii. 190–1: Lady Mary Wortley Montagu to Lady Mar [Aug. 1725].
9. BL Egerton MS 2540, fo. 570: Clarke to Nicholas, 3 Feb. 1726.
10. BL Add. MS 61451, fo. 133: narrative by SM; Add. MS 61449, fo. 102: SM to Duchess of Bedford, 8 Nov. 1726.
11. BL Add. MS 61445, fo. 11: SM to Fish, 21 Jan. 1728.
12. BL Add. MSS 61436, fos. 68, 81, 86, 94, 120, 124; 61437, fos. 8–10: Godolphin to SM, 13 Nov. 1723–Feb. 1726. Dickson, *Financial Revolution*, 432, 434, and J. H. Plumb, *Sir Robert Walpole: The King's Minister* (1960), 129, both state that Marlborough money was not lent to the treasury at this period; this correspondence with Godolphin makes it clear that the cycle of loans was continuous.
13. *PC* ii. 458–9: SM to Hare [Aug. 1726]; *Memoirs*, 299; BL Add. MS 61446, fo. 167: SM to Marlborough, 25 Jan. 1740[/1].
14. Coxe, *Walpole*, ii. 262: Walpole to Townshend, 30 Aug. 1723.
15. BL Add. MS 61437, fo. 8: Godolphin to SM, 13 Feb. 1726; *PC* ii. 458: SM to Hare [Aug. 1726].
16. BL Add. MS 61464, fo. 83: Hare to SM, 24 Sept. 1726.
17. BL Add. MS 61437, fos. 30–1: Godolphin to SM, 3, 4 Feb. 1727.

18. H. Phillips, *Mid-Georgian London* (1964), 49–51, maintains that Walpole deliberately thwarted her in this matter, but on her own evidence he did grant her all the leases she wanted; see BL Add. MS 61437, fo. 95: Godolphin to SM, 21 June 1728; Bank of England RO Private Drawing Office Ledger 77/3279, 21 Feb. 1729; BL Althorp Papers D18: will, 1729; Add. MS 61471, fo. 38: SM to Wilmington, 9 Oct. 1742.

19. *PC* ii. 452–72: Hare to SM, 26 Aug. 1726, with reply.

20. BL Add. MS 61445, fo. 11: SM to Fish, 21 Jan. 1728.

21. *PC* ii. 455, 469–70; BL Add. MS 61464, fo. 84: Hare to SM, 26 Aug., 24 Sept. 1726, with reply.

22. BL Add. MS 61464, fo. 81: SM to Hare [Sept. 1726].

23. BL Add. MS 61444, fo. 147: SM to Fish, 31 July 1727.

24. Longleat, Portland MSS, Misc. Box 1: extracts from a narrative by SM.

25. BL Add. MS 61447, fo. 142: anon. letter to SM, 16 Sept. [1727].

26. Christ Church, Evelyn MSS: diary of Sir John Evelyn, 11 Oct. 1727.

27. BL Add. MS 61447, fo. 144: anon. letter to SM [Oct. 1727].

28. Graham, ii. 223: SM to Stair, 15 June 1734.

29. BL Add. MS 61444, fos. 94, 97, 110: SM to Fish, 15 Jan., 1 Feb., 13 Mar. 1727.

30. BL Add. MS 61477, fo. 89: Pulteney to SM, 24 Nov. 1734.

31. BL Add. MS 61444, fo. 165: SM to Fish, 24 Oct. 1727.

32. BL Egerton MS 2540, fo. 464: Clarke to Nicholas, 5 Oct. 1725; HMC, *Portland MSS*, vii. 442: Stratford to Oxford, 15 Oct. 1726; Hearne, *Remarks and Collections*, ix. 34, x. 53; BL Add. MS 61468, fos. 65–143: Diston to SM, 1726–8.

33. BL Add. MS 15931, fo. 164: SM to ?, 6 July 1727.

34. Rowse, *Later Churchills*, 14–15.

35. BL Add. MS 61466, fo. 128: SM to Lady Cairnes, 25 Feb. 1725.

36. BL Add. MS 61444, fo. 80: SM to Fish, 16 Nov. 1726.

37. BL Add. MS 61466, fos. 32–51: *An Account of Mr. Guidott's Proceedings* [1726]; Add. MS 61476, fo. 173: SM to King [Jan. 1727].

38. BL Add. MS 61477, fos. 1, 40: Pulteney to SM, 1 March 1728; SM to Chesterfield [1732].

39. BL Add. MS 61457, fo. 38: Somerset to SM, 29 Oct. 1723.

40. BL Add. MS 61440, fo. 64: Mann to SM, 12/23 Sept. 1724; Egerton MS 2540, fo. 457: Clarke to Nicholas, 19 Sept. 1725; Add. MS 61437, fo. 24: Godolphin to SM, 16 Sept. 1726.

41. BL Add. MS 61469, fo. 42: Macclesfield to SM, 3 Nov. 1727; Stowe MS 750, fo. 434: SM to Macclesfield, 31 Jan. 1727[/8].

42. Green, *Blenheim Palace*, 174; BL Add. MS 38056, fos. 20–1: SM to Pengelly, 10 Sept., 3 Oct. 1728; *Letters to and from Henrietta, Countess of Suffolk*, [ed. J. W. Croker] (1824), i. 406: Pulteney to Berkeley [Aug. 1728].

43. BL Stowe MS 751, fos. 129–30: SM to Craggs, 1 Sept. 1716.

44. Suffolk, *Letters*, i. 406.

45. BL Add. MS 38056, fo. 21: SM to Pengelly, 3 Oct. 1728; Add. MS 61468, fo. 177: SM to Lady Abingdon, 12 July 1727.

46. BL Add. MSS 61444, fo. 171; 61445, fo. 11: SM to Fish, 27 Dec. 1727, 21 Jan. 1728.

47. BL Add. MS 61437, fo. 78: Godolphin to SM, 16 Feb. 1728.

48. BL Add. MS 61445, fos. 19, 72: SM to Fish, 15 Feb., 3 Aug. 1728.

49. Ibid. fo. 41: 1 May 1728.

50. BL Add. MS 61444, fo. 171: SM to Fish, 27 Dec. 1727; *Boswell's Life of Johnson*, ed. G. B. Hill, 2nd edn. (Oxford, 1964), v. 175 n. 2.

51. BL Add. MS 61445, fo. 82: SM to Spencer, 14 Sept. 1728; Add. MS 61437, fo. 123: Godolphin to SM, 28 Nov. 1728.

52. BL Add. MS 61447, fo. 18: SM to Lord ?, 13 Aug. 1732.

53. BL Add. MS 61444, fo. 155: SM to Fish, 12 Oct. 1727; Add. MS 61440, fo. 115: SM to Blandford, 24 Aug. 1728.

54. BL Add. MS 61437, fo. 100: Godolphin to SM, 30 July 1728; Add. MS 61440, fo. 109: Blandford to SM, 6/17 Aug. 1728.

55. BL Add. MS 61440, fos. 112–15: SM to Blandford, 24 Aug. 1728.

56. Bristol, *Letter-books*, iii. 30: Lady to Lord Bristol, 7 Jan. 1729.

57. BL Add. MS 61437, fo. 124: Godolphin to SM, 16 Mar. 1729; Add. MS 38056, fo. 22: SM to Pengelly, 12 Apr. 1729.

58. Yale UL Osborn Collection: SM to Lady ?, 21 Apr. 1731; BL Add. MS 38056, fo. 38: SM to Pengelly, 4 Dec. 1729.

59. BL Add. MS 63650, fo. 70: SM to Lady Longueville, 18 Mar. 1728[/9].

60. BL Add. MS 38056, fos. 22–4: SM to Pengelly, 12 Apr., 5 June 1729; BL Althorp Papers D17: SM's lists of her estates; D18: draft wills, 1729.

61. BL Add. MS 61444, fo. 15: SM to Stanhope, 20 Sept. 1729; O. Colville, *Duchess Sarah* (1904), 309–11: SM to [Winchilsea], 22 Sept. 1729; Montagu, i, p. li: SM to Lady Mary Wortley Montagu, 25 Sept. 1729.

62. BL Add. MS 61440, fo. 128: SM to Blandford, 8 Feb. 1729[/30].

63. Ibid. fos. 130–2, 137; Lever, *Godolphin*, 260: Blandford to SM, 10/21 Mar., 24 Mar./4 Apr. 1730, with replies, 17, 27 Mar. 1730.

64. BL Add. MS 61440, fo. 168: narrative by SM.

65. Hervey, 80: to Stephen Fox, 26 Aug. 1731; A. L. Rowse, *The Early Churchills*, Penguin edn. (1969), 430–1.

66. History of Parliament, *House of Commons 1715–1754*, ii. 67; *The Douai College Diaries . . . 1715–1778*, Catholic Record Society, 28 (1928), 143; Windsor Castle, Stuart Papers 142/141: Nathaniel Mist to D. O'Brien, 28 Jan./8 Feb. 1731.

67. Lever, *Godolphin*, 261.

68. BL Add. MS 61467, fo. 115: Holloway to SM, 19 Dec. 1730.

69. HMC, *Verulam MSS*, 121–2: SM to Gape, 27 Feb. 1730; History of Parliament, *House of Commons 1715–1754*, ii. 58–9.

Chapter 19: 1730–1733

1. BL Add. MS 61447, fo. 144; this letter is in the same hand, probably that of a servant, as another anonymous letter of 1732, which certainly did come from Lady Bateman or one of her circle; see ibid. fo. 145 and pp. 289–90 above.

2. BL Add. MS 38056, fo. 37: SM to Pengelly, 20 Oct. 1729.

3. BL Add. MS 61447, fo. 135: SM to Lady Bateman, 14 June 1727.

4. Ibid. fo. 29: SM to Spencer, 2 Dec. 1732.

5. BL Add. MS 61451, fos. 120–1, 151: narratives by SM.

6. BL Althorp Papers B8: Lady to Lord Burlington, 3, 8 July [1730].

7. Christ Church, Evelyn MSS: SM to Mrs Boscawen, 21 July 1730.

8. BL Add. MS 61454, fos. 174–89: correspondence with Lady Rich, Aug.–Sept. 1730.

9. HMC, *Hastings MSS*, iii. 3: Lady Strafford to Lady Huntingdon, 27 Sept. 1730.

10. Walpole, *Reminiscences*, 75–7.

11. Christ Church, Evelyn MSS: SM to Mrs Boscawen, 21 July 1730.

12. Hervey, 59: to Stephen Fox, 9 Sept. 1730; BL Add. MS 28052, fo. 293: Duchess of Newcastle to Mary Godolphin, 7 Jan. 1731.

13. R. Halsband, *Lord Hervey* (Oxford, 1973), 102: Hervey to Lady Bristol, 9 Sept. 1730.
14. Devon RO Seymour MSS L18, 30/6: SM to Somerset, 13 Oct. 1730.
15. BL Add. MS 28052, fo. 293: Duchess of Newcastle to Mary Godolphin, 7 Jan. 1731.
16. BL Althorp Papers D18: draft will, 1729.
17. Bank of England RO Private Drawing Office Ledger 91/3255, 3259: 12 May, 2 Nov. 1731.
18. BL Add. MS 28052, fos. 293, 295: Duchess of Newcastle to Mary Godolphin, 7 Jan., 2 Feb 1731.
19. BL Add. MS 61477, fos. 12–21: SM to Lady Fane, Feb. 1731.
20. BL Add. MS 61449, fo. 108: Bedford to SM, 15 Apr. 1731.
21. HMC, *Hastings MSS*, iii. 8: Lady Strafford to Lady Huntingdon, 25 Oct. 1731.
22. Hervey, 85: to Stephen Fox, 4 Sept. 1731.
23. BL Add. MS 61440, fo. 170: narrative by SM; Hearne, *Remarks and Collections*, xi. 450; A. Dryden, *Memorials of Old Warwickshire* (1908), 28–9.
24. Hervey, 83: to Stephen Fox, 4 Sept. 1731.
25. Green, *Blenheim Palace*, 160; Hearne, *Remarks and Collections*, xi. 454; Christ Church, Evelyn MSS: J. Sparrow to Mrs Boscawen, 29 Aug., 6 Sept. 1731.
26. Suffolk RO Ickworth MSS 941/47/4, fo. 248: Hervey to Stephen Fox, 19 Oct. 1731.
27. Montagu, i, p. lii: SM to Lady Mary Wortley Montagu, 28 Sept. 1731. Torrismond was the hero of Dryden's *Spanish Friar*.
28. Dryden, *Memorials*, 28–9.
29. BL Add. MS 61451, fo. 148: narrative by SM.
30. BL Add. MS 51386, fo. 16: SM to Henry Fox, 30 Nov. 1732; Add. MS 61447, fos. 8, 19, 60: SM to Spencer, 1 July, 13 Aug. 1732, 31 May 1735.
31. Hervey, 80; Suffolk RO Ickworth MSS 941/47/4, fo. 173: Hervey to Stephen Fox, 26 Aug., 4 Sept. 1731.
32. BL Add. MS 61451, fo. 150: narrative by SM; Hervey, 291: SM to Henry Fox, 23 Nov. 1732.
33. BL Add. MS 61451, fo. 151: narrative by SM.
34. BL Add. MS 61447, fo. 13: narrative by SM; Add. MS 61446, fos. 17–18: SM to Sunderland, 3 May 1732.
35. Green, *Sarah*, 287–8; BL Add. MS 61446, fo. 21: Sunderland to SM [May 1732].
36. Ibid. fo. 21: SM to Sunderland, 8 May 1732.
37. BL Add. MS 61447, fos. 16, 19: narrative by SM; SM to Lord ?, 13 Aug. 1732; HMC, *Egmont Diary*, i. 279.
38. D. Adamson and P. B. Dewar, *The House of Nell Gwyn* (1974), 36.
39. BL Add. MS 61447, fo. 2: SM to Spencer, 29 June 1732; Walpole, *Reminiscences*, 90.
40. Bedford Office: SM to Duchess of Bedford (21), 14 Aug. 1732.
41. BL Add. MS 61477, fo. 38: SM to Yorke, 24 May 1732.
42. *LG* 34–5: SM to Duchess of Bedford, 3, 4 July 1732.
43. BL Add. MS 61451, fos. 123, 134: narratives by SM.
44. *LG* 41, 45–6, 48–9, 57–9; SM to Duchess of Bedford, 9, 11, 14, 26 July 1732.
45. HMC, *Hastings MSS*, iii. 15: Lady Strafford to Lady Huntingdon, 25 Aug. 1732.
46. *LG* 61: SM to Duchess of Bedford, 30 July 1732.
47. Ibid. 83: 18 Nov. 1732; BL Add. MS 61447, fos. 19–20: SM to Lord ?, 13 Aug. 1732; to Spencer, 12 Sept. 1732.

48. *LG* 30, 35, 73: SM to Duchess of Bedford, 24 June, 24 July, 23 Sept. 1732.
49. Hervey, 149, 294: to Stephen Fox, 11 Nov. 1732; SM to Mrs Strangways-Horner, 1 Mar. 1733.
50. BL Add. MS 61448, fo. 76; *LG* 83: SM to Duchess of Bedford, 18 Nov. 1732.
51. Hervey, 121: SM to Henry Fox, 8 Dec. 1731.
52. BL Add. MS 61447, fo. 145: anon. letter to SM [Nov. 1732].
53. Ibid. fos. 21, 25, 29: SM to Spencer, 12 Sept., 2 Dec. 1732; Spencer to SM, 30 Nov. 1732.
54. BL Add. MSS 61447, fo. 35: SM to Spencer, 13 Dec. 1732; 61448, fo. 77: SM to Duchess of Bedford, 5 Dec. 1732.
55. BL Add. MS 61447, fo. 39: Spencer to SM, 14 Dec. 1732.
56. *LG* 86: SM to Duchess of Bedford, 3 Jan. 1733.
57. BL Add. MS 61446, fo. 34: SM to Sunderland, 10 May 1733.
58. BL Add. MS 61447, fo. 8: SM to Spencer, 1 July 1732.
59. BL Add. MS 61446, fos. 33, 47: Sunderland to SM, 25 Feb. 1733 and n.d. [1733]; Add. MS 29549, fos. 120–2: SM to [Winchilsea, 1733].
60. Bedford Office: SM to Duchess of Bedford (44, 48), 25, 29 June 1733.
61. Hervey, 295: SM to Mrs Strangways-Horner, 1 Mar. 1733; *LG* 89: SM to Duchess of Bedford, 29 June 1733.
62. Bristol, *Letter-books*, iii. 108: Lady to Lord Bristol, 3 Nov. 1733.
63. *LG* 96: SM to Duchess of Bedford, [26] Oct. 1733.
64. BL G.14844: *An Account of the Conduct of the Dowager Duchess of Marlborough* (1742), 'Postscript', 43: Marlborough to SM, 26 Oct. 1733.
65. Ibid. 44: SM to Marlborough, 27 Oct. 1733.
66. *LG* 97, 99, 104: SM to Duchess of Bedford, 1, 5, 6 Nov. 1733.
67. Ibid. 97: 1 Nov. 1733.

Chapter 20: 1733–1735

1. Hervey, 180: to Henry Fox, 19 Nov. 1733.
2. Bedford Office: SM to Duchess of Bedford (57), [?27 Nov. 1733]; BL Add. MS 61448, fo. 131: note by SM.
3. BL Add. MS 61451, fo. 151: narrative by SM; Rowse, *Later Churchills*, 32–4.
4. Bedford Office: SM to Duchess of Bedford (60), 22 'Oct.' [Nov.] 1733; BL Add. MS 54225, fo. 145: SM to Malleson, 7 Dec. 1733.
5. Bedford Office: SM and Stephens to Duchess of Bedford (73, 74), [1]8, 20 Dec. 1733.
6. BL Add. MS 61447, fo. 35: Spencer to SM, 16 Dec. 1733.
7. BL Add. MS 61448, fo. 146: Duchess of Bedford to SM, 21 Dec. 1733.
8. BL Add. MS 61466, fo. 128: SM to Lady Cairnes, 25 Feb. 1725; Bedford Office: SM to Duchess of Bedford (69, 74), 4, 20 Dec. 1733.
9. *LG* 110: SM to Duchess of Bedford, 25 Dec. 1733.
10. BL Add. MS 61446, fo. 108: SM to Malleson, 24 Jan. 1734.
11. HMC, *Egmont Diary*, ii. 34–5.
12. Rose, ii. 19.
13. Huntington Library, RB 284482: verses interleaved in Alison's *Life of Marlborough*, v. 4.
14. BL Add. MS 61477, fo. 36: SM to Stephens, 28 Apr. 1732; Add. MS 61438, fos. 61–3, 72: Godolphin to SM and Stephens, 25 Apr., 2 May, 15 June 1732.
15. P. Langford, *The Excise Crisis* (Oxford, 1975), 53–4.

16. BL Add. MS 61477, fo. 52: Sir William Chapman to SM, 31 Aug. 1733.
17. Lady Wyndham, *Chronicles of the Eighteenth Century* (1924), i. 33–5: SM to Sandby, 26 Aug. 1733; Bedford Office (44); *LG* 92: SM to Duchess of Bedford, 25 June, 24 Aug. 1733.
18. HMC, *8th Report*, pt. 2, 110: SM to Manchester, 24 Aug. [1733]; Wyndham, *Chronicles*, i. 34: SM to Sandby, 26 Aug. 1733.
19. Windsor Castle, Stuart Papers 163/57: Pretender to SM, 12 July 1733.
20. HMC, *Egmont Diary*, ii. 407; *LG* 109: SM to Duchess of Bedford, 11 Nov. [1733].
21. BL Add. MS 61477, fo. 56: SM to Onslow, 10 Sept. 1733.
22. *LG* 95: SM to Duchess of Bedford [Sept. 1733].
23. Graham, ii. 208: Stair to Grange, 2 Mar. 1734.
24. BL Add. MS 61448, fo. 121: Bedford to SM, 9 Nov. 1733; Add. MS 61446, fo. 62: Marlborough to SM [Nov. 1733].
25. *LG* 114: SM to Duchess of Bedford, 19 Apr. 1734.
26. Ibid. 113.
27. Pierpont Morgan Library: SM to Sir John Hynde Cotton, 13 Sept. 1740.
28. Bedford Office: SM to Duchess of Bedford (81), 17 Apr. 1734.
29. Ibid.
30. Graham, ii. 225: SM to Stair, 15 June 1734.
31. Bedford Office: SM to Duchess of Bedford (84, 85), 13, 23 May 1734; Graham, ii. 223: SM to Stair, 15 June 1734.
32. BL Add. MS 61447, fo. 54: SM to Spencer, 9 Dec.1733.
33. BL Althorp Papers D39: *1st Duke's Trustees* v. *3rd Duke*, 5 June 1738, fos. 10–12, listing the estates bought by the trustees.
34. BL Add. MS 61438, fo. 21: Godolphin to SM, 8 Sept. 1730; Bedford Office: SM to Duchess of Bedford (56) [summer 1733].
35. G. E. Mingay, 'The Agricultural Depression 1730–1750', *Economic History Review*, 2nd ser. 8 (1955–6), 323–30.
36. East Sussex RO Frewen Papers 6763–5: SM to Hanbury, Sir Joseph Jekyll and Charles Frewen, 10, 24 Oct., 8 Nov. 1732
37. BL Add. MS 61477, fo. 43: SM to John Bennet, 15 July 1733; Pierpont Morgan Library: SM to an unnamed steward, 1 May 1739.
38. BL Add. MS 61470, fo. 101: SM to Norgate, 19 Apr. 1733; Add. MS 54225, fo. 145: SM to Malleson, 7 Dec. 1733.
39. BL Add. MSS 61437, fos. 76, 134; 61438, fo. 42: Godolphin to SM, 12 Feb. 1728, 20 July 1729, 15 Dec. 1730.
40. BL Add. MS 61356, fos. 194–5: SM's notes on Talbot's decree; Add. MS 61446, fo. 120: SM to Marlborough, 19 Sept. 1734.
41. Bedford Office: SM to Duchess of Bedford (57) [27 Nov. 1733].
42. Bank of England RO Private Drawing Office Ledger 105/3289: 17 Apr. 1734; BL Add. MS 61439, fo. 6: SM to Godolphin [Feb. 1735].
43. BL Add. MS 61447, fo. 62: SM to Spencer, 7 June 1735; Add. MS 61451, fos. 148–9: narrative by SM.
44. Lord Hervey, *Some Materials towards Memoirs of the Reign of George II*, ed. R. Sedgwick (1931), 246.
45. *LG* 124; Bedford Office (100, 104): SM to Duchess of Bedford, 21 June, [19 July,] 4 Aug. 1734.
46. *LG* 135: SM to Duchess of Bedford, 13 July 1734.
47. Bedford Office: SM to Duchess of Bedford (100), [19 July] 1734; BL Add. MS 61356, fo. 194: narrative by SM.

48. *LG* 138–41: SM to Duchess of Bedford, 20, 22 July, 2, 5 Aug. 1734.

49. S. Markham, *John Loveday of Caversham* (1984), 209; L. Whistler, *The Imagination of Vanbrugh and his Fellow Artists* (1954), 173–4: SM to Herbert, 29 Mar. 1732; *LG* 52: SM to Duchess of Bedford, 21 July 1732; Bank of England RO Private Drawing Office Ledgers 91/3261, 98/3313, 3317, 105/3289: 4 Apr., 25 Sept. 1732, 6 July 1733, 8 Apr. 1734.

50. M. P. G. Draper, 'When Marlborough's Duchess Built', *Country Life*, 132 (July–Dec.1962), 248–50; *LG* 142: SM to Duchess of Bedford, 5 Aug. 1734.

51. BL Add. MS 61448, fo. 154: Duchess of Bedford to SM, 24 Aug. [1734].

52. Bedford Office: SM to Duchess of Bedford (56) [summer 1733]; BL Add. MS 61438, fo. 97: Godolphin to SM, 30 Dec. 1733.

53. BL Add. MS 61439, fo. 19: narrative by SM; Add. MS 61470, fo. 118: SM to Sharpe, 6 May 1736.

54. BL Add. MSS 61438, fos. 133–61; 61439, fos. 1–22: letters between SM and Godolphin, Sept. 1734–Mar. 1735.

55. BL Add. MS 61446, fos. 118, 122: Marlborough to SM, 25 July, 23 Sept. 1734; Bedford Office: SM to Duchess of Bedford (117), 19 Oct. 1734.

56. *LG* 148; Bedford Office (118, 123): SM to Duchess of Bedford, 21 Oct., 16 Nov. 1734.

57. BL Add. MS 61477, fos. 87–9: Pulteney to SM, 22, 24 Nov. 1734.

58. Bedford Office: SM to Duchess of Bedford (122), 12 Nov. 1734.

59. BL Add. MS 61448, fos. 156–7: SM to Duchess of Bedford, 27 Dec. 1734.

60. *LG* 176–7: SM to Duke of Bedford, 16 Mar. 1737[/8].

61. Ibid. 162: SM to Duchess of Bedford, 30 July 1735.

62. Bedford Office: SM to Duchess of Bedford (83), 9 May 1734.

63. Rose, ii. 57, 60, 62; Hervey, *Memoirs*, 408–10.

64. BL Add. MS 61457, fos. 125–7: SM to Somerset, [13] Feb. 1735, with reply; HMC, *Egmont Diary*, ii. 152.

65. Bedford Office: SM to Duchess of Bedford (92) [22 June 1734].

66. Delany, 1st ser. i. 478.

67. BL Add. MS 61447, fos. 62, 66: SM to Spencer, 7 June, 15 July 1735.

68. *LG* 150: SM to Duchess of Bedford, 5 June 1735.

69. BL Add. MS 61447, fos. 58–66: SM to Spencer, May–July 1735.

70. BL Althorp Papers D22: will, 23 May 1735.

71. BL Add. MS 61447, fos. 60–2: SM to Spencer, 31 May, 7 June 1735.

72. Bedford Office: SM to Duchess of Bedford (128) [9 July 1735].

73. Rose, ii. 70–1: SM to Marchmont, 31 Dec. 1735.

74. Wyndham, *Chronicles*, i. 35: SM to Sandby, 26 Aug. 1733.

75. Bedford Office: SM to Duchess of Bedford (128) [9 July 1735].

76. BL Add. MS 61447, fos. 58, 60, 62, 65: SM to Spencer, [May,] 31 May, 7 June, 15 July 1735; Bedford Office: SM to Duchess of Bedford (127), 7 June 1735.

77. BL Add. MS 61451, fo. 137: narrative by SM.

78. Bedford Office: SM to Duchess of Bedford (136), 19 July [1735].

79. *LG* 160: SM to Duchess of Bedford, 30 July 1735; BL Add. MS 61451, fo. 137: narrative by SM.

80. Bedford Office: SM to Duchess of Bedford (36) [5 Aug. 1735].

81. BL Add. MS 61448, fo. 180: Duchess of Bedford to SM, 10 Aug. 1735; *LG* 164, 166–7: SM to Duchess of Bedford, 7 [?22 Aug.] 1735.

82. Adamson and Dewar, *House of Nell Gwyn*, 33–5.

83. *PC* ii. 476–7; BL Add. MS 61441, fo. 62; Thibaudeau, 1st ser. iv. 156–7: letters

between SM and Newcastle, 1–25 Aug. 1735; Bedford Office: SM to Duchess of Bedford (149), 25 Aug. 1735.

84. BL Add. MS 61451, fo. 137: narrative by SM; *LG* 177: SM to Bedford, 16 Mar. 1737[/8].

85. BL Add. MS 61451, fo. 137.

86. Christ Church, Evelyn MSS: Lady Medows to Lady Evelyn, 2 Oct. 1735; BL Add. MS 61448, fo. 186: Bedford to SM, 10 Oct. 1735; *LG* 175–8: SM to Bedford, 16 Mar. 1737[/8]; Longleat, Portland MSS, Misc. Box 2: notebook by Duchess of Portland; Hervey, 231: to Mrs Digby, 6 Oct. 1735.

87. Delany, 2nd ser. iii. 167.

Chapter 21: 1736–1741

1. Rose, ii. 71: SM to Marchmont, 31 Dec. 1735.
2. Montagu, iii. 145: Lady Mary Wortley Montagu to Lady Bute, 30 Sept. 1757.
3. BL Add. MS 61451, fo. 149: narrative by SM; Delany, 1st ser. i. 545.
4. BL Add. MS 61451, fo. 151ᵛ: narrative by SM; Add. MS 61446, fos. 139–46: Marlborough to SM, Nov–Dec. 1735.
5. Delany, 1st ser. i. 553.
6. HMC, *Egmont Diary*, ii. 254.
7. Rose, ii. 70: SM to Marchmont, 31 Dec. 1735.
8. BL Add. MS 61439, fo. 68: SM to Godolphin [9 Feb. 1736].
9. Ibid. fos. 64–70: letters between Godolphin and SM, 8–11 Feb. 1736.
10. BL Add. MS 61463, fos. 55–6: narrative by SM; Add. MS 61439, fos. 90–6: Godolphin to SM, 22–31 July 1736, with her notes; Add. MS 9199, fo. 123: notes by Etough.
11. Yale UL Osborn Collection: SM to Stair, 30 Jan. 1736[/7].
12. BL Add. MS 61467, fo. 24: Stair to SM, 22 June 1736; Rose, ii. 75: Marchmont to Stair, 21 Nov. 1736; Add. MS 47012 B, fo. 13: SM to Mrs Southwell, 5 Sept. 1736.
13. Harris, 'Accounts of the Conduct', 27–8.
14. Christ Church, Evelyn MSS: SM to Lady Evelyn, 17 Oct. 1736.
15. Yale UL Osborn Collection: SM to Stair, 30 Jan., 6 Feb., 6 June 1737; cf. *Memoirs*, 313–15, 280.
16. Undated excerpts were printed under subject-headings in 1788 as *The Opinions of Sarah, Duchess Dowager of Marlborough*, and reprinted in *Memoirs*, 273–332; the originals are now in Yale UL Osborn Collection.
17. Rose, ii. 102: Marchmont to Montrose, 12 May 1738.
18. Yale UL: SM to Stair, 6 June 1737.
19. BL Add. MS 61467, fo. 24: Stair to SM, 22 June 1736.
20. Yale UL: SM to Stair, 6 Feb., 3 March 1736[/7]; cf. *Memoirs*, 293, 316–17.
21. Ibid.: 6 June 1737; cf. *Memoirs*, 299.
22. Ibid.: 6 June, 15 July 1737, 29 Jan. 1737[/8]; cf. *Memoirs*, 282–5.
23. Bank of England RO Private Drawing Office Ledgers 119/3299, 126/3273: 27 May, 14 June 1737.
24. Butler, *Rule of Three*, 339: SM to Thomas Cooke, 26 Nov. 1741. Green, *Sarah*, 295, disposes of the tale that she once saved Child's Bank at the expense of the Bank of England. Child's family connections with William Guidott caused her to transfer her main current account from there to the Bank in 1725.
25. Yale UL: SM to Stair, 25 Nov. 1738, 20 Nov. 1739; cf. *Memoirs*, 289.

26. Yale UL: SM to Stair, 16 Feb. [1742]; BL Add. MS 61447, fo. 85; BL Althorp Papers D49: SM to Spencer, 28 Dec. 1738, 8 Sept. 1742.

27. BL Add. MS 61471, fo. 32: warrant of George II, 16 June 1737; Yale UL: SM to Stair, 15 July 1737.

28. Ibid.: 6 June 1737; cf. *Memoirs*, 299; BL Add. MS 61439, fo. 103: Godolphin to SM, 5 Sept. 1737.

29. Hervey, *Memoirs*, 778–9; BL Add. MS 61467, fo. 5: Lyttelton to SM [5 Aug. 1737]; Yale UL: SM to Stair, 17 Aug. 1737; cf. *Memoirs*, 318–20.

30. BL Add. MS 61467, fo. 14: Lyttelton to SM [18 Sept. 1737]; HMC, *Egmont Diary*, ii. 435.

31. Yale UL: SM to Stair, 30 Oct. 1737; cf. *Memoirs*, 315.

32. Ibid.: 15 July, 17 Aug. 1737.

33. Ibid.: 1, 24 Dec. 1737; cf. *Memoirs*, 279, 309.

34. Ibid.: 24 Feb. 1737[/8].

35. *Transactions of the Birmingham and Midland Institute, Archaeological Section*, 12 (1884–5), 15: SM to Townesend, 8 Aug. 1738; *LG* 152: SM to Duchess of Bedford, 24 June 1735.

36. Yale UL: SM to Stair, 30 May 1738; cf. *Memoirs*, 273–6; Longleat, Portland MSS, Misc. Box 2: extracts from a narrative by SM; Green, *Blenheim Palace*, 176; M. I. Webb, *Michael Rysbrack, Sculptor* (1954), 164.

37. Yale UL: SM to Stair, 24 Feb. 1737[/8].

38. Ibid.: 4, 18 Feb. 1737[/8].

39. Rose, ii. 99–101: Marchmont to Montrose, 12 May 1738.

40. Yale UL: SM to Stair, 17 Apr. 1738.

41. History of Parliament, *House of Commons 1715–1754*, i. 193; Yale UL: SM to Stair, 19, 27 Mar. 1738; cf. *Memoirs*, 327–31.

42. BL Add. MS 61446, fo. 151: Marlborough to SM [30 Mar. 1738].

43. BL Add. MS 61451, fo. 152: narrative by SM; Yale UL: SM to Stair, 31 Mar. 1738.

44. Ibid.; Walpole, *Reminiscences*, 89–90; Windsor Castle, Stuart Papers 206/106: Carte to O'Brien, 4 May 1738.

45. BL Add. MS 61446, fo. 149: SM to Marlborough, 5 Jan. 1737[/8].

46. Ibid. fos. 153–4, 167: SM to Marlborough, 3 May 1738, 25 Jan. 1740[/1]; the hiatus in lending between 1737 and 1738 is not apparent from the table printed in Dickson, *Financial Revolution*, 432.

47. Yale UL: SM to Stair, 27 May 1738; BL Althorp Papers D22: wills, 2 July 1736, May 1738.

48. BL Add. MS 61451, fos. 149–50: narrative by SM; BL Althorp Papers D49: SM to Spencer, 8 Sept. 1738; Walpole, *Reminiscences*, 90.

49. Yale UL: SM to Stair, 31 Mar. 1738.

50. Ibid.: 27 Apr., 27 May 1738; cf. *Memoirs*, 281.

51. BL Althorp Papers D39: *1st Duke's Trustees* v. *3rd Duke*, 5 June 1738; Add. MS 61451, fos. 146, 152–3: narrative by SM.

52. BL Add. MS 61447, fo. 87: SM to Spencer, 31 Dec. 1738.

53. BL Add. MS 61451, fo. 154: narrative by SM; HMC, *Hare MSS*, 243: Hare to Naylor, 15 Feb. 1739.

54. Yale UL: SM to Stair, 12, 20, 27 Feb. 1739.

55. Ibid.: 3, 6 Mar. 1739.

56. Ibid.: 3, 10 Mar. 1739.

57. Ibid.: 5 Apr. 1739.

58. Ibid.: 23 May 1739.
59. Rose, ii. 162–3: Erskine to Marchmont, 8 Sept. 1739.
60. Yale UL: SM to Stair, 20 Nov. 1739.
61. Ibid.: 20 May 1740.
62. Ibid.: 8 Jan. 1739[/40].
63. Rose, ii. 207: SM to Marchmont [27 Feb. 1740].
64. BL Althorp Papers D14: Lady Sunderland to SM, 12 June 1713; Add. MS 61443, fo. 174: Lady De La Warr to SM, 17 Oct. 1734.
65. Ibid. fo. 177: Lady De La Warr to SM [c.1734]; *A True Copy of the Last Will . . . of . . . Sarah, Late Duchess Dowager of Marlborough* (1744), 41; BL Add. MS 61451, fo. 146: narrative by SM; Bank of England Archives: SM to the cashiers, 17 May 1733, 25 June 1736, 20 Mar. 1744.
66. BL Althorp Papers D49: SM to Spencer, 27 May, 5 June 1740.
67. Ibid.; BL Add. MS 61446, fos. 164–5: Marlborough to SM, 26, 28 May 1740.
68. BL Althorp Papers D49: SM to Spencer, 5 June 1740; Add. MS 61447, fo. 93: Spencer to SM, 12 June 1740.
69. BL Althorp Papers D51–D55: *Spencer's Executors* v. *Janssen*, concerning a debt of 17 May 1738; Althorp Papers D49: bond from Spencer to Duncombe, 13 Apr. 1739.
70. *The Greville Memoirs*, ed. H. Reeve (1903), v. 69; *The Complete Letters of Lady Mary Wortley Montagu*, ed. R. Halsband (Oxford, 1965–67), iii. 254: to Lady Bute [Feb. 1761].
71. *LG* 110: SM to Duchess of Bedford, 25 Dec. 1733.
72. Pierpont Morgan Library: SM to [Sir J. Hynde Cotton], 31 Jan. 1741.
73. BL Althorp Papers D53: depositions in *Spencer's Executors* v. *Janssen*, fos. 75, 145, 169.
74. Montagu, i. 81.
75. BL Add. MS 61451, fos. 143, 161, 188: narratives by SM.
76. BL Althorp Papers D39: decree, 20 June 1740.
77. BL Add. MS 61451, fo. 188: narrative by SM; Montagu, i. 80; Walpole, *Reminiscences*, 90.
78. BL G.14844: *An Account of the Conduct of the Dowager Duchess of Marlborough* (1742), 'Postscript', 22–3.
79. John Wilson, *Catalogue 56* (1985), no. 93: SM to Nicholas Fazackerley, 16 Oct. 1740.
80. P. C. Yorke, *The Life and Correspondence of Philip Yorke, Earl of Hardwicke* (Cambridge, 1913), ii. 241: SM to Lady Hardwicke, 22 July 1740.
81. Graham, ii. 264: Crighton to Stair, 26 Aug. 1740; Yale UL Osborn Collection: SM to A. Hume Campbell, 30 July 1741.
82. BL Add. MS 61478, fo. 59: SM to Cornbury, 29 Oct. 1741.
83. *The Works of Alexander Pope*, eds. W. Elwin and W. J. Courthope (1881), iii. 76–89.
84. *The Correspondence of Alexander Pope*, ed. G. Sherburn (Oxford, 1956), iv. 177: to Swift, 17 May 1739.
85. Ibid. iv. 265: Pope to SM, 5 Sept. [1740].
86. Rose, ii. 233–4: SM to Marchmont, 29 Aug. 1740.
87. Ibid.; Pierpont Morgan Library: SM to Cotton, 20 Sept. 1740; BL Add. MS 33963, fo. 113: SM to Lady Fane, 23 Oct. 1740; Huntington Library, RB 284482: SM to [Cotton?], 20 Jan. 1740[/1], in Alison's *Life of Marlborough*, v, aft. 318.

88. Pierpont Morgan Library: SM to Cotton, 30 Sept., 11 Oct. 1740; National Library of Wales, Brogyntyn MSS 620: Mary Godolphin to Mrs Owen, 18 Nov. 1740.

89. Yale UL: SM to Stair, 21 Feb. 1741; cf. *Memoirs*, 304–6, 292, 327.

90. Pierpont Morgan Library: SM to Cotton, 20 Sept. 1740; Yale UL: SM to Stair, 21 Feb. 1741; cf. *Memoirs*, 306.

91. History of Parliament, *House of Commons 1715–1754*, i. 262, 422; BL Althorp Papers D49: SM to Spencer, 12 Jan. 1743.

92. BL Add. MS 61478, fo. 153: draft letter by SM, [c. early 1740s].

93. Yorke, *Life of Hardwicke*, ii. 275: SM to Hardwicke, 3 Oct. 1741.

94. Chesterfield, *Letters*, ii. 449: to Marchmont, 24 Apr. 1741.

95. BL Add. MS 61451, fos. 161, 171: narratives by SM.

96. Pope, *Correspondence*, iv. 358–60, 366: to SM, 13, 15 Aug., 22 Oct. 1741.

97. Yale UL, Osborn Collection; Butler, *Rule of Three*, 338–9: SM to Cooke, 20 Oct., 26 Nov. 1741.

98. National Library of Wales, Brogyntyn MSS 636: Mary Godolphin to Mrs Owen, 7 Dec. 1741; E. J. Climenson, *Elizabeth Montagu* (1906), i. 94–5; [Henry Fielding], *A Full Vindication of the Dutchess Dowager of Marlborough* (1742), 38.

99. Yale UL: SM to Stair, 20 Jan., 16 Feb. 1742.

100. Ibid.: 16, [?23] Feb. [1742].

101. *Miscellaneous Works of the . . . Earl of Chesterfield . . . to which are Prefixed Memoirs of his Life by M. Maty* (Dublin, 1777), i. 115–16.

102. Harris, 'Accounts of the Conduct', 7, 28–31.

103. *PC* ii. 482: SM to Cooke, 6 Apr. 1742. It may have been Lyttelton who arranged for his protégé Fielding to produce a defence; for this see M. C. and R. Battestin, *Henry Fielding* (1989), 343–5.

104. Bristol, *Letter-books*, iii. 278: to Dr Monsey, 16 Mar. 1742.

105. BL Add. MS 61467, fo. 180: SM to Scrope, [26 Apr. 1744].

106. O. Ruffhead, *The Life of Alexander Pope* (1769), 490; Pope, *Correspondence*, iv. 383: to Allen, 19 Jan. [1742].

Chapter 22: 1742–1744

1. BL Add. MS 61451, fos. 134–5: narrative by SM; Add. MS 61450, fo. 216: Duchess of Manchester to SM, 22 Feb. 1741[/2].

2. BL Add. MSS 61450, fos. 155, 160; 61451, fo. 126: narratives by SM; Add. MS 61450, fos. 177–8: Duchess of Montagu to SM [28 Dec. 1739]; SM to Mrs Hammond, 29 Dec. 1739.

3. BL Add. MS 61450, fo. 180: SM to Duchess of Montagu, 5 Jan. 1742.

4. Ibid. fo. 182: Duchess of Montagu to SM [May 1742].

5. Ibid. fos. 183–7: SM to Duchess of Montagu, 17 May 1742.

6. Ibid. fos. 189–91: Duchess of Montagu to SM [May 1742].

7. BL Add. MS 61451, fo. 161.

8. Yorke, *Life of Hardwicke*, ii. 224: Hardwicke to Newcastle, 4 Aug. 1739.

9. Graham, ii. 255: SM to Stair, 3 Aug. 1739; Yorke, *Life of Hardwicke*, ii. 224: SM to Lady Hardwicke, 5 Aug. 1739.

10. E. Marshall, *The Early History of Woodstock Manor* (Oxford, 1873), 268: SM to Clancarty, 6 Sept. 1739.

11. BL Add. MS 36052, fo. 113^{v}: decree, 3 Aug. 1742.

12. BL Add. MS 61439, fo. 123: SM to Godolphin, 4 Aug. 1742.

13. Ibid. fo. 125: Godolphin to SM, 5 Aug. 1742.

14. Ibid. fos. 128–38: 10 Aug.–7 Oct. 1742.

15. Butler, *Rule of Three*, 336: SM to Spencer, 30 Aug. 1742.

16. BL Add. MS 61451, fo. 161: narrative by SM; National Library of Wales, Brogyntyn MSS 214: Mary Godolphin to Mrs Owen, 8 Oct. 1740.

17. BL Add. MS 61441, fos. 77–81: Leeds to SM, 2 Oct. 1741, 25 Nov. 1742, 19 Aug. 1743.

18. BL Add. MS 61472, fo. 145: notes by SM; BL Althorp Papers D49: SM to Spencer, 12 Mar. 1742[/3], 18 Aug. 1744.

19. BL Add. MS 61467, fo. 171: SM to Scrope, 7 June 1742; Add. MS 61471, fos. 36–8: SM to Wilmington, 9 Oct. 1742.

20. BL Add. MS 35455, fo. 48: SM to Stair, 23 Dec. 1742.

21. Pope, *Correspondence*, iv. 419: to SM, 16 Sept. 1742, and note.

22. BL Add. MS 61478, fos. 88–90, 96: Lewis to SM, 31 Aug., 4 Sept. 1742; Glover to SM, 11 Nov. 1742.

23. J. Kenworthy-Browne, 'Portrait Busts by Rysbrack', *National Trust Studies* (1980), 67–8; K. Esdaile, *The Life and Works of Louis François Roubiliac* (Oxford, 1928), 55; Pope, *Correspondence*, iv. 421: to SM, 13 Oct. 1742; BL Add. MS 61478, fo. 98: Rysbrack to SM, 17 Nov. 1742.

24. BL Althorp Papers D49: SM to Spencer, 12 Jan. 1743.

25. John, Lord Campbell, *The Lives of the Chief Justices of England*, 2nd edn. (1858), ii. 343–4.

26. BL Althorp Papers D49: SM to Spencer, 20, 25 Jan. 1742[/3]; Add. MS 61440, fos. 173–80: notes by SM.

27. BL Althorp Papers D49: SM to Spencer, 20 Jan. 1742[/3].

28. BL Add. MS 61446, fos. 182–6: Marlborough to SM, 31 Jan., 4, 9 Feb. 1743.

29. Yale UL Osborn Collection: Stephens to Waller, 4 Dec. 1741; BL Add. MS 61470, fo. 122: 'An Account of Gardiner's Cause' [July 1742].

30. BL Althorp Papers D49: SM to Spencer, 8 Sept. 1742; Add. MS 61467, fo. 173: SM to Scrope, 7 Dec. 1743.

31. Rose, ii. 272: SM to Marchmont, 15 Mar. 1742[/3].

32. Ruffhead, *Life of Pope*, 490.

33. Pope, *Correspondence*, iv. 432, 381: to SM, 22 Dec. [1742]; 18 Jan. [1742/3] (misdated 1741/2 by editor).

34. Rose, ii. 265–7: SM to Marchmont, 3 Mar. 1742[/3].

35. Pope, *Correspondence*, iv. 444–5: Marchmont and Pope to SM, 13 Mar. 1743.

36. Rose, ii. 268–72: SM to Marchmont, 15 Mar. 1742[/3].

37. Pope, *Works*, eds. Elwin and Courthope, iii. 76–92; V. A. Dearing, 'The Prince of Wales's Set of Pope's Works', *Harvard Library Bulletin*, 4 (1950), 327–36; *The Twickenham Edition of the Works of Alexander Pope*, iii. pt. 2, ed. F. W. Bateson (1951), pp. xii–xiv, 57–60, 155–164 (which understates the resemblance to Sarah).

38. Pope, *Correspondence*, iv. 382, 457–8: to SM, 18 Jan. [1743], [? June 1743]; Bank of England RO Private Drawing Office Ledger 140/3299, 3301: 9 Dec. 1741, 1 Jan., 19 Feb. 1742. But for the bitter aftermath, see Maynard Mack, *Alexander Pope* (New Haven, 1985), 746–8, 922.

39. BL Add. MS 61478, fos. 53, 59, 79–83: correspondence between SM and Cornbury, Oct. 1741–July 1742.

40. Rose, ii. 304–5: SM to Marchmont, 16 Aug. 1743; Pope, *Correspondence*, iv. 466: to SM, 6 Aug. 1743.

41. Pope, *Correspondence*, iv. 459: to Marchmont, [July 1743].

42. [A. C. H. Seymour], *The Life and Times of Selina, Countess of Huntingdon* (1839), i. 25–6. I am grateful to Mr Edwin Welch for evidence of the unreliability of this work in other matters. Sarah was acquainted with Lady Huntingdon's aunt, Lady Fanny Shirley, at Twickenham (BL Add. MS 61477, fo. 170), but there is no evidence of a close relationship with her niece.

43. Pope, *Correspondence*, iv. 498: to SM [Feb. 1744].

44. BL Althorp Papers D49: SM to Spencer, 20 Aug. 1743.

45. Ibid: 26 Nov. 1743.

46. Delany, 1st ser. ii. 228.

47. BL Add. MS 61443, fo. 189: Clancarty to SM, 26 Dec. 1743; Add. MS 61446, fos. 190–1: Marlborough to SM, 29 Jan. 1744, with her notes.

48. Rowse, *Later Churchills*, 47.

49. BL Add. MS 61446, fo. 191: notes by SM.

50. BL Althorp Papers D59: defendants' answer in *Furnese* v. *Spencer's Executors*, 1750, fo. 18.

51. BL Add. MS 61467, fo. 173: SM to Scrope, 10 Dec. 1743.

52. Dickson, *Financial Revolution*, 432–3.

53. BL Althorp Papers D14: SM to Pelham, and reply, [Apr.,] 14 Apr. 1744.

54. BL Add. MS 61467, fos. 173, 180–1, 194: SM to Scrope, 10 Dec. 1743, [Apr. 1744]; Scrope to SM, 13 Sept. 1744; Thomson, ii. 550–2, 555, 559: Scrope to SM, 26 Apr. 1744, SM to Scrope, 4, 7, 11, 21 Sept. 1744. For Scrope, see History of Parliament, *House of Commons 1715–1754*, ii. 413–14.

55. BL Add. MS 61443, fos. 189–90: Clancarty to SM, 26 Dec. 1743; BL Althorp Papers D49: instructions by SM for Spencer's will [Apr.–May 1744].

56. BL Add. MS 61467, fo. 196: SM to Scrope, 13 Sept. 1744.

57. BL Althorp Papers D14: SM to Mallet, Sept.–Oct. 1744.

58. BL Add. MS 61467, fo. 200: SM to Scrope, 17 Sept. 1744.

59. *A True Copy of the Last Will . . . of . . . Sarah, Late Duchess Dowager of Marlborough* (1744), 80; Churchill, i. 999: SM's 'Instructions' [1744]; Thomson, ii. 558: SM to Scrope, 20 Sept. 1744.

60. BL Althorp Papers D59: defendants' answer in *Furnese* v. *Spencer's Executors*, 1750, fo. 18.

61. BL Add. MS 62709 A: Duchess of Montagu to B. Fairfax, 25 Oct. [1744].

62. BL Add. MS 61467, fo. 200: SM to Scrope, 17 Sept. 1744.

Epilogue

1. App. II above; BL Althorp Papers D32: Chancery report on SM's estate, 1769.

2. Ibid. D51: Spencer to Janssen, 29 Nov. 1745.

3. Ibid. D45–D48: trustees' account-books, 1744–64.

4. R. H. Eden (comp.), *Reports of Cases in the High Court of Chancery, from 1757 to 1766*, 2nd edn. (1827), i. 403–24.

5. BL Althorp Papers D36–D38: Chancery proceedings concerning the papers in Stephens's custody, 1760–1.

6. BL Althorp Papers D14: Mallet to Stephens, 25 Oct. 1751; Add. MS 61479, fos. 183–206: Mallet's receipt, 2 Nov. 1751.

7. *The Letters of David Hume*, ed. J. Y. T. Greig (Oxford, 1932), i. 370, 387, 460, 501; ii. 162–3; BL Althorp Papers D14: legal opinion, 1781.

8. History of Parliament, *The House of Commons 1754–1790*, eds. Sir L. Namier and J. Brooke (1964), ii. 460.

9. M. Brock, *The Great Reform Act* (1973), 218.

BIBLIOGRAPHY

MANUSCRIPT SOURCES

Bank of England Archives and Record Office: letters of Sarah, Duchess of Marlborough to the cashiers, and her account in the Private Drawing Office Ledgers, 1725–44.

Bedford Office, London: letters of Sarah, Duchess of Marlborough, chiefly to Diana, Duchess of Bedford (numbered 1–150).

Bodleian Library, Oxford: MSS Add., Lister, Rawlinson, Top. Oxon.

British Library: Additional MSS, particularly 61101–61710; Egerton MSS; Lansdowne MSS; Stowe MSS; Althorp and Trumbull Papers (unincorporated).

Cambridge University Library: Houghton (Cholmondeley) MSS.

Child's Bank, Fleet Street: Marlborough accounts, 1676–92, 1721–5.

Christ Church, Oxford: Evelyn MSS, Letters 'Evelyn Period' and '1706–1763' (alphabetically boxed): diary of Sir John Evelyn, 1st Bart.

Churchill College, Cambridge: Erle–Drax MSS.

Devon Record Office: Seymour of Berry Pomeroy MSS (1392M L18), letter of Sarah, Duchess of Marlborough to the 6th Duke of Somerset.

Dr Williams's Library, London: Roger Morrice's 'Entring Books'.

East Sussex Record Office: Frewen MSS 6761–6773 (letters of Sarah, Duchess of Marlborough concerning Crowhurst estate).

Hertfordshire Record Office: Manorial Records 40857–40999 (Sandridge and St Albans), Inventory A25/3792 (Holywell), Panshanger (Cowper) MSS (D/EP F).

Hoare's Bank, Fleet Street: privy purse accounts kept by Abigail Masham, 1711–14; accounts of Sarah, Duchess of Marlborough, and her executors, 1740–69.

Hove Public Library: Wolseley MSS.

Huntington Library, San Marino, California: Ellesmere (Bridgwater) MSS; Hastings (Huntingdon) MSS; HM 16600–16635 (letters of Sarah, Duchess of Marlborough to James Waller); HM 44710 (letters to Hanover, 1713); Loudoun MSS; Stowe (Brydges) MSS; RB 284482.

Kent Archives Office, Maidstone: Stanhope MSS.

Leicestershire Record Office: Finch MSS.

Longleat: Coventry, Portland, and Thynne MSS (British Library Microfilms 863, 921, 904).

National Library of Wales: Brogyntyn MSS (Godolphin–Owen letters); MSS 18091 D (Queen Anne letter and privy purse accounts).

Newberry Library, Chicago: Case MS E5 M3827 (Esther Masham's letterbook).

Northamptonshire Record Office: Spencer Estate Papers.

Pierpont Morgan Library, New York; Rulers of England, Box XI (Anne), letters of Sarah, Duchess of Marlborough.

Public Record Office, London: Baschet's transcripts of French diplomatic dispatches (PRO 31/3); Chancery Records (C); Prerogative Court of Canterbury Wills (PROB); State Papers, Foreign and Domestic (SP).

Suffolk Record Office, Bury St Edmunds branch: Ickworth MSS.

Westminster Public Libraries: parish registers of St Martin-in-the-Fields.
Windsor Castle: Stuart Archives (University of London Microfilm 150).
Yale University Library, Osborn Collection: letters of Sarah, Duchess of Marlborough to Lord Coningsby, James Waller, the 2nd Earl of Stair, and others.

PRINTED SOURCES

(The place of publication is given only where it is not London.)

ADAMSON, D., and DEWAR, P. B., *The House of Nell Gwyn* (1974).

AILESBURY, THOMAS BRUCE, 2nd EARL OF, *Memoirs* [ed. W. E. Buckley], Roxburghe Club (2 vols., 1890).

ANDREWS, H. C., 'Notes on the Rowlett and Jennings Families', *Miscellanea Genealogica et Heraldica*, 5th ser. 8 (1932–4), 88–108.

ANNE, QUEEN, *Letters and Diplomatic Instructions*, ed. B. Curtis Brown (1935).

ASHDOWN, C. H., 'The Accounts of St Albans Grammar School', *Home Counties Magazine,* 6 (1904), 52–9, and 7 (1905), 266–75.

BATHURST, B., ed., *Letters of Two Queens* (1924).

BATTESTIN, M. C. and R., *Henry Fielding* (1989).

BAXTER, S., *William III* (1966).

BEATTIE, J. M., *The English Court in the Reign of George I* (Cambridge, 1967).

BENNETT, G. V., 'Robert Harley, the Godolphin Ministry, and the Bishoprics Crisis of 1707', *EHR* 82 (1967), 726–46.

——, *The Tory Crisis in Church and State: The Career of Francis Atterbury, Bishop of Rochester* (Oxford, 1975).

BLACK, W. H., ed., *Catalogue of the Ashmole Manuscripts* (Oxford, 1845).

BOLINGBROKE, HENRY ST JOHN, VISCOUNT, *Letters and Correspondence*, ed. G. Parke (4 vols., 1798).

BONFIELD, L., *Marriage Settlements 1601–1740* (Cambridge, 1983).

BOSWELL, E., *The Restoration Court Stage* (Cambridge, Mass., 1932).

BOSWELL, JAMES, *Life of Johnson*, ed. G. B. Hill (2nd edn., 6 vols., Oxford, 1964).

Bouchain: in a Dialogue between the Medley and the Examiner (1711).

BOYER, ABEL, *The History of Queen Anne* (1735).

BRAMSTON, SIR JOHN, *Autobiography*, Camden Society, 32 (1845).

BRIGG, W., ed., *The Parish Registers of St Albans Abbey 1558–1689* (Harpenden, 1897).

BRISTOL, JOHN HERVEY, 1st EARL OF, *Letter-books* [ed. S. A. H. Harvey] (3 vols., Wells, 1894).

BROCK, M., *The Great Reform Act* (1973).

BROWNING, A., *Thomas Osborne, Earl of Danby* (3 vols., Glasgow, 1944–51).

BUCKINGHAM, JOHN SHEFFIELD, 1st DUKE OF, *Works* (2 vols., 1726; 3rd edn., 1740).

BURNET, GILBERT, *History of his own Time*, ed. M. J. R[outh] (6 vols., Oxford, 1833).

——, *Supplement to Burnet's History of my own Time*, ed. H. C. Foxcroft (Oxford, 1902).

BUTLER, I., *Rule of Three: Sarah, Duchess of Marlborough and her Companions in Power* (1967).

CAMPBELL, JOHN, LORD, *The Lives of the Lords Justices of England* (2nd edn., 2 vols., 1858).

CARSWELL, J., *The South Sea Bubble* (1960).

CARTWRIGHT, J. J., ed., *The Wentworth Papers* (1883).

CHAMBERLAYNE, E. (continued by J. Chamberlayne), *Angliae Notitia* (1st–23rd edns., 1669–1710).

CHAUNCY, SIR HENRY, *The Historical Antiquities of Hertfordshire* (1700).

CHESTERFIELD, PHILIP DORMER STANHOPE, 2nd EARL OF, *Letters* (1829).

CHESTERFIELD, PHILIP DORMER STANHOPE, 4th EARL OF, *Miscellaneous Works . . . to which are Prefixed Memoirs of his Life by M. Maty* (2 vols., Dublin, 1777).

—— , *Letters*, ed. B. Dobrée (5 vols., 1932).

CHILDS, J., *The Army, James II and the Glorious Revolution* (Manchester, 1980).

—— , *The British Army of William III* (Manchester, 1987).

CHRISTIE, W. D., ed., *Letters Addressed . . . to Sir Joseph Williamson*, Camden Society, new ser. 8 (2 vols., 1875).

CHURCHILL, W. S., *Marlborough: His Life and Times* (2 vols., 1947).

CIBBER, C., *An Apology for the Life of Mr Colley Cibber* (2nd edn., 1740).

CLARENDON, HENRY HYDE, 2nd EARL OF, *Correspondence*, ed. S. W. Singer (2 vols., 1828).

CLARK, R., *Anthony Hamilton* (1921).

CLARKE, J. S., *The Life of James the Second* (2 vols., 1816).

CLAVERING, SIR JAMES, *Correspondence*, ed. H. T. Dickinson, Surtees Society, 178 (1967).

CLIMENSON, E. J., *Elizabeth Montagu* (2 vols., 1906).

COHEN, S. J., 'Hester Santlow', *Bulletin of New York Public Library*, 64 (1960), 95–106.

COLERIDGE, H. J., *St Mary's Convent, Micklegate Bar, York* (1887).

COLLEY, L., *In Defiance of Oligarchy: The Tory Party 1714–1760* (Cambridge, 1982).

COLVILLE, O., *Duchess Sarah* (1904).

CONINGSBY, THOMAS, LORD, 'Account of the State of Political Parties', *Archaeologia*, 38 (1860), 3–18.

COOPER, W. D., ed., *Savile Correspondence*, Camden Society, 71 (1858).

COWBURN, P., 'Christopher Gunman and the Wreck of the *Gloucester*', *Mariner's Mirror*, 42 (1956), 113–29.

COWPER, MARY, COUNTESS, *Diary*, ed. S. Cowper (1865).

COWPER, WILLIAM, 1st EARL, *The Private Diary*, ed. E. C. Hawtrey, Roxburghe Club (1833).

COXE, W., *Memoirs of . . . Sir Robert Walpole* (3 vols., 1798).

—— , *Memoirs of the Duke of Marlborough* (Bohn edn., 3 vols., 1847).

CUSSANS, J. E., *History of Hertfordshire* (3 vols., 1870–81).

DALRYMPLE, SIR J., *Memoirs of Great Britain and Ireland* (3 vols., Edinburgh, 1771–88).

DAWE, P. N., 'The Dorset Churchills', *Notes and Queries for Somerset and Dorset*, 27 (1958), 185–92.

DEARING, V., 'The Prince of Wales's Set of Pope's Works', *Harvard Library Bulletin*, 4 (1950), 327–36.

[DEFOE, DANIEL], *A Short Narrative of the Life of . . . John, Duke of Marlborough* (1711).

DELANY, MARY, *Autobiography and Correspondence*, ed. Lady Llandover, 1st and 2nd ser. (6 vols., 1861–2).

DENNY, H. L. L., *Memorials of an Ancient House* (Edinburgh, 1913).

DICKINSON, H. T., *Bolingbroke* (1970).

DICKSON, P. G. M., *The Financial Revolution in England* (1967).

DILLON, VISCOUNT, ed., 'Some Familiar Letters . . . addressed to . . . the Countess of Lichfield', *Archaeologia*, 58 (1902), 153–88.

DOUAI COLLEGE, *The Douai College Diaries . . . 1715–1778*, Catholic Record Society 28 (1928).

DOWNIE, J. A., *Robert Harley and the Press* (Cambridge, 1979).

DRAPER, M. P. G., 'When Marlborough's Duchess Built', *Country Life*, 132 (July–Dec. 1962), 248–50.

[DUNCOMBE, J., ed.], *Letters by Several Eminent Persons . . . including the Correspondence of John Hughes* (2 vols., 1773).

EDEN, R. H., comp., *Reports of Cases in the High Court of Chancery, from 1757 to 1766* (2nd edn., 2 vols., 1827).

ELLIS, F. H., ed., *Poems on Affairs of State 1704–14* (New Haven, 1975).

ELLIS, G. A., ed., *The Ellis Correspondence* (2 vols., 1829).

ESDAILE, K., *The Life and Works of Louis François Roubiliac* (Oxford, 1928).

EVELYN, JOHN, *The Life of Mrs Godolphin*, ed. H. Sampson (Oxford, 1939).

—— , *Diary*, ed. E. de Beer (Oxford, 1959).

The Examiner, [eds. Jonathan Swift, Delariviere Manley, et al.], 1710–12.

FEVERSHAM, LOUIS DURAS, EARL OF, 'Account of the Battle of Entzheim—1674', *JSAHR* 1 (1921), 35–43.

[FIELDING, HENRY], *A Full Vindication of the Dutchess Dowager of Marlborough* (1742).

FITZMAURICE, LORD, *The Life of William, Earl of Shelburne*, (2nd edn., 2 vols., 1912).

FOLEY, H., *Records of the English Province of the Society of Jesus* (7 vols., 1877–83).

FOOT, M., *The Pen and the Sword* (1957).

FORNERON, H., *Louise de Kéroualle, Duchesse de Portsmouth* (Paris, 1886).

FORRESTER, E. G., *Northamptonshire Elections and Electioneering 1695–1832* (1941).

FOXCROFT, H. C., *The Life and Letters of Sir George Savile, 1st Marquis of Halifax* (2 vols., 1898).

FRANCIS, D., 'Marlborough's March to the Danube', *JSAHR* 50 (1972), 78–100.

GEIKIE, R., and MONTGOMERY, I. A., *The Dutch Barrier 1705–1719* (Cambridge, 1930).

GOSLINGA, SICCO VAN, *Mémoires relatifs à la Guerre de Succession de 1706–1709 et 1711* (Leeuwarden, 1857).

GRAHAM, J. M., ed., *Annals and Correspondence of the Viscount and 1st and 2nd Earls of Stair* (2 vols., Edinburgh, 1875).

GREEN, D., *Blenheim Palace* (1951).

—— , *Sarah, Duchess of Marlborough* (1967).

GREENBERG, J., 'The Legal Status of the English Woman in Early Eighteenth Century Common Law and Equity', *Studies in Eighteenth Century Culture*, 4 (1975), 171–81.

GREGG, E., 'Marlborough in Exile 1712–1714', *Historical Journal*, 15 (1972), 593–618.

—— , *Queen Anne* (1980).

—— , *The Protestant Succession in International Politics* (New York, 1986).

GREVILLE, C., *The Greville Memoirs*, ed. H. Reeve (8 vols., 1903).

GROVESTINS, BARON DE, *Histoire des luttes . . . entre les puissances maritimes et la France* (8 vols., Paris, 1851–4).

HAILE, M., *Queen Mary of Modena* (1905).

HALSBAND, R., *The Life of Lady Mary Wortley Montagu* (Oxford, 1956).

—— , *Lord Hervey* (Oxford, 1973).

HAMILTON, ANTHONY, *Memoirs of Count Grammont*, ed. Sir W. Scott (1896).

HAMILTON, SIR DAVID, *Diary*, ed. P. Roberts (Oxford, 1975).

HARCOURT, E. W., ed., *The Harcourt Papers* (14 vols., Oxford [1880–1905]).

HARDWICKE, PHILIP YORKE 2nd EARL OF, ed., *Miscellaneous State Papers from 1501 to 1726* (2 vols., 1778).

HARRIS, F., 'Accounts of the Conduct of Sarah, Duchess of Marlborough', *British Library Journal* 8 (1982), 7–35.

—— , 'Holywell House, St Albans', *Architectural History*, 28 (1985), 32–6.

—— , 'Parliament and Blenheim Palace', *Parliamentary History*, 8 (1989), 43–62.

HATTON, R., *George I* (1978).

HEARNE, THOMAS, *Remarks and Collections*, ed. C. E. Doble, Oxford Historical Society (11 vols., 1885–1921).

[HEATHCOTE, R., ed.], *Sylva, or the Wood* (1786).

HEINSIUS, ANTHONIE, *De Briefwisseling . . . 1702–1720*, ed. A. J. Veenendal (The Hague, 1976–[in progress]).

HERVEY, JOHN, LORD, *Some Materials towards Memoirs of the Reign of George II*, ed. R. Sedgwick (1931).

—— , *Lord Hervey and his Friends*, ed. Lord Ilchester (1950).

HILL, B. W., *Robert Harley* (New Haven, 1988).

HISTORICAL MANUSCRIPTS COMMISSION (for full details, see HMSO Sectional List 17), *5th, 7th, 8th, 9th*, and *10th Reports*; *Ailesbury MSS, Atholl MSS, Bath MSS, Bathurst MSS, Beaufort MSS, Buccleuch MSS, Cowper MSS, Dartmouth MSS, Downshire MSS, Egmont MSS, Finch MSS, Hare MSS, Hastings MSS, Portland MSS, Rutland MSS, Stuart MSS, Various Collections*, and *Verulam MSS*.

HISTORY OF PARLIAMENT, *The House of Commons 1660–1690*, ed. B. D. Henning (3 vols., 1983).

—— , *The House of Commons 1715–1754*, ed. R. Sedgwick (2 vols., 1970).

—— , *The House of Commons 1754–1790*, ed. Sir L. Namier and J. Brooke (2 vols., 1964).

HOLMES, G. S., *British Politics in the Age of Anne* (1967).

—— , *The Trial of Doctor Sacheverell* (1973).

—— , and SPECK, W. A., 'The Fall of Harley in 1708 Reconsidered', *EHR* 80 (1965), 673–98.

HORWITZ, H., *Parliament, Policy and Politics in the Reign of William III* (Manchester, 1977).

HOSFORD, D. H., 'Bishop Compton and the Revolution of 1688', *Journal of Ecclesiastical History*, 23 (1972), 209–18.

—— , *Nottingham, Nobles and the North* (Hamden, Conn., 1976).

HUDSON, H., *Cumberland Lodge* (Chichester, 1989).

HUGHES, H. S., *The Gentle Hertford* (New York, 1940).

HUME, DAVID, *Letters*, ed. J. Y. T. Greig (2 vols., Oxford, 1932).

HUYGENS, CONSTANTIJN VAN, *Journaal . . . 1673–1678 (1688–1696)*, Werken van het Historisch Genootschap gevestigd te Utrecht, new ser, 25, 32 (1877, 1881).

JAPIKSE, N., ed., *Correspondentie van Willem III en van Hans Willem Bentinck* (5 vols., The Hague, 1927–37).

JESSE, J. H., *Memoirs of the Court of England during the Reign of the Stuarts* (4 vols., 1840).

—— , *Memoirs of the Court of England from the Revolution in 1688 to the Death of George II* (3 vols., 1843).

JONES, J. R., *The Revolution of 1688 in England* (1972).

KEELER, M. F., *The Long Parliament* (Philadelphia, 1954).

KEMBLE, J. M., ed., *State Papers and Correspondence Illustrative of the . . . State of Europe from the Revolution to the Accession of the House of Hanover* (1857).

KENWORTHY-BROWNE, J., 'Portrait Busts by Rysbrack', *National Trust Studies* (1980), 67–8.

KENYON, J. P., *Robert Spencer, Earl of Sunderland* (1958).

—— , *The Popish Plot* (1972).

KLOPP, O., *Der Fall des Hauses Stuart* (14 vols., Vienna, 1875–88).

LANGFORD, P., *The Excise Crisis* (Oxford, 1975).

LAUDER, SIR J., *Historical Notices of Scotish Affairs*, Bannatyne Club, 87 (1848).

LEVER, SIR T., *Godolphin* (1952).

LEWIS, JENKIN, *Queen Anne's Son*, ed. W. J. Loftie (1881).

LLOYD, E. M., 'Marlborough and the Brest expedition', *EHR* 9 (1894), 130–2.

LOCKHART, GEORGE, *The Lockhart Papers*, ed. A. Aufrere (2 vols., 1817).

LUKE, J., *Tangier at High Tide: The Journal of John Luke*, ed. H. Andrews (Geneva, 1958).

LUTTRELL, NARCISSUS, *A Brief Historical Relation of State Affairs* (6 vols., Oxford, 1857).

MACK, M., *Alexander Pope* (New Haven, 1985).

MACPHERSON, JAMES, *Original Papers . . . from the Restoration to the Accession of the House of Hanover* (2 vols., 1775).

MANCHESTER, 7th DUKE OF, ed., *Court and Society from Elizabeth to Anne* (2 vols., 1864).

MARCH, LORD, *A Duke and his Friends* (2 vols., 1911).

MARKHAM, S., *John Loveday of Caversham* (1984).

MARLBOROUGH, JOHN CHURCHILL, 1st DUKE OF, *Letters and Dispatches*, ed. Sir G. Murray (5 vols., 1845).

—— , *The Marlborough–Godolphin Correspondence 1701–1711*, ed. H. L. Snyder (3 vols., Oxford, 1975).

MARLBOROUGH, SARAH CHURCHILL, DUCHESS OF, *An Account of the Conduct of the Dowager Duchess of Marlborough* (1742) (BL G.14844, with 'Postscript').

—— , *A True Copy of the Last Will . . . of . . . Sarah, Late Duchess Dowager of Marlborough* (1744).

—— , *Private Correspondence* (2 vols., 1838).

—— , *Letters of Sarah, Duchess of Marlborough . . . at Madresfield Court* (1875).

—— , 'Some Unpublished Letters of Sarah, Duchess of Marlborough, Relating to the Building of Blenheim Palace', *Transactions of the Birmingham and Midland Institute, Archaeological Section*, 12 (1884–5), 5–15.

—— , *Memoirs*, ed. W. King (1930); this reprints *An Account of the Conduct of the Dowager Duchess of Marlborough* (1742), 'Characters of her Contemporaries' (extracts from a version of her memoirs compiled by Bishop Hoadly in 1715, now BL Add. MS 61426), and *Opinions of Sarah, Duchess Dowager of Marlborough* (1788) (extracts from her letters to Lord Stair, 1736–42).

—— , *Letters of a Grandmother 1732–1735*, ed. G. Scott Thomson (1942).

MARSHALL, E., *The Early History of Woodstock Manor* (Oxford, 1873).

MARY II, *Memoirs of Mary, Queen of England 1689–1693*, ed. R. Doebner (Leipzig, 1886).

The Medley, [eds. A. Maynwaring *et al.*], 1710–11.

MICHAEL, W., *England under George I: the Beginnings of the Hanoverian Dynasty* (1936).

MILLER, J., *James II* (1989).

MINGAY, G. E., 'The Agricultural Depression 1730–1750', *Economic History Review,* 2nd ser. 8 (1955–6), 323–30.

——, *English Landed Society in the Eighteenth Century* (1963).

MONTAGU, LADY MARY WORTLEY, *Letters and Works,* ed. Lord Wharncliffe (2nd edn., 3 vols., 1837).

——, *Complete Letters,* ed. R. Halsband (3 vols., Oxford, 1965–7).

NATIONAL LIBRARY OF WALES, *Calendar of Wynn (of Gwydir) Papers 1515–1690* (Aberystwyth, 1926).

O[LDMIXON], J[ohn], *The Life . . . of Arthur Maynwaring* (1715).

PAULI R., *Aufsätze zur Englischen Geschichte,* new ser. (Leipzig, 1869–83).

PEPYS, SAMUEL, *The Tangier Papers,* ed. E. Chappell, Navy Records Society, 73 (1935).

PHILLIPS, H., *Mid-Georgian London* (1964).

PINTO, V. DA SOLA, *Sir Charles Sedley* (1920).

PLUMB, J. H., *Sir Robert Walpole: The Making of a Statesman* (1956).

——, *Sir Robert Walpole: The King's Minister* (1960).

POPE, ALEXANDER, *Works,* eds. W. Elwin and W. J. Courthope (10 vols., 1871–89).

——, *Correspondence,* ed. G. Sherburn (5 vols., Oxford, 1956).

——, *Twickenham Edition of the Works,* iii, pt. 2, ed. F. W. Bateson (1951).

RANKE, L. VON, *A History of England* (6 vols., Oxford, 1875).

REALEY, C. B., *The Early Opposition to Sir Robert Walpole* (Lawrence, Kansas, 1931).

REID, S. J., *John and Sarah, Duke and Duchess of Marlborough* (1914).

ROSE, SIR G. H., *A Selection from the Papers of the Earls of Marchmont* (3 vols., 1831).

ROWSE, A. L., *The Early Churchills* (Penguin edn., 1969).

——, *The Later Churchills* (Penguin edn., 1971).

RUFFHEAD, O., *The Life of Alexander Pope* (1769).

SCHWOERER, L. G., *The Declaration of Rights 1689* (Baltimore, 1981).

SERGEANT, P. W., *Little Jennings and Fighting Dick Talbot* (2 vols., 1913).

[SEYMOUR, A. C. H.], *The Life and Times of Selina, Countess of Huntingdon* (2 vols., 1839).

SHEENAN, J. H. and M., 'The Protestant Succession in English Politics, April 1713– September 1715', in R. Hatton and J. S. Bromley, eds., *William III and Louis XIV* (Liverpool, 1968), 252–70.

SHREWSBURY, CHARLES TALBOT, DUKE OF, *Private and Original Correspondence,* ed. W. Coxe (1821).

SIMMS, C. J., 'Churchill Court and Manor', *Somersetshire Archaeological Society Proceedings,* 30 (1885).

SIMMS, J. G., *The Williamite Confiscations in Ireland* (1956).

SIMPSON, A. W. B., *An Introduction to the History of the Land Law* (Oxford, 1961).

SNYDER, H. L., 'Daniel Defoe, the Duchess of Marlborough, and the *Advice to the Electors of Great Britain*', *HLQ* 29 (1965–6), 53–62.

—— , 'Godolphin and Harley: A Study of their Partnership in Politics', *HLQ* 30 (1966–7), 241–71.

—— , 'The Duke of Marlborough's Request of his Captain-Generalcy for Life', *JSAHR* 45 (1967), 67–83.

—— 'The Defeat of the Occasional Conformity Bill and the Tack', *BIHR* 41(1968), 172–87.

—— , 'Queen Anne versus the Junto', *HLQ* 35 (1971–2), 323–42.

SPECK, W. A., *Tory and Whig: The Struggle in the Constituencies* (1970).

—— , 'The Whig Schism under George I', *HLQ* 40 (1976–7), 171–9.

—— , ' "The Most Corrupt Council in Christendom": Decisions on Controverted Elections 1702–1742', in C. Jones, ed., *Party Management in Parliament 1660–1784* (Leicester, 1984), 107–21.

SPRAT, THOMAS, BISHOP OF ROCHESTER, *A Relation of the Late Wicked Contrivance of . . . Robert Young* (2 pts, 1692–3).

STANHOPE, 5th EARL, *History of England . . . 1713–1783* (3rd edn., 7 vols., 1853–4).

STEINMAN, G. S., *Althorp Memoirs* (n.p., 1869).

SUFFOLK, HENRIETTA HOWARD, COUNTESS OF, *Letters to and from Henrietta, Countess of Suffolk* [ed. J. W. Croker] (2 vols., 1824).

SUTHERLAND, J., *Background to Queen Anne* (1939).

SWIFT, JONATHAN, *Correspondence*, ed. H. Williams (5 vols., Oxford, 1963).

TEMPLE, J. A., *Temple Memoirs* (1925).

THIBAUDEAU, A. W., ed., *Catalogue of the Collection . . . of Alfred Morrison*, 1st ser. (6 vols., 1883–92) and 2nd ser. (6 vols., 1882–93).

—— , *The Bulstrode Papers* (1897).

THOMPSON, E. M., ed., *Correspondence of the Family of Hatton*, Camden Society, new ser. 23 (1878).

THOMSON, K., *Memoirs of Sarah, Duchess of Marlborough* (2 vols., 1839).

TREVELYAN, G. M., *England under Queen Anne* (Fontana edn., 3 vols., 1965).

TRUMBACH, R., *The Rise of the Egalitarian Family: Aristocratic Kinship and Domestic Relations in Eighteenth Century England* (New York, 1978).

VANBRUGH, SIR JOHN, *Complete Works*, ed. B. Dobreé and G. Webb (4 vols., 1928).

VERNEY, LADY, *Verney Letters of the Eighteenth Century* (2 vols., 1930).

VERNON, JAMES, *Letters Illustrative of the Reign of William III*, ed. G. P. R. James (3 vols., 1841).

VICTORIA COUNTY HISTORY, *Hertfordshire* (4 vols., 1902–14).

WALPOLE, HORACE, *Reminiscences*, ed. P. Toynbee (Oxford, 1924).

WEBB, M. I., *Michael Rysbrack, Sculptor* (1954).

WHISTLER, L., *The Imagination of Vanbrugh and his Fellow Artists* (1954).

WILLIAMS, B., *Carteret and Newcastle* (Cambridge, 1943).

WILSON, J. H., *Court Wits of the Restoration* (Princeton, 1948).

WOLSELEY, VISCOUNT, *The Life of John Churchill, Duke of Marlborough* (2 vols., 1894).

WYNDHAM, LADY, *Chronicles of the Eighteenth Century* (2 vols., 1924).

YORKE, P. C., *The Life and Correspondence of Philip Yorke, Earl of Hardwicke* (3 vols., Cambridge, 1913).

INDEX

Waller, James 341
Walpole, Horace 252, 280, 333
Walpole, Sir Robert 171, 185, 214, 231, 239, 277, 280–1, 295, 302, 328
advises SM about her memoirs 188–9
SM alienates him by joking of his beggary 207–8
and the Whig schism 216, 229
takes over treasury 234
SM's opposition to 236, 237–8, 241–2, 260, 265–6, 268–9, 297–300, 304, 306–8, 310, 316–17, 319, 324–5, 329, 330
and SM's loans to the treasury 250, 255, 264–5, 314–15, 318, 321–2
lures 3rd Duke of Marlborough from opposition 321–2
fall from power 332–3, 342
Walter, Peter 214
Water End 10
Watkins, Henry 184
Webb, Gen. John 152
West, Charlotte (Maccarty), Lady De La Warr 109, 225, 248, 258, 303, 326
West, John, 1st Earl De La Warr 248, 303, 324
Weymouth, see Thynne
Wharton, Thomas, Marquess of Wharton 150, 152, 207

William III (William of Orange) 23, 24, 41, 43–65, 69, 72, 74–86, 89
Willoughby, Francis, 5th Baron, of Parnham 9
Wills, Gen. Charles 210
Wilmington, see Compton
Wimbledon 255–6, 275, 284, 303–4, 309, 310, 315, 318–19, 325, 329, 331, 339, 349
Winchilsea, see Finch
Windsor Park and Lodge 19, 76, 87, 99, 100, 103, 111, 143, 206, 221, 242–3, 249, 266, 275, 280–1, 299–300, 302–3, 311, 313, 314–15, 318, 321, 322, 337–8, 339, 346, 349
Woodstock 114–15, 117, 120, 128–9, 145, 163, 174, 196, 214, 222, 237–8, 247, 257, 269–70, 272, 283, 290, 299, 306, 331
see also Blenheim Palace
Wren, Sir Christopher 119, 149, 154–5, 184
Wren, Christopher, jr. 155, 184
Wright, Sir Nathan 111–12, 116
Wyndham, Sir William 308–9, 314

Young, Robert 66–8
York, James, Duke of, see James II
Yorke, Philip, 1st Earl of Hardwicke 286, 310, 327–8, 331, 336, 340, 344, 345